CONGRESS RECONSIDERED

CONGRESS RECONSIDERED

Sixth Edition

✧ ✧ ✧

Edited by

LAWRENCE C. DODD

University of Florida

BRUCE I. OPPENHEIMER

Vanderbilt University

A Division of Congressional Quarterly Inc.
Washington, D.C.

1414 22nd Street, N.W., Washington, D.C. 20037

Printed in the United States of America

Cover and book design: Paula Anderson

Library of Congress Cataloging-in-Publication Data

Congress reconsidered / edited by Lawrence C. Dodd,
Bruce I. Oppenheimer. -- 6th ed.
p. cm.
Includes bibliographical references and index.
ISBN 1-56802-203-4 (alk. paper)
1. United States. Congress. I. Dodd, Lawrence C., 1946- .
II. Oppenheimer, Bruce Ian.
JK1021.C558 1997
328.73--dc20 96-38960

Contents

✧ ✧ ✧

Tables, Figures, and Boxes

✧ ✧ ✧

Tables

Figures

Boxes

Contributors

✧ ✧ ✧

John B. Bader is assistant professor of political science and associate director of the UCLA Center for American Politics and Public Policy in Washington, D.C. He received his Ph.D. from the University of Wisconsin–Madison in 1994. He has been a Fulbright Scholar to India and a Research Fellow at the Brookings Institution. He is the author of *Taking the Initiative: Leadership Agendas in Congress and the "Contract with America"* (1996) and is writing a new book on leadership in the Senate.

Eileen Burgin is associate professor of political science at the University of Vermont. She received her Ph.D. from Harvard University and, before that, worked in the House of Representatives as a congressional staff person. She has written numerous articles in the general area of Congress and foreign policy.

Joseph Cooper is professor of political science at Johns Hopkins University. He has served as Autrey Professor of Social Sciences at Rice University, staff director of the U.S. House Commission on Administrative Review, and president of the Southwestern Political Science Association. He is currently president of the National Capital Area Political Science Association and a member of the U.S. Commission on the Records of Congress. He is the author of several works on the development of the committee system and numerous articles on congressional structures, processes, parties, and policy making.

Lawrence C. Dodd is the Manning J. Dauer Eminent Scholar in Political Science at the University of Florida in Gainesville. He received his Ph.D. from the University of Minnesota in 1972 and has served as a Congressional Fellow (1974–1975) and a Hoover Fellow (1984–1985). His books include *Coalitions in Parliamentary Government* (1976), *Congress and the Administrative State* (1979), *Congress and Policy Change* (1986), *New Perspectives on American Politics* (1994), and *The Dynamics of American Politics* (1994).

Robert S. Erikson is the Dr. Kenneth L. Lay Professor of Political Science at the University of Houston. He received his Ph.D. from the University of Illinois. He has written numerous articles on congressional elections and is coauthor of *American Public Opinion*, 5th ed. (1995), and *Statehouse Democracy: Public Opinion and Policy in the American States* (1993). He is a former editor of the *American Journal of Political Science.*

C. Lawrence Evans is associate professor of government at the College of William and Mary, where he also serves as associate director of the Thomas Jefferson Program in Public Policy. A former Brookings Institution Fellow and APSA Congressional Fellow, he served on the Joint Committee on the Organization of Congress from 1992 to 1994 as the staff representative of Rep. Lee H. Hamilton. His publications include *Congress Under Fire: Reform Politics and the Republican Majority* (1997), *Leadership in Committee* (1991), and numerous articles on congressional organization.

Richard L. Hall is associate professor of political science and public policy at the University of Michigan. He is the author of *Participation in Congress* (1996) and has published numerous articles on legislative politics.

Susan Webb Hammond is professor of political science at American University. She has worked on congressional committee and personal office staffs. Her publications include *Congressional Staff: The Invisible Force in American Lawmaking* (1977), *Congressional Caucuses in National Policymaking* (forthcoming, 1997), and articles on congressional organization and reform.

Paul S. Herrnson is professor of government and politics at the University of Maryland, College Park. He earned his Ph.D. at the University of Wisconsin–Madison in 1986. He is the author of *Congressional Elections: Campaigning at Home and in Washington* (1995) and *Party Campaigning in the 1980s* (1988). He is coeditor of several edited volumes, including *The Interest Group Connection: Electioneering, Lobbying, and Policy Making in Washington* (1997), *Multi-Party Politics in America* (1997), and *Risky Business? PAC Decisionmaking in Congressional Elections* (1994). He has served as an APSA Congressional Fellow.

John R. Hibbing, professor of political science at the University of Nebraska–Lincoln, received his Ph.D. from the University of Iowa in 1981. He is a former editor of the *Legislative Studies Quarterly* and the author of several articles on Congress. His books include *Choosing to Leave* (1982), *Congressional Careers* (1991), and *Congress as Public Enemy* (1995). The latter was awarded the Richard F. Fenno Prize for the best book on legislatures published in 1995.

Eric D. Lawrence, a Ph.D. candidate at the University of Minnesota, is currently a Research Fellow at the Brookings Institution. His research interests include institutional change, congressional elections, and political methodology.

Gary J. McKissick is assistant professor of political science at Emory University. He has published articles on committee decision making and is currently completing a study of interest group lobbying in Congress.

Walter J. Oleszek is senior specialist in American national government at the Congressional Research Service. In 1993 he served as policy director of the Joint Committee on the Organization of Congress. His publications include

Congress Under Fire: Reform Politics and the Republican Majority (1997), *Congressional Procedures and the Policy Process,* 4th ed. (1996), *Congress and Its Members,* 5th ed. (1996), *Governing: Readings and Cases in American Politics,* 2d ed. (1991), and *Congress Against Itself* (1977), as well as numerous articles.

Bruce I. Oppenheimer is professor of political science at Vanderbilt University. He earned his Ph.D. at the University of Wisconsin. He currently serves as chair of the Legislative Studies Section of the American Political Science Association. His publications include *A History of the Committee on Rules* (1983), *Oil and the Congressional Process* (1974), and numerous articles. His current research focuses on the impact of the apportionment scheme of the U.S. Senate. Articles on this project appeared in the November 1996 issue of the *American Journal of Political Science* and the February 1997 issue of the *Legislative Studies Quarterly.*

Norman J. Ornstein is a resident scholar at the American Enterprise Institute for Public Policy Research. He is also an election analyst for CBS News and writes columns for *USA Today* and *Roll Call.* His books include *Vital Statistics on Congress, 1995–1996, Debt and Taxes: How America Got into Its Budget Mess and What to Do About It,* and *Intensive Care: How Congress Shapes Health Policy.*

Robert L. Peabody has recently retired as professor of political science at Johns Hopkins University after more than three decades of service. He served as associate director of the American Political Science Association's Study of Congress project. He is the author of numerous books on Congress, including *Leadership in Congress* (1976). He is the coauthor of *Congress: Two Decades of Analysis* (1969) and *To Enact a Law: Congress and Campaign Finance* (1972), editor of *Education of a Congressman* (1972), and coeditor of *New Perspectives on the House of Representatives,* 4th ed. (1992).

David W. Rohde is University Distinguished Professor of Political Science at Michigan State University. He received his Ph.D. from the University of Rochester and has written numerous articles and books about internal congressional politics and congressional elections. He is the author of *Parties and Leaders in the Postreform House* (1991) and coauthor of *Change and Continuity in the 1992 Elections,* rev. ed. (1995). He is former editor of the *American Journal of Political Science,* chairman of the Legislative Studies Section of the American Political Science Association, and APSA Congressional Fellow.

Barbara Sinclair is Marvin Hoffenberg Professor of American Politics, University of California, Los Angeles. She received her Ph.D. from the University of Rochester. Her publications include *Congressional Realignment* (1982), *Majority Leadership in the U.S. House* (1983), *The Transformation of the U.S. Senate* (1989), *Legislators, Leaders, and Lawmaking: The U.S. House of Representatives in the Postreform Era* (1995), and *Unorthodox Lawmaking: New Legislative Processes in the U.S. Congress* (forthcoming, 1997). She served as an APSA Congressional Fellow in the office of the House Majority Leader in 1978 and 1979 and was a participant-observer in the office of the Speaker in 1987 and 1988.

Steven S. Smith is Morse–Alumni Professor of Political Science at the University of Minnesota. He is author or coauthor of *Politics or Principle: Filibustering in the United States Senate* (1997), *Committees in Congress,* 3d ed. (1997), *The American Congress* (1995), *Call to Order: Floor Politics in the House and Senate* (1989), and *Managing Uncertainty in the House of Representatives* (1988).

Carol M. Swain is associate professor of politics and public affairs at Princeton University. She received her Ph.D. from the University of North Carolina at Chapel Hill. She is the author of *Black Faces, Black Interests: The Representation of African Americans in Congress* (1993) and editor of *Race Versus Class: The New Affirmative Action Debate* (1996). She won the 1994 Woodrow Wilson Foundation Award for the "best book published in the United States during the prior year on government, politics or international affairs." She is the co-winner of the 1994 V. O. Key Award for the best book published on southern politics and of the D. B. Hardeman Prize for the best scholarly work on the U.S. Congress.

Elizabeth Theiss-Morse is associate professor of political science at the University of Nebraska–Lincoln. She received her Ph.D. from the University of Minnesota in 1989. She has published research on citizenship, political tolerance, public opinion, and methodology and is coauthor of two books: *Congress as Public Enemy: Public Attitudes Toward American Political Institutions* and *With Malice Toward Some: How People Make Civil Liberties Judgments.*

James A. Thurber is professor of government and director of the Center for Congressional and Presidential Studies at American University. His books include *Remaking Congress: Change and Stability in the 1990s* (1995), *Campaigns and Elections: American Style* (1995), and *Rivals for Power: Presidential-Congressional Relations* (1996). He received American University's Teacher-Scholar of the Year Award for 1996.

Gerald C. Wright is professor of political science at Indiana University and was formerly the political science program director at the National Science Foundation. He received his Ph.D. from the University of North Carolina at Chapel Hill. His publications include *Electoral Change in America* (1974) and numerous articles in professional journals. He coedited *Congress and Policy Change* (1986) and is coauthor of *Statehouse Democracy: Public Opinion and Policy in the American States* (1993).

Garry Young is assistant professor of political science at the University of Missouri, Columbia. He received his Ph.D. from Rice University in 1994. His interests include the development of congressional organization and presidential decision making.

Preface

✧ ✧ ✧

If anyone had told us when the first edition of *Congress Reconsidered* was published in 1977, that there would be a sixth edition of the book twenty years later, it would not have required false modesty to react with total disbelief. As two young faculty members, we were nervous about the reaction to the first edition and had not even contemplated that there might be a second, let alone a sixth edition.

We opened the preface to the first edition with a question: "Why reconsider Congress?" Although we provided a somewhat more elaborate answer, much of it could be boiled down to a single sentence that reflected our concerns after completing the 1974–1975 academic year as APSA Congressional Fellows and returning to our respective universities to teach about Congress. We wrote, "The Congress we observed and worked in ourselves was indeed substantially different from the one about which we had read and taught." The purpose of the book was to provide the reader with up-to-date knowledge and insights through a series of articles by many of the best congressional scholars researching the contemporary institution and its historical development.

With subsequent editions, some friends, colleagues, and students have asked us with a mix of good-natured ribbing and seriousness, "Why do you keep reconsidering Congress?" We have had suggestions that we retitle the book *Congress Reconsidered Again* or *Congress Re-reconsidered,* or *Child of Congress Reconsidered.* The motive for subsequent editions of the book is not monetary. Granted, we do earn some royalties after our contributors' fees are paid, but we recognize that we could earn more if we spent our time bagging groceries at the local supermarket rather than working on this book. At least *Congress Reconsidered* involves no "heavy liftin'."

The real reason for new editions is that despite a certain institutional stability Congress continues to change. Naturally, there are times, such as the early and mid-1970s and the Republican revolution of the 104th Congress, when the changes and reforms are more numerous and consequential than at other times. During those periods, providing a good description of the changes and some expert assessment of their potential impact is a major undertaking. But even during periods of consolidation, Congress is not unchanging. Sometimes there is a reaction to an earlier reform period, such as the consolidation of leadership power in the late 1970s in response to the excesses of subcommittee government. Frequently, the consequences of change, especially the unanticipated consequences, surface years later. For example, the campaign finance reforms of the 1970s set in motion the growth of PACs, which analysts identify as the source of many current problems with Congress. Similarily, changes that were at first seen as modest may prove to have great significance for the operation of the institution. The use of multiple referrals in the House is a classic example.

We have always tried to recognize that a useful focus on change can be achieved only if a sense of broader institutional and historical context is maintained. The contributors to *Congress Reconsidered* have been particularly sensitive to the need to go beyond cross-sectional analysis and have refrained from the assumption that all change must be consequential. Rather, they have endeavored to place their findings in a historical and dynamic context and to provide compelling arguments and evidence that suggest the real impact of change.

The sixth edition, more than the others, is like the first edition. Both follow immediately on the heels of what many rank as revolutionary changes in Congress. The results of the midterm elections of 1974 and 1994 were critical for these changes to be realized, although the groundwork for change had already been laid. As in the mid-1970s, the magnitude and immediate effect of the changes were greater in the House than in the Senate. But the Senate in gradual and more subtle ways followed the House's lead. Moreover, the sixth edition, like the first, placed an unusual burden on the contributors. Not only did they provide careful and accurate description of the reforms of the 104th Congress, but also they took great pains to assess the impact of these changes after a relatively short period of time. In the first edition there was considerable certainty that the Democrats would remain the majority party after the 1976 election. The contributors to this edition had no such luxury. In fact, as this book was going to press, some 1996 House races were still undecided.

The articles in the sixth edition do not simply document the Republican revolution of the 104th Congress. To be sure, there is considerable attention to detailing the reforms that constituted the revolution and to explaining the circumstances that made the Republican takeover possible. But beyond tracking the changes and reforms, the contributors attempt to place the developments of the 104th Congress in the context of the long-term evolution of the modern Congress. Readers should be able to assess which changes break new ground and which provide continuity with previously developing trends. Many of the articles evaluate the impact the changes have on the current power relationships within Congress and on the relationship between Congress and the executive branch. And some are willing to offer a view of how these changes will affect future Congresses.

This edition also has a number of features in common with the earlier editions. Again, we are fortunate to have contributions from an outstanding group of congressional scholars. The success of this book has always depended on the willingness of the writers to produce first-rate manuscripts that make cutting-edge scholarly research accessible and yet challenging to a broad audience. The quality of the contributors over the years has greatly facilitated our job as editors.

The sixth edition, like its predecessors, is essentially a new book. Most of the articles in it are new, and others are so substantially revised that for all practical purposes they too are new contributions. All of the articles were written for this book. Like us, our contributors understand that the success of *Congress Reconsidered* rests in part on its offering the reader new material. Some adopters inevitably are disappointed that favorite articles from a previous edition have not made their way into the new edition. Perhaps one day we might produce a volume called *The Best of Congress Reconsidered,* even though the task of making the selections might be impossible. For now, *Congress Reconsidered* will continue to avoid an "oldies but goodies" craze.

This edition of the book is divided into six parts. The first, Patterns and Dynamics of Congressional Change, again includes an overview piece on the Senate by Norm Ornstein, Bob Peabody, and Dave Rohde and our overview piece on the House. The two articles offer a useful contrast between the more gradual alteration of the Senate and the more abrupt alteration of the House in the wake of the Republican takeover. In addition, a third article by John Hibbing and Beth Theiss-Morse focuses on the reasons for public disaffection with Congress and examines whether the Republican revolution has altered public attitudes.

Part II contains three articles on elections and constituencies. For the first time, we have included a chapter that focuses on issues of structural representation in Congress. Carol Swain provides a historical overview to the recruitment and representation of women and blacks in Congress, assesses future trends, and discusses the policy impacts caused by increases in minority representation. In a piece on PAC contributions in House elections, Paul Herrnson looks at the contribution advantages the Republicans achieved upon becoming the majority party and their effect on future control of the House. Bob Erikson and Jerry Wright attend to the representational linkages between voter policy preferences and the decisions they make in congressional elections, particularly as they played out in 1994. In an inventive presentation, they demonstrate that voters know little about their House members and senators but nevertheless constitute "smart and discerning" electorates.

Congressional committees, especially in the House, were most notably affected by the Republican takeover in 1995. Part III offers three chapters that provide differing perspectives on committee reform and its effects. Steve Smith and Eric Lawrence contrast the erosion of standing committee independence in the House with the more gradual impact on committee activity in the Senate and discuss the short-term and long-term implications of these changes. Larry Evans and Walter Oleszek examine the efforts at committee reform in the House and Senate in the 1990s. These reforms solidified after the Republican takeover, and Evans and Oleszek ask why the Republicans were more willing to make major reforms and assess their likely durability. From an alternative perspective, Rick Hall and Gary McKissick analyze whether the institutional changes produced by committee reforms have affected the behaviors of committee chairs and members to a lesser extent than one might have anticipated.

Three articles that delve into the workings of parties and leaders in Congress make up Part IV. Barbara Sinclair details what she sees as a "new legislative process" in which leaders and parties play a far greater role in the management of major legislation than before. Her findings force us to reconsider the accuracy of the traditional textbook description of how a bill becomes a law. Joe Cooper and Garry Young give a new perspective on the ebbs and flows of party voting in the House and Senate. Their newly developed method for measuring the degree to which party structures congressional roll call behavior offers fresh insights into our understanding of parties in Congress. Finally, in the aftermath of reforms that threatened not just the influence but the very existence of congressional caucuses, Sukie Hammond's research finds that caucuses continue to thrive. She discusses why this is the case and how caucuses have adapted.

Chapters contributed by Eileen Burgin, Jim Thurber, and John Bader are found in the section called Congress, the Executive, and Public Policy. In a significant update to her essay in the fifth edition, Burgin evaluates the conflicting arguments about the proper role for Congress in the making of foreign policy in light of the reversal to a Republican Congress and a Democratic executive. The ongoing struggle to reduce the nation's budget deficit provides the backdrop for Thurber's evaluation of congressional budget politics. Bader presents a detailed analysis of the Republicans' Contract with America, from the motivations behind its design to the enactment of many of its provisions in the 104th Congress, and evaluates its success in partisan and institutional terms.

Two of the overriding issues that concern congressional scholars now and will in the future—the balance of governing influence between Congress and the president and the nature and effects of partisanship within Congress—are addressed in Part VI, Congress and Political Change. Bruce Oppenheimer presents a nonconventional view of the Republican revolution, arguing that the long-term effect of the reforms of the 104th Congress will be to diminish the power of Congress and strengthen the president. In the concluding essay, Larry Dodd and Oppenheimer examine the various directions partisanship in Congress may now take. The chapter considers whether the model of "conditional party government" that dominated the 103d and 104th Congresses will persist in the 105th and beyond and argues that Republicans now may have to pursue a strategy of "constructive partisanship."

Once again, we are indebted to the staff at CQ Press for their role in *Congress Reconsidered.* They do more than simply compensate for our shortcomings as editors. From finding just the right image for the cover to going the extra mile in assisting the contributors to holding off until the last minute so that the election results can be incorporated into the book, in this edition as in the past they have gone beyond what we have any reasonable right to expect. Brenda Carter remained in contact with us throughout the four-year cycle since publication of the fifth edition. She offered innovative suggestions about the content, organization, and timing of the book and ensured that we maintain the quality that has made this book successful. We were pleased to work again with Carolyn Goldinger, who was the manuscript editor on the fourth edition as well the sixth. She deserves credit for molding the styles and approaches of the seventeen essays so that they are consistent in presentation and accessible to a varied audience. Julie Rovesti and Kathryn Suárez were vital in bringing the sixth edition to the attention of the broader profession in a most effective manner. We thank Sabrina Salcito for performing many of the administrative tasks necessary for completion of the project. Most important, all maintained good humor even as deadlines approached.

In tangible and intangible ways, our professional colleagues at our respective institutions offered guidance during our work on this edition. In particular, John Geer and Frances Lee offered valuable comments on draft materials.

Our personal relationships were again crucial to the completion of another edition. Leslie, Susan, and Anne not only tolerated our time commitments to this project but also understood when we were unable to leave *Congress Reconsidered* at the office. Finally, our working relationship and friendship has lasted through a Democratic revolution of the 1970s and a Republican revolution of the 1990s. We remain very different individuals with differing tastes. Dodd enjoys his country music, but nods off watching University of Florida football games. Oppenheimer has season tickets to Vandy basketball and football, but has yet to attend the Opry. But there are important areas of common ground, especially in our appreciation, tolerance, and respect for each other. These have allowed us to make room for professional moves and changing lives over the course of producing six editions and still retain the commitment to this ongoing enterprise.

CONGRESS RECONSIDERED

Part I
Patterns and Dynamics of Congressional Change

1. The U.S. Senate: Toward the Twenty-First Century

Norman J. Ornstein, Robert L. Peabody, and David W. Rohde

In an era of major political upheaval, the election of 1994 brought even more change to the U.S. Senate. The Republicans gained a net of twelve seats, recapturing the majority they had lost eight years earlier. The election propelled Robert Dole of Kansas back into the position of majority leader he had been forced to relinquish in 1986 and changed dramatically the power structure and agenda of the institution. Under other circumstances, the Republicans' retaking the Senate would have been huge political news. It barely raised a ripple on November 7, because more startling news came from the other side of the Capitol. The House of Representatives also saw an incoming Republican majority, but for the first time in forty years, not eight. And Speaker-elect Newt Gingrich of Georgia was a more earth-shaking story than Majority Leader Dole.

The last time the Republicans had captured a majority in the Senate—and they had to wait a quarter century for it—was in 1980, when Ronald Reagan was elected president. Through the succeeding 97th Congress and the two that followed, the Senate Republicans set the congressional agenda, including taking the lead on tax matters, which usurped a treasured House congressional role.[1]

In 1995 the situation was very different. The House became the nation's policy initiator, acting almost like a parliament, with Speaker Gingrich behaving more like a prime minister than a traditional Speaker.[2] The Senate seemed like a junior partner, lagging behind the House on policy, and reacting rather than leading.

The Senate was not, however, irrelevant—not the American equivalent of the British House of Lords. As 1995 progressed, especially after the excitement of the first hundred days generated by the House's Contract with America, the Senate's role became more central—and more like the Founders envisioned it—than we had seen in decades. The House acted swiftly and broadly, while the Senate adopted a more deliberative pace and a caution reinforced by less-sweeping changes in its membership. As is always the case in the Senate, two-thirds of its members had not been up for election in 1994. Just over a fifth of its new majority were freshmen. The reversal in attitudes caused by the switch in party majorities was also interesting to observe. Democrats in the Senate, who had complained for years about Republicans' use of obstructionist tactics to block action on their favorite initiatives, suddenly found merit in the availability of the "hold" (an informal practice that enabled any senator anonymously to block action on any bill or nomination) and in the weapon of the filibuster (which often required sixty votes, not a simple majority of fifty or fifty-one, to achieve results). The Republicans, who had used these tactics frequently during their years in the Senate minority, now found their priorities frustrated by them.

But the contrast between House hyperactivity and Senate sloth also underscored another reality. The individualistic nature of the Senate, ingrained in its rules and culture, had become even more oriented toward the prerogatives and whims of its individual members and less to the collective needs of the body. Efforts to reform the Senate, to streamline its processes, strengthen its leadership, and create a more collective sense of responsibility, foundered in 1994.

In 1996 change in the Senate took on another twist with a partisan overlay. The second session of the 104th Congress saw the Senate struggle to achieve a balance between debate and action, the role of individuals and the needs of the institution. But from March until June, when Dole resigned to campaign full time for the presidency, the Senate's efforts were shaped by the unusual dual roles of its majority leader. For the first time in American history, a Senate party leader became a presidential nominee—and played both parts simultaneously. The intertwining of, and conflicts between, the Senate's policy-making role and partisan political interactions underscored how dynamic the politics of the Senate had become in the 1990s. The nature of that change is the subject of this essay.

The Membership

With six-year terms and only about a third of the seats available for contest in any election year, alteration in the Senate membership does not follow any set pattern. Some change has been gradual. At times, however, it has occurred in large jolts—as in the elections of 1980, 1986, and 1994, which brought the only shifts of partisan control of the Senate since the early 1950s.

Some segments of the public have an image of the Senate as an institution filled with thirty-year veterans of the seniority system. For the body in general, that image is anything but accurate. Large portions of the membership have turned over a number of times since Donald R. Matthews and Ralph K. Huitt wrote brilliant portraits of the Senate in the 1950s.[3] When the 104th Congress convened in January 1995, only five of the hundred senators had served thirty years or more, and just twenty had served twenty years or more. Indeed, fifty-three senators—a majority of the membership—had been elected in the decade since Reagan won his second term in 1984.

Membership change is more than just the substitution of one person for another. With respect to a variety of attributes, a different mix of senators sets the character of the institution at any given moment. The pattern of this turnover, moreover, has substantially affected the operation of the Senate and the policies it has produced. We consider here three attributes that characterize the aggregate membership: division by party, sectional party affiliation, and the partisanship of members.

The most obvious and visible changes in the Senate's membership are in party affiliation. From the end of World War II through most of the 1950s, the partisan division of the Senate was very close; neither party controlled the body by more than a few votes. In the election of 1958, however, Democratic membership jumped from forty-nine seats to sixty-four, and through the 1970s the number of Democrats was usually sixty or more. The 1980 election brought a stunning reversal of the Democrats' twenty-six years of unbroken control and replaced it with a narrow Republican majority that persisted for the next six years. In 1986 Democrats won back control and held it until the GOP tidal wave of 1994. For the last decade and a half, the Senate has experienced relatively close division between the parties, coupled with uncertainty about which party would prevail in the next election.

A second notable change involves the regional character of the two parties. Through the 1950s Democratic membership was concentrated in the South and West, while Republicans came primarily from the East and Midwest. In 1957, for example, the Democrats held every seat from the South and thirteen of twenty-two seats from the West, but they controlled only five of twenty eastern seats and three of twenty-two midwestern seats. By the 1970s, however, these regional patterns were different; Democrats had gained ground in the regions of GOP strength, and vice versa. Indeed, in the 1994 election, history reversed itself: the strongest Democratic regions were in the East and Midwest, while the strongest for the Republicans were in the South and West. More important, however, was that the pronounced regional deviations in party affiliation were gone: in no region did the Republican majority hold more than 62 percent of the seats, and in none did it hold less than 45 percent. Across the country, national electoral forces had produced a more similar mix of Democrats and Republicans from region to region. Another result of this process is that the policy positions of senators within each party across different regions became more similar over time. That development leads us to the final attribute we consider.

The amount of partisanship in the Senate—or in other legislative bodies—is the consequence of two interacting factors: the similarity of the policy views of members within each party and the degree of difference on those policies between the parties. In the 1960s and 1970s there was considerable disagreement over legislative issues within both parties, with northern and southern Democrats often in conflict, and northeastern Republicans frequently disagreeing with the rest of the GOP senators. As a result, there was significant overlap between the parties, with a number of the Democratic senators on the conservative side of the policy spectrum and a number of Republicans on the moderate to liberal side. The overlap muted conflict between the parties, so that majorities of the parties voted the same way more often than not. More specifically, in the seven Congresses between 1963 and 1976, the percentage of the roll call votes on the Senate floor on which majorities of the parties were opposed (usually called "party-unity votes") ranged between 33 percent and 43 percent.[4] The average was 39 percent. During the next six Congresses (1977–1988), the frequency of party conflict increased somewhat, ranging between 41 percent and 51 percent, with an average of 45 percent. In the most recent period, conflict grew again, with party unity votes accounting for 63 percent, 51 percent, and 60 percent of the Senate roll calls between 1989 and 1994, and jumping to 69 percent in the first session of the 104th Congress (1995).

The frequency of interparty conflict in the 1980s and 1990s reflected the growing homogeneity within each party on those issues where Democrats and Republicans disagree. This pattern resulted not only from the replacement of members, but also from senators modifying their positions in response to changing electoral conditions. Southern Democrats found themselves less often in opposition to their northern colleagues, and Republican members from the northeast disagreed less frequently with other GOP senators.[5] These changes are illustrated by the data on senators' level of support for party positions in six selected Congresses displayed in Table 1-1.

In the 85th Congress (1957–1959), more than four-fifths of Democrats were relatively strong supporters of their party's positions, while this was true for only two-thirds of Republicans. In the 1960s and the 1970s, about the same proportion (approximately 25 percent) of both parties fell in the moderate category, and a small proportion of both were strong supporters of the opposite party. During this period, party lines were blurred, and the Democrats from the South were overwhelmingly in the moderate or pro-Republican categories. At the beginning of the 1980s, the GOP regained the Senate majority, and the proportion of Republicans in the moderate range dropped. This change produced a set of scores that was roughly a mirror image of the 85th Congress. In the 101st Congress (1989–1990), majority control and the pattern switched again, with Democratic moderates decreasing and GOP moderates increasing a bit.

The first session of the 104th Congress (1995) exhibits the starkest pattern: only seven of the one hundred senators were in the moderate category, and 93 percent of each party were strong supporters. The separation of members by party is almost complete.[6] It is likely that these developments will be reinforced further. Two Democratic senators, Richard Shelby of Alabama and Ben Nighthorse Campbell of Colorado, switched their affiliation to the Republican Party after the 1994 elections. Moreover, of the seven moderate members in 1995, three announced their retirement in 1996.[7] It is likely that their replacements will be more partisan, regardless of their party.

In addition to affecting voting patterns on the Senate floor, the intensification of partisan divisions has affected the internal politics of the parties. Individual senators are still free to vote their conscience or their constituency, but a pattern of deviation from party positions can risk negative consequences. For

Table 1-1 Support for Party Positions in the Senate, Selected Congresses from the 85th to the 104th (in percentages)

Congress	Northern Democrats	Southern Democrats	All Democrats	Repub-licans	All members
85th Congress (1957–1959)	(27)	(22)	(49)	(47)	(96)
Pro-Rep	—	—	—	66	32
Moderate	7	32	18	32	25
Pro-Dem	93	68	82	2	43
89th Congress (1965–1966)	(46)	(20)	(66)	(34)	(100)
Pro-Rep	2	5	3	68	25
Moderate	7	70	26	24	25
Pro-Dem	91	25	71	9	50
93d Congress (1973–1974)	(43)	(16)	(59)	(41)	(100)
Pro-Rep	—	13	3	59	26
Moderate	7	75	25	29	27
Pro-Dem	93	13	71	12	47
97th Congress (1981–1982)	(35)	(12)	(47)	(53)	(100)
Pro-Rep	—	8	2	83	45
Moderate	14	67	28	17	22
Pro-Dem	86	25	70	—	33
101st Congress (1989–1990)	(40)	(15)	(55)	(45)	(100)
Pro-Rep	—	—	—	71	32
Moderate	13	27	16	29	22
Pro-Dem	88	73	84	—	46
104th Congress (1995)	(37)	(9)	(46)	(54)	(100)
Pro-Rep	—	—	—	93	50
Moderate	3	22	7	7	7
Pro-Dem	97	78	93	—	43

Sources: The scores for the 85th through the 97th Congresses were computed from data provided by the Inter-University Consortium for Political and Social Research (ICPSR 7645: Voting Scores for Members of the United States Congress (1945-1982)). Those for the 101st Congress and the first session of the 104th were computed from data in *Congressional Quarterly Weekly Report.*

Note: The classification is based on a variation of the party unity scores computed by Congressional Quarterly. The support score of a member was divided by the sum of that member's support and opposition scores, which removes the effect of absences. Then Republican scores were subtracted from 100, to give their support for Democratic positions. Members whose scores were 0–29 were classified as pro-Republican, 30–70 as moderate, and 71–100 as pro-Democratic. The number of senators used to compute each percentage is shown in parentheses.

example, Sen. Charles S. Robb, D-Va., was dropped from the Budget Committee in 1991, a move many observers saw as a result of his fiscal conservatism and his support for authorizing President Bush to use force in the Persian Gulf crisis.[8]

Among Republicans, one manifestation of partisanship has been the replacement of members of the existing party leadership with new people. At the beginning of the 103d Congress, the Senate GOP decided to dump the moderate John H. Chafee of Rhode Island, chairman of the conference, the group of all Senate Republicans. They selected Thad Cochran of Mississippi, a much more conservative member. Chafee had sided with the Democrats on a number of important legislative conflicts. Conservative senator Dan Coats, R-Ind., said that the leadership election "may reflect the fact that there is a sense that business as usual is not going to serve us in 1992. We need an aggressiveness in defining differences between the two parties."[9] At the beginning of the 104th Congress, the leadership transformation continued when Alan K. Simpson of Wyoming, the GOP Senate whip (the second-ranking post), was replaced by Trent Lott of Mississippi (who then became the majority leader when Dole resigned). While Simpson was certainly more conservative than Chafee, he was also frequently involved in working out compromise legislative solutions with the previous Democratic majority, and he was pro-choice on abortion. Lott, who had been a Gingrich ally in the House, was always more aggressively partisan and identified with the GOP "hard right." The selection did not necessarily imply significant legislative effects, but it reflected the changing character of the Senate Republicans. As former GOP senator John C. Danforth of Missouri, who did not seek reelection in 1994, said, "I think it has to do with the self-identity of the Republican Party. . . . It's symbolic more than anything else. . . . Does the Republican Party view itself as sharply ideological or does it view itself as being a more pragmatic party."[10]

Another indication that the Republicans had chosen the "sharply ideological" self-image was the pressure on GOP committee chairs to support party positions. Because chairs are determined by seniority, in a number of instances these senators were more moderate than the Republican Conference generally. For example, when Mark Hatfield of Oregon, chairman of the Appropriations Committee, provided the deciding vote against the constitutional amendment to require a balanced federal budget—and was the only GOP senator to oppose it—his party tried to strip him of his chairmanship. There is speculation whether moderate Jim Jeffords, R-Vt., who is next in line to be chair of the Labor and Human Resources Committee, will be allowed by the conference to take the post in the Republican-controlled Senate.[11]

The Republican Conference chose not to take a formal vote on the effort to depose Hatfield, but at the meeting where the vote was scheduled to take place a number of GOP freshmen suggested "that the leadership look at ways to strengthen its authority over Members on key votes."[12] In response, Dole appointed a task force—chaired by conference secretary Connie Mack of Florida—to study possible rules changes. The task force proposed a variety of ideas, many of which were adopted. These included six-year term limits on committee chairs and a restriction on their also chairing subcommittees and similar term limits on all leaders except the party leader and the president pro tempore. Also passed were secret-ballot votes on proposed committee chairs, both among committee Republicans and in the full conference, and a plan to adopt a formal GOP agenda at the beginning of each Congress (before the votes on committee chairs). The task force also proposed permitting their leader to nominate committee chairs and to appoint a senator to a committee when two or more vacancies occurred, but those ideas were defeated.[13]

Despite those setbacks, the new rules mark an important move in equalizing power among senior and more junior Republican members and in strengthening the impact of the party organization on the behavior of committee chairs. Because of the increased partisanship between the parties and the increased homogeneity within them, the patterns of policy making in the Senate have become noticeably different from those of earlier decades.

Norms and Rules

The Senate is a decision-making institution, and as such it has extensive formal rules that regulate its activities. It is also a collection of individuals, and "just as any other group of human beings, it has its unwritten rules of the game, its norms of conduct, its approved manner of behavior."[14] While there has been significant continuity in the Senate's formal and informal rules over the last forty years, major changes also have occurred.

The unwritten rules, or norms, of the Senate are patterns of behavior senators think the body's members ought to follow. In established organizations, most members share similar expectations about some aspects of behavior. In an institution that permits great leeway in the written rules for its members' behavior, these norms can be very important. Matthews, in his study of the Senate in the mid-1950s, cited six norms or "folkways": legislative work, specialization, courtesy, reciprocity, institutional patriotism, and apprenticeship.

The first norm required that senators devote a major portion of their time to their legislative duties in committees and on the floor, and not seek personal publicity at the expense of these legislative obligations. Under the second norm, specialization, each senator was expected to concentrate on matters pertaining to his or her committee business or directly affecting constituents. The courtesy norm required that political conflicts within the Senate not become personal conflicts. References to colleagues in legislative situations should be formal and respectful, and personal attacks were deemed unacceptable. Reciprocity, the fourth folkway, meant that senators were expected to help colleagues whenever possible and were to avoid pressing their formal powers too far (for example, by systematically objecting to unanimous consent agreements). A senator was to understand the problems of colleagues, and to keep bargains once they were struck. The fifth norm of institutional patriotism required that a member protect the Senate as an institution, avoiding behavior that would bring it or its members into disrepute. Finally, new senators were expected to serve a period of apprenticeship, waiting a substantial amount of time before participating fully in the work of the Senate. During this time, freshmen were to learn about the Senate and seek the advice of senior members.

Many of these folkways provided benefits to the collective membership, and it is not surprising that some of them are still recognized in the Senate today. But, as patterns of power and ambition inside and outside the Senate have changed, both normative expectations and the degree to which they are observed changed as well. During the 1960s and 1970s, the frequency of behavior that seemed to violate the norms increased, and by the 1980s a number of them had disappeared as expectations or had become significantly altered. As Barbara Sinclair concluded from her analysis of Senate change, "Both in terms of expectations and behavior, the norms of apprenticeship, specialization, and legislative work are defunct; reciprocity and institutional patriotism have undergone major changes; courtesy is still a Senate norm but is more frequently breached in practice."[15]

Expansion in the size and scope of the federal government provided electoral incentives for senators to become involved in a wide range of issues, a tendency that was reinforced in many instances by their personal policy interests. This trend undermined the norm of specialization. Both Sinclair and Steven S. Smith have shown that the percentage of floor amendments coming from senators who were not members of the committee of jurisdiction has risen somewhat.[16] This increase, moreover, occurred at a time when the committee assignments of senators had grown. In terms of expectations, Sinclair drew the following conclusion from her interview data: "That a senator will be broadly involved in a number of issues, some of which do not fall within the jurisdiction of his committees, is taken as a matter of course."[17]

Even before the specialization norm disappeared, senators had ceased to expect junior members to serve a period of apprenticeship. This norm had provided little benefit to the general membership; rather, it was a way for the senior conservatives of both parties, who dominated the institution's positions of power, to control the behavior of the more liberal junior members. Beginning with the 1958 election, liberal northern Democrats entered the Senate in greater numbers, and the conservative dominance began to decline. Consequently, junior members had less incentive to observe the norm; and, as these members gained seniority, the expectations regarding apprenticeship became less widely shared.

The Republican gains of the late 1970s and early 1980s brought a resurgence of conservative influence, but the new members had no interest in restoring the norm of apprenticeship. Instead, they had electoral and policy interests in quickly attempting to reverse the liberals' legislative gains over the previous two decades. Interviews at that time showed that junior senators felt no need to serve an apprenticeship, nor did senior members expect them to do so. For example, a junior Republican said, "Well, that [apprenticeship] doesn't exist at all in the Senate. The senior senators have made that very clear, both Democrats and

Republicans." A senior conservative GOP senator agreed: "We now hope and expect and encourage the younger guys to dive right into the middle of it."[18]

This pattern of immediate, extensive participation by new members persists in the Senate of the 1990s, as was demonstrated by the active role played by the eleven GOP freshmen elected in 1994. They organized the "Freshman Focus," which sought to increase the visibility of important parts of the Republican agenda though twice-weekly speeches by their group.[19] Collectively and individually they pursued a wide variety of legislative initiatives, including constitutional amendments to impose term limits and to require a balanced budget. Many observers believe that the freshmen's vigorous approach stems from the fact that six of them came directly from the House, where they were used to a more combative and partisan approach to legislating. One of the former representatives, Rick Santorum of Pennsylvania, was the original proponent of the idea of stripping Hatfield of his chairmanship. Santorum showed that his view of his role was antithetical to apprenticeship: "I have a lot of respect for Mark Hatfield and the service he's provided for this country, but he's an equal to me—in that we're both United States senators. I have every right to be heard and make things happen as much as anybody else."[20]

Santorum's remark demonstrates that the Senate in the 1990s, considered along seniority lines, is a more egalitarian institution than it used to be. Junior members play important roles, and this change in the Senate's informal rule structure has contributed to alterations in the formal rules. In 1970, for example, a rule was adopted that limited members to service on only one of the Senate's four most prestigious committees: Appropriations, Armed Services, Finance, and Foreign Relations. The limit prevented senior members from monopolizing these important committee posts and made it easier for junior senators to receive appointments to them earlier in their careers. Over the last twenty-five years, both parties adopted measures limiting the role of seniority in the selection of committee chairs, and, as we mentioned, in 1995 Senate Republicans imposed term limits on chairs and barred committee chairs from also heading a subcommittee.

In the 1960s, as junior members became more active, they began to feel more intensely the disparity of resources between themselves and senior senators, particularly with regard to staff. These members sponsored a resolution, adopted in 1975, that permitted them to hire additional legislative staff to assist in their committee duties. Although the Senate cut back its spending on staff in 1995, the distribution of funds is more equal across the membership than it was in the late 1960s.

Changes in the amount and distribution of staff resources among members also helped to undermine another folkway: legislative work. In the Senate of the 1950s, when members had relatively little staff, members did the "great bulk of the Senate's work [that] is highly detailed, dull and politically unrewarding."[21] The wide dispersion of substantial staff resources made this type of work less necessary; and senators could devote more time to other matters, including the pressures of electoral competition and its accompanying demand of fund-raising.

In addition, several members sought their party's presidential nomination—in 1995 and 1996 Phil Gramm of Texas, Richard Lugar of Indiana, and Arlen Specter of Pennsylvania, in addition to Dole—or they sought the media attention that would, they hoped, make a candidacy possible. These pursuits further reduced the time available for detailed legislative work.

Regarding the norm of institutional patriotism, members are still interested in protecting the Senate's reputation and integrity. This interest is intensified by the recurrence of partisan division (and, therefore, of institutional competition) between the Senate and the presidency. However, the period of partisan division between the House and Senate in the 1980s and the negative attitudes of the public toward Congress have made it easier for senators to criticize the Senate.

The courtesy norm also continues to serve the interests of members, but it too is violated more frequently than in the past. Courtesy permits political conflict to remain depersonalized, allowing yesterday's opponent to be tomorrow's ally. As one Republican senator said, "It's the catalyst that maintains a semblance of order." The ideological divisions in the contemporary Senate, however, have frequently pitted one or more of the extreme liberals or the staunch conservatives against their colleagues on the opposite side in public and often bitter exchanges. These personal conflicts also occur within partisan or ideological groups. For example, William S. Cohen, R-Maine, reported that Lowell P. Weicker, R-Conn., responded to a statement by John Heinz, R-Pa., by saying, "Anyone who would make such a statement is either devious or an idiot. The gentleman from Pennsylvania qualifies on both counts."[22]

More intense partisan conflict over legislation has increased the frequency and intensity of verbal departures from the courtesy norm. For example, in February 1995, Sen. Robert C. Byrd, D-W.Va.—himself a former Senate majority leader—labeled a motion by Majority Leader Dole to recess the Senate while he sought one more vote to pass a GOP measure as a "sleazy, tawdry effort" to save the proposal.[23] On the other side of the fence, Byrd complained in December about statements by two Republicans that charged that President Clinton was deliberately lying with regard to disputes over balancing the federal budget. Senator Mack said that Clinton "broke his word," and Senator Santorum claimed that the president was telling "bald-faced untruths" and that Democratic senators were portraying GOP tax cuts as targeted to the wealthy "when they know that is a lie." Byrd asked whether "civility and common courtesy and reasonableness [had] taken leave of this chamber." Mack, serving his second term, subsequently apologized to the Senate, but freshman Santorum did not. Byrd, he said, "is entitled to his opinion and I am entitled to mine. . . . I was sent here by the people of Pennsylvania who want me to push for big changes. I intend to continue."[24]

Under the final norm, reciprocity, it was expected that members would not press their individual prerogatives too far. During the past three decades the Senate has seen, despite its benefits to the institution, more frequent violations of this folkway as well. The Senate's expanding workload and the increase in amending activity on the floor led to substantial pressures on floor time.[25] This altered context, in turn, created strategic opportunities for opponents of legislation to use filibusters (extended debate to prevent a proposal from coming to a vote) to extract concessions from a bill's supporters, especially late in a session when the press of legislation is greatest. More frequent use of the filibuster in the early 1970s resulted in a change in the number of votes required to formally end debate, a procedure called cloture, from two-thirds of those present and voting (sixty-seven votes for the full Senate) to three-fifths of the entire membership or sixty votes. In the years immediately after the rules change, cloture was more often sought and imposed than in earlier years.[26]

During the 1980s, however, the advent of a Republican majority and growing partisanship within the Senate increased the inclination of members to use filibusters, and the tactic often succeeded. Barbara Sinclair analyzed the thirty-seven filibusters waged between 1981 and 1986. She found that fifteen "ultimately rendered the Senate's decision on the measure at issue more favorable to the filibusterers than it would have been otherwise. When the chance of having an impact is 40 percent, the incentives to engage in extended debate are obvious."[27] Moreover, the frequency and success of filibusters made even the threat of one an important bargaining chip in the legislative struggle. To keep the schedule of legislation on track, Senate leaders had to rely more often on unanimous consent agreements among the members before bringing a major bill to the floor. Such agreements usually specify the length of time for debate, the time of a final vote, and the amendments that may be considered. Because the agreements must be unanimous, to secure them leaders often have to make concessions to a bill's opponents.[28]

The restoration of a Democratic Senate majority in the 1986 election increased Republican conservatives' incentives to use their individual prerogatives to block liberal initiatives. Christopher Bailey noted, "A small group of 'New Right' senators believed that obstructionism was not only a right, but a duty. Sen. Jake Garn, R-Utah, summed up this attitude when he stated: 'If I'm against a bill in committee, I try to keep it there. If I can slow down a mark-up, or find some tactic to keep it off the floor, I'll do it. . . . I don't particularly have a loyalty to tradition.'"[29] In the 1990s, as majority control shifted again, both parties and both ends of the ideological spectrum found the filibuster useful, so it was employed more often. In the last week of the Senate's session before the 1994 election, the body took seven cloture votes on six different legislative measures, as the GOP made a maximum effort to block Democratic proposals. (The Senate agreed to four of the motions for cloture.) With the Republicans back in the majority in 1995, the Democrats frequently used filibusters to delay Republican initiatives and extract concessions. There were cloture votes on five different measures during the first hundred days of the 104th Congress; only one was successful, and that was unanimous.

One result of these changes in Senate norms and behavior has been frequent calls to alter the institution's rules to deal with their consequences. In the 103d

Congress (1993–1994), the House and Senate created a Joint Committee on the Organization of Congress. It recommended a number of changes in separate reports for the two houses. Among the Senate recommendations were proposals to adopt a two-year budget cycle, streamline floor procedures, and reduce the size of some committees. However, efforts to bring the bill to the floor late in 1994 were blocked by a minority of senators. At the beginning of the 104th Congress, two Democrats, Tom Harkin of Iowa and Joseph Lieberman of Connecticut, proposed a four-step procedure on efforts to obtain cloture, with the number of votes required dropping at each step, from sixty to fifty-one. The proposal was tabled (killed), however, on a 77–19 vote. Too many senators in both parties regarded their own interest in being able to block legislation through a filibuster to be more important than the benefits that would flow from making it easier to pass bills.

It is also important to remember that the rules of the full Senate are not the only consequential rules the body has. Each party regulates its own activities, and—as we pointed out—the Senate GOP adopted some important changes in their conference's rules in 1995. The Senate's norms and rules, and the patterns of behavior they relate to, continue to evolve as the individual incentives and preferences of members also change. The Senate is not only more egalitarian and open than it was but also more partisan and conflictive.

Leadership

The formal leadership of legislatures often determines the policy directions taken, modified, or rejected. In the U.S. Senate, party leadership can determine the degree of partisan conflict or consensus, the success or failure a president has in relating to the Senate, and the efficiency or slowness with which the nation's policy agenda is considered. The 1995–1996 budget impasse is an example of how contentious such matters can become.

The top party leaders, especially the majority and minority leaders, are selected in secret-ballot votes by their party colleagues in caucus or conferences. Who they are and how and why they are selected can reveal a great deal about the nature of the Senate over the past several decades. Matthews's classic analysis, *U.S. Senators and Their World,* continues to provide a historical baseline for analyzing Senate party leadership in the post–World War II era. "Democratic party leadership," he argued, "is highly personalized, informal, centralized in the hands of the floor leader." In contrast, "even when compared to a Democratic party under a relatively weak leader, the Republican leadership is more formalized, institutionalized and decentralized."[30] These generalizations about differences between the two Senate party leadership structures held up remarkably well through the 1970s, although they underwent considerable modification in the 1980s and 1990s.

When Robert Byrd was elected majority leader in December 1977, he also presided over committee assignments as chairman of the Democratic Steering Committee, directed party strategy and the scheduling of legislation as chairman of the Democratic Policy Committee, and presided over the Democratic caucus, which includes all senators elected under the Democratic banner. Authority was concentrated in his hands. When George Mitchell of Maine won a three-way contest for majority leader in 1988, he not only rewarded his followers but also reached out to his rivals. For example, he appointed Sen. Daniel K. Inouye of Hawaii, his most senior rival, as chairman of the Steering Committee. He also appointed freshman senator Tom Daschle of South Dakota as co-chairman of the Democratic Policy Committee. Mitchell continued to serve as chairman of his party's caucus. Mitchell's turning to Daschle demonstrated his willingness to share party leadership with junior members, some fifteen to eighteen of whom had been crucial to his election as majority leader.

Mitchell's sharing power did not signal weakness or lack of desire to assert his power as majority leader. In keeping with Senate Democratic efforts to show an assertive and partisan presence in the face of continued Republican dominance of the White House, from 1989 to late 1992 Mitchell served as a major spokesman for the Democratic Party, especially as a counterpoint to President Bush. He also used his position as majority leader to help shape a policy agenda during President Clinton's first two years, 1993–1995.

In contrast to the Democrats' flexible organization, Senate Republicans, whether in the majority or in the minority, divide their leadership into seven offices. They are floor leader, assistant floor leader (or whip), chairman of the Republican Policy Committee, chairman of the Republican Conference, secretary of the conference, chairman of the National Republican Senatorial Committee, and chairman of the Republican Committee on Committees. These offices are frequently contested. The one exception is the chairman of the Committee on Committees, who is appointed by the chairman of the Republican Conference after consultation with the floor leader.

Because of the differences in organizational style, Senate Democrats have, in most cases, greater potential for strong, concentrated leadership than do Senate Republicans. Even so, Democrat Mike Mansfield of Montana, who served as majority leader longer—from 1961 to 1977—than anyone in the history of the Senate, was among the least assertive of Senate floor leaders. Strong GOP leaders such as Robert A. Taft of Ohio (1953), Everett McKinley Dirksen of Illinois (1959–1969), Howard Baker of Tennessee (1977–1985), and Robert Dole (1985–1996) were able to centralize power and transform the contributions of lesser party officers into mainly supportive roles.[31]

Two other formal Senate leadership positions, both constitutionally designated, require brief mention. First, the vice president of the United States is also president of the Senate but has "no vote unless [the Senate] be equally divided." (Article I, section 3, paragraph 4.) In the absence of the vice president, the president pro tempore or a designee presides over the Senate. By long tradition, the president pro tempore is the most senior member of the majority party; after Republicans regained control following the 1994 midterm elections, the venerable Strom Thurmond of South Carolina took over the position. The usual practice is for members of the majority party to take turns presiding over the Senate in fifteen-minute to half-hour stints.

From the early 1950s through the mid-1990s, five men, Lyndon Johnson (1953–1961), Mansfield (1961–1977), Byrd (1977–1989), Mitchell (1989–1995), and Daschle (1993–), served as Democratic floor leaders in the Senate. Except for Johnson in his first two years, Byrd (who had a mid-career minority stint), and Daschle, they all served only as majority leader. In contrast, the six Republican floor leaders, Taft (1953), William Knowland of California (1953–1959), Dirksen (1959–1969), Hugh Scott of Pennsylvania (1969–1977), Baker (1977–1985), and Dole (1985–1996), have frequently had to compensate for minority status and the inability to move their legislation unless they could persuade Democratic senators to cross over. This prolonged minority status—all but the 83d Congress (1953–1955), the 97th through 99th Congresses (1981–1987), and the 104th Congress (1995–1997)—has been substantially offset, however, by Republican control of the White House under Presidents Eisenhower, Nixon, Ford, Reagan, and Bush. Because presidents mostly set the legislative agenda, even Senate minority leaders of the president's party can play pivotal roles.

Democrats Johnson, Mansfield, and Byrd

The mid- to late 1950s are remembered as years of strong, individual leaders in the Senate—especially Johnson in the majority and Knowland and Dirksen in the minority. As observers have noted, their floor leadership helped to centralize what was a much "flatter" hierarchy, with power more evenly distributed, compared with that of the House.[32] Even incoming freshmen of the majority party were likely to obtain a subcommittee chairmanship. With the election results of 1958, which brought in large Democratic majorities, Johnson's ability to persuade (if not to strong-arm) his fellow Democrats suffered. All congressional leaders have to rely heavily on persuasion, one-on-one.

In 1960, after John Kennedy and Johnson were elected president and vice president, respectively, the Democrats promoted Majority Whip Mansfield to succeed Johnson as floor leader. Austere, highly intelligent, a conciliator by temperament, Mansfield found it difficult to be unpleasant to any of his colleagues. He was much more interested in influencing foreign policy (from a continuing position on the Foreign Relations Committee) than in establishing a tight rein over the Kennedy-Johnson legislative programs. In general, Mansfield backed off from exercising the power he had inherited until 1966, when he began to take issue with President Johnson's Vietnam War policies. His style of leadership also reflected the independent and decentralized trends that characterized the Senate of the 1960s and 1970s. Mansfield's gentle leadership was complemented by the equally gentlemanly style of the moderate minority leader, Hugh Scott. In 1977 both leaders retired from the Senate after forty years or more of congressional service.

Even before this, the counterrevolution in Senate norms was under way. In the early 1970s senators on both sides of the aisle had begun to complain about a lack of formal direction. Byrd, who had won the whip position by upsetting the Chappaquiddick-plagued Edward Kennedy of Massachusetts in 1971, succeeded Mansfield as floor leader in 1977. Almost immediately, he set out to restore the floor leader's traditional position of dominance. Still, there would be no return to Johnson's concentrated leadership style. As Byrd commented in a 1979 interview:

> I could not lead the Senate as Johnson did . . . Johnson could not lead this Senate [the 96th]. These are different times. He had cohesive blocs; he had the southern senators. When Johnson was the majority leader, both senators from Texas were Democrats; both senators from Virginia, from South Carolina, and so on. Now you have a host of Republican senators from the South. The members are younger now, they tend to be more independent. We are living in different times.[33]

If Byrd lacked Johnson's dominating techniques of personal persuasion, he was nevertheless a master of parliamentary procedure and indefatigable in attending to legislative detail. Above all, he looked after the day-to-day needs of other senators, Republicans as well as Democrats.

Republican Howard Baker

While Byrd was ascending to the floor leadership in January 1977, minority Republicans were having their own leadership contests. Robert Griffin of Michigan, the incumbent whip since 1959, was considered the favorite, but he was defeated in a last-minute challenge by Howard Baker on a 19–18 vote. In 1980 Republican senatorial candidates piggybacked the Reagan electoral victory and won control of the Senate for the first time since 1954.

Sidestepping a possible challenge from the right after the Republican surge, Baker and his assistant floor leader, Ted Stevens of Alaska, advanced to majority status in their posts. In the 97th and 98th Congresses (1981–1985), Baker demonstrated considerable legislative acumen working closely with President Reagan and his White House staff. In January 1983, however, after sixteen years in the Senate, the last six as Republican floor leader, Baker announced he would retire at the end of the term. His plans were to join a law firm and give strong consideration to running for the presidency himself. Baker's bid for the Republican nomination for the presidency in 1988 was set aside, however, when President Reagan, plagued by the Iran-contra scandal, selected him to become White House chief of staff.

Republican Robert Dole

In the elections of 1984, despite Reagan's landslide victory over former vice president Walter Mondale, Senate Republicans suffered a net loss of two seats.

They returned to Washington in November to organize and select a replacement for Baker. The campaign to succeed him had gone on for nearly two years, ever since he announced he would retire. Two strong contenders emerged: Ted Stevens, the assistant majority leader, who had served under Baker since 1977, and Bob Dole, a vice-presidential candidate on the Ford ticket in 1976 and chairman of the powerful Senate Finance Committee since 1981. Three other senators with less seniority also declared their candidacies: James A. McClure of Idaho, chairman of the Energy and Natural Resources Committee; Pete V. Domenici of New Mexico, chairman of the Budget Committee; and Richard Lugar, chairman of the National Republican Senatorial Committee.

In November 1984 Senate Republicans, fifty-three members strong, elected Dole as their majority leader for the 99th Congress (1985–1987). Dole won on the fourth secret ballot over Stevens, 28–25. On earlier votes, first McClure, then Domenici, and finally Lugar were eliminated on a "low-man out" procedure. Never before in the history of the Senate had as many candidates competed in a single contest for floor leadership in either party.

As is true for all party leadership contests, Dole won for a combination of reasons. Chief among them were his national prominence, the Finance Committee chairmanship, and his media skills. In selecting Dole, Senate Republicans clearly wanted a more assertive and independent leader, freer from White House influence and less conciliatory than Baker. Senate Republicans knew that the 1986 elections, when their class of 1980 would be up for reelection, would be the major test of their majority status. They wanted a leader who would protect their interests and would be an attractive public spokesman and an aggressive legislative tactician. The volatile, sometimes hot-tempered Stevens filled the latter requirements, but Dole was seen by a majority of his colleagues as having a better combination of traits beneficial to Republican senatorial goals.

Throughout the 99th Congress, Dole had the delicate task of demonstrating his assertiveness without excessively antagonizing the White House or plunging Senate Republicans into further disarray. In May 1985, for example, he won a dramatic late-night, one-vote victory on the budget by having Sen. Pete Wilson (later governor of California) brought from the hospital and wheeled onto the floor, intravenous hookup and all, to achieve a tie vote. The tie gave Vice President Bush the opportunity to cast the winning vote for the Republican plan.

Picking his issues carefully, usually siding with the president, but sometimes opposing his programs or seeking modifications, Dole won a number of legislative battles. Despite taking every opportunity to put Republican freshmen forward, Dole's intensive campaign efforts in behalf of his colleagues fell short of the mark in the 1986 elections. Democratic candidates picked up nine of the twenty-two contested seats held by Republicans and lost only one of their own seats. After six uneasy years in the minority, Democrats once again controlled the Senate, this time by a 55–45 margin.

Marked by intense partisanship and increasing legislative stalemate, the 100th Congress (1987–1989) was also characterized by speculation about who would be the two major party presidential nominees in 1988. When Dole, a major contender, lost to Bush in the critical New Hampshire primary, he resumed his Senate leadership post. Meanwhile, Byrd, who had served as Democratic floor leader (majority or minority) since 1977, announced in April 1988 that, although he would seek his sixth Senate term, he did not want to be reelected majority leader. Instead, at the urging of his West Virginia constituents, he would opt for the chairmanship of the Senate Appropriations Committee and take over the position of president pro tempore. His decision set in motion an intense three-way competition for the majority leader position.

Democrat George Mitchell

Three Senate Democrats sought to replace Byrd as majority leader: Daniel Inouye, first elected to the Senate in 1962; J. Bennett Johnston of Louisiana, first elected in 1972; and George Mitchell, a relative newcomer, appointed to the Senate in May 1980. Mitchell replaced Edmund Muskie, who had resigned to become President Carter's secretary of state.

Fifty-five Democrats entered the Democratic Conference in mid-December 1988 before the 101st Congress convened. A majority of twenty-eight would secure election. Mitchell won handily, with twenty-seven first ballot votes to fourteen each for his two opponents. Johnston immediately moved to make the election unanimous, a motion seconded by Inouye. Why did Mitchell, with only eight years of Senate experience, win so handily? First, his opponents probably split the votes of most senior Democrats. Second, Mitchell, as chair of the Democratic Senatorial Campaign Committee (DSCC), had led his party to impressive victories in the 1986 elections. Two senators acknowledged, in independent interviews, that as many as nine of the eleven incoming freshmen voted for Mitchell, who promised reforms to improve the "quality of life" of Senate members. But as important as anything else was the sense that Mitchell would be the strongest public spokesman for the Democratic majority. As the party out of the White House, Democrats wanted a leader who could be an attractive and persuasive counterweight to the Republican president. At the same time, they wanted a senator who would personify an image of the Senate and its Democratic majority as judicious, reasonable, and forward looking. The "inside" skills that mattered most in selecting earlier leaders such as Johnson and Byrd were less significant in an era of divided government and more intense television coverage. Despite his junior status, Mitchell fit these leadership requirements best, in the eyes of a majority of his colleagues.

Through the 101st and 102d Congresses (1989–1993) Mitchell and Dole generally worked well together, although they had their share of conflict. Much more than in the partisan and fractional House of Representatives, Senate leaders with lesser formal powers are dependent upon one another, especially in matters of legislative scheduling. In the 103d Congress, with a Democrat in the White House, Dole became less cooperative, especially as he began to maneuver for the 1996 Republican presidential nomination. Then in the 104th Congress, with Republicans controlling both houses, intense partisanship became the norm. By late 1995, President Clinton began to use his veto powers as Republicans fought for a seven-year balanced-budget commitment.

Democrat Thomas Daschle

Tom Daschle served four terms as a mainstream Democratic liberal in the House (1979–1987) before he was elected to the Senate in 1986. Daschle got there by beating James Abdnor, a legendary farmer and former House member who was elected in the Reagan sweep in 1980, but was no match for Daschle's youth and vigor six years later. Beholden to DSCC Chairman Mitchell for financial support in 1986, Daschle became one of Mitchell's prime supporters in the 1988 contest for Senate majority leader. As noted, Mitchell appointed Daschle co-chairman of the Democratic Policy Committee. Daschle quickly became a Mitchell favorite and confidant and an integral part of the leadership team.

When Mitchell opted to retire in 1994, Daschle became locked in an intensive year-long leadership struggle with James R. Sasser of Tennessee, chairman of the Budget Committee. Eleven years older than Daschle, with three terms behind him, Sasser was upset in the 1994 Republican sweep. A bid by Connecticut's Christopher C. Dodd, backed by Byrd and other senior Democrats, came within one vote of upsetting Daschle's candidacy. Dodd settled for the consolation prize of Democratic National Committee chair. With no opposition, sixty-four-year-old Wendell H. Ford of Kentucky retained his position as Senate Democratic party whip.

Daschle got off to a shaky start as Senate minority leader, partly because of his relative youth, lack of seniority, and his close margin of victory. His early days were marred by a charge of political favoritism back home. Weathering these media criticisms, Daschle began to make more of his uneasy position as spokesman for forty-five disparate colleagues and a "centrist" Democratic president. His task was far from easy. Nevertheless, by the end of the first year of the Republican-controlled 104th Congress, Daschle was rallying his troops rather effectively. At times he mobilized them to block cloture; at other times he cooperated with Dole.

As the first session of the 104th Congress built to a climax, the Democrats, often working closely with six or seven Republican moderates, were strategically placed to offer important amendments to major GOP-proposed reforms on Medicare, Medicaid, and the deficit limit, and to frustrate efforts to achieve a balanced budget on Republican terms. By the end of the year, there was deadlock over the budget, and nearly 300,000 federal workers were furloughed. Daschle devised a Democratic plan that would produce a balanced budget in seven years using Congressional Budget Office numbers. President Clinton embraced the plan, which enabled him to trump the congressional Republicans. Daschle's deft parliamentary maneuvering also forced Dole to withdraw an immigration bill from the Senate floor, and consequently to endorse a plan to vote on a proposal to increase the minimum wage. Maintaining strong party unity in the minority, using the Senate rules to great advantage, and securing a good working relationship with the White House, by the second session of the 104th Congress, Daschle had become an extremely effective legislative leader.

The presidential election of 1996 brought one more change to the Senate leadership. When Dole resigned to campaign full-time for the presidency, the Senate GOP chose Whip Trent Lott over fellow Mississippian Thad Cochran to replace him. As we noted, Lott had been a Gingrich ally in the House and had advocated a more aggressive partisanship in the Senate than was Dole's style. Some observers wondered whether Lott's selection might augur an even more partisan Senate that would mirror the confrontational House. Commenting on this speculation, Lott said: "We will work very hard to have a good relationship with the House. . . . I do have friends there. But we will in no way try to make the Senate like the House."[34]

Committees

From its earliest days, the U.S. Senate, like the House of Representatives, has used a division of labor in a committee system to organize its work. The committee system remains the single most important feature affecting legislative outcomes in the Senate; and, not surprisingly, it has changed as other aspects of the Senate—workload, membership, power—have changed.

Committee Assignments

Shortly after being sworn in, each senator is assigned to several committees. When vacancies occur on attractive committees, senators can switch assignments. The assignment process and the selection of committee and subcommittee chairs are crucial to the Senate: they can determine the policy orientation and activity of the committees, and they are pivotal in the career directions of individual senators.

The two parties handle their members' assignments differently. The Republicans have a nine-member Committee on Committees, including the majority leader as an ex officio member and with an elected chairman—in the 104th Congress, Larry Craig of Idaho. The Democrats use a twenty-five member—more than half their members—Steering and Coordination Committee, chaired in the 104th Congress by John Kerry of Massachusetts, who was appointed to the post by Minority Leader Daschle. The parties also have different procedures for filling their slots on committees. Republicans use a system based firmly on seniority: when a vacancy occurs, Republican senators, in order of seniority, are given the option of filling it, consistent with other assignment limitations. Democrats take seniority into account, but are more flexible in filling their slots.

In many ways, committee assignments exhibit important aspects of the broader institution. In the 1940s and early 1950s committee assignments reflected the apprenticeship norm, with freshmen assigned only to minor committees. When Lyndon Johnson became majority leader in 1955, he instituted the "Johnson Rule," which guaranteed every Democrat, no matter how junior, a major committee assignment. Johnson, however, ran the Steering Committee as a one-man show, personally controlling the assignments. Under Mansfield the process became more democratic, with assignments to all committees becoming more open to junior and liberal Democrats. But because of the importance members attach to committee posts, the process frequently generated attempts to give more of a say to the Democratic membership as a whole.

After Byrd announced that he would step down as Democratic leader before the 101st Congress convened, the contenders for the post began to discuss the option of doing as the Republicans historically have done, separating the party leader position from the chairmanships of the Steering and Policy committees. Mitchell accomplished this reform in December 1988, and, although the committees' names and functions have changed, the separation of responsibilities continues under Daschle.

The Republicans' process of relying more automatically on seniority created some stresses and strains when they took the majority in the Senate in 1980. Despite the huge freshman class (sixteen) that rivaled the 1958 Democratic group, the change in party ratios on committees did not allow for many vacancies on the blue-chip committees such as Finance and Armed Services. Within a few years, however, junior members were able to move up. With election changes and turnover, Senate committees moved in a more conservative direction. The Democratic recapture of the Senate in 1986 swung the makeup of the committees back to the liberal side, but they changed again in 1994 with the Republicans in the majority. As in 1980, ideological shifts were accentuated by the large freshman class, in this case a dozen members who were all Republican and nearly all staunchly conservative.

The ideological changes between the 103d Senate, with a Democratic majority, and the 104th Senate, run by the Republicans, were particularly pronounced on the Environment and Labor Committees, with the freshmen providing the impetus. While none of the freshmen secured assignments on the powerful money committees of Appropriations or Finance, three won assignments to the Budget Committee along with two to Commerce, Science, and Transportation; five to Foreign Relations; four to Judiciary; and four to Labor and Human Resources, increasing the ideological polarization especially on the latter three panels.

Chairmanships

For many decades, no matter which party is in the majority, Senate committee chairmanships and ranking minority memberships have been selected through the process of seniority, even though there are no formal requirements for seniority to rule. The process is not entirely clear and consistent, however. Because some senators with longevity become senior on more than one committee, they can choose which one to chair, creating an occasional pattern of musical chairs. In the 100th Congress, for example, Edward Kennedy chose the Labor and Human Resources Committee chairmanship over that of the Judiciary Committee, which he had chaired in the late 1970s. Kennedy's move enabled Joseph R. Biden Jr. of Delaware to take over Judiciary and blocked Howard Metzenbaum of Ohio from chairing Labor. Kennedy did not make his choice either to help Biden or hinder Metzenbaum, but his choice shaped the agendas and directions of the two committees.

In 1981 conservative Republicans persuaded Strom Thurmond to choose the Judiciary Committee chairmanship over that of Armed Services, where he was also senior, specifically to keep liberal Charles Mathias, R-Md., from assuming the Judiciary reins. In 1993 Thurmond reasserted his seniority on Armed Services to become ranking member there, unseating John Warner of Virginia from that position; and Thurmond chose to keep Armed Services after the Republican takeover of the Senate in the 1994 elections, becoming chairman there and leaving Warner without a leadership post when the 104th Congress began. (Warner got a chairmanship, that of the Senate Rules Committee, when Bob Packwood's resignation in 1995 caused a round of musical chairs among Senate committees: William Roth of Delaware took Packwood's position as chair of the Finance Committee; Ted Stevens then replaced Roth as chair of Governmental Affairs; and Warner replaced Stevens as chair of Rules.)

The seniority process became particularly controversial for Republicans after the 1986 election. Jesse Helms, the ultraconservative senior Republican on both Agriculture and Foreign Relations, had chosen for constituency reasons to chair Agriculture in the 99th Congress, leaving Foreign Relations to the more junior and more moderate Lugar. But after the Republicans lost the Senate in 1986, Helms decided to assert his seniority rights and make the switch to become the ranking Republican on Foreign Relations. Lugar, who had been an effective and well-respected chairman, vigorously contested Helms. Despite the sharp ideological differences between the two, the overriding issue became the sanctity of the seniority system. Liberal Republican Lowell Weicker, afraid of what breaking the seniority precedent would do to his own future chances of chairing the Appropriations Committee, came out publicly for his arch foe Helms, as did several other senior Republicans, both moderates and liberals. Helms won, solidifying the seniority principle in the GOP.

A different kind of challenge to the principle came early in the 104th Congress. Mark Hatfield, the liberal Republican chairman of the Appropriations Committee, voted against a constitutional amendment to balance the budget—the only one of the fifty-four Republicans to do so—and the proposal went down to defeat by a single vote. Outraged conservatives, including freshman senator Rick Santorum, along with the more senior Connie Mack, demanded that sanctions be applied to Hatfield, including removing him from the Appropriations chairmanship for defying a clear party priority. But most Republican senators, including Dole, fearing the precedent of punishing a chairman for a vote of conscience, declined to take any action. The possibility that Hatfield might be challenged for the chairmanship in the next Congress evaporated when several weeks later Hatfield announced his retirement, effective at the end of the 104th Congress.

The preference for seniority over ideology held true in the Senate for Democrats in the 1970s, for Republicans during their majority status from 1981 through 1986, for the Democrats again in the 100th through the 103d Congresses, and for the Republicans again in the 104th. In the House, by contrast, during the 1989–1991 period, several chairmen were forced out of their positions for being too old, conservative, or passive; and, when the Republicans secured their first majority in forty years for the 104th Congress, Gingrich, the new Speaker, conspicuously bypassed several senior members for chairmanships of committees, including Appropriations, Commerce, and Judiciary.

The decentralization of the power structure of the Senate—in the 104th Congress 82 percent of majority senators chaired at least one subcommittee or committee—contributed to the chamber's friendly attitude toward the seniority process. But one effect of seniority was to skew powerful chairmanships toward members who were not broadly representative of the overall majority. In both periods of Republican majority, in the 1980s and 1990s, the seniority process limited the effectiveness of the conservative trend in American politics and within the Senate. The senior majority members in the Republican Senate in 1981 and in 1995 were less conservative than their colleagues: nearly half the major committee chairs, including Appropriations and Foreign Relations in the 97th Congress, and Appropriations, Finance, Labor and Human Resources, and Environment and Public Works in the 104th, were less conservative than their committee colleagues.

Workload

With its small membership, the Senate is profoundly affected by its workload.[35] The 1960s and 1970s saw that workload burgeon, leading to calls for reform, some of them successful. Although the workload stabilized and in some ways even declined in the 1980s, senators' level of satisfaction with their output and lifestyle deteriorated—leading to more calls for reform. The early 1990s saw an uptick in activity, which turned into a torrent in the first session of the 104th Congress. But the hyperactivity in the first part of the 104th Congress did not translate into many public laws or other enactments. Overworked and undernourished, a particularly large group of senators opted out via voluntary retirement, with a number of them suggesting the need for fundamental change in the way the Senate does its business.

Increases in Senate workload were particularly striking in the early 1970s. There were five times as many roll call votes on the Senate floor in the 95th Congress as there were in the 84th (1,151 compared with 224); the huge number of votes was matched by increases in the number of bills introduced and hearings held.

Responding to the number and complexity of decisions senators had to make, the Senate expanded the committee system. In 1957 there were 15 standing committees with 118 subcommittees; by 1975 there were 18 standing committees with 140 subcommittees. Counting the special, select, and joint committees raises the totals to 31 committees and 174 subcommittees.

More important, perhaps, the size of the panels also increased. Because the Senate had barely increased in size, going from ninety-six in the mid-1950s to its present one hundred with the addition of Alaska and Hawaii in 1959, each member took on more committee assignments. In 1957 each senator averaged 2.8 committees and 6.3 subcommittees. But by 1976 senators on average served on 4 committees and 14 subcommittees.

A reform panel chaired by Adlai Stevenson III, D-Ill., issued a plan in 1976 to streamline the system; an amended version passed the Senate early in 1977. It eliminated 3 standing committees and 5 select and joint committees, rearranged several others, and resulted in a dramatic drop in the number of subcommittees (from an overall total of 174 to 110), and it reduced the number of assignments for each senator (from an average of 4 committees and 14 subcommittees to 3 committees and 7.5 subcommittees). In a trend typical for an individualized, democratized institution, however, the assignments immediately began to escalate again. By the 98th Congress the average number of assignments had risen to nearly twelve, and forty senators had violated, in one way or another, the chamber's rules on assignment limitations.

In 1992 yet another reform committee was created, this one a joint committee co-chaired by two highly respected senators, Republican Pete Domenici and Democrat David Boren of Oklahoma. They were joined by two equally respected House members, Democrat Lee Hamilton of Indiana and Republican Bill Gradison of Ohio. (David Dreier of California replaced Gradison, who retired from the House in early 1993.) The Joint Committee on the Organization of Congress deliberated throughout the 103d Congress, recommending major reductions in the numbers of committees and subcommittees and in member assignments, among other things. The recommendations were not considered in the final weeks of the 103d Congress. When the 104th Congress convened in 1995 with a Republican majority, there were some significant cutbacks in the number of subcommittees, from 86 down to 68, which translated into a reduction in average subcommittee assignments from 7.8 to 6.2. But no serious change in the jurisdiction, number, or size of full committees was undertaken, leaving larger reform for some future date.

In the meantime, the remarkably full agenda and rapid timetable of the Republican House's Contract with America increased the overall workload of the Senate dramatically in 1995. The Senate had 613 yea-and-nay votes that year, compared to 395 the first session of the 103d Congress and 280 the first year of the 102d. It was in session 211 days (1,839 hours), compared to 153 days (1,269 hours) during the first session of the 103d Congress. But it also saw only twenty-eight of its public bills enacted into law—compared to eighty-three in the previous Senate's first session.

Growth in the workload had led to an increase in Senate committee staff members. They went from roughly 300 in the 85th Congress to well over 1,200, including permanent and investigative staff, by the 95th. The numbers stabilized and even declined thereafter, settling to just under 1,100 in the 100th Congress, and declining to 900 in the 103d Congress. The Republican majority in the 104th Congress pledged to cut staffs further.

Increase in staff has enabled senators to cope better with their heavy workload and responsibilities, but entrepreneurial, active, and ambitious staffs also have created more work by promoting ideas, writing amendments, and drafting bills and speeches. Large staffs also contributed to the democratization and decentralization of the Senate. Staff resources were allocated increasingly through subcommittees rather than full committees, accentuating the spread of power to junior senators; but this change also made it easier for the 104th Senate to cut committee staffs as it cut the number of subcommittees.

The cutbacks in staff in 1995 were a part of a broader effort to cut the costs and size of the congressional establishment and the federal government more generally, efforts that had included a highly publicized 25 percent cutback in the White House staff in 1993 and 1994. But the timing was unfortunate: the cuts came as the workload of the Senate increased. They added to the burden of senators, justifying their complaints about the overloaded and unpredictable schedule of the Senate, and probably contributed to the large number of announced retirements.

What takes place in committee rooms, subcommittee rooms, and on the Senate floor also has changed significantly. During the 1970s the legislative struggle shifted from the committees to the floor, while the functions of agenda setting and legislative oversight moved from the committees to the subcommittees. As workloads waned in the 1980s and increased again in 1995 and 1996, the basic patterns of legislative initiation and the relative importance of Senate institutions remained the same. Committees continue to be highly important: all legislation is referred to them, as are all executive and judicial nominations, and they retain the authority either to kill or to report out bills and nominations. But today's Senate is a more open, fluid, and decentralized body than it was in the 1950s or even in the 1980s. The personal style and savvy of individual senators, including committee chairs, is relatively more important, and the role of institutional positions, relatively less, than in past decades. Power, resources, and decision-making authority have become more diffuse. The combined effects of changes in membership, norms, leadership, workload, and committees, along with partisan shifts and the nature of television coverage, have produced a markedly different Senate.

The Senate and Its Broader Environment

As we have pointed out, the Senate does not operate in a vacuum. It has been and is affected by trends within the broader political system and society. In turn, it has impacted American politics, and nowhere is its effect been felt more strongly than in presidential nominations. From 1960 to 1972 the Senate was dominant. Since then, Senate candidates have lost some luster, but it continues to turn out many presidential contenders and to attract many who aspire to the Oval Office.

During the "golden era" of 1960 to 1972 the two parties nominated either senators (John Kennedy, Barry Goldwater, and George McGovern) or former senators who had become vice presidents (Richard Nixon, Lyndon Johnson, and Hubert Humphrey). Why this crucial role for the Senate? The near-revolutionary growth in media influence over politics, particularly through television, focused public attention on Washington and especially on the Senate. Television contributed to, and was affected by, the growing nationalization of party politics. A national attentiveness to foreign affairs heightened the importance of the Senate, with its well-defined constitutional role in foreign policy.

Some of these trends and conditions continued beyond 1972. But after the Watergate scandal, a somewhat negative attitude about national government enabled Jimmy Carter, a young former governor of Georgia with little Washington exposure, to capture the Democratic nomination in 1976. He won by campaigning against Washington politics. Despite the presence of senators and former senators as candidates in 1980 (Howard Baker, Bob Dole, and Edward Kennedy) and in 1984 (Gary Hart, John Glenn, Alan Cranston, and Ernest Hollings), another former governor, Ronald Reagan of California, was the GOP nominee in 1980, and he won easily. Former vice president (and senator) Walter Mondale bested a more contemporary set of contenders for the Democratic nomination in 1984.

George Bush, Reagan's vice president for eight years, won over Massachusetts governor Michael Dukakis in 1988, only to lose to another governor, Bill Clinton of Arkansas, in 1992. Senators entered most of the 1988 and 1992 primary contests, but were undone by charges of Washington "insiderism." In 1988, for example, Dole got off to a good start in Iowa, only to be blindsided by Bush in New Hampshire. Both Bush and Dukakis turned to senators to round out their presidential tickets—Dan Quayle of Indiana and Lloyd Bentsen of Texas, respectively.

In 1992 some of the most prominent senators mentioned as presidential prospects (Al Gore, Bill Bradley, George Mitchell, and Lloyd Bentsen) chose not to run. Two other senators did run—Democrats Tom Harkin of Iowa and Bob Kerrey of Nebraska—along with former senator Paul Tsongas of Massachusetts. But continuing the recent record of senatorial futility, they all dropped out by March, with Gore eventually becoming Clinton's running mate. In 1996 a senator again achieved success in the presidential nomination process when Dole quickly triumphed over the rest of the Republican field. That group included two other senators, Phil Gramm and Richard Lugar.

Despite senators' decidedly mixed record of success in presidential contests in the last four decades, the Senate remains an institution that receives national and international attention and produces numerous serious presidential contenders. Many senators consider themselves presidential possibilities, or they are mentioned as such in the media or polls. Senators tailor their behavior in accord with their presidential ambitions, spreading their legislative interests more broadly, and increasing their levels of activity and media visibility.

Conclusion

The Senate of the 1990s is a very different institution from the Senate of the 1950s, and it is different in important ways from the Senate of just a decade ago. The composition of the Senate went from a close partisan balance during the Truman and Eisenhower presidencies in the 1950s, to dominant Democratic party control in the 1960s and 1970s, to a narrow Republican majority in the early and mid-1980s, back to narrow Democratic control after 1986, and back to the Republicans after 1994. Close partisan competition is likely to be the pattern into the first decade of the twenty-first century.

Whatever the partisan makeup of the Senate, it has become a more fluid, more decentralized, and more democratized chamber. Individual senators, from the most senior to the most junior, have benefited—but also have become frustrated with the institutional consequences of these trends. The Senate has become preoccupied for extended periods of time with a small number of issues, especially the budget, which never seem to be resolved satisfactorily. Filibusters, once rare and reserved for the weightiest of issues, now routinely tie up the institution. The hold has become a routine method to block action indefinitely on important bills or nominations, or even to kill them without a vote.

The lack of progress on many issues and the preoccupation with talk over action have not brought a return to the leisurely, "clublike" atmosphere of the past, nor have they greatly increased the role or quality of debate. Although televised sessions improved floor attendance, they have not done much to make the Senate fulfill its motto as the world's greatest deliberative body. Today's Senate shows no clear institutional direction or identity. Neither a great deliberative body nor an efficient processor of laws, the Senate, after years of dramatic change, is an institution in search of an identity.

In the mid-1990s the Senate faced another problem. Even with its many partisan changes, the Senate remained through most of the 1980s and 1990s an institution that gravitated to the middle of the political process, in significant part because of the nature of the seniority system. During the eras of Democratic control, more centrist and conservative majority senators, mainly from the South, retained important committee leadership positions by virtue of their tenure; during the GOP eras, more centrist and moderate Republicans took a disproportionate share of pivotal committee chairs. Major legislative decisions tended to be bipartisan, as a consequence. But the turnover in the institution, including the influx of the conservative freshman class of Republicans in 1994 and the departure through resignation and retirement of many moderate Democrats and Republicans in 1994 and 1996, created a more polarized environment in the 104th Congress, a trend likely to continue in the 105th and perhaps beyond. Partisan tension and ideological division became a more regular part of the daily life of the institution, itself contributing to the decision by prominent centrist legislators like Nancy Kassebaum, Bill Bradley, Alan Simpson, and Bennett Johnston to retire. Whether their replacements, and the other new senators to come, can find a stable and satisfying role for their institution in future years—satisfying not just to them but to the public—remains to be seen.

Notes

1. See, for example, Jeffrey Birnbaum and Alan Murray, *Showdown at Gucci Gulch: Lawmakers, Lobbyists, and the Unlikely Triumph of Tax Reform* (New York: Random House, 1987); and John H. Makin and Norman J. Ornstein, *Debt and Taxes: How America Got into Its Budget Mess and What to Do About It* (New York: Times Books, 1995).
2. See, for example, Norman J. Ornstein and Amy L. Schenckenberg, "The 1995 Congress: The First Hundred Days," *Political Science Quarterly* 110 (1995): 183–207.
3. See Ralph Huitt's collection of essays in *Congress: Two Decades of Analysis,* ed. Ralph K. Huitt and Robert L. Peabody (New York: Harper and Row, 1969); and Donald R. Matthews, *U.S. Senators and Their World* (Chapel Hill: University of North Carolina Press, 1960).
4. Data on party unity votes through the 100th Congress (1987–1988) are taken from David W. Rohde, "Electoral Forces, Political Agendas, and Partisanship in the House and Senate," in *The Postreform Congress,* ed. Roger H. Davidson (New York: St. Martin's Press, 1992), 27–47. Data from 1989 through 1995 are taken from annual compilations in *Congressional Quarterly Weekly Report.*
5. See Rohde, "Electoral Forces," 29–31.
6. For an excellent discussion of the theoretical implications of this situation, see John H. Aldrich, *Why Parties? The Origin and Transformation of Party Politics in America* (Chicago: University of Chicago Press, 1995), especially chap. 7.
7. The three are Sam Nunn, D-Ga., William Cohen, R-Maine, and Howell Heflin, D-Ala.
8. See Helen Dewar and Kent Jenkins Jr., "Party Squalls Pose Test for Robb," *Washington Post,* March 26, 1991, A4.
9. Quoted in Janet Hook, "Senate Republican Conference Takes a Step to the Right," *Congressional Quarterly Weekly Report,* Nov. 17, 1990, 3871.
10. Quoted in Jackie Koszczuk with Alissa J. Rubin, "With Lott, Senate GOP Chooses a Bolder Approach," *Congressional Quarterly Weekly Report,* Dec. 3, 1994, 3437.
11. See Gabriel Kahn, "Kassebaum's Retirement Opens Door for Jeffords To Take Labor Gavel. Will Conservatives Close It?" *Roll Call,* Dec. 7, 1995, 10.
12. Mary Jacoby, "GOP Calls Off Hatfield Fight," *Roll Call,* March 9, 1995, 1.
13. See David S. Cloud, "GOP Senators Limit Chairmen To Six Years Heading Panel," *Congressional Quarterly Weekly Report,* July 22, 1995, 2147; and Mary Jacoby, "Senate GOP Bars Panel Chairmen From Heading Subcommittees, Too," *Roll Call,* Aug. 7, 1995, 3.

14. Matthews, *U.S. Senators and Their World,* 92.
15. Barbara Sinclair, *The Transformation of the U.S. Senate* (Baltimore: Johns Hopkins University Press, 1989), 101.
16. Ibid., 82. Steven S. Smith, *Call to Order: Floor Politics in the House and Senate* (Washington, D.C.: Brookings, 1989), 143.
17. Sinclair, *Transformation of the U.S. Senate,* 101.
18. These quotations and the other unattributed quotations in this essay are taken from semistructured taped interviews, conducted between 1973 and 1979, with more than sixty sitting and former senators. The interviews were part of a broader study of the Senate conducted by the authors with the help of a grant from the Russell Sage Foundation.
19. See Graeme Browning, "Shaking Up the Senate," *National Journal,* April 29, 1995, 1035.
20. Quoted in Kevin Merida, "The Freshman Who Raised the Fuss," *Washington Post,* March 9, 1995, A27.
21. Matthews, *U.S. Senators and Their World,* 94.
22. William S. Cohen, *Roll Call: One Year in the United States Senate* (New York: Simon and Schuster, 1981), 238.
23. Quoted in Mary Jacoby, "Dole Ploy Brings Senate to Halt," *Roll Call,* March 2, 1995, 21.
24. All of the quotations in this description are taken from Richard Sammon, "Byrd Urges Return of Civility," *Congressional Quarterly Weekly Report,* Dec. 23, 1995, 3866. For a more general treatment of the decrease in civility, see Eric Uslaner, *The Decline of Comity in Congress* (Ann Arbor: University of Michigan Press, 1993).
25. See Bruce I. Oppenheimer, "Changing Time Constraints on Congress: Historical Perspectives on the Use of Cloture," in *Congress Reconsidered,* 3d ed., ed. Lawrence C. Dodd and Bruce I. Oppenheimer (Washington, D.C.: CQ Press, 1985), 393–413.
26. Ibid., 398. Under the revised cloture rule, efforts to change the Senate's rules are still governed by the old two-thirds requirement.
27. Sinclair, *Transformation of the U.S. Senate,* 136.
28. See Smith, *Call to Order,* 94–119, for a discussion of cloture and the use of unanimous consent agreements.
29. Christopher J. Bailey, "The United States Senate: The New Individualism and the New Right," *Parliamentary Affairs* 39 (July 1986): 357–358.
30. Matthews, *U.S. Senators and Their World,* 123–124.
31. Robert L. Peabody, *Leadership in Congress* (Boston: Little, Brown, 1976), 332–333; Peabody, "Senate Party Leadership: From the 1950s to the 1980s," in *Understanding Congressional Leadership,* ed. Frank H. Mackaman (Washington, D.C.: CQ Press, 1981), 56; and Sinclair, *Transformation of the U.S. Senate,* 45.
32. See William S. White, *Citadel: The Story of the U.S. Senate* (New York: Harper, 1967); Matthews, *U.S. Senators and Their World*; Huitt and Peabody, *Congress: Two Decades of Analysis*; and Rowland Evans and Robert Novak, *Lyndon B. Johnson: The Exercise of Power* (New York: New American Library, 1966).
33. Interview with authors, July 13, 1979.
34. Quoted in Jerry Gray, "Lott Defeats Fellow Mississippian as Republican Leader of Senate," *New York Times,* June 13, 1996, A15.
35. Figures in this section come from Norman J. Ornstein, Thomas E. Mann, and Michael J. Malbin, *Vital Statistics on Congress, 1995–1996* (Washington, D.C.: Congressional Quarterly, 1996).

2. Revolution in the House: Testing the Limits of Party Government

Lawrence C. Dodd and Bruce I. Oppenheimer

The Republican revolution of the mid-1990s activated a period of significant upheaval and transition in the House of Representatives. Prior to the revolution, the Democratic Party had controlled the House continuously since 1954. President Bill Clinton's election and the coming of united party government in 1992 presented the Democrats with an opportunity to further consolidate their hold over the House through enactment of major legislation such as national health care. The Republicans seemed fated to remain the permanent minority party. But only two years later the Republicans captured control of Congress, extensively restructured the operation of the House, and pursued an aggressive partisan agenda devoted to reducing the role of the national government in American society. In their first year the House Republicans voted together in a cohesive manner not seen since the early twentieth century and attempted a style of party government reminiscent of the days of Speaker "Uncle Joe" Cannon. At the end of the first year of control, however, the Republican Party vastly overreached in its effort to dominate national policy making, found itself blamed by the public for two lengthy government shutdowns, and then suffered the collapse of its governing momentum. Thereafter, the Republicans struggled to regain their political footing and retain control of the House while the Democratic president and his congressional party enjoyed a political resurgence that had seemed almost unimaginable in November 1994.

The purpose of this chapter is to present these developments in greater detail and historical context and then to assess their significance for the modern House. In doing so, we consider the factors that enabled the Republicans to capture House control and describe how they restructured the House during the 104th Congress. We then detail their historic effort to institute party government during 1995 and describe the Democratic resurgence that occurred in 1996. We close with a brief assessment of the implications these developments have for the future of the House. We also consider their significance for scholarly arguments, such as those presented by Gary Cox and Mathew McCubbins, that stress the power of Speakers and the preeminence of party government in the House.[1] We begin with a discussion of the decades of Democratic control that set the stage for the Republicans' dramatic revolution.

The Era of Democratic Control

Long-term Democratic control of the House began with the Great Depression of 1929 and the election of a Democratic majority in 1930.[2] With the subsequent election of President Franklin Roosevelt and a Democratic Senate in 1932, the party used its unified control of government to create a powerful governing legacy. In 1933 congressional Democrats enacted Roosevelt's One Hundred Days legislative program, which was designed to address immediate problems such as the collapse of the nation's banking system. Over the next four years the party passed a wide range of New Deal legislation that laid the foundations of the modern social service state. The Democrats' activist response to the depression created broad popular support that sustained the party's dominance of congressional elections for six decades. Indeed, the Democrats controlled the House for sixty of the next sixty-four years, losing their majority only in the 1946 postwar election and in the 1952 victory of President Dwight Eisenhower.

When the Democrats came to power in 1930, they inherited an organizational structure based on committee government. In the late nineteenth century both parties had moved to solidify an activist committee system under the strong control of the House Speaker.[3] As a result, the Speaker controlled the appointments of committee members and committee chairs, dominated the Rules Committee, and exercised extensive authority over floor proceedings. The office grew so powerful that Speaker Cannon could seriously challenge the policy leadership of President Theodore Roosevelt. This system came to an end in 1910, when deep disagreements over policy and the distribution of power within the Republican Party led GOP progressives to turn against Cannon and his conservative allies and unite with House Democrats to challenge his power. The insurgency formally stripped the office of the Speaker of its historic prerogatives and helped shift power to House committees.[4] The Democrats during the Wilson years and the Republicans during the roaring twenties solidified committee control of the House and regularized the role of seniority in committee chair selections, thereby creating a complex and decentralized structure of policy making. This structure fostered a system of policy expertise and stabilized policy-making processes, but it also hindered rapid, coordinated policy activism by the parties.

The history of Democratic control of the House over the subsequent six decades was in many ways a continuing effort to use the policy-making expertise of the standing committees while overcoming the obstacles to party government created by the committee system. During the first four to six years of Franklin Roosevelt's presidency, the House Democratic leadership used the extensive public support for the New Deal, enormous House majorities, and the resources of the presidency to generate committee and floor support among Democratic members. But in the late 1930s public support for the New Deal ebbed, and conservative Democrats, particularly southern Democrats, began to unite with Republicans to oppose New Deal legislation in committees and on the floor. Even though the conservatives were a minority within the Democratic Party, they were protected in their committee appointments and chairmanships by seniority. Southern Democrats had dominated the party prior to the 1930s and, as senior members, occupied many of the Democratic power positions. When allied with Republicans in the so-called conservative coalition, as they often were from the late 1930s into the early 1960s, the southern Democrats were a substantial force in the House. As a result, one cannot equate Democratic control of the House during those years with liberal or Democratic Party dominance of congressional policy making. Those years were characterized by coalitional politics, conservative policies, and strong committee government.[5]

With the liberal successes in the 1958 election and the subsequent election of John Kennedy in 1960, House Democrats began a sixteen-year process that would restrict the power of seniority, bring greater authority to party leaders, and constrain the conservative coalition.[6] The early reform process began in the late 1950s with the creation of the Democratic Study Group, a liberal caucus devoted to House reform, and continued in 1961 with increased leadership control of the House Rules Committee, a feat engineered in his last year of service by a legendary Speaker, Sam Rayburn. Liberal dominance of House policy making surged forward with the presidential landslide of 1964 and the subsequent Great Society legislation of the 89th Congress. But a sustained period of moderate to liberal control of the House Democratic Party began in earnest only with reforms enacted in the 1970s and with regional shifts in the distribution of major committee and party leadership positions.

While the Democrats were in the majority, the Republicans pursued influence through strategies provided them by the decentralized structure of the House and factional divisions within the Democratic Party.[7] As long as the conservative coalition of southern Democrats and Republicans dominated policy making in the House, the Republicans played a relatively active, significant, and rewarding institutional role. During the first thirty years of Democratic control, the Rules Committee, which establishes the terms of floor debates, was responsive to Republican and southern Democratic concerns and often hostile to policy concerns of the Democratic majority.[8] In his classic study, *Congressmen in Committees,* Richard Fenno concluded that it was crossparty coalitions and consensus building among relatively conservative members from both parties that shaped the decisions of the Appropriations Committees in these years.[9] And even in the House Ways and Means Committee, members of both parties often stressed loyalty to the committee rather than to their party in making revenue policy.[10] These committee patterns allowed the Republicans to play strong roles in policy making. They embraced conciliatory and cooperative relations with the majority party Democrats rather than pursuing aggressive and combative tactics in House deliberations.

The conservative coalition began to collapse in the 1970s, in part because of congressional reforms and in part because of the changes in southern Democratic representation in Congress resulting from the Voting Rights Act. With the registration of large numbers of black voters, Democratic candidates moderated their views on social policy. The Republican Party then became more competitive in many southern districts by attracting conservative white voters. The distinctiveness between southern and northern congressional Democrats waned, and interparty differences increased. While over the long run these shifts laid the foundation for growing Republican representation in the South, in the short run they increased unhappiness among Republicans over their isolation in the House and their lack of a strong institutional role.[11]

No longer did Republicans exercise considerable hidden influence in House policy making. Their consequent frustration mounted when the Reagan landslide of 1980 failed to produce Republican control of the House, despite success in winning some conservative districts previously controlled by Democrats. During this period the Democrats appeared to have learned to use the benefits of incumbency and majority party control so effectively in campaigning for reelection, and they had become so adept at raising money even from conservative business PACS, that Republicans began to doubt whether a "natural" alteration in party control of the House would ever occur.[12] House Republicans then began to consider a more aggressive assault on Democratic dominance, a move that was reinforced by the party's failure to gain control even in the Reagan tidal wave of 1984. The impetus for this attack came from the younger and more conservative Republicans and was led by Newt Gingrich of Georgia.

In the 98th Congress (1983–1985), Gingrich and other junior Republicans united informally into an organization called the Conservative Opportunity Society and began to challenge the Democrats on procedural, policy, and political grounds.[13] They pushed reform issues such as the balanced budget amendment, reform of House rules, and the line-item veto, and social issues such as abortion and school prayer. Many of their concerns would form the basis of the Contract with America a decade later. The young Republicans used televised coverage of House debates so effectively that they provoked Speaker Tip O'Neill into an outburst against them in 1984, which led the House to take the extraordinary step of striking a Speaker's words from the House record. This action also garnered publicity for the young Republicans and encouraged them to continue their attack. Over the next decade, Gingrich and his supporters mounted a direct assault on Speaker Jim Wright, who eventually resigned under an ethics investigation. They pushed for an examination of the House Bank, which exposed a highly damaging public scandal over bank overdrafts that particularly discredited the governing Democrats. In addition, they continuously called for reform and reorganization of the House rules.

The Republicans argued that House Democrats had used the advantages of incumbency and majority party status to insulate themselves from the public and focus on their personal careers. When the term limits movement began to gain momentum in the late 1980s and early 1990s, a number of House Republicans embraced the idea as the solution to the careerism and insulation of the House Democrats. Republicans promised they would enact term limits if they became the majority party in Congress.

During the late 1980s, Gingrich became a visible force in his party and in the House Republican Conference. In 1988 he became head of GOPAC, a Republican political action committee, and he began to use it to recruit conservative Republicans to run for state and local office. He focused on recruiting conservative ideologues who would be committed to implementing an aggressive party agenda and who would work passionately in behalf of the "party cause." In so doing he was creating a "farm team" of experienced politicians who could run for the House in the 1990s. While he achieved considerable success around the country, his greatest inroads came in the South and Southwest, where GOPAC helped reinforce the growing Republican strength. In March 1989 House Republicans elected Gingrich as their minority whip over a more moderate candidate and positioned him as the most obvious successor to their long-term minority leader, Bob Michel of Illinois. As minority whip and prospective party leader, Gingrich pushed the House Republicans closer to confrontation with the Democrats.

The election of President Clinton and the return of unified party control of government in 1992 offered the Democrats a historic opportunity to solidify again their hold on national politics, as well as a chance to defuse the Gingrich-led Republican challenge.[14] But Clinton, new to the ways of Washington and uncertain in his use of presidential power, provided weak leadership to his congressional party. His efforts to draft and push national health care reform relied on an executive task force, led by Hillary Rodham Clinton, that left many House members uninvolved and uncommitted. Within Congress, the senior House Democrats opposed congressional reforms, even though passage might have dulled the ongoing Republican attack. In the face of these developments, House Republicans effectively opposed the health care reform, pushed for radical reform of Congress, and began planning for a united effort to win control of the House and Senate.

Gingrich and the House Republicans built their 1994 campaign around a united national agenda, the Contract with America, which is discussed by John Bader in Chapter 15. The contract was dedicated to extensive reform of the House and the implementation of a conservative policy agenda. Just two years earlier, the nation had completed a reapportionment process that created a number of southern, southwestern, and western districts with conservative leanings. Those districts had gone narrowly to Democrats during the rout of President George Bush in 1992; Republicans now hoped they might capture them. A large number of long-term Democrats had retired prior to the 1994 elections, creating open seats that Republicans hoped to win. But most important, the Republicans believed that they had a compelling message that the voters would embrace. They believed that the time had come when voters would end the long era of Democratic control and try Republican party government in Congress.

The 1994 Election in Historical Context

On November 8, 1994, the American voters elected a Republican majority in the House for the first time since 1952.[15] The Republicans defeated the Democratic Speaker, two senior committee chairmen, and thirty-one other Democratic incumbents. No Republican incumbents lost, making the party's fifty-two seat gain the largest net partisan swing since 1948. There could be no doubt that the Republicans had scored a major victory. The party proved particularly successful in the South, picking up nineteen House seats in Dixie and turning a 54–83 southern deficit into a 73–64 advantage. The party held a 230–204 majority in the House. The victory was clearly a testament to the hard work that Gingrich and others had done over the previous decade to prepare the groundwork for a serious challenge to Democratic dominance. But why did they succeed?

Much attention has focused on the 1994 defeat of long-term Democratic incumbents like Speaker Tom Foley and committee chairs Dan Rostenkowski and Jack Brooks, but the Republican majority was built largely on winning open seats and on the defeat of junior Democratic incumbents. For all the campaign rhetoric about term limits and long-term, out-of-touch incumbents, the defeat of senior members played a minor role in the Republican victory. Of the thirty-four seats Republicans won by defeating incumbents, sixteen were held by freshmen Democrats, and six others were held by members completing their second or third terms. (Even allowing for the partisan swing of the election, the sophomore surge did not seem to exist for the Democrats.) Republicans were particularly successful in defeating Democrats who had won open seats during the Clinton presidential victory. Thirteen of the sixteen freshmen Democrats who lost to Republican challengers in 1994 had won open seats in 1992. Most important, Republicans won thirty-nine of fifty-two (75 percent) of open seat contests. In the 103d Congress, they had held only twenty-one of those seats. The continuation of the Republican majority in the 1996 election hinged largely on their ability to win enough open Democratic seats to offset any Democratic gains derived from defeating junior Republicans.

For years Republicans had argued that their failure to be competitive for control of the House could be traced to the Democrats' incumbency advantage, but they were correct only to a modest degree. Incumbency advantage seemed to insulate the Democratic members from the short-term partisan forces of given elections. In the Reagan landslides, Democrats had suffered net losses of twenty-four seats held by incumbents in 1980 and ten in 1984. In fact, the longer-term problem the Republicans faced was their failure to do much better in open seat contests than in those where incumbents were running.[16] Much of the failure has been attributed to the Republicans' inability to recruit quality candidates for open seat contests and Democratic dominance of state legislatures from which many congressional candidates are recruited. Moreover, Democrats had benefited from having relatively few open seats vacated by their incumbents during election years when the partisan forces favored the Republicans.[17] For example, in 1984 there were only twenty-seven open seat contests (thirteen with previous Democratic incumbents and fourteen with previous Republican incumbents). Although Republicans won eighteen of those seats, the result was a net loss of only four Democratic seats. In contrast, 1982, a good year for the Democrats, was one with a large number of open seats (thirty-seven where the previous incumbent was not running and another twenty-two new seats created

Figure 2-1 Ebb and Flow Patterns in House Membership, 83d–104th Congresses

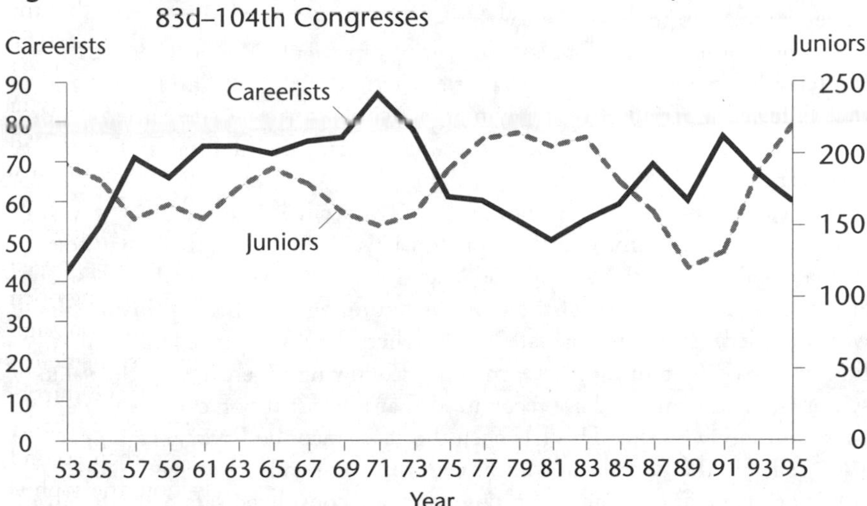

Source: The data used for creation of this figure come from Norman J. Ornstein, Thomas E. Mann, and Michael J. Malbin, *Vital Statistics on Congress, 1995–1996* (Washington, D.C.: Congressional Quarterly, 1996), 19.

by reapportionment and redistricting). Democrats won 61 percent of those contests. The 1994 election changed all that: Republicans not only won three-quarters of the open seat contests, but also did it when there was a large number of them.

Important for Republicans, 1992 and 1994 were years of high membership turnover, but only slightly higher than in previous waves. When one examines the data from the post–World War II period, one sees a series of ebbs and flows in turnover. The patterns are illustrated in Figure 2-1. The right axis of this figure traces the number of junior members, by our definition those serving their third term or less. The left axis traces the number of careerists, those serving their tenth term or more.[18] This figure demonstrates that what occurred in the early 1990s was a continuation of the periodic increase of new members and decline in careerists.[19] During the late 1940s and early 1950s, the number of new members grew, but then membership turnover dropped and careerism increased. At the start of the 83d Congress in 1953, there were 193 (44 percent) junior House members and only 42 (10 percent) careerists. Despite some fluctuation along the way, by 1971 junior members had declined to 150 (34 percent) and careerists had increased to 87 (20 percent). A new wave of membership turnover in the 1970s brought the number of junior members above 200 in four consecutive Congresses (95th-98th), and the number of careerists hit a low of 50 (11 percent) at the start of the 97th Congress in 1981. The four elections from 1984 to 1990 produced low turnover. Relatively few members retired or were defeated. The number of junior members reached a low of 120 (28 percent) in 1989, and by 1991 careerists were up to 76 (17 percent).

The House was ripe for another wave of turnover by the early 1990s. In fact, the term limits movement was in part a reaction to the ebb in House turnover that followed a period of relatively high activity. Only a decade earlier, political scientists had been writing articles trying to explain the high rates of voluntary turnover.[20]

Clearly, House turnover does not have to occur in fairly regular waves. In much of the nineteenth century, it was consistently high. But there may be contextual conditions of the post–World War II era that have resulted in these ebbs and flows. First, for most of the period, continuing membership in the House was rewarded. Except for the late 1970s, when there was considerable disaffection expressed by retiring House members following an erosion in the value of seniority, most members have recognized that the institution extends power and perks to those who stay. This has been the case since the Reorganization Act of 1946 reduced the number of committees, making committee chairs more valuable. Second, a large number of House seats are considered safe by both parties. With the exception of the increased use of the House as a stepping-stone to other offices, there have been few incentives to leave the institution, and reelection rates for incumbents have remained around 90 percent and above, even in 1992 and 1994. From this statistic one might expect a certain stability, with the number of junior members to be relatively low (less than 40 percent) and the number of careerists to be relatively high (above 15 percent).

Although the ingredients are present for consistently low membership turnover, and, accordingly, one might expect steady levels of junior members and careerists, we instead find that members tend to enter and leave the House in waves. Some of this movement results from elections with large partisan swings such as 1948, 1964, 1974, 1980, and 1994. And often the party on the short end in these elections recoups a sizable number of seats two years later. In addition, reapportionment and redistricting occur at ten-year intervals, resulting in a spurt in voluntary and involuntary retirements. Between 1952 and 1994, the number of first-term House members was more than one-third higher in the five Congresses that followed reapportionments than in the seventeen other Congresses. The reasons for this difference are fairly obvious. States gaining seats elect new members to the House. New district lines may make some incumbents more vulnerable. Some incumbents may retire or be defeated, especially those senior members who may not want to reenter what Fenno describes as an "expansionist" home style phase.[21] Therefore, reapportionment and redistricting are bound to bring a departure of some and the influx of others.

Careerists may be better insulated than junior members from partisan swings (the data on this are mixed) and have greater influence with those drawing new district maps, but they do not control aging.[22] Many of those who enter the House will be between forty and fifty years of age. Having entered in waves, those who stay will tend to reach careerist status in clusters and may also exit in clusters.

Taken together, these factors have led to ebbs and flows in the seniority mix of the House. The elections of 1992 and 1994 brought a large number of new members to the House and ended four consecutive elections in which House turnover averaged under 10 percent. (And the 1996 election produced more than seventy new members, a higher than average number for modern Congresses, but fewer than in 1992 and 1994.) However, unless there are a number of strong partisan swings, or the members who favor term limits voluntarily exclude themselves, or more individual House districts become party competitive, another period of lower turnover and growing careerism is likely to begin in 1998.

Compared to the membership turnover that resulted in Republican control of the House, the 1994 election had a far smaller impact on its race and gender composition (see Carol Swain's chapter). After the 50 percent increase in the number of African American House members at the start of the 103d Congress, the number of black members remained at thirty-nine. The overwhelming number of black House members come from majority-minority districts. In an effort to comply with the Voting Rights Act in redistricting for 1992, states created an increased number of black (and Hispanic) majority districts. But until black candidates become competitive in more majority white districts, their numbers in the House are not likely to increase. Moreover, with successful court challenges to the use of race as a criterion for drawing district lines, the number of minority members of the House may well decline over the next few Congresses.

In contrast, there were no similar impediments to the continued growth in the number of women in the House, but, after increasing from twenty-eight to forty-eight between the 102d and 103d Congresses, there was no net gain for women in the 104th Congress. However, the number of Republican women rose from twelve to seventeen, while the Democratic women dropped from thirty-six to thirty-one. Six first-term Democratic women were among those defeated in 1994. With six women incumbents retiring (a seventh was defeated for renomination) at the end of the 104th Congress and with relatively few women nominated in open seat contests, one analyst described the prospects for an increase of women serving in the 105th Congress as "dim" and suggested that the number may well drop.[23] In fact, there was a net gain of two women House members in 1996. Moreover, the gender gap that exists in the electorate continues to be reflected in the composition of the two parties in the House. Until 1990 there was relative balance between the number of Republican and Democratic women House members. Since then, the Democrats have had the advantage. As the Republican Party works to address issues of diversity, we might expect an increase in women House members.

It is difficult to predict whether the freshmen of the 104th Congress will behave differently from their predecessors as they progress through their House careers. A large freshmen class creates the potential for change because few members have a political stake in the preexisting norms. Their background data suggest that a higher than usual proportion of them were political amateurs who had not previously held office, although some had nonelective political experience.[24] Perhaps they are more policy oriented and less service and reelection oriented than previous classes. Or their election may reflect the growing distinctiveness of the parties and the nationalization of the 1996 campaign. Whether they will be the foundation of conditional party government during Republican periods of House control, however, is not yet clear.

What is clear is that the Republicans benefited from the timing of their historic challenge. The results were not only an indication of voter hostility toward the Democrats, or voter support of the Contract with America, but also a stage in the recurring cycles of generational turnover in the modern House. The Republican victory resulted from the combination of the determined Republican assault on the Democrats and the large number of Democratic freshmen and open seats that existed in 1994. Gingrich and the party activists interpreted the election as a mandate for the Republican agenda, even though polls indicated that the majority of voters had never heard of the Contract with America. Gingrich announced that the Republicans would move to implement the contract and would do so, as they had promised, within the first hundred days of Republican rule. They focused first on reform and restructuring of the House.

Restructuring the House

If the electoral turnovers of 1994 were partially a product of recurring cycles in congressional change, so too were the reforms that followed.[25] Since the overthrow of Speaker Cannon in 1910, concern with reform has seldom been absent from Capitol Hill. In both the 1940s and 1970s, Congress went through extensive reform efforts. With the Legislative Reorganization Act of 1946 Congress moved to streamline its committees and create expanded staffs for committees and members, and it embraced some symbolic efforts to strengthen party policy making. In the early 1970s House Democrats restricted committee power and increased the autonomy and resources of subcommittees; they followed these moves in the mid-1970s by strengthening the Speaker and party leadership and creating a new congressional budget process. These reforms created a bifurcated power structure, especially for the majority party, with more power going to subcommittee chairs and party leaders. The formal authority of most committee chairs was weakened. The change in the power structure not only gave the Democratic central leaders more resources and opportunity with which to coordinate party activity, but also provided members greater resources that they could use in pursuing their autonomous career interests separate from party leaders.[26] In this way, the reforms increased expectations of party leaders but compromised their chances of success.

The calls for additional reforms continued in the 1980s and early 1990s.[27] Perhaps the most important was the proposal to strengthen the speakership and make it the central manager of the House, as it was before the revolt against Speaker Cannon. Additional proposals concerned modernizing the jurisdictions of standing committees; revising floor procedures and scheduling practices to increase the efficiency and fairness of House activities; limiting the members' perks, salaries, and pensions; increasing minority party rights; and controlling proxy voting and other devices that undermine the integrity of congressional decision making. Some, including members of Congress, also called for the passage of constitutional amendments that would limit the legislature's power and strengthen the presidency—for example, term limits for members, requiring a balanced budget, and a line-item veto for the president. In addition, there were repeated calls for campaign finance reform. The bank scandal and the growing public dissatisfaction with Congress led to two organized reform efforts in 1992, but as Lawrence Evans and Walter Oleszek detail in *Congress Under Fire,* both were blocked by senior Democrats who feared that real reform would undercut their personal power in the House.[28]

When the Republicans took control of the House, their effort to fulfill the Contract with America led to far more extensive reforms than the Democrats had considered in the previous quarter-century. The Republican reforms addressed leadership power, the jurisdictions and decision processes of House committees, and floor deliberations and scheduling procedures; additional reforms focused heavily on the "institutional integrity" of the House.

The most critical reforms were those that strengthened the power and prerogatives of the Speaker. The Republicans had a small majority that could be upended by the defections of a few members. Such defections seemed possible because some Republican moderates had doubts about the party's policy initiatives. As a result, a strong Speaker was deemed essential to the cohesion of the party and its enactment of the contract and other policy initiatives. And in Newt Gingrich the party had an aggressive, willful leader who had built the organizational and electoral foundations that produced the 1994 victory, and who wanted to play an assertive leadership role. The Republicans decided to allow Speaker Gingrich to appoint committee chairs (and to remove chairs); gave him additional leverage over the assignment of Republican members to committees; permitted him to name the chair and Republican members of the House Oversight Committee, which monitors the internal administrative operations of the House; and enhanced his administrative and procedural authority. The reform effort, however, did not focus solely on strengthening the Speaker. The Republican freshmen, concerned that the power of the Speaker might itself become an oppressive force within the House and an obstacle to their revolution, insisted that an eight-year term limit be imposed on the occupant of the office. The result was that the Republicans gave the Speaker substantial new power but put him on a very short leash.

The Contract with America also had called for six-year terms for chairs of the standing House committees. The Republicans enacted this reform, but at the same time strengthened the power of committee chairs, which in turn strengthened the Speaker who appointed them. This new control came through the repeal of the subcommittee bill of rights, which the Democrats had enacted in the 1970s, and the enactment of procedures that allowed committee chairs to name the subcommittee chairs and members, hire majority staff for committees and subcommittees, and control subcommittee budgets. The Republicans also enacted modest changes in committee jurisdictions and imposed new rules on committee proceedings and members' personal prerogatives within committees, including a ban on proxy voting. Not wanting to cause controversy within its own conference that might undermine momentum, Republicans refrained from major reform of committee jurisdictions beyond abolishing three minor panels with constituency links to the Democratic Party.

They also addressed some concerns they had when they were the minority party. They promised to increase the use of open rules on the House floor, to protect procedural rights of minority party members, to encourage greater clarity from the House Rules Committee with respect to major actions by the committee, and to establish a "family-friendly" schedule for House proceedings. The party also enacted changes designed to enhance public support for the institution. For example, the House would now abide by laws governing workplace regulations in the private sector. To make the institution more responsive to the new majority party, the Republicans reduced committee staffs by one-third and in ways that forced turnover of long-term Democratic staffers. By abolishing legislative service organizations, the Republicans restricted resources that Democrats had amassed over the years through their use of such organizations.

The Republican reforms altered the institution in substantial and potentially historic ways. It would be a mistake, however, to see their changes as a transforming and permanent consolidation of the power of the Speaker and party leaders. The Republicans enacted these changes when a large number of members were beginning their first or second terms and were not yet fully attentive to personal career interests within the House power structure. In addition, some of the appearance of leadership power may have owed as much to the momentary influence that Gingrich enjoyed as the architect of the Republican victory as it did to the actual grants of new authority to the Speaker. The Speaker's power, therefore, was subject to reversal with shifts in context. These reforms were not without their debilitating long-term implications for leadership power.

The Republicans addressed some of the constraints on party leaders that the Democrats had left in place or imposed during the 1970s, but the new majority party also created its own complications for leadership power. First, as with the Democrats, the Republicans sought to strengthen the Speaker through reforms in caucus and House rules rather than through constitutional expansion of his power, which left the Speaker dependent for his prerogatives on the members he was trying to manage. Although the Speaker was given considerable authority on paper, in reality his power still rested in the willingness of party members to support a powerful speakership. The Speaker could be crippled at any point by a successful revolt within the party or the House, as Speaker Cannon discovered, or by tepid support during a crisis, as Speaker Wright experienced. Second, the eight-year term limit meant that maneuvering to replace a sitting Speaker could begin in the incumbent's fourth or fifth year of service and undercut leadership authority.

Enhancing the power of committee chairs meant that substantial power centers could arise within the party if the Speaker was embattled or nearing the end of his term and unable to assert his authority. Moreover, by imposing a six-year limit on committee chairs, the new rules created incentives for strong, popular, and ambitious chairs to challenge a vulnerable Speaker before the end of his eight years. In sum, on the surface the new rules seemed to strengthen the Speaker and make committee leaders his secure lieutenants, but over the long run the new rules may have created a more complex and less stable leadership structure.

The overall pattern of power distribution created by the Republicans meshed in interesting ways with the changes the Democratic Party had developed over the previous two decades. In the 1970s the Democrats' bifurcated structure had spread power downward to subcommittees, upward to party leaders, and away from committees and committee chairs. In the 1980s this formal bifurcation had been magnified by the growth of caucuses that spread resources more widely among House members, as discussed by Susan Webb Hammond in Chapter 12, and by the emergent authority of a new governing oligarchy that broadened the relevant participants' leadership power.[29] The new oligarchy, which came in response to the need for better coordinated party policy making in a period of divided government and deficit politics, was centered primarily in the money committees of Congress and in the party leadership. In the 1990s the Republicans succeeded in lessening the formal bifurcation of power in the House and shifting formal authority toward the Speaker. They reined in the subcommittees and caucuses and put committee chairs under the Speaker's control. It is possible, however, that the powers given to the committee chairs—and assumed to strengthen the Speaker who appointed them—may actually have created the possibility of a governing oligarchy not unlike the one evident in the Democratic House. Moreover, the term limits imposed on the Speaker gave considerable potential leverage to the Republican Party caucus and to its rank and file members.

The Republican reforms therefore can be seen as magnified continuations of previous trends within the Democratic House toward a formal strengthening of the Speaker, an informal emergence of a governing oligarchy, and the continued empowerment of rank and file members. Also evident was a weakening of the routinized processes of committee deliberation and decision making that had characterized the House through much of the twentieth century. And, as discussed above, embedded within the new structure was the possibility of contentious future struggles over institutional power and leadership succession. Yet, whatever long-term developments flow from these reforms, there can be little doubt that in the short run they fueled the move toward united party government in the House.

Republican Rule

The high point of the Republican revolution came during the first hundred days of the 104th Congress, from January through early April 1995, when House Republicans acted on the major promises of the Contract with America and propelled Speaker Gingrich into a role as policy leader on a par with the president. The low point came during December 1995 and January 1996 as a conflict between the president and Congress over the national budget resulted in two lengthy and unpopular government shutdowns. The public blamed the shutdowns on the House Republicans and began to turn against the revolution, propelling the party into a period of floundering and reassessment. Renewed activism came during the spring and summer of 1996 when the congressional Republicans and the president began to work together to pass major legislation such as welfare reform. But the party never fully recovered its momentum, and this loss was attributed particularly to Speaker Gingrich and the party leadership. To understand why the Speaker and party elders were held responsible for such a failure, and why they fell prey to it, we examine the structure of power within the party at the beginning of the 104th Congress and the subsequent policy decisions the leadership confronted.

The Structure of Leadership Power

When Gingrich became Speaker, he benefited in critical ways from the earlier Democratic efforts to strengthen majority party leadership.[30] By the 1980s the House Democrats had gained substantial control over the management of their legislative program. On major legislation, party task forces monitored and guided the decision process from the subcommittee level through final passage; an expanded party whip system ensured cohesion on important votes; the Rules Committee designed complex procedures to facilitate floor consideration and to protect against minority party amendments and obstruction; experimentation with multiple referral procedures opened an expanded role for party leaders to craft the substance of legislation; and the budget process and budget summits became tools for directing the standing committee agendas. All of these elements in party leadership ascendancy predated the Republican takeover.[31] They were particularly evident during the speakership of Jim Wright, who not only had mobilized a Democratic policy agenda but had also challenged presidential leadership on policy toward Nicaragua. Even a less aggressive Speaker, Tom Foley, had successfully forced President Bush into negotiating a compromise budget in 1990.

It was evident after the Republican victory in 1994 that Gingrich would continue to strengthen the speakership and that his party would support his efforts. The two large classes of Republicans elected in 1992 and 1994 in some degree owed their election to Gingrich; they supported his policy goals and leadership style; and they constituted a majority of the Republican Conference. The conference appeared even more homogeneous on policy than the Democratic Party and more amenable to centralized guidance. The Contract with America gave the Republicans a policy direction to pursue and a mandate to assert, and the promise to vote on it in one hundred days justified strong leadership control. The Republicans perceived that they were facing a "liberal" Democratic president and wanted to present a united front against him. These factors, combined with

Gingrich's aggressive personality, contributed to a strong speakership. Gingrich also benefited from the decision of House Republicans to elect Dick Armey of Texas as majority leader. Armey supported a conservative revolution in government, but seemed less concerned with personal power than with policy success. Likewise, the elected majority whip, Tom DeLay of Texas, was a strong conservative ideologue committed to the revolution and closely attuned to the Republican freshmen. These decisions, which placed three southerners in the top three leadership posts, minimized the possibility of internal struggles over power and reinforced the move toward centralized power.[32]

To shape the party's legislative program, Gingrich created a kind of Speaker's cabinet, called the Speaker's Advisory Group (SAG).[33] SAG, composed of the Speaker, the majority leader, the majority and deputy whips, the Republican Conference chair, and the National Republican Congressional Committee chair, met weekly to set party direction. Gingrich also created task forces, eventually numbering thirty, to develop legislation independently of committees and committee chairs and oversee the passage of the legislation. The Democrats had used task forces during the previous two decades, but they had done so primarily for building floor support for bills; the Republicans used them to bypass standing committees and to pursue a centralized party agenda.

What Gingrich put in place was a highly centralized leadership structure that placed responsibility for policy success directly on his shoulders. His goals as Speaker were to reshape the direction of the nation's policy agenda, to consolidate his party's hold over the House, to pave the way for Republican control of the White House in 1996, and then to institute a new Republican era in American politics. He seemed to view the speakership as a place for visionary leadership and programmatic policy direction, roughly as powerful as the presidency.[34] By consolidating organizational power within the speakership, Gingrich provided himself with the critical tools for realizing his expansive goals. He saw himself as the chief executive officer of the House rather than its presiding officer.[35] He was prepared to leave much of the day-to-day operations to subordinates while he set policy directions and controlled the critical levers of power. In their influential book, *Legislative Leviathan*, Gary Cox and Mathew McCubbins argue that any Speaker of the House in fact has the power to be an authoritative leader bending the legislative party to his will.[36] Gingrich appeared to be the virtual manifestation of the party leader theorized by Cox and McCubbins. Others drew the analogy between Gingrich and prime ministers in parliamentary governments.[37]

To assist in managing the House, Gingrich turned to his two elected assistants, particularly Armey, with whom he entrusted the passage of the contract.[38] Following that successful venture, Gingrich further relied on Armey to oversee House operations while the Speaker took on an even more public role in representing the House Republicans to the nation. In addition to charting his party's policy direction, Gingrich recruited candidates and raised money for the 1996 elections. As whip, Tom DeLay was responsible for advising the Speaker as to fellow Republicans' vote sentiments and for gathering votes on critical leadership issues. DeLay was somewhat hampered by his extreme positions on some issues, such as environmental regulation, and for his reputed tendency to use his office to promote his own policy agenda rather than the leadership's. Nevertheless, he was popular with large segments of House Republicans, especially the conservatives and freshmen.

Backed by a united party and trusted assistants, Gingrich presented the House Republicans as an aggressive, cohesive, and irresistible force that could not fail to create a new Republican era in Congress, which would go on to transform the nation.[39] The size of the 1994 victory seemed to provide the justification for this Republican confidence, and the Contract with America provided the policy agenda that Republicans claimed the public had mandated in the election. National polls showing initial support by the public reinforced these expectations, as did the demoralization of the House Democrats and the disarray in the Clinton White House.[40] Moreover, there was a widespread expectation that the Republicans would now inherit the incumbent advantages that the Democrats had long enjoyed. Perhaps they would receive an even larger share of PAC money than the Democrats because of the natural affinity of business for the GOP.[41] House passage of the bulk of the Contract with America within one hundred days, always with remarkable levels of Republican voting cohesion—except on term limits—added to the sense of inevitability.[42]

Their early success was a heady experience for Gingrich and the Republicans. It seemed to foretell a new era of Republican cohesiveness that would sweep away the remnants of Democratic control and an activist national government. Following the first hundred days, the leadership used its power to push a number of policy initiatives that would dismantle the Democrats' policy legacy. Drafting and negotiating major legislation were carried on by the party leadership and selected members outside the confines of the standing committees, and committee hearings were occasionally dispensed with altogether. Legislation was presented to the appropriate committee for its approval with limited opportunity for consideration of alternatives. A Republican majority on the Rules Committee would then craft terms for debate that ensured Republican dominance in floor consideration and helped sustain Republican control of the policy process. Using these processes, complex legislation like welfare reform, a tax cut bill, regulatory overhaul, a budget resolution, and environmental legislation all passed the House as products of party leadership negotiations rather than committee deliberations.

Despite such success, the real test of the House Republicans' ability to govern was still to come.[43] Much of their apparent cohesion and momentum had come on early votes that the party leadership had planned because of their popularity and their ease. Some of the most important and visible of these reform votes dealt only with issues directly related to the House, so that "success" did not involve negotiations with the president or the Senate. As controversial legislation came forward, House bills began to be substantially altered by the Senate, or vetoed by the president, as with the welfare reform legislation passed in 1995. It remained to be seen whether Gingrich and the Republican leadership could actually use their cohesive control of the House to reshape the nation's policy agenda and assert congressional governance. The Senate, in particular, was an irritant to House Republicans because Republican senators were more moderate than their House counterparts, and Senate leaders could not seek a level of control aspired to by House leaders. In some cases, Senate Republicans were unwilling to support Gingrich's policy initiatives because they thought them too extreme; in other cases, bills that passed the Senate languished in conference committee. Moreover, individual members could threaten filibusters, and a fairly cohesive Democratic Party in the Senate could prevent cloture. Long before conservative legislation passed by the House could reach the president's desk, it might come unraveled in the Republican-controlled but more moderate and deliberative Senate.

Perhaps most critical, it was not clear whether the House Republicans could enact a 1996 federal budget by the October 1 beginning of the fiscal year. This question was particularly pressing with respect to appropriations legislation. Prior to the revolution, the Democrats had sought to make the Appropriations Committee a relatively nonpartisan body where the major emphasis was on the timely passage of spending legislation, rather than on ideological conflict over the programs. The Republicans chose to inject tough partisanship and ideological fervor into the appropriations decisions by slashing spending on authorized programs and placing in appropriations bills riders that would control how agencies implemented programs. These efforts slowed the appropriations process and raised serious questions as to whether the Republican Party could handle the most essential role of the House of Representatives, drafting and passing the nation's taxing and spending legislation.

Testing the Power of the Speakership

The greatest tests of a party's ability to govern the House and shape national policy are the annual and unavoidable decisions that deal with the budget, taxes, and spending.[44] These issues directly affect the lives of every individual and group and necessarily involve the Senate and the executive. Taxing and spending decisions take center stage in late summer and early fall, as the new fiscal year approaches, and they must be settled as early as possible if the government is to function in an orderly, predictable manner. A delay in House passage of the necessary bills or the failure to reach sensible compromise with the Senate and the president raises questions about a majority party's ability to govern.

In pursuing the Contract with America almost to the exclusion of other policy concerns, Gingrich and the House Republicans gambled that their early successes would create such momentum for the Republican agenda that when they turned to fiscal matters they would prevail here as well.[45] However, the Republicans soon discovered that appropriations and revenue bills were far more difficult to draft and debate than the items in the contract. More than other policy areas, these bills rely on the expertise of committee and subcommittee members and staff. The time lost during the first four months of 1995 was almost impossible for the money committees, particularly the Appropriations Committee, to make up during the summer and early fall, and the leadership could not easily step into the void and produce appropriations and revenue legislation on its own. Ideological and partisan conflict within the committees, particularly Appropriations, slowed the process further.

The overall design of the budget was critical to the success of the Republican revolution because the party had called for significant budget cuts, a large tax cut, and movement toward a balanced national budget. It needed a 1996 spending and taxing program that reflected these commitments. Most of all, Gingrich and the House leadership saw the 1996 budget as a political opportunity. It would force the president either to accept a conservative budget—and cripple his support within his own party and liberal constituencies—or to veto it and lose support with the majority of the nation's citizens who backed a balanced budget. For Gingrich and other party leaders, the defeat of a sitting Democratic president in this manner was the key to gaining control of policy making during the 104th Congress, winning the White House in 1996, and consolidating a Republican era in American politics.

In fall 1995 the most dramatic and visible policy struggle in recent times erupted between the president and Congress. The Republicans demanded that the president accept their seven-year balanced budget plan as part of the annual appropriations and revenue legislation. When he refused, much of the government was left with no appropriations. Congress refused to provide short-term funding for government programs, except those deemed "essential," and the government was shut down. The Republican effort might have succeeded had the party been able to move on its strategy in mid-September, prior to the October 1 deadline. The previous year the Democrats had enacted all thirteen appropriations bills on time, but the Republicans had cleared only two appropriations bills by the start of the 1996 fiscal year. They took until November to mount their challenge to the president, so that pressure for a 1996 budget was growing on all sides. By then, Congress could be made to look responsible for the slowness of the process. Moreover, the House Republicans were demanding reductions in the expected level of Medicare and Medicaid benefits, and related social services, that would have adverse effects on millions of citizens. At this point the president, who only months earlier had seemed overshadowed by the Speaker, began a masterful effort to use the bully pulpit of the White House to attack the priorities of the House Republicans as extremist and to blame their leadership for the government shutdowns.

Through two months, two government shutdowns, and countless meetings involving the president, congressional leaders, and staffers, the standoff continued. Public opinion swung toward the president's position. As Clinton's resolve and the damage to the Republican Party became clear, Speaker Gingrich and

Senate majority leader Bob Dole sought a compromise with the president that would serve Republican interests by producing a conservative national budget. Because Clinton had repeatedly called for a balanced budget and had supported cuts in expected spending on Medicare, Medicaid, and other programs, he was not in a strong position to resist a compromise. In addition, the president knew that a significant number of House Democrats were tilting toward support of the Republican budget and might help the Republicans override a presidential budget veto. It is not inconceivable that he would have accepted a face-saving compromise, even if it benefited the Republican agenda and reinforced their political momentum. But, in the end, the president and the House Democrats prevailed, not the House Republicans and Speaker Gingrich.

Ironically, it was the House Republicans, particularly the conservative freshmen and sophomores whom Gingrich had recruited and helped elect, who refused to support his effort at compromise in mid-December and forced him to hold out for White House acquiescence.[46] Steeped in a belief that compromise was the main problem with Washington politics, and that only total victory on the budget showdown would fulfill their mandate to transform government, the conservative members of the Republican Conference kept the government shutdown in place until late January. Overwhelming constituent demand for a reopening of government, particularly in Republican districts with large numbers of government employees, forced the conservatives to relent.[47] The Republicans then moved to enact partial appropriations without a seven-year balanced budget agreement. Various Republican budget priorities had won the day in the previous three months, as spending and taxing levels shifted during negotiations toward the Republican positions, which became law during the winter and spring of 1996. But in twice shutting down the government and refusing to compromise on a seven-year balanced budget, the Republicans had diverted public attention from their many victories to one great tactical error and one highly visible legislative defeat. By using extreme tactics, they handed President Clinton and the Democrats a huge political, if not substantive, victory. More important, they revealed the Speaker's inherent weakness.

Despite all the formal power Gingrich had amassed in the House in 1995, he still had to rely for his position on the daily support of his own caucus. When the decisive moment came in negotiations with the president, Gingrich found the speakership a highly constrained office and himself the captive of the ideologues he had recruited. Confronted by Clinton with yet another proposal that he knew the conservative freshmen would oppose, Gingrich reportedly blurted out that if he took the offer to the Republican Conference, "the next time you'll be dealing with Speaker Armey."[48] Faced with the critical test of his power as Speaker, Gingrich found that, unlike the president (who is guaranteed a four-year term except under extraordinary circumstances), he could be stripped of power should his caucus choose to remove him as Speaker. He decided not to take the risk, while President Clinton gambled that Gingrich and the House Republicans would fold. The power and momentum of the Gingrich speakership and the Republican revolution was broken. In the process, Gingrich and the Republicans demonstrated the limits of party government in the House, as well as the constitutional vulnerabilities of the speakership that Joseph Cannon had discovered eight decades earlier.

Creating a Legislative Record

The months following the budget battle tested the ability of Speaker Gingrich and the House Republicans to resuscitate their revolution and retain control of the House in the 1996 elections.[49] They faced a difficult challenge. Under investigation for serious ethics violations and hurt by widely publicized verbal gaffes, Gingrich had become unpopular with the public during 1995. The budget battle with the president reinforced the public's hostility toward him. Moreover, as a result of the budget fiasco, the public was also questioning the judgment of rank and file Republicans, and polls showed that party control of the House could be in jeopardy. In contrast, President Clinton's popularity increased following the budget battles. It seemed possible that he might win a landslide reelection and provide coattails for Democratic congressional candidates. Perhaps most critical, the House Republicans lacked a sense of direction and suffered growing internal dissension and mutual recrimination over the budget defeat. At this point Gingrich altered his leadership strategy.

Political scientists have long debated whether the approach to governance taken by legislative leaders stems primarily from their individual personality and skill or is a product of the context within which they are operating.[50] The difficulty of unraveling this puzzle is perhaps nowhere better illustrated than in the speakership of Newt Gingrich, especially in the adjustments in his leadership style following the budget battle. From November 1994 until January 1996 Gingrich was clearly the dominant ministerial leader, seeking to impose Republican party government and a new conservative era on the House and the nation. In the spring of 1996 this emphasis on confrontation and dominance subsided, and Gingrich became a less visible but more attentive and conciliatory party leader focused on creating a legislative record that would help reelect Republicans. The shift was subtle but significant. In fact, Gingrich's speakership can be divided into two phases: the first, which lasted until February 1996, focused on party governance, while the second focused on enacting legislation.

In shifting leadership styles, Gingrich reflected a new political environment not only in the House but in the nation. In the House, his party had placed clear limits on his power. In the nation, he had become one of the most unpopular political figures of recent history. Gingrich chose not to fight back aggressively, as Jim Wright had done, and as the pugnacious Gingrich of earlier days might have done. Instead, after some initial recriminations against noncooperative freshmen, Gingrich embraced a strategy that few would have expected from his performance during the first phase of his speakership. He adopted a low profile as a party spokesman, avoided extensive television coverage, and plotted strategy for the revival of Republican fortunes. He also redoubled his efforts at fund-raising and support for his party's congressional candidates.

Although the need to shift styles was dictated by context, the choice of a low-key legislative style reflected Gingrich's pragmatism and self-control and considerable experience at adjusting to new contexts in ways that would serve his long-term goals of power and influence.[51] As he made the shift, Gingrich moved his party colleagues toward less combative and more moderate policy positions. He encouraged Republicans to separate themselves from the party and himself and even to run against him, if that would enhance their reelection chances. In addition, he and his party lieutenants focused attention on the passage of significant legislation dealing with issues such as farm policy, telecommunications regulation, and welfare reform. While such legislation was perhaps less epochal in nature than the budget initiatives, their passage would demonstrate the Republicans' ability to govern. To achieve this goal, moreover, he and his lieutenants insisted that these programs be moderate enough for the president to sign or risk appearing to be politically motivated and hypocritical by not signing them. The party leadership also insisted that the spending and taxing committees move swiftly through their hearings and markups so that acceptable revenue and appropriations legislation would be passed by October 1996. The Republicans were trying to avoid any possibility of a government shutdown during the fall campaigns.

As the House Republicans refocused their attention on building a legislative record, the battleground shifted away from confrontations with the president, which made the news every night, and toward the committee rooms and the House floor. Throughout 1995 and the early months of 1996, the Republican task forces and standing committees had worked on policy innovations designed to restructure critical aspects of the federal programs that Democrats had built since the New Deal. Between March and October, when the 104th Congress adjourned, House Republicans, working more cooperatively with the Senate and the Clinton administration, achieved important legislative policy results in agriculture, welfare, and communications. In other areas such as campaign finance and similar political reform initiatives, they floundered.

By fall 1996 the Republican Party had reformed and restructured the House. It had substantially altered the national debate over the budget and pushed the president toward Republican budget priorities. In the process, the GOP had asserted a level of institutional activism and party government unique in the modern Congress. In the first session of the 104th Congress, the House took more recorded votes, and members voted a higher percentage of the time (96.5 percent), than at any time in the institution's modern history.[52] Likewise, in the first session the Republicans maintained a voting cohesion that approached the high levels witnessed under Speaker Cannon.[53] To their party discipline, in the second session the House Republicans added cooperation with the president, the Senate, and House Democrats and made historic alterations in major policy programs.

Such accomplishments would appear more than sufficient to warrant substantial support from the public and an expanded mandate in 1996. Nevertheless, the party entered the elections dispirited and concerned that, rather than achieve the seat gains that would consolidate party control of the House, it might lose seats and even forfeit control.[54] One reason was Bob Dole's lackluster presidential campaign and the good economic times that were benefiting the Democratic incumbent. Another reason was the public's continuing hostility toward Gingrich, despite his role in the budget cuts that may have promoted the good economic times the country was enjoying. But the primary reason was the momentum the budget battle had given to the Democratic president and his resurgent congressional party.

The Democratic Resurgence

Following the 1994 elections, House Democrats appeared to be on the verge of disintegration as a cohesive congressional party. In the previous two years they had helped to defeat their president's national health care initiative, which might have resolidified Democratic dominance of national politics. They had suffered a decisive electoral defeat. They had watched their president move close to collapse as a forceful national leader. Most important, they had come to look like liberal political anachronisms painfully out of sync with the national mood. While the country appeared to be favoring more conservative policies, the House Democrats were dominated by leaders whose urban, poor, and unionized constituencies committed them to an expansive liberal agenda. These leaders were deeply entrenched within the power structure of the party caucus by virtue of their seniority, and they appeared committed to using their power to protect the liberal programs that benefited their constituents. The party also had a declining but significant number of moderate to conservative members from the South, Southwest, and West who were facing considerable electoral pressure from Republicans. Some of these members were so unhappy in the House Democratic caucus that they were prepared to support popular Republican initiatives and were even tempted to switch parties.

The last six weeks of 1994 and the first months of 1995 constituted a period of considerable danger for the Democratic Party. Several House Democrats switched parties and became Republicans. Perhaps more ominous, the ideological divisions within the party raised the possibility that a new conservative coalition of Republicans and conservative Democrats might arise in the House, this time reliant on Republican control of the institution and additional votes from Democrats. This possibility was reinforced by the decisions of House Democrats to sustain liberal control of the caucus during the 104th Congress by selecting Richard Gephardt as minority leader and David Bonier as minority whip.[55] When conservative and moderate Democrats supported Republican leaders on some important votes early in the session, a new conservative coalition appeared possible. And yet influential conservative Democrats—Charles Stenholm of

Texas, for example—held back from a full embrace of Gingrich and the House Republicans. Rather, most conservative and moderate Democrats chose to move cautiously, to organize themselves informally into a group called the Blue Dog Democrats to propose policy compromises distinct from both the Republican and Democratic leaders, and to keep their long-term options open.[56] The Blue Dogs were concerned that by allying themselves with the Republicans they might alienate their traditional Democratic constituents who cared about issues such as Medicare, but not gain subsequent support from Republican activists. They were also encouraged to stay in the Democratic caucus by reassurances they would not be punished for selective votes with Republicans.

Despite the defection of the conservatives on some important votes, throughout 1995 the House Democrats struggled to hold together as a functioning congressional party.[57] Their leaders, particularly Bonior, attacked the ethical lapses of Speaker Gingrich and filed repeated charges against him to fuel the sort of public disillusionment with him that Gingrich had directed toward Jim Wright. The leaders also highlighted what they saw as the Republicans' political and procedural abuses of the minority party and attempted to unite fellow Democrats by obstructing House operations. At this point, political analysts were estimating that the Republicans would gain at least twenty to thirty additional seats in the 1996 elections and solidify their majority. Despite such dire predictions, the House Democrats were unable to find any new policy proposals that would be popular enough to counter the momentum of the Republican revolution. However, as the Republicans pushed for spending cuts in critical areas such as Medicare and Medicaid, liberal and conservative Democrats discovered that they could unite in defense of traditional and popular Democratic programs and slow down the Republicans.

As with the Republican Party, the pivotal moment for the House Democrats came in the struggle over the budget at the end of 1995. When the budget talks began, the Blue Dog Democrats' position was closer to the general spending cuts of the Republicans than to the budget positions of the president and the Democratic congressional leaders. But, as the Republicans held firmly to upper income tax cuts and Medicare reductions and demanded that the president and the Democrats acquiesce, the conservative Democrats began to distance themselves from the Republicans and reach out to their president and party leaders. The unpopularity of the first government shutdown solidified the opposition of conservative and moderate Democrats to the House Republicans. A united Democratic Party then provided the essential—if fragile—support base on which President Clinton relied during his budget negotiations with the Republicans.

When public sentiment swung to the president during the second government shutdown, House Democrats began a period characterized by greater internal cooperation and external assertiveness.[58] The increased popularity of the president and his party in Congress appeared to benefit the Democrats in their home districts. In particular, it increased the prospect that southern conservatives might survive Republican challenges in the 1996 elections. To sustain the momentum of the party and reinforce its renewed cohesion, party leaders looked for issues that would again unite liberals and conservatives, put the Republicans on the defensive, and shape visible policy accomplishments that Democrats could run on. The leaders focused on an increase in the minimum wage.[59] Democrats experienced growing success in such efforts as the election approached and Republican moderates began to split from their party on some issues.[60]

By mid-summer, Democratic members were uniting behind their leaders, while the patience of many Republicans with their party leadership had become exhausted. As one "leadership aide" within the Republican camp said, "The sense is most [Republican] members have reached their breaking point." With a narrow House majority, and the Democrats on the assault, Republican leaders discovered they had little leeway. Defection by a small number of Republican members could turn the party's governing majority into a struggling minority. Clinton and the congressional Democrats exploited the Republicans' vulnerability and forced them to accept many of the president's spending priorities in areas such as education.[61] During the summer the Democrats also crafted their own national agenda, called Putting Families First, that took a more modest approach to policy innovations than had Democrats in the 103d Congress or the Republicans at the beginning of the 104th.

Their success in obtaining passage of the minimum wage and crafting a shared agenda allowed the Democrats during the summer and fall to present a more successful and united appearance to the nation than had seemed possible at the beginning of the 104th Congress.[62] This image was somewhat muddied by President Clinton's decision to sign a modified welfare bill in August 1996, after vetoing two earlier versions, over the objection of his party leaders in Congress. But the welfare bill also had its subtle advantages for the Democrats. Its enactment with the support of the president and conservative-to-moderate House Democrats appeared to convince some segments of the public that a new Democratic Party was emerging that would require citizens to work for a living and then reward workers by protecting their retirement and medical benefits. This perception helped the electoral fortunes of Democrats in the more conservative constituencies within the nation as well as in open southern seats. At the same time, the harsher elements of the welfare bill, particularly its consequences for children and legal immigrants, created pressure on voters in more liberal areas to support the president and congressional Democrats to obtain the improvements of welfare reform that Clinton promised when he signed the legislation. In surprising ways, the passage of the welfare bill solidified the Democratic base and removed welfare reform as an issue in the 1996 elections, allowing a focus on issues more favorable to Democrats.

The Democrats now appeared well positioned on visible policy debates confronting the nation and entered the general elections with a realistic opportunity to pick up additional seats and even regain control of the House. Their efforts were reinforced by generous financial support from labor unions and other Democratic interest groups that particularly targeted freshman Republicans for defeat.[63] The Democrats had come so far in their resurgence, in fact, that by the fall the question facing the nation was whether it wanted to return to united Democratic control of government, as it had experienced during Clinton's first two years in office, or sustain divided control and the restraint it brings to government.[64]

Conclusion

By the end of the 104th Congress, the majority and minority parties had experienced a significant reversal in party fortunes. The surge and decline in Republican fortunes and, indeed, the pattern of surge and decline in majority party government over the past several Congresses, suggest that there are strong pressures for assertive leadership in House policy making, but that sustaining strong party leadership is extraordinarily difficult. The desire for strong party leadership mirrors the public demand that the House overcome its fragmented policy processes and the members' preoccupation with their careers and address the nation's policy problems. These demands are particularly pronounced in periods of divided government. Such concerns made possible Jim Wright's effort to create a strong Democratic speakership in the late 1980s, Tom Foley's assertiveness in the budget struggles with President Bush in 1990, and Newt Gingrich's virtual transformation of the speakership into a dominant position of national policy leadership in 1995. The difficulty of sustaining such leadership, ironically, resulted from the very fragmentation of the House and the careerist calculations of members that generated the demands for it in the first place. Wright's fall, the collapse of Foley's authority during debate over the health care initiatives of President Clinton, and Gingrich's stunning political defeat during the budget battle were rooted in the Speakers' inability to maintain support of their party members at the critical moments of testing.

These developments point to a powerful constraint on strong, autonomous party government in the House: in the end, the individual members have resources in the committee system and careers in their legislative districts distinctly separate from the Speaker's. These personal resources and autonomous careers allow them, and perhaps even propel them, to exercise collective constraint over a Speaker's leadership behavior.[65] When majority party members restrain a Speaker, as they did with Gingrich during the budget battle, they demonstrate the limits of party governance in the House, underscoring the substantial differences between the Speaker and the prime minister in a British-style parliamentary system. In a parliamentary system, the fall of the prime minister can bring down a government and even initiate new elections that members may fear, but in the House the collapse of a speakership simply leads to a new person in the post and may increase the autonomy of party members to follow their own interests. House members have positions on standing committees and resources of personal office staffs that are far more significant and substantial than analogous positions controlled by individual members of a parliament. Although they may owe their institutional positions to a Speaker, the threat of a sudden and united move against him neutralizes any power he has to restrict their personal resources, as Gingrich discovered in December 1995. Moreover, the members can move against a Speaker without facing immediate elections. These difficulties are increased by the Speaker's need to win support not only in the House but also from the Senate with its distinctly separate power relations. Even if the Speaker gains the solid support of a Senate majority, he still is not in charge of the government, as is a prime minister. He is a legislative leader who then must contend with a president who commands the power of government and exercises veto rights over all legislation, including taxing and spending bills.

Autonomous party government in the House, therefore, is inherently difficult to create in a system based on the separation of powers. This fact is not only misunderstood by those politicians who occasionally seek to pursue a parliamentary model of party government in the House, but also by scholars such as Cox and McCubbins who treat House Speakers as virtual legislative dictators and compare House parties to organized leviathans. In truth, congressional parties in the House are not cartel-like syndicates that dominate policy making at the behest of the Speaker and with the subservience of party members. Rather, they more nearly resemble collective cooperatives among equal partners who have considerable autonomy in their career behavior and policy choices. It is the members who choose the momentary leader of their party cooperative, establish its organizational rules and leadership resources, set its broad policy directions, and ultimately decide the level of group cooperation required for members to receive the benefits of membership in the party. Speakers in such parties can be seen more as collegial power brokers who negotiate with members from a position of significant but constrained authority, rather than as authoritative power wielders controlling and directing member behavior. Party members can grant such leaders extensive resources and leadership opportunities, but the leaders are always dependent on their ability to maintain support of party members and therefore always subject to a change in the rules that grant them leadership resources, or even to removal as Speaker.

Lacking the autonomous power to impose authoritative party government on the House, much less on the nation, Speakers may find themselves humiliated by junior members of the minority party, as were O'Neill and Wright; defeated for reelection, as was Foley; or crippled by junior members of the majority party, as was Gingrich. Such vulnerability has substantial implications not just for Speakers as individuals, but for their parties during periods of policy transition and divided government such as the late twentieth century.

Majority parties attempt to create strong party government during periods of policy upheaval to stabilize, energize, and coordinate policy-making processes. The limits on the power of Speakers and the House parties, however, ultimately constrain their success. Certainly, skillful leaders can bridge disagreements among members and forge effective policy coalitions that promote solutions to tough problems. They can also help ensure that decision-making processes at the committee and subcommittee levels proceed efficiently and even vigorously, and they can invent strategies for overcoming organizational and political deadlock. They can push the House to complete its most critical business, such as spending and taxing legislation, in a timely and responsive manner. They can, in short, help ensure that the House functions as a viable and constructive partner in the nation's separation of powers system. But when Speakers try to control House policy making and use such control to dominate the government, they set in motion polarizing conflicts that can undermine constituent support of House members. In pursuing such efforts, moreover, a Speaker necessarily relies on strategies of institutional control that threaten the resources, autonomy, and power of individual members. As the members face mounting electoral pressures and dwindling personal autonomy, the Speaker, who is beholden to them for his office, discovers the limits of party government. The members remind the Speaker who, in a collegial assembly, is truly in charge.

The resulting pattern of surge and decline in party governance during such times can create a fluid and unpredictable congressional policy process and generate sudden shifts in the power relations within the House, between the House and the Senate, and between Congress and the president. This pattern has been witnessed progressively over the past decade and demonstrated vividly during the Republican revolution. In the first phase of Gingrich's speakership, he appeared to control the House, the House appeared to dominate the Senate, and Congress appeared to overshadow the president. But Gingrich's apparent dominance generated concern among citizens about him, particularly because he had not been elected by the nation at large, as had the president. These doubts led to quick judgments when the Republicans overreached in ways he could not then control and fueled his rapid loss of support in his party and the nation. The pattern of rise and fall would seem almost inherent in the effort to create a strong majority party government in the House in an era of careerist legislators and a professionalized Congress.

Creating effective majority party government would appear particularly difficult in the absence of a strong, experienced, and committed majority party president who could support the Speaker with substantial resources and pressures from the Oval Office. Moreover, the difficulty of creating and sustaining assertive party government separate from a strong president, or in conflict with one, would seem increased by the experiments of the Republican revolution and Speaker Gingrich. The future prospects for autonomous majority party government in the House would seem undercut both by the failure of Speaker Gingrich in the 104th Congress, which may by itself restrain the ambitions of Speakers in the future, and by the new rules such as leadership term limits and the enhanced power of committee chairs, should the rules remain in place. Certainly, the creation of strong party government in the House is a considerable challenge rather than a normal occurrence.

The pressure for effective party government and the inherent difficulties in achieving it will now play themselves out in the 105th Congress and beyond. While the voters returned the Republican Party to control of the House in the 1996 elections, they gave the party a reduced majority and pitted it against a Democratic president who won a landslide in the electoral college. Moreover, the defeat of junior Republicans and the closeness of many of the races the Republicans won demonstrated that the Democratic congressional party remains a force to be reckoned with. The Republicans must decide whether to attempt a renewed effort at strong party government in opposition to the president and congressional Democrats—and risk being held accountable in future elections should such efforts fail—or to attempt a more muted partisan strategy. A more restrained partisanship might lead to some cooperation with the president and the Democrats and to legislative successes that might appeal to the public. It could also frustrate the Republican Party's more ideological members, split its ranks in the House, and undercut its momentum as a conservative governing party. As we discuss more fully in Chapter 17, there are considerations that could lead the party in either direction. Whatever tack the Republicans take, their assertiveness is likely to be constrained by the limits on party government that they discovered in the 104th Congress.

Notes

1. Gary W. Cox and Mathew D. McCubbins, *Legislative Leviathan: Party Government in the House* (Berkeley: University of California Press, 1993).
2. For a more extensive discussion, see Randall B. Ripley, *Party Leaders in the House of Representatives* (Washington, D.C.: Brookings, 1967); and Ripley, *Majority Party Leadership in Congress* (New York: St. Martin's, 1969).
3. An excellent discussion of the development of the speakership is Ronald M. Peters Jr., *The American Speakership* (Baltimore: Johns Hopkins University Press, 1990).
4. See Kenneth W. Hechler, *Insurgency: Personalities and Politics in the Taft Era* (New York: Columbia University Press, 1940).
5. James T. Patterson, *Congressional Conservatism and the New Deal* (Lexington: University of Kentucky Press, 1967); John Manley, "The Conservative Coalition," *American Behavioral Scientist* 17 (November-December 1973); and David W. Brady and Charles S. Bullock, III, "Coalitional Politics in the House of Representatives," in *Congress Reconsidered,* 2d ed., ed. Lawrence C. Dodd and Bruce I. Oppenheimer (Washington, D.C.: CQ Press, 1981).
6. Arthur Stevens, Arthur Miller, and Thomas Mann, "Mobilization of Liberal Strength in the House, 1955–1970," *American Political Science Review* 68 (June 1974): 667–681.
7. Charles O. Jones, *The Minority Party in Congress* (Boston: Little, Brown, 1970).
8. Bruce I. Oppenheimer, "The Rules Committee: New Arm of Leadership in a Decentralized House," in *Congress Reconsidered,* 1st ed., ed. Lawrence C. Dodd and Bruce I. Oppenheimer (New York: Praeger, 1977).
9. Richard F. Fenno Jr., *Congressmen in Committees* (Boston: Little, Brown, 1973).
10. Ibid.; and John F. Manley, *The Politics of Finance* (Boston: Little, Brown, 1970).

11. David W. Rohde, *Parties and Leaders in the Postreform House* (Chicago: University of Chicago Press, 1991); and John B. Bader and Charles O. Jones, "The Republican Parties in Congress: Bicameral Differences," in *Congress Reconsidered,* 5th ed., Lawrence C. Dodd and Bruce I. Oppenheimer (Washington, D.C.: CQ Press, 1993).
12. Morris P. Fiorina, *Congress: Keystone of the Washington Establishment* (New Haven: Yale University Press, 1977); and William F. Connelly Jr. and John J. Pitney Jr., *Congress' Permanent Minority? Republicans in the U.S. House* (Lanham, Md.: Rowman and Littlefield, 1994).
13. For a thorough discussion of these developments within the House Republican Conference, see the excellent studies by Douglas L. Koopman, *Hostile Takeover: The House Republican Party, 1980–1995* (Lanham, Md.: Rowman and Littlefield, 1996); and Dan Balz and Ronald Brownstein, *Storming the Gates: Protest Politics and the Republican Revival* (Boston: Little, Brown, 1996).
14. Haynes Johnson and David S. Broder, *The System* (Boston: Little, Brown, 1996).
15. For excellent analyses of the 1994 election, see the essays in *Midterm: The Elections of 1994 in Context,* ed. Philip A. Klinkner (Boulder: Westview, 1996).
16. Bruce I. Oppenheimer, "Split Party Control of Congress, 1981–86: Exploring Electoral and Apportionment Explanations," *American Journal of Political Science* 33 (August 1989): 653–669.
17. Ironically, this seems to run counter to Jacobson and Kernell's view of strategic candidacies. One would expect high incumbent retirements in a party when its prospects for success in an upcoming election were poor. Gary C. Jacobson and Samuel Kernell, *Strategy and Choice in Congressional Elections* (New Haven: Yale University Press, 1983).
18. The concepts of careerism and its operationalization are borrowed from Charles S. Bullock, III, "House Careerists: Changing Patterns of Longevity and Attrition," *American Political Science Review* 66 (1972): 1295–1305.
19. This trend will continue for another two years because the number of open seats created by the departures of nonjunior members going into the 1996 election exceeds the number of members who will start their fourth terms in the House in 1997 and will no longer be categorized as juniors. Even if no incumbents had been defeated in the 1996 election, the 105th Congress would have had more junior members than the 104th. However, it is likely that the trend will end in the 106th Congress because the huge freshman class elected in 1992 will then leave the junior ranks.

    Retirements of careerists exceed the number of members who will be entering their tenth term in 1997. Even if careerists suffer no reelection defeats, the number of careerists will decline to 13 percent in the 105th Congress.
20. Joseph Cooper and William West, "The Congressional Career in the 1970s," in *Congress Reconsidered,* 2d ed., 83–106.
21. Richard F. Fenno Jr., *Home Style: House Members in Their Districts* (Boston: Little, Brown, 1978).
22. For analysis and discussion of the relationship between length of tenure and reelection success, see John R. Hibbing, *Congressional Careers* (Chapel Hill: University of North Carolina Press, 1991), 25–56.
23. Debra L. Dodson, "Whatever Happened to the 'Year of the Woman'?" *The Public Perspective,* August-September 1996, 32.
24. Linda L. Fowler, "Who Runs for Congress?" *PS* 29 (September 1996): 432.
25. For discussions of the link between electoral and organizational cycles, see Evelyn C. Fink and Brian D. Humes, "Party Conflict and Institutional Change in the United States House of Representatives, 1st-99th Congresses" (paper delivered at the annual meeting of the American Political Science Association, San Francisco, Aug. 29–Sept. 1, 1996); and Lawrence C. Dodd, "A Theory of Congressional Cycles," in

Congress and Policy Change, ed. Gerald C. Wright Jr., Leroy N. Rieselbach, and Lawrence C. Dodd (New York: Agathon Press, 1986).

26. For more extensive discussion of the reforms and their effects, see Leroy N. Rieselbach, *Congressional Reform: The Changing Modern Congress* (Washington, D.C.: CQ Press, 1994). See also the essays in *Congress Reconsidered,* 1st and 2d eds.
27. For a more extended discussion of these reform proposals and the subsequent Republican changes in the 104th Congress, see the excellent coverage in C. Lawrence Evans and Walter J. Oleszek, *Congress Under Fire: Reform Politics and the Republican Majority* (Boston: Houghton Mifflin, 1997).
28. Ibid.
29. Lawrence C. Dodd and Bruce I. Oppenheimer, "Consolidating Power in the House: The Rise of a New Oligarchy," in *Congress Reconsidered,* 4th ed., ed. Lawrence C. Dodd and Bruce I. Oppenheimer (Washington, D.C.: CQ Press, 1989), 48–50.
30. Barbara Sinclair, *Majority Party Leadership in the U.S. House* (Baltimore: Johns Hopkins University Press, 1983).
31. Steven S. Smith, *Call to Order* (Washington, D.C.: Brookings, 1989); and Barbara Sinclair, *Legislators, Leaders, and Lawmaking: The U.S. House of Representatives in the Postreform Era* (Baltimore: Johns Hopkins University Press, 1995), analyze these developments.
32. Catalina Camia, "Texans Top List of Aides Picked to Help Gingrich," *Congressional Quarterly Weekly Report,* Dec. 10, 1994, 3490–2.
33. Ronald M. Peters Jr., "The Republican Speakership" (paper prepared for delivery at the annual meeting of the American Political Science Association, San Francisco, Aug. 29–Sept. 1, 1996).
34. David S. Cloud, "Speaker Wants His Platform to Rival the Presidency," *Congressional Quarterly Weekly Report,* Feb. 4, 1995, 331–335.
35. Gingrich acknowledges his debt to the writings of Peter Drucker on executive management and models himself in many ways after the executive strategies proposed by Drucker. See the discussion in John J. Pitney Jr., "Understanding Newt Gingrich" (paper prepared for delivery at the annual meeting of the American Political Science Association, San Francisco, Aug. 29–Sept. 1, 1996), 13–16.
36. Cox and McCubbins, *Legislative Leviathan.*
37. Based on interview material and public documents, Ron Peters suggests that Gingrich sees himself as a leader similar to Benjamin Disraeli, the British prime minister in the 1870s who created a new party majority in the House of Commons and dominated British politics. See Peters, "The Republican Speakership," 9. Former senator Eugene J. McCarthy concluded from his observations of the Speaker, "Gingrich seems to think of himself as a kind of Prime Minister, chosen by the House of Representatives, as a U.S. equivalent of the British Parliament." See McCarthy's comments in Cloud, "Speaker Wants His Platform to Rival the Presidency," 331. See also the discussion in William F. Connelly Jr., "Newt Gingrich: Speaker as Educator and Intellectual" (paper prepared for delivery at the annual meeting of the American Political Science Association, San Francisco, Aug. 29–Sept. 1, 1996). Connelly concludes, "Strong, disciplined, party-oriented congressional government made Gingrich a veritable Prime Minister in 1995" (page 9).
38. Jennifer Babson, "Armey Stood Guard Over Contract," *Congressional Quarterly Weekly Report,* April 8, 1995, 987; Jackie Koszczuk, "With Humor and Firm Hand, Armey Rules the House," *Congressional Quarterly Weekly Report,* March 2, 1996, 523–528; and Koszczuk, "Hard-Charging GOP Whip Seeks a Softer Image," *Congressional Quarterly Weekly Report,* April 13, 1996, 977–979.
39. See Daniel Stid, "Transformational Leadership in Congress?" (paper prepared for

delivery at the annual meeting of the American Political Science Association, San Francisco, Aug. 29–Sept. 1, 1996).

40. Robert W. Merry, "Voters' Demand for Change Puts Clinton on Defensive," *Congressional Quarterly Weekly Report,* Nov. 12, 1994, 3207–9.
41. Gary Jacobson and Thomas P. Kim, "After 1994: The New Politics of Congressional Elections" (paper prepared for delivery at the annual meeting of the Midwest Political Science Association, Chicago, April 18–20, 1995); and Jonathan D. Salant and David S. Cloud, "To the '94 Election Victors Go the Fundraising Spoils," *Congressional Quarterly Weekly Report,* April 15, 1995, 1055–9.
42. Donna Cassata, "Swift Progress of 'Contract' Inspires Awe and Concern," *Congressional Quarterly Weekly Report,* April 1, 1995, 909–912; David S. Cloud, "House GOP Shows a United Front In Crossing 'Contract' Divide," *Congressional Quarterly Weekly Report,* Feb. 25, 1995, 577–579; Jennifer Babson, "House Rejects Term Limits; GOP Blames Democrats," *Congressional Quarterly Weekly Report,* April 1, 1995, 918; and Donna Cassata, "Republicans Bask in Success of Rousing Performance," *Congressional Quarterly Weekly Report,* April 8, 1995, 986–1006.
43. Jeffrey L. Katz, "GOP Faces Unknown Terrain Without 'Contract' Map," *Congressional Quarterly Weekly Report,* April 8, 1995, 979–983.
44. Daniel P. Franklin, *Making Ends Meet* (Washington, D.C.: CQ Press, 1993).
45. The struggle over the nation's budget during 1995 and early 1996 is described extensively by Elizabeth Drew in *Showdown: The Stuggle Between the Gingrich Congress and the Clinton White House* (New York: Simon and Schuster, 1996).
46. Jackie Koszczuk, "Gingrich Struggling to Control Revolts Among the Troops," *Congressional Quarterly Weekly Report,* Dec. 23, 1995, 3864–5.
47. Jackie Koszczuk, "House Republicans Abandon Confrontational Tactics," *Congressional Quarterly Weekly Report,* Jan. 27, 1996, 210–212; and George Hager, "Republicans Throw in Towel on Seven-Year Deal," *Congressional Quarterly Weekly Report,* Jan. 27, 1996, 213–216.
48. Drew, *Showdown,* 352.
49. Jackie Koszczuk, "GOP Faces Campaign Year Adrift in Roiled Waters," *Congressional Quarterly Weekly Report,* Jan. 20, 1996, 139–141; and Koszczuk, "For Embattled GOP Leadership, A Season of Discontent," *Congressional Quarterly Weekly Report,* July 20, 1996, 2019–23.
50. Joseph Cooper and David Brady, "Institutional Context and Leadership Style: The House from Cannon to Rayburn," *American Political Science Review* 75 (June 1981): 411–425; and David W. Rohde and Kenneth A. Shepsle, "Leaders and Followers in the House of Representatives: Reflections on Woodrow Wilson's Congressional Government," *Congress and the Presidency* 14 (Autumn 1988): 111–133.
51. On the pragmatic streak in Gingrich's personality, see Peters, "The Republican Speakership," 15–17; and Pitney, "Understanding Newt Gingrich," 24–26.
52. Melissa Weinstein Kaye, "Most Votes Ever Were Taken, With Fewer Votes Missed," *Congressional Quarterly Weekly Report,* Jan. 27, 1996, 205.
53. Dan Carney, "As Hostilities Rage on the Hill, Partisan-Vote Rate Soars," *Congressional Quarterly Weekly Report,* Jan. 27, 1996, 199–201.
54. Richard E. Cohen, "Doom and Gloom Plague the Republicans," *National Journal,* May 4, 1996, 1003; and Paul Starobin, "Divided They Fall?" *National Journal,* Aug. 10, 1996.
55. Jonathan D. Salant, "Retrenching House Democrats Seek Solace in Seniority," *Congressional Quarterly Weekly Report,* Dec. 17, 1994, 3543–6.
56. David S. Cloud, "Conservative Democrats Band Together to Try to Maximize Their Influence," *Congressional Quarterly Weekly Report,* Feb. 18, 1995, 496–497.

57. David S. Cloud, "Democrats Find Their Footing in Minority Party Trenches," *Congressional Quarterly Weekly Report,* July 1, 1995, 1893.
58. Jackie Koszczuk, "Democrats' Resurgence Fueled by Pragmatism," *Congressional Quarterly Weekly Report,* May 4, 1996, 1205–10.
59. Jonathan Weisman, "Minimum Wage: Maximum Effect," *Congressional Quarterly Weekly Report,* May 4, 1996, 1206.
60. Jonathan D. Salant, "House Republicans Stray from 'Contract' Terms," *Congressional Quarterly Weekly Report,* July 6, 1996, 1929–33.
61. George Hager, "Eager to Deal and Leave, GOP Yields to Clinton," *Congressional Quarterly Weekly Report,* Sept. 21, 1996, 2655–6.
62. Paul Starobin, "Hanging Together," *National Journal,* Aug. 24, 1996; and Richard E. Cohen, "On Capitol Hill, Togetherness for Now," *National Journal,* Aug. 24, 1996.
63. Jonathan Weisman, "Republicans Battle Unions on Hill and on Airwaves," *Congressional Quarterly Weekly Report,* Aug. 10, 1996, 2250–2.
64. For a discussion of the preference distributions and voter calculus that could lead citizens to produce divided government and political moderation, see Morris Fiorina, *Divided Government,* 2d ed. (Boston: Allyn and Bacon, 1996), 72–81.
65. Or as Barbara Sinclair puts it, "Members of the House expect their party leaders to advance the members' goals of reelection, policy and influence . . . but without imposing unacceptable constraints on members' pursuit of their goals through individualist strategies. . . . What members consider the optimal balance will vary over time as a function of the costs and benefits to members of assertive versus restrained central leadership." See Barbara Sinclair, *Legislators, Leaders, and Lawmaking,* 18. See also the discussion in Lawrence C. Dodd, "Congress and the Quest for Power," in *Congress Reconsidered,* 1st ed.

3. What the Public Dislikes About Congress

John R. Hibbing and Elizabeth Theiss-Morse

To state the obvious, the 1990s have not been a time of public satisfaction with politics. Americans, we are told, "hate politics"[1] and are experiencing a "crisis of confidence."[2] But the precise nature and causes of this disapprobation remain uncertain. Efforts to account for public sourness include diverse arguments such as E. J. Dionne Jr. blaming the parties, Alan Ehrenhalt blaming ambitious professional politicians, the Kettering Foundation blaming a detached system, and politicians blaming the people.[3] At the same time, nearly all commentators agree that at the center of the public's unrest is Congress, the first branch of government. Year in and year out, Congress is easily the least popular institution.[4] Americans, it is reported, "hate Congress."[5]

Our major purpose in this chapter is to provide an overarching theory for understanding public attitudes toward political institutions, focusing primarily on public opinion toward Congress. This choice of institutions is appropriate not only because of the prominent place Congress is accorded in the American system of government but also because of the continuing "crisis" of approval engulfing Congress, which attracts extensive discussion and speculation in both popular and scholarly writings.

Our theoretical argument focuses on the importance of political processes in public opinion. Many observers of American politics assume that people find procedural matters boring and beyond their zone of interest. Policy outcomes are what matter to people, not political processes.[6] Lewis Froman and Randall Ripley, for example, describe how members of Congress follow the party line more often on matters of process than on matters of substance largely because the public is less likely to follow, to appreciate, and to understand procedural nuances.[7] House Minority Leader Richard Gephardt, D-Mo., in explaining the public's lack of understanding of Congress, notes that people tend to get lost in the day-to-day process stories inevitable during the lengthy congressional consideration of bills.[8]

While it is true that people are not particularly attuned to day-to-day maneuverings on specific legislation, it should not be concluded that they are unaware of the process. In fact, we contend that the cornerstone of public disapprobation of Congress is grounded in process. Institutional approval, in other words, is largely contingent upon perceptions of the processes in and around those institutions. Disapprobation for a particular institution, we believe, is often produced not by public dissatisfaction with what that institution did but by dissatisfaction with how the institution is perceived to have done it.

To help us understand attitudes toward political institutions, we use two novel data sets, expressly collected for the purpose of discovering the subtleties of public approval of Congress and other political institutions. One data set comes from thirty-minute nationwide telephone interviews of 1,400 randomly selected adults. The other data set comes from eight focus group sessions held in four states: Nebraska, Minnesota, Texas, and New York. Both data sets were collected in the summer of 1992.[9]

People Love Congress but Hate Members

Before we investigate who is most likely to approve or not approve of Congress, we need to clarify what we mean by Congress. Richard Fenno's often-repeated point that people approve of their own member of Congress but disapprove of Congress generally is correct.[10] This precise configuration of the situation, however, obscures what people really think about Congress. The truth is people disapprove of members of Congress as a *collectivity* while approving of Congress as an *institution,* just as they disapprove of the leaders of Congress while approving of their own member.

Our national survey instrument included questions on people's attitudes toward the 1992 membership of Congress, the congressional leadership, their own member of Congress, and Congress as an institution. Figure 3-1 shows how important specification of the referent is. People's attitudes toward Congress vary dramatically depending upon the particular aspect of Congress mentioned. The general membership and the leadership receive poor marks, with only about one in four respondents approving. As Fenno pointed out long ago, people's attitudes toward their own members are much more favorable, with two-thirds of Americans approving. Yet approval of one's representative is not a core feature of public sentiment toward Congress generally; rather, it is a somewhat special feature of the American form of government—representation in single-member districts with relatively independent legislators.

Perhaps the most notable aspect of Figure 3-1 is the strong level of support for Congress *as an institution.* Eighty-eight percent of the respondents expressed approval of Congress in the rather abstract version referenced in our question.[11] To be sure, when ordinary people think of Congress, they think of a collection of 535 members and not an institution, so the high level of support for the institution does not mean that the public actually likes Congress. Instead, the point is that statements such as "the people hate Congress" ignore the fact that Congress is many different things. When people think of Congress as an institution with history, buildings, and a constitutional role, they tend to be highly approving of it, but when they think of it as an amalgamation of hundreds of breathing, fallible human beings, approval dwindles. The fact that public opinion toward Congress generally is so negative indicates that when the public thinks of Congress, it thinks of Congress the collection of members, not Congress the institution.

With this clarification behind us, we now turn to the challenge of explaining why some people are more approving of Congress than others, for it is in these patterns that we can discern the nature and causes of attitudes toward Congress and political institutions more generally. We start by examining some pop-

Figure 3-1 Evaluations of Congressional Referents, 1992

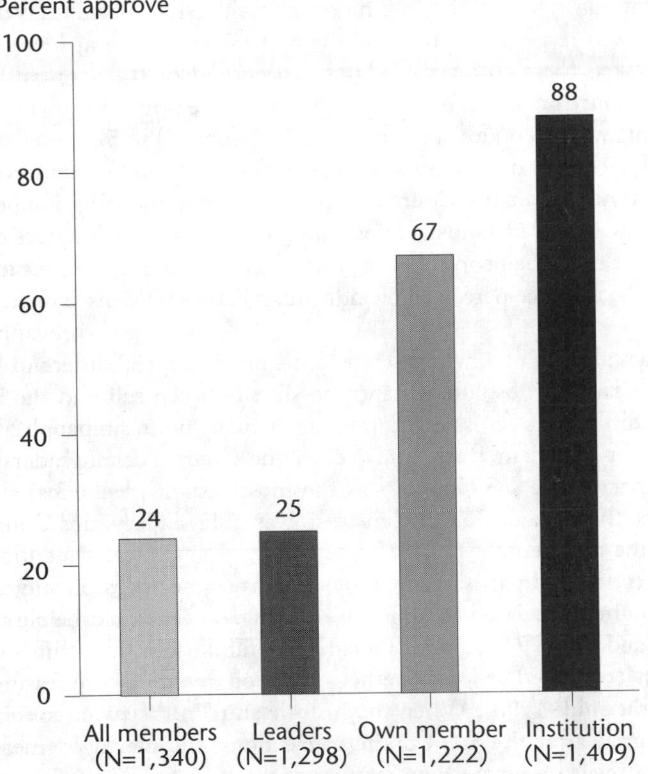

Source: Perceptions of Congress Survey, 1992.

ular explanations, then move to our preferred explanation before concluding with a multivariate investigation of these various hypotheses.

Conventional Wisdom on Who Approves of Congress: Ideology, Partisanship, and Education

It has long been held that a major reason for Congress's unpopularity is that the American people believe it is out of step with them ideologically. Remember that our survey was conducted in 1992, before the Republicans ended forty years of congressional dominance by the Democrats. Perhaps Congress's unpopularity at that time derived from the perception that it was in the clutches of a liberal Democratic leadership and membership while the American people were more centrist or perhaps even right of center. How accurate is such speculation?

The first condition necessary for this explanation to work is that the people must believe they are more ideologically distant from Congress than from political institutions of which they are more approving. To determine if this was the case, we asked respondents to place themselves on a 5–point ideological scale. We also asked them to place Congress, the president (George Bush), and the Supreme Court on the same scale. The mean ideological self-placement for respondents was 3.3 on a scale running from 1 (liberal) to 5 (conservative) while the mean placement of Congress was 2.5, of Bush, 3.9, and of the Court, 3.6 (the standard deviation for the Court was extremely high, meaning the people really do not know where it stands ideologically). Congress, on average, is only a little more distant from the people, but the important consideration is not mean placement but the distance perceived by individuals between themselves and the institutions.

On a scale of 0 to 4, where 0 represents no ideological difference and 4 represents the farthest absolute distance possible between self and the institution, the mean differences across institutions are actually quite similar—2.0 for Congress, 1.7 for President Bush, and 1.8 for the Court. Although these numbers indicate that people see Congress as the most distant ideologically from their own views, the distance, in 1992 at least, was only slightly greater than for the Court or the president.

The concept of partisanship, often seen as connected to ideology and policy, is undoubtedly related to approval of Congress. It would be surprising if it were not, and the 1994 elections provide a useful illustration of this relationship. Democrats controlled at least one house of Congress—usually two—from the 1950s to the mid-1990s. When the historic shift in the party control of Congress occurred after the 1994 midterm elections, the media covered Congress extensively, focusing on the new Speaker of the House, Newt Gingrich, R-Ga., the reforms proposed in the Contract with America, and the incoming class of freshman Republicans. It makes sense to think that approval of Congress would increase when a different group of people come into power with a desire to shake up the system, especially given people's disgust with "politics as usual" prior to the 1994 election. The attitude that anything that is different is good should have led to an increase in Congress's overall approval level in 1995. It is surprising, therefore, that overall approval of Congress increased only a little after the new party leadership took control.

Using *New York Times*/CBS News poll data, Figure 3-2 compares people's approval of the 103d Congress with their approval of the 104th Congress. While the increase in approval from December 1994, the end of Democratic control, to February 1995, the beginning of Republican control, is 16 percentage points, the honeymoon period, such as it was, was short-lived. By December 1995 approval of the Republican Congress had dropped to 26 percent, very similar to the rating given the Democratic Congress.[12] One might have thought that a new majority party and leadership team in both houses would have produced an impressive and less-transient increase in support, but it never materialized.

Figure 3-2 Approval of Congress, 103d and 104th Congresses

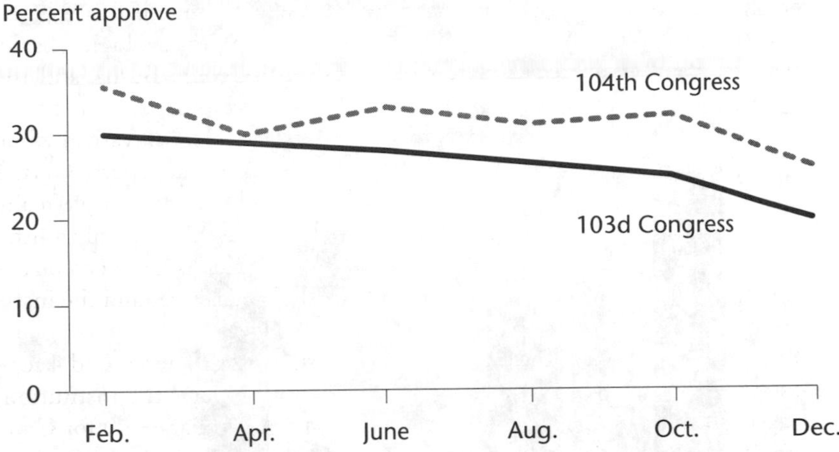

Sources: *New York Times*/CBS News poll, Dec. 9–11, 1995; Richard Berke, "Clinton's Ratings Over 50% in Poll as G.O.P. Declines," *New York Times*, Dec. 14, 1995, A1, B17.

These overall approval ratings, however, may hide intense partisan patterns in approval or disapproval of Congress. Democrats may have adored the Democratic-controlled Congress but detested the Republican-controlled Congress. Republicans may have had the opposite reaction. We were surprised to learn that the effect of partisanship on approval is relatively modest. When we conducted our survey in 1992, and the Democrats were still in control of both houses of Congress, we found that 41 percent of Democrats approved of Congress, 34 percent of independents approved, and 32 percent of Republicans approved. The difference between Democrats and Republicans (9 points) is not great because nearly 60 percent of all Democrats disapproved of the institution their party had dominated for so long.

To what extent did the situation reverse after the Republicans took over both houses in early 1995? With all of the fanfare that attended the changing of the guard, we would expect that partisanship would be more strongly related to approval of Congress in the post–1994 era than was the case in 1992. Figure 3-3 shows that this expectation is accurate to a point. Data from a *New York Times*/CBS News poll conducted in February 1996 indicate that public approval of Congress declined dramatically among Democrats and independents, and rose slightly among Republicans, between 1992 and 1996. These low approval ratings may be due in part to the raised expectations Americans had for the new Congress and the subsequent realization that Congress was back to business as usual a year after the Republicans gained power. Figure 3-3 also shows that party shifts occurred as we expected. In 1992 Democrats were more approving of the Dem-

Figure 3-3 Shift in Partisan Approval of Congress, 1992–1996

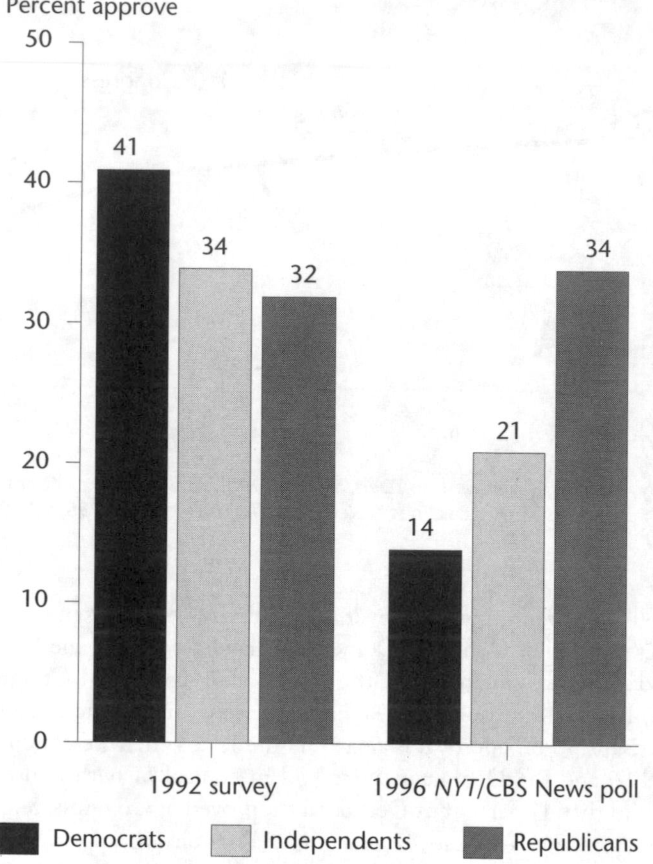

Sources: Perceptions of Congress Survey, 1992; and *New York Times*/CBS News poll, Feb. 22–24, 1996.

ocratic Congress than Republicans, and in 1996 Republicans were more approving of the Republican Congress than Democrats. When party control shifts, so does support across partisans, but perhaps not as much as might be expected. Only a year after the Republicans seized control of Congress, almost 60 percent of Republicans continued to disapprove, and independents' approval declined by more than 10 percentage points between 1992 and 1996. Large majorities of all party groups, both before and after the 1994 elections, disapproved of Congress.

Once the effects of partisanship are controlled, using the 1992 data, the effects of perceived ideological distance from Congress are revealed to be small, as can be seen in Figure 3-4. For each partisan group, it would appear that approval of Congress diminishes slightly as perceived ideological distance increases from

Figure 3-4 Approval of Congress by Ideological Distance, Party, 1992

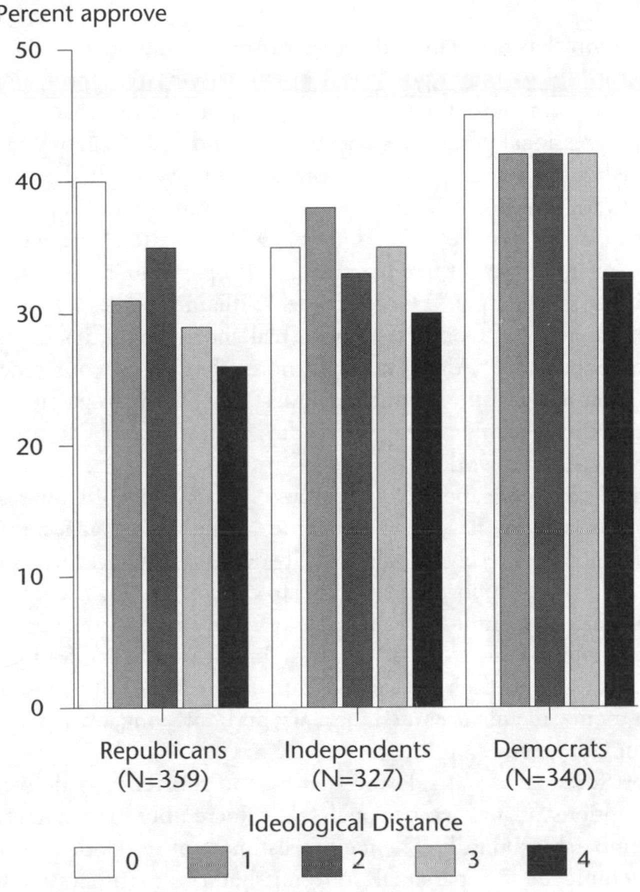

Source: Perceptions of Congress Survey, 1992.

0 to 4. But the pattern is not strong, achieving significance for Democrats and Republicans but not for independents, and even for partisans explaining less than 3 percent of the variance in approval of the congressional membership. Moreover, a large chunk of the population (302 of our 1,400 respondents) is unwilling to try placing Congress on the ideological spectrum.[13] Even so, these people are still unsupportive of Congress, with approximately 62 percent either disapproving or strongly disapproving.

Clearly, it is not necessary for people to believe Congress is out of step with them ideologically for them to disapprove of Congress. Like partisanship, perceived ideological distance is not irrelevant to public approval of Congress, but the notion that this perceived distance is at the root of Congress's problems with the public is erroneous. Only a little more than a third of those people who believe Congress is a perfect match with their own ideological preferences approves of the congressional membership.

Another explanation that has achieved the status of conventional wisdom, particularly on Capitol Hill, is that a good deal of the public's disapprobation comes from a lack of information about what Congress does, from inaccurate information about congressional perquisites and the like, and from negative stories that the media delight in sending into the homes of the people. If the public just knew the facts, this argument holds, they would be much more supportive of Congress. For example, Rep. Peter J. Visclosky, D-Ind., states, "I've gotten letters saying we get free food, we get free haircuts. . . . People write half-truths, and all of a sudden it becomes gospel." His colleague, William Goodling, R-Pa., believes that "if we [members of Congress] have a real shortcoming, it's in the area of educating the populace."[14] Alan Ehrenhalt notes that "every conference on the subject of legislatures and their future includes at least one impassioned plea from an elected official to his colleagues to do a better job of educating reporters on the way legislatures work."[15]

The "if they only knew more about us they would like us" view of Congress is not totally false, but is seriously flawed. For example, giving people an accurate picture of the benefits members receive would actually decrease support for Congress. How can this be? Public support for proposals to cut congressional salaries, reduce congressional staffs, and limit the time members can remain in Congress is overpowering, often approaching three to one. In light of these strong feelings, we asked respondents to give us their best guess as to how many staffers members had, how much money members earned in salary, and how long, on average, members had been in Congress.

Is public support for smaller staffs, lower salaries, and shorter stays derived from erroneous perceptions of massive personal staffs, incredibly high salaries, and a permanent membership? Hardly. The median estimate of respondents was that each member employed 7.5 personal staffers, that the members made $99,000, and that they had been in Congress for eight years. When we conducted the survey, House members actually employed an average of 17.4 personal staffers, made $130,000, and had served in Congress an average of eleven years.

It is easy to see that if the people knew more about the situation in Congress, they would almost certainly be *more* supportive of term limits and *more* supportive of efforts to cut salary and reduce staff. Public misperceptions in this instance work to Congress's advantage. It should not be assumed that objective information about Congress and perquisites will turn citizens from surly to supportive; it will instead quite likely make them grumpier.

We will see later that, in a more general sense, traditional education and information are not related to public approval of Congress. Sad to say, a citizenry informed about the specifics of the congressional benefits package or about the political scene generally is not going to improve the status of Congress in American society. Those who believe the central problem of Congress's image has to do with an uninformed, misinformed, or uneducated citizenry are perpetuating a myth. Certain kinds of information would likely improve Congress's image, but simply having a more informed citizenry would not do the trick.

Our Preferred Explanation: The Democratic Wish in Modern Liberal Democracy

If not conventional wisdom, then upon what can a theory of institutional approval be built? Institutional approval is more than public appreciation of policy outputs. It is more than liking one's own representative. It is more than being informed about politics. American democracy has evolved over time both in terms of public expectations and institutional structures. We contend that public disaffection with institutions is largely the result of frustration with the way democracy is practiced in those institutions.

Public disgust is manifested when the people's pristine "democratic wish" confronts the gritty reality of the current practice of American liberal democracy.[16] The democratic wish "imagines a single, united people, bound together by a consensus over the public good, which is discerned through direct citizen participation."[17] Do Americans really believe such a consensus exists? They do. While our survey did not contain questions useful for eliciting attitudes about the extent to which such values are shared, the focus group discussions provided sufficient evidence to support this argument.

Most of the participants fell comfortably into talking about the wishes of "the people" or "the American people" as if there were a united public mind. If members of Congress would only pay attention to "the people," they argued, the United States would be better off. Even though a few focus group participants were reluctant to lump all people together, they still made a strong distinction between the majority of people and the extremes. The following exchange is illustrative.

> Sally: I think the vast majority of Congress's members have no idea really what the people's wishes are.
>
> Don: They are in touch with the extreme. Those are the people that they listen to and they're the ones that pull their strings, right? But the majority. . . .
>
> Jack: I think the problem is that the majority isn't getting what it wants.

Participants talked easily about the wishes of "the people" or "the majority," but they almost never connected these wishes to actual substantive content. For most people, the public good is *not* specific policy outputs; rather, it is a feeling that the government goes about its business in a manner that is sensitive to the public interest. As such, the public good is as much procedural as substantive.

Writings on the democratic wish for consensus often use the community as the unit of analysis—a level at which some degree of consensus *may* be possible.

At the national level, particularly in a large, complex, and diverse society, the public's belief in the existence of consensus seems naive. James Madison, for example, in *The Federalist Papers,* No. 10 and No. 51, argued that in populous democracies diverse interests are natural and "the regulation of these various and interfering interests forms the principal task of modern legislation and involves the spirit of party and faction in the necessary and ordinary operations of government."[18] The structure of government, the two houses of Congress and a separate executive, ensures that the process of government will be slow and deliberate, providing multiple and conflicting access points to take into account various factions without allowing the majority to infringe upon private interests.

By our reading, the people could hardly be less Madisonian on this count. Belief in the existence of popular consensus is firmly embedded, even at the national level, which makes it extremely difficult for national political institutions to gain public respect. Why do we need clackety Rube Goldberg-like contraptions for political institutions when they only stand in the way of the public will—at best slowing it down, at worst diverting the public will in favor of nefarious special interests? The public has a sense that if things were working properly, institutions would be silent processors of the public consensus; they would be whirring, taken-for-granted parts of the black box.

The reality of diverse special interests, partisan divisions, a ponderously slow political process, debate, and compromise all seems strangely out of place to a public convinced that deep down we all agree on most things. Hostility naturally arises toward these counterproductive political institutions. The professionalization of institutions that usually comes with maturation and the more impersonal representation that accompanies populous democracies add to the feeling that the government ignores the people's wishes.

Feelings of hostility are likely to be directed most vehemently at the institution that exhibits these procedural characteristics most publicly and is thereby perceived to be the most powerful obstruction to the democratic wish. That institution is Congress. Its procedures are public by nature so people can see Congress openly hindering efficient decision making, listening to special interests, and building a large infrastructure. Because Congress is so visible, the people see it as powerful. It is, after all, the major dam obstructing what would otherwise be a smooth flow from public consensus to public policy.

The Importance of Power and Process Perceptions

Our theory of institutional approval focuses on Congress and the interplay of popular expectations and liberal democratic processes.[19] We test this theory empirically in two stages. We first investigate whether people do in fact perceive Congress to be a powerful institution. Such a finding would be consistent with our process-based theory, but would contradict the accepted wisdom in political science that the presidency is the most powerful institution. In the second stage, we examine whether people's awareness of and attitudes toward liberal democratic processes are related to hostility toward Congress. If our argument is correct, the public nature of congressional processes contributes much to people's disgust with their national legislature.

Congressional Power

A typical textbook on the presidency leads off by saying that nothing "haunts Americans as persistently as the illusion that the president of the United States is an all-powerful, all-knowing, one-man government."[20] In fact, the thesis of the book is that belief in the power of the president is so great that people are setting themselves up for inevitable disappointment and disillusionment. Numerous other works on the president and on American politics are predicated on the belief that citizens see the president as omnipotent, and professional observers of the political scene usually concur. Morris Fiorina notes that "certainly on the national level most analysts have viewed the presidency as stronger than the Congress at least since the time of FDR."[21]

Whether the president is actually more powerful than Congress is not our concern here; neither is whether people *want* the president to be more powerful. But we would like to issue a direct challenge to the conclusion that the American people *believe* the president is more powerful than Congress. It simply is not true. Consider the following. We asked respondents, "Which part of the government is more responsible for the massive budget deficits currently facing the U.S. government?" The three options provided were Congress, the president, or both. It seemed likely that people would gravitate toward the "both" response or, if the speculation about an all-powerful president is correct, would say the president was the most powerful. This was not the case. About one in four respondents (27 percent) believed both institutions were equally responsible, and only one in five (21 percent) believed the presidency was the more responsible, leaving a remarkable 52 percent to register the belief that Congress was the institution responsible for the budget deficits.

What about people's perceptions of the budget impasse in late 1995 and early 1996 that led to the longest government shutdown in recent U.S. history? The Republican leadership pointed the finger of blame at President Clinton for the impasse, while he in turn blamed the Republicans in Congress. Whom did the public blame? A *New York Times*/CBS News poll conducted in early January 1996 found that 44 percent of respondents placed more blame on the congressional Republicans for the budget impasse compared to 33 percent who blamed President Clinton more.[22] The results from both the 1992 and 1996 surveys suggest that the public believes Congress is more powerful than the president and therefore calls the shots in Washington, especially on budget matters. In fact, a *New York Times*/CBS News poll taken in early December 1995 found that 58 percent of respondents said congressional Republicans would have more influence over the direction the country was heading compared to only 32 percent who chose President Clinton.[23]

Figure 3-5 Perceptions of Institutional Power, 1992

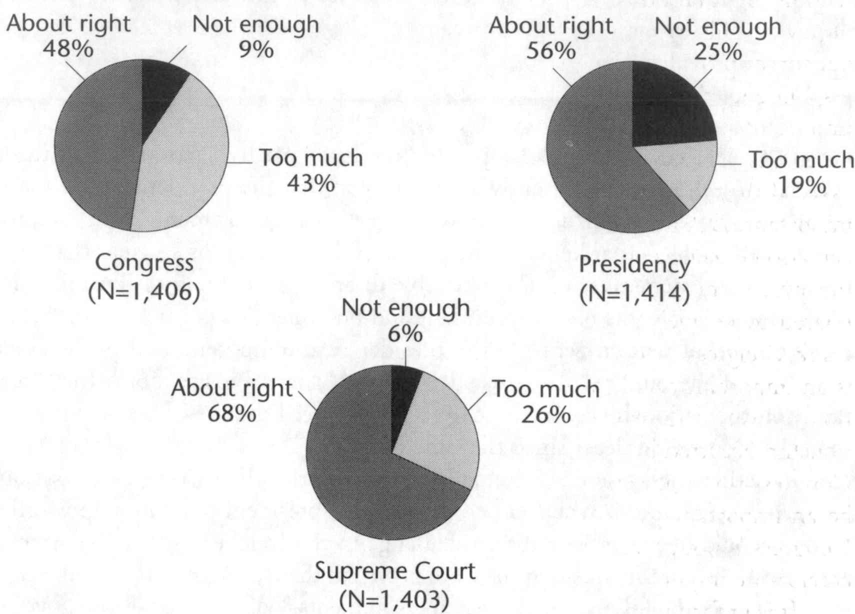

Source: Perceptions of Congress Survey, 1992.

But these perceptions of congressional power could be due to the understanding that Congress controls the nation's spending and is therefore more powerful than the president on an issue such as the budget deficit. A second approach is to ask people if they believe in a general sense that each institution has too much, about the right amount, or not enough power. Asking whether an institution has too much or too little power is not the same as asking how much power it has. Nonetheless, it is unlikely that respondents would say that a weak institution should have less power or that an incredibly powerful institution should have more power.

While Figure 3-5 reveals that the percentage of people believing the Supreme Court and the presidency have too much power is relatively modest (26 percent and 19 percent, respectively), a much more substantial 43 percent believes Congress has too much power. More people believe the presidency has too little power than believe it has too much, but when asked about Congress, nearly five times as many people believe it has too much power than believe it has not enough.[24] Political analysts may assume that people believe the president is omnipotent, but someone forgot to tell this to the public. Most people see Congress as much more powerful than the president.

Moreover, people perceive Congress to have a certain kind of power, a negative power by which it keeps things from getting done by talking issues to death. People who are particularly disapproving of a "talk" rather than an "action" orientation are especially likely to see Congress as having a great deal of power. This hypothesis was tested in the following manner. One question on our survey provides a rough measure of perceptions of obstructionism. We asked respondents the extent to which they considered six different tasks to be an important part of a representative's job. One task, relevant to our discussion here, was "discussing and debating controversial issues." Respondents were asked if they thought the task was not important, somewhat important, or very important. Debating issues is part of the democratic process in Congress, but can also be seen as obstructionist. In essence, people can see Congress spending too much time *talking* and not enough time *doing*. Is obstructionist process related to people's perceptions of congressional power? It is. The less people think Congress is too powerful, the more likely they are to believe that debate is an important task in which representatives should be involved. (The correlation between the two sentiments is –.08, and the likelihood that such a relationship occurred by chance is less than 5 percent.) Among people who believe Congress is too powerful, 53 percent do *not* think debate and discussion should be an important part of a representative's job, but among people who believe Congress is not powerful enough, only 40 percent do not think debate and discussion are important in the job of a representative.

It is unfortunate that the public's perception of congressional power and the extent to which this power is seen as the power to obstruct has been so unappreciated by analysts, because these perceptions have important implications and must be placed at the core of any serious attempt to come to grips with public disapproval of the institution. The importance can be seen in the strong relationship between perceptions of congressional power and support for Congress. Approval of Congress is highest among respondents who think Congress does not have enough power (48 percent) and fairly high among those who think it has about the right amount of power (34 percent). Congressional approval is extremely low (only 9 percent), however, among those who think Congress has too much power. Unhappiness with Congress stems from two perceptions—first, that Congress has more to do with shaping the governmental process than do the other institutions and, second, that its power is manifested primarily through obstructionism. If the public is upset when nothing seems to get done, it usually vents its spleen at the institution it believes possesses but does not use the ability to affect significantly those conditions: Congress. In the eyes of the people, Congress's power actually keeps things from getting done.

Professionalization and Representation

In addition to perceptions of power, our process-based explanation for congressional support holds that unrest with Congress will be unusually acute among those who dislike the way Congress goes about its business. Two of the most visible components of modern congressional processes are professionalization—the

Figure 3-6 Process Perceptions and Approval of Members of Congress, 1992

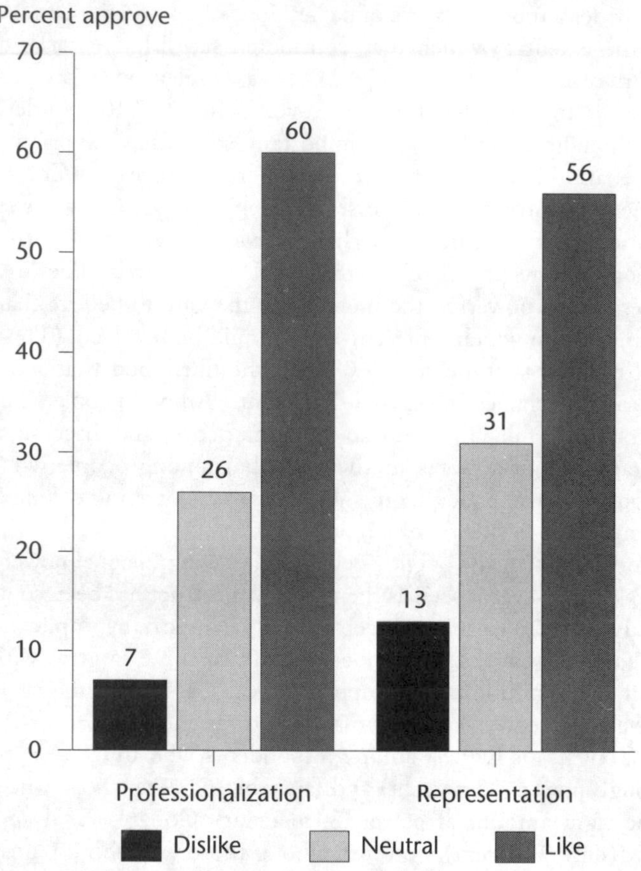

Source: Perceptions of Congress Survey, 1992.

extent to which members stay a long time, are attractively remunerated, and are faced with a complex, multidimensional institution—and the tendency of Congress to represent (in the public eye) interests rather than people. Is it the case that those who are unfavorable toward legislative professionalization and interest group representation are, other things being equal, the least approving of Congress? Our results are presented in Figure 3-6.

Our specific measure of attitudes toward a professionalized Congress is the combination of responses to questions on attitudes toward the number of staffers in Congress, the division of labor (committees), the degree of power concentration in Congress, and the degree to which members are perceived to concentrate on their world in Washington.[25] Professionalization has a natural tendency to increase the perceived distance between the citizenry and the government, thereby loosening the public's control over government. Because one of the hallmarks of the modern Congress is professionalization, those people least supportive of professionalization should also be the people least supportive of Congress.

The second procedural variable we include is perceptions of the kind of representation provided by Congress. This variable is the combination of responses to questions on the degree to which Congress is influenced by interest groups, the degree to which it fails to represent diverse groups, and the degree to which it has become detached from ordinary people. The democratic wish is that the government represent the public good as expressed by the people, and not by special interests that reflect atypical opinions and values. Obviously, the expectation is that the more people believe Congress is not influenced inordinately by interest groups, is representing diverse groups, and is not detached from ordinary people (all coded with higher values), the more favorable they should be toward Congress.

Like the perceived power of Congress, these two crucial process variables behave just as we expected (see Figure 3-6). Approval of Congress is considerably higher among people who do not mind legislative professionalization and who are not especially bothered by the way Congress is seen to represent various interests. This is strong preliminary evidence that we are on the right track in stressing the perceived processes of Congress as a reason for public disapproval. Many people, it would seem, dislike Congress because of how it does things.

Before putting stock in this belief, we must test it in a multivariate fashion. Many bivariate relationships have been known to fade away once other known influences are allowed to work at the same time. Therefore, we offer our attempt to marshal a more complete model of variations in public evaluations of Congress. Our measure of approval ranges from 0 to 100 and combines equally weighted responses to a feeling thermometer for members of Congress and a standard approval question for the same, which means that our approval score is the combined effect of people's evaluation of the job Congress has done and the extent to which people like or dislike Congress. This dependent variable focuses on the congressional membership rather than the institution because, as we noted earlier, for so many people Congress *is* its membership. Explaining variations in approval of Congress as the congressional membership constitutes the core of our analysis.

In addition to the three central variables—power of Congress, professionalization, and representation—Table 3-1 includes ten other variables ranging from obvious controls such as gender, age, income, efficacy (one's feeling of political effectiveness), and party identification to variables more relevant to topics raised earlier in this essay, such as ideology, approval of Congress as an institution, approval of one's own member of Congress, perceptions of how well Congress is handling the nation's most important problem, and level of political knowledge. Approval of Congress was regressed (ordinary least squares) on all these independent variables.[26]

Table 3-1 Causes of Approval of Members of Congress, 1992

Independent variable	Regression coefficient	Standard error	t-ratio
Demographic features			
Sex	−0.58	0.93	−0.6
Age	1.04	2.25	0.5
Income	−4.74	1.86	−2.6**
Political attitudes			
External efficacy	5.17	1.26	4.1**
Party identification	−3.98	1.45	−2.7**
Ideology	−2.71	1.45	−1.9
Congress's handling of most important problem	9.59	2.06	4.7**
Political knowledge	−3.41	1.31	−2.6**
Approve institution	7.73	2.36	3.3**
Approve own member	12.74	2.12	6.0**
Perceptions of Congress			
Power of Congress	−8.55	1.54	−5.5**
Professionalization	19.34	3.68	5.2**
Representation	15.00	3.26	4.6**
Constant	25.20	3.01	8.4**

$F_{(13,810)} = 49.0$
Adj. $R^2 = .43$
* $p < .05$
** $p < .01$

Gender, age, and ideology seem not to have strong effects on approval of Congress, although, as we saw in the bivariate results, being more liberal may boost support marginally, as does being a Democrat. In addition, and with other variables held constant, feelings of effectiveness and having a low income contribute to approval of Congress. Evaluations of Congress as an institution, although much different from approval of the congressional membership, are related to the latter just the same, and those people who are very satisfied with their own member are also more likely to approve of Congress as a whole,[27] as are those (rare) people who believe Congress has done a good job on the country's most important problem. Disconfirming evidence for the argument that political knowledge boosts approval of Congress is provided in the form of the variable recording respondents' ability to answer correctly a battery of general political information questions. As it turns out, the better people did on this test, the *less* they approved of Congress. The politically knowledgeable are not necessarily friends of Congress, even with other variables (such as partisanship) controlled.[28]

It is important to emphasize that we do not claim that policy concerns are unimportant. Clearly, they are. Approval of Congress would obviously go up if all of society's most important problems were solved and if Congress adopted the precise partisan coloring of each individual respondent. Setting aside the fact that these goals are not achievable, we maintain that in addition to these traditional variables, public perceptions of congressional procedures exert a strong and independent influence on evaluations of Congress.

We believe the more complete specification presented in Table 3-1 provides the most compelling evidence yet that this is the case. As our theory predicts, those who see Congress as having much power relative to other parts of the polity and those most disturbed by the nature of representation and by aspects of professionalization in Congress are much less likely to approve of Congress. In fact, these three variables are among the most powerful in the equation. A movement from very negative to very positive views of congressional professionalization, for example, is predicted to increase approval by 19 points on a scale running from 0 to 100. Views of congressional representation have almost as strong an impact, with predicted approval increasing 15 points.

Even after we have controlled for everything from partisanship to efficacy, from ideology to political knowledge, those people who are most disapproving of professionalized politics and the perceived nature of representation in the modern Congress and those believing Congress to be powerful are the most disapproving of Congress. Attitudes toward the way Congress goes about its business are powerful predictors of overall attitudes toward Congress. The core disapproving segment of the population consists not so much of the politically uninformed or conservatives in 1992 or liberals in 1995, but of those who dislike the processes and features of Congress.

The public sees Congress as extremely powerful and extremely ponderous. The public sees Congress as being loaded with staffers, committees, and perquisites that add to the expense and confusion but do not solve important societal problems. The public sees Congress as representing special interests but not ordinary people, and for an institution built on the representation of the public's interests to be viewed as representationally flawed is a serious problem. These complaints with Congress are more procedural and structural than they are substantive and issue-based, and in this sense procedural matters are anything but outside the purview of ordinary citizens.

A lively literature has developed on the topic of procedural justice,[29] and in Congress the people believe they see processes that are not just, processes that are not equitable. A minority—the extremists, the special interests—are seen as having more access and influence than "the people." Lobbyists are in and ordinary people are out, so there is a clear injustice present. But this is only part of the problem. People also see procedural inefficiencies with large numbers of members, staffers, and administrative units all milling around not doing much of substance or, if they do get something done, taking forever to do it. This inefficiency is a perceived problem that is quite separate from procedural injustice.

The American People and Democratic Processes

People are highly supportive of democracy as an abstract concept but quite negative toward the democratic processes that they can see and hear. The most frequently registered complaints about Congress in the focus group sessions involved the "bickering," the influence of special interests, the incessant bargaining and compromising, the over-abundance of talk, and the slow pace and inability of the body to "get anything done." Even though it seems inevitable that liberal democratic processes in a populous, technologically advanced, and heterogeneous society would involve debate, a measured pace, disagreements, and brokered solutions to these disagreements, people express an aversion to all of this.

People do not wish to see uncertainty, conflicting options, lengthy debate, competing interests, confusion, and bargaining, leading to compromised, imperfect solutions. They want institutions to do what "the people" want, quietly and efficiently, without conflict or fuss. Accomplishing this seems quite straightforward and easy to them: "the people" are united behind the public good, so why should there be so much conflict and foot-dragging? The public shows little appreciation for the fact that interests are naturally divided and cannot be accurately represented without representatives coming into conflict and attempting to resolve these conflicts by debating, disagreeing, and compromising. The "open canvassing of rival interests" that Bernard Crick quite rightly takes to be the essence of democracy in realistic polities is not appreciated by the American people.[30]

We argue that approval of Congress would be enhanced more by changes in attitudes toward process than by Congress passing particular substantive policies. Specifically, approval of Congress would be enhanced if people could be convinced that political professionalization is not all bad, that Congress represents the views of real people, and that democracy in a society like that of the United States rightly involves debate, disagreement, and compromise. The democratic wish is just that—a wish. Very diverse popular interests and beliefs are the reality that Congress must try to represent—and it must be done in a sometimes embarrassingly open fashion. The people are upset with political institutions and the political system not just because H.R. 2 rather than H.R. 1 became law but because they do not have a good feeling about the process employed in passing H.R. 2 and in not passing H.R. 1. Until this basic fact is appreciated, understanding of the public's interaction with and orientation toward the modern Congress will be sadly and unnecessarily incomplete.

Notes

Financial support for this project was provided by the National Science Foundation (SES–91–22733).

1. E. J. Dionne Jr., *Why Americans Hate Politics* (New York: Simon and Schuster, 1991).
2. Dan Balz and Richard Morin, "An Electorate Ready to Revolt," *Washington Post National Weekly Edition,* Nov. 11–17, 1991, 6–7.

3. Dionne, *Why Americans Hate Politics*; Alan Ehrenhalt, *The United States of Ambition: Politicians, Power, and the Pursuit of Office* (New York: Times Books, 1991); Kettering Foundation, *Citizens and Politics: A View from Main Street America* (Dayton: Kettering Foundation, 1992); and see, for example, the quotations in Phil Duncan, "Defending Congress, The Institution," *Congressional Quarterly Weekly Report,* Nov. 30, 1991, 3551.
4. For example, since Harris began in the 1960s to ask questions about confidence in the leadership of the institutions, the public has consistently expressed less confidence in Congress than the other institutions (the mean percent with a great deal of confidence was 29 percent for the Supreme Court, 24 percent for the presidency, and 17 percent for Congress).
5. Richard Morin and David S. Broder, "Why Americans Hate Congress," *Washington Post National Weekly Edition,* July 11–17, 1994, 6–7.
6. See James Fallows, "Why Americans Hate the Media," *Atlantic Monthly,* February 1996, 45–64.
7. Lewis A. Froman Jr. and Randall B. Ripley, "Conditions for Party Leadership," *American Political Science Review* 59 (March 1965): 52–63.
8. Paraphrased by Morin and Broder in "Why Americans Hate Congress."
9. See John R. Hibbing and Elizabeth Theiss-Morse, *Congress as Public Enemy: Public Attitudes Toward American Political Institutions* (Cambridge: Cambridge University Press, 1995), for details.
10. Richard F. Fenno Jr., "If, as Ralph Nader Says, Congress is 'The Broken Branch,' How Come We Love Our Congressmen So Much?" in *Congress in Change: Evolution and Reform,* ed. Norman J. Ornstein (New York: Praeger, 1975).
11. We attempted to distinguish clearly between the membership of an institution and the institution itself in our survey questions. We prefaced questions on the institutions with the following: "Now, I've asked you to rate some people in government, but sometimes when we talk about the parts of the government in Washington, like the Supreme Court, the presidency, and the Congress, we don't mean the people currently serving in office, we mean the institutions themselves, no matter who's in office. These institutions have their own buildings, historical traditions, and purposes laid out in the Constitution." The approval question on Congress as an institution asked, "In general, do you strongly approve, approve, disapprove, or strongly disapprove of the U.S. Congress, no matter who is in office?"
12. Overall, 22 percent of the respondents approved of Congress and 70 percent disapproved. President Clinton's approval rating in the same poll was 52 percent.
13. The inability of so many people to place Congress ideologically makes this variable an inappropriate candidate for inclusion in our multivariate regression equation (see Table 3-1).
14. Both quoted in Duncan, "Defending Congress."
15. Alan Ehrenhalt, "An Embattled Institution," *Governing,* January 1991, 32.
16. Political scientists have long recognized that the values promoted by the communitarian and liberal traditions are at odds, but they have focused their discussion of these conflicting values specifically on citizen participation in politics. See, for example, Pamela Johnston Conover, Stephen Leonard, and Donald Searing, "Duty Is a Four-Letter Word: Democratic Citizenship in the Liberal Polity," in George Marcus and Russell Hanson, eds., *Reconsidering the Democratic Public* (University Park: Pennsylvania State University Press, 1993); Robert Bellah, Richard Madsen, William Sullivan, Ann Swidler, and Steven Tipton, *Habits of the Heart* (Berkeley: University of California Press, 1985); and Richard Merelman, *Partial Visions* (Madison: University of Wisconsin Press, 1991). The effects of these competing values, however, may also be felt much more widely, especially on institutional support.

17. James A. Morone, *The Democratic Wish* (New York: Basic Books, 1990), 7.
18. James Madison, Alexander Hamilton, and John Jay, *The Federalist Papers,* with an introduction by Clinton Rossiter (New York: Mentor, 1961), 79.
19. On the importance of expectations, see David C. Kimball and Samuel C. Patterson, "Living Up to Expectations: Public Attitudes Toward Congress" (paper presented at the annual meeting of the American Political Science Association, Chicago, Aug. 31–Sept. 3, 1995).
20. Harold M. Barger, *The Impossible Presidency* (Glenview, Ill.: Scott Foresman, 1984), 9.
21. Morris Fiorina, *Divided Government* (New York: Macmillan, 1992), 79; see also Samuel Popkin, *The Reasoning Voter* (Chicago: University of Chicago Press, 1991), 90.
22. Adam Clymer, "Battle over the Budget," *New York Times,* Jan. 5, 1996, A1.
23. Richard L. Berke, "Clinton's Ratings Over 50% in Poll as G.O.P. Declines," *New York Times,* Dec. 14, 1995, A1, B17.
24. Actually, evidence that the people believe Congress is more powerful than the president has been present but largely ignored for quite some time. See Jack Dennis, "Public Support for American National Political Institutions" (paper presented at the Conference on Public Support for the Political System, Madison, Wis., August 1973); and Glenn R. Parker, "Some Themes in Congressional Unpopularity," *American Journal of Political Science* 21 (February 1977): 93–110.
25. All of these characteristics are parts of professionalization or institutionalization as commonly conceived. See S. N. Eisenstadt, "Institutionalization and Change," *American Sociology Review* 29 (April 1964): 235–247; Samuel P. Huntington, "Congressional Responses to the Twentieth-Century," in *Congress and America's Future,* David B. Truman, ed. (Englewood Cliffs, N.J.: Prentice-Hall, 1965); and Nelson Polsby, "The Institutionalization of the U.S. House of Representatives," *American Political Science Review* 62 (March 1968): 144–168.
26. We recoded all of our independent variables to range from 0 to 1. See Gary King, "How Not to Lie with Statistics," *American Journal of Political Science* 39 (August 1986): 666–687; and Robert Luskin, "*Abusus non tollit usum:* Standardized Coefficients, Correlations, and R^2s," *American Journal of Political Science* 35 (November 1991): 1032–46.
27. See Richard Born, "The Shared Fortunes of Congress and Congressmen," *Journal of Politics* 52 (November 1990): 1223–41.
28. The same absence of a relationship is present if we substitute years of education for the political knowledge variable. This despite the overwhelming theoretical expectation in the literature. Dennis writes that "we would expect . . . that people high in education . . . would be those most supportive of the existing set of political institutions." Dennis, "Public Support for American National Political Institutions," 319. Patterson, Hedlund, and Boynton believe that legislative support will be "strongest among those high in levels of education." Samuel C. Patterson, Ronald D. Hedlund, and G. Robert Boynton, *Representatives and Represented: Bases of Public Support for the American Legislatures* (New York: Wiley, 1975), 56. While these expectations are hardly atypical, they also are not supported by the data—theirs or ours.
29. See, for example, Tom Tyler, *Why People Obey the Law* (New Haven: Yale University Press, 1990).
30. Bernard Crick, *In Defense of Politics,* 4th ed. (Chicago: University of Chicago Press, 1993), 18.

Part II
Elections and Constituencies

4. Women and Blacks in Congress: 1870–1996

Carol M. Swain

Since 1789 the U.S. Congress has been dominated by well-educated, white males of middle class to upper class status. But times are changing. Unprecedented numbers of retirements, resignations, and incumbent defeats in the 1990s opened the way for larger numbers of women and minorities in Congress. Blacks in the House of Representatives have seen their numbers leap from thirteen in 1970 to thirty-eight (excluding delegates) in 1992 and 1994 (see Figure 4-1). Blacks lost one member in 1996. The number of Latinos has risen from five in 1970 to eighteen in 1994 and 1996. Between 1990 and 1994, the number of women representatives rose from twenty-nine to forty-seven, and their totals in the Senate jumped from two to eight.[1] In 1996 women gained ten in the House and one in the Senate.

But the more things change, the more they stay the same. The demographic makeup of the institution has changed in important ways; whether it continues to show greater diversity is far from certain. In this chapter I examine the experiences and backgrounds of African Americans and women in Congress. In particular, I consider whether existing theories of candidate recruitment adequately explain the observed patterns.

Congressional Candidates: The Pool of Eligibles

Studies show that the pool of potential congressional candidates is dominated by people drawn from a relatively narrow social base. In regard to education, for instance, members of Congress, regardless of their race or gender, tend to have far more years of schooling than the vast majority of other Americans.[2] While only 30 percent of the U.S. population has a four-year college degree, more than 90 percent of the members of Congress do.[3] Indeed, most legislators have advanced degrees and are overrepresented in certain types of professions. In the 104th Congress, 54 percent of the Senate had a background in law, and a career in business or banking applied to 38 percent of the House.[4] As William J. Keefe and Morris Ogul have observed, "Formal educational attainment . . . appears as one of the central criteria in the winnowing-out process under which legislative candidates are recruited and elected. An invitation to legislative candidacy is not likely to come unbidden to those whose credentials fall short."[5]

Figure 4-1 Women and Minorities in Congress, 1970–1994

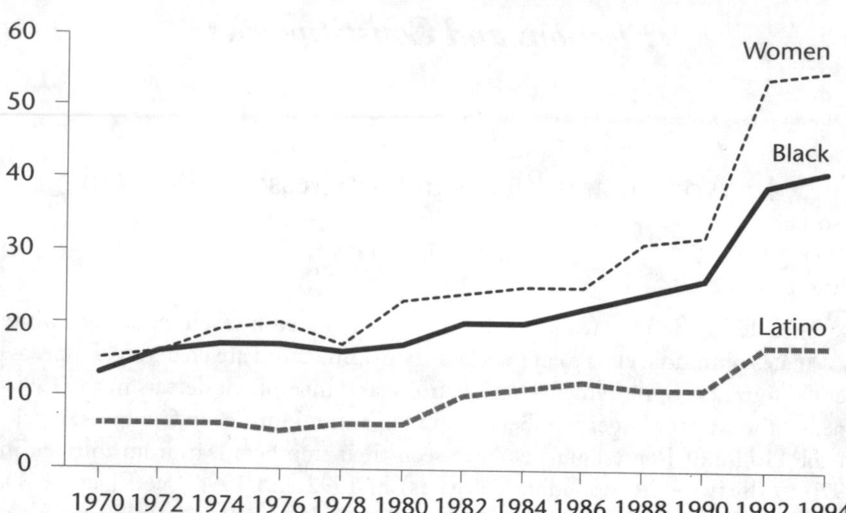

Sources: *Statistical Record of Hispanic Americans,* 1993: Center for the American Woman and Politics (CAWP), "Voices, View, Votes," 1995; *Congressional Quarterly Weekly Report,* various issues.

Credentials in education are important for entrance into the pool of eligibles, but other considerations matter, too. There are many personal attributes that make some individuals much stronger candidates than others. For example, prior experience in an appointive or elective office, previous congressional bids, celebrity status, a history of party activism, and large financial resources can turn some individuals into "quality" challengers with an enhanced chance of winning.[6] Quality challengers are more likely than others to weigh carefully when and where they make their first run for office. These candidates are usually in a better position than other candidates to assess their odds accurately before they enter a congressional race. Such strategic decision making increases their probability of success.

The ability (or lack of it) to raise lots of money plays a major role in the decision to run for Congress, and it influences the results. Congressional campaigns are very expensive ventures indeed. According to Gary Jacobson, challengers need to spend more than $400,000 to have a 20 percent chance of beating an incumbent.[7] In 1992 the average congressional nominee spent more than $400,000 for a House race and almost $3 million for the Senate. The ease or difficulty of raising money often depends on a candidate's perceived chances of winning. Incumbents and nominees for open-seat races tend to raise far more money than challengers because potential contributors, as rational actors, typically assess the probability of a win before they contribute their dollars.

In addition to money and background, several other considerations are relevant in the decision calculus of most would-be candidates. It is well known, for instance, that local factors create opportunities for some candidates and deterrents for others. Local factors include the racial composition of the district, the presence or absence of an incumbent, and perceived incumbent vulnerability. An example of a relevant local factor might be a redistricting plan that substantially reduces or increases the district's minority population; another example is a plan that alters its partisan distribution.

National factors such as the economy or the popularity of the president are also known to affect the quality of the candidate pool. More candidates run for office when they think it will be a good year for their party. But these same national factors may count for less in the decision calculus of minority candidates because most run in minority-dominated districts. Voters in minority districts have not shown any strong inclination to throw out incumbents for a failing economy or to punish members of the president's party for their poor performance. Consequently, minority incumbents and challengers may weigh matters differently from members of the majority group.

Linda Fowler and Robert McClure have shown that for every congressional candidate who enters the fray there are countless other "unseen candidates" who might have competed but chose not to run.[8] In recent years, however, something has changed in the political milieu of racial and political minorities that has had a positive effect on their willingness to put themselves forward as political candidates. More and more women and minorities seem to be leaving the ranks of "unseen" candidates and entering congressional races.

In 1996, 217 women filed as House candidates, and 22 as Senate candidates. Ninety-seven of the House candidates lost their primaries along with eight of the senatorial candidates.[9] The number of women running was higher than in 1994 when 203 women filed as House candidates, with 112 winning their party's nominations, and 47 prevailing in the general election.[10] Twenty-seven women filed for the Senate in 1994, with nine winning their primaries, and three winning general elections, bringing the number of women senators to eight.[11] Fewer women ran for their party's nomination in 1994 than the 218 who ran in 1992, but the 1992 figure was an enormous increase over the previous high of 134 women who filed in 1986. Forty-one women survived the 1992 primary season to run as challengers, and thirty-nine obtained major party nominations for open seats. Two women defeated incumbents, and twenty-two won their open-seat bids.[12] Women ran against women in five races in 1992. In 1996 women were surprisingly successful at defeating House incumbents. Although they comprised only 14 percent of all candidates, they were 25 percent of those defeating challengers.

As we shall see, African Americans and women have quite different experiences in getting themselves elected and reelected to Congress.

African American Representatives

The earliest black members of Congress were all Republicans and mostly drawn from the socioeconomic elite of the African American community (see

Table 4-1 Characteristics of the First Twenty-Two African Americans in Congress, 1870–1901

Member	Party/State/Service	Occupation/ Political Experience	Education
Senate			
Hiram Revels	R-Miss., 1870–71	Public office	Some college
Blanche K. Bruce	R-Miss., 1875–81	County sheriff	College degree
House			
Joseph H. Rainey	R-S.C., 1870–79	State senator	
Jefferson F. Long	R-Ga., 1870–71	Party official	
Robert C. DeLarge	R-S.C., 1871–73	State House	
Robert B. Elliot	R-S.C., 1871–74	State House	Legal training[1]
Benjamin S. Turner	R-Ala., 1871–73	City council	
Josiah T. Walls	R-Fla., 1871–76	State Assembly	
Richard H. Cain	R-S.C., 1873–75; 1877–79	Minister	
John R. Lynch	R-Miss., 1873–75; 1882–83	State House	Legal training
Alonzo J. Ransier	R-S.C., 1873–75	State House	
James T. Rapier	R-Ala., 1873–75	Public service	Some college
Jeremiah Haralson	R-Ala., 1875–77	State senator	
John A. Hyman	R-N.C., 1875–77	State senator	
Charles E. Nash	R-La., 1875–77	Bricklayer	
Robert Smalls	R-S.C., 1875–79; 1882-83; 1884–87	State House	
James E. O'Hara	R-N.C., 1883-87	Lawyer	Legal training
Henry P. Cheatham	R-N.C., 1889-93	Public official	College degree
John M. Langston	R-Va., 1890-91	Town clerk	College degree
Thomas E. Miller	R-S.C., 1890-91	State Assembly	Legal training/ college degree
George W. Murray	R-S.C., 1893–95; 1896-97	Party official	College degree
George White	R-N.C., 1897–1901	Public official	Legal training

Sources: Black Americans in Congress, 1870–1989 (Washington, D.C.: U.S. Government Printing Office, 1990); *American Leaders, 1789–1994* (Washington, D.C.: Congressional Quarterly, 1994).

[1] Some representatives gained legal educations by reading law and then passing the state bar exams.

Table 4-2 Characteristics of African Americans in the 104th Congress

	Number	%[1]		Number	%
Occupation before election			Education[2]		
Business/Entrepreneur	7	17.1	Some college	1	2.4
Education	4	9.8	B.A./B.S.	13	31.7
Law	11	26.8	Master's/ Graduate degree	8	19.5
Minister	1	2.4	J.D.	14	34.1
Politics	26	63.4	Ph.D.	1	2.4
Public service/Nonprofit	3	7.3	LL.B./LL.D.	4	9.8
			Party affiliation		
Elective experience			Democrat	38	92.7
Appointed office/ State government	5	12.2	Republican	2	4.9
Candidate governor	1	2.4	Independent	1	2.4
Candidate mayor	2	4.9	Office		
Candidate U.S. House	3	7.3	Delegate	2	4.9
City council	6	14.6	Representative	38	92.7
County government	2	4.9	Senator	1	2.4
Mayor	1	2.4			
No previous office	9	22.0	Region[3]		
Party position	1	2.4	South	17	41.5
School board	2	4.9	Midwest	9	22.0
State House	14	34.1	West	3	7.3
State Senate	11	26.8	East	9	22.0

Source: Congressional Quarterly Weekly Report, various issues, 1994.

1 Percentages include delegate. Some members qualify for more than one category; total may exceed 100 percent.

2 Indicates highest level of education attained. Ed. S. included as a graduate degree.

3 Region definitions are taken from the *Congressional Quarterly Weekly Report.* Delegates are not included.

Table 4-1). In fact, a majority of the twenty-two black men who served in Congress between 1870 and 1901 were politically experienced and well educated. No less than seventeen had previously held an elective office, such as tax assessor, sheriff, or state legislator. Half had at least some college experience, five were college graduates, and five had legal training of one kind or another.[13] At the time, only 1.8 percent of the U.S. adult population had ever attended college, and only 3.1 percent of males held a bachelor's degree.[14] In financial terms, too, black members of Congress were quite well off. Only one black representative had an estate worth less than $1,000, while five had estates ranging in value from $5,000 to $20,000—very respectable fortunes for the time.[15] Black Congress members in the nineteenth century, therefore, fit the standard profile of quality candidates. Just like white members then and now, these black legislators were not socially, economically, or educationally representative of their constituents.[16]

Since 1870 somewhat less than one hundred blacks have served in Congress. Almost half, 46 percent, have come from southern states, with the greatest proportion of the remainder coming from the Midwest. The overwhelming majority of them served in some type of public service job before they were elected to Congress. Among their occupations, the most common were teacher, minister, entrepreneur, and business manager. Compared to their white counterparts, a far smaller percentage of black Congress members have had legal training, although this situation seems to be changing rapidly in the modern Congress.

In the 104th Congress, all the black representatives except Rep. Cardiss Collins, D-Ill., had college degrees, and more than 80 percent had some type of prior political experience in an elective office. Almost half had law degrees, and seven had been business owners or business managers (see Table 4-2). In contrast to an earlier era, only one member of the 104th Congress, Rep. Floyd Flake, D-N.Y., came from the ministry. These data suggest that contemporary black representatives share backgrounds quite similar to those of the white males in Congress, with perhaps one major exception: a greater percentage of black representatives appear to have had prior electoral experience.

Candidate Emergence

Not much research has been done on the psychological and motivational backgrounds of black representatives and how they might compare to those of whites. Examining the career path of former representative Mike Espy, D-Miss., who in 1986 defeated a two-term white incumbent, Linda Fowler noted that our existing theories of political ambition and career progression would not have predicted Espy's success.[17] He had never served in an elective office and, surprisingly as a challenger, he was able to raise and spend more money than the incumbent. Although African American leaders had given up hopes of claiming the district, Espy saw an opportunity and successfully exploited it.

Black representatives have entered Congress under a variety of circumstances. During the early twentieth century, the majority, including men such as Oscar De Priest, R-Ill., and Arthur Mitchell, D-Ill., appear to have been recruited by political machines seeking to reward party loyalists for service in districts that had grown majority black.[18] William Dawson, D-Ill., a party faithful who succeeded Mitchell, was chosen in much the same manner. However, Rev. Adam Clayton Powell Jr., D-N.Y., who became one of the most influential black congressmen, emerged from his pulpit in a Harlem church to defeat the candidate preferred by the Tammany Hall political machine. Powell was regarded as a maverick. Many of the black representatives in Congress have had histories of involvement in local politics and were favored by the dominant political power brokers in their area.

Reverse recruitment, in which party leaders actively discourage blacks from running, is also a part of the experience of black politicians. Ron Dellums,

D-Calif., elected in 1970, speaks of having been recruited and urged to run for his first political office, a city council seat. He has also reported, however, that some people tried to discourage him from seeking a congressional seat in an overwhelmingly white district. When Alan Wheat, D-Mo., first sought election in a white-majority district, some party leaders tried to pressure him into abandoning the race. Both Dellums and Wheat persisted and have been among the relatively few blacks elected from nonblack constituencies. Others include Gary Franks, R-Conn., and J. C. Watts, R-Okla., both elected from districts more than 80 percent white.

Open seats have been rare in black-majority districts, so black candidates have fewer electoral opportunities than white candidates. Because few other districts would seem to offer them realistic chances of getting into Congress, the prospect for many would-be black candidates is limited. When Rep. Kweisi Mfume, D-Md., resigned from Congress in 1996 to head the NAACP, thirty-two people filed for his open seat, indicating the frustrations of some black would-be candidates.

Black incumbents often have safer seats than white incumbents. Since the 1950s, the reelection rate for incumbent House members has rarely dipped below 90 percent. For 1988 and 1990 it was 98.4 and 96.9 percent, respectively.[19] The reelection rate was 82.1 percent in 1992, and 92.3 percent in 1994. Most black incumbents, however, have enjoyed a 100 percent reelection rate in general elections, even in 1994. Despite Democratic losses of fifty-two House seats and two Senate seats, blacks had a 100 percent reelection rate. In fact, only a handful of black incumbents have ever been defeated—De Priest (1934), Powell (1970), Robert Nix, D-Pa. (1978), Katie Hall, D-Ind. (1984), Bennett Stewart, D-Ill. (1981), Alton Waldon, D-N.Y. (1986), Lucien Blackwell, D-Pa. (1992), and Barbara-Rose Collins, D-Mich., and Gary Franks (1996)—and most of these were defeated in primaries, not in the general election. The one black Republican senator, Edward Brooke of Massachusetts, was defeated in a general election, but only after having served in the Senate for twelve years.

Campaign Finance

When it comes to campaign dollars, black challengers and incumbents are often at a disadvantage. On average, African American candidates receive lower amounts of money from individual contributors and political action committees (PACs) than white candidates. Table 4-3 shows average contributions for the sixty-six black challengers and incumbents who competed for congressional seats during the 1993–1994 election cycle by race and party. These data show that blacks are receiving slightly fewer PAC dollars than nonblacks. Black incumbent Democrats are raising far more money than black Republicans, which should be expected because there are so few competitive black districts. Many black candidates are self-starters who enter races poorly financed and with little chance of defeating an incumbent.[20]

Table 4-3 Average Contributions to Candidates by Race and Party, 1993–1994

Race of Candidate	Net Receipts	PAC	Individual	Candidate
Black challengers	$289,983	$139,620	$132,983	$ 3,720
Nonblack challengers	433,512	158,476	229,546	26,973
Black Republicans	152,501	34,733	99,161	8,165
Nonblack Republicans	397,887	106,255	240,159	34,407
Black Democrats	370,499	201,985	153,093	1,077
Nonblack Democrats	471,994	215,607	217,365	18,916

Source: Compiled from data provided by the Center for Responsive Politics and the Joint Center for Political and Economic Studies.

Note: $N = 66$. Data include challengers and incumbents.

Some black incumbents have no difficulty raising adequate funds. In 1996 the media dubbed Rep. Louis Stokes, D-Ohio, the king of campaign fund raising, after his committee reported almost $200,000 on hand at the end of 1995. Most of Stokes's money came from generous PAC donations. His success in a year in which Republicans controlled the House represents an improvement from previous elections.[21] Using data from the 1980 and 1982 election cycles, Allen Wilhite and John Theilmann found that black candidates were less successful than white candidates when it came to PAC contributions. They report that "blacks faced a funding disadvantage of almost $60,000 in 1980 and over $67,000 in 1982."[22] Using a regression analysis and 1994 data of candidates and incumbents, Archis Parasharami examined race, candidate status (incumbent versus challenger), and type of election (open seat or not) and found that black candidates received about $151,000 less than white candidates after controlling for the other variables.[23] Nonblack candidates received more than twice the amount in individual contributions than blacks. In addition, lacking substantial personal wealth, blacks generally contribute substantially less of their own money to their campaigns than do white candidates.

When black challengers run against other candidates, regardless of race, they are usually on a shoestring budget. Consequently, many of the blacks who challenged incumbents in 1994 reported zero campaign receipts and expenditures. Again, there are exceptions even among political novices. In 1996 Jesse Jackson Jr., D-Ill., was able to outraise and outspend three veteran state legislators. Jackson raised $420,677, took out loans of $45,000, and spent $469,538. His closest rival raised less than $60,000 and took out loans of $1,000.[24] Jackson was able to cash in on his father's name and connections, which worked for Jackson the same way the Kennedy name and connections have facilitated the elections of Joseph Kennedy II, D-Mass., and Patrick Kennedy, D-R.I.

Perhaps those harmed the most by the disparity in campaign receipts are blacks seeking election in majority-white districts. Most report difficulty in raising money and lose decisively. Believing that these candidates cannot win against white opponents, potential contributors are reluctant to invest in them. Because all candidates need money to run successful campaigns, blacks' inability to raise adequate amounts of money can set in motion a self-fulfilling prophecy. One such case may have occurred in Washington State's 1994 Senate race in which a black Democrat, Ron Sims, came within striking distance of toppling the incumbent, Republican Slade Gorton. Although Gorton outspent Sims more than three to one, Sims won 44 percent of the vote in a state that is less than 4 percent black. A similar situation occurred in Missouri's Fifth District. Black House candidate Ron Freeman, a Republican, raised $458,373 and won 43 percent of the vote in a 73 percent white district, while his Democratic opponent, Karen McCarthy, raised and spent $866,808.[25] It was widely believed that these black candidates might have prevailed had they been better financed at the beginning of their candidacies. As we shall see, the financial situation for women candidates differs significantly from that of blacks.

Women in Congress

Between 1916 and 1996, 172 women have served in Congress: 23 in the Senate and 153 in the House, with 4 serving in both chambers.[26] The West has sent the most women to Congress, followed by the Northeast. While most states have elected at least one female U.S. representative, as of 1996, seven states—Alaska, Delaware, Iowa, Mississippi, New Hampshire, Vermont, and Wisconsin—had never elected any.[27] The percentage of women in the House has increased from 4 percent in 1984 to almost 11 percent in 1996, but women remain disadvantaged in terms of their proportional representation relative to white men and black men. Although 51 percent of the population is female, only 10.8 percent of the House and 8 percent of the Senate is female. White men, in contrast, represent 36 percent of the population and 78 percent of the House, and black men represent 5.7 percent of the population and almost 6 percent of the House (see Figure 4-2). In the United States the percentage of women in the national legislature has lagged significantly behind that of several other Western democracies including Austria, Germany, and the Netherlands.[28]

The relatively poor representation of women in the U.S. Congress has yet to be adequately explained. Many reasons have been advanced to account for this dismal record: bias among voters, discrimination by the media, disadvantages in raising early money, lack of ambition, male incumbency advantage, the U.S. system of single-member districts, stereotyping by voters, the supply of candidates, and a reluctance of party leaders to recruit women aggressively.[29] While many hypotheses have been explored, few have been substantiated. In fact, gender may be an advantage under some circumstances. For example, voter name recall and name recognition have sometimes worked to favor women.[30] Barbara Burrell and

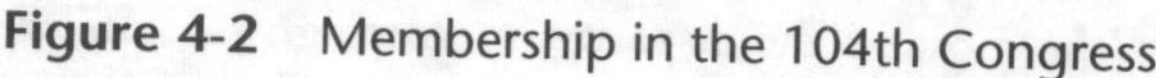

Figure 4-2 Membership in the 104th Congress

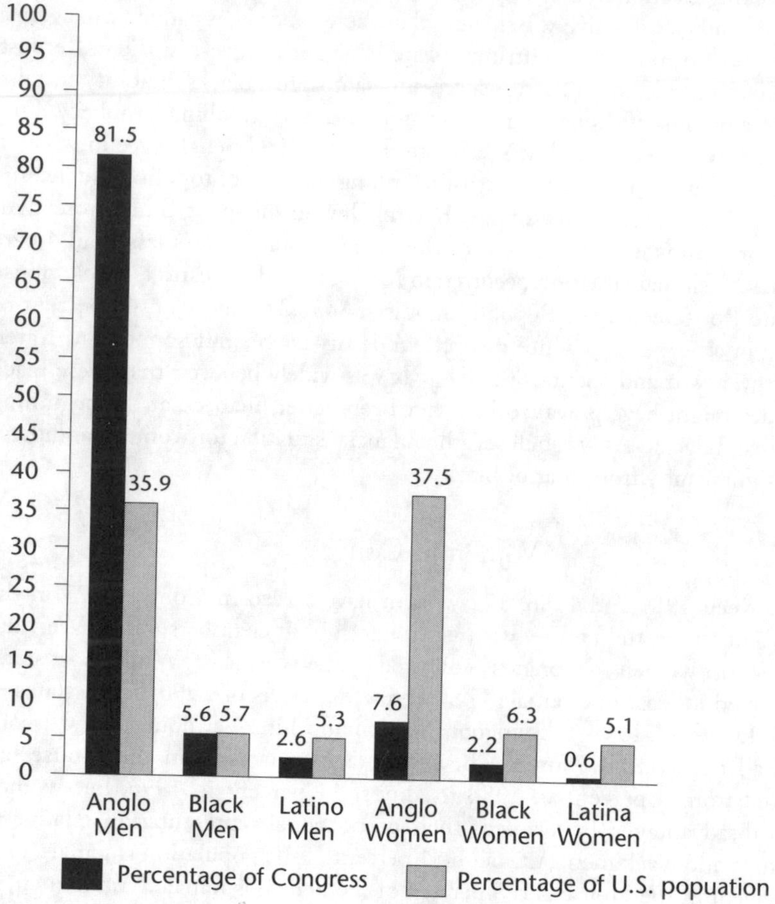

Sources: *CAWP News and Notes,* Winter 1994; *Congressional Quarterly Weekly Report,* various issues; U.S. Bureau of the Census, *Residential Population of the United States,* 1996.

Linda Fowler are among the scholars who argue that the problem is supply—not enough women chose to run. "To increase their numbers in the national legislature," Burrell contends, "women first have to enter primary elections."[31]

The best explanation seems to come from an examination of institutional barriers such as type of electoral system—single-member districts—and the male incumbency advantage. Research into comparative government by Wilma Rule and Pippa Norris shows that in other countries more women are elected in multimember districts than single-member.[32] Richard E. Matland and Deborah D. Brown argue that the number of seats per district can greatly reduce the barriers affecting whether women choose to enter legislative races and their probability of gaining voter support. Rather than sticking with the zero-sum nature of contests in single-member districts, slating women in multimember districts enables the party to appease women voters and reduces the likelihood that a woman candidate will confront an ambitious male one-on-one.[33] The solution for women candidates, however, seems to work to the disadvantage of African American candidates who traditionally have performed worse in multimember districts.[34]

Background Characteristics

Fifty-six percent of the women elected to Congress in the period before the Second World War had attended or completed college. By contrast, between 1917 and 1940, only 6.3 percent of men and 4.3 percent of women nationally had bachelor's degrees. Irwin Gertzog reports that the majority of women elected during this era came from wealthy families or families with long histories of political involvement. They include Frances P. Bolton, R-Ohio, Edith Norse Rogers, R-Mass., Ruth McCormick, R-Ill., Ruth Pratt, R-N.Y., and Ruth Owen, D-Fla., who was the daughter of William Jennings Bryan. Few had prior legal training, and fewer than 20 percent had previous political experience. These women served an average of two and a half terms, whereas those elected between 1940 and 1964 served from three and a half to four and a half terms.[35]

Fourteen of the first twenty-five women who served in Congress came through the matrimonial link in which widows were selected to fill the unexpired terms of their deceased husbands. This practice was set in motion in 1923 when Republican leaders recruited Ella Mae Hunt Nolan, R-Calif., to run for the House seat previously held by her husband.[36] The first woman senator, Rebecca Latimer Felton, D-Ga., entered Congress in 1922 after the death of her husband, but served for only one day. Twenty-six years later, Margaret Chase Smith, R-Maine, became the first woman to serve in the Senate without having been appointed to the position. Smith entered the House in 1940 through the matrimonial link, but she won her 1948 Senate seat on the strength of her own record.

Thirty years later in 1978, Nancy Landon Kassebaum, R-Kan., daughter of Republican presidential candidate Alfred Landon, became the first woman elected to the Senate without having served an unexpired congressional term. More recently, Barbara Boxer, D-Calif., Carol Moseley-Braun, D-Ill., Dianne Feinstein, D-Calif., Kay Bailey Hutchison, R-Texas, Barbara Mikulski, D-Md., and Olympia Snowe, R-Maine, have been elected to the Senate on the strength of their own candidacies.[37]

According to Gertzog, the degree of competition in the election and the woman's prior involvement in politics have been major factors in determining whether party leaders would recruit and support the widow of a deceased Congress member. A woman who has been considered important to her husband's election and political career generally has been seen as more worthy of the nomination than a woman who has not participated.[38]

For African American women, however, widowhood has never been a common mode of entry into Congress. All but one of the black women who have served in Congress were highly educated, experienced politicians before arriving on Capitol Hill.[39] Rep. Shirley Chisholm, D-N.Y., had a master's degree from Columbia University and had served in the state assembly. Rep. Barbara Jordan, D-Texas, and Yvonne Burke, D-Calif., both elected in 1972, had law degrees and had previously served in their state legislatures. Cardiss Collins is the only black woman to enter Congress through widowhood.

Surprisingly, three of the first five women in Congress did not enter through widowhood. These women were activists with their own political agendas. The first, Jeannette Rankin, R-Mont., elected in 1916, entered politics through her participation in the suffrage movement. Rankin, a college graduate, won one of Montana's two at-large seats and served two nonconsecutive terms more than twenty years apart. She was a pacifist who became the only member of Congress to vote against U.S. involvement in both world wars. Rankin was followed in 1921 by the election of an antifeminist candidate, Alice M. Robertson, R-Okla., who defeated a three-term incumbent. Unlike Rankin, Robertson disassociated herself from women's groups. In fact, reports state that Robertson "refused to support legislation central to the political agendas of many women. In 1921 she spoke out against the Sheppard-Towner bill which provided the Labor Department's Children's Bureau with $1 million annually to promote maternity and infant child care."[40] Mary T. Norton, D-N.J., was the first Democratic woman to serve in the House. A former business owner, she was recruited by Jersey City party boss Frank Hague and loyally served her party organization during her twenty-six years in Congress.[41]

The political backgrounds of the first twenty-five women to serve in Congress, many of whom had never held political office, can be contrasted with those of women who served in the 104th Congress. With very few exceptions, the latter group was composed of experienced legislators (see Table 4-4). Sixty-seven percent of the women in the 104th Congress served in one or more elective offices before being elected to Congress—more than 40 percent were state representatives. Twenty of the women in the 104th Congress served as mayors or city council members; three served on county boards; seven served in a statewide offices; and two were judges.[42] Among the ten women who list no previous political experience are several who worked as White House aides or congressional aides. Almost all of the forty-seven women in the House and eight women in the Senate fit our definition of "quality" candidates.

Although law has always been the predominant background of the white males who served in Congress, only two of the women elected before 1940 had legal training. That proportion climbed to one in three women serving their first terms between 1965 and 1982. However, beginning in 1983 only five of forty-one were lawyers.[43] Of the 183 lawyers serving in the 102d Congress, only three of the twenty-eight women (and four of the twenty-five blacks) had law degrees. Among women candidates contesting seats in 1992, less than 10 percent had

Table 4-4 Characteristics of Women in the 104th Congress

	Number	%[1]		Number	%
Occupation before election			Education[2]		
Business/Entrepreneur	13	23.2	High school	1	1.8
Education	17	30.4	Community college	1	1.8
Homemaker	1	1.8	Some college	5	8.9
Journalism	3	5.4	B.A./B.S./LL.B.	21	37.5
Judge	2	3.6	Master's/ Graduate degree	17	30.4
Law	11	19.6	J.D.	11	19.6
Politics	25	44.6			
Public service/Nonprofit	4	7.1			
Research	2	3.6	Party affiliation		
			Democrat	36	64.3
Elective experience			Republican	20	35.7
Appointed office/ State government	7	12.5	Office		
Candidate governor	2	3.6	Delegate	1	1.8
Candidate mayor	1	1.8	Representative	47	83.9
Candidate U.S. House	7	12.5	Senator	8	14.3
Candidate U.S. president	1	1.8			
Candidate U.S. Senate	4	7.1	Race		
City council	17	30.4	Asian	1	1.8
County government	3	5.4	Black	11	19.6
Judge	2	3.6	Latina	3	5.4
Mayor	3	5.4	White	41	73.2
Party position	3	5.4			
School board	5	8.9	Region[3]		
State House	18	32.1	East	13	23.2
State Senate	12	21.4	Midwest	11	19.6
U.S. House	3	5.4	South	12	21.4
No previous office	10	17.9	West	19	33.9

Sources: Philip D. Duncan and Christine C. Lawrence, eds., *Politics in America, 1996* (Washington, D.C.: Congressional Quarterly, 1995); Center for the American Woman and Politics, *CAWP News and Notes* (New Brunswick, N.J.: Eagleton Institute of Politics, 1992–1994).

[1] Percentages include delegate. Some members qualify for more than one category; total may exceed 100 percent.

[2] Indicates highest level of education attained. Ed.S. included as a graduate degree.

[3] Region definitions are taken from the *Congressional Quarterly Weekly Report*. Delegates are not included.

backgrounds in law. Instead, the most common professions cited were business, government and community service, education, and media and public relations.[44]

Since the 1970s, changing patterns of recruitment have become evident among women. More women have acquired some of the qualifications that make them quality candidates, including prior elective experience, party service, and professional training. In 1994, for instance, 21 percent (1,526) of the nation's 7,424 state legislators were women, a dramatic increase over the 1960s when women were rarely to be seen in state legislatures. In 1969 there were only 300 women serving in state legislatures, just 4 percent of all the seats. However, a disproportionate number of women serve in the legislatures of small states like New Hampshire and Delaware, where chances to go to Congress are very rare. Larger states with professional legislatures, such as New York and California, have noticeably fewer women in office.[45]

Democratic women outnumber Republican women in state legislatures, but the gap is closing. The percentage of Republican women increased from 38 percent in 1994 to 44 percent in 1995, and, over the same period, the proportion of Democratic women dropped from 62 percent to 55 percent. These partisan disparities among women in state legislatures may give the Republican Party an advantage when it comes to recruiting strong women candidates for Congress. Already Republican women candidates appear to fare better than Democrats. In 1994 Democratic women challengers won only 4 percent of their congressional races, compared with 25 percent for Republican women.

Leaders of both parties have become interested in recruiting more women for congressional service. After a 1993 study conducted by the Republican Network to Elect Women showed Republican women more likely to attract crossover votes than Republican men, Newt Gingrich, R-Ga., stepped up his recruitment of women.[46] In the 1994 elections, Gingrich's efforts paid off for the Republicans. Seven new Republican women won election, and three defeated incumbents.

As early as 1984, Democratic Party leaders were seeking women to run for open seats. Among those approached was Louise Slaughter of New York, a former state legislator, who declined to run when first recruited, but two years later entered the race and defeated an incumbent.[47] Slaughter's experience can be contrasted with that of Rep. Patricia Schroeder, D-Colo., a community activist and attorney elected twelve years earlier. Schroeder's candidacy came after an antiwar group decided to run a woman against a "hawkish" male incumbent.[48] She was not recruited by party leaders, and she had few of the attributes normally associated with quality challengers. Yet, Schroeder defeated the incumbent and became dean of the congressional women. In 1995, after the Republican takeover of the House and years of fighting battles, Schroeder announced her retirement.

Campaign Finance

Although a female candidate may have the attributes campaign contributors value, there is no strong evidence that gender has an independent effect on a candidate's ability to raise money.[49] Women can raise as much money as men in comparable races—for example, contests in which challengers run against incumbents or challengers against challengers for open-seat races.

In 1994 female incumbents and open-seat candidates raised more than their male counterparts regardless of party. Democratic women challengers raised almost $40,000 more than the mean for challengers within their party. Only Republican women challengers raised less than the mean for all candidates, $96,000 compared to $118,000. Among female candidates, Democratic women consistently raised more than Republicans whether running as incumbents, challengers, or for an open seat.[50]

Women incumbents raised more than their opponents in 93 percent of their races. Eleven women lost despite raising more than their opponents, and only one woman who raised less was victorious. Women seeking open seats raised more money than their opponents in 72 percent of the races. In fact, two of the five top fund raisers in Senate races were Feinstein and Hutchison.

Women also appear to be garnering a fair share of PAC contributions. In this regard, they are doing considerably better than African American candidates. The rise of women's PACs has played an important role in helping candidates raise early money to get their campaigns off to a good start. Among the women's PACs formed for this purpose are EMILY's List (Early Money is Like Yeast) for pro-choice Democratic women and the Republican counterpart WISH (Women in the Senate and House).

Impact of Blacks and Women on Public Policies

Does the presence of more blacks and women in Congress make a difference in terms of legislative outputs? The answer is a qualified yes. Researchers have documented that men and women in state legislatures pursue different priorities, especially on issues affecting women and children, health care, discrimination, and sexual harassment.[51] Their studies show that women are more likely than men to favor open decision making, inclusion, and general legislative responsiveness. Some anecdotal evidence suggests the same may be true in the national legislature. Marjorie Margolies-Mezvinsky, D-Pa., elected in 1992 and defeated in 1994, reported that the women who served with her in the 103d Congress shared similar issue preferences that cut across party lines.[52]

Any unanimity among Democratic and Republican women, however, surely disappeared after the November 1994 elections ushered in seven new Republican women. Hanna Rosin reports, "The old class of Republican women, such as Connie Morella [Md.], Nancy Johnson [Conn.], and Susan Molinari [N.Y.], served as a moderating influence . . . [and] made their names during the 1992 Year of the Woman, joining Democratic women to pass legislation like the Family Leave Act, Violence Against Women Act, and bills authorizing federal funding of abortion. The new women break that mold. None ran on a platform of women's issues."[53] On most issues, Republican women vote along party, rather than gender lines. Among their main priorities are government reform, crime policy, and protecting the civil rights of devout Christians. Two of the seven Republican women are openly hostile towards gays and lesbians.[54]

A Congress member's political party and manner of recruitment are usually accurate predictors of legislative performance. The newly elected Republican women were recruited by Gingrich, and most were trained by Republican mentoring networks. Consequently, they have been loyal to the Republican leadership and its Contract with America.[55] Only one Republican woman decided to join the remnants of the Congressional Caucus for Women's Issues, which the Republican Party defunded in 1995 along with twenty-seven other caucuses.[56]

Manner of recruitment also affects the type of representation that black members of Congress provide. Through the Congressional Black Caucus, black Democrats have established reputations as the most left-oriented Democrats in Congress. Significant differences with Republicans appear in their interest in serious government spending on redistribution, social welfare policy, and urban problems. Political party affiliation, however, seems as important as race in explaining their legislative priorities. When the voting records of the two black Republicans are examined, it becomes apparent that they are almost indistinguishable from the white Republicans: both gave the Contract with America almost 100 percent of their support. The differences in the types of districts from which black representatives are elected explain the voting patterns. Unlike black Democrats, who, with few exceptions, represent heavily minority districts, black Republicans represent districts that are less than 10 percent black. Consequently, their policy views are likely to be similar to those of their more conservative constituents.

Regardless of their policy views, many think it is important for the U.S. Congress to look like the American people. Michael Preston has argued that descriptive representation is essential for African Americans. According to Preston, "Blacks need role models in government; they need representatives that they believe will represent their interests; they need to know that good leadership (or bad) is not dominated by one race or group."[57] The same argument can be made for other groups.

Significant growth in the number of women and minorities in Congress is not certain. Nine women who served during the 104th Congress retired, including five of the most senior women.[58] Unlike in African American or Latino voting districts, when women resign or retire from Congress, there is no reason to assume that they will be replaced by women. Two black incumbents with long-term seniority retired: Rep. Collins and Rep. Harold Ford, D-Tenn. They were both replaced by blacks. Rep. Cleo Fields, D-La., decided against running for reelection after his district was redrawn. His replacement is a white Republican. Representative Franks was defeated in the 1996 general elections.

Blacks fared better than anticipated given recent U.S. Supreme Court decisions ruling that the race of voters cannot be the "predominant" factor in a redistricting plan. Congressional districts in several states, including Florida, Georgia, North Carolina, and Texas, have been invalidated by state and federal courts. Civil rights leaders had predicted a sharp decline in the number of black representatives. What actually happened surprised many observers. All the black Democrats were reelected by respectable margins, including five whose districts had been invalidated by the courts. The latter were elected in majority-white districts, along with Julia Carson, D-Ind., whose district has only a 27 percent black voting-age population.

Notes

1. Linda L. Fowler, *Candidates, Congress, and the American Democracy* (Ann Arbor: University of Michigan Press, 1993), 125.
2. Donald R. Matthews, "Legislative Recruitment and Legislative Careers," in Gerhard Loewenberg, Samuel C. Patterson, and Malcolm Jewell, eds., *Handbook of Legislative Research* (Cambridge: Harvard University Press), 1985.
3. Ibid.
4. Leroy N. Rieselbach, *Congressional Politics,* 2d ed. (Boulder: Westview, 1995), 67.
5. William J. Keefe and Morris S. Ogul, *The American Legislative Process,* 7th ed. (Englewood Cliffs, N.J.: Prentice-Hall, 1989), 117.
6. Jonathan Krasno and Donald Philip Green, "Preempting Quality Challengers in House Elections," *Journal of Politics* 5 (November 1988): 4; Gary C. Jacobson and Samuel Kernell, *Strategy and Choice in Congressional Elections,* 2d ed. (New Haven: Yale University Press, 1983), chap. 3; Gary C. Jacobson, *The Politics of Congressional Elections,* 3d ed. (New York: HarperCollins, 1992), 47–48.
7. Jacobson, *Politics of Congressional Elections,* 53.
8. Linda L. Fowler and Robert D. McClure, *Political Ambition* (New Haven: Yale University Press, 1989).
9. Center for the American Woman and Politics, "Women Candidates 1996 Summary," *Fact Sheet,* June 10, 1996. Updated by the author.
10. Center for the American Woman and Politics, Eagleton Institute of Politics, Rutgers University, personal communication, Feb. 28, 1996.
11. Center for the American Woman and Politics, "Summary of Women Congressional and Statewide Candidates in 1994," *CAWP News and Notes* 10 (Winter 1994): 1.
12. Clyde Wilcox, "Why Was 1992 the 'Year of the Woman'? Explaining Women's Gains in 1992," in Elizabeth Adell Cook, Sue Thomas, and Clyde Wilcox, *The Year of the Woman: Myths and Realities* (Boulder: Westview, 1992), chap. 1; Fowler, *Candidates, Congress, and the American Democracy,* 131.
13. Maurine Christopher, *America's Black Congressmen* (New York: Crowell, 1971); Edward Clayton, *The Negro Politician* (Chicago: Johnson, 1964), 32.
14. Compiled from census data found in *Historical Statistics of the United States: Colonial Times to 1970* (Washington, D.C.: Department of Commerce, Bureau of the Census), Series H., 689–699.
15. Terry Seip, *The South Returns to Congress* (Baton Rouge: Louisiana State University Press, 1983), 27–29.
16. Carol M. Swain, *Black Faces, Black Interests: The Representation of African Americans in Congress* (Cambridge: Harvard University Press, 1993), chap. 2.
17. Fowler, *Candidates, Congress, and the American Democracy,* 1–10.
18. Harold F. Gosnell, *Negro Politicians: The Rise of Negro Politics in Chicago* (Chicago: University of Chicago Press, 1935); Dianne Pinderhughes, *Race and Ethnicity in Chicago Politics: A Reexamination of Pluralist Theory* (Urbana: University of Illinois Press, 1987).
19. "Warning Shots Fired by Voters More Mood than Mandate," *Congressional Quarterly Weekly Report,* Nov. 10, 1990, 3797.
20. See David A. Bositis, "African Americans and the 1994 Midterms: What Hap-

pened?" (paper, Joint Center for Political and Economic Studies, Washington, D.C., 1994).

21. Halle Shilling, "Stokes Rolling in Campaign Dough," *State News Service,* Feb. 8, 1996.
22. Allen Wilhite and John Theilmann, "Women, Blacks, and PAC Discrimination," *Social Science Quarterly* (1986): 283–298.
23. Archis Parasharami, "Black Candidates and the Campaign Finance System" (paper, Princeton University, Fall 1995).
24. Anne Hazard, "Weller Leaves Democratic Opponents Far Behind," *State News Service,* Feb. 7, 1996.
25. Michael Barone and Grant Ujifusa, *The Almanac of American Politics 1996* (Washington, D.C.: National Journal, 1995).
26. Barbara Boxer, D-Calif., Margaret Chase Smith, R-Maine, Barbara Mikulski, D-Md., and Olympia Snowe, R-Maine, served in both chambers.
27. Center for the American Woman and Politics, "Women in Congress 1995," April 1995.
28. Robert Darcy, Susan Welch, and Janet Clark, *Women, Elections, and Representation* (New York: Longman, 1987), 74–103.
29. The following authors provide a review and discussion of these factors: Susan J. Carroll, *Women as Candidates in American Politics* (Bloomington: Indiana University Press, 1985); Darcy, Welch, and Clark, *Women, Elections and Representation*; Fowler, *Candidates, Congress, and the American Democracy,* 127–136.
30. Darcy, Welch, and Clark, *Women, Elections, and Representation,* chap. 4.
31. Barbara C. Burrell, *A Woman's Place Is in the House* (Ann Arbor: University of Michigan Press, 1996), 184.
32. Wilma Rule and Pippa Norris, "Anglo and Minority Women's Underrepresentation in the Congress: Is the Electoral System the Culprit," in Wilma Rule and Joseph Zimmerman, eds., *United States Electoral Systems: Their Impact on Women and Minorities* (New Haven: Greenwood, 1992).
33. Richard E. Matland and Deborah D. Brown, "District Magnitude's Effect on Female Representation in U.S. State Legislatures," *Legislative Studies Quarterly* 16 (November 1992), 4, 471.
34. Bernard Grofman, Lisa Handley, and Richard G. Niemi, *Minority Representation and the Quest for Voting Equality* (New York: Cambridge University Press, 1992), chap. 5.
35. Irwin Gertzog, *Congressional Women: Their Recruitment, Integration, and Behavior,* 2d ed. (New York: Praeger, 1995), 20–21.
36. Ibid.
37. Center for the American Woman and Politics, "Women in the U.S. Senate 1922–1994," *Fact Sheet,* February 1994.
38. In addition, Gertzog notes a regional difference in the frequency of widow recruitment and reelection. Southern states have been much more likely to recruit a widow to fill an unexpired term, but they have also been less likely than other regions to support her beyond the one term. The Northeast has ranked second behind the South in recruiting widows to serve unexpired terms, but unlike their southern counterparts, many northeastern women have stayed in Congress and have had lengthy careers.
39. Charles S. Bullock III and Patricia Heys, "Recruitment of Women for Congress: A Research Note," *Western Political Quarterly* 25 (September 1972): 416–423; Gertzog, *Congressional Women.*
40. Commission on the Bicentenary of the U.S. House of Representatives, *Women in Congress, 1916-1990* (Washington, D.C.: U.S. Government Printing Office, 1991), 218.
41. Ibid., 183–184.

42. Ibid.
43. Gertzog, *Congressional Women,* 42–43.
44. Fowler and McClure, *Political Ambition,* 15–126.
45. Ibid., 131–132.
46. Jennifer Gonnerman, "The Femi-Newties: GOP Congresswomen Up Front and Center," *Village Voice,* Jan. 31, 1995.
47. Fowler and McClure, *Political Ambition,* chap. 5.
48. Barone and Ujifusa, *The Almanac of American Politics 1996,* 239.
49. Carole J. Uhlaner and Kay Lehman Schlozman, "Candidate Gender and Congressional Receipts," *Journal of Politics* 48 (February 1986): 46.
50. Katheryne McCormick and Lucy Baruch, "Women Show Strength as Fundraisers," *CAWP News and Notes* 10, Center for the American Woman and Politics (Winter 1994): 16-17.
51. Ruth Mandel and Debra Dodson, "Do Women Officeholders Make a Difference?" in Paula Ries and Anne J. Stone, eds., *The American Woman: 1992–93 Status Report* (New York: Norton, 1992). See also Kay Schlozman, Nancy Burns, and Sidney Verba, "Gender and Citizen Participation: Is There a Different Voice?" *American Journal of Political Science* 39 (May 1995): 267–293; Sue Thomas, *How Women Legislate* (New York: Oxford University Press, 1994); Arturo Vega and Juanita Firestone, "The Effects of Gender on Congressional Behavior and the Substantive Representation of Women," *Legislative Studies Quarterly* 20 (May 1995): 213–222; Edith J. Barrett, "The Policy Priorities of African American Women in State Legislatures," *Legislative Studies Quarterly* 20 (May 1995): 223–247.
52. Marjorie Margolies-Mezvinsky, *A Woman's Place* (New York: Random House, 1994), 34.
53. Hanna Rosin, "Invasion of the Church Ladies," *New Republic,* April 24, 1995.
54. Ibid.
55. Gonnerman, "The Femi-Newties."
56. Under the institutional rules of the House, caucuses are called legislative service organizations (LSOs). They have been positioned to wield considerable influence over the public policy process. For more information, see R. A. Champagne and Leroy N. Rieselbach, "The Evolving Congressional Black Caucus," in Huey L. Perry, ed., *Blacks in the American Political System* (Gainesville: University of Florida Press, 1995); A. Fiellin, "The Functions of Informal Groups in Legislative Institutions," *Journal of Politics* 24 (February 1995): 72–91; Susan W. Hammond, "Congressional Caucuses and Party Leaders in the House of Representatives," *Political Science Quarterly* 106 (Summer 1991): 277–294; and Burdett A. Loomis, "Congressional Caucuses and the Politics of Representation," in Lawrence C. Dodd and Bruce I. Oppenheimer, eds., *Congress Reconsidered,* 2d ed. (Washington, D.C.: CQ Press, 1981), 204–220.
57. Michael Preston as cited in Swain, *Black Faces, Black Interests,* 217.
58. Women who had announced their retirements as of June 1996 were Sen. Nancy Kassebaum, R-Kan., and the following representatives: Cardiss Collins, D-Ill., Blanche Lambert Lincoln, D-Ark., Jan Meyers, R-Kan., Patricia Schroeder, D-Colo., Barbara Vucanovich, R-Nev., and Enid Greene Waldholtz, R-Utah. Two women lost their primaries: Sen. Sheila Frahm, R-Kan., and Rep. Barbara-Rose Collins, D-Mich.

5. Money and Motives: Spending in House Elections

Paul S. Herrnson

Politicians run for Congress for many reasons. The chance to shape the country's agenda, address serious problems, and serve constituents back home, to say nothing of the trappings and prestige of high political office, are powerful incentives for making a serious effort to win. Occasionally, individuals run for office knowing they have little chance of getting elected, using the campaign to publicize an issue. Campaigns are expensive undertakings, and the political parties, political action committees (PACs), and individuals who help finance them also have a variety of motives for offering financial support. The goals of these groups and individuals are not set in stone, but they are fairly consistent: most contributors invest money in politics because they want to influence the policy process. This objective has a major impact on the way money flows into congressional campaigns, with most of it going to incumbents and candidates in competitive contests.

From the mid-1950s until election day 1994, the two major elements of the context within which individuals and groups contributed to campaigns—high reelection rates for congressional incumbents and Democratic dominance of the Congress—were fairly stable. The regulations governing the financing of congressional elections were also, for the most part, unchanged from the late 1970s through 1994. The combination of consistent goals and a relatively unchanging environment fostered a campaign finance system that overwhelmingly favored incumbents and, to a somewhat lesser degree, benefited Democrats.

The 1994 elections drastically altered that environment. Nearly one-fifth of those elected to the House were first-termers. The Senate, which is more immune to rapid change because of its six-year, staggered terms, became the workplace of nine new members. Perhaps more important, the Republicans won majorities in both chambers. Whether the 1994 elections marked the beginning of a long-term Republican Congress is an open question, but the fact remains that it ended Democratic dominance of the House and ushered in a period of more competitive congressional elections.

The 1994 elections introduced a new set of realities on Capitol Hill, in congressional districts, and in the states. How will these realities affect the financing of House elections? This question can be best addressed by examining the environment in which the financiers of congressional elections operate; analyzing their resources, goals, and strategies; assessing the impact the political context has on campaign contributions and expenditures; and examining how the decisions of different participants in the campaign finance system affect the resources the candidates have at their disposal. This chapter analyzes the dynamics of party,

PAC, and individual contributions in the 1994 House elections and speculates about changes in the flow of campaign money that are likely to emerge in future battles for control of the House.

The Context of Congressional Elections

The United States has a candidate-centered system of congressional elections.[1] Instead of the political parties, candidates and the organizations they assemble are the major players: they are responsible for campaign management, fund-raising, public opinion polling, issue and opposition research, advertising, voter mobilization, and virtually every other campaign activity. The relegation of political parties to a supporting role in national elections is unique among modern democracies. The high degree of professionalism and specialization of congressional campaign organizations is also somewhat unusual.[2]

The candidate-centered nature of congressional campaigns elevates the importance of candidate fund-raising and spending. Candidates must raise huge sums of money to assemble organizations, communicate their messages, and mobilize voters. Fund-raising is especially important to congressional challengers, who may be waging uphill battles against entrenched incumbents. Money is more critical to challengers than incumbents because most House members already enjoy high levels of name recognition and popularity with voters and have easy access to the press.[3] A healthy campaign war chest enables a challenger to gain visibility among voters, publicize campaign themes and issues, and attract media coverage.[4] Candidates for open seats also need large campaign accounts. Although open-seat candidates usually begin their campaigns on a more equal footing than do incumbents and challengers, many have little visibility at the beginning of the campaign and need to spend large sums to disseminate their messages.

Campaign spending usually has a major impact on the number of votes won by challengers and open-seat candidates, but it has less influence on the votes garnered by incumbents.[5] Ironically, raising money is easy for incumbents and difficult for challengers. During the 1994 elections, incumbents collected, on average, more than $615,000 in campaign funds, more than two and a half times the amount for challengers. Candidates for open seats raised an average of just under $646,000. Most two-party open-seat races were financially competitive.

The financing of federal elections is regulated by the Federal Election Campaign Act of 1974 and its amendments (collectively referred to as FECA). The law, which was passed in response to the Watergate scandal, represents an attempt to restrict the flow of money in federal elections, broaden the base of campaign contributors, increase public awareness of how campaign money is raised and spent, and prevent individuals, corporations, and other groups from having undue influence in the political process. The FECA effectively restructured the funding of federal elections.

The FECA limits contributions by individuals to $1,000 per candidate for each stage of the election cycle: primary, runoff, and general election. The law also caps individual contributions at $5,000 per year to a single PAC or state party committee and at $20,000 per year to a national party committee; the law imposes an aggregate contribution limit of $25,000 per year for individual contributions in federal elections. Congressional candidates are allowed to make unlimited contributions to their own campaigns.

The FECA allows national, congressional, and state party campaign committees to contribute up to $5,000 each to individual House candidates at the different stages of the election.[6] Parties can also spend larger sums of money on behalf of individual candidates. This spending, often referred to as "coordinated expenditures" because it can be made in direct coordination with a candidate's campaign, typically consists of campaign services that a congressional or senatorial campaign committee or some other party organization gives to an individual candidate or purchases from a political consultant for the candidate.

Coordinated expenditures can be polls, radio advertisements, television commercials, fund-raising events, direct mail solicitations, or issue research. They differ from campaign contributions in that both the party and the candidate have some control over them, giving the party the ability to influence some aspects of how the campaign is run. Originally set at $10,000 each for a state and national committee, the limits for coordinated expenditures on behalf of House candidates are adjusted for inflation and reached $29,300 per committee in 1994.[7] Although state and national party committees are authorized to spend the same amount in coordinated expenditures, the committees often create "agency agreements" that allow the parties' congressional campaign committee or national committee to take over a state party's share of the expenditures in situations where a state party committee lacks adequate funds. Doing so enables national parties to double the amount they can spend in congressional races.

The FECA also bans corporations, trade associations, labor unions, and other organized interests from giving money from their treasuries to congressional candidates. It does not prevent these groups from participating in congressional elections, but it results in most of their financial election activities being channeled through political action committees. The telecommunications giant AT&T sponsors a PAC, as do the National Association of Realtors and the AFL-CIO.[8] Nonconnected PACs, such as the National Committee for an Effective Congress, which have no sponsoring group, pay their expenses out of money they raise from contributors and have greater autonomy than those with sponsors.[9] PACs can contribute up to $5,000 per candidate in each stage of the election. PACs also are allowed to make unlimited expenditures for or against candidates so long as they are made without the candidates' knowledge or consent. In June 1996, in the middle of the primary season, the Supreme Court ruled in a controversial decision that party committees could also make independent expenditures in federal election campaigns.[10]

While the FECA regulates the flow of money to and from congressional campaigns, a loophole in the law allows parties and other groups to raise and spend huge sums of money outside of the federal limits. These funds, commonly referred to as "soft" money, are subject only to the limits imposed on them by state laws. Collected mainly from wealthy individuals, corporations, unions, and other groups, soft money is used to help finance national party operations, strengthen state and local party committees, carry out voter-mobilization drives, and pay for party-focused television advertisements.[11] Most soft money is raised at the national level, transferred to state party committees, and spent in ways that help a party's candidates for federal, state, and local offices.

Soft money and "hard" money, which is raised and spent in accordance with the FECA, are not interchangeable. Although both can be spent on party operations and election-related activities, soft money cannot be directly contributed to or spent to directly advocate the election of individual congressional candidates. The parties have found ways to help their congressional candidates despite this distinction. In some situations when a national party organization has an abundance of soft money, but not hard dollars, and a state party committee is flush with hard dollars, the national organization encourages the state committee to spend its hard dollars in congressional races by promising to replace those funds with an equivalent amount of soft money. Also, as a result of several court decisions, soft money can be spent on "issue advocacy" campaigns that mention the names of federal candidates in connection with specific issues but do not expressly call for a candidate's election or defeat.[12] Court rulings have weakened the FECA, allowing party committees, PACs, and other interest groups a larger role in communicating politically relevant information during election years.

The Political Environment of the 1994 House Elections

Few political scientists, journalists, or political practitioners anticipated the tidal wave that gave the Republicans a net gain of fifty-two House seats and eight Senate seats and placed the GOP in control of both chambers for the first time in forty years.[13] But there were some early signs that the 1994 elections would be unusual. The first and perhaps most important sign was the closeness of the 1992 elections. Despite their party's success in capturing the White House for the first time in twelve years, Democrats suffered a net loss of ten House seats. More than one-third of those Democrats who beat their GOP opponents won with less than 55 percent of the vote, indicating that many Democrats would be vulnerable in future elections.

Other signs had to do with national political and economic conditions. For the first time since Jimmy Carter occupied the White House, Democrats were in control of both the legislative and executive branches of the federal government. The end of divided government meant that Democrats would be held accountable for the federal government's performance and the state of the nation. Despite two years of economic growth under the Clinton administration, more than half of all voters still believed that the economy was in bad shape and their financial situation had not improved.[14] Because most of the economic growth mainly benefited the wealthiest segments of the population, middle-income breadwinners felt insecure about their prospects for a better life for themselves and their children.

The Democrats' failure to pass health care reform or a middle-class tax cut—two of their major promises from the 1992 election—caused the president to decline in the polls and led to widespread public discontent with Washington. Discontent with Congress reached an all-time high prior to the 1994 elections: roughly three-fourths of all Americans disapproved of its performance.[15] Prompted by the rhetoric of Ross Perot and GOP leaders, many Americans came to believe the government was controlled by corrupt politicians who were either out of touch with ordinary people or did not care about their needs. As the governing party, Democrats were in a position to feel the wrath of the voters.

These were promising conditions for Republicans, and the GOP was poised to take advantage of them. Prior to the 1990s, the National Republican Congressional Committee (NRCC) had only limited success in recruiting candidates who either had held elective office or had significant unelective experience in politics. The Republicans' lack of a congressional "farm team," particularly the small numbers of Republican state legislators and municipal officials, was thought by many to be a major reason for the GOP's minority status in the House.[16] However, through party-building and candidate recruitment and training by the Republican National Committee (RNC), GOPAC, and reinvigorated Republican state and local party organizations, the GOP had increased the number of Republicans occupying state and local offices. The NRCC encouraged many of these politicians and others experienced in politics to run for Congress in 1994.

The NRCC turned to other talent pools in search of House candidates in 1994. Although previous officeholding experience is thought by many to be the mark of a well-qualified Democratic House challenger, strong Republican candidates traditionally have come from more diverse backgrounds. Political aides, party officeholders, previously unsuccessful candidates, administration officials, and other "unelected politicians" have long been an important source of strong Republican House candidates.[17] Wealthy individuals often have been viewed by GOP and Democratic strategists as good candidates because they can finance significant portions of their own campaigns.

The GOP's long-term party-building and short-term recruitment efforts resulted in its fielding record numbers of challengers and open-seat contestants in 1994. This election was the first in recent history in which more Republicans than Democrats ran for the House and more Republican-held than Democratic-held House seats went uncontested.[18] Moreover, the GOP fielded a fairly talented group of candidates. Nearly 20 percent of all Republican nonincumbents in two-party contested races had once held elective office, and another 10 percent had some form of nonelective political experience. The percentages were smaller than in 1992, but higher than during most of the 1970s and 1980s. In addition, fifty-four GOP nonincumbents (more than 20 percent) were able to invest more than $50,000 in their own campaigns, and thirty-four (roughly

13 percent) invested at least $100,000. A combination of political talent, money, and national conditions laid the foundation for the Republican takeover of the House in 1994.[19] The Republicans' Contract with America provided an issue platform for achieving that goal.[20] Some, but not all, campaign contributors reacted to the unique circumstances that appeared in 1994.

Political Parties and the Redistribution of the Wealth

Parties play an important supporting role in contemporary congressional elections. Party organizations in Washington, D.C.—mainly the NRCC and the Democratic Congressional Campaign Committee (DCCC)—help House candidates, especially nonincumbents, cope with the costs and complexities of waging campaigns. These organizations, sometimes referred to (along with their Senate counterparts) as the "Hill committees," have developed into major repositories of campaign money and expertise for congressional candidates.[21] They provide candidates with assistance in campaign management, fund-raising, issue and opposition research, communications, and other election activities that require in-depth research or technical expertise. In addition to money, the Hill committees also help candidates obtain election services from political consultants, congressional incumbents, PACs, and other groups.[22] Some state party committees provide congressional candidates with similar kinds of assistance, but most state and local parties concentrate their efforts on voter registration and get-out-the-vote activities and participate less in congressional elections.[23]

Party finances, strategies, and campaign expenditures are influenced by many factors, including the parties' wealth and the political circumstances of a given election year. During the 1994 elections, the DCCC raised in excess of $19.4 million, and the NRCC just under $26.7 million in hard money that could be spent directly in connection with congressional campaigns. In addition, the two committees took in $5.2 million and $7.6 million, respectively, in soft money. The Democratic National Committee (DNC) raised roughly $41.8 million in hard money and $41.3 million in soft money, while the RNC raised $87.4 million in hard and $46.1 million in soft money.[24]

Some of the Republicans' fund-raising success in 1994 can be attributed to the possibilities brought on by the political environment, but some of the GOP's advantage is more permanent. The Republicans' superior direct mail fund-raising list and wealthier constituency enable the party to solicit small and medium-sized donations from people of moderate means as well as to raise large sums from the rich. Many business executives and entrepreneurs, who are accustomed to paying dues to civic groups and making political and charitable contributions, are more comfortable contributing to the GOP than to the Democrats. The same is true of many corporate and trade association executives who agree with the Republicans' free market ideology. Some of these individuals and groups contribute to the Democratic Party out of a desire to facilitate access to members of the party that controlled Congress, but many feel more at home supporting the GOP.

Table 5-1 Party Spending in the 1994 House Elections

Party Group	Contributions	Coordinated Expenditures
Democratic		
DNC	$58,693	$18,755
DCCC	974,239	7,730,815
DSCC	10,000	0
State and local	458,288	705,500
Total Democratic	$1,501,220	$8,455,070
Republican		
RNC	$539,069	$4,607,337
NRCC	705,382	3,926,641
NRSC	122,500	0
State and local	669,761	317,897
Total Republican	$2,036,712	$8,851,875

Source: Federal Election Commission, "FEC Reports on Political Party Activity for 1993–94," press release, April 13, 1995.

The party organizations' goal—to win the maximum number of seats—encourages them to target their resources to candidates in closely contested races. Protecting incumbents facing strong opposition is a major priority, followed by winning open seats and challenging weak incumbents from the opposing party. Both parties' decision makers maintain that candidate ideology does not influence the distribution of money. Pressures from nervous incumbents, the leadership aspirations of Hill committee chairs and members, and other political considerations inside Congress and the Hill committees themselves can skew the distribution of party resources, often to the advantage of safe incumbents and the disadvantage of competitive challengers. Changing political and economic conditions and the overall uncertainties of election politics can also result in some competitive campaigns being overlooked, while some uncompetitive races are deluged with resources.

In their spending in the 1994 House elections, the parties followed several patterns from earlier elections: Republican Party committees slightly outspent their Democratic counterparts (see Table 5-1). Both parties distributed most of their money in coordinated expenditures, reflecting the higher ceilings allowed by the FECA. Most party expenditures originated at the national level rather than the state and local levels. Some "crossover" spending from the two senatorial campaign committees to House candidates also occurred. One unusual development was the large amount of RNC spending in House races. In earlier elections, spending in House races by either national committee rarely reached $1.5 million, but in 1994 RNC spending exceeded $5.1 million. The RNC's large investment reflects both the opportunities offered by the electoral environment and the

Table 5-2 Distribution of Party Money in the 1994 House Elections

Contest Type	Democrats	Republicans
Incumbents		
Competitive contests	41%	6%
	(112)	(18)
Uncompetitive contests	5	8
	(99)	(107)
Challengers		
Competitive contests	9	51
	(18)	(112)
Uncompetitive contests	17	6
	(107)	(99)
Open seats		
Competitive contests	20	21
	(33)	(33)
Uncompetitive contests	7	8
	(19)	(19)
Total (in thousands)	$9,440	$10,157
	(388)	(388)

Source: Compiled from Federal Election Commission data.

Notes: Incumbents in competitive contests are those who won or lost by 20 percent or less of the two-party vote, and incumbents in uncompetitive contests are the remainder. Challengers in competitive contests are those who won or lost by 20 percent or less of the two-party vote, and challengers in uncompetitive contests are the remainder. Open-seat candidates in competitive contests are those who won or lost by 20 percent or less of the two-party vote, and uncompetitive open-seat candidates are the remainder. The figures include only party contributions and coordinated expenditures to general election candidates in two-party contested races. They do not include soft money expenditures.

fact that the NRCC was unable spend much of the money that it had raised during the 1994 election cycle because it was still paying off the large debt it had incurred in 1992.[25]

Both the Democrats and the Republicans responded to the political environment of the 1994 elections (see Table 5-2). The Democrats were on the defensive, using 41 percent of their money to protect incumbents in competitive contests. The Republicans went on the offensive, spending 51 percent of their funds on challengers involved in these same races. Both parties also spent heavily in open-seat contests. Overall, the GOP delivered a greater portion of its funds to candidates in competitive races, but the Democrats improved in their ability to deliver resources to these contests over previous elections.[26]

Party committees also influence the flow of money distributed by others. One of the major tasks carried out by congressional campaign committee members and staffs is to persuade PACs, individuals, and congressional incumbents to support the party's most competitive challengers and open-seat contestants. This task is difficult because it requires incumbents to donate some of the resources they would normally devote to their own reelection efforts to other campaigns. The fear of losing their own seats, which is chronic among most politicians, makes it extremely challenging to get candidates to work in behalf of others.[27]

In recent years, however, the parties have persuaded many congressional incumbents to help raise funds for those who aspire to a House seat. The parties worked to redistribute the wealth among candidates in several ways. First, they solicited contributions and fund-raising assistance from House incumbents to amass the resources needed for promising challengers and open-seat contestants, as well as incumbents in jeopardy. In 1994, ninety-eight GOP House members involved in two-party contested races contributed almost $930,000 from their own reelection accounts to Republican party committees. One hundred and seven incumbent Democrats contributed just under $737,000 to Democratic party organizations.[28] Nearly 85 percent of the funds contributed by Democratic and Republican candidates went to the NRCC and the DCCC. Most of the money was contributed by senior House members, such as Rep. Gerald Solomon, R-N.Y., who gave $65,000, Rep. Joseph McDade, R-Pa., who gave nearly $68,000, and House Speaker Thomas Foley, D-Wash., who gave $30,000. The biggest contributor from either party was Rep. James McDermott, D-Wash., who gave $108,000, most of it to the Washington State Democratic Committee. House members in uncontested races, retiring members, a few nonincumbent contestants, and some senators contributed additional funds.

Second, the parties encouraged House incumbents to contribute money directly from their campaign treasuries to other candidates.[29] In 1994, 78 House Republicans contributed $1.17 million from their campaign treasuries to 204 Republican general election candidates; 104 House Democrats gave $708,000 to 191 Democrats.[30] Rep. Robert Livingston of Louisiana, Rep. Newt Gingrich of Georgia, and Rep. Tom DeLay of Texas were the leading Republican candidate-to-candidate contributors, giving roughly $139,000, $125,000, and $122,000, respectively, to GOP House candidates. Leading the Democrats were Reps. Robert Matsui and Nancy Pelosi of California, as well as James McDermott, with contributions to other candidates of $133,000, $43,450, and $30,500, respectively.

About two-thirds of the campaign funds that candidates redistributed to other candidates went to nonincumbents. Republicans were more supportive of challengers and open-seat candidates than were Democrats, who were somewhat more inclined to support incumbents. These patterns reflect the challenges and opportunities that emerged from the political environment in which the 1994 elections occurred. Members of both parties were highly supportive of compatriots in close races. More than three-quarters of all candidate-to-candidate contributions were spent in general elections decided by vote margins of 20 percent or less.

Third, the parties encouraged those incumbents—mostly congressional leaders—who headed leadership PACs, sometimes referred to as member PACs, to support fellow partisans who are in need. Leadership PACs sponsored by House Democrats distributed more than $1.6 million to 249 general election House candidates, while GOP-sponsored leadership PACs distributed $263,000 to 371 candidates in 1994.[31] Topping the Democratic leadership PACs' donations was Missouri representative Richard Gephardt's Effective Government Committee, followed by the Leadership America PAC, headed by Rep. Charlie Rose of North Carolina, and California representative Vic Fazio's Victory USA PAC. These three PACs contributed roughly $702,000, $504,000, and $130,000 to Democratic candidates.[32] The top GOP PACs were Representative DeLay's Americans for a Republican Majority, Representative Gingrich's GOPAC, and California representative Jerry Lewis's Future Leaders PAC, which distributed about $227,000, $20,000, and $16,000 to House Republican contestants. Nearly 60 percent of all funds given by leadership PACs went to House incumbents. Democratic leadership PACs were far more incumbent-oriented in their contributions than Republican PACs. As was the case with member-to-member contributions, more than three-fourths of all leadership PAC contributions were spent in contests decided by margins of 20 percent or less.

Candidate-to-party, candidate-to-candidate, and leadership PAC-to-candidate contributions accounted for more than $5.3 million of the funds spent in the 1994 House races. Some House members redistribute the wealth solely to help their party win or maintain control of the chamber; some give to strengthen their holds on party leadership posts and committee chairmanships; others give to build the support needed to win these positions. Policy entrepreneurs use campaign contributions to create good will that could someday be useful in passing their legislative priorities. Not surprisingly, the most active redistributors of the wealth were the formal and informal party leaders.

The greatest beneficiaries of the redistribution of party wealth were candidates who ran in competitive elections. Candidates whose races were decided by margins of 20 percent of the vote or less received 75 percent of the money that was redistributed by formal party committees and 79 percent of the money redistributed by House members and membership PACs. The fact that most candidate-to-candidate and leadership PAC-to-candidate contributions went to the same candidates who received the lion's share of the money distributed by party committees highlights the importance of the party connection in the redistribution of campaign funds.

A fourth way parties help candidates in close contests raise funds is by influencing the decisions of PACs and individuals who make large campaign contributions. Parties help challengers, open-seat candidates, and House members in marginal seats raise money through direct mail and telemarketing solicitations. The Hill committees also organize "meet and greet" sessions for candidates and PACs on Capitol Hill and regularly update PACs on the campaigns of candidates in competitive districts. Party leaders and Hill committee staffs routinely twist the arms of PAC managers to get them to contribute to their candidates. Party committees also host high-dollar fund-raisers in Washington, D.C., and in other major metropolitan areas. Congressional party leaders, committee chairs, and other celebrities encourage PAC members and generous donors to attend these events.[33]

By participating in "buddy system" and "adopt a candidate" programs that match nonincumbents with committee chairs and other congressional leaders, influential House members help financially needy candidates. During the 1994 elections, House Republicans, who did not perceive themselves to be nearly as vulnerable as did their Democratic counterparts, were more aggressive in this area. One NRCC staffer credited a GOP incumbent who had never before lifted a finger on behalf of a House challenger with raising more than $50,000 in PAC money for his "buddy" in just one afternoon.[34] It is difficult to measure the impact that party and incumbent fund-raising assistance has on candidates' receipts. However, the efforts that many House members and party aides undertake on behalf of promising nonincumbents and incumbents in jeopardy further show the parties' strong commitment to redistributing the funds that are spent in congressional elections. They demonstrate how party activities have contributed to the nationalization of campaign finance.

Political Action Committees: Ideology and Access

PACs contributed a total of $131.8 million in the 1994 congressional elections. Corporate PACs gave approximately $38.2 million, and trade association PACs gave $34.4 million. Labor unions donated roughly $33 million in an attempt to counter some of the money pumped into elections by these business-sponsored groups. An additional $4.9 million was contributed by PACs sponsored by cooperatives and corporations without stock. Ideological PACs, referred to as nonconnected PACs by the Federal Election Commission because of their lack of a separate sponsoring organization, accounted for about $12 million in PAC dollars.

PACs are commonly divided into three types, depending on whether they are motivated by ideological, access-oriented, or mixed objectives.[35] Ideological PACs tend to be the most issue- or cause-oriented, and they mainly pursue electoral goals. EMILY's List, which tries to elect pro-choice Democratic women, and Jesse Helms's National Congressional Club, which helps their opponents, are among the best known ideological committees. Because their overriding goal is to elect politicians who share their views, rather than gain access to members or change their positions, ideological PACs most often donate to candidates in close contests. These groups are also more supportive of nonincumbents than are other kinds of PACs. In 1994, 65 percent of the contributions that ideological PACs made in connection with House races was spent in competitive elections, and 35 percent went to nonincumbents (see Table 5-3). Liberal PACs contributed two-thirds of their money to Democratic

Table 5-3 Distribution of PAC Contributions in the 1994 House Elections

Contest Type	Nonconnected	Corporate	Trade Association	Labor
Democrats				
Incumbents				
Competitive contests	36%	35%	33%	44%
Uncompetitive contests	13	19	18	26
Challengers				
Competitive contests	2	—	1	5
Uncompetitive contests	2	—	1	7
Open seats				
Competitive contests	8	2	5	11
Uncompetitive contests	3	1	1	4
Republicans				
Incumbents				
Competitive contests	3	4	4	—
Uncompetitive contests	12	26	23	3
Challengers				
Competitive contests	10	6	6	—
Uncompetitive contests	1	—	—	—
Open seats				
Competitive contests	6	4	5	—
Uncompetitive contests	3	3	3	—
Total (in thousands)	$10,520	$38,213	$34,411	$30,110

Source: Compiled from Federal Election Commission data.

Notes: The figures include only PAC contributions to general election candidates in two-party contested races. An empty cell indicates that PACs spent less than 1 percent of their funds in these races. The candidate categories are the same as those in Table 5-2. Some columns do not add to 100 percent because of rounding.

incumbents, while conservative committees gave more than one-quarter of their donations to promising Republican challengers. These patterns bear a striking resemblance to those for 1992, except that liberal PACs gave slightly more to Democratic incumbents and conservative PACs gave slightly more to Republican challengers. It is clear that nonconnected committees react to the opportunities offered by the political environment of a particular election cycle, but they do not respond as strongly as party committees.

Ideological PACs also make more independent expenditures than do other PACs. In 1994 groups such as the National Right to Life PAC, the Minnesota

Citizens Concerned for Life Committee, and the National Taxpayers Union spent $1.61 million, which accounted for 73 percent of the total independent expenditures PACs made in connection with contested House races. More than one-fourth of all independent expenditures were negative, consisting of attack ads aimed at bringing about the defeat of some House incumbents. The most visible independent expenditures take the form of television and radio ads designed to arouse the interest of the general public. Other expenditures are made for ads in trade magazines or mailings targeted at specific audiences.

Their lack of a corporate or union sponsor gives ideological PACs the freedom to make independent expenditures. These groups rarely worry about incurring the wrath of a congressional incumbent whom they publicly oppose because they do not seek special benefits for a sponsoring group. They also recognize that the causes they support, including abortion rights and prayer in school, are not likely to convert many legislators. In addition, independent expenditures and the publicity that often accompanies them help ideological PACs gain greater visibility and raise funds.

Access-oriented PACs, which include most business-oriented committees, rarely make independent expenditures; they are more interested in laying a foundation for influencing the policy process than in replacing those involved in the process.[36] Their overriding concern is with keeping open to their lobbyists the doors of powerful legislators.[37] Given the high reelection rates enjoyed by House incumbents—higher than 90 percent between 1950 and 1994—contributing to incumbents is an ideal strategy. Many of these PACs, which include United Parcel Service's UPSPAC, Federal Express's PAC, and AT&T PAC, view a contribution as the price of guaranteeing that their lobbyist's telephone calls are among the few that members of Congress return.[38] Because special tax breaks, government appropriations, or federal regulations can be worth millions or even billions of dollars to a corporation or other business enterprise, the costs of forming and maintaining a PAC are viewed as a sound investment.

In 1994 all but 16 percent of the funds corporate PACs spent in House elections went to incumbents and less than 7 percent went to challengers. As has been the case for most of the 1980s and early 1990s, House Democrats received significantly more corporate PAC money than their Republican counterparts. This bias does not result from an affinity that business groups have for the Democratic Party: on the contrary, Republicans have been and continue to be more sympathetic to the concerns of business. Instead, the Democrats' control over the chamber, which gave them the ability to set the legislative agenda and appoint committee and subcommittee chairs, made it important for business interests wishing to influence legislation to contribute to Democratic House members, including some with whom the groups disagreed on fundamental issues. Incumbents of both parties flaunted their legislative influence to leverage large contributions from corporate PACs.[39] Powerful party leaders, committee and subcommittee chairs, ranking members, and policy entrepreneurs, many of whom faced only weak challenges, capitalized on these PACs' access-oriented goals to take in many contributions.

Access-oriented goals tend to be so important for most corporate committees that they ignore considerations of electoral competitiveness and do not respond to the political environment. During the 1994 election cycle, corporate PACs contributed only 2 percent more funds to candidates in close races than they did to candidates in one-sided contests. These PACs paid little attention to competitive House challengers and open-seat contestants, allocating to them only 12 percent of the money they spent in House races. Corporate PACs, concerned with solidifying their relations with those who ran the established order in Congress, invested little in the campaigns of those attempting to bring that order down.

PACs that use mixed strategies make some contributions to maintain access to the policy-making process and others to influence the composition of Congress. They give not only to incumbents who can promote their legislative priorities but also to candidates in competitive elections, including some challengers. Many trade association PACs, such as the Realtors' PAC, and labor PACs, such as the National Education Association's PAC, use mixed strategies.[40] In 1994 trade PACs made contributions to many of the same candidates as did corporate PACs, but favored Democrats and contestants in close races somewhat more than did their corporate counterparts.

One thing that distinguishes trade association PACs from corporate committees is that trade PACs make more independent expenditures. Trade groups have greater freedom to make these expenditures because they have many backers, and there is no single sponsoring organization that could face the retribution of angry incumbents. Trade association committees made independent expenditures of $418,000 in 1994, about 19 percent of the total independent expenditures made by PACs during that election.

Labor PACs also follow mixed strategies, but their contributions and independent expenditures traditionally have a decidedly pro-Democratic tilt. In 1994 labor PACs gave Democrats 97 percent of all their contributions in House races. Organized labor's response to the political environment was visible through these contributions. About 73 percent of all labor PAC money went to incumbents, including 44 percent spent to help reelect Democratic House members in close contests and 26 percent spent to ensure continued access to House members of both parties who were involved in lopsided races. More than a quarter of all labor PAC contributions went to nonincumbents, mostly to Democrats in close races. Labor PACs also made about $17,000 worth of independent expenditures in 1994 (less than 1 percent of the total independent expenditures made by all PACs), and virtually all were intended to help Democrats. The financial activities of organized labor in 1994, as in previous elections, clearly reflect labor's twin goals of courting influence with powerful congressional Democrats and seeking to maximize the number of seats the Democratic Party controls.

Individual Contributors

Individuals gave $172.9 million dollars to candidates in contested House races during the 1994 elections. Some individual contributors are motivated by a desire to maintain or change the composition of Congress. Others pursue material concerns: their donations are intended to secure access to influential politicians who are already in the legislature. Still others contribute for what are often referred to as solidary goals. They donate money because they enjoy rubbing elbows with members of Congress and other political elites. Some individual contributors are also motivated by the desire to support candidates who share their racial, ethnic, or religious identification.[41]

Just as PACs tend to favor incumbents, so do individuals. In 1994 incumbents in contested House races raised $98.4 million from individuals, $46.6 million more than their challenger opponents. These figures account for 57 percent and 24 percent of all individual contributions (see Table 5-4). Open-seat candidates received 19 percent of all individual contributions. Republicans raised $91.6 million in individual contributions, while Democrats raised $81.3 million. Candidates in close races received 56 percent of all individual money spent in House races. Competitive Republican challengers took in substantially more in individual funds than other groups of challengers in 1994 and slightly more than Republican challengers in 1992. Democratic incumbents in close contests collected more in individual dollars than other incumbents in 1994 and slightly more than their counterparts in the 1992 election cycle. These patterns show that individual contributors reacted, at least to some extent, to the political environment. Democratic contributors tried to help Democratic House members in jeopardy, and Republican contributors tried to better the chances of the GOP candidates challenging them. Incumbency, partisanship, competition, and electoral conditions all had a major impact on the flow of individual contributions in 1994.

The impact of these factors was somewhat less than uniform across different sizes of individual contributions. Republican candidates collected 58 percent of all small contributions (those of $200 or less), 16 percent more than the Democrats, but the gap largely disappears for contributions of $200 or more. The fund-raising gap between candidates in competitive and one-sided races is fairly consistent, however, favoring those in close contests across the four contribution categories. Individual small contributions are slightly more challenger-oriented than larger contributions. Individuals who gave small contributions to Republicans were either less concerned about or less able to judge the competitiveness of GOP members' reelection contests than were those who donated larger amounts. Their relative indifference toward electoral competition is due in part to their stronger ideological views. Large contributors' access-oriented motives and better sources of information also account for the differences in giving patterns.[42] The parties and PACs they support furnish many large contributors with campaign information they can use when deciding how to give money to congressional contestants.[43]

Table 5-4 Distribution of Individual Contributions in the 1994 House Elections

Contest Type	All	Under $200	$200-499	$500-749	$750-1,000
Democrats					
Incumbents					
Competitive contests	21%	19%	20%	23%	22%
Uncompetitive contests	12	8	13	14	14
Challengers					
Competitive contests	3	3	3	2	2
Uncompetitive contests	3	4	3	2	3
Open seats					
Competitive contests	6	6	6	6	6
Uncompetitive contests	3	2	3	3	3
Republicans					
Incumbents					
Competitive contests	4	5	4	4	4
Uncompetitive contests	20	24	20	20	16
Challengers					
Competitive contests	16	17	15	15	16
Uncompetitive contests	2	2	2	2	3
Open seats					
Competitive contests	6	6	6	6	7
Uncompetitive contests	4	4	4	4	4
Total (in thousands)	$172,878	$63,085	$25,564	$30,975	$53,255

Source: Compiled from Federal Election Commission data.

Notes: The figures include only individual contributions to general election candidates in two-party contested races. The candidate categories are the same as those in Table 5-2. Some columns do not add to 100 percent because of rounding.

Candidate Receipts

Candidates are not passive players in the money chase. They develop strategies and tactics and mount sophisticated campaigns for resources. Almost all incumbents hire professional consultants to carry out direct mail and telephone solicitations and organize fund-raising events. Once they identify a national financial constituency, the professionals develop a pitch that is designed to remind PACs and individuals who make large contributions of the candi-

Table 5-5 Sources of Support for Candidates, 1994

Sources of Support	Democrats			Republicans		
	Incumbent	Challenger	Open Seat	Incumbent	Challenger	Open Seat
Individual contributions	$266,725 (41%)	$77,648 (45%)	$294,049 (47%)	$336,969 (59%)	$151,404 (56%)	$337,218 (51%)
PAC contributions	$318,314 (50%)	$39,022 (22%)	$171,498 (27%)	$194,995 (34%)	$27,270 (10%)	$125,200 (19%)
Party contributions and coordinated expenditures	$20,623 (3%)	$19,634 (11%)	$50,653 (8%)	$11,613 (2%)	$27,201 (10%)	$57,043 (9%)
Candidate contributions	$8,456 (1%)	$31,406 (18%)	$88,730 (14%)	$4,625 (1%)	$54,213 (20%)	$125,652 (19%)
Miscellaneous	$28,813 (4%)	$6,509 (4%)	$21,546 (3%)	$20,767 (4%)	$8,441 (3%)	$20,437 (3%)
Total (*N*)	$642,931 (211)	$174,219 (125)	$626,476 (52)	$568,969 (125)	$268,529 (211)	$665,550 (52)

Source: Compiled from Federal Election Commission data.

Notes: Figures are the averages for general election candidates in major party contested races. Candidate contributions include loans candidates made to their own campaigns. Some columns do not add to 100 percent because of rounding.

dates' legislative goals, accomplishments, committee assignments and other sources of influence, and of the amount of money they need to win reelection.[44]

Incumbents are almost always able to meet their financial goals. In 1994, as in many previous elections, House Democratic incumbents in two-party contested races raised approximately half their funds from PACs and more than 40 percent from individuals (see Table 5-5). Their control of the House gave Democratic members tremendous advantages in soliciting PAC money. Republican incumbents raised significantly more from individuals. Few incumbents needed to turn to their parties for substantial help, but Democratic incumbents received more party money than did Republican incumbents.

Fund-raising is a much more difficult task for challengers than for incumbents. Challengers lack the political clout of incumbents. Many contributors do not give to challengers because they see them as longshots and fear alienating a powerful incumbent. The campaigns that many challengers wage, which tend to rely heavily on volunteers for fund-raising and most other activities, often do not instill much confidence in access-oriented contributors.[45] For these reasons, challengers typically receive far less from them and need to rely on contributions from individuals and parties. In 1994 Democratic challengers raised 45 percent of their funds from individuals, 22 percent from PACs, and 11 percent from parties, while their Republican counterparts raised significantly more from individuals and much less from PACs. Challengers from both parties dug deeper into their own pockets than did incumbents, supplying roughly one-fifth of their own campaign funds.

However, it is important to note the tremendous variation in challenger fund-raising. Successful challenger fund-raising efforts usually begin at home. Challengers who succeed in raising money from individuals in their districts and states are then able to raise more money from parties, PACs, and political elites in Washington, D.C., and individuals in the nation's major metropolitan centers.[46] Challengers with significant political experience (either as elected officials or in unelective political posts) and the services of professional fund-raisers are usually more successful in collecting money than inexperienced candidates who wage amateur campaigns.[47] Although few challengers raised significant PAC funds, Democratic control of Congress gave that party's challengers an advantage over their GOP counterparts in raising PAC money in the 1982 through 1994 elections.[48]

Candidates for open seats have few of the disadvantages of challengers and few of the advantages of incumbents. Because open-seat contests tend to be the most competitive races, party committees, many individuals, and some PACs invest money in them. During the 1994 congressional elections, open-seat candidates raised substantial sums from a variety of sources, including PACs. The Democrats' advantage in raising PAC money came from their party's control of the chamber—an advantage that has belonged to the Republicans since the 1994 elections. The Republicans' advantage in raising money from party committees and individuals is due mainly to the greater wealth of the GOP's constituency, just as the large sums GOP candidates contributed to their own campaigns reflect their personal wealth.

The stunning successes enjoyed by Republican nonincumbents in 1994 had less to do with where their money came from than with the amounts they raised. Republican challengers and open-seat candidates increased the sizes of their war chests by about 45 percent and 56 percent, respectively, between 1992 and 1994, as opposed to the 10 percent and 23 percent increases enjoyed by their Democratic counterparts. Moreover, an exceptionally large number of Republican challengers collected sufficient resources to wage competitive campaigns: fifty-one (24 percent of the candidates) raised $400,000 or more in direct contributions and party coordinated expenditures, and thirty-six (17 percent) raised $500,000 or more. Eighteen (14 percent) of the Democratic challengers reached the lower threshold, and only eight (6 percent) reached the higher. Well-funded Republican challengers were able to overcome the "invisibility problem" that plagues most House challengers, enabling many of them to disseminate their messages and win their races.

Prognostications for the Post-Democratic Congress

The 1994 elections ushered in a new era of congressional politics. Republican successes across the country and at many levels of government show that the 1994 GOP victory was both deep and wide. In addition to their gains in the House and Senate, the Republicans won eleven governorships, hundreds of state legislative seats, and captured control of fifteen state legislative chambers. Not one incumbent Republican House member, senator, or governor was defeated. GOP candidates for the House, Senate, and state and local offices enjoyed victories in every region. Republican successes in the South, which had long been a Democratic stronghold, indicate the end of Democratic dominance over that region. Party switching by five Democrats in the House, two in the Senate, and scores holding local office in the South and elsewhere suggest that at least some politicians anticipated that 1994 was an enduring change rather than a fluke.

The reapportionment and redistricting of House seats after the 1990 Census contributed to the political changes. Reapportionment increased the number of congressional districts in the South and Southwest, which tend to lean Republican, at the expense of the more liberal and more Democratic Northeast and Midwest. The redistricting that increased the number of majority-minority districts in several states also created some competitive and Republican-leaning districts out of adjacent seats that were once controlled by the Democrats. Even though many of the minority-majority districts were overturned in the courts and most reelected Democratic incumbents in 1996, the Democrats were not able to reclaim many of the seats that were adjacent to these minority-majority districts.[49]

Retirements, deaths, and other career moves also affected the balance of power in the House. Before the 1996 election, twenty-one Democrats retired, eight sought higher office, and one—Barbara Rose Collins of Michigan—lost her primary. On the Republican side, thirteen retired, eight sought another office, Rep. Greg Laughlin of Texas lost his primary, and Rep. Bill Emerson of Missouri died. The large number of GOP victories in the 1994 state and local elections enabled the Republicans to recruit experienced candidates to run for many of these open seats, helping the party to capture twenty-nine of fifty-three.[50]

The Republicans' electoral success in 1996 also depended on how well they governed. Once they took control of Congress, the Republicans became vulnerable to charges that they were extremists, caused gridlock, favored special interests, and did not care about ordinary citizens—some of the same charges that played a role in bringing down the Democrats. Speaker Gingrich's attempts to make the Republican-led Congress the locus of national policy making caused the outcome of the 1996 elections to turn at least in part on the GOP's conservative political agenda. Although local factors such as the partisan composition of congressional districts, whether an incumbent was seeking reelection, the quality of House challengers and open-seat contestants, and the kinds of campaigns the candidates waged were crucial, national tides were important in some close contests and are believed to have contributed to the shrinkage of the GOP House majority.

Both parties and some interest groups spent record amounts on party and issue-oriented public relations campaigns to ensure that national issues played a significant role in the 1996 elections. The DNC, RNC, the four Hill committees, several large labor unions, and a number of business-oriented groups mounted television, radio, mail, and grassroots voter-mobilization campaigns to encourage voters to assess the performance of the Republican Congress and the Clinton White House when voting. Having been allowed by the Supreme Court to make independent expenditures in congressional campaigns, party committees spent unprecedented amounts directly advocating their candidates' election and their opponents' defeat. A number of party committees and several large PACs also took advantage of the Court's decision allowing them to wage issue advocacy campaigns. The AFL-CIO, for example, spent $35 million trying to help the Democrats retake control of Congress. The Coalition, a group of thirty-one business groups headed by the U.S. Chamber of Commerce, spent several millions to counter the unions' advocacy campaign.

Whether the 1994 elections were a harbinger of forty years of Republican hegemony over Congress, or a prelude to many years of revolving partisan control or some other pattern of competition, one thing is clear: 1994 ushered in the era of the post-Democratic Congress. The iron-clad hold that Democrats once had over the House of Representatives has been broken.

Off-Year Party Activity

How did the parties, PACs, and individuals who finance congressional elections respond to the new environment? The activities leading up to the 1996 elections make possible some informed observations. The early figures on national party fund-raising indicated that the Republicans capitalized on their majority status in Congress. During the first year after the GOP took control of the House, its congressional campaign committee raised almost $26 million in hard money, roughly three times as much as their Democratic rivals (see Table 5-6). The NRCC raised 180 percent more in 1995 than it had in 1993, a level of growth that dwarfs that of the DCCC, but both committees set fund-raising records. Most of the NRCC's money came in the form of individual contributions, but the committee also raised a record $2.3 million from PACs. The disparity in the realm of soft money is even more impressive: NRCC fund-raising rose by nearly 400 percent, while DCCC fund-raising fell by 16 percent.

The numbers for the other Washington party committees were not so impressive. Both DNC and RNC fund-raising went up, reflecting the fact that 1996 was a presidential election year. The progress that the DNC made in raising funds, particularly hard money, was due to Democratic control of the White House. Hard money fund-raising at both senatorial campaign committees was

Table 5-6 National Party Receipts for the First Half of the 1994 and 1996 Election Cycles

Party Group	Hard Money			Soft Money		
	1994 Election	1996 Election	Percentage Change	1994 Election	1996 Election	Percentage Change
Democratic						
DNC	$18,619,657	$33,544,073	+80	$17,034,180	$25,260,996	+49
DCCC	6,661,467	8,433,618	+27	2,706,490	2,281,635	−16
DSCC	10,420,123	10,086,688	−3	345,055	925,386	+168
Total	$35,701,247	$52,064,379	+46	$20,085,725	$28,468,017	+42
Republican						
RNC	$34,197,814	$46,150,824	+35	$10,581,731	$21,158,110	+100
NRCC	9,238,015	25,937,136	+180	1,369,219	6,650,915	+385
NRSC	29,098,083	23,550,626	−19	2,190,980	7,518,203	+229
Total	$72,533,912	$95,638,586	+32	$14,141,930	$35,327,228	+150

Sources: Federal Election Commission, "Democratic Party Narrows Fundraising Gap," press release, March 4, 1994; and FEC, "Fundraising Increases for National Party Committees," press release, March 13, 1996.

Note: The figures are for party receipts collected between January 1 and December 31 for each nonelection year.

down, even though the committees increased their soft money receipts. The off-year figures suggest that the National Republican Senatorial Committee had not taken full advantage of its majority status. This somewhat puzzling phenomenon can be attributed to two factors. First, the House and the presidency—not the Senate—were considered to be the major battlegrounds early in the 1996 elections. Republican donors, well aware that their party was predicted to retain control of the upper chamber, chose to contribute more early money to the NRCC and RNC, which were waging the nation's most important electoral battles. Second, the absolute number of competitive Senate races was much smaller than the number for the House. Even if their early fund-raising lagged behind that of their House counterparts, both senatorial campaign committees eventually raised more than enough money to spend the legal maximum on every Senate candidate involved in a hotly contested race.

The patterns for early NRCC and DCCC fund-raising prove the old adage: to the victors go the spoils—or more accurately, most of the spoils. Following in the tradition of former DCCC chairman Tony Coelho, D-Calif., NRCC Chairman Bill Paxon, R-N.Y., exploited his party's majority status to raise money for the committee he heads. Paxon used a steering committee of the managers of thirty leading PACs representing every major industry to solicit funds for the NRCC. As of June 1995, 225 corporations and PACs had spent $5,000 each to join the committees' "House Council," and another 150 spent between $15,000 and $20,000 to join its "Congressional Forum."[51] The NRCC's successful fund-raising, especially its big dollar fund-raising from individuals and PACs, was a product of the new order on Capitol Hill. Members of the business community, who previously contributed to the Democrats for pragmatic reasons, were able to pursue both pragmatic and ideological objectives by giving most of their money to Republicans.

Paxon also persuaded virtually every Republican House member to meet a quota for NRCC fund-raising as a way to bring in additional party money. Party leaders and the chairs of major committees were asked to contribute (or raise) $7,500 per year, subcommittee chairs were asked to contribute $6,500, and other Republican members to contribute $2,500.[52] The DCCC also raised large sums from its House members and other groups. However, the Democratic committee's fund-raising pace was unimpressive compared to the Republicans'.

The vast sums that the NRCC collected enabled it to hire additional staff, modernize its computers, refurbish its television and radio studios, and enhance other elements of its operation in preparation for the 1996 elections. Some of the money was used to establish a new team of Washington-based political advisers to focus solely on assisting incumbents with their reelection efforts. The team held special seminars to teach Republican House freshmen how to raise money, defend their roll call votes, and exploit the perquisites of office for reelection purposes.[53] The balance of the funds went into a special fund designated to help reelect Republican members, reflecting a recognition that incumbent retention was the committee's priority for 1996.

The Republicans also expanded the web of leadership PACs and fund-raising activities that extend out from the NRCC. Gingrich's new Monday Morning PAC raised more than $460,000 in the first twelve months of its existence. Rep. Dick Armey's Majority Leader's Fund and DeLay's Americans for a Republican Majority raised roughly $379,000 and $289,000, respectively, in the first half of the 1996 election cycle. DeLay confronted lobbyists with a list that described the four hundred largest PACs as friendly or unfriendly, depending on the proportion of their contributions that went to Republicans in the 1994 elections.[54] DeLay used this list to hammer home the message that he expected business interests to support his party's pro-business agenda by giving most of their contributions to Republican candidates. Gingrich, Armey, and other Republican leaders, as well as celebrity members, such as Rep. Sonny Bono, R-Calif., traversed the country to raise money for Republican freshmen and party switchers who joined the GOP after the 1994 elections. Gingrich was said to have persuaded more than 150 members from safe seats to raise $50,000 each for competitive nonincumbents and for colleagues who were in jeopardy. He is also estimated to have raised more than $9.3 million for Republican House candidates over the course of the 1996 election cycle.[55]

The DCCC also reoriented its programs. The committee stepped up its candidate-recruitment efforts, a difficult undertaking for a minority party headed by a controversial president. It enlarged its field staff to better assist Democratic open-seat contestants and challengers in their districts. But the need to make do with limited resources forced the DCCC to reduce the number of employees in its Washington headquarters.

Democratic leaders also stepped up their fund-raising efforts in anticipation of a chance to take back the House. Minority Leader Gephardt's Effective Government Committee raised more than $417,000 during the first half of the 1996 election cycle, and Democratic Caucus Chairman Fazio's Victory USA PAC raised nearly $78,000. Democratic incumbents also helped Democrats in marginal districts and nonincumbents to raise funds.

Early PAC Contributions

Most PACs that make early contributions do so to gain access to House members. A few make early contributions for ideological reasons, giving money to encourage politicians who share their policy goals to run and backing incumbents and nonincumbents in close primaries. PACs contributed slightly more than $43 million to House candidates during the first half of the 1996 election cycle, roughly $9 million more than they had contributed during the first half of the 1994 election cycle. All but a tiny fraction of these funds went to incumbents (see Table 5-7). A few nonconnected and labor PACs invested in challengers or open-seat candidates, but most of their early efforts benefited incumbents.

The Republican takeover of the House had a profound impact on the distribution of early PAC money. The pattern of contributions from corporate and

Table 5-7 Distribution of PAC Contributions to House Candidates During the First Half of the 1994 and 1996 Election Cycles

Contest Type	Nonconnected		Corporate		Trade Association		Labor	
	1994 Election	1996 Election	1994 Election	1996 Election	1994 Election	1996 Election	1994 Election	1996 Election
Democrats								
Incumbents	70%	39%	60%	27%	61%	31%	92%	77%
Challengers	—	2	—	—	1	—	1	5
Open seats	2	—	—	—	—	—	1	2
Republicans								
Incumbents	27	57	39	72	38	67	6	16
Challengers	1	1	—	—	—	1	—	—
Open seats	—	1	—	1	—	1	—	—
Total (in thousands)	$2,011	$3,151	$13,669	$17,729	$9,639	$12,280	$7,616	$8,047

Source: Compiled from Federal Election Commission data.

Note: The figures are for receipts raised between January 1 and December 31 for each nonelection year. They include only the receipts of candidates who reported raising some funds during these periods. The *N* for the 1994 figures is 737; the *N* for the 1996 figures is 762. Some columns do not add to 100 percent because of rounding.

trade association PACs in the first half of the 1996 election cycle was almost the opposite of the pattern during the first half of the 1994 elections. Following the 1992 elections just over 60 percent of the money distributed by business-oriented PACs went to Democrats; after the 1994 elections roughly two-thirds went to Republicans. These PACs' support for the GOP's pro-business agenda and their concern with gaining access to powerful members are principally responsible for the dramatic switch. Many business-oriented PACs made early contributions as a way of "introducing themselves" to new Republican committee and subcommittee chairs. Some business-oriented PACs also made early contributions to GOP House freshmen in an attempt to make amends for having backed their Democratic opponents in 1994. Raw numbers—the increase in the number of Republican incumbents and the corresponding decrease in Democrats—contributed to the change, but are of secondary importance.

Business-oriented PACs did not completely abandon the Democrats. Despite pressure from Republican House leaders, many of these groups continued to give incumbent Democrats money. The possibility that the Democrats could retake control of the House in the near future, a recognition that Democratic leaders still wield influence in the legislative process, and Democratic control of the White House motivated many of these groups to support Democratic members. Other business PACs contributed to Democrats who supported their policy goals. Democratic party leaders and ranking committee members continued to enjoy strong support from business PACs, but the early figures suggested that many Republican backbenchers and freshmen were also big winners in business PAC fund-raising.

The patterns for early contributions by nonconnected PACs indicated that a desire to maintain GOP control of the House mobilized many conservative ideological groups. Conservative groups contributed three times as much money in the first half of the 1996 election cycle as in the first half of the 1994 contest. Virtually all of the money distributed by ideological groups went to incumbents, but this pattern changed significantly once the primaries were over and the general election season began.

Even some labor PACs, which traditionally have been among the staunchest supporters of Democratic candidates, changed their early giving patterns in an attempt to secure access to newly empowered Republican House members. The Seafarers Union is an example. The PAC gave $51,100 or 10 percent of its House contributions to fourteen Republicans in the entire 1994 election cycle, but gave $73,000 or 29 percent of its funds to twenty-nine GOP members in the first half of the 1996 cycle.

Early Individual Contributions

The patterns for early individual contributions were also influenced by the Republicans' becoming the majority party in the House. Democratic incumbents' share of all early individual contributions fell by 14 percent, reflecting both their

Table 5-8 Distribution of Individual Contributions to House Candidates During the First Half of the 1994 and 1996 Election Cycles

Contest Type	All		Under $200		$200–499		$500–749		$750–1,000	
	1994 Election	1996 Election	1994 Election	1996 Election	1994 Election	1996 Election	1994 Election	1996 Election	1994 Election	1996 Election
Democrats										
Incumbents	41%	27%	34%	24%	42%	27%	46%	27%	45%	28%
Challengers	4	8	5	10	4	8	4	6	4	7
Open seats	5	3	4	2	4	3	4	3	7	3
Republicans										
Incumbents	39	50	45	47	41	51	38	55	32	50
Challengers	7	9	8	14	5	6	5	6	6	8
Open seats	4	4	4	3	4	4	4	4	6	4
Total (in thousands)	$14,855	$20,520	$6,143	$8,468	$8,354	$11,804	$13,740	$22,777	$43,000	$663,219

Source: Compiled from Federal Election Commission data.

Note: The figures are for receipts raised between January 1 and December 31 for each nonelection year. They include only the receipts of candidates who reported raising some funds during these periods. The *N* for the 1994 figures is 737; the *N* for the 1996 figures is 762. Some columns do not add to 100 percent because of rounding.

Table 5-9 Average Receipts Collected by House Candidates During the First Half of the 1994 and 1996 Election Cycles (in thousands)

Candidate Type	1994 Election	1996 Election	Percentage Change
Democrats			
Incumbents	$186,979	$203,319	+9
(*N*)	(228)	(172)	
Challengers	36,173	63,680	+76
(*N*)	(68)	(105)	
Open Seats	54,977	80,924	+47
(*N*)	(55)	(43)	
Republicans			
Incumbents	178,192	269,654	+51
(*N*)	(158)	(221)	
Challengers	43,328	55,370	+27
(*N*)	(162)	(156)	
Open Seats	42,372	52,249	+23
(*N*)	(66)	(65)	

Source: Compiled from Federal Election Commission data.

Note: The figures are for receipts raised between January 1 and December 31 for each nonelection year. They include only the receipts of candidates who reported raising some funds during these periods.

smaller numbers and diminished status in the House (see Table 5-8). In contrast, Republican incumbents' individual fund-raising grew by 11 percent. The changes were far from uniform. Contributions of under $200 were the least affected by the turnover in partisan control. The relationship is not perfect, but it shows that those who made larger contributions were more strongly affected than were those who gave smaller amounts. The big givers' pragmatic approach to politics and support for the GOP's pro-business agenda were apparent in their early giving patterns.

Early Candidate Receipts

How did the change in party control of the House and the early responses of campaign contributors influence the receipts of House candidates? The answer to this question provides insight into the kind of election political elites anticipated in 1996. The increase in candidate receipts indicated that many contributors rightly predicted that the 1996 elections would be competitive and that control of the House was at stake (see Table 5-9). In the first half of the 1996 election cycle, Republican incumbents raised an average of $91,500 more than they raised in the first half of the 1994 cycle—an increase of more than 51 percent. Republican freshmen, many of whom anticipated stiff challenges to their bids for reelection, brought in a significant portion of those funds. Rep. Jon Christensen, R-Neb., led the GOP first-term lawmakers, raising more than $686,000, including nearly $266,000 from PACs, during his first year in office. A dozen Republican freshmen raised more $400,000 during their first year, and fifteen GOP freshmen received more than half their funds from PACs. Although they may have campaigned for "change" and made pledges to "clean up" politics, these first-termers appeared to have embraced politics as usual when it came to campaign finance.

The patterns for Democrats were quite different. The typical Democratic incumbent's receipts increased by a mere $16,300 or 9 percent. The average Democratic challengers' and open-seat candidates' receipts, however, increased by 76 percent and 47 percent, respectively, more than their Republican counterparts. The figures for both parties' nonincumbents and House members showed the broad outlines of what promised to be a tight battle for control over the House. Democratic House candidates and their supporters prepared an offensive strategy, funneling resources to open-seat contestants and candidates challenging House Republicans, especially GOP freshmen. The Republicans and their backers, on the other hand, took a complementary defensive posture, investing most of their funds in incumbent races and giving extra support to GOP first-termers.

Conclusion

The 1994 elections were events of seismic proportions in American politics. They brought to an end forty years of Democratic control of the House and introduced a new and more competitive era in the politics of congressional elections. Evidence from the first half of the 1996 election cycle suggests that the flow of campaign money is among those aspects of congressional elections most heavily affected by the GOP takeover.

This analysis of contributor motives and giving patterns suggests that party committees, congressional incumbents, and leadership PACs, which tend to be motivated primarily by electoral considerations, will continue to serve as vehicles for the redistribution of wealth. These individuals and groups will target most of their resources to candidates in close races. Some House members will continue to use their contributions to lay the groundwork for winning their legislative colleagues' support for future leadership bids or legislative votes. PACs and individuals who are motivated by access will probably continue to distribute the vast majority of their funds to powerful incumbents, including members of the majority party and minority party members in positions of influence. Should the current balance of power extend beyond 1998, most contributions that are motivated by access will probably favor Republicans, but powerful Democrats will not be totally abandoned. Ideological contributors will more than likely distribute their funds in ways that are consistent with their past giving: liberals will support Democrats, and conservatives will support Republicans.

The flow of early money foreshadowed the fund-raising records that GOP incumbents and party committees set during the 1996 elections. Democrats also set some fund-raising records in anticipation of the hotly contested battle for control of the House, but they fell far short of the fund-raising levels reached by the Republicans.

The motives of most contributors and the early campaign receipts reported by the candidates indicated that one critical aspect of the campaign finance system remained unchanged: most campaign contributions flowed to House incumbents and away from House challengers. This suggests that most incumbents will continue to raise huge war chests, while their opponents remain starved for campaign funds. As it did for most of the elections held between 1980 and 1996, a skewed distribution of campaign resources will more than likely continue to provide House incumbents with tremendous advantages in future elections.

Notes

I would like to thank Robert Biersack and Michael Dickerson for their assistance with the Federal Election Commission data and for their helpful comments. Joseph Cantor, Jim Gimpel, and Ric Uslaner also provided helpful comments and suggestions.

1. See Frank J. Sorauf, "Political Parties and Political Action Committees: Two Life Cycles," *Arizona Law Review* 22 (1980): 445–464; Paul S. Herrnson, *Party Campaigning in the 1980s* (Cambridge: Harvard University Press, 1988), chaps. 2 and 3.
2. See, for example, Paul S. Herrnson, *Congressional Elections: Campaigning at Home and in Washington* (Washington, D.C.: CQ Press, 1995), chap. 3.
3. Gary C. Jacobson, *The Politics of Congressional Elections* (New York: HarperCollins, 1992), 116-145.
4. Peter Clarke and Susan Evans, *Covering Campaigns: Journalism in Congressional Elections* (Stanford, Calif.: Stanford University Press, 1983), 60–62; Edie N. Goldenberg and Michael W. Traugott, *Campaigning for Congress* (Washington, D.C.: CQ Press, 1984), 127; Anita Dunn, "The Best Campaign Wins: Coverage of Down Ballot Races by Local Press" (paper presented at the Conference on Campaign Management, The American University, Washington, D.C., Dec. 10–11, 1992); Herrnson, *Congressional Elections,* 193.
5. Gary C. Jacobson, *Money in Congressional Elections* (New Haven: Yale University Press, 1980); Jacobson, "The Effects of Campaign Spending in House Elections: New Evidence for Old Arguments," *American Journal of Political Science* 34 (1990): 334–362; Donald P. Green and Jonathan S. Krasno, "Salvation for the Spendthrift Incumbent," *American Journal of Political Science* 32 (1988): 844–907; Green and Krasno, "Rebuttal to Jacobson's 'New Evidence for Old Arguments,'" *American Journal of Political Science* 34 (1990): 363–372.
6. Party committees, however, usually give contributions only to general election candidates.
7. Coordinated expenditure limits for states with only one House member were set at $58,600 in 1994.
8. For a detailed analysis of how these PACs operate, see Robert E. Mutch, "AT&T PAC: A Pragmatic Giant," in Robert Biersack, Paul S. Herrnson, and Clyde Wilcox, eds., *Risky Business? PAC Decision Making and Strategy in Congressional Elections*

(Armonk, N.Y.: M. E. Sharpe, 1994); Anne H. Bedlington, "The National Association of Realtors PAC: Rules or Rationality?" in *Risky Business?* and Clyde Wilcox, "Coping with Increased Business Influence: The AFL-CIO's Committee on Education," in *Risky Business?*

9. On this PAC, see Paul S. Herrnson, "The National Committee for an Effective Congress: Liberalism, Partisanship, and Electoral Innovation," in *Risky Business?*
10. *Colorado Republican Federal Committee v. Federal Election Commission,* No. 95–489 (1996).
11. The term "soft" money was coined by Elizabeth Drew, *Politics and Money: The New Road to Corruption* (New York: Macmillan, 1983), 15. See also Frank J. Sorauf, *Inside Campaign Finance: Myths and Realities* (New Haven: Yale University Press, 1992), 147–151; and Herbert E. Alexander and Anthony Corrado, *Financing the 1992 Election* (Armonk, N.Y.: M. E. Sharpe, 1995), chap. 6.
12. The most notable of these cases is *Federal Election Commission v. Massachusetts Citizens for Life, Inc.,* 479 U.S. 238 (1986).
13. As will be noted later, the Republicans picked up five House seats and two Senate seats as a result of Democratic incumbents who switched parties after the election. The GOP also increased its margin when Tom Campbell won a special election to replace Rep. Norman Mineta, D-Calif., who resigned from Congress during the middle of his term.
14. Gary Langer, "Vote '94: Republicans Seize the Reins of Discontent," ABC News Analysis, November 11, 1994, cited in Gary C. Jacobson, "The 1994 House Elections in Perspective" (paper presented at the annual meeting of the Midwest Political Science Association, Chicago, April 6–8, 1995).
15. David B. Magleby, Kelly D. Patterson, and Stephen H. Wirls, "Fear and Loathing of the Modern Congress: The Public Manifestation of Constitutional Design" (paper presented at the annual meeting of the Midwest Political Science Association, Chicago, April 14–16, 1994). See also Jacobson, "The 1994 House Elections in Perspective."
16. See Alan Ehrenhalt, *The United States of Ambition: Politicians, Power, and the Pursuit of Office* (New York: Random House, 1991), 225–226.
17. David T. Canon, *Actors, Athletes, and Astronauts: Political Amateurs in the United States Congress* (Chicago: University of Chicago Press, 1990); Green and Krasno, "Salvation for the Spendthrift Incumbent"; Herrnson, *Congressional Elections,* 34–35; and Herrnson, "Congress's Other Farm Team: Congressional Staff, *Polity* 27 (1994): 135–156.
18. Federal Election Commission, "1994 Congressional Fundraising Climbs to New High," press release, April 28, 1995.
19. For the impact of the political environment on the decisions of campaign contributors, see Gary C. Jacobson and Samuel Kernell, *Strategy and Choice in Congressional Elections* (New Haven: Yale University Press, 1983), esp. chap. 4.
20. Although fewer than one-third of the general public had heard of the Contract with America by election day, many Republican House candidates relied on the contract and the issue materials that accompanied it when waging their campaigns. See James G. Gimpel, *Fulfilling the Contract: The First 100 Days* (New York: Allyn and Bacon, 1996); and Paul S. Herrnson, "Directing 535 Leading Men and Leading Ladies: Party Leadership in the Modern Congress," in Herbert F. Weisberg and Samuel C. Patterson, eds., *Great Theatre: The American Congress in the 1990s* (New York: Cambridge University Press, forthcoming).
21. The term "Hill committees" probably originates from the fact that the congressional and senatorial campaign committees were originally located in congressional office space on Capitol Hill. On these committees see Herrnson, *Party Campaigning in the 1980s,* esp. chaps. 3 and 4.

22. Herrnson, *Congressional Elections,* 87–96; Herrnson, *Party Campaigning in the 1980s,* 66–91; Larry J. Sabato, *PAC Power: Inside the World of Political Action Committees* (New York: Norton, 1984), 144–149.
23. Cornelius P. Cotter, James L. Gibson, John F. Bibby, and Robert J. Huckshorn, *Party Organizations in American Politics* (Pittsburgh: University of Pittsburgh Press, 1989), 20–25, 45–54; Cornelius P. Cotter and John F. Bibby, "Party Organization at the State Level," in *The Parties Must Respond: Changes in the American Party System,* ed. L. Sandy Maisel (Boulder: Westview, 1990), 21–40; Robert Huckfeldt and John Sprague, "Political Parties and Electoral Mobilization: Political Structure, Social Structure, and the Party Canvass," *American Political Science Review* 86 (1992): 70–86; Herrnson, *Congressional Elections,* 96–98.
24. Federal Election Commission, "FEC Reports on Political Party Activity for 1993–94," press release, April 13, 1995.
25. The NRCC was more than $7.9 million in debt as of December 30, 1992, and nearly $2.6 million in debt as of March 31, 1994, while its Democratic counterpart reported debts of under $2.1 million and $65,000 on the same dates. Federal Election Commission, "Democrats Narrow Financial Gap in 1991–1992," press release, March 11, 1993; and "FEC Reports on National Party Finances," press release, June 15, 1994.
26. On the distribution of party funds in 1982, see Gary C. Jacobson, "Party Organizations and Campaign Resources in 1982," *Political Science Quarterly* 100 (1985–1986): 604–635; on the distribution of party funds in 1984, see Paul S. Herrnson, "National Party Decision Making, Strategies, and Resource Distribution in Congressional Elections," *Western Political Quarterly* 42 (1989): 301–323; on the distribution of party funds in 1992, see Herrnson, *Congressional Elections,* 85–87.
27. Gary C. Jacobson, "The Misallocation of Resources in House Campaigns," in *Congress Reconsidered,* 5th ed., ed. Lawrence C. Dodd and Bruce I. Oppenheimer (Washington, D.C.: CQ Press, 1993), 116-118.
28. These funds do not include money that was contributed by congressional incumbents who had no major party opposition in the general election, money contributed by those who retired in 1994, contributions from the campaign coffers of incumbents who had retired earlier, or money contributed by Senate candidates. They also exclude contributions that candidates gave from their personal funds.
29. On candidate-to-candidate contributions, see Clyde Wilcox, "Share the Wealth: Contributions by Congressional Incumbents to the Campaigns of Other Candidates," *American Politics Quarterly* 17 (1989): 386–408.
30. These funds do not include money that was contributed by House incumbents who had no major party opposition in the general election, money contributed by those who retired in 1994, money that came from the campaign coffers of incumbents who had retired earlier, money contributed by Senate candidates, or money that was given to candidates who were defeated in congressional primaries (which totalled roughly $500,000). They also exclude contributions that candidates gave from their personal funds.
31. On member PACs, see Ross K. Baker, *The New Fat Cats: Members of Congress as Political Benefactors* (New York: Priority Press, 1989).
32. See note 30.
33. Herrnson, *Congressional Elections,* 92–96; and Herrnson, *Party Campaigning in the 1980s,* 71–77.
34. Interview with Deb Flavin, Finance Division, National Republican Congressional Committee, Oct. 30, 1995.
35. On PAC strategies see, for example, Theodore J. Eismeier and Philip H. Pollock III, *Business, Money, and the Rise of Corporate PACs in American Elections* (New York: Quorum Books, 1988), 27–30; J. David Gopoian, "What Makes PACs Tick? An Analy-

sis of the Allocation Patterns of Economic Interest Groups," *American Journal of Political Science* 28 (May 1984): 259–281; Sorauf, *Inside Campaign Finance,* 64–65, 74–75; and Biersack, Herrnson, and Wilcox, eds., *Risky Business?*

36. Corporate PACs accounted for a minuscule portion of the independent expenditures made during the 1994 House elections.
37. See, for example, Laura Langbein, "Money and Access: Some Empirical Evidence," *Journal of Politics* 48 (1986): 1052–62; Richard Hall and Frank Wayman, "Buying Time: Moneyed Interests and the Mobilization of Bias in Congressional Committees," *American Political Science Review* 84 (1990): 797–820; and Dan Clawson, Alan Neustadtl, and Denise Scott, *Money Talks: Corporate PACs and Political Influence* (New York: Basic Books, 1992), 169–173.
38. On AT&T PAC, see Robert E. Mutch, "AT&T PAC: A Pragmatic Giant.
39. Sorauf, *Inside Campaign Finance,* 61–71; Brooks Jackson, *Honest Graft: Big Money and the American Political Process* (New York: Knopf, 1988), 69–70, 77–81, 90–93.
40. Bedlington, "The National Association of Realtors PAC," in *Risky Business?* and Denise L. Baer and Martha Bailey, "The Nationalization of Education Politics: The National Education Association PAC and the 1992 Elections," in *Risky Business?*
41. Gary C. Jacobson, *Money and Congressional Elections* (New Haven: Yale University Press, 1989), 66–72; James Guth and John C. Green, "Faith and Politics: Religion and Ideology Among Political Contributors," *American Politics Quarterly* 14 (1986): 186–200; James Guth and John C. Green, "God and the GOP: Varieties of Religiosity Among Political Contributors," in Ted Jelen, ed., *Religion and American Political Behavior* (New York: Praeger, 1991); Clifford W. Brown Jr., Lynda W. Powell, and Clyde Wilcox, *Serious Money: Fundraising and Contributing in Presidential Nomination Campaigns* (Cambridge: Cambridge University Press, 1995), chap. 5.
42. Brown, Powell, and Wilcox, *Serious Money,* 98.
43. Robert Biersack, Paul S. Herrnson, Wesley Joe, and Clyde Wilcox, "The Allocation Strategies of Congressional High Rollers: A Preliminary Analysis" (paper presented at the annual meeting of the Midwest Political Science Association, Chicago, April 14–16, 1994).
44. Herrnson, *Congressional Elections,* 65–68, 133–140.
45. Ibid., 65–68.
46. Robert Biersack, Paul S. Herrnson, and Clyde Wilcox, "Seeds for Success: Early Money in Congressional Elections," *Legislative Studies Quarterly* 18 (1993): 535–553.
47. Herrnson, *Congressional Elections,* 142–145.
48. See, for example, David B. Magleby and Candice J. Nelson, *The Money Chase: Congressional Campaign Finance Reform* (Washington, D.C.: Brookings, 1990), 81–84.
49. With the exception of Rep. Cleo Fields, D-La., who decided not to run for reelection when his district was obliterated by a federal three-judge panel, all of the Democrats who had represented minority-majority districts were reelected.
50. More than half of the GOP candidates elected to fill open seats in 1996 had previously held elective office or had some other significant political experience.
51. David Maraniss and Michael Weisskopf, "Speaker and His Directors Make the Cash Flow Right," *Washington Post,* Nov. 27, 1995.
52. Interview with Ruth Burns, Incumbent Services Division, NRCC, Nov. 5, 1995.
53. Ibid.
54. Maraniss and Weisskopf, "Speaker and His Directors Make the Cash Flow Right."
55. Juliet Eilperin and Ed Henry, "Leaders Barnstorm; Gingrich Won't Take Top Job in Minority," *Roll Call,* Oct. 28, 1996.

6. Voters, Candidates, and Issues in Congressional Elections

Robert S. Erikson and Gerald C. Wright

The Founders designed the House of Representatives to be the popular branch of government. Elections for the House were expected to reflect the ebb and flow of public preferences. And even though the Senate has also become responsive to public opinion, analysts and journalists continue to watch House elections for what they say about what the public wants and the future directions of U.S. public policy. In taking the biennial national pulse in House elections, interest generally centers on the partisan split of seats and the mood of the electorate that underlies that resulting party balance in the House.

For most of the last fifty years, this balance has consistently favored the Democratic Party. The only question was how large or small the Democrats' advantage in seats would be. The 1994 election provided a thunderous exception to the years of Democratic dominance of the House. The Republican Party won a clear majority, and it did so by nationalizing the election. As such, the 1994 election nicely demonstrates the changing mixture of national and local forces that have always been at work in contests for the House and Senate alike, and the 1996 election generally reaffirms that decision with continuing Republican control of both houses. In this essay, we first examine the national forces in House elections and their influence on partisan divisions of the national vote and House seats. Next, we look at the role of candidates in individual House contests. Finally, we compare elections for the House with elections for the Senate.

The National Verdict in House Elections

The public's verdict in House elections is cast in terms of votes, but it has its effect in terms of the seats won by each party. The partisan division of seats receives the most attention because it reflects the parties' actual balance of congressional power. Naturally, the seat division is largely a function of how many votes the two parties receive nationwide. It would seem "fair" that if a party won 1 percent more of the national vote than in the last election that it would get an additional 1 percent of the seats. However, such a one-to-one relationship is the exception rather then the rule. How vote changes nationwide actually translate into seat changes depends on a number of factors. These include where the votes are won and lost as well as the levels of competitiveness of the seats. For example, if one party gains most of its votes where the other party is already winning by large margins, these votes may not turn over any seats. If the same votes are gained where the other party barely squeaked by in the last election, they can gain many more seats for the same number of votes.

Figure 6-1 House Seats and Votes, 1952–1994

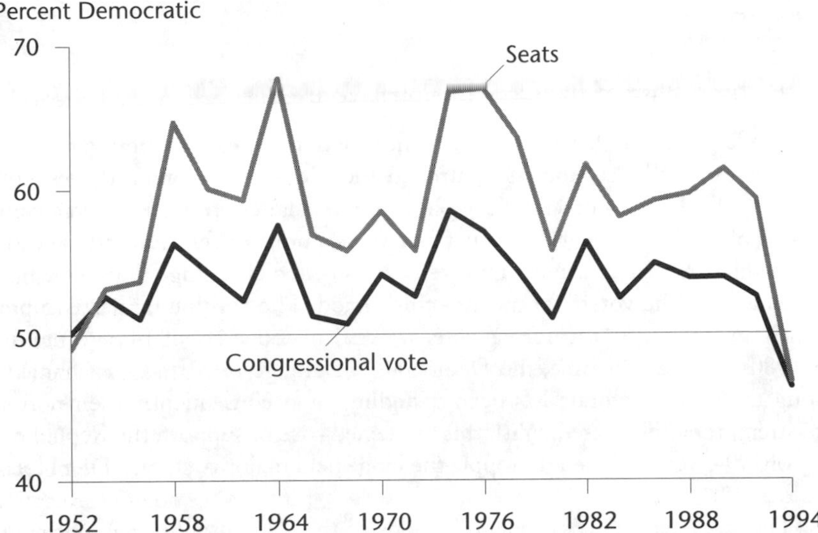

Source: Compiled by the authors.

There is a formula called the swing ratio that translates votes to seats. For much of the post–World War II period, the swing ratio was about 2.0, meaning that for every percentage point a party gained in votes, an additional 2 percent of the seats switched to its column.[1]

Figure 6-1 shows the pattern of the two-party vote and the two-party division since 1952. Between 1952 and 1992 the seat division varied from about an even split between the Republicans and Democrats to a Democratic edge of more than two-thirds of the seats. These seat changes were in reaction to much smaller vote changes, varying from about 50 percent Democratic to about 58 percent Democratic.

In general, we see a dampening of the swing ratio through the 1960s; a given vote gain led to a smaller reward in seats, dipping in some years to 1.0.[2] What caused the swing ratio to drop was the greater insulation from electoral tides that incumbents achieved during this period. Incumbents separated themselves from their national parties. This separation was due in part to their own behavior, but was assisted by the breakdown of strong partisan ties among the electorate, which freed voters to base their choices on the individual candidates rather than feelings of party loyalty or judgments about presidential performance.

Notice the last time point in Figure 6-1, representing the Republican takeover of the House in 1994. There we see a change from 1992 of 6.4 percent of the vote leading to a decisive change of 12.6 percent of the seats. The resulting swing ratio of almost 2.0 reflects the nationalization of the election and was crucial for the Republican success at taking control of the House for the first time in forty years.

The Partisan Base of the Congressional Vote

While the Republican Party has generally dominated contemporary presidential politics, the Democrats controlled the House of Representatives from 1953 to 1995. That Democratic edge in congressional elections reflected a combination of their advantage in the partisan dispositions of the electorate and the growing power of incumbency. The Democrats held a clear edge in party identification among the voters for most of this period. The continuing partisan predisposition, known as "the normal vote," was calculated at about 54 percent until the 1980s.[3] Since that time, the Democrats' advantage in partisan attachments among the mass electorate has been dwindling, and consequently their normal vote strength has decreased. With this weakened base of support, the Republican tides of 1994 were sufficient to topple the long-held majority status of the House Democrats.

The long-term partisan identifications of the electorate form a continuing base for the congressional vote. Election outcomes that depart from this base stem from defections and turnout failures by partisans and temporary vote movement by independents. These temporary deviations from base partisan strength are attributable to short-term partisan forces of the campaign. These can be of two sorts: national short-term forces that have an impact across the nation in a given election and local short-term forces that reflect the idiosyncratic personalities, issues, and campaigns in individual contests. When national forces are weak, which they have been most of the time in recent decades, election outcomes are propelled by differences in local contests. In the rare times when national forces are large—and 1994 was such a year—we see a clearer national verdict in congressional elections. But even in 1994 local factors played a large role.

Presidential Election Years

In presidential years the short-term forces of the presidential election and forces of the House election run in the same partisan direction, and the party that wins more than its normal vote for president wins more than its normal vote in the congressional contests. Whether this happens because the House vote and the presidential vote are influenced by the same national issues or because people decide their congressional vote on the basis of their partisan choice for president is not clear. Whatever the cause, this phenomenon is known as the coattail effect. Some House candidates seem to be carried into office by riding the coattails of their party's popular presidential candidate. Democratic coattails were at their strongest in 1964, when President Lyndon B. Johnson's landslide victory created an overwhelming 295–140 Democratic majority in the House of Representatives. Republican coattails were particularly strong in 1980, when Ronald Reagan won the presidency. At other times the presidential coattails are virtually nonexistent: when Bill Clinton was elected in 1992, the Democrats actually lost seats in the House of Representatives.

The size of the coattail effect is decidedly irregular. One statistical estimate for post–World War II elections puts it at +0.31 congressional votes nationally for every percentage point of the vote gained by the party at the presidential level.[4] Put another way, every added percentage point of the vote gained by a presidential candidate also adds almost one-third of a percentage point to the totals of the presidential candidate's congressional running mates. Before World War II presidential coattails appeared to be stronger than they are today; the national presidential vote and the national congressional vote marched more in lockstep. One consequence of the weakening of the coattail effect is the increase in divided control of government, with one party controlling the presidency and the other party controlling at least one house of Congress.

Midterm Years

One regular pattern of House elections is that the party that wins the presidency suffers a net loss of votes and seats in the following midterm election. Of the twenty-three midterms of the twentieth century, in only one (1934) did the president's party gain seats, and in only one (1926) did the president's party increase its share of the House vote. What accounts for this regularity?

Among political scientists, the conventional explanation for midterm loss has been the withdrawal of presidential coattails. The argument goes as follows: in presidential years the congressional vote for the president's party is inflated by presidential coattails. At the next midterm the congressional vote reverts toward the "normal" vote outcome. The result is a decline for the president's party.[5]

Although this argument is appealing, it is wrong. The size of the midterm loss does not depend on the size of the presidential year victory, as the coattail argument would predict. The midterm loss is not a return to a normal vote. Rather, the congressional vote for the president's party drops 4 percent to 5 percent in the midterm, and this seems to occur regardless of how the economy is doing or how the public feels about the president. It is as if the midterm electorate chooses to punish the president's party, no matter what the circumstances. In fact, both congressional parties average their best performance in midterm elections when the other party has power. In other words, over the last fifty years, the midterm loss has outweighed the gains made from presidential coattails.[6] These results lead to the strange conclusion that part of the Democratic Party's dominance of the House can be attributed to its failure at the presidential level and vice versa. More midterms have occurred with Republicans in the White House with predictable results for the Republican congressional party.[7]

Why would the electorate regularly vote against the presidential party in midterm elections? According to one controversial theory, the electorate "punishes" the presidential party as an ideological hedge. Moderate voters, seeing themselves ideologically between the Democratic and Republican positions, have some incentive to balance the president's ideology with a congressional vote for the "out" party.[8] The process encourages divided government, with one party controlling the presidency and the other controlling Congress.

Electoral Change as a Search for Policy Direction

Every two years the national vote for Congress produces a change in its party composition. When the voters send a different person to Washington, do they have a specific policy purpose? What do congressional election results indicate about the electorate's policy preferences?

The popular view, often propounded by pundits at election time, is that partisan tides reflect the electorate's changing ideological mood—as if Democratic congressional gains signify growing liberal sentiment and Republican gains signify growing conservative sentiment. For example, the major Democratic gains associated with Johnson's landslide victory in 1964 were interpreted at the time as a mandate for a new liberal agenda. A conservative mood switch is identified with Reagan's surprise win in 1980. More recently, the Republican takeover of Congress in 1994 was proclaimed by the victors and media to indicate a sharp rejection of the liberalism of President Clinton and the Democratic majority. In each case, Congress responded with legislation that matched the purported public cries for change.

But it can be dangerous to read turns in the electorate's ideological preference from election returns. Public opinion research shows there is usually little more than a trace of ideological movement over the short span between elections.[9] Even so, this trace can be important: recent statistical analyses suggest that small shifts in the electorate's ideological mood actually do correlate with election returns.[10]

Still, even if election results respond to small changes in the public mood, other variables are more important as determinants of election results. In presidential elections, evaluations of the candidates as potential national leaders loom large in the electorate's choice. These presidential evaluations involve the candidates' ideologies to some extent, with most voters preferring moderates to liberal or conservative ideologues. The evaluations also involve nonpolicy considerations such as character and competence. The national economy represents one aspect of competence; voters hold the presidential party accountable for economic prosperity.

At the national level, electoral changes in the congressional partisan balance are largely a byproduct of presidential politics. In presidential years, short-term forces from the presidential contest reverberate down to the congressional level as a coattail effect. At the midterm, two years later, the partisan tide predictably moves away from the presidential party, and the strength of the tide is a function of the electorate's evaluation of presidential performance and changes in the

Figure 6-2 Democratic and Republican Candidate Spending Preferences for Different Programs, 1994

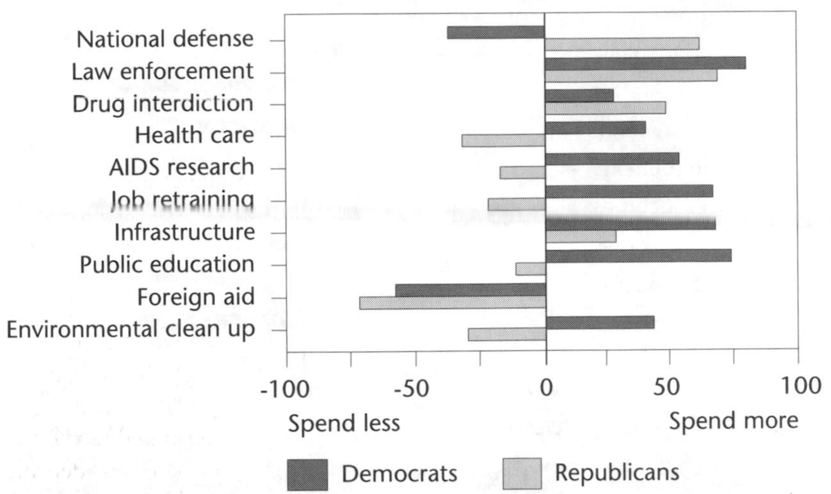

Source: Compiled by the authors. Data are from the Project Vote Smart congressional survey.

Note: Each bar represents the percentage of candidates wanting to spend more minus the percentage wanting to spend less.

economy. Although policy and ideological considerations play a role in the process, rarely is it the case that electoral change is a straightforward translation of changed public attitudes into new membership in Congress.

The Policy Consequences of Electoral Change

Election outcomes matter because the candidates who run under the two party banners generally stand for very different policy agendas. We begin by showing how the parties differ on some representative issues, drawing on a survey of candidates in the 1994 election done by Project Vote Smart.[11] Among other questions, House candidates were asked whether they wanted changes in spending on a number of programs. In Figure 6-2 we plot the percentage wanting an increase minus the percentage wanting a decrease by party for ten programs. A bar to the left of the vertical line indicates more party members wanted to cut spending than wanted to increase it; a bar to the right of the vertical line represents greater preferences for spending increases.

We see at the top of Figure 6-2 that many more Democratic candidates wanted to cut defense spending than wanted to increase it, while a majority of the Republican candidates wanted to increase defense spending. In contrast, the

Figure 6-3 Democratic and Republican House Candidate Spending Preferences on Tax Changes, 1994

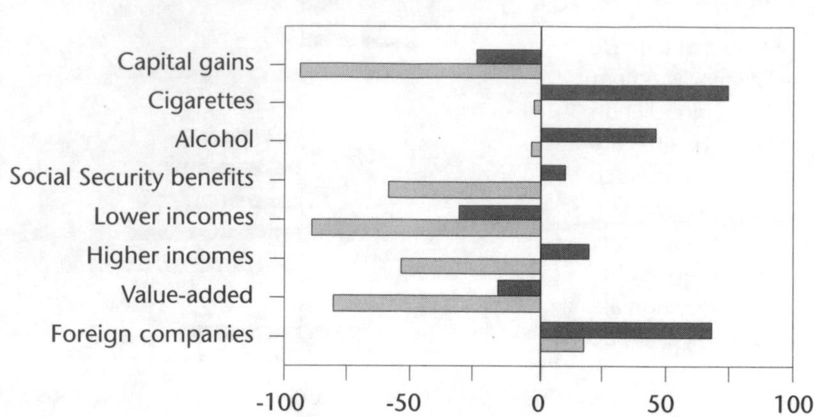

Source: Compiled by the authors. Data are from the Project Vote Smart congressional survey.

Note: Each bar represents the percentage of candidates wanting to raise each tax minus the percentage wanting to cut the tax.

candidates of both parties called for increases in spending for law enforcement and decreases in foreign aid. The two parties' candidates would take the nation in very different directions in several areas of domestic policy. The Democrats strongly favored expansion of the federal role in health care, AIDS research, funding for education, and environmental protection. The Republican candidates favored decreasing federal spending in these areas.

Party differences also extended to how federal funds should be raised. Figure 6-3 shows party differences in preferences for handling different types of taxes. The parties are on the same side in favoring cuts in the capital gains tax—but with Republicans almost unanimously so—and both favor cutting income taxes for the middle class (families with incomes of less than $140,000 per year)—again with Republicans more eager for tax cuts. The parties diverge in their willingness to tax the wealthier citizens: on both taxing the Social Security benefits of those with incomes higher than $40,000 and increasing income taxes on families with incomes higher than $140,000, the Republicans want tax decreases, and majorities of Democratic candidates want increases. The Democrats were also much more willing to increase taxes on cigarettes and alcohol.

The accumulated Democratic and Republican differences over specific issues can be seen in their overall ideological tendencies. To examine these dif-

Figure 6-4 Distributions of Candidate Ideology by Party, 1994

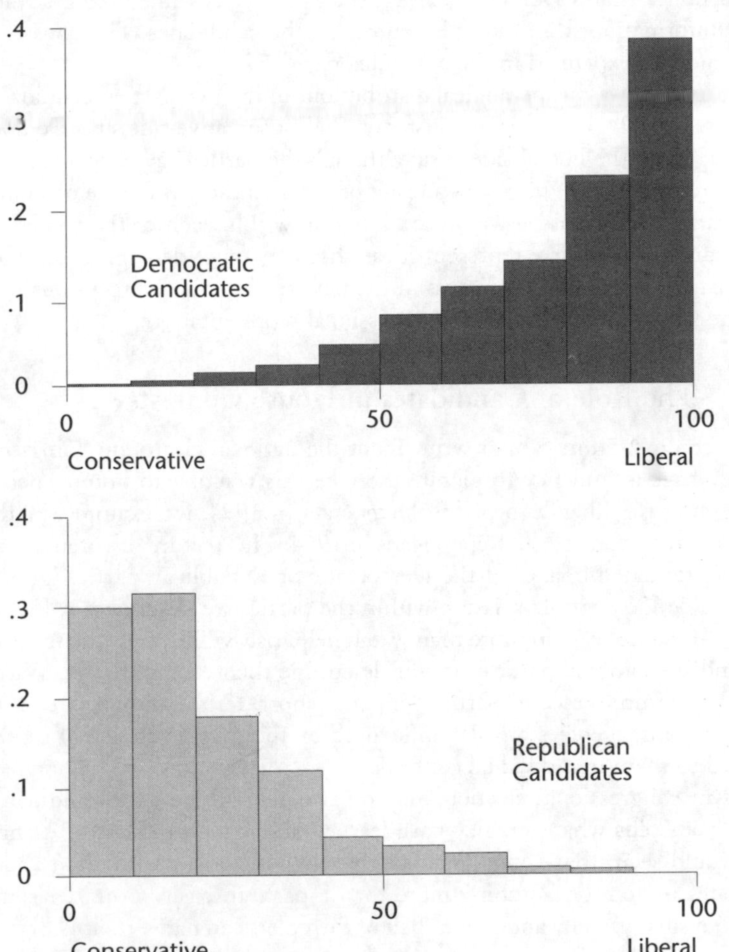

Source: Compiled by the authors. The scores are our candidate ideology index derived from the ADA and ACU roll call ratings for 1993 and 1994, Congressional Quarterly, and Project Vote Smart congressional surveys.

ferences we developed an index of candidate ideology, which measures the general policy liberalism - conservatism of House candidates. It is based on a combination of roll calls from two well-known ideological groups and two 1994 campaign surveys. We used the Americans for Democratic Action and the American Conservative Union ratings for roll calls, and we drew on surveys of the 1994 House candidates carried out by Congressional Quarterly and by Project Vote Smart. The overall candidate ideology index ranges from 0 to 100, with higher scores indicating greater liberalism. It allows us to compare incumbents and challengers, Republicans and Democrats all on the same scale, while taking advantage of the information from multiple sources on the candidates. The construction of the index is explained in the appendix, page 157.

Figure 6-4 shows the ideological distributions of the two parties' candidates for the House in 1994. Republicans cluster on the conservative side, and Democrats are grouped on the liberal side. And although the parties have become more polarized in recent years—largely as a result of the dwindling presence of southern conservative Democrats—we do see variation within each of the parties so that some candidates clearly represent ideas that are some ideological distance from their party's norm. As we discuss in the next section, these exceptions play a significant role in the dynamics of congressional representation.

The Role of Candidates in House Contests

When commentators talk or write about the national electorate doing this or that, they have a tendency to picture the voters as reacting to homogeneous parties, rejecting the liberalism of the Democrats in 1994, for example, or the Goldwater conservatism of the Republicans in 1964. This picture of voters reacting to undifferentiated images of the Democratic or Republican parties ignores the considerable ideological variation within the parties we described in Figure 6-4. Local candidates can do more than watch helplessly while constituency partisanship and the national partisan trends determine their electoral fates. Without denying the importance of partisanship and short-term national forces, we maintain that constituencies are also influenced by the specific choice of candidates offered to them in individual contests.

Voters in congressional elections rely on two sets of cues: the candidates' party affiliations plus whatever they have learned about the candidates. At first glance, it would seem that voters generally have insufficient information about the candidates to vote on anything more than a partisan basis. Consider some evidence from surveys: only about one-half of the voters can name their U.S. representative, and slightly fewer claim to have "read or heard" something about him or her. The content of this information is generally vague ("He is a good man." "She knows the job.") and rarely touches on policy issues or roll call votes. Only by the generous criterion of *recognition* of the representative's name does the electorate perform well. More than 90 percent claim to recognize their representative's name when supplied with it. Candidates for open seats are even less visible than incumbent candidates. Challengers trying to defeat incumbent representatives are the least visible of all. Typically, only about 20 percent of the voting electorate can recall the challenger's name or anything else about this person. Only about half will claim to recognize the challenger's name when supplied with it.[12]

Although voters generally are not well informed about their local House candidates, it does not follow that the candidates have little impact on election outcomes. Movements by relatively few voters in a constituency can create a major surge for or against a candidate. This movement, the "personal" vote, results from the constituency's reaction to the specific candidates, as opposed to the "partisan" vote, which results from the constituency's partisanship. The personal vote is about as important as the partisan vote in deciding elections.

The Success of House Incumbents

One amazing fact about House elections is the success rate of incumbents. In recent years about 95 percent of incumbents have been reelected. Even in 1994, the year of the "Republican revolution," more than 90 percent of all incumbents running in the general election won.[13] Why do House incumbents do so well at the ballot box? Actually, there are several factors contributing to their electoral popularity, and only a few have to do with being an incumbent.

District partisanship. Partisanship is an important factor in how candidates fare with the voters. Some districts are more Democratic in their predispositions, others more Republican. These leanings can be based on both the predominant partisan attachments people feel (party identification) and the ideological preferences of voters in different areas. Given how the parties have separated themselves on the issues, it makes sense for more conservative areas to favor Republican candidates, and more liberal areas to favor Democratic candidates.

We can illustrate this point by looking at the parties' success rates in different types of districts. Here, we use a baseline of *presidential partisanship,* which is the average of the 1988 and 1992 two-party presidential vote for the Democratic candidates for president (Dukakis and Clinton) in each House district. It represents a combination of enduring partisan attachments and local ideological preferences. The association between presidential partisanship in the districts and House outcomes is striking. Democrats had only a 12 percent success rate in 1988 and 1992 in the districts that averaged at least 55 percent for Bush. In contrast, they won 94 percent of the seats in the districts that averaged at least 55 percent for Dukakis and Clinton. In districts with balanced presidential partisanship (45 percent to 55 percent), the parties divided the seats just about evenly, with the Republicans winning 52 percent in 1994.

Notice that these are tendencies. The relationship between district partisanship and election outcomes has declined since the mid-1960s. One reason for the decline is that the electorate has become less partisan. In the early 1960s, for example, only 21 percent to 23 percent of the electorate claimed to be independent. By the early 1990s about 35 percent identified themselves as independent.[14] The effect of these loosened partisan ties is that other factors now operate with greater influence on the congressional vote.

Electoral selection. One simple but sometimes overlooked reason incumbents win is that incumbency status must be earned at the ballot box. Apart from district partisanship and partisan trends, elections are won on the basis of which

Table 6-1 Challenger Quality in the 1994 House Elections and Incumbent Safety

1992 Electoral Margin	Democratic Incumbents	Republican Incumbents
Safe: won by 60% or more	9% (137)	5% (61)
Competitive: won by less than 60%	24% (68)	31% (58)

Note: Cell entries are the percentages of incumbents running for reelection who faced experienced challengers. The numbers of incumbents are in parentheses.

party can field the stronger candidate. Strong candidates tend to win and by winning become incumbents. They survive until they falter or lose to even stronger candidates. Retirement of a successful incumbent starts the process again.

The process of electoral selection is independent of any incumbency advantage, but the two factors may reinforce each other. For instance, unusually strong candidates, with the help of a favorable partisan tide, can win in districts with adverse partisanship. Then, as the favorable partisan tide recedes, the strong candidates can stay elected by using the advantage of incumbency to enhance their personal appeal even further.

Weak challengers. Incumbents also tend to win because they draw weak opposition. Candidates and their supporters behave strategically in most instances, so they are reluctant to expend funds and political reputations in races they are likely to lose.[15] Strong, high-quality candidates conserve their political resources and tend to run in races they can win, either because the incumbent is vulnerable, the national short-term forces favor their party, or they have a shot at an open seat.

The tendency for candidates to behave strategically can be seen in the patterns of opposition incumbents faced in the 1994 election. Incumbents with safe margins in 1992 were much less likely to have to run against experienced challengers in 1994 than were those who had tough 1992 races (see Table 6-1). More experienced or higher-quality candidates are deterred by strong incumbents, resulting in weak challengers, who hand even larger victories to the incumbents.

Strategic retirements. One reason why incumbents rarely lose is the process of "strategic retirements." When incumbents are threatened by an imminent loss, they generally announce their retirement rather than face the verdict from the voters. In general, incumbents retire with about the same frequency as their objective probability of defeat. For instance, House members facing a 60 percent chance of losing will retire about 60 percent of the time. Strategic retirement is one reason why there were not more incumbents defeated in 1992 following the House check-bouncing scandal. Rather than face risky reelection battles, about one-third of the House members with overdrafts at the House bank chose to quit.[16]

The incumbency advantage. Finally, there are electoral benefits that accrue to candidates as incumbents. More precisely, there are opportunities that incumbents have to strengthen their electoral position by virtue of serving in the House, and most incumbents exploit these resources, although some more energetically than others.

By the incumbency advantage we mean the increment to the vote margin that a candidate gains by virtue of being the incumbent. There are several ways to measure this, but arguably the best is known as the sophomore surge, the percentage of the vote that candidates gain between their first victory and their first reelection attempt. Averaged across elections and adjusted for the national partisan trend, the sophomore surge is a simple but accurate measure of the typical vote share gained from incumbency.

The value of incumbency has increased substantially. The sophomore surge ran only about two percentage points in the 1950s when partisanship was the dominant consideration in congressional elections. By the 1970s the sophomore surge had reached about 7 percent, where it remains today.[17]

This increase in the incumbency advantage coincides with two important trends. One is the loosening of individual voter party ties that we have already discussed. Weaker party identification and more independents in the electorate mean other forces can have more sway. The other trend is that the slack has been taken up by the members and their ability to make their offices into reelection machines.[18] In the mid-1960s Congress changed the rules to bestow on its members several increases in the resources of their offices, the perquisites of office, or "perks." These perks included free mailing privileges (the frank), increased travel allowances to visit their districts and build constituent favor, and increased staff to handle constituents' growing concerns with the federal bureaucracy.[19] The result is that incumbents are well thought of by their constituents, often for reasons that have nothing to do with policy-making considerations at all.

It may seem surprising that an incumbency advantage that averages only seven percentage points can ensure success for most incumbents. The explanation is that the incumbency advantage is not a simple seven points across-the-board for all incumbents, but an average. Some incumbents work harder than others to please their constituents. Members trying to stay elected in districts with adverse partisanship have the greatest incentive to build constituency support with casework and getting the district its share of government largesse—keeping attention away from possible party support positions in the House that may not be electorally beneficial. Moreover, very safe members do not need extra votes to stay in office. As long as the districts vote close to their partisan predispositions, the members should be fine. In this case, we expect such members to earn little or no incumbency advantage at all. In contrast, the more threatened members

Figure 6-5 The Incumbency Advantage in the House, 1994

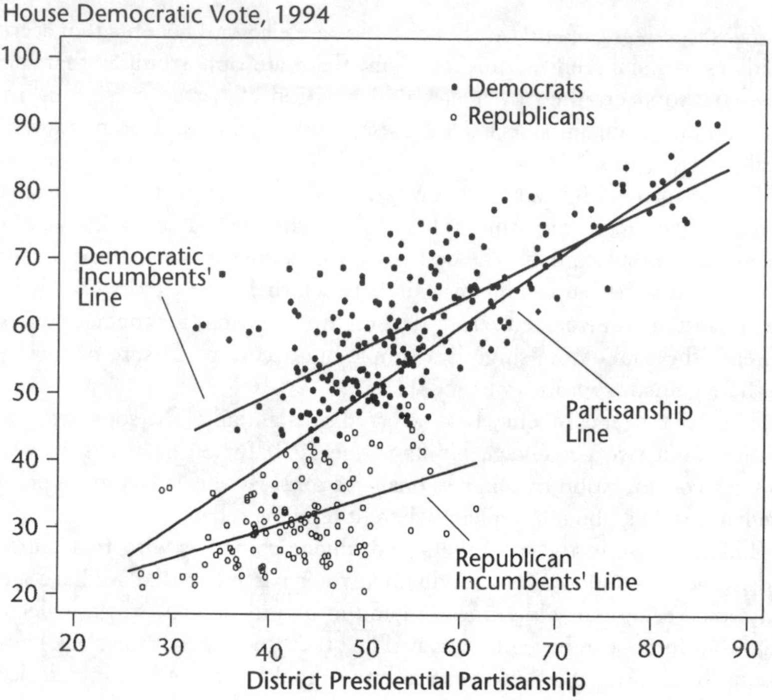

need to work to earn every extra ballot that vigorous use of the perks of office can produce.

Figure 6-5 shows that this logic works. It shows the electoral outcomes for Democratic (black dots) and Republican (white dots) incumbents in the 1994 election. If the only systematic force in congressional elections were partisanship, we would expect the points for both parties' incumbents to be scattered more or less randomly around the presidential partisanship line. Two additional lines are shown. These are best-fit regression lines, here termed incumbency lines, one for each party. The distance between the incumbency line and the partisanship line can be interpreted as a rough indicator of the incumbency advantage relative to partisanship. We expect Democratic incumbents to run above the line, Republican incumbents below. And this is what we find. Incumbents of both parties generally beat a straight partisan vote.

The incumbency advantage over straight partisanship is not uniform. At the party extremes, the best-fit lines for each party indicate that safe incumbents get about what we would expect based on district partisanship. In the competitive areas and areas of adverse partisanship—where we expect incumbents to work the hardest—the incumbency line for each party departs from the straight partisanship line as we expect. Threatened incumbents have a larger incumbency advantage.

We also see evidence of the 1994 short-term national forces. Notice that a considerable number of Democratic incumbents fall below where we expect them to be based on district partisanship, and in a number of cases they lost their jobs: all the Democratic incumbents below 50 percent on the vertical axis lost in 1994. In contrast, hardly any Republican incumbents rose above the partisanship line, and even those who did were in safe enough districts that they still won.

The incumbency advantage as an investment. Because incumbents almost always win, it might seem that incumbents can ignore their constituents' concerns. But that impression would be quite mistaken. A central source of the incumbency advantage is the careful tending to district interests. Incumbents like to stay elected, and they know that providing constituents with what they want is the way to do this. Incumbents are well aware that their long-term electoral security depends on satisfying their constituencies. Even though House members know they are unlikely to lose the next election, they also understand that their chances are roughly one in three that they will eventually lose. After all, roughly one in three got to Congress in the first place by defeating a sitting incumbent.[20]

If House members ignored their districts, we would see no incumbency advantage and, instead, rapid turnover. House members, we have argued, do not get their incumbency advantage automatically; they earn it by hard work. Part of the work is constituency service and bringing home the pork in the form of government construction projects, local government contracts, and the like. But there is also a policy component to the incumbent's investment. One way House members earn their incumbency advantage is by representing their districts' policy interests. Often, these interests can be expressed as an ideological preference. As we shall see in the next section, House members add to their vote margins by representing the ideological preferences of their constituents.

Candidates, Issues, and the Vote

In this section we explore the impact of candidates and their issue stances on vote outcomes. We first look at a simple question: "Do the candidates matter?" Survey researchers long have found that only a handful of the congressional electorate has any but the most rudimentary information about incumbents, and they typically know next to nothing about challengers and candidates in open seat contests.

In spite of individual voter ignorance, candidates make a huge difference in the elections, as can be seen by looking at the dramatic nature of shifts in the vote from one election to the next when the candidates change. Figure 6-6 shows three scatter plots of the 1994 congressional vote against the vote in the same districts in 1992. The top graph plots the relationship for those contests in which

Figure 6-6 Effects of Candidate Pairings on Electoral Change, 1992–1994

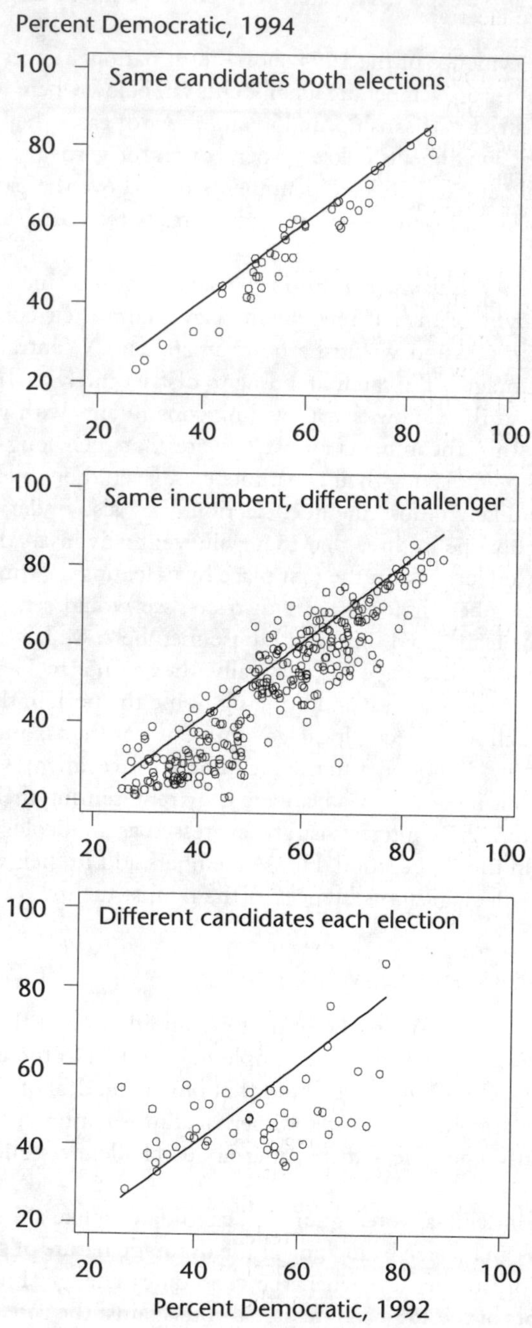

the same individuals ran against one another. When voters were given the same choice in the two elections, they tended to make the same decision, except for a shift down (in the Republican direction) reflecting the short-term national forces of 1994. The 1992 to 1994 outcomes are closely related as indicated by the high correlation (r =.97). The middle graph shows the relationship between 1992 and 1994 outcomes when one candidate—usually the incumbent—remained the same, but ran against a different opponent from the other party. Here the picture is a bit fuzzier (r =.90), showing that challengers make a difference in voters' choices. The strong continuity, however, suggests that the incumbents are the most visible stimulus in these elections.

The third graph shows what happens when an incumbent did not run in the 1994 general election because of retirement or defeat in the primary, so that voters face an entirely new choice. There is now only a modest relationship between the 1992 and 1994 decisions (r =.48), and in almost all cases the 1994 outcomes have moved toward a more competitive outcome. These results reflect the loss of the incumbency advantage in the later election.

Now that we have shown that candidates matter, we can turn our attention to how candidates take issue stances to influence the voters and win elections. As noted earlier, Republican candidates tend to be conservative and Democratic candidates tend to be liberal. The average constituent is caught in the middle, located between the two candidates on the ideological spectrum. When voters respond to ideology and issues, candidates gain votes by moving away from their party's ideological norm and toward the center of the spectrum. In principle, each candidate would maximize his or her general election votes by moving in the direction of the opponent. If both candidates were to do so, they would meet in the center of the local ideological spectrum.[21]

In reality, candidates do not converge. In 1994 the Democrat was more liberal than his or her Republican opponent in more than 99 percent of the races.[22] The average difference between candidates on our ideology index is fifty-eight points out of an absolute maximum possible difference of one hundred. Candidates do not converge because of the countervailing forces of their own liberal or conservative beliefs and those of their contributors and ideological supporters, which operate to pull candidates toward the ideological extremes.[23] Still, within each party, the candidates do vary in their ideological positions, and the degree to which they moderate their stands by moving toward their opponents influences the vote.[24]

In terms of their personal ideological views, most House members are probably comfortable with the typical position of their congressional party—quite conservative for Republicans and quite liberal for Democrats. Those members who represent safe districts tend to reflect such views in their roll call voting. Their constituents allow this "ideological extremism" for the simple reason that often those positions are not far from the average voter in those districts. What appears to be extremely conservative in metropolitan California, for instance, may seem only reasonable in rural Mississippi.

Table 6-2 Regressions of Democratic Vote on Candidate Ideology and Presidential Partisanship, 1994 House Elections

Independent Variable	Regression Coefficient	t-ratio	Beta	
Democratic incumbents				
Incumbent ideology	−.201**	−6.7	−.34	
Challenger ideology	.127**	4.8	.22	R^2 = .676
Presidential partisanship	−.845**	15.5	.86	
Constant	27.2			N = 188
Republican incumbents				
Incumbent ideology	−.113**	−2.7	−.26	
Challenger ideology	−.027	−0.8	−.07	R^2 = .25
Presidential partisanship	.557**	6.1	.59	
Constant	11.55			N = 107
Open seats				
Democrats' ideology	−.049	−0.2	−.03	
Republicans' ideology	−.021	−1.0	−.09	R^2 = .79
Presidential partisanship	.947**	7.5	.95	
Constant	4.95			N = 31

Source: Compiled by the authors.

Note: Candidate ideology is an index based on roll calls in the 103d Congress and issue surveys of candidates by Congressional Quarterly and Project Vote Smart. The index is scored in units of typical congressional ratings on a 0–100 scale with higher values indicating greater liberalism. Presidential partisanship is the average Democratic percentage of the two-party vote for president, 1988 and 1992.

**sig. at p<.01; * sig. at p<.05.

All candidates have an incentive to gain votes as a hedge against unexpected adverse short-term forces, whether they come in the form of national tides or an unexpectedly strong challenger. This incentive is particularly strong for candidates in competitive districts or in districts where the opposition party has stronger support among the voters. One way these candidates can win and hold such seats is to represent the ideological preferences of the district. A Republican attempting to hold a competitive or Democratic district can take a moderate or liberal posture on issues. A Democrat trying to hold a competitive or Republican district can take a moderate or conservative posture.

We show the effects of ideological positioning in examining the relationship among voting outcomes, district ideology, and the candidates' issues stances. The analysis is presented in three parts, one for Democratic incumbents, one for Republican incumbents, and one for open seat contests. We examine the effects of both candidates' ideology while controlling for presidential partisanship.

For all candidates we use our index of ideology to measure issue positions. Working with similar data from previous Congresses, we found that candidate moderation is consistently rewarded by voters.[25] The 1994 data generally support this finding, but with an interesting twist due to the proconservative short-term forces of that year (see Table 6-2).

First, the impact of Democratic incumbent ideology is as expected and it is statistically significant. The negative sign indicates that the more liberal the voting record the lower the vote for the Democrat when presidential partisanship is controlled. The size of the coefficient indicates that the electoral costs of running as an extreme liberal rather than a moderate (scores of 100 and 50 respectively) is a loss of about 10 percent of the vote.[26] The coefficient for the Republican challengers, however, is a surprise. It is highly significant, but the effect is opposite of what we expect. It appears that in the conservative tide of 1994, strong conservative positions among the Republican freshmen carried the message in Democratic incumbent contests that the best way to reject the (liberal) status quo was to vote for those who offered the clearest alternative—or those who used the strongest rhetoric in rejecting the Democrats and the Clinton administration.

The usual pattern of moderation being rewarded holds for Republican incumbents. The effects of a very conservative voting record is a lower vote. Perhaps because of the proconservative short-term forces of 1994, however, the effect of ideological extremism here is less than in previous Congresses and less than the effect of ideological extremism for Democrats in 1994. Controlling for presidential partisanship, the difference between a moderate (score of 50) and extreme Republican (0) was between 5 percent and 6 percent of the vote in 1994. The issue stances of Democratic challengers to Republican incumbents did not seem to matter. The effect has the right sign, but it does not reach statistical significance.

Finally, the picture for open seats suggests the dominance of presidential partisanship. The ideology coefficients have the right sign, but neither reaches statistical significance. This result could be caused by the smaller number of cases—we have data on only thirty-one of fifty-nine pairs of candidates in open seat contests—but the magnitude of the coefficients also suggests a smaller effect than we find for incumbents. The smaller effects of ideology in open seat contests is to be expected because the candidates are much less well known than are incumbents who have had years to build their reputations.

The Republicans' efforts to nationalize the campaign by linking all Democratic candidates with the purported liberalism and failings of the Clinton administration seemed to work in the open seat races particularly. The large coefficient of .947 there underlines the overwhelming importance of attitudes toward the parties and the president in these open seat contests.

We find, then, that what the candidates—particularly incumbents— stand for influences how well they do at the polls. In 1994, with liberalism under a concerted attack, Democratic ideology mattered, and Democratic incumbents who stuck with their party's liberal tradition paid the price electorally.

Naturally, candidates have a pretty good idea of what it takes to get votes,

Figure 6-7 Candidate Liberalism with District Presidential Partisanship, by Party, 1994

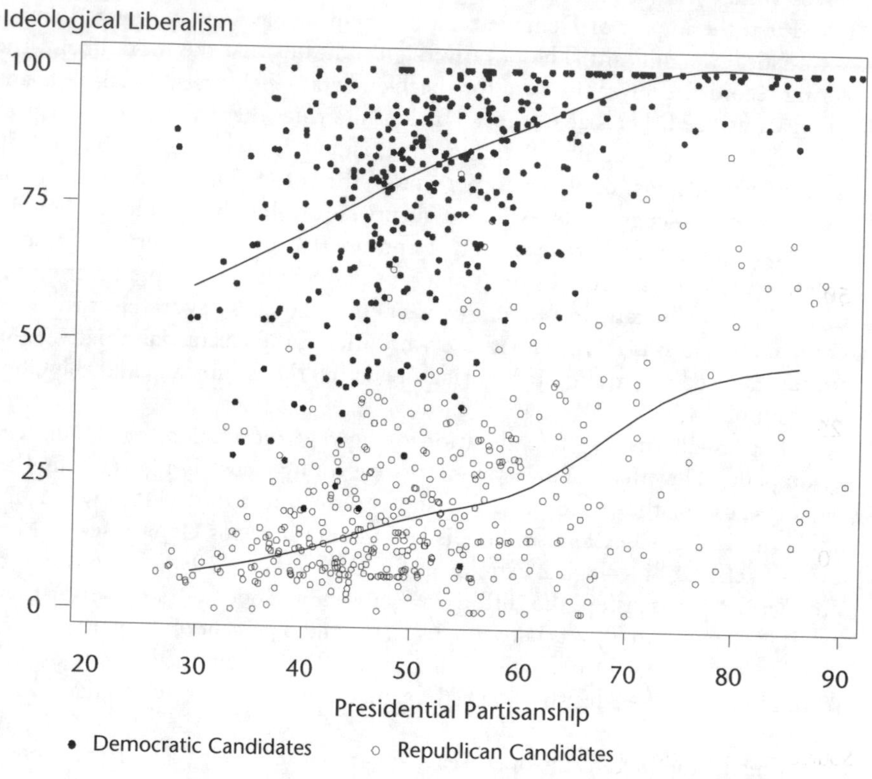

Source: Compiled by the authors.

Note: Points represent all Democratic and Republican scores on the candidate ideology index.

and we suspect that they know when an issue stance is too liberal or conservative for their districts. There should be a tendency for both Democrats and Republicans to heed district preferences. Figure 6-7 shows the relationship between our index of candidate ideology and presidential partisanship. Notice that there is a tendency for each party's most liberal candidates to run in the areas where Clinton and Dukakis had their strongest support, and the most conservative members to run in areas of highest Bush support. Candidates shade their positions to match local coloration. But the lines in Figure 6-7 also show that at any level of presidential partisanship, there is a clear ideological distance between competing candidates. Both parties' candidates demonstrate a tendency to veer in a moderate direction when they are running in districts that are competitive or even friendly to the opposite party.

Figure 6-8 Winner's Ideology (1994) by District Presidential Partisanship

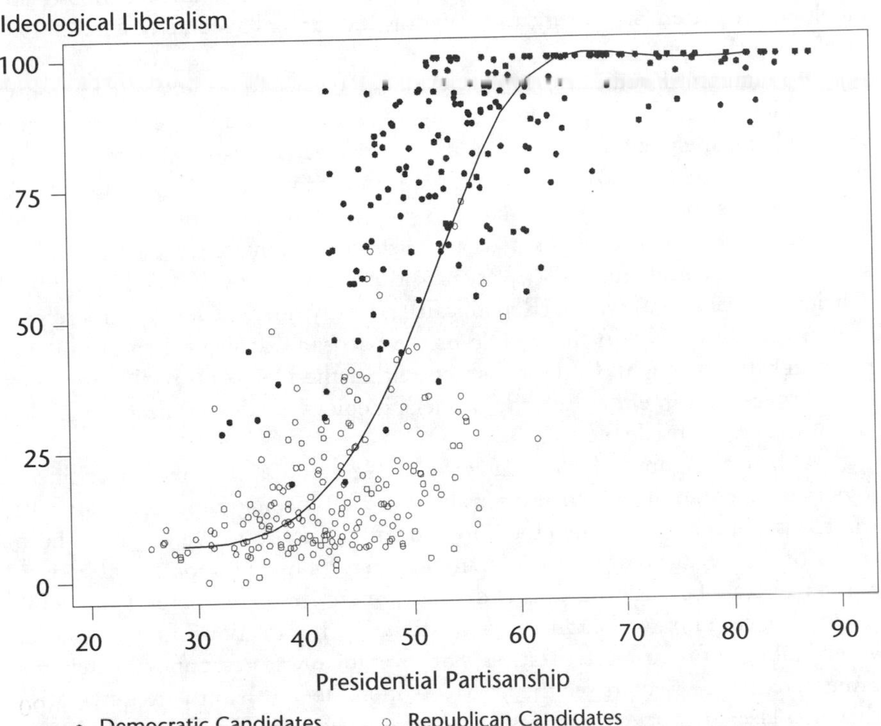

Source: Compiled by the authors.

Note: Candidate ideology scores are derived from roll calls and surveys of candidates as described in the text. Presidential partisanship is the average percent Democratic in the 1988 and 1992 presidential elections.

Congressional Elections and Representation

The political parties and the candidates provide the mechanisms by which constituencies can electorally determine the policy views of their representatives in Congress. First, consider the role of political parties. Democratic and Republican congressional candidates are sufficiently divergent from each other on the liberal-conservative spectrum to provide their constituencies with a clear choice. Liberal districts generally vote Democratic and elect liberals, while conservative districts generally vote Republican and elect conservatives.

Second, consider the role of the individual candidates. Candidates for Congress sometimes deviate from their party's ideological orthodoxy. By moving toward a more moderate position, one that is closer to the constituency's prevailing view, the candidate enhances his or her electoral chances and by doing so can enhance the representation of constituency views. When a candidate chooses an ideologically extremist strategy, the constituency can enhance its representation by electing the opponent.

As Figure 6-8 indicates, the net result is a clear pattern whereby the most liberal House members represent the most liberal districts and the most conservative House members represent the most conservative districts. Here we plot the winning candidates' ideology index scores on the vertical axis; the horizontal axis represents constituency preferences as measured by presidential partisanship. Representatives' ideological positions and district opinion are represented with a strong positive correlation (+.77). Very pro-Bush and very pro-Dukakis/Clinton districts get very conservative (Republican) and very liberal (Democratic) representation, respectively. In the middle of the partisan-ideological spectrum the partisan battle is fought. In these districts, either the Democrat or the Republican may win, but in either case the winner's ideology tends to reflect the gradient of the presidential vote.

Although Figure 6-8 shows a considerable amount of district-level ideological representation, we can also ask about the net ideological representation of the House. Specifically, is the House too liberal, too conservative, or just right in terms of the net taste of the American electorate? This question is not easy to answer directly because roll calls and voter preferences cannot readily be compared on a common scale. One way of estimating the relationship is to consult voters' ratings of their representatives. For several Congresses, approximately the same percentage of voters see themselves as more liberal than the representative they just elected as see themselves as more conservative. This balance indicates that, at least perceptually, Congress has been neither too liberal nor too conservative for the general electorate. This pattern can be seen in Table 6-3. There we see that a slightly greater percentage of reasonably informed respondents see themselves as more conservative than their representatives. However, the reason for this perception is simply that the people who have difficulty sorting out the parties in abstract ideological terms tend to be less well educated and vote Democratic. In spite of the rhetoric of the parties and pundits, the public does not see Congress as too liberal or too conservative overall.

But what if the voters wanted electoral change from Congress? Ideological changes follow shifts in the House's party composition, but, as we have seen, the forces behind these partisan changes do not often involve collective public desire for an ideological shift of direction. Normally the American public is rather static in its collective position on the ideological scale. But if the national electorate were to shift ideologically, could it get the House of Representatives to change with it? The evidence from 1994 is an emphatic yes.

An examination of the National Election Studies data by Alan Abramowitz and Suzie Ishikawa is quite revealing.[27] They argue convincingly that the Republican House victories did not result just from voter angst with President Clinton. Rather, the 1994 elections brought a clear ideological shift: voters in 1994, com-

Table 6-3 Voter Perceptions of the Ideological Positions of Winning House Candidates Relative to the Voter's Preferences

Percentage of respondents who	1978	1980	1982	1986	1990	1994
See themselves as more liberal than their representative	27%	33%	31%	37%	37%	34%
See themselves at same place as their representative	26	26	27	24	21	26
See themselves as more conservative than their representative	47	41	42	40	42	41
(N)	(132)	(133)	(139)	(161)	(104)	(274)

Note: Calculated by the authors from National Election Studies. Responses pertain to the candidate who just won in the district. Percentages are based on voters who saw Democrats left of Republicans and the Democratic candidate to the left of the Republican candidate.

pared to 1992, were clearly more conservative; they saw themselves as distinctly closer to their perceptions of the Republican Party's positions on issues; and they even shifted in the Republican direction in overall partisanship. Their analysis provides a clear policy basis for the electoral change that occurred in 1994. When the electorate wants a change, it can bring it about.

It is important to note that the electorate can also reverse itself. The changes in public opinion that occurred in 1994 may not signal a long-term trend. Gary Jacobson and Thomas Kim provide ample evidence from trends in responses to various surveys to suggest that 1994 could be a fluke.[28] If the electorate does not like what it has brought about, it can change its course—as it has done numerous times in the past. Republicans in the House significantly moderated their stance in the waning months of the 104th Congress, which allowed for the passage of several significant pieces of legislation. This willingness to work together seems to have been rewarded at the polls: the electorate in 1996 voted to continue Republican control of Congress while returning President Clinton to the White House for another four years. The linkage between electoral response and governing, so essential for democratic government, appears to be in good working order in elections for the House of Representatives.

House-Senate Differences in Electoral Representation

The Framers of the Constitution intended the Senate to be an elite chamber, isolated from the popular demands on the House. Regardless of how well or poorly this intention has been realized, there are fundamental constitutional differences between the two chambers. The most remarkable difference has been eliminated. Before 1913 and ratification of the Seventeenth Amendment, state legislatures selected their state's senators. Today, voters elect their senators directly. Because senators have six-year terms, they are relatively free from the never-ending campaigns carried on by representatives. And, for the most part, the constituencies senators represent are larger and much more diverse than those of representatives.

Election Results and the Senate

In terms of national election results, the party composition of the Senate reflects the same forces that determine the party composition of the House. The division between Democrats and Republicans in the Senate is influenced by presidential coattails in presidential years and the bounce to the out party at midterm. The Senate's partisan division responds more sluggishly to national trends, however, because only one-third of the senators are up for reelection in any election year.

As a general rule, Senate elections are more competitive than House elections. Senate races with no incumbent are almost always sharply contested by both parties, and an incumbent senator who seeks reelection has a considerably greater chance of defeat than does an incumbent House member who seeks reelection. Incumbent senators are reelected at about a 78 percent rate, compared with 92 percent for House incumbents. One reason for closer Senate races is that the statewide Senate constituencies are rarely dominated by one political party as the smaller House districts are. Another major factor is that Senate races attract strong challengers. A senator is far more likely than a House member to face a politically seasoned and well-financed election opponent. Finally, senators seem unable to obtain the strong incumbency advantage that House members enjoy, averaging no better than a few percentage points as their average sophomore surge. (Evidently, senatorial challengers find it easier to generate visibility for their campaigns than do challengers to House incumbents.) Senators perform well electorally, compared with nonincumbent candidates of their party, partly because they had to be good candidates to be elected the first time.

Although reelection to the Senate is more difficult than reelection to the House, senators need to run only once every six years. The appropriate comparison of electoral security is a comparison of survival rates over the same period of time. Measured over six years, House members seeking reelection have a survival rate of approximately 78 percent—about the same as the reelection rate for senators.[29]

Therefore, the six-year term for senators almost exactly offsets the greater incumbency advantage of the House. Senators run less often but at higher risk. The long-run survival rates for the two houses would appear to be roughly equal.

Is the Senate any less responsive to popular opinion than the House? Six-year terms would seem to provide senators with ample freedom from electoral concerns, except for the final run up to election. Moreover, when senators decide to be attentive to their electorates, their diverse constituencies make full representation difficult.

Like House members, senators are sensitive to constituency opinion, with each party's most conservative senators found in conservative states, and most liberal members found in liberal states. In terms of partisan politics, the states are competitive enough that each party has a chance at a Senate seat. As a result, many states send both a Republican and a Democrat to the Senate, a pattern that baffles some observers. In a pattern similar to that of the House, senators from states in which the other party dominates often are ideologically atypical for their party.[30]

State Populations and the Senate

Although states vary considerably in population, each has two senators. California's 31 million people get the same number of senators as Alaska's 600,000. To some extent, this constitutionally designed "malapportionment" favors political conservatism. Indeed, state population correlates rather strongly (+.34) with our measure of citizen liberalism, based on pooled CBS News/*New York Times* surveys.[31] Small, politically conservative states enjoy an extra margin of representation in the Senate.

During the Reagan years, when the Republicans enjoyed a six-year Senate majority, the Senate was the more conservative chamber. One is tempted to attribute this senatorial conservatism to the Senate's overrepresentation of small states. However, in the immediate aftermath of the Republican takeover of both houses of Congress in 1994, the Senate was the more moderate of the two chambers. The greater responsiveness of the House to national forces in that year brought in a crew of conservative freshmen legislators that, coupled with vigorous conservative leadership, put the House distinctly in the lead of the Republican revolution launched by the 1994 election.

The Six-Year Term

Because the next election for representatives is never more than two years away, electoral considerations are always an important consideration for members of the House. For senators, the six-year term can provide some leeway. Voters—so it sometimes seems—are electorally myopic, forgetting what senators do early in their terms and remembering only what they do close to the election.

Whether this view of the electorate is valid, there is a good deal of evidence that senatorial roll call voting responds to the six-year cycle.[32] In the year or two before they must run again, incumbents move away from their party's extreme. Democrats inch in a conservative direction, and Republicans edge over to the left. The purpose in each instance is to appeal to moderate voters.

Because senators moderate their ideological positions as reelection approaches, they presumably have good reason to do so: senators must believe that moderation enhances their chances of electoral success. Earlier we saw evidence that House members are more likely to be reelected with moderate ideological positions. Is the same true for senators?

Candidates' policy positions affect their election chances. For the Senate, candidates do better if they avoid their party's ideological extremes. Gerald Wright and Michael Berkman estimated the effect of candidates' issue positions by comparing different pairings of ideological positions while statistically controlling for the effects of several constituency characteristics and attitudes.[33] They estimated that whether a Senate candidate represents the party's moderate wing or more extremist wing creates a difference ranging from five to eight percentage points. This effect is similar to that observed for House elections. The evidence suggests that the same electoral connection leading to representation exists in the Senate as in the House, with the added twists of the larger, more heterogeneous constituencies and the latitude of the six-year Senate term.

Conclusion

Along with presidential elections, congressional elections provide citizens with their main opportunity to influence the direction of national policy. When elections bring about significant changes in the party composition of Congress, we can be fairly confident of two things. The first is that the new Congress will have a different ideological cast. Democratic and Republican candidates for House and Senate stand for quite different things. Therefore, electing more Democrats or more Republicans increases the likelihood of policy movement in the ideological direction of the advantaged party. Ironically, the second is that such changes do not always stem from the electorate's desire for new policy directions. The big change in 1994 did coincide with an increase in conservative Republican sentiments in the mass electorate. Other, less substantial changes, however, have stemmed from factors such as presidential coattails or the usual slump the presidential party experiences at midterm.

We see the electorate's influence on policy direction most clearly in the relationship between constituencies and their elected representatives. In terms of ideological direction, individual House and Senate members respond to their constituencies. In turn, ideological direction matters when constituencies decide which candidates they will elect and which they will not.

The average voter knows little about his or her representative and only a bit more about his or her senators. House challengers are almost invisible, and only a portion of the electorate has even a modest amount of information about senatorial challengers. Nevertheless, the electorates that candidates and parties face are smart and discerning, and they reward faithful representation. Candidates, generally desirous of attaining and staying in office, heed their electorate's wishes and work to give them what they want. Elections bring about much higher levels of policy representation than most observers would expect based on the low levels of citizen awareness.

Appendix: The Candidate Ideology Index

The candidate ideology index is formed from three data sets: roll call votes and two excellent surveys of congressional candidates, but none is complete. Our goal is to achieve comparable information on as many incumbents and challengers as possible. Using any data set alone loses many cases for the analysis, but the combined measure allows systematic analysis across a larger subset of all the candidates involved in the 1994 contest.

The first component of our candidate ideology index combines the roll call ratings of House incumbents from a liberal group, the Americans for Democratic Action, and a conservative group, the American Conservative Union. Each of these ratings runs from 0 to 100 depending on the percentage of the time a member voted with the positions the group favors. We combined the scores to form a conservative (0) to liberal (100) roll call ideology index. Roll call ideology = (ADA - ACU)/2+50.

We use candidate responses to issue surveys conducted during the 1994 campaign by Congressional Quarterly and by Project Vote Smart (PVS). Our strategy was to first construct general liberal-conservative issue position indices from these two sources, and then to combine the roll calls, the CQ, and the PVS measures into a grand index of candidate ideology.

Congressional Quarterly solicited responses from candidates concerning positions on sixteen issues. Thirteen of these come together to form a good measure of overall liberal-conservative orientation as shown in the factor structure in Table 6–A.

The second set is the PVS data. That survey was quite long, and only the forced choice options are included in the measures examined here. (We do not examine in this analysis the long series of policy options in which candidates were allowed to check only those positions they supported. The problem is that when an option is not checked we do not know if this means opposition or no preference—and candidates varied greatly in their frequency of taking positions when given a choice.) The factor structure and items making up the PVS liberal-conservative index are shown in Table 6–B.

For both data sets, principal factor components were extracted based on the set of Democratic and Republican candidates who provided usable answers to all questions (332 in the CQ survey, 350 in the Project Vote Smart Survey). Rather than throw out candidates who failed to answer a small number of the questions, these full-information indices were used as a basis for imputing values based on items respondents did answer, as long as they provided answers to at least half the questions. The imputation was done by a missing values regression. This regression estimates the value for the dependent variable (the estimated PVS and CQ scale scores) based on regressions using the available information (*Stata Reference Manual,* Release 5, vol. 2, [College Station, Texas: Stata Press, 1997: 214–218]; Richard J. A. Little and Donald B. Rubin, *Statistical Analysis with Missing Data* [New York: Wiley, 1987]). The procedure

Table 6-A Factor Structure of the Items from the Congressional Quarterly Congressional Survey, 1994

Question	Factor Loading
Legislation establishing a woman's right to obtain an abortion in most cases	.69
Federal funding for abortions in cases of rape, incest, or when the life of the mother is in danger	.67
Reversing a Supreme Court ruling allowing employers to permanently replace striking workers	.66
Government-mandated universal health coverage for all Americans	.86
Requiring employers to pay for a portion of their employees' health care benefits	.81
A Canadian-style, single-payer health care system in the U.S.	.70
Partial federal funding of congressional candidates who comply with spending limits	.75
Taxpayer-supported school vouchers for private schools	-.72
Legislation prohibiting discrimination against gays in employment and housing	.78
Limiting the number of terms members of Congress may serve	-.58
A constitutional amendment requiring a balanced federal budget	-.68
Banning the manufacture, sale, and possession of certain semi-automatic weapons	.72
Defense spending levels proposed by President Clinton	-.63

Note: The options for all items but the last (and their scoring) are "support" (1) and "oppose" (2); the options on the last item, were "too high" (1), "adequate" (2) and "not enough" (3).

increased the Ns to 420 respondents in the CQ data and 436 respondents in the PVS data.

The final step was to create an overall index of ideology based on all available information: roll calls (ADA and ACU for the 103d Congress) and the CQ and PVS surveys. Here the strategy of aggregation and imputation was the same. First an overall factor was created based on full information respondents with the following factor (principal components) structure:

Roll Calls	.98
Project Vote Smart	.88
CQ	.97

This yields one factor with an eigenvalue of 2.67. Clearly, the three scales are measuring the same underlying liberal-conservative policy dimension.

Next, we extract factor scores for those respondents who had usable information on all three measures (N = 67). Final scores for the ideology index were then imputed using missing values regression based on all patterns of responses.

Table 6-B Factor Structure of the Items from the Project Vote Smart Congressional Survey, 1994

Question	Loading
Support increase of the minimum wage?	.74
Spending	
National defense	−.65
Federal health care program	.72
AIDS research	.71
Job retraining programs	.80
Public education	.75
Environmental clean up and enforcement	.72
Taxes	
Capital gains	.65
Social Security benefits of retirees with incomes more than $40,000	.62
Income taxes on families earning less than $140,000	.67
Income taxes on families earning more than $140,000	.79
Value-added taxes on U.S. businesses	.64

We end up with scores for 769 candidates, based on responses to all three data sets (N = 67), two of the data sets (N = 344) or just one data set (N = 358). The metric is then set to match the 0–100 scale of the combined ADA and ACU roll calls with its mean of about 50 and standard deviation of 35.

By combining ideological measures from different sources, we lose some ground in terms of measurement precision, but we gain lots of cases for analysis. Following traditional procedures and doing the analysis only on the cases available for the specific components of our ideology index would greatly attenuate our working N. When the analysis is replicated using the original measures on the partial subsets of cases that then result, we found patterns that support our conclusions here in every substantively significant respect.

Notes

1. Gary C. Jacobson and Samuel Kernell, "Strategy and Choice in the 1982 Congressional Elections," *PS* 15 (Summer 1982): 426; John A. Ferejohn and Randall L. Calvert, "Presidential Coattails in Historical Perspective," *American Journal of Political Science* 28 (February 1984): 131.
2. Stephen Ansolabehere, David Brady, and Morris Fiorina, "The Marginals Never Vanished?" Research paper 970, Graduate School of Business, Stanford University, December 1987.
3. Philip E. Converse, "The Concept of the Normal Vote," in *Elections and the Political Order*, ed. Angus Campbell, Philip E. Converse, Warren E. Miller, and Donald E. Stokes (New York: Wiley, 1966), 9–39.

4. Ferejohn and Calvert, "Presidential Coattails."
5. Angus Campbell, "Surge and Decline: A Study of Electoral Change," in *Elections and the Political Order,* 40–62.
6. Robert S. Erikson, "The Puzzle of the Midterm Loss," *Journal of Politics* 50 (November 1988): 1011–29.
7. Robert S. Erikson, "Why the Democrats Lose Presidential Elections," *PS* 22 (March 1989): 30–35.
8. Alberto Alesina and Howard Rosenthal, "Partisan Cycles in Congressional Elections and the Macroeconomy," *American Political Science Review* 83 (June 1989): 373–398.
9. Robert S. Erikson and Kent L. Tedin, *American Public Opinion: Its Origins, Content and Impact,* 5th ed. (Boston: Allyn and Bacon, 1991), chap. 4.
10. James A. Stimson, Michael B. MacKuen, and Robert S. Erikson, "Dynamic Representation," *American Political Science Review* 89 (September 1995): 543–564.
11. Project Vote Smart is the major program of the Center for National Independence in Politics, a national nonpartisan organization focused on providing citizens with information about the political system, issues, candidates, and elected officials. Information about Project Vote Smart and access to much of the data it collects can be found on the World Wide Web at http://www.vote-smart.org/
12. On voters' awareness of candidates, see Thomas E. Mann, *Unsafe at Any Margin: Interpreting Congressional Elections* (Washington, D.C.: American Enterprise Institute, 1978); Donald E. Stokes and Warren E. Miller, "Party Government and the Saliency of Congress," *Public Opinion Quarterly* 26 (Winter 1962): 531–546.
13. The balance of incumbents' success, however, was decidedly in favor of GOP incumbents who won at an amazing 100 percent rate compared to the Democrats who lost their majority status but still managed an impressive 84 percent success rate.
14. Based on National Election Studies data presented in Harold W. Stanley and Richard G. Niemi, *Vital Statistics on American Politics,* 5th ed. (Washington, D.C.: CQ Press, 1995).
15. Gary C. Jacobson and Samuel Kernell, *Strategy and Choice in Congressional Elections,* 2d ed. (New Haven: Yale University Press, 1983).
16. Susan A. Banducci and Jeffrey A. Karp, "Electoral Consequences of Scandal and Reapportionment in the 1992 House Elections," *American Politics Quarterly* 22 (January 1994): 3–26; Gary C. Jacobson and Michael A. Dimock, "Checking Out: The Effects of Bank Overdrafts on the 1992 House Elections," *American Journal of Political Science* 38 (February 1994): 601–624; Timothy Groseclose and Keith Krehbiel, "Golden Parachutes, Rubber Checks, and Strategic Retirements from the 102d House," *American Journal of Political Science* 38 (February 1994): 75–99.
17. Robert S. Erikson, "Estimating the Incumbency Advantage in Congressional Elections" (paper presented at the annual meeting of the Political Methodology Society, St. Louis, July 1990). For earlier estimates of the growth of the incumbency advantage, see Robert S. Erikson, "Malapportionment, Gerrymandering, and Party Fortunes in Congressional Elections," *American Political Science Review* 66 (December 1972): 1234–45; David Mayhew, "Congressional Elections: The Case of the Vanishing Marginals," *Polity* 6 (Spring 1973): 295–318; John A. Ferejohn, "On the Decline of Competition in Congressional Elections," *American Political Science Review* 71 (March 1977): 166–176.
18. David Mayhew, *Congress: The Electoral Connection* (New Haven: Yale University Press, 1974).
19. Morris Fiorina, *Congress: Keystone of the Washington Establishment,* 2d ed. (New Haven: Yale University Press, 1989).
20. Robert S. Erikson, "Is There Such a Thing as a Safe Seat?" *Polity* 8 (Summer 1976): 613–632.

21. Anthony Downs, *An Economic Theory of Democracy* (New York: Harper and Row, 1957), chap. 8.
22. In only 2 of 327 contests (0.6 percent) for which we have information on both candidates' ideological stands was the Democrat more conservative than the Republican House opponent.
23. Gerald C. Wright, "Policy Voting in the U.S. Senate: Who Is Represented?" *Legislative Studies Quarterly* 14 (November 1989): 465–486.
24. Robert S. Erikson, "The Electoral Impact of Congressional Roll Call Voting," *American Political Science Review* 65 (December 1971): 1018–32; Gerald C. Wright, "Candidates' Policy Positions and Voting in U.S. House Elections," *Legislative Studies Quarterly* 3 (August 1978): 445–464; Robert S. Erikson and Gerald C. Wright, "Policy Representation of Constituency Interests," *Political Behavior* 1 (Summer 1980): 91–106.
25. See our analyses of the 1974, 1978, 1982, and 1990 congressional elections in the fourth and fifth editions of *Congress Reconsidered,* ed. Lawrence C. Dodd and Bruce I. Oppenheimer (Washington, D.C.: CQ Press, 1989 and 1993).
26. This estimate is achieved by multiplying the coefficient for Democratic incumbents by the ideological distance: -.201 x 50 = -10.05.
27. Alan I. Abramowitz and Suzie Ishikawa, "Explaining the Republican Takeover of the House of Representatives: Evidence from the 1992–1994 NES Panel Survey" (paper delivered at the annual meeting of the American Political Science Association, Chicago, Aug. 31–Sept. 3, 1995).
28. Gary C. Jacobson and Thomas P. Kim, "After 1994: The New Politics of Congressional Elections" (paper presented at the annual meeting of the Midwest Political Science Association, Chicago, April 18–20, 1996).
29. Amihai Glazer and Bernard Grofman, "Two Plus Two Plus Two Equals Six: Tenure of Office of Senators and Representatives, 1953–1983," *Legislative Studies Quarterly* 12 (November 1987): 555–563.
30. Robert S. Erikson, "Roll Calls, Reputations, and Representation in the U.S. Senate," *Legislative Studies Quarterly* 15 (November 1990): 623–642.
31. Robert S. Erikson, Gerald C. Wright, and John P. McIver, *Statehouse Democracy* (New York: Cambridge University Press, 1993), chap. 2.
32. Richard F. Fenno Jr., *The United States Senate: A Bicameral Perspective* (Washington, D.C.: American Enterprise Institute, 1982); Martin Thomas, "Electoral Proximity and Senatorial Roll Call Voting," *American Journal of Political Science* 29 (February 1984): 96–111; Gerald C. Wright, "Representation and the Electoral Cycle in the U.S. Senate" (paper delivered at the annual meeting of the Midwest Political Science Association, Chicago, April 15–17, 1993).
33. Gerald C. Wright and Michael B. Berkman, "Candidates and Policy in U.S. Senatorial Elections," *American Political Science Review* 80 (June 1986): 576–590.

Part III
Committee and Subcommittee Politics

7. Party Control of Committees in the Republican Congress

Steven S. Smith and Eric D. Lawrence

In November 1995 Speaker Newt Gingrich put his views about the future of the committee system in writing for *Roll Call,* a Capitol Hill newspaper. The Speaker made the case for task forces—ad hoc groups of members drawn together to develop specific pieces of legislation—as the means for formulating legislation. He asserted that

> the committee system remains an important resource as we draft legislation. However, I believe as the world is changing, we need to be flexible and find ways to get people with competence in a room together to solve problems. . . .
>
> The creation of task forces represents something other than mere rearrangement. The 104th Congress believes that while committees must continue to be used as the base of expertise for consideration of legislation, they can be augmented. We can assemble others who have an interest and expertise to focus on the specific issues at hand. . . .
>
> In balancing the use of committees and task forces, we should avoid considering them in a static "either/or" model, but instead use a dynamic, creative "both/and" formulation.[1]

The Speaker's comments were a response to criticism that the majority party Republicans of the 104th Congress, under the direction of the Speaker, might be subverting the House committee system by handing the responsibility to write legislation to task forces of the majority party. These task forces excluded minority party members, held no public hearings, made policy choices in meetings behind closed doors, left no formal record that can be reviewed, and made choices without the benefit of a full set of policy alternatives and full deliberation. The not-so-hidden fear was that the task forces would be dominated by the hand-picked political allies of the Speaker and not represent the wider range of opinion typically found on standing committees.[2]

In this chapter, we stay out of the argument about whether the House (or the Senate, for that matter) should center its policy-making activities in task forces or in standing committees. Instead, we ask whether the developments in the 104th Congress (1995–1996) were consistent with what we would have expected, given the character of the new Republican majority in both houses and other features of that Congress. To address the issue, we need a theory about the role of congressional committees in legislating that yields some predictions about the 104th Congress. We begin with the outline of such a theory and note its implications for the 104th Congress. We then review the record of the first half of the 104th to determine whether committee activities were consistent with our expectations.

We find that the 104th Congress substantially eroded the independence of standing committees in the House, extending a trend that was well under way before the Republicans assumed majority control. But the situation in the Senate was different. No substantial change occurred in the role of Senate committees. Senate committees have long had less influence over policy choices because of the ease with which policy alternatives are proposed and opposed on the Senate floor.

Theorizing About the Legislative Process

The legislative process is the product of choices made by the members. The Constitution does not detail the internal decision-making processes of either the House or the Senate beyond identifying presiding officers and requiring majority votes for legislation to be adopted. It does not mention parties, committees, or any of the organizational units that define the complex structure of the modern Congress. Instead, the Constitution allows each house to determine its own rules. Over more than two centuries of development, the two houses have developed similar but not identical decision-making processes through formal rules and informal practices.

Styles of Decision Making

The decision-making process of the House and Senate has three major components: committees, parties and their leaders, and the full chamber. The standard view of the modern legislative process is that parties and their leaders organize the committees and set the floor agenda; committees draft the details of legislation; and the full chamber reviews the work of committees and parties before voting final approval on the floor. The relative importance of the three components for policy making has varied. At times, central party leaders and the majority party caucus have been able to set a policy direction, formulate legislation, and gain chamber approval with only token participation by committees and without serious challenge on the floor. At other times, committees have set the agenda within their jurisdictions, written bills, and pushed them to final passage without change. Occasionally, however, the handiwork of committee and parties is set aside and completely reworked while the legislation is pending on the floor.

Historically, the Senate's rules, which allow extended debate and nongermane amendments on the floor, have produced a far more floor-oriented process than the House rules. This floor-oriented process has been labeled *collegial* because all members have an opportunity to debate, offer amendments, and vote on the floor. A more committee-oriented, *decentralized* process has characterized House decision making throughout most of the twentieth century. House committees and their subcommittees have assumed the initiative in policy making, and their work has been granted some deference in the formal rules and informal norms of the chamber. But at times, such as in the 104th Congress under a Republican majority, House decision making has appeared more *centralized,* with the agenda directed by the Speaker and major policy choices made within the councils of the majority party. Explaining these differences—the more centralized process of the House and the continuation of a more collegial process of the Senate of the 104th Congress—requires a theory of the legislative process.

Alternative Theories of the Legislative Process

Social scientists have developed two classes of theory about institutional arrangements.[3] *Efficiency* theories of institutions assume that the members' views about what is in the best interest of the institution, or perhaps of the larger political system, produce a choice of one set of institutional arrangements over other possibilities. An institution evolves as conditions change and require new arrangements because the members seek to maintain an well-adapted institution. For Congress, we might interpret Speaker Gingrich's rationale for an expanded use of task forces as an argument for an efficient institution. Task forces or some other arrangements, it could be argued, are the efficient solution to organizational problems that members within the same institution share.

Redistributive theories of institutions treat institutional arrangements as the product of competing interests among members. Factions and parties seek to establish rules and structures that further their interests, perhaps at the expense of the interests of other factions or parties. The political interests may concern enacting good public policy, electoral objectives, or other goals. But whatever the nature of the interest, it is the dominant coalition's interest that underpins choices about the rules and structures that give order to behavior in institutional contexts. An institution evolves as the balance of forces changes among the competing factions or parties. For Congress, we might consider competition between the parties to be a basis for the adoption of rules that advantage one party over the other. A new rule may redistribute parliamentary advantages between the parties.

The redistributive perspective does not imply that the general welfare or public interest should have no part in an explanation of institutional arrangements. For Congress, members' personal goals may be shaped by what they consider to be the best interest of the country or the institution. Moreover, political competition between parties may lead them to promise to serve the nation's larger interests and follow through on their promises. And at other times, the well-being of the institution or the nation is so closely connected to members' personal political interests that disentangling one from the other is nearly impossible. But the presence of public-regarding members does not eliminate conflict. To the contrary, competing views about the public interest may produce competition for control over the houses of Congress and motivate the selection of rules and structures that serve those views. In this way, redistributive theories consider service of the general welfare of the institution or nation to be a by-product more than a direct cause of institutional change and development.

We favor the redistributive perspective. Members of Congress treat most of the procedural and structural details of their institution as means to an end—perhaps as the means for enacting desirable public policy. Their differences over policy, or even their competing electoral interests, shape their views about the most desirable institutional arrangements. For example, senators' views about the filibuster seem to flip back and forth as their parties change from majority to minority status and back again. The "where you stand depends on where you sit" principle seems to apply to most of the rules governing Congress. To be sure, most members are genuinely committed to some rules—those few rules specified in the Constitution, for example—but members appear to place little intrinsic value on most of the internal rules of their institution. In our view, members' views of most chamber rules are utilitarian. If principle enters their calculations about the legislative process, it is by influencing their policy goals, which in turn shape their views about the best structure of the decision-making process within their chambers.

Redistributive theory suggests that we look beyond the public rationales offered by members for the institutional choices they make and consider the costs and benefits of the choices for members, factions, and parties. A good explanation of changes in the legislative processes is one that identifies those factors that alter members' calculations about the costs and benefits of organizing the decision-making process in one way rather than some other way. Three factors—the inherited rules, the nature of the issue agenda, and the alignment of policy preferences—shape those calculations and strategies in fundamental ways. The importance of each factor for the role of committees deserves a brief discussion.

Inherited Rules

Legislative battles are fought under rules that set many important features of the policy-making process: who gets to participate at what stage in the process, the number of votes required to adopt a motion or pass a bill, the nature of a permissible proposal or amendment, and even how proposals are packaged into larger bills. Rules of the modern House and Senate are quite different in many important respects—a product of decades of choices about their organization, formal precedents, and informal practices.

These institutional arrangements may place constraints on future choices. Members advantaged by inherited rules fight to retain them and often are able to bring considerable power acquired under the old rules to bear in the struggle. Sometimes the rules themselves affect future choices about rules. In the Senate, a change in the rules is subject to filibuster (unlimited debate), which can be cut off only with the vote of a two-thirds majority of the Senate. In the House, a rule change can be imposed by a simple majority. Consequently, proponents of reform in the Senate have little chance of success if their proposals disadvantage a sizable number of senators, such as the senators who comprise the minority party, but a House majority party can reshape the rules to suit its members' interests.

At the start of the 104th Congress, the leaders of the new Republican majority in the House knew that they would be operating under rules that allowed them to set the floor agenda, make informal alterations in the decision-making process, and even adopt new rules as long as the party was cohesive. The leaders of the new Republican majority in the Senate knew that their legislation could be long delayed, or even killed, by Democrats' parliamentary maneuvers and that there was no chance of gaining new rules that would add to their advantage in getting legislation passed. As both houses passed to Republican control, therefore, we would expect the more substantial changes in the rules and practices that shape the influence of committees over policy choices to occur in the House.

Issue Agenda

The size and salience of the congressional agenda affect the importance of committees to the parties and most members. If members want to process a large volume of legislation, some division of labor is required, which the committee system provides. Standing committees—committees with jurisdictions that carry over from Congress to Congress—are particularly useful if many of the policy questions are separable and recurring so that committee members and staff can develop expertise and expedite the creation of legislation. Over its two-hundred-year history, Congress's enlarging policy agenda has produced a nearly continuous elaboration of its committee systems.

At the start of the 104th Congress, House Republicans already had a policy agenda in the form of the Contract with America, drawn up under the guidance of Representative Gingrich, who was soon to become Speaker. Most of the substantive policy items in the contract concerned reducing the size and responsibilities of the federal government. Republicans saw them as closely connected issues. Moreover, most of the contract items would make lasting changes in federal policy, so would not be recurring. The Republicans also had a store of detailed legislative proposals that were ready to be considered without delay. These features of the House Republicans' agenda reduced the need for active committees exercising their own judgment about the best legislative approach to policy problems.

Perhaps more important, the centerpiece of the Republican program was to reduce federal spending, eliminate many federal programs, and cut taxes. These elements of the program could be accomplished, at least in theory, in a single bill—the budget reconciliation bill. Under the Budget Act of 1974 (an inherited rule), Congress can fold dozens of program changes into the reconciliation bill, which is constructed of proposals designed by authorizing committees and debated on the House and Senate floor under strict time limits. Republicans were expected to use the reconciliation process to send to the president a large bill that reordered federal policy priorities in a fundamental way. As in the past, the reconciliation process would place committee action under the direction of central party and budget leaders of the majority party of the House.[4]

Senate Republicans had not participated in the Contract with America, so their political commitment to it, although substantial, was much weaker than that of their House colleagues. But Senate Republicans would also avail themselves of the reconciliation process to package the many changes in spending priorities they held in common with House Republicans.

Alignment of Policy Preferences

When most members have a stake in the legislative outcome on a controversial issue, they are not likely to defer to a committee that does not share their policy views. Under such circumstances, the committee's role will depend on the balance of preferences in the parent chamber and parties. If members care about the outcome and the majority party is cohesive, the majority party has both the incentive and the votes to control committees. Central party leaders will be encouraged to see that committees either have little influence over outcomes or are stacked with friendly members. If issues are salient to most members and either preferences are not aligned by party or the majority party lacks sufficient cohesiveness, coalitions cutting across the parties—perhaps different coalitions on different issues—may assert themselves on the floor and determine policy outcomes.

The partisanship of policy alignments is quite variable. Highly partisan alignments have followed dramatic shifts in the coalitions supporting the two major parties, shifts that have been labeled "realignments." The timing of realignments in the Civil War years, the 1890s, and the 1930s gives congressional partisanship a cyclical cast that contrasts sharply with the more monotonic increases in the size and complexity of the congressional agenda. A pattern of periodically centralized party leadership appears to overlay a more linear pattern toward more elaborate committee systems.

Partisanship interacts with inherited rules to produce different outcomes in the House and Senate. In the House, a cohesive majority party can alter the legislative process to meet its needs without concern for the reaction of members of the minority party. In the Senate, unless the majority party is very large, even a cohesive majority party must be mindful of the minority party's ability to obstruct floor action on rules changes and substantive legislation.

Partisanship reached another peak in the 104th Congress. According to Congressional Quarterly, partisanship in roll call voting reached its highest point in more than four decades in the first session of the 104th in 1995.[5] In the House, we would expect this extraordinary cohesiveness within the majority party to be associated with a powerful Speaker who, in representing the party's perspective, receives House support for rules that advantage his party, sets an agenda, and directs the activities of committees on major legislation. Committees would exhibit little independence of the majority leadership. In the Senate, we would expect the majority to push forward with its agenda, but to be unable to alter the decision-making process to its advantage. The more floor-oriented process would remain.

Organizing the Committee System

Between the mid-1970s and mid-1990s, the committee systems of the House and Senate retained fairly stable structures and jurisdictions. The House had twenty-two standing committees, while the Senate had sixteen. House committees were more formally decentralized into subcommittees. These panels enjoyed certain rights to legislation and staff, and much of the initiative for new legislation came from them. Senate committees were not subject to as many constraints in the rules of the chamber or the majority party and therefore exhibited wider variation in their internal organization than House committees. Over time, members of both houses and both parties became more concerned that jurisdictional conflicts among committees had become serious and that scheduling problems (with so many committees and subcommittees) had become difficult. But a joint House-Senate effort to address these concerns in the 103d Congress (1993–1994) failed to produce any changes in the committee systems.

The switch in party control of the House yielded the most important changes in that chamber's committee system since the early 1970s. The Republicans were able to gain House approval of several rules changes that altered the structure of the committee system and the operating procedures of committees. But no significant changes were made in the Senate, where the new majority party Republicans chose not to stimulate long floor fights that might divide the party or filibusters that would obstruct action on substantive legislation.

Following the 1994 elections, Speaker Gingrich asked Rep. David Dreier, R-Calif., to produce a reform plan similar to the one Dreier had advocated as his party's vice chairman of the Joint Committee on the Organization of Congress in the 103d. Dreier proposed radical surgery on the structure of the committee system. His plan would have stripped the powerful Energy and Commerce Committee of its jurisdiction over securities, railroads, and energy policy and transferred the Ways and Means Committee's jurisdiction over welfare and health care to other committees. The plan would have eliminated four committees (District of Columbia, Merchant Marine and Fisheries, Post Office and Civil Service, and Small Business), given their jurisdictions to other committees, and combined two committees (Ethics and House Administration) into one. Nearly all other authorizing committees would have gained or lost jurisdiction in some way.[6]

Senior Republicans whose committees were slated to lose jurisdiction were quick to resist. In fact, the objections were so strong that Speaker Gingrich decided to avoid a fight on Dreier's proposal. Instead, the leadership proposed

Table 7-1 Standing House Committees, 1996

Committee	Republicans/ Democrats	Number of Subcommittees
Agriculture	27/22	5
Appropriations	32/24	13
Banking and Financial Services	27/22	5
Budget	24/18	0
Commerce	25/21	5
Economic and Educational Opportunities	24/19	5
Government Reform and Oversight	27/22	7
House Oversight	7/5	0
International Relations	22/19	5
Judiciary	20/15	5
National Security	30/25	5
Natural Resources	25/20	5
Rules	9/4	2
Science	27/23	4
Select Intelligence	9/7	2
Small Business	22/19	4
Standards of Official Conduct	5/5	0
Transportation and Infrastructure	33/28	6
Veterans' Affairs	18/15	3
Ways and Means	21/15	5

Note: Rep. Bernard Sanders (I-Vt.) is assigned to Banking and Government Reform and is counted against the Democrats.

the elimination of the committees on the District of Columbia, Post Office and Civil Service, and Merchant Marine and Fisheries and the transfer of their jurisdictions to other panels. Small Business was spared, in part because the Republicans did not want to be blamed for eliminating a committee supported by an important constituency group and in part because it was the only committee slated to be chaired by a woman. A few other jurisdictional transfers were included, as were changes in the names of several committees.[7] These changes were approved by the House (committees of the 104th Congress are listed in Tables 7-1 and 7-2). The promise of later action on a more comprehensive reform did not bear fruit by the end of the Congress.

House Republicans devised a set of additional rules changes that were approved by the House when it convened January 4, 1995, which are summarized in Box 7-1. We discuss several of these changes later in the chapter. Here, we

Table 7-2 Standing Senate Committees, 1996

Committee	Republicans/ Democrats	Number of Subcommittees
Agriculture, Nutrition and Forestry	10/8	4
Appropriations	15/14	13
Armed Services	11/10	6
Banking, Housing, and Urban Affairs	9/7	5
Budget	12/10	0
Commerce, Science, and Transportation	10/9	6
Energy and Natural Resources	11/9	5
Environment and Public Works	9/7	4
Finance	11/9	6
Foreign Relations	10/8	7
Governmental Affairs	8/7	3
Indian Affairs	9/7	0
Judiciary	10/8	6
Labor and Human Resources	9/7	4
Rules and Administration	9/7	0
Small Business	10/9	0
Veterans' Affairs	7/5	0
Select Committee on Ethics	3/3	0
Select Committee on Intelligence	9/8	0

note only that House Republicans followed through on their promise to cut the number of committee staff and committee budgets. They did so by consolidating the guaranteed "statutory" and the specially funded "investigative" staffs into one budget, cutting funding by 30 percent overall, and setting new caps on the total number of staff allowed.[8] Deep funding cuts for some committees, such as Ways and Means and Commerce, forced particularly sharp cutbacks in support for staff serving subcommittees and the minority party's staff and left a much higher proportion of staff under the direct supervision of full committee leaders.

In addition to the reforms of House rules pushed through by the Republican majority, both parties adopted rules that affected committee organization and operations. The Republican leadership imposed a plan that gave the Speaker "supervisory" authority over all Republican staff in the House. The effort by House Democratic leader Richard Gephardt of Missouri to adjust to his party's new minority status included a proposal, approved by the Democratic Caucus, that made the hiring of all Democratic committee staff subject to the approval of the minority leader. Rep. Louise Slaughter, D-N.Y., the chair of the party's

Major Rules Changes Affecting...

Standing Committee System

- eliminated three committees: District of Columbia, Merchant Marine and Fisheries, and Post Office and Civil Service
- renamed several committees
- newly named Committee on Government Reform and Oversight, previously called Government Operations, gained the jurisdiction of the District of Columbia and Post Office and Civil Service committees
- eliminated joint referrals (referring a measure to more than one committee simultaneously), but retained sequential and split referrals

Internal Organization and Procedure of Committees

- limited the number of subcommittees on a committee to five, except for Appropriations (thirteen), Government Reform and Oversight (seven), and Transportation and Infrastructure (six)
- cut the number of committee staff by one-third of its level in the previous Congress
- placed all committee staff under the control of full committee chair, eliminating the authority of subcommittee chairs and ranking minority members to appoint one staff member each

Box 7-1

Committee on Organization, Study, and Review, explained that the rule was designed to help the party make the committee staffing cuts imposed by new House rules. Rep. Bob Wise, D-W.Va., added that committee staff should know that they are working for the party caucus as well as committee chairs.[9]

The new majority party's rules related to committee governance lacked some of the provisions found in the old majority party's rules. For example, the so-called subcommittee bill of rights, adopted by House Democrats in 1973, guaranteed that legislation would be referred to subcommittees in most committees, that subcommittees would have fixed, written jurisdictions, that subcommittee leaders could appoint staff, and that means were established for the election of subcommittee chairs. The Republicans entered majority status without such rules and did not create them.[10]

The immediate political effect of these developments was to reverse many of the practices the Democrats had adopted in the 1970s. Republican subcom-

... House Committees, 104th Congress

- required committee and subcommittee meetings to be open to the public, unless an open meeting would endanger national security, eliminating the ability of a committee or subcommittee majority to close a meeting without cause
- required committees and subcommittees to allow still photography and electronic broadcasts at open meetings
- required committees to publish members' votes for or against all measures and amendments
- prohibited a chair or other member from casting proxy votes—votes cast for an absent member
- prohibited committees from using rolling quorums—indefinitely holding open a vote so that members could vote at their convenience to get around a quorum requirement

Committee Assignments and Leadership Selection

- limited chairs of committees and subcommittees to three consecutive terms
- limited members to two full committees and four subcommittees, except for chairs and ranking minority members, who may serve on more subcommittees as ex officio members
- increased the number of terms members may serve on the Committee on the Budget and the Select Committee on Intelligence

mittee chairs, appointed by the full committee chairs, no longer enjoyed the independence that their Democratic predecessors did. Even full committee chairs, operating with much smaller budgets, lost some of their independence from central party leaders in their formal authority over committee staff. While not fully centralized, committee operations and staffing became less formally decentralized than under the Democrats.

Republicans in the Senate also indicated their intention to cut committee staff by 15 percent. The Rules and Administration Committee proposed the cut, and the Senate adopted the 15 percent cut in staff budgets, but only after adjusting them for a cost-of-living increase.[11] But the Senate Republicans did not attempt to devise a committee reform plan before the start of the new Congress. Instead, a Republican task force later proposed that major Senate committees be limited to five subcommittees in the 104th Congress and four subcommittees in the 105th Congress. The task force also recommended that any committee that dropped below 50 percent of the membership it had in the 102d Congress be abolished. Neither the Republican leadership nor the Committee on Rules and Administration had acted on the task force's recommendations in these respects.[12]

Naming Committees and Committee Chairs

In 1995 the process of appointing committee chairs and members was subjected to the most important changes since the early twentieth century. As we would expect, the changes were more radical in the House, but the Senate Republicans put in place new rules that may have lasting effects as well. If the changes last, they mean a substantial weakening of the seniority norm, under which the party member with the most seniority on a committee assumed each party's top leadership spot on it. The House also set new limits on the number of committee assignments that its members may hold.

The majority parties of the two houses handled disputes over committee assignments very differently, reflecting the changes in the political circumstances of the leadership in the two houses. House Republicans led the way: they created a new twenty-six-member Steering Committee, which took over the duty of making committee assignments from the old Committee on Committees. Chaired by the Speaker, the new committee consisted of a representative from each of nine regions, a representative of the small-state Republicans, two sophomores and three freshmen appointed by Gingrich, the chairs of the Appropriations, Budget, Rules, and Ways and Means Committees, and the top six party leaders. To give the central leaders more weight in the assignment process, the Speaker could cast five votes and the majority leader two votes. All other Steering Committee members cast one vote.[13] Gingrich was instrumental in the appointment of freshmen to top committees—three of ten new Republicans on Ways and Means, seven of the eleven on Appropriations, and nine of the ten on Commerce were freshmen. Gingrich also asked for and received conference approval of rules changes that allowed him to appoint the Republican members of the new Oversight Committee (the old House Administration Committee).[14]

Even before he was endorsed for the speakership by his party conference, Gingrich exercised extraordinary influence. During the transition period following the election, he named new committee chairs—who then felt confident enough to hold press conferences announcing their plans—weeks before the Steering Committee and party conference met in early December to vote on chairmanships. For three committees, Gingrich bypassed the most senior committee Republican and appointed a more assertive, conservative, and loyal member as chair. These new appointees owed their chairmanships to the Speaker, a circumstance that had not been present in the House since the first decade of the twentieth century.

Gingrich went beyond the appointment of full committee chairs to influence the choice of a few subcommittee chairs as well. For example, he asked the new chair of the Government Reform and Oversight Committee to name freshmen Republicans to subcommittee chairmanships. The appointment of two freshmen—ranked thirteenth and fourteenth in seniority on the committee among Republicans—was a sharp break even from recent Democratic practice. In the last two decades, Democrats frequently prevented the most senior member from taking a subcommittee chairmanship, but then normally went to the next most senior member. Gingrich's intervention represented a significant change from the hands-off approach of recent Democratic Speakers.

House Republicans also sponsored, and the House approved, a rule, effective with the 104th Congress, that limited to three consecutive terms a member's service as chair of a committee or subcommittee. The rule was complemented by a Republican Party rule that applied the three-term limit to service as either a chair or ranking minority member. House Democrats considered, but chose not to impose, term limits on their committee leaders.

House Republicans also proposed, and the House adopted, limits on members' assignments. House members could not hold more than two full committee assignments or more than four subcommittee assignments. For years, critics had charged that House members' multiple committee and subcommittee assignments were responsible for frequent scheduling conflicts and the lack of attention some members could give to the work of a committee or subcommittee. Until 1995 the House did not have a rule limiting the number of assignments its members could hold. Only party rules applied limits, and members were frequently granted exemptions when it suited their interests or the party's. Beyond adding the new House rule, the Republicans also changed an important party rule by adding the Commerce Committee to the exclusive category, which included Appropriations, Rules, and Ways and Means. Members of these committees could not sit on another committee.[15]

No significant changes in the appointment of committee chairs or members occurred in the Senate at the start of the 104th Congress (see Box 7-2), but the Republicans eventually adopted a rule limiting the party's full committee chairs (or ranking members) to six-year terms. Senate Republicans had long allowed the party's members on a committee to nominate a committee chair or ranking member, who was nearly always the senior party member and who would easily gain endorsement from the party conference. Reformers hoped to give their floor leader more power by granting to the leader the right to name chairs, subject to the approval of the conference, but objections from some senior Republicans killed that proposal. Instead, Republicans adopted a rule requiring that committee members, and then the full party conference, cast secret ballots when choosing a chair.[16]

In a move that could have set a powerful precedent for Senate parties in the modern Congress, many Senate Republicans—particularly the more conservative and junior Republicans—sought to remove Sen. Mark Hatfield, R-Ore., from the chairmanship of the Appropriations Committee. Not since 1924, when

Senate Republican Committee Assignment Practices

Republicans make committee assignments on the basis of seniority—the most senior Republican requesting a vacant seat receives the seat. In most circumstances, this practice reduces conflict and eliminates politicking for or against senators seeking coveted seats. In some circumstances, a senator can be prevented from gaining a committee seat if a more senior senator is drafted to request it. At the beginning of a Congress, when many senators are seeking assignments, it is often difficult to tell whether a senator was drafted by leaders to block a more junior senator. At other times, drafting is quite conspicuous, as when Sen. Phil Gramm, R-Texas, sought a Finance Committee seat in late 1995.

Gramm wanted the Finance post to pursue his interests in tax policy. He also was a candidate for the presidency, running against Republican leader Bob Dole, R-Kan., who had an interest in preventing Gramm from gaining the platform of the Finance Committee to advertise himself and his ideas. According to press reports, Dole successfully blocked Gramm's appointment at the start of the Congress by finding more senior Republicans to request Finance. But Dole failed the second time. No Republican senator stepped forward to so conspicuously block Gramm's appointment, and he got the seat. It did not help his presidential campaign, however. He dropped out of the race after the New Hampshire primary.

In the 104th Congress, Senate Republicans adopted party rules that (1) set a term limit of six years on committee chairs or ranking members, (2) prevent a senator from reclaiming seniority once he or she has left a committee, (3) provide for secret ballots for election of committee chairs by committee Republicans and then by the full party, and (4) limit senators to just one full or subcommittee chairmanship, except on the Appropriations Committee.

Box 7-2

Sen. Robert LaFollette, R-Wis., was stripped of a chairmanship after running for president against his party's nominee, had a chairmanship been taken away from a senator. Hatfield was the only Republican who voted against the balanced-budget amendment in March 1995, a vote that angered Republicans who believed that a committee chair was obligated to follow the party line on such an important matter. However, even some conservative Republicans balked at the idea of deposing Hatfield, perhaps wondering who would be next. The move against Hatfield failed, but may have lasting effects. Observers noted that chairs became aware that many of their party colleagues believed that chairmanships were contingent on supporting the party on major issues.[17]

Setting Committee Agendas

Several influences representing a break with established patterns shaped House committee agendas in the 104th Congress.[18] The Contract with America provided a more explicit license for leadership assertiveness than is usually found in Congress. Speaker Gingrich, with the assistance of Majority Leader Dick Armey, demonstrated a willingness to take legislation away from committees or to overrule committees when they did not meet the leadership's expectations in acting on contract legislation. Once the Republicans decided to pass a seven-year balanced budget plan, the budget constraints substantially limited what actions could be taken by individual committees. We discuss these developments and then turn briefly to developments in the House Democratic caucus and changes in the Senate.

Setting the Agenda

The ambitious one-hundred-day schedule for the Contract with America placed immediate pressure on the House leadership. To expedite House action and maintain leadership supervision of the process, Speaker Gingrich created five task forces—crime, regulatory reform, term limits, legal reforms, and welfare reform—to deal with contract items.[19] Gingrich chaired an additional task force on Medicare reform. Although committee leaders were also on the various task forces, some committee autonomy was lost by having separate decision-making units. According to a Gingrich aide, task forces are a way of "finessing some institutional obstacles to decision making."[20] "Institutional obstacles," no doubt, included committees composed of members of both parties, committee practices that include hearings and markups that are open to the public, and committee rules that give the minority some opportunity for delay.

Majority Leader Armey was in charge of holding House committees to a schedule to meet the one-hundred-day deadline for House action on contract items. Armey said, "Newt has the contract; I have the schedule."[21] Armey asked for and received commitments from committee chairs to adhere closely to his schedule for contract measures: failure to keep to the schedule risked Rules Committee action on a resolution to discharge a measure from the committee and bring it to the floor in a form designed by the leadership and its task force. Armey pursued a lengthy list of initiatives, mainly program cuts, even soliciting support from other Republicans when committee Republicans resisted his suggestions.[22]

The relationship between House committees and the central party leadership was reinforced at the staff level. Senior committee staff met with leadership staff on a regular basis in formal meetings—a sharp contrast to the rather loose relationship between leadership and committee staffs under the Democrats.

Moreover, leadership aides played a significant role in the appointment of numerous committee aides. One of Armey's top aides, Ed Gillespie, was responsible for recommending the appointment of at least five press secretaries to their positions on major committees. The group met frequently with Gillespie to plan unified Republican public relations strategies.[23] The closer relationship between leadership and committee staff provided the leadership with timely intelligence about potential trouble spots in committee action, enhanced coordination of the flow of legislation to the floor, and reduced the possibility that intraparty differences would be spilled to the press.

Shaping the Content of Legislation

The issue of Medicare reform provides a striking example of party control over committee action. By placing himself at the head of his party's Medicare task force and taking charge of the details of the Republican plan on the issue, Speaker Gingrich assumed the initiative that otherwise would have belonged to the Committee on Ways and Means and its chair, Bill Archer, R-Texas.[24] Gingrich believed that winning the rhetorical war over Medicare would be crucial for passing legislation and that he was in the best position to be an effective communicator for the Republican Party. In addition, Gingrich felt that using a task force was the best way to coordinate the interests of the party.[25] According to the Speaker, "It's more than just centralization. It's an effort to pull together a task force, to hear the whole [party] Conference. You can't let [Medicare] be an isolated effort."[26] Gingrich's "design team on Medicare" was composed of eight members including the party leadership, Chairman Archer, Chairman Thomas Bliley, R-Va., of the Commerce Committee; Chairman Bill Thomas, R-Calif., of the Ways and Means Subcommittee on Health; and Chairman Michael Bilirakis, R-Fla., of the Commerce Committee's Subcommittee on Health and the Environment. The design team met frequently, and the committee chairs were involved in the decision-making process. But by taking the issue from the committees and using the task force, the Speaker avoided the usual committee review, where open hearings and markups, minority party participation, and the need to coordinate the work of multiple committees would have slowed the process and created more media coverage of the politically sensitive Republican plans.

The structure of the Medicare design team left the subcommittees of jurisdiction with less to do and frustrated the minority Democrats. Subcommittee chairman Thomas, like Pete Stark, D-Calif., before him, had his staff start drafting legislation on Medicare. In Thomas's case, however, the leadership asked him to stop work on his bill until they decided what they wanted to do. This interference may have worried Thomas, but he still believed that the leadership would allow the subcommittee to use its expertise during the decision-making process and let Thomas make the "right" policy choices.[27] Some Democrats were skeptical about whether policy considerations would take precedence over party needs.

James McDermott, D-Wash., who had led the fight for a single payer plan in the health care debate in the previous Congress, asserted, "I expect ultimately that they will take the issue away from him and do it at the full committee. The Speaker won't tolerate anyone who doesn't toe the line and whack the hell out of Medicare. Gingrich has his lieutenants and his sub-lieutenants, and you either deliver or you are stripped of your rank. So, I think he's going to get stripped of his rank."[28] Henry Waxman, D-Calif., typified Democratic frustration, when he commented, "In the Commerce Committee, the subcommittees are practically irrelevant."[29] Although the minority Democrats can hardly be considered disinterested observers, the views they expressed indicate a significant change in the way committees conduct business.

The handling of Medicare may be the most conspicuous case of leadership influence over committee decision making, but the House Republican leadership organized itself to more easily exert influence over many issue areas. At the start of the 104th, Gingrich created the Speaker's Advisory Group (SAG) composed of himself, Majority Leader Armey, Majority Whip DeLay, Conference Chairman John Boehner, R-Ohio, and a top aide to each leader. SAG met at least twice a week to plan tactics, work out the schedule and agenda, and discuss problematic amendments. While the leadership provided the core of SAG, other members regularly participated, including Bill Paxon, R-N.Y., chair of the party's campaign committee, Dennis Hastert, R-Ill., chief deputy majority whip, and Robert Walker, R-Pa., a longtime friend of Gingrich. By having regular meetings and by communicating frequently with important committee chairs, the leadership was able to direct the committee agendas and head off surprises that might embarrass the party.[30]

Assertive central leadership greatly affected the role of committee chairs. As noted, Speaker Gingrich appointed party loyalists to most of the important chairmanships, in a few cases passing over more senior members. On the Commerce Committee, Gingrich chose Bliley over Carlos Moorehead, R-Calif. Likewise, Gingrich appointed Robert Livingston, R-La., as chair of the Appropriations Committee, passing over three more senior Republicans. Some committee Democrats, such as David Skaggs of Colorado, felt that because Livingston had leapfrogged more senior Republicans, he would be more beholden to the party leadership.[31]

Democrats expressed a quite misanthropic view of the relationship between the Speaker and many committee chairs. Stark complained about Ways and Means Committee Chairman Archer: "It's as if the committee doesn't exist—it's a conduit for Gingrich's ideas. Bill, left to his own devices, might run it differently, but he's a toady to Gingrich."[32] But even Henry Hyde, R-Ill., chairman of the Judiciary Committee, which handled term limits and the balanced budget amendment, complained in 1995 that the leadership orders made him into a "subchairman."[33]

The fingerprints of the Speaker and majority leader could be found on many measures. Consider these items:

- On both term limits and welfare reform, the House leadership overruled policy decisions made by the committees and had the Rules Committee bring to the floor a somewhat different version of the measures.
- After the House Appropriations Subcommittee on the District of Columbia passed a bill that would give Congress more power over the District, Gingrich forced the appropriators to meet with city officials who opposed the measure to negotiate a compromise.[34] Effectively, the subcommittee was compelled to rewrite legislation it had already passed.
- Gingrich overruled Ways and Means Chairman Archer on tax breaks for ethanol. Archer's committee had eliminated nearly $1.8 billion in tax breaks for the ethanol industry, a measure that would help the gas and oil interests in Archer's home state. When legislators from states with ethanol interests complained to Gingrich, he told them that if they could demonstrate majority Republican support for the ethanol tax breaks, they could then use the Rules Committee to keep the tax breaks at the status quo. After Commerce Chairman Bliley put together a giant telecommunications bill that had bipartisan support, Gingrich interceded and forced changes that would ease the Baby Bells' entry into the long-distance market.
- After Appropriations Chairman Livingston complained about controversial riders being tacked onto spending bills, Gingrich again had the final word, this time clearly reflecting the view of most Republicans, and the riders remained in the bills.

By so frequently overruling chairs of major committees, Gingrich broke sharply from the leadership styles of most modern Democratic Speakers.

Nevertheless, leadership assertiveness did not always produce leadership success, as illustrated by the 1995 action on the reform of farm programs. The Republican leadership, especially Armey and Agriculture Chairman Pat Roberts, R-Kan., favored radical reform of the farm programs, with Roberts's "Freedom to Farm Act" as the legislative vehicle. The changes favored by the Republican leaders would impose losses on several farm states, and some members from those states were resisting the measure. When two Agriculture Committee Republicans, Larry Combest of Texas and Bill Emerson of Missouri, opposed parts of the reform bill, Gingrich initially sided with Chairman Roberts, but a Republican leadership memo was leaked that changed the political environment. A staff member for Majority Whip Tom DeLay mistakenly sent an e-mail message containing details of a Republican leadership meeting to a Democratic office, which gleefully leaked the memo to the press. In the memo, Gingrich laid out the possibility of stripping Combest and Emerson of their committee assignments. Once the memo became public, Gingrich denied that he would threaten the two dissidents and agreed to help reach a compromise between them and the chairman. Although Gingrich was willing to interfere with committee deliberations in the name of the party, he still needed to maintain support from the rank

House Subcommittee Assignments as Punishment

In late 1995 House Republican freshman Mark Neumann of Wisconsin voted against a conference report for the defense appropriations bill that was favored by Speaker Gingrich and Appropriations Committee Chairman Robert Livingston, R-La. Livingston, after consulting Gingrich, responded by stripping Neumann of his assignment to the National Security Subcommittee, where the legislation originated, and giving him a less important Appropriations subcommittee assignment in its place. Livingston gave Neumann's subcommittee seat to a loyal Republican.

Many House Republican freshmen took offense at the leadership's action against Neumann and rallied to his support. One was quoted in the press as saying, "This was an attempt to deal with Mr. Neumann that was also an attempt to send a message to the freshmen. We weren't sent here to kowtow to anybody. We were sent here to vote our conscience." The freshmen were appeased only after Gingrich gave Neumann a Budget Committee seat, which is temporary, and arranged with Livingston to allow Neumann to maintain seats on three Appropriations subcommittees.

Source: Quote from Donna Cassata, "GOP Leaders Walk a Fine Line To Keep Freshmen on Board," *Congressional Quarterly Weekly Report,* Oct. 14, 1995, 3122.

Box 7-3

and file Republicans. Once the memo became public, he risked appearing heavy-handed and capricious if he punished the dissidents by taking away their committee assignments.[35]

The controversy surrounding the Freedom to Farm Act illustrates the tension between the central leadership and the committee system. On many issues, the House Republican leaders believed that placing primary responsibility for legislation in the hands of senior committee leaders might jeopardize radical reform. Gerald Solomon, R-N.Y., chair of the Rules Committee, asserted that for major legislative changes "you can't depend on the committee system" and therefore the leadership "needs to pick up the slack." Before the Agriculture Committee met to vote on Freedom to Farm, the Republican leaders sent a letter to the committee, warning that if the committee did not pass the bill, "we will feel compelled" to respond, with the possibility of "bringing a farm bill to the floor within the next two weeks" with no restrictions on amendments. Similarly, John Boehner, chair of the Republican Conference and a member of the Agriculture Committee, told the committee that unless a bill was passed that the leadership supported, "the future of this committee is seriously in doubt." Later, after the bill failed to pass in committee, Boehner reiterated this stance, saying the inability to pass the bill "puts doubts in people's minds as to the value of the committee." These threats echoed early proposals by the leadership to abolish the Agriculture Committee, an idea that was abandoned for the sake of maintaining civility within the party.[36]

The farm bill controversy exposed the tension that arises between party-based and committee-based policy making when members of the majority party do not share basic policy views (see Box 7-3). Chairman Roberts said, "I understand marching orders, deadlines and ideology. But the proper policy decisions are equally important."[37] Combest registered similar frustrations: "If the people who are going to write ag policy are not on the committee, then why have a committee?" The conflict between Roberts (and the Republican leaders) and the dissident Republicans was eventually resolved after the farm program legislation became part of the omnibus budget reconciliation bill. During the reconciliation bill negotiations, Roberts met with Gingrich and came up with a compromise to placate the dissident farm district Republicans, including Emerson and Combest. After the leadership agreed to address the dissidents' reservations in conference, Emerson and thirteen colleagues agreed to vote for the budget plan.[38]

The Budget Process

As it had been used since 1981, the reconciliation process was used in 1995 to order committees to report legislation achieving specified deficit-reduction targets, thereby reducing the committees' freedom to initiate legislation as they saw fit. And, as in the recent past, the House and Senate budget committees, working with the majority party leadership, fashioned reconciliation instructions for committees with specific policy changes in mind. The House Republicans' seven-year balanced budget plan, which Gingrich devised after the demise of the proposed constitutional amendment to require a balanced budget, was implemented through the budget reconciliation process.[39]

In 1995 the deep spending cuts and the assertive central leadership combined to sharply restrict the options of committees in fashioning their reconciliation packages. In addition to the changes in farm subsidies, the leadership made alterations in many other areas. During the preparation of the budget reconciliation bill for floor consideration, Majority Leader Armey and Budget Chairman John Kasich, R-Ohio, killed or modified several provisions drafted by authorizing committees. For example,

- a Natural Resources Committee provision to sell off the Southeastern Power Administration was dropped;
- a Natural Resources Committee provision to create a National Parks Commission was dropped;
- a Government Reform and Oversight Committee proposal for changes in federal workers' pension plans was blocked; and

- a Ways and Means Committee provision to renew fast-track authority on trade agreements was killed.

In each case, a committee majority had approved the provision.[40]

House Democrats

While the House Republicans were responsible for the most dramatic changes in setting committee agendas, the House Democrats also took steps to reorganize to more effectively consider party policy and strategy. Tom O'Donnell, the chief of staff for Minority Leader Gephardt, observed that the Republicans "are certainly more centralized than we were" but "we're a lot more centralized than before, too, because of the challenges we face as a minority."[41] In fact, among the four congressional parties, the House Democrats made the most significant changes in their internal organization. Gephardt received caucus approval to split the old Steering and Policy Committee into two committees, and he appointed a new nine-member Leadership Advisory Group. The new Steering Committee was selected the same way as the old Steering and Policy Committee (top leaders, elected regional representatives, and a few leadership appointees), while the new Policy Committee was composed of the elected leaders, six appointed vice chairs, and the members of the Leadership Advisory Group. Gephardt chaired both committees. The Steering Committee was given jurisdiction over committee assignments, while the Policy Committee conducted research, wrote policy proposals, and devised communications strategies. The importance of these changes was limited in the 104th Congress because of the Democrats' minority status and the Republicans' cohesiveness, but they provided an infrastructure that could facilitate greater centralization of policy making should Democrats regain majority status in the near future.

And the Senate

In the Senate both parties tried to adjust to the shift in party control by altering their previous ways of conducting business. In July 1995, for example, the Senate Republicans adopted a rule that provided for adoption of a formal legislative agenda by the party at the start of each Congress, with positions on issues determined by a three-fourths vote of their members. The Republican senators were not involved in writing the Contract with America but were obliged to act on the legislation coming from the House. Their new rule could be the way to gain more effective party control over the legislative agenda, although it did not, by itself, make the party leader more powerful. In any event, the new rule was to take effect at the start of the 105th Congress. Both Senate parties, but more the minority Democrats than the majority Republicans, continued the trend toward greater use of task forces.

As should be expected, the Senate leadership was able to exert less centralized control over the reconciliation process. During Senate negotiations, a group of moderate Republicans persuaded Majority Leader Dole to modify the reconciliation bill by threatening to vote against it unless changes were made on Medicaid, health care for the elderly, and education funding.[42] The threats of even small groups of senators are serious because these factions can use individual parliamentary rights to slow down or stop the business of the Senate. Although the substance of policies passed in the Senate changed as a result of the swing in majority control, the shifts were much more dramatic in the House.

Leaders and Subcommittees

Since 1946, when the modern system of about fifteen Senate and twenty House standing committees was set, subcommittees gradually have become a more important part of the legislative process. Because of the House Democrats' subcommittee bill of rights and other developments, in the 1970s standing committees became more formally decentralized, with growing numbers of subcommittees and greater independence for their chairs. The ascendancy of the Republicans in 1994 brought significant changes to the internal decision-making processes of committees and subcommittees.

In accordance with one of the items in the Contract with America, both the House and Senate cut the number of subcommittees to their lowest levels in decades. House Republicans imposed a new rule to limit the number of subcommittees to five on most standing committees. Senate Republicans limited subcommittee assignments so that some subcommittees had to be disbanded for lack of a sufficient number of eligible members.

Moreover, the new House majority had no party rules that guaranteed subcommittees a substantive role in committee decision making. The full committee chairs exercised substantial control over their panels' internal affairs: they appointed subcommittees and their chairs, controlled all staff, and, on most committees, personally approved subcommittee activities. Subcommittees and their chairs, therefore, lost most of the ability to independently initiate hearings and legislation, which their Democratic predecessors had enjoyed. So, while the full committee chairs lost much of their independence from the central party leadership, the subcommittee chairs lost most of their independence from full committee chairs.

The balance of full committee and subcommittee hearings and meetings is one way to gauge the importance of subcommittees. During the 1970s and 1980s, more meetings and hearings occurred in subcommittees than in full committees. To assess the possible changes, we counted the number of full committee and subcommittee hearings and meetings held in the House and Senate during the first session of the 104th Congress (see Table 7-3). The most obvious conclusion is that there were bigger changes in the House than in the Senate, although the effects are clearer for meetings than for hearings. Also, the numbers reveal that it is still the case that more business is conducted at the full commit-

Table 7-3 Percentage of Committee Meetings and Hearings Held in Subcommittees

	100th Congress	104th Congress, 1st Session
House		
Meetings	52.0%	31.7%
Hearings	95.1	76.4
Senate		
Meetings	18.6	18.1
Hearings	64.4	50.4

Source: 100th Congress from Steven S. Smith and Christopher J. Deering, *Committees in Congress,* 2d ed. (Washington, D.C.: CQ Press, 1990); 104th Congress from the *Daily Digest* of the *Congressional Record.* House Appropriations Committee and subcommittee meetings and hearings are excluded.

tee level in the Senate. Although these figures should be regarded as preliminary, as we have counted only the first session, they give us more confidence in concluding that the changes in committee decision making were larger in the House than in the Senate.

The membership of conference committees also gives clues about the importance of subcommittees. Because conferees are usually the last members to alter the details of a bill before its final approval by the House and Senate, members seek appointments to conference delegations. The presiding officer of the Senate and the Speaker of the House generally follow the recommendations of the committee leaders. Under the Democrats, House subcommittees gained a central place in policy making in part because of the special access subcommittee members gained to conference delegations. By the late 1970s, most House conference delegations had become quite large and were composed primarily of members from the subcommittee where the legislation originated. Senate delegations generally have been much smaller than House delegations, regardless of the party in the majority, and the 104th Congress was no exception.

In their first year in the majority, House Republicans tended to appoint smaller conference delegations, sometimes only the top committee and subcommittee leaders. Perhaps most important, the Republicans left conference negotiations over the large budget reconciliation bill (their seven-year budget plan) to the three top committee leaders—the top two Republicans and the ranking Democrat—for most of the committees with titles in the bill. Only seventy different representatives were appointed to the 1995 reconciliation conference, about half as many as participated in the 1993 reconciliation. It is reasonable to speculate that the House Republicans of the 104th were so cohesive and so strongly led by the party leadership that representation of Republican diversity on conference delegations was not a major consideration. A small group of committee leaders was sufficient, even desirable, for the pursuit of such purposes.

The Democrats continued to select their subcommittee leaders as they did when they were in the majority—in order of seniority. Democratic committee members chose the subcommittees on which they would serve as ranking minority members, subject to the approval of the Democrats on the committee. No significant controversies arose as House Democrats reinstated the senior members as the ranking minority members in all committees. However, the Democrats, like the Republicans, barred the ranking full committee Democrats from assuming the ranking position on a subcommittee. Democrats also followed the Republican lead by eliminating subcommittee leaders' right to appoint staff. The full committee ranking minority member appointed all committee staff in consultation with subcommittee leaders, subject to the approval of a majority of a committee's Democrats.

The sharp change in House committee practices was not mimicked in the Senate. In fact, an effort by one Senate chair to centralize control over committee activities was quickly reversed. Early in the 104th Congress, several members of the Armed Services Committee complained when Chairman Strom Thurmond, R-S.C., failed to appoint subcommittees, apparently with the intention of retaining control over all legislation. All early hearings were held at the full committee level and, for the most part, Thurmond set the committee's agenda without consulting his party colleagues. Only when Thurmond learned that many of his fellow Republicans intended to force votes on naming subcommittees and assigning legislation to them did he relent and reestablish subcommittees.[43] Nevertheless, some recentralization of committee decision making occurred in Armed Services and other Senate committees. Cutbacks in staff funding forced some personnel to be recentralized so that staff time could be allocated more efficiently across the subcommittees. And the focused agenda, driven by House action on Contract with America items, reduced incentives for a diversity of subcommittee-based initiatives.

Appropriations Versus Authorizations

Conflict between appropriations committee members and authorizing committee members has been nearly continuous since control over spending bills was consolidated under the two appropriations committees early in this century. Authorizers' most common complaint over the years is that appropriators undercut programs by providing less than adequate funding. More recently, the major complaint has been that appropriators attach to appropriations bills various legislative provisions that alter programs and policies, which otherwise are within the jurisdiction of the authorizing committees. To be sure, authorizers sometimes encourage legislating in an appropriations bill when that bill appears to be the best vehicle for getting the legislative provisions enacted. But disputes between appropriators and authorizers have often become personal and intense, particularly when serious policy differences exist between them.

Under the current House rule, "no provision changing existing law shall be reported in any general appropriation bill except germane provisions which retrench expenditures by the reduction of amounts of money covered by the bill." The rule can be waived by the House when it approves a special rule providing for floor consideration of an appropriations bill. The rule does not apply to continuing appropriations resolutions that are adopted when the regular, general appropriations bills are not passed. Nor does the rule apply to "limitations," which provide that "none of the funds shall be used for" some specified purpose, thereby altering the effect of current law. These possibilities, combined with the fact that general or continuing appropriations measures eventually get passed, make legislating in appropriations measures irresistible for a faction, party, or chamber that may not be able to pass a freestanding measure containing the desired legislative provisions.

In the 104th Congress, House Republicans, often with the direct involvement of the Speaker, used appropriations to sharply reduce, and sometimes nearly eliminate, dozens of federal programs. For the Republicans, retrenchment often provided a basis for including substantial changes in existing law in appropriations, but they also used special rules to waive the rule on legislative provisions and took advantage of the multiple continuing appropriations resolutions to enact legislative provisions. Among other things, House Republicans sought to limit federal regulatory activity affecting automobile fuel economy, unfair labor practices, and on-the-job safety. The Senate resisted a number of these changes, and some were dropped or greatly modified in conference, but many were enacted.

The traditional complaints of authorizing committee leaders about such practices were largely absent. The usual public hearings that would be held by authorizing committees on such changes were not held. In some cases, authorizers worked closely with appropriators to craft the legislative provisions of appropriations bills. In other cases, it appeared that authorizers favored the legislative provisions but did not want to be closely associated with them and so had little role in writing law that fell under the jurisdiction of their committees. Yet, the Speaker and the Appropriations Committee chair were actively involved in designing legislative provisions for appropriations measures, which reflected the House majority party's control over the procedural means of passing its agenda.[44] The Speaker's involvement was particularly important because it served to insulate appropriators from potential criticism from party colleagues on the authorizing committees.

Conclusion

The party-oriented, centralized policy-making process in the House of the 104th Congress reduced the independence of House committees to a lower point than at any time since the second decade of the twentieth century. Within the Republican-led committees of the House, subcommittees were stripped of the independence they had enjoyed under Democratic majorities. Committee staffs were reduced and put under the control of full committee leaders; and they now have a formal connection to central party leaders. Full committee chairs were made more accountable to the majority party leadership. Just how long this new decision-making process lasts depends on how long the focused agenda and cohesive parties remain in the House.

Caution is in order when interpreting the developments in the House of the 104th Congress. A natural tendency is to assert that all power rested in the hands of Speaker Gingrich, perhaps by force of his personality. The Speaker enjoyed power to the extent that his party tolerated his exercise of it. His influence originated in the like-mindedness of his party colleagues and consequent ease with which he could set party strategy.

Yet, it is equally mistaken to assume that the policy cohesiveness of the House Republicans was a fully sufficient condition for the centralization of policy and strategy making in the speakership. The institutional context inherited by the Republicans—a majoritarian body of rules and practices—was essential to the success of the narrow Republican majority. Moreover, Gingrich's skill had at least a marginal effect on the decision-making process in the House. It was Gingrich's own judgment that asserting control over party affairs—even before his conference met and chose him as its leader—would be important to his gaining control over committee chairs. Gingrich quickly demonstrated his willingness to listen to his party colleagues, worked endlessly with the larger team of party and top committee leaders, actively courted the assertive freshman class, and sometimes backed down from policy positions, parliamentary tactics, and party matters as a consequence of pressure from party colleagues and factions. Still, the remarkably cohesive Republicans clearly wanted a strong leader who could keep the party's collective efforts focused and coordinated, and they got him.

The Senate was more party-oriented in the 104th, reflecting the greater cohesiveness of the parties in both chambers, but the Senate's decision-making process did not change nearly as much as the House's. In the House, the ability of simple majorities to bring up bills, fend off unfriendly amendments, and pass legislation enables a cohesive majority, even a small one, to rule the chamber as it sees fit. In the Senate, the ability of senators to offer nearly any amendment to nearly any bill limits the majority leader's control of the agenda. And the ability of senators to filibuster often requires that more than a simple majority of senators be found to pass legislation. Consequently, policy choices made within committees and parties are more likely to be challenged successfully on the Senate floor, and members of the minority party have effective sources of leverage with the majority party leadership.

In the midst of the sweeping changes that occurred on Capitol Hill since the 1994 elections, the basic institutional characteristics of the House and Senate remained unchanged. The House is still majoritarian; the Senate is still individualistic. The House is capable of great swings in its decision-making processes with changes in majority control; for the time being, it is far less committee-oriented than it was just a few years ago. The Senate changes infrequently and incrementally, even with changes in majority control.

Notes

1. Newt Gingrich, "Leadership Task Forces: The 'Third Wave' Way to Consider Legislation," *Roll Call,* Nov. 16, 1995, 5.
2. Norman J. Ornstein, "Is Speaker Gingrich Plotting to Overthrow the Committee System?" *Roll Call,* Nov. 9, 1995, 5, 30.
3. George Tsebelis, *Nested Games: Rational Choice in Comparative Politics* (Berkeley: University of California Press, 1990). Also see Jack Knight, *Institutions and Social Conflict* (New York: Cambridge University Press, 1992).
4. On budgeting and committee power, see Steven S. Smith and Christopher J. Deering, *Committees in Congress,* 2d ed. (Washington, D.C.: CQ Press, 1990), chap. 5.
5. Dan Carney, "As Hostilities Rage on the Hill, Partisan-Vote Rate Soars," *Congressional Quarterly Weekly Report,* Jan. 27, 1996, 199–201.
6. "A GOP View of House Committees," *Congressional Quarterly Weekly Report,* Nov. 19, 1994, 3325.
7. The jurisdictions of the old District of Columbia and Post Office and Civil Service Committees were folded into the new Government Reform and Oversight Committee, along with the jurisdiction of the old Government Operations Committee. Merchant Marine and Fisheries' jurisdiction over fisheries went to Natural Resources; its jurisdiction over the Coast Guard went to Transportation and Infrastructure; and its jurisdiction over the merchant marine went to National Security. Among other changes was the distribution of Commerce's jurisdiction over railroads and inland waterways to Transportation and Infrastructure; its jurisdiction over the Glass-Steagall Act (antimonopoly policy) to Banking and Financial Services; and its jurisdiction over energy research to Science.
8. The Republicans also changed committee funding from an annual to a two-year budget period. See Paul Nyhan, "House Approves Cuts in Committee Funds," *Congressional Quarterly Weekly Report,* March 18, 1995, 788.
9. Gabriel Kahn, "Democrats Nix All Reform Ideas But One: More Power for Leader," *Roll Call,* Dec. 19, 1994, 3.
10. House Democrats also eliminated their caucus rule that guaranteed subcommittee leaders the right to appoint staff.
11. Janet Hook, "Dole Pledges Quick Pace," *Congressional Quarterly Weekly Report,* Dec. 10, 1994, 3489; Janet Hook and Paul Nyhan, "Task Force Recommends Steep Senate Cuts," *Congressional Quarterly Weekly Report,* Jan. 28, 1995, 265. The Senate has adopted two-year budgets for its committees since 1989.
12. Kenneth J. Cooper, "GOP Plans Shake-Up of House Committees," *Washington Post,* Dec. 3, 1994.
13. This arrangement reduced the influence of large-state delegations, which previously had cast votes according to the number of Republicans in the delegations. It increased the influence of the Republican leader in the making of committee assignments. See Mary Jacoby, "Big States Big Losers in Gingrich's Plan for Committee on Committees," *Roll Call,* Dec. 1, 1994, 3; and Jonathan D. Salant, "New Chairmen Swing to Right; Freshmen Get Choice Posts," *Congressional Quarterly Weekly Report,* Dec. 10, 1994, 3493–4.
14. The Democrats also gave their party leader authority to appoint the party's members on the Oversight Committee.
15. Committee sizes and party ratios became unusually controversial in the House before the start of the 104th Congress. The new Republican majority trimmed committee sizes and allocated themselves a disproportionate share of seats on most committees. While Republicans constituted 52.9 percent of the House, they gave themselves 55 percent or more of the seats on most committees. As Democrats have done in the past, the Republicans reserved an even larger share of the seats for themselves on

Appropriations, Budget, Rules, and Ways and Means. Republican leaders' decisions about the size of some committees forced some Democrats to give up committee assignments that they had held for some time. Fourteen Democrats were bumped from the top committees—Appropriations, Rules, and Ways and Means. The loss of their disproportionate share of seats on the exclusive committees, combined with the small discriminations exacted on other committees, produced a shortage of about twenty seats for the new minority party (assuming Democrats on the nonexclusive committees wanted two assignments). The Select Intelligence Committee was made an exclusive committee, although its members rotate on and off and may return to their original committees. Commerce was made an exclusive committee for new members, and Democrats who had been granted waivers of the party's two-assignment limit in the past had to give up their extra assignments. The Democratic Steering Committee decided to allow members bumped from Appropriations and Ways and Means to take other assignments, but permitted them to maintain their seniority ranking on the committee that they were forced to leave, which allows them to regain the exclusive committee assignments when vacancies occur in the future. See Gabriel Kahn, "Democrats: 'This Is Outrageous,'" *Roll Call,* Dec. 5, 1994, 3.

16. David S. Cloud, "GOP Senators Limit Chairmen to Six Years Heading Panel," *Congressional Quarterly Weekly Report,* July 22, 1995, 2147.
17. Donna Cassata, "GOP Retreats on Hatfield, But War Far From Over," *Congressional Quarterly Weekly Report,* March 11, 1995, 729–731.
18. In addition to the changes discussed below, the House Republicans changed the rule governing the referral of legislation to committees. Since 1974, the House has permitted the referral of legislation to multiple committees. Multiple referral has become more common over time, especially on major legislation, growing from 6 percent of all referrals in 1975 and 1976 to 18.2 percent in 1989 and 1990. Multiple referrals have never gained much significance in the Senate, where intercommittee negotiations are routine as the Senate prepares for floor debate. As a way to mitigate the problem of cross-committee turf battles, the Republicans in the 104th House abolished joint referrals—referrals in which a whole bill is sent to two or more committees simultaneously. To replace joint referrals, the Republicans created a new form of multiple referral, the "additional initial referral." Under the new rule, the Speaker must refer legislation to a primary committee of jurisdiction, but can also refer the same legislation to additional committees with jurisdiction over parts of the bill. The Speaker may apply time limits for acting on the bill by the additional committees, and the primary committee may revise the handiwork of the other committees. The record of the first session of the 104th shows that the pattern of increasing use of multiple referral, established under the Democratic Speakers of the 1980s and early 1990s, continued in the 104th Congress. We collected data on bill referrals in the 104th Congress as follows: using Legislate, an online information retrieval service, we selected all bills that passed the House during the first session of the 104th. Of those 492 measures (bills, resolutions, joint resolutions, and continuing resolutions), 261 were singly or multiply referred. Of the referred measures, 40 of 261, or 15.1 percent, were multiply referred. This figure is greater than the *Passed as a percentage of total measures* figures for the 100th and 101st Houses reported by Garry Young and Joseph Cooper, "Multiple Referral and the Transformation of House Decision Making," in *Congress Reconsidered,* 5th ed. (Washington, D.C.: CQ Press, 1993), 214. Young and Cooper's numbers for the 100th and 101st Houses are 11.3 percent and 8.9 percent, respectively. Whether the small differences between the earlier Congresses and the 104th Congress will hold up once the current session of Congress is over remains to be seen. See Roger Davidson, "Multiple Referral in the Senate," *Legislative Studies Quarterly* (1989): 375–392; and Young and Cooper, "Multiple Referral."

19. C. Lawrence Evans and Walter Oleszek, "Congressional Tsunami? Institutional Change in the 104th Congress" (paper delivered at the annual meeting of the American Political Science Association, Chicago, Aug. 31–Sept. 3, 1995), 12.
20. Ibid., 13.
21. Jennifer Babson, "Armey Stood Guard Over Contract," *Congressional Quarterly Weekly Report,* April 8, 1995, 987.
22. Jackie Koszczuk, "With Humor and Firm Hand, Armey Rules the House," *Congressional Quarterly Weekly Report,* March 2, 1996, 525.
23. Richard E. Cohen, "Republican Leaders Have Instructed Their Aides to Revamp the Operations of Capitol Hill," *National Journal,* June 17, 1995, 1438.
24. Alissa J. Rubin, "Archer: A Quiet Conservative With an Explosive Agenda," *Congressional Quarterly Weekly Report,* Aug. 12, 1995, 2432.
25. Jackie Koszczuk, "Gingrich Puts More Power Into Speaker's Hands," *Congressional Quarterly Weekly Report,* Oct. 7, 1995, 3050.
26. Marilyn Webber Serafini, "Who's in Charge Here?" *National Journal,* July 1, 1995, 1710.
27. Ibid.
28. Ibid.
29. Koszczuk, "Gingrich Puts More Power," 3050.
30. Walter Pincus, "Centralized Republican Power House: Weekly Strategy Sessions Give Gingrich and Company the Right Stuff to Handle Congress," *Washington Post,* Sept. 9, 1995.
31. Jon Healy, "Livingston, Hatfield: Different Styles But Pragmatists at Heart," *Congressional Quarterly Weekly Report,* Feb. 4, 1995, 346–347.
32. Rubin, "Archer: A Quiet Conservative," 2432.
33. Cohen, "Republican Leaders," 1438.
34. All of the examples in this discussion are drawn from Koszczuk, "Gingrich Puts More Power," 3050–1.
35. Guy Gugliotta, "Democratic Tactics Prove Useful to GOP Leaders: Omnibus Bill Revives Rejected Agriculture Cuts," *Washington Post,* Oct. 8, 1995.
36. Quotes from ibid.
37. Ibid.
38. See Eric Pianin and Ann Devroy, "Clinton Pledges to Veto GOP Budget: President Points to Shrinking Deficit in Defending his Policy," *Washington Post,* Oct. 26, 1995.
39. The first item in the Contract with America, the Fiscal Responsibility Act, promised a vote on a balanced budget amendment and on a presidential line-item veto. The Republicans did not specify what they would do about the budget if the balanced budget amendment did not pass (it failed by one vote in the Senate), but the deficit hawks pressed for passing a balanced budget even absent a constitutional amendment.
40. Although committees found themselves highly constrained by central party and budget leaders, even Speaker Gingrich found that he was not free to operate independently of his party conference. Freshman Republicans were especially resistant to particular forms of compromise. Some of the deficit hawks pointed to Gingrich's opposition to the 1990 budget compromise and noted that the Speaker risked similar rebellion if he abandoned the balanced budget plan. As Christopher Shays, R-Conn., asserted, if Gingrich gave up on a seven-year plan, "He'd have 'junior Newts,' and he'd have more than one of us doing to him what he did" to Bush. The existence of a faction unwilling to compromise on the budget deal and the negotiating stance of President Clinton put pressure on the leadership from both sides of the balanced budget debate. See George Hager, "Historic Votes Add Momentum as Conferees Start Work," *Congressional Quarterly Weekly Report,* Oct. 28, 1995, 3282; and Hager, "To Deal or Not To Deal," *Congressional Quarterly Weekly Report,* Oct. 14, 1995, 3120.

41. Quoted in Pincus, "Centralized Republican Power House."
42. Alissa Rubin, "Senate GOP Appeases Moderates, Gets Majority Behind Bill," *Congressional Quarterly Weekly Report,* Oct. 28, 1995, 3290.
43. Janet Hook and Donna Cassata, "Low-Key Revolt May Spur Thurmond to Give Colleagues Freer Hand," *Congressional Quarterly Weekly Report,* Feb. 11, 1995, 466.
44. George Hager, "As They Cut, Appropriators Add a Stiff Dose of Policy," *Congressional Quarterly Weekly Report,* July 29, 1995, 2245–8.

8. Congressional Tsunami? The Politics of Committee Reform

C. Lawrence Evans and Walter J. Oleszek

Following the landmark 1994 congressional elections, Republican leaders unveiled the most sweeping reforms of House operations in several decades.[1] These reforms dealt with the policy responsibilities, leadership, and internal processes of the House committee system—traditionally the locus for most legislative work in the chamber. Former representative Dan Rostenkowski, D-Ill., longtime Democratic chair of the House Ways and Means Committee, observed that the new Republican majority was making "basic changes that are a virtual guarantee that the House at the turn of the century will be significantly different than it was at the beginning of this decade, irrespective of how long the Republicans retain control."[2] On the other side of the Capitol, Senate Republican leaders were less quick to embrace committee reform, but by summer 1995 GOP senators also were adopting potentially significant changes in their committee system.

What were the changes in the House and Senate committee systems adopted by the Republican-controlled 104th Congress (1995–1996), and why should we care? Why were Republicans willing to pass major committee reforms, whereas previous Democratic majorities had considered and rejected similar proposals? Are the GOP committee reforms likely to be maintained in future years, particularly if Democrats regain control of one or both chambers? What does the committee reform experience of the 1990s reveal about the nature of congressional procedure and structure? Addressing these questions is the purpose of this chapter.

Rationales for Reform

Under Article I of the Constitution, members of Congress are responsible for determining the internal rules, procedures, and structures of their respective chambers. The internal organization of Congress matters profoundly because it shapes the distribution of power on Capitol Hill and therefore the content of legislation. Members are well aware of the importance of congressional rules and structure. According to veteran Democratic representative John Dingell of Michigan, "If you let me write the procedure, and I let you write the substance, I'll [beat] you every time."[3]

By most accounts, the committee system is the central element of congressional organization and the major arena for legislative work in both bodies. Since the 1960s, however, House and Senate committees have received less deference from their parent chambers. Floor challenges to committee bills are more common now, and important legislative decisions are increasingly made by the majority leadership or in the majority party caucus. Still, on most bills in both chambers, legislation is usually drafted and publicized by members of the committee of jurisdiction, and much of the coalition-building process occurs in committee.

It is no surprise, then, that lawmakers periodically attempt to alter, or reform, aspects of the House and Senate committee systems. The term "reform" is somewhat ambiguous, but it is usually interpreted as meaning change for the better. Because of the linkages between process and policy, lawmakers often disagree about what constitutes an improvement in congressional operations. Even though lawmakers differ about reform specifics, there is considerable agreement on Capitol Hill about the range of reform alternatives that affect committees significantly. We treat a suggestion to alter the committee system as a reform proposal if lawmakers and congressional observers view it as such.

Committee reform initiatives are pursued in a number of different settings in Congress. One forum has been the annual process through which committees are allocated funds for staff and other resources. The biennial revision of House rules that occurs at the beginning of each new Congress provides another opportunity to alter committee structure or procedures. And over the past few decades, the House and Senate have periodically created temporary commissions or committees for the purpose of studying the committee system and providing recommendations for reform.

In 1973, for instance, the House created the Select Committee on Committees—informally called the Bolling committee after its chair, Richard Bolling, D-Mo.—which recommended a major overhaul of the House committee system. The following year, the chamber adopted a watered-down version of the Bolling proposals. In 1976 the Senate created its own select panel, chaired by Adlai Stevenson, D-Ill., to consider major committee reforms. The Stevenson committee recommended important changes in jurisdictional boundaries, many of which were adopted by the full Senate in 1977. Prior to the GOP-controlled 104th Congress, no fewer than six different panels had been created by the House or Senate to consider comprehensive committee reform.

In August 1992 Congress established the Joint Committee on the Organization of Congress and charged it with providing recommendations for reform by the end of 1993.[4] Early backers of the reform panel had argued that a comprehensive reorganization effort was necessary to confront a number of institutional ills, but initial efforts to establish the panel were impeded by the indifference or hostility of influential lawmakers who wanted to protect their power bases. However, by spring 1992 public outrage over the House bank scandal, which revealed that hundreds of members had "bounced" checks, mobilized public opinion in favor of reform, and Democratic leaders endorsed the creation of the Joint Committee. It was the main arena for the consideration of committee reform in the early 1990s.

Discerning the forces that shape congressional organization, particularly the structure of the committee system, is one of the most important and controversial topics for contemporary scholars of Congress. Three competing perspectives have dominated recent academic studies: clientele rationales, partisan rationales, and institutional rationales. In this chapter, we evaluate the relevance of these perspectives for committee reform politics in the 1990s. We also explore two additional factors: public opinion and the personal power agendas of individual lawmakers.

One perspective is that the House and Senate committee systems are designed to promote the policy goals of outside clientele groups.[5] From campaign contributions to the mobilization of voters, organized constituencies such as the veterans' community, labor unions, and agricultural groups control resources that are highly valued by reelection-minded legislators. Not surprisingly, members of Congress promote the legislative agendas of the groups and constituencies most important to their electoral fates. The committee system may be structured to facilitate such legislative exchanges. Clientele groups usually want their issues to be considered by committees that are supportive of their aims. Farm policy, for example, is consolidated within the jurisdictions of the House and Senate Agriculture committees, which traditionally have functioned as important advocates for farmers.

Another perspective is that the House and Senate committee systems are primarily designed to promote the policy interests of the majority party.[6] Although the partisan attachments of voters have declined in recent decades, parties remain the central organizational units on Capitol Hill, particularly in the House. The standing rules of the House, which codify the basic structure of the committee system, are typically adopted at the beginning of a new Congress on a straight party-line vote. And important elements of the committee system do appear to reflect the interests of majority party members. For instance, in both chambers the majority controls at least twice as many committee staff resources as does the minority, and full and subcommittee membership ratios are tilted toward the partisan majority.

Yet another approach to understanding committee organization emphasizes the collective benefits that a committee system can generate for the institution as a whole, rather than for outside groups or the majority party.[7] Some congressional scholars have argued that the committee system is designed so that individual panels are not dominated by narrow interests, but instead reflect diverse viewpoints on the issues they consider. Such "heterogeneous" committees are more likely to produce balanced policy recommendations and provide the institution as a whole with accurate information about policy alternatives. Indeed, a perennial goal of committee reformers has been to realign jurisdictions to promote a "balance of interests" within individual panels.[8] Many reformers argue that such a committee system would be more responsive to the policy and informational needs of the parent chamber.

Under certain conditions, the general public can mobilize behind proposals to alter committee organization. Ordinary citizens seldom develop firm preferences about specific aspects of the House or Senate committee systems: the

Major House Committee Reforms, 104th Congress

Committee Assignments

- Limit members to two full committee assignments and four subcommittee assignments
- Reduce committee sizes
- Increase leadership influence over GOP committee assignments

Powers of the Chair

- Allow Speaker Gingrich to appoint committee chairs
- Limit full and subcommittee chairs to six-year terms
- Allow members to chair only one full committee or subcommittee
- Allow the Speaker to appoint GOP members and chair of the Committee on House Oversight
- Give full committee chairs the power to appoint subcommittee chairs on their panels
- Abolish independent subcommittee staffs

Jurisdictions

- Restructure the committee system by abolishing the District of Columbia, Merchant Marine and Fisheries, and Post Office and Civil Service Committees and shifting their jurisdictions to other panels; transferring certain items from the jurisdiction of the Commerce Committee to other committees
- Limit most committees to five subcommittees
- Rename many committees to reflect Republican policy priorities
- Abolish the joint referral of legislation and authorize the Speaker to designate a primary committee of jurisdiction upon initial reference of measures
- Make systematic use of ad hoc party task forces

Internal Procedures

- Prohibit proxy voting in committees and subcommittees
- Prohibit rolling quorums
- Open all public committee meetings to radio/TV coverage unless deliberations would expose sensitive information
- Include committee voting records in committee reports

Staff Resources

- Reduce committee staff by one-third
- Increase percentage of committee staff allocated to minority party

Source: C. Lawrence Evans and Walter J. Oleszek, *Congress Under Fire: Reform Politics and the Republican Majority* (Boston: Houghton Mifflin, 1997), 88, 92, 106.

Box 8-1

details of committee structure and procedure tend to be arcane and far removed from the experiences and concerns of most Americans. However, if some aspect of the committee system is widely viewed as wasteful, corrupt, or fundamentally unfair, substantial public momentum for change can arise. Particularly given the highly negative public attitudes toward congressional operations that have characterized the 1990s, public opinion is an important factor in the reform process.[9]

Analysts of earlier reform periods have mentioned another influence on the committee system: the personal power agendas of individual lawmakers. Securing power helps members advance their electoral and policy agendas; political power also is valued for its own sake.[10] Important elements of the committee system may be shaped by the "quest for power" by ambitious lawmakers.[11] For example, attempts to alter committee jurisdictions often are stymied by shifting coalitions of committee chairs who fear that realigning committee boundaries will reduce their clout.

The committee reforms implemented by congressional Republicans in 1995 reflect two decades of discussions among lawmakers, congressional scholars, and pundits about whether and how the committee system should be altered. Most of the GOP reforms were considered and rejected by previous Democratic majorities on Capitol Hill. In evaluating the relevance of the five perspectives on congressional change, it is important that we consider reform politics under both partisan majorities.

Specific reform proposals also should be distinguished by the aspect of committee organization that is targeted for change. Congressional committees are microcosms of the institution as a whole. Proposals to alter the committee system can touch on disparate elements of congressional operations, from leadership selection to the distribution of resources between the two political parties. We examine the 1990s reform experience as it relates to the following aspects of committee operations: the assignment process; the powers of the chair; jurisdictions; internal procedures; and staff resources. For each element of committee reform, we explore the incentives for and against change.

We begin by analyzing committee reform politics in the House. A summary of the major committee changes adopted by the House Republican majority is provided in Box 8-1. The Senate committee reforms of 1995 were less significant and wide-ranging. They are examined in a separate section of this chapter.

Committee Assignments

Members of Congress receive their committee assignments through a process of constrained self-selection, in which individual lawmakers submit requests to their party/chamber "committee on committees."[12] There is a House Republican committee on committees, a Senate Republican committee on committees, and so on—each typically has its own special name. In the House, for instance, the GOP assignment committee is called the Steering Committee. Committee assignments help party leaders and individual lawmakers pursue their reelection, policy, and power goals. As a result, the various assignment panels attempt to satisfy as many member requests as possible. Not surprisingly, there is a tendency toward inflation in the number of assignments, as well as in committee sizes.

In the 103d Congress (1993–1994), House Democrats were restricted to just two full committee and five subcommittee assignments unless they were on the so-called exclusive committees—Appropriations, Rules, or Ways and Means—in which case their limit was one full committee. Waivers from this Democratic Caucus rule were so common, however, that dozens of members were on three or more committees. Reform-minded lawmakers argued that the assignment limitations should be tightened so that members would be spread less thinly.

The growth in committee assignments also translated into larger committees. In the House, the average committee size rose from twenty members in 1946 to almost forty in 1992; some panels had sixty or more members.[13] Many lawmakers, particularly committee chairs, argue that coalition building is more difficult in larger panels because the policy interests of more individuals must be balanced and aggregated. Party leaders, on the other hand, may override the interests of committee chairs in smaller committees because they want to accommodate the assignment requests of their partisan colleagues and build a cache of political IOU's.

An assignment issue emphasized by House Republicans throughout their minority status was the ratio of committee positions between the two political parties. On most panels, the distribution of seats was roughly proportional to the partisan makeup of the House, with a slight bias toward the majority. On certain panels, however, the disparity was substantial. On the important Rules Committee, for example, Democrats controlled nine of the thirteen seats—a two-to-one plus one ratio. While in the minority, Republicans backed proposals to equate committee ratios with the partisan composition of the House. They even brought suit in federal court to achieve this objective. Their demands were rebuffed by both the Democratic majority and federal judges.

The 1993 Joint Committee—after months of difficult deliberations, including a partisan blow-up among its House members—reported packages of House and Senate reform recommendations that offered tighter limits on committee assignments and, implicitly, smaller committee sizes. These proposals, along with the other reform initiatives recommended by the panel, went nowhere during the Democratic-controlled 103d Congress. Although most lawmakers recognized the benefits of tighter assignment limits, individual members opposed restrictions that would limit their own ability to take on additional assignments. Moreover, Democratic leaders believed that reform in general would be disruptive for the majority party and do little to improve the institution's public standing.

The prospects for internal reform changed markedly in November 1994, when voters elected GOP majorities in both chambers. In the House, an array of important changes, including committee assignment reforms, were quickly implemented by the new majority. House members were limited to two full committee and four subcommittee assignments. About a dozen committees were reduced in size, four grew larger, and the others were left unchanged from the 103d Congress. The thrust toward smaller panels was intended to facilitate prompt consideration of the Contract with America, the House Republicans' campaign manifesto.[14] As under the Democratic majority, the GOP maintained a nine-to-four margin on the Rules Committee, which they argued was necessary for the new majority to manage deliberations on the floor.

The most significant committee assignment reform adopted by House Republicans dealt with the makeup of their committee on committees. Prior to November 1994, the members of the House GOP assignment panel cast votes in proportion to the number of Republican members from their state. At the instigation of the incoming Speaker, Newt Gingrich, party rules were altered so that he controlled, directly or indirectly, 25 percent of the votes on the panel. The change was part of Gingrich's broader effort to consolidate his influence over the committee system, to which our attention now turns.

Powers of the Chair

For party leaders in Congress, the chairs of the standing committees are rivals for power. The chairs traditionally have significant discretion over which bills are scheduled for committee consideration and therefore over which bills are reported to the full chamber. Committee chairs also have significant informational advantages relative to other members because of their control over committee staff resources. They play a prominent role when legislation from their panel is considered on the House or Senate floor, and they also influence the selection of lawmakers to conference committee deliberations with the other body.

Individual committee chairs are usually responsive to their party leaders, but they also consider their own policy preferences and the views of other committee members, which can diverge from the party's legislative agenda. Reforms that strengthen the prerogatives of party leaders (who act as agents for the party rank and file) relative to the committee chairs tend to reduce the likelihood that recalcitrant chairs will impede, or not fully support, the majority party's program. Such reforms typically are adopted when (1) majority party lawmakers have relatively homogeneous policy preferences on major issues and (2) there is concern that the committee chairs may not be sufficiently supportive of the party agenda.[15] Unified congressional parties tend to shift power from committee to party leaders; conversely, divided parties usually prefer to center power in the committee system.

In the Democratic House, proposals regularly surfaced to transfer power from committee to party leaders. Some Democrats proposed that Speaker Thomas Foley, D-Wash., be granted the authority to select and remove committee chairs. Others argued that the terms of committee chairs should be limited to preclude the gradual accumulation of power by long-serving committee leaders.

Preference homogeneity within the Democratic Caucus did increase somewhat during the 1980s and 1990s, and Democratic Speakers became more active and influential in the legislative process during this period.[16] However, serious policy divisions remained in the Democratic Caucus. As a result, rank-and-file lawmakers were unwilling to significantly constrain the committee chairs. Speaker Foley opposed efforts within the caucus to increase his formal powers relative to committee leaders.

The incoming GOP majority was highly cohesive on policy matters. House Republicans had promised to bring the ambitious Contract with America to the floor within the first one hundred days of the 104th Congress. After forty years in the minority wilderness, they wanted their party to succeed and to maintain its majority status. But certain senior Republicans on important committees were viewed by their colleagues as insufficiently committed to the party's agenda. As a result, the new majority adopted several reforms aimed at making the committee chairs more accountable to party leaders and the majority rank and file.

First, Gingrich assumed the authority to name the committee chairs, rather than continue to rely solely on seniority. The incoming Speaker passed over more senior committee Republicans to place ideological loyalists at the helms of the Appropriations, Commerce, and Judiciary panels. Second, the terms of full and subcommittee chairs were limited to six years to keep chairmanships from developing into personal fiefdoms. The Speaker's term also was limited, but to eight years. Third, committee chairs were not allowed to head subcommittees unless granted a waiver by the GOP Conference. This change was intended to distribute power more broadly in committee. Fourth, the Speaker was formally given the authority to appoint the chair and other GOP members of the House Oversight Committee, which has jurisdiction over campaign finance reform and the administrative functions of the chamber, thereby transforming the committee into a leadership panel like the Rules Committee. Together, these reforms helped constrain the legislative discretion of the House chairs throughout the 104th Congress. One Republican lawmaker would later complain, "Being a chairman in the Newt Congress means not being in the room when the deals are done."[17]

The new Republican majority also adopted reforms that effectively repealed the Democrats' subcommittee bill of rights, thereby increasing the prerogatives of full committee chairs relative to other committee members. In the early 1970s, rank-and-file members of the majority party had also confronted committee chairs unsympathetic to their party's agenda. During this period, however, the backbenchers were liberal Democrats and the recalcitrant chairs were party conservatives. The Democrats were much less unified than their Republican successors; for them, *fundamentally* shifting power to party leaders was not a viable option, although more incremental increases in the Speaker's authority over the Rules Committee and bill referrals were adopted. Instead, Democrats weakened the chairs relative to other committee members by increasing the prerogatives of subcommittees and of subcommittee leaders. Collectively, the 1970s Democratic Caucus changes were called the subcommittee bill of rights. Subcommittees were guaranteed their own jurisdictions and staffs, and subcommittee chairs were to be chosen by the majority party members of the committee, rather than hand-picked by the full committee chair. By devolving power to the subcommittee level, Democratic reformers hoped to make the committee system more responsive to the policy aims of the liberal majority within their caucus.

The House Republicans also sought to make the committee system more responsive to the majority party agenda—but they chose to reverse the Democratic subcommittee reforms. Full committee chairs were given the power to appoint subcommittee chairs and control subcommittee staffs and budgets.

The factor that triggered this power shift was the greater preference homogeneity within the Republican majority. A united GOP was willing to cede substantial new authority to the Speaker and did not need strong subcommittees to constrain obstructionist committee chairs. Indeed, the majority Republicans viewed the subcommittee bill of rights as a potential impediment to prompt consideration of the Contract with America; independent subcommittees would add another layer to the decision-making process. Therefore, the GOP reforms increasing the prerogatives of committee chairs should be viewed in conjunction with the changes that strengthened the party leadership. Rather than provide chairs with the leverage necessary for independent action, these reforms largely enabled the Speaker, who could hire and fire the chairs, to reach down into the middle management of the committee system and ensure that it served the interests of the majority party.

Jurisdictions

The legislative role of a committee is rooted in its jurisdiction, the array of policy matters for which it has special responsibility. Formal jurisdictional boundaries are delineated in the standing rules of the House and Senate, and derive mostly from the Legislative Reorganization Act of 1946.[18] Since the 1940s, however, new issues have emerged that do not fall neatly into existing jurisdictions, and complex mega-issues such as health care, transportation, or the environment often touch on the policy domains of many different panels. A 1970s rule change further muddied the division of labor among committees by permitting the House Speaker to refer individual bills to multiple committees. As a result, initiatives to realign committee boundaries have been perennial items on the House's reform agenda. Jurisdictional reform was the most controversial topic considered by the 1993 Joint Committee on the Organization of Congress. And proposals to redraw committee boundaries created intense conflict during the transition to a Republican House.

Although members generally favor jurisdictional reform in the abstract (a 1993 survey indicated that 80 percent of House members supported some changes), specific proposals to reshuffle jurisdictions are opposed by the chairs and other committee members who stand to lose turf. Outside clientele groups, not to mention committee staff in danger of losing their jobs, also fight jurisdictional changes that would reduce the value of their contacts in the existing committee system. In addition, the lawmakers who stand to gain turf typically do not fight for reform as strongly as the opposing forces try to block it. Committee leaders usually prefer the jurisdiction they already have to the uncertainty of a major overhaul. Such factors have impeded most attempts to realign committee boundaries, and they were operative throughout the 1990s.

During the Democratic-controlled 103d Congress, members of the Joint Committee on the Organization of Congress considered a number of proposals to revamp jurisdictions. The panel's co-chairs, Rep. Lee Hamilton, D-Ind., and Sen. David Boren, D-Okla., initially urged their Democratic colleagues to support major jurisdictional change, citing the need to rationalize outdated committee boundaries and to distribute turf more equitably. The Renewing Congress Project, supervised by political scientists Thomas Mann and Norman Ornstein, enlisted the scholarly community to develop a congressional reform plan that included a well-publicized realignment proposal.[19] The Republican leaders of the Joint Committee, Rep. David Dreier of California and Sen. Pete Domenici of New Mexico, drafted their own comprehensive proposals for overhauling the committee system.

These attempts to mobilize support behind committee realignment were swamped by the organized and vocal opposition of committee chairs, party leaders, and other powerful Democrats. In the House, the committee chairs agreed to stand together against any jurisdictional shifts. When rumors surfaced that Hamilton was considering the Renewing Congress plan, Ways and Means Committee Democrats demanded, and received, a private meeting with Speaker Foley to protest any reductions in their turf. Foley urged Hamilton not to consider any committee realignment, predicting that the issue would create a firestorm within the Democratic Caucus. In the end, Hamilton and Boren decided that including major jurisdictional changes in the Joint Committee's recommendations would endanger the entire reform effort. They instead endorsed an attrition approach whereby panels that lost 50 percent or more of their members due to tighter assignment limits would be considered for abolition. This proposal died in 1994, along with the rest of the Joint Committee's reform plan.[20]

In the months preceding the 1994 elections, Representative Dreier tried to convince House Republican leaders that they should overhaul the committee system if their party won majority status. Like Foley, Gingrich was concerned that a comprehensive realignment would sharply divide his party. As a result, he did not include a proposal for major jurisdictional change in the Contract with America. Instead, the contract pledged to reduce the number of committees, without mentioning which might be abolished. During a telephone conversation with GOP leaders the morning after the election, Dreier once again argued for a comprehensive realignment of House committee boundaries. There was some support for Dreier's position among the leadership, and he was asked to draft four options for their consideration, ranging from incremental adjustments to a complete revamping of the committee system. Dreier presented his four options to the GOP transition team during a pivotal meeting on November 16, and he urged the adoption of one plan that would have significantly altered committee jurisdictions.

Dreier argued that his preferred option would promote a number of objectives important to the new majority.[21] First, it would abolish five full committees, fulfilling the contract pledge to reduce the number of panels. Second, it would consolidate jurisdiction over major issues within single committees, facilitating GOP efforts to move the contract items to the floor. For example, Dreier recommended the creation of a new Committee on Empowerment, which would have sole jurisdiction over the GOP welfare reform initiative. Third, committees would be formed to highlight Republican, rather than Democratic, policy priorities. Fourth, certain Democratic power centers, such as Representative Dingell's wide-ranging Commerce Committee, would be dismantled. The plan also would have distributed the legislative workload more equitably among committees.

Dreier's initiative caused intense conflict within the Republican Conference. Incoming leaders of committees that would have lost turf, particularly Thomas Bliley, R-Va., the new Commerce chair, vigorously opposed it. Clientele groups, such as the securities industry, also worked against realigning jurisdictions. Already ambivalent about the benefits of shuffling committee boundaries, and faced with a brewing insurrection within Republican ranks, GOP leaders decided within days of the November 16 transition meeting that a comprehensive jurisdictional overhaul would not be included in the party's reform slate.

Instead, the GOP leadership endorsed an alternative Dreier plan that advocated incremental jurisdictional reform. Three committees were eliminated—District of Columbia, Merchant Marine and Fisheries, and Post Office and Civil Service—with their jurisdictions transferred to other panels. All three committees considered issues that were primarily of interest to traditionally Democratic constituencies. Small Business—the other committee regularly mentioned as a candidate for abolition—was maintained because it served a traditionally Republican constituency and because it would have the only female full committee chair in the 104th House. A few items within the huge Commerce Committee jurisdiction also were parceled out to other panels, and committee names were altered to better reflect Republican themes and priorities. To cite one example, the Education and Labor Committee was renamed the Committee on Economic and Educational Opportunities, dropping the reference to organized labor. Most committees were limited to five subcommittees, adding credence to GOP claims that they were streamlining the system. Overall, the House Republican jurisdictional reforms were significant, but fell short of a comprehensive realignment.

In addition to abolishing panels and formally altering some committee boundaries, House Republicans modified the process for referring legislation to committee; this change affected committees' jurisdictional prerogatives. When Democratic Speakers referred legislation to multiple committees, they typically used open-ended joint referrals in which entire bills were sent to more than one panel. Republicans believed that this practice exacerbated jurisdictional tensions among committees. The GOP majority abolished joint referrals, mandating instead that the Speaker designate a "primary," or lead, committee of jurisdiction upon initial reference. Other committees receiving the same measure would be granted what the parliamentarians call an "additional initial referral," and would play a secondary role.

A final change relating to committee jurisdictions was first mentioned by GOP leaders during the transition, but did not require a formal alteration of chamber rules. Gingrich pledged that the new majority would routinely use temporary task forces to consider major legislation, rather than follow the Democratic practice of relying on standing committees. In the 104th House, Republican leaders formed a large number of mostly partisan task forces to help draft legislation and mobilize support on major issues. Examples include task forces on health, immigration reform, and even one on the entertainment industry chaired by Rep. Sonny Bono, R-Calif. The systematic use of task forces was part of the general strategy of shifting power from the committee system to the Republican leadership. It is worth noting that the reduced role of standing committees during the 104th Congress helped diminish jurisdictional strife among panels. Turf was less important in 1995 and 1996 because committees in general were somewhat less important.

Internal Procedures

Other elements of committee organization are the internal procedures and rules that guide the panels' deliberations. In both the House and Senate, committees have substantial discretion over their internal procedures, as long as their rules are consistent with chamber rules. As a result, internal committee procedures vary somewhat from panel to panel. Under the Democratic majority, there were no chamberwide rules banning proxy voting, a practice whereby members can miss a committee meeting but still participate in committee votes by letting a colleague in attendance vote for them. Only four standing committees prohibited proxy voting—Appropriations, Ethics, Rules, and Veterans' Affairs.

The minority Republicans had opposed the practice of proxy voting, arguing that it promoted absenteeism (or "ghost" voting), undermined deliberation, and gave the chair, who typically controlled the most proxies, excessive influence over committee outcomes. Democratic committee leaders responded that attendance at committee meetings was not essential for a member to cast an informed vote and that proxies made it easier for them to schedule bill-writing sessions.

In 1970 and 1974, the full House voted to abolish proxy voting as part of broader reform packages. Both times, the proxy bans were reversed in the Democratic Caucus. The abolition of proxy voting was included in the House GOP reform agenda throughout the 1980s, with Republican members of the 1993 joint reform committee considering it an important minority party initiative. However, without a cross-partisan coalition of sufficient strength to extend minority party prerogatives, proxy bans went nowhere in the Democratic House.[22]

In January 1995 the new Republican majority abolished proxy voting in House committees. House Republicans had publicly campaigned against the practice for so long that reversing their position would have provoked charges of hypocrisy from the media. GOP reform leaders such as David Dreier and Robert Walker of Pennsylvania also opposed proxy voting on the merits. Moreover, Republicans believed that their majority status might be short-lived, providing further incentive for them to abolish proxies while they had the votes. For similar reasons, House Republicans also banned use of the "rolling quorum" in committee. Under this practice, Democratic committee chairs were able to report legislation to the floor without a quorum being physically present: the chairs simply held the votes open, allowing members to come to the committee room, answer to their names, and then leave.

Finally, the House GOP majority adopted a number of procedural changes aimed at opening up committee proceedings to enhanced public scrutiny. Most of these changes were included in the Contract with America and were intended to increase public support for the GOP's program and congressional candidates.

Under Democratic control, committee meetings were usually open to the public, with radio and television broadcast permitted. There were some important exceptions, however, which created considerable partisan tension. Republicans regularly protested that meetings of the Appropriations, Rules, and Ways and Means panels were insufficiently open. In 1995 the Republican majority mandated that all committee meetings be open to the public and that radio/TV coverage be automatically allowed for all committee meetings unless the deliberations would expose sensitive information, such as classified material. The GOP House also adopted rules requiring that transcripts of committee meetings be a full and accurate account of the proceedings and that a record of how members vote in committee be included in the explanatory reports that accompany legislation to the floor. The purpose of these reforms was to address widespread public demands for a more open Congress.

Staff Resources

Information is the crucial ingredient in committee deliberations.[23] Lawmakers typically know where they stand on the main ideological issues of the day, but often there is significant uncertainty about the political and policy implications of specific legislative proposals, especially for complex issues. Committee staff are valuable sources of expertise.

By the early 1990s the number of House committee aides was approximately two thousand, or about 18 percent of total House staff; the number of Senate committee staff was somewhat smaller.[24] After almost doubling in the 1970s, the number of committee staff, and of congressional staff in general, had been relatively stable since 1980. Still, the notion persisted that congressional staffs were exploding in size, and that slashing the congressional bureaucracy was a reform priority with the public. The 1993 joint reform committee, for instance, proposed that congressional staff be cut by an amount equal to ongoing reductions in executive branch personnel. And for a decade, actions were taken during consideration of the legislative branch appropriations bill to reduce staff and curb staff expenditures.

House Republican leaders included in the Contract with America a proposal to cut committee staffs by one-third. Why did the GOP focus on committee staff, which accounts for less than 20 percent of total House staff? During the years of Democratic control, the vast majority of committee aides—80 percent or more in some cases—on most panels were controlled by the majority. Republicans viewed these staffing ratios as unfair and argued that majority party staffing was excessive. GOP lawmakers recognized that if they assumed majority status in 1995 the number of committee staff they hired would increase dramatically—even if total committee personnel was slashed. Republicans replaced staff with people of their choosing and reduced the absolute numbers.

Another potential target for reduction was the personal staffs of individual members, which constitute almost 60 percent of total House employees. However, personal staff are equitably distributed among members regardless of party, and they are primarily responsible for the casework, letter writing, and other constituency services so important to reelection-minded members. Aiming the axe at committee aides enabled the GOP majority to claim credit for what appeared to be a significant staff reduction while minimizing the damage to the majority's program and to individual lawmakers. For similar reasons, Republicans also were able to increase the proportion of committee staff allocated to the minority party. By spring 1996, however, some committee chairs were telling GOP leaders that they lacked the staff necessary to process Republican bills expeditiously and to exercise aggressive oversight over the Democratic-controlled executive branch.

Senate Committee Reforms

Compared to what the Republicans did in the House, their efforts to alter the internal operations of the Senate were less bold and less successful. Differences in rules, chamber size, and chamber traditions mean that the Senate is not as committee centered as the House. Senators have more committee assignments than House members, and they can more easily amend committee bills on the floor. Nevertheless, in summer 1995 partisan incentives led Senate Republicans, who had been in the minority for eight years, to adopt reforms that mirrored somewhat the more dramatic changes that were occurring in the House. The critical event was the vote by Mark Hatfield, R-Ore., chair of the Senate Appropriations Committee, against a proposed constitutional amendment requiring a balanced federal budget. Hatfield was the sole Republican senator to oppose the balanced budget amendment, and his vote determined the negative outcome.

Major Senate Committee Reforms, 104th Congress

- Limit terms of committee chairs and ranking minority members to six years
- Establish a Republican legislative agenda at the beginning of each Congress, with passage requiring a three-fourths vote
- Allow Republican members of a committee to select the chair by secret ballot, to be followed by a secret ballot vote in the Republican Conference
- Limit members to no more than one full or subcommittee chairmanship, except on Appropriations

Source: C. Lawrence Evans and Walter J. Oleszek, *Congress Under Fire: Reform Politics and the Republican Majority* (Boston: Houghton Mifflin, 1997), 155.

Box 8-2

Backbench GOP senators responded by threatening to strip Hatfield of his chairmanship, but the Republican Conference did not vote on the matter.

Instead, the majority leader, Robert Dole, R-Kan., formed a task force, chaired by Sen. Connie Mack, R-Fla., to devise reforms that would make committee chairs more responsive to the party leadership. A modified version of the task force's plan was adopted by the Senate Republican Conference in July 1995. The changes amended Republican Party rules but did not alter chamber rules.

Certain of the Senate GOP reforms directly affected the committee system, and they are summarized in Box 8-2. Like their House counterparts, Senate chairs would be limited to six-year terms. Prior to the beginning of a new Congress, Republican senators would vote on a legislative agenda for the GOP Conference. Three-quarters support was needed to place a policy proposal on the agenda, and the agenda would not be binding. However, votes on items to be included in the agenda would occur before Republican senators selected their committee chairs. Party moderates expressed concern that these votes might serve as a litmus test for the selection of committee leaders. The Senate committee reforms were to be implemented at the beginning of the 105th Congress; their impact on committee politics and committee power is potentially significant.

Conclusion

The committee reform experience of the 1990s has implications for our understanding of reform politics on Capitol Hill, the foundations of committee organization, and the likely direction of future change in the committee system.

All five of our organizational rationales explain significant aspects of committee reform politics during the decade. The relative importance of these rationales varies, depending on the aspect of committee structure or procedure targeted for change. For instance, clientele factors shaped the politics of jurisdictional reform, but not initiatives to increase the Speaker's leverage over the committee chairs.

Even though diverse factors can shape the politics of committee reform, partisan rationales clearly dominated during the 1990s. The impact of clientele groups was mostly felt during Democratic and Republican attempts to revamp committee jurisdictions. Under both majorities, interest group pressure and the opposition of important committee chairs precluded a major committee realignment. Certain proposals were drafted to create panels more representative of the chamber as a whole, but such proposals were quickly discarded. The changes in the GOP committee assignment process primarily served to strengthen party leaders, rather than promote a diversity of viewpoints on the major panels. There is little evidence that the 1990s reforms enhanced the informational efficiency of the committee system, and institutional rationales in general are of limited relevance for the committee reform effort.

Partisan factors were critical to understanding the reform process. While the Democrats were in the majority, significant preference heterogeneity within their caucus kept Democrats from substantially increasing the power of party leaders over committee chairs. In the 104th House, a highly unified GOP majority did shift power from the committee system to the centralized party leadership—and to the Republican Conference as a whole. From committee assignments to staff resources, the impact of partisan incentives was apparent in all elements of committee reorganization.

Still, a proper understanding of how partisan factors shaped committee reform requires that we look beyond the degree of preference homogeneity within the majority party. Many partisan incentives influenced committee reform politics, incentives that were conditioned by public opinion and the personal power agendas of individual members. House Republicans had included certain of their 1995 committee reforms dealing with congressional streamlining and openness in the Contract with America. Partisan motivations were behind the contract reforms, but they mostly took the form of position-taking for electoral gain, rather than a desire to redesign the House to advance GOP legislation.

The personal power agendas of individual lawmakers also conditioned committee reform politics during the 1990s. As mentioned, forceful opposition from committee chairs and other committee members blocked a comprehensive jurisdictional overhaul. But the pivotal reform actor throughout the period was Newt Gingrich, who used procedural and structural change to tighten his grip over the committee system. It is difficult to gauge how the Republican transition would have proceeded without Gingrich at the helm, but our conversations with members and staff, as well as close observation of the reform process, lead us to believe that he exerted a significant and independent impact on the procedural and structural innovations of the 104th House. Remarking on the new environment,

Robert Michel of Illinois, the GOP leader Gingrich succeeded, said, "I didn't crave power when I was leader—I don't know if it would have changed if I were Speaker. I just hope it doesn't go to our newly elected leaders' heads."[25]

Compared to the House, the pace and scope of committee reform was less extensive in the Senate. But even in the Senate, potentially significant reforms were adopted to make committees more accountable to GOP leaders. Partisan factors also shaped committee reform politics in that chamber, as many junior Republicans backed initiatives to promote party solidarity and cohesion.

How long lasting are the Republican committee reforms likely to be? By 1996 GOP lawmakers were urging Gingrich to delegate more responsibility to other party leaders and rank-and-file Republicans. With his public approval ratings plummeting, the Speaker agreed to decentralize power somewhat, but the Republican leadership as a whole remained highly involved in determining the day-to-day governance of the House. Power may shift back to committee chairs and rank-and-file committee members. However, the days of committee-based legislative fiefdoms appear to be gone on Capitol Hill.

What if Democrats regain control of one or both chambers in 1998 or beyond? In August 1996 Democratic leader Richard Gephardt of Missouri suggested that most of the Republican reforms would not be reversed if his party regained majority status. He promised to maintain the ban on proxy voting, asserting that it increased the efficiency of committee operations. Most important, from increased party leadership authority to enhanced congressional openness, the GOP reforms of the 104th Congress largely built on institutional trends that were already in place. The Republican reorganization should be lasting because the GOP reformed Congress in the direction in which it already was evolving.

Notes

1. An in-depth analysis of the congressional reform process during the 1990s is provided in C. Lawrence Evans and Walter J. Oleszek, *Congress Under Fire: Reform Politics and the Republican Majority* (Boston: Houghton Mifflin, 1997).
2. David Rosenbaum, "Strong Speaker, Strong House? One Doesn't Necessarily Follow the Other," *New York Times,* Dec. 4, 1994, 32.
3. *National Review,* Feb. 27, 1987, 24.
4. For an in-depth analysis of the Joint Committee's work, consult C. Lawrence Evans and Walter J. Oleszek, "The Politics of Congressional Reform: The Joint Committee on the Organization of Congress," in *Remaking Congress: Change and Stability in the 1990s,* ed. James A. Thurber and Roger H. Davidson (Washington, D.C.: CQ Press, 1995), 73–98.
5. David R. Mayhew, *Congress: The Electoral Connection* (New Haven: Yale University Press, 1974). See also Morris P. Fiorina, *Congress: Keystone of the Washington Establishment,* 2d ed. (New Haven: Yale University Press, 1989).
6. Gary Cox and Mathew McCubbins, *Legislative Leviathan: Party Government in the House* (Berkeley: University of California Press, 1993); David W. Rohde, *Parties and Leaders in the Postreform House* (Chicago: University of Chicago Press, 1991).

7. Consult Keith Krehbiel, *Information and Legislative Organization* (Ann Arbor: University of Michigan Press, 1991). See also Joseph Cooper, *The Origins of the Standing Committees and the Development of the Modern House* (Houston: Rice University Studies, 1970).
8. Evans and Oleszek, *Congress Under Fire.*
9. Ibid.
10. Richard F. Fenno Jr., *Congressmen in Committees* (Boston: Little, Brown, 1973).
11. See Lawrence C. Dodd, "Congress and the Quest for Power," in *Congress Reconsidered,* 1st ed., ed. Lawrence C. Dodd and Bruce I. Oppenheimer (New York: Praeger, 1977).
12. Kenneth Shepsle, *The Giant Jigsaw Puzzle* (Chicago: University of Chicago Press, 1978).
13. From 1946 to 1992, Senate committee sizes increased from an average of fifteen to more than eighteen.
14. The shift to majority status, combined with the influx of new members, also increased the total number of committee slots available to House Republicans, thereby making it easier to limit committee sizes.
15. Joseph Cooper and David W. Brady, "Institutional Context and Leadership Style: The House from Cannon to Rayburn," *American Political Science Review* 75 (June 1981): 411–425. See also Rohde, *Parties and Leaders in the Postreform House.*
16. Barbara Sinclair, *Legislators, Leaders, and Lawmaking* (Baltimore: Johns Hopkins University Press, 1995).
17. Charles Cook, "Lack of Leadership, Followership Produces House GOP Paralysis," *Roll Call,* March 11, 1996, 6.
18. In an interesting article, David King argues that committee jurisdictions change primarily because of new precedent created when the parliamentarians refer legislation to committee, rather than through formal reform efforts. See David C. King, "The Nature of Congressional Committee Jurisdictions," *American Political Science Review* 88 (March 1994): 48–62. King's conclusion is overdrawn. Consider the impact of the 1974 House reforms on the distribution of health care jurisdiction between the Commerce Committee and the Ways and Means Committee. King states that these reforms "maintain the preexisting distinction between the committees and that the net effect of the 1974 reforms was to write down in the Rules Manual the established common law jurisdictions governing bill referrals on health issues." This assertion is simply inaccurate. The 1974 House reforms shifted to Commerce jurisdiction over those health titles of the Social Security Act not financed by payroll deductions, including portions of Medicare. In the Congress immediately preceding implementation of the 1974 reforms, the Commerce Committee received exactly zero referrals of legislation dealing with the Medicare program. In the Congress immediately following implementation of the reforms, the panel received 31 exclusive referrals and 230 joint referrals in the issue area. See Carol P. Hardy, Paul S. Rundquist, and Judy Schneider, "House Committee Jurisdiction over Medicare," *Congressional Research Service,* 1986. Precedent matters, but formal reforms also are an important source of jurisdictional change on Capitol Hill.
19. Thomas E. Mann and Norman J. Ornstein, *Renewing Congress: A Second Report* (Washington, D.C.: American Enterprise Institute and Brookings, 1993). Also consult Mann and Ornstein's *Renewing Congress: A Progress Report,* a 1994 evaluation of the Joint Committee's reform package. Matt Pinkus ably assisted in the preparation of these studies.
20. Evans and Oleszek, "The Politics of Congressional Reform."
21. C. Lawrence Evans and Walter J. Oleszek, "Reform Redux: Jurisdictional Change

and the Republican House" (paper presented at the annual meeting of the Midwest Political Science Association, Chicago, April 6–8, 1995).
22. Sarah A. Binder and Steven S. Smith, "Acquired Procedural Tendencies and Congressional Reform," in *Remaking Congress,* 53–72. See also Evans and Oleszek, "The Politics of Congressional Reform."
23. C. Lawrence Evans, *Leadership in Committee* (Ann Arbor: University of Michigan Press, 1991), chap. 2.
24. Joint Committee on the Organization of Congress, *Background Materials,* Senate Print 103–55, 1993, 103d Cong., 1st sess., 1393.
25. "On Way Out, Michel Stops to Warn GOP," *Washington Times,* Nov. 26, 1994, A2.

9. Institutional Change and Behavioral Choice in House Committees

Richard L. Hall and Gary J. McKissick

Over the last two decades, congressional scholars have shown a greater interest in the ways institutional arrangements shape legislative decision making. The allocation of parliamentary rights and prerogatives, embedded in the rules of each chamber of Congress, helps transform the institution from the simple majoritarian assembly it appears to be on constitutional parchment to the contemporary assembly we observe, where influence over legislation varies from member to member and issue to issue. Simply put, the Jeffersonian principle that each member is the equal of every other appears infrequently in the practice of legislative choice. Why? Among other reasons, the rules do not treat everyone the same at every stage of the legislative game.

Significant changes in those rules therefore deserve careful study. If institutional arrangements channel and constrain members' behavior in significant ways, then reform-induced rearrangements ought to generate significant behavioral change. This premise appears central in the extensive literature generated by the reforms of the early 1970s. Indeed, those reforms were considered so important that they gave designation to a congressional era: from the mid-1970s through the mid-1990s Congress was universally labeled postreform.[1] This premise, in turn, underpins the considerable attention that students of Congress have paid to the House reforms of 1995. Participant observers have described these internal rearrangements as "historic," "monumental," or "revolutionary." The best congressional scholars have described them as "profound."[2]

However dramatic the descriptions, systematic research on the behavioral changes fostered by institutional reform is somewhat thin. Institutional arrangements, one can rightly theorize, count as an important class of variables that structure individual behavior in a process of collective legislative choice. But what specific behavioral changes do we observe in the aftermath of institutional reform? And to what extent do those changes flow from changes in institutional arrangements?

To answer these questions, we begin with this premise: members of Congress make two types of choices for every issue that comes before them. First, they must decide what position they will take, positions most often expressed in their various votes on recorded roll calls. Second, they must also decide how active they will be—how much they will participate in legislative deliberations on any given bill.

While the first type of behavior has been widely studied, it is difficult to overestimate the importance of the second. Taken together, members' participation decisions prefigure the range of views and values that receive representation and stand to matter on the particular issues under consideration. This is especially true at the earliest and typically most important stages of decision making, namely, the deliberations in and around the committees of jurisdiction. Writing the provisions of a bill, offering amendments, deploying obstructionist tactics, negotiating with outside actors, persuading colleagues to adopt one's point of view—all these activities weigh heavily in the decision-making calculus of most bills. David Mayhew states the general principle: "In small working units, formal voting tends to recede in importance as a determinant of outcomes, and what individuals do with their time and energy rises in importance."[3]

We investigate changes in committee decision making brought about by the 1995 House reforms, taking Mayhew's principle as our point of departure. Conventional accounts to the contrary, we argue that there is little theoretical reason to expect that even these historically dramatic reforms have dramatic behavioral effects. We evaluate this argument using data from before and after the reforms. We conclude that less changed as a result of the 1995 reforms than meets the eye.

The Intentions of the 1995 Committee Reforms

As other chapters in this volume describe, many of the most important institutional rearrangements sought to alter troublesome patterns of decentralized decision making. In particular, the 104th House reorganized committee jurisdictions to cut by three the number of standing committees and by twenty-one the number of standing subcommittees. In addition, the leadership cut back the use of multiple bill referrals so that duplicative reviews would eat up less of members' time and provide fewer occasions for conflict and delay. House members, whose frustration with the inefficiency of the chamber had grown since the 1970s, would serve on fewer panels and consider fewer bills, allowing them to concentrate on matters falling within their committees' newly delineated jurisdictions. This tendency, in turn, would be reinforced by procedural changes that gave members greater incentives to tend to their committee work, namely, an abrupt ban on proxy voting in committee and a new requirement that committee votes (and the failure to vote) be officially published.

A second important impulse of the 104th reforms was to recentralize power within the committee system. Members and critics of House organization had come to lament the extent to which power had devolved to the scores of subcommittees over the previous two decades. House subcommittees had become "new channels for policymaking," according to one of the most knowledgeable students of the institution.[4] Members of Congress saw them as the principal venues for legislative participation. "The most important thing is getting a seat at the table," one committee staffer commented in the mid-1980s. "If you're on the subcommittee, you've got that." Such decision-making patterns led three prominent scholars to advocate a return to earlier days when a "full committee maintaining a broader representation of interests could mute the excessive enthusiasms of each of its subcommittees."[5]

The 1995 reforms attempted to do just that. According to the new rules, subcommittees would be stripped of their own budgets and staff; they would lose their nearly automatic right of referral and therefore first review of bills within their jurisdictions; members would lose some of their ability to place themselves on subcommittees, a process that allegedly had led to the overrepresentation of those with "excessive enthusiasms"; and subcommittee chair selection would no longer follow a simple seniority rule. In short, the opportunities of subcommittee members to participate, the resources to participate, and the level of interest motivating participation were to diminish as a result of the reforms.

A third organizational change involved substantial cutbacks in committee staff. The growth in staff since the mid-1970s had raised concerns about an increasingly bureaucratic Congress and whether staffs were becoming too powerful. Staff cuts were not new with the 104th Congress, however. The Democratic 103d Congress had cut staff by about 10 percent. But the reformers of the 104th imposed cuts of an additional 30 percent. Subcommittee staffs were eliminated altogether, and committee staff payrolls were slashed across the board. Subcommittee chairs, in particular, would be constrained to legislate (or not) more on their own rather than delegating their constitutional work to unelected representatives.

These, at least, were some of the goals of the 1995 House reforms. But were they realistic goals? To answer that question requires careful attention to behavioral theory, which raises two other questions that must be answered first: What are the factors that affect members' participation in committee decision making, and to what extent do the reforms manipulate those factors? Stated somewhat differently, we need a theory of behavior before we can make informed speculations about how specific organizational and procedural changes might affect that behavior.

The components of such a theory have been elaborated elsewhere and form the basis for our analysis here.[6] Why do members participate (sometimes and not others) in the time-consuming, tedious business of legislating? We will briefly sketch some of the most important factors, so we can then assess how the Republican reforms of 1995 might affect important behavioral patterns in committee.

Participation in Committee: An Overview

Participation in Congress is seldom universal; it is never equal.[7] This fact is obvious to the most casual observer of the House floor, where even the most important debates typically involve only a handful of members. But it is also true in committee. Within these specialized workgroups, the nominal specialists who actively legislate on any given bill are few in number, sometimes only two or three.

That the majority of committee members do not faithfully attend to all of their committee work does not reflect member indolence. It has been a constant of legislative life for some time that lawmakers have too much to do and too little time to do it. "I feel like I'm spread thin all the time," one House member observed in 1984. "There's never any time to read or think an issue through or anything like that." A member elected in 1994 expressed a similar frustration. "I had big plans when I got here. I wanted to do everything; I had about six different areas. But there just isn't time. I can't even keep up with the health stuff." Elizabeth Drew quotes one representative who summarizes the almost universal frustrations of the job:

> There are just too many votes, too many issues, too many meetings, too many attention-demanding situations. We're going to committee meetings, subcommittee meetings, caucuses—a caucus of the class with which you were elected here, the rural caucus, the steel caucus, you name it—and we're seeing constituents and returning phone calls and trying to rush back and forth to the district, and then we're supposed to understand what we're voting on when we get to the House floor.[8]

Such observations were systematically confirmed in a survey administered by the House Commission on Administrative Review in 1977. Analyzing data drawn from that survey, Thomas O'Donnell concluded that House members' "ability to concentrate time on any single activity is severely constrained by the abundance and complexity of the demands that confront them."[9] If anything, the time pressures have increased in the two decades since. Studies of congressional organization in the 1980s and again in the 1990s came to similar conclusions.

In sum, it is an organizational fact of life that individual members of Congress act in some areas, but mostly abdicate in others. The member and her staff are constantly pulled between the lure of legislative opportunities and the limits on what they can do. They cannot be involved in every issue, even those issues that come before the committees and subcommittees on which the member sits. She must choose. The choices are made on a case-by-case basis as the office decides whether a particular issue is, as one staffer put it, "worth our time."

Participation and Interest

Several factors influence those determinations. Perhaps the most important is the perception that an issue affects the member's interests. In a word, member behavior is purposive.[10] Serving one's constituents is among the purposes most often mentioned, even on committees that are not normally thought to be constituency oriented. Historically, House Education and Labor was one of the most ideologically charged committees in Congress, but constituency motivations frequently and systematically affect member participation there. For instance, the legislative assistant to a senior member of the committee explained her boss's role in reauthorizing the Older Americans Act:

> Older Americans is so important to the district for demographic reasons. The district is the tenth most senior district in the country, the other nine being in Florida. It's a very stable community of immigrants, and [the Older Americans] programs affect them directly.

More generally, however, members and their staffs cite a variety of interests that affect their participation in committee work. Many of these interests influence their decisions about which committees and subcommittees they seek, so that they put themselves in a good institutional position to pursue those interests. In particular, the member's personal policy views, partisan loyalties, and concern with chamber reputation count as important motives. For example, in pushing President Clinton's National Service bill through the House during the 1993–1994 session, Rep. William Ford, D-Mich., was concerned with both prosecuting the agenda of a Democratic president and making a mark on important legislation.[11] Because Ford planned to retire in 1994, reelection considerations did not matter. Likewise, the Republican members who led the assault on agricultural subsidies in 1995 did so out of faith in free markets and their distaste for federal deficits, not their desire for electoral dividends.

In short, while members may seldom take the lead on issues that will do them direct political harm, concern with reelection is only one of several important interests that affect their committee participation. One senior Republican member explained his participation on the House Education and Labor Committee:

> First, you look at how it affects your district. What legislation would be beneficial to your constituents. Second, there's personal interests. I'm a former school superintendent, so I'm going to be involved in education matters. Even within education, I have some real pets. If you're talking about the training of administrators, that's something I'd be interested in. If you're talking about recruiting teachers, that's something I'd be interested in. If you're talking about school lunch or child nutrition, the same. Because that's something I feel strongly about.

Legislative Resources

Participation in committee tends to be interest-driven, but few members are able to pursue their interests on more than a few bills with any efficacy. Procedural prerogatives and institutionally provided budgets and staff are unevenly distributed. These resources count as important subsidies to members' investments in legislative activity. Their reallocation through organizational reforms, one might surmise, should affect who makes the laws in House committees.

Both before and after reform, official committee leaders could claim a number of legislative advantages. First, committee chairs and, to a lesser extent, ranking minority members enjoy certain procedural prerogatives not available to the average backbencher. They have considerable control over the committee's agenda, the scheduling of meetings, and the progress of legislation. If committee action is likely to conflict with other business that the chair finds important or otherwise violates some strategic purpose, the chair can adjust the nature and timing of committee events.

Rep. John Dingell, D-Mich., who chaired the House Commerce Committee from 1981 to 1994, provides a case study in how such prerogatives can be exploited to the leader's advantage. The 1984 Natural Gas Policy Act involved the deregulation of natural gas prices and therefore the transfer of billions of dollars from one region of the country to another and from consumers to natural gas corporations.[12] For almost a year during the 98th Congress, Dingell avoided bringing the bill to committee markup, fearing that proponents of deregulation had the votes to push through amendments that benefited the gas industry and hurt energy-consuming areas such as Dingell's home state. When Dingell finally convened a full committee markup, one member walked over to him and boasted, "John, we've got the votes." Dingell replied, "Yeah, but I've got the gavel." He soon illustrated the difference. When markup began, he first allowed consideration on two amendments that would reveal the strength of his coalition. When he lost on both test votes, Dingell simply adjourned the markup, delaying consideration indefinitely.[13] He did not bring the bill up again until the following year, after he had managed to negotiate a less pro-industry substitute. The committee then reported the substitute package over the vigorous objections of members from gas-producing states.[14]

Second, beyond their procedural prerogatives, committee leaders of both parties have important resources that defray the costs of legislative involvement. Given their relative seniority and the repetitious nature of most committees' agendas, leaders are more likely to have greater experience in the politics and substance of legislation that comes before their panel. Many have dealt with the same issues, heard the same arguments, and even questioned the same witnesses in previous sessions. If leaders start with superior expertise, they also have greater resources to pay the marginal information costs. Most important is their greater access to and control over professional staff. Prior to the 1995 reforms at least, a leadership position on either a committee or subcommittee greatly expanded a member's opportunities for involvement. As one member put it upon his retirement in 1994, "The [subcommittee] staff carries everything. Once I became chair, [the staff] made it possible for me to take up issues I'd left alone my whole career."

Finally, members with a formal institutional position occupy a central place in an information network that extends beyond the confines of the committee, but plays a crucial role in the legislative process. Given their control over the committee's agenda space, for instance, committee leaders and their staffs become the focal points for outsiders wishing to press their ideas, analysis, and demands upon the government. A case in point is the Federal Insecticide, Fungicide, and Rodenticide Act (FIFRA), a bill to regulate the agricultural use of potentially harmful chemicals. While not likely to enthrall the average voter, passage of FIFRA would have important implications for the environmental quality of lakes, rivers, and groundwater; for farmers and fruitgrowers who use chemicals in raising their crops; for agricultural workers whose health might be affected by exposure to such products; and for private companies that manufacture and market them. The act had been up for reconsideration in every Congress for fifteen years, generating countless studies and endless controversies among the various interest groups and policy specialists. An aide to Rep. George Brown,

D-Calif., who chaired the subcommittee of jurisdiction for more than a decade, described the drafting of one version of the bill:

> We spent weeks pouring over all these reports and recommendations, and we finally put together a draft. But the environmentalists didn't like it, and there were fractures on the chemical industry's side—one side wanted some proposals relating to the release of health and safety data and the pesticide registration process. . . . So Brown said, "You guys sit down with my staff and go through this thing, point by point, and figure out where you want to be." That was the beginning of four months of protracted negotiations with EPA, the industry, the environmentalists—sitting down, going back and forth, drafts and redrafts. Finally, we got a negotiated settlement between the industry and the environmental groups and only then moved a bill, that comprehensive compromise, up to subcommittee markup.

The Consequences of Reform

In making choices about whether and to what extent they invest time in any given bill, then, legislators are what economists call "constrained optimizers." Each member "contemplating involvement in a particular matter entertains certain interests, possesses behavioral alternatives, chooses among the latter with an eye to the former, and is constrained in her choices by the information and other resources available to her and by the institutionally provided opportunities to act."[15] With this account in view, what behavioral changes might we expect from the committee reforms of 1995? We examine several specific reforms and assess their impact using behavioral data pre- and postreform.

Jurisdictional Consolidation

The official rules of the House, adopted at the beginning of each Congress, define in considerable detail the jurisdictions of the standing committees, and these jurisdictions are thought to define the chamber's formal organizational structure. Jurisdictional boundaries, in turn, have a tremendous impact on what policies eventually emerge from committee rooms.[16] It is not surprising, then, that the Republican reformers of 1995 included jurisdictional consolidation as part of their reform package. The 104th House abolished three of the twenty-two standing committees: Post Office and Civil Service, District of Columbia, and Merchant Marine and Fisheries. And it cut the number of subcommittees by almost 20 percent, from 115 to 84.

Along with reforms that scaled back the use of multiple referrals, these changes were intended to diminish the duplication and inefficiency of overlapping panels and to cut the number of panel assignments in each member's portfolio. Some issues were reallocated to different committees to make committee responsibilities more coherent. The intention was to permit members to better tend to matters before their panels and improve deliberation.

Is there good theoretical reason to believe that such effects would materialize in postreform decision making? Not really. As we have noted, the increasing demands on members' time over the last several decades have exacerbated the tendency of committee members to participate selectively. The growth in the number of panel assignments per member probably increased the frequency of scheduling conflicts, causing members to sometimes choose between competing responsibilities. But the jurisdictional reforms did not diminish the sum of demands on members' time. Areas of legislative action were not somehow banished from the agenda; they were simply reallocated across panels. Nineteen committees now had to do the work of twenty-two. Eighty-four subcommittees had to cover the policy turf formerly covered by 115.

More generally, it is not obvious that formal jurisdictional reforms change jurisdictional practices. In an important essay, David King developed a new view of the way institutions change.[17] Committee jurisdictions, King argues, are not static institutional facts, subject to alteration only during rare moments of reform. Rather, King distinguishes between a committee's *statutory* jurisdiction and its *common law* jurisdiction. The former refers to the specific issues delegated to a committee that are codified in the House rules; and this is what students of Congress normally have in mind when they speak of committee jurisdictions. Change in statutory jurisdictions is episodic, taking the form of major turf battles or the enactment of formal reforms, such as those passed in 1946, 1974, and 1995. But King demonstrates that the most important jurisdictional changes do not follow from formal reforms; rather, they emerge from entrepreneurial behavior of committee leaders responding to new issues that arise on the national agenda. Unlike statutory jurisdictions, common law jurisdictional change tends to be incremental, not episodic. More important, King shows that formal jurisdictional revisions track the common law patterns that had evolved over the period since the previous reform. Statutory reform, in other words, mostly codifies prior behavioral patterns.

King's thesis is nicely confirmed by the jurisdictional changes of 1995. While the changes were touted as "bold and dynamic," perhaps "the greatest in half a century," King shows that the changes on parliamentary parchment made little practical difference.[18] The major committee most affected by jurisdictional rearrangements was Energy and Commerce, which would be renamed simply Commerce in the 104th. According to critics, Energy and Commerce was one of the worst organizational culprits. One of twenty-two standing committees in the 103d, it claimed jurisdiction on two of every five House bills, with many of those bills multiply referred to other committees. The 104th reforms stripped it of jurisdiction in six areas, which according to reformers was a "monumental" 20 percent of its jurisdiction.[19]

In behavioral practice, however, very little changed. Figure 9-1 shows that the six policy areas that Commerce lost in 1995 were taking up very little of members' time and energy in the years leading up to reform. Some issues, such as inland waterways and food inspections, had barely appeared on the commit-

Figure 9-1 Commerce Committee Activity on Issues Lost in 1995 Reforms

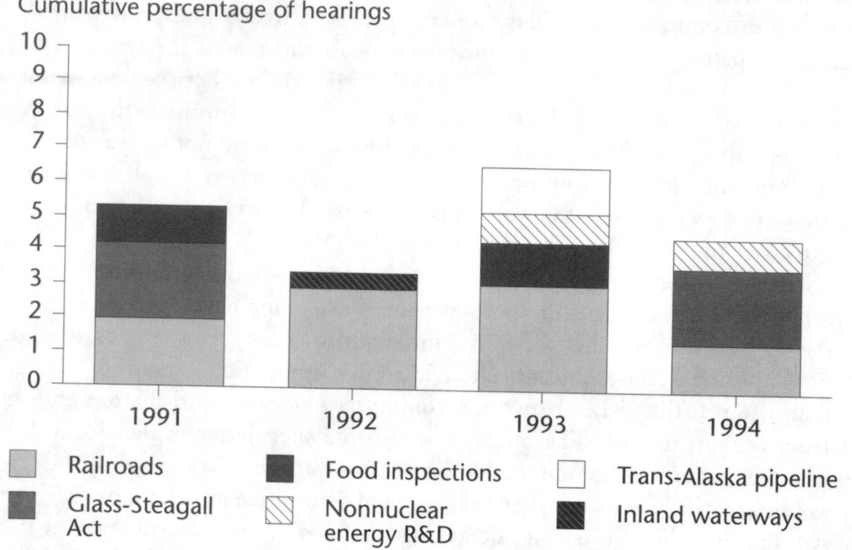

Source: David C. King, "What Happens When Jurisdictions Are Reformed," John F. Kennedy School of Government, Harvard University, April 1996, 31.

tee's agenda during the previous four years. Looking at actual activity rather than formal procedure, we see that the reformed Commerce Committee lost less than 5 percent, not 20 percent, of its jurisdiction.

If one looks at activity in the 104th Commerce Committee, even this estimate appears high. Committee members continued to actively consider issues they had supposedly lost! Statutorily speaking, Commerce had lost food inspection to House Agriculture, but nevertheless considered the Food Quality Protection Act. Commerce also had lost jurisdiction over nonnuclear energy research to the Science Committee, but still considered the Propane Education and Research Act in the 104th, just as it had in the 103d. Commerce had been stripped of jurisdiction over the Glass-Steagall Act, but it held hearings on the Financial Services Competition Act, a proposal to reform Glass-Steagall. A systematic review of Commerce's agendas in prereform and postreform Congresses reveals that the committee held as many hearings in the 104th Congress in the areas of officially "lost" jurisdiction as it had in the 103d.

But even if legislative demands were diminished for some committees, it still does not follow that such changes would noticeably affect members' participation in committee deliberations. Cutting back in some areas of committee work would enhance participation in other areas only if we assume that the competing committee demands had depressed it. This is not a good behavioral assumption. The simple fact is that the demands of any given panel represent only a small fraction of the everyday claims on a member's time and resources. Such claims are varied and numerous—meetings with constituents, votes on the floor, trips to the district, party meetings, caucus meetings, staff meetings, fundraising events, and more. And as we have already discussed, participation is interest-driven as well as demand-constrained. If members are not interested in a bill, they are unlikely to participate, whether they have committee conflicts or not. There are always politically profitable alternatives. According to a survey conducted in the 1980s, members of three major House committees had little or no interest in fully a third of all bills marked up in their delegated areas of specialization.[20] At best, then, competing committee demands are only a small part of the behavioral story.

Committee Voting Reforms

A second reform intended to enhance participation in committee deliberations was the ban on proxy voting. For at least two decades, Republicans had complained about the provision in House standing rules that allowed committees to decide whether they would allow members to vote by proxy. Most committees did so. But the practical effect of proxy voting was not to preserve the voting authority of the absent member; rather, it augmented the power of those who were present and active. Members typically gave their proxies to their committee or subcommittee chairs without specific instructions as to how the votes should be cast. The committee leaders could thereby prevail on contested votes governed by majority rule, even if they had no majority present. One study of House committees during the early 1980s showed that members typically missed more than a third of their committee votes.[21]

The ban on proxy voting was intended to bring absentee legislators back into the committee mix. Is there good theoretical reason to think that this reform would have that effect? Not much. Members who missed votes in the past in favor of more profitable activities would be inclined to miss them again. In those instances where a vote was likely to be close, so that one vote might well make a difference, members would be more inclined to show up. But the reform most likely to enhance voting participation was not the ban on proxy voting per se. Rather, it was the ancillary reform that all committee votes would be made public, letting the electorate know not only how members voted but also whether they voted.

Unlike committee participation, attendance for floor votes tends to be high, mainly because members want to avoid the appearance that they are neglecting their duties, which might threaten their reelection. But that was not always so. Before 1973, when the House began recording votes in the Committee of the Whole, rates of floor voting were about 50 percent, lower than the rates for committee voting. But when the House began reporting teller votes in the *Congressional Record,* voting participation doubled almost over night.[22] We should expect

Table 9-1 Voting in House Committees Before and After the 1995 Reforms

	Agriculture		Economic and Educational Opportunities		Commerce	
	97th	104th	97th	104th	98th	104th
Voting (in person)	45.0%	94.4%	36.7%	87.9%	45.1%	87.8%
Votes sampled	35	13	20	35	47	67

Source: Minutes and transcripts of committee markup sessions.

Note: Data for the 97th (1981–1982) and 98th (1983–1984) Congresses include votes from samples of bills drawn from the entire Congress. Data for the 104th Congress include votes from samples of bills marked up in committee from June 1, 1995, to June 1, 1996. Prior to the 104th Congress, the official name of the Commerce Committee was Energy and Commerce, and the official name of Economic and Educational Opportunities was Education and Labor.

the same incentives to operate in committees of the 104th Congress. The midwestern member whose service on the House Agriculture Committee boosted her standing with rural constituents might find it hard to explain why she missed half that committee's votes.

Did the reporting requirements affect voting practice? Yes. Although we do not have data on the rates of proxy voting in the 103d Congress, such data were available for a period in which the committee voting rules were identical to those in 1993 and 1994. Table 9-1 shows the respective rates at which members voted in person before and after the rules changes of 1995. Prior to those changes, members showed up and voted in committee markups less than half the time. They were just as likely to abdicate their voting authority and relinquish their proxy to a more interested colleague as they were to cast the votes themselves. The behavioral change apparent in the 104th Congress is striking. Voting participation roughly doubled for all three committees, and the members cast roll call votes in committee about as often as they did on the floor. The question that remains is whether mere changes in voting rates made any difference.

Efficiency Reforms

As we noted in the opening section, voting is only one, and seldom the most important, form of legislative participation. And as one staffer observed, most committee members would "hustle in and take their cue from the same member they used to give their proxy to, then leave again." Is there good theoretical reason to expect that more committee members would get actively into the deliberative mix as a result of the 104th House reforms? We have described a number of changes that were intended to cut back on competing committee demands and duplicative work, freeing members to focus their time and attention on the mat-

Table 9-2 Participation in House Committees Before and After the 1995 Reforms

	Agriculture		Economic and Educational Opportunities		Commerce	
	103d	104th	103d	104th	103d	104th
Players in bill-specific games						
Players	24.1%	28.6%	34.7%	38.3%	19.7%	11.7%
Nonplayers	75.9	71.4	65.3	61.7	80.3	88.3
Number of observations (Member x on bill y)	730	528	619	574	924	846

Source: Minutes and transcripts of committee markup sessions.

Notes: The data for the 103d Congress are based on samples of bills from the entire Congress. Data for the 104th Congress are based on samples of bills drawn from June 1, 1995, to June 1, 1996. Prior to the 104th Congress, the official name of the Commerce Committee was Energy and Commerce, and the official name of Economic and Educational Opportunities was Education and Labor. The number of observations in the dataset is the number of members observed multiplied by the number of bills.

ters before their panels. But those reforms diminished the demands on members' time minimally, if at all. Moreover, other changes cut rather than increased members' staff capacity—an important determinant of the breadth and depth of members' issue-to-issue participation. And the reforms did nothing to heighten members' interests in issues that did not interest them before. If anything, efforts to curtail self-selection onto panels should diminish members' personal motivations to participate.

Table 9-2 compares the patterns of participation in committee deliberations in the Congresses immediately before and after the 1995 reforms.[23] The statistics summarize the number of members actively involved in samples of bills marked up in each of the three committees.[24] While the changes in voting participation were striking, more general changes in committee participation appear slight. For the Agriculture and the Economic and Educational Opportunities Committees, the average number of participants increased about four percentage points, but we cannot conclude with confidence that these differences are statistically different from zero, even using generous standards. And participation in the Commerce Committee actually dropped—this despite the fact that mostly low-salience issues had been removed from the committee's jurisdiction. In sum, there is no clear evidence that the institutional reforms, which were applicable to all committees, had any consistent effect on collective patterns of participation.

Ending Subcommittee Government

In the early 1970s, a different cohort of House newcomers had supported what were labeled "democratizing" reforms in the chamber's organizational structure. Committee chairs were then reputed to be oligarchs, controlling schedules and agendas, vetoing legislation, controlling committee staff, and dictating the creation of and assignment to subcommittees. The reforms of the 1970s diminished these powers by creating standing subcommittees with fixed jurisdictions, rights of referral, separate budgets, separate staff, and other subcommittee rights. Subcommittee leaders and members pursued legislative—sometimes conflicting, sometimes overlapping—agendas of their own.[25]

In 1995 the impulse of the new House majority was to reverse this tendency, to undo what House reformers had done circa 1974. Where the earlier generation had put in place a subcommittee bill of rights, the latter-day reformers effectively deratified it.[26] Subcommittee prerogatives were shifted in procedural principle to the full committee chairs, the formal leaders once spurned as oligarchs. The principal losers under the new arrangements were House subcommittees and subcommittee chairs. Full committee leaders and members would play a newly expanded role in committee decision making.

Is there good reason to expect that these reforms would have their intended effect? Yes, for the most part. As we have stated, procedural prerogatives and staff capacity are important factors in determining how much and how often members can participate. If these advantages are redistributed from subcommittee to committee actors, then we ought to see more participation by the latter relative to the former. At the same time, members tend to participate more on bills that interest them, and the self-selective nature of the subcommittee assignment process prior to reform served to align members' panel portfolios to their respective interests. After reform, position self-selection could give way to the preferences of full committee chairs, who would be empowered to choose subcommittee chairs and assign members to the groups.

The only remaining question is whether the actual practices of staff allocation, subcommittee chair selection, and subcommittee assignment changed as a result of statutory change. While chairs were empowered in certain ways, their authority remained contingent on the good will and support of the committee and subcommittee rank and file, the claims of some committee chairs notwithstanding. If committee chairs indulged their personal preferences too much, committee majorities still retained parliamentary authority to reject subcommittee chair appointments and panel assignments.[27] As in the decades prior to 1995, a chair who did not anticipate the reactions of panel members could find that her power on parchment became powerlessness in practice.[28] Table 9-3 reports the incidence of participation in committee markups, broken down by committee and subcommittee position. Here we find some evidence of behavioral differences consistent with the intentions of reform. The redistribution of staff, budgets, and parliamentary prerogatives apparently diminished the legislative roles

Table 9-3 Subcommittee Participants in House Committees Before and After the 1995 Reforms

	Agriculture		Economic and Educational Opportunities		Commerce	
	103d	104th	103d	104th	103d	104th
Players in bill-specific games						
Subcommittee members	32%	34%	47%	48%	29%	14%
Subcommittee nonmembers	18	25	23	32	15	9
Subcommittee chairs	73	73	94	80	95	64
Full committee chairs	100	100	100	100	100	100
Number of observations (Member x on bill y)	730	528	619	574	924	846

Source: Minutes and transcripts of committee markup sessions.

Notes: The data for the 103d Congress are based on samples of bills from the entire Congress. Data for the 104th Congress are based on samples of bills drawn from June 1, 1995, to June 1, 1996. Prior to the 104th Congress, the official name of the Commerce Committee was Energy and Commerce, and the official name of Economic and Educational Opportunities was Education and Labor. The number of observations in the dataset is the number of members observed multiplied by the number of bills.

played by subcommittee members relative to members not serving on the subcommittee. For the Agriculture and Economic and Educational Opportunities Committees, subcommittee members remained about as active in the committee mix in the 104th Congress as they had been in the 103d. But on both committees, the incidence of participation by subcommittee nonmembers increased. And although participation by subcommittee nonmembers went down in the 104th Commerce Committee, it dropped off even more rapidly among members of the reporting subcommittee.

We find some evidence of a diminution in the role of subcommittee leaders as well. Subcommittee chairs on House Agriculture were just as likely to be major players in the 104th Congress as in the 103d. On the other two committees, however, reporting subcommittee chairs proved considerably less likely to participate in the 104th Congress. Taken together, the records suggest that in more than 25 percent of the cases, the reputed subcommittee oligarchs were not major players in bills within their own jurisdictions. It does appear that the resource redistributions enacted as part of the 1995 reform package made a behavioral difference. Although members do not participate much more in committee deliberations, the mix of members participating appears somewhat different, with full committee members and chairs better able to "mute the enthusiasms" of the respective subcommittees.

Conclusion

The behavioral change we might reasonably attribute to institutional reform is not trivial, but neither is it dramatic or profound. When set against the claims of reformers and close observers, in fact, the practical effects appear underwhelming.

The "momentous" jurisdictional reforms simply did not amount to much. Likewise, the centralizing reforms did not suddenly resuscitate committee chairs as major institutional players. The evidence, here and elsewhere, consistently shows that these actors were major players before their alleged empowerment in 1995—across almost all bills, arising out of all subcommittees, across all committees.[29] Indeed, full committee chairs of the 103d Congress were more likely to get into the legislative game than the reporting subcommittee chairs, and this during a period when the rules of subcommittee government were still in place. Despite being formally stripped of staff and procedural prerogatives, in turn, postreform subcommittee chairs remained two to four times more likely to be major players than subcommittee backbenchers.

In sum, the 1995 committee reforms made at most a modest behavioral difference. As other chapters in this volume testify, there was much more to the Republican package of reforms than those discussed here. Changes in other institutional arrangements, especially affecting the powers of the Speaker and party leadership in their dealings with committees and committee chairs, appeared more dramatic.[30] The newly elected Republican leadership was building a Republican regime. As the 104th Congress came to a close, however, it became less clear that these new powers were the result of structural rearrangements. As the popularity of Speaker Newt Gingrich and his program waned, so too did his support among the Republican rank and file. And as support waned, so too did the Speaker's discretion to exercise his formal prerogatives. In this respect, too, the practical meaning of institutional reforms may prove mostly contingent on the behavioral impulses of purposive members.

Notes

All unattributed quotations are from interviews conducted by the authors. The authors thank Kim Hill, Dave King, and John Kingdon for their comments and assistance.

1. See, for instance, the collection of essays in Roger H. Davidson, ed., *The Postreform Congress* (New York: St. Martin's Press, 1992).
2. See especially C. Lawrence Evans and Walter Oleszek, *Congress Under Fire: Reform Politics and the Republican Majority* (Boston: Houghton Mifflin, 1997).
3. David R. Mayhew, *Congress: The Electoral Connection* (New Haven: Yale University Press, 1974), 95.
4. Roger H. Davidson, "Subcommittee Government: New Channels for Policymaking," in *The New Congress,* ed. Thomas Mann and Norman Ornstein (Washington, D.C.: American Enterprise Institute, 1981).

5. Clifford Hardin, Kenneth Shepsle, and Barry Weingast, "Government by Subcommittee," *Wall Street Journal,* June 24, 1983.
6. The following discussion derives from Richard L. Hall, "Participation and Purpose in Committee Decision Making," *American Political Science Review* 81 (March 1987): 105–127; Hall, "Participation, Abdication, and Representation in Congressional Committees," in *Congress Reconsidered,* 5th ed., ed. Lawrence C. Dodd and Bruce Oppenheimer (Washington, D.C.: CQ Press, 1993); and Hall, *Participation in Congress* (New Haven: Yale University Press, 1996).
7. Hall, *Participation in Congress,* 2.
8. Quoted in Thomas O'Donnell, "Managing Legislative Time," in *The House at Work,* ed. Joseph Cooper and G. Calvin Mackenzie (Austin: University of Texas Press, 1981), 128.
9. Ibid., 138.
10. See especially Richard F. Fenno Jr., *Congressmen in Committees* (Boston: Little, Brown, 1973); John W. Kingdon, *Congressmen's Voting Decisions* (New York: Harper, 1989); and Mayhew, *Congress: The Electoral Connection.*
11. See Steven Waldman, *The Bill* (New York: Viking, 1995).
12. See David Maraniss, "Power Play: Chairman's Gavel Crushes Gas Decontrol Vote," *Washington Post,* Nov. 20, 1983, A1.
13. Ibid.
14. For a case study that reveals both the value and the limits of a chair's procedural control over his committee's agenda, see Richard Cohen, *Washington at Work: Back Rooms and Clean Air* (New York: Macmillan, 1992).
15. Hall, *Participation in Congress,* 12. See also Kenneth Shepsle, *The Giant Jigsaw Puzzle* (Chicago: University of Chicago Press, 1978), esp. 6–7.
16. David C. King, "The Nature of Congressional Committee Jurisdictions," *American Political Science Review* 88 (March 1994): 48. See also Bryan D. Jones, Frank R. Baumgartner, and Jeffrey C. Talbert, "The Destruction of Issue Monopolies in Congress," *American Political Science Review* 87 (1993): 657–671.
17. King, "The Nature of Congressional Committee Jurisdictions." See also King, "What Happens When Jurisdictions Are Reformed," John F. Kennedy School of Government, Harvard University, April 1996; and especially King, *Turf Wars* (Chicago: University of Chicago Press, 1997).
18. See King, *Turf Wars,* chap. 3, esp. 29–30.
19. Ibid., 30.
20. Hall, *Participation in Congress,* 81–84.
21. Hall, "Participation, Abdication, and Representation in Congressional Committees," 168.
22. Steven S. Smith, *Call to Order* (Washington, D.C.: Brookings, 1989), 22.
23. The data for the 103d Congress were drawn from dense samples of bills marked up in the three committees during the entire two-year Congress. The data for the 104th Congress include all bills that saw significant markup action in the middle period of the Congress, namely, June 1, 1995, to June 1, 1996. Our purpose is to assess the extent to which the institutional rearrangements created a new equilibrium in behavioral patterns. We therefore focused on bills considered after the extraordinary period of action on the Republican Contract with America and the writing of the first Republican budget resolution.
24. A member was coded as actively involved if she (1) was a major participant in markup debate; or (2) played a significant role in writing the bill, in writing a substitute bill, or in setting the markup agenda, as revealed by records available through the on-line data service, *Legi-Slate.* Bills were sampled from the entire list of bills that saw significant markup action in the 103d Congress in each of the three committees. All bills

that saw significant markup action between June 1, 1995, and June 1, 1996, were included in the 104th Congress samples. See note 23.

25. See Davidson, "Subcommittee Government"; Lawrence C. Dodd and Bruce I. Oppenheimer, "The House in Transition," in *Congress Reconsidered,* 3d ed., ed. Lawrence C. Dodd and Bruce I. Oppenheimer (Washington, D.C.: CQ Press, 1985); and Hardin, Shepsle, and Weingast, "Government by Subcommittee." But see Richard L. Hall and C. Lawrence Evans, "The Power of Subcommittees," *Journal of Politics* 52 (May 1990): 335–354.
26. Evans and Oleszek, *Congress Under Fire,* 91.
27. Ibid., 92.
28. See John F. Manley, "Wilbur Mills: A Study in Congressional Influence," *American Political Science Review* 63 (1969): 442–464; and Hall and Evans, "The Power of Subcommittees."
29. See Hall, *Participation in Congress,* esp. chap. 6.
30. See John H. Aldrich and David W. Rohde, "Conditional Party Government Revisited: Majority Party Leadership and the Committee System in the 104th Congress," and Roger H. Davidson, "Building a Republican Regime on Capitol Hill," in *Extension of Remarks: The New Republican Congress: Explanations, Assessments, and Prospects,* ed. Lawrence C. Dodd, Legislative Studies Group, American Political Science Association, December 1995.

Part IV
Congressional Leadership and Party Politics

10. Party Leaders and the New Legislative Process

Barbara Sinclair

As 1995 drew to a close, President Bill Clinton, Speaker of the House Newt Gingrich, and Senate Majority Leader Bob Dole sat face-to-face attempting to negotiate a comprehensive budget agreement, a task that entailed making a host of major changes in policy. That this mode of policy making did not strike Americans as particularly out of the ordinary indicates just how much the legislative process has changed in recent years. Although it received less media attention, the legislative process on the budget bill in the months before the summit talks was also far from what would have been considered normal only a few years ago. In both chambers a large number of committees had a hand in drafting the legislation, and the resulting bill was an enormous omnibus measure. In the House, floor procedure was tailored especially to the specific problems this bill raised, and in both chambers majority party leaders were intensely involved throughout the process.

As this example suggests, the how-a-bill-becomes-a-law diagram that is a staple of American government textbooks in reality describes the legislative process on fewer and fewer of the major measures Congress considers. Rather than being sent to one committee in each chamber, a measure may be considered by several committees, and some measures bypass committees altogether. In addition, after a bill has been reported, but before it reaches the floor, substantive changes are often worked out via informal processes. Omnibus measures of great scope are a regular part of the legislative scene, and formal executive-congressional summits to work out deals on legislation are no longer considered extraordinary. On the House floor, most major legislation is considered under complex and usually restrictive rules, often tailored to deal with problems specific to that bill. In the Senate, bills are regularly subject to large numbers of not necessarily germane floor amendments, and filibuster threats are an everyday fact of life, affecting all aspects of the legislative process and making cloture votes a routine part of the process.[1]

This essay explores how and why the legislative process in the U.S. Congress has changed and examines the consequences of that change. Because of their role in the development and deployment of a number of these unorthodox processes, majority party leaders are a special focus of the essay.

The Sources of Change

Why has the legislative process changed in such major ways? I hold that the modifications and innovations are responses to problems and opportunities that members of Congress—as individuals or collectively—confronted, problems and opportunities that arose from changes in institutional structure or challenges in the political environment. Majority party leaders' strivings to meet their members' expectations for legislation were an important but not the only source of procedural innovation, and many but by no means all of the special processes are used at their discretion.

Although the evolution of a new, more varied legislative process was complex, several factors can be isolated as pivotal: internal reforms that changed the distribution of influence in both chambers in the 1970s and a political environment in the 1980s and early 1990s characterized by divided control, big deficits, and ideological hostility to the legislative goals of congressional Democrats.

During the 1970s both the Senate and House distributed internal influence more broadly.[2] As the incentives to exploit fully the great powers Senate rules confer on the individual senator increased in the 1960s and 1970s, the restraint senators had exercised in the use of their prerogatives gave way, and they began to offer more floor amendments and use extended debate—filibusters—more often. As a result, the Senate floor became a more active decision-making arena, and filibusters, or the threat of them, became a routine part of the legislative process.

The change in the Senate's legislative process brought about by senators' greater individualism and activism put heavy demands on party leaders, especially on the majority leader, who is in charge of scheduling legislation for the floor. The majority leader is also expected to help party members pass the legislation they need and want. The change in process increased the majority leader's involvement, often casting him in the role of head negotiator. But the Senate gave the majority leader no new powers to carry out his job.

In the House, reformers redistributed influence through a number of rules changes mostly instituted between 1969 and 1975.[3] Powers and resources were shifted from committee chairs not only down to subcommittee chairs and rank and file members but also up to the party leadership. Junior members gained resources, especially staff, that boosted their ability to participate in the legislative process. The Speaker, as leader of the majority party, was given the power to select the Democratic members of the Rules Committee, a greater say in the assignment of members to other committees, and new powers over the referral of bills.

By reducing the power of the committees and facilitating greater participation by the rank and file, the reforms made legislating more difficult for the majority Democrats. Republicans quickly became adept at using floor amendments to make political points, confronting Democrats with a stream of politically difficult votes. Compromises carefully crafted in committee were being picked apart on the floor, and floor sessions were stretching on interminably.

Democrats began to look to their party leaders, the only central leaders in the chamber, to counter these problems. The leaders responded by innovating in ways that led to alterations in the legislative process. The leadership became more involved with legislation before it reached the floor, at times negotiating post-committee adjustments to ease its passage. To respond to the barrage of amendments offered on the floor, the leadership developed special rules into devices for structuring floor decision making.

In the 1980s both the House and Senate were feeling the results of the changes in their internal distribution of influence. The highly individualistic Senate, in which each senator was accorded extraordinary latitude, was very good at agenda setting and publicizing problems, but poorly structured for legislative decision making. The House, which had expanded junior members' opportunities for participation, also had problems legislating, although its central leadership had begun to develop reasonably effective responses.

The political climate of the 1980s and early 1990s exacerbated the problems of legislating, especially for the Democratic House. Ronald Reagan was a conservative, confrontational president with policy views far from those of congressional Democrats. George Bush's policy preferences were not much closer. After 1981 large deficits became chronic and severely restricted the policy options seen as feasible. Partisan conflict and stalemate in Washington fed public cynicism about government's ability to handle effectively the problems facing the country. In such a climate the majority Democrats found it difficult to pass legislation they considered satisfactory. Just enacting the legislation necessary to keep the government going was often arduous, first, because of the ideological gulf between the congressional Democrats and the Republican president and, second, because of the unpalatable decisions they had to make.

In the 1980s and 1990s the battles over priorities and deficits were waged within the context of the budget process. Although instituted by the Budget and Impoundment Control Act of 1974, the budget process did not move to center stage until the early 1980s. Since then, the budget process, governed by complex rules and procedures, has had far-reaching effects on the legislative process. One reason is that the Reagan administration's use of it in 1981 showed that the mechanism could be used by central leaders to bring about comprehensive policy change.

The tough climate of the 1980s forced further innovation in the legislative process, especially in the House. Party leaders, as they tried to engineer passage of legislation that would satisfy their members, were more and more drawn into the substantive legislative process; in the House, leaders developed special rules into powerful and flexible tools for structuring floor decisions.[4]

By the early 1990s the usefulness of many of the special processes for enacting legislation had become widely recognized, and congressional leaders continued to use them even though political circumstances changed. As the partisan climate intensified, individuals, especially in the Senate, stepped up their use of processes under their control. The 103d Congress (1993–1994) was the first in twelve years in which both houses of Congress and the White House were controlled by the same party. The 104th (1995–1996) was the first in forty years in which Republicans controlled both chambers. The two Congresses were similar in that both were under intense pressure to produce legislation; in the 103d, Clinton and congressional Democrats needed to show that the Democratic Party could govern; in the 104th, Gingrich and House Republicans needed to deliver on their promises in the Contract with America. The changes in the legislative process discussed here contributed significantly to their considerable success in the House and their lack of it in the Senate.

Omnibus Legislation, the Budget Process, and Summits

Omnibus legislation—bills with great substantive scope often involving, directly or indirectly, many committees—is now a regular part of the congressional agenda. Such measures increased as a proportion of the congressional agenda of major legislation from zero in the 91st Congress (1969–1970) to 8 percent in the 94th (1975–1976)—all budget resolutions—to 20 percent in the 97th (1981–1982) and 100th (1987–1988). In the Congresses of the 1990s, omnibus measures made up about 11 percent of major measures.[5]

Some omnibus measures are the result of the 1974 budget act. The act requires an annual budget resolution and, in the 1980s and 1990s, the budget resolution often called for a reconciliation bill.[6] Beyond that, the decision to package legislation into an omnibus measure is discretionary, and it is principally the majority party leadership that decides. Measures may be packaged into an omnibus bill for several reasons: to pass unpalatable but necessary legislation; to force the president to accept legislative provisions that, were they sent to him in freestanding form, he would veto; or to raise the visibility of popular legislation and garner partisan credit. During the Reagan and Bush administrations, for example, House Democratic leaders packaged legislation on issues such as trade and drugs into high-profile omnibus measures to compete with the White House for media attention and public credit and to protect favored provisions from a veto. During the 103d Congress, congressional leaders did not need to pressure President Clinton into signing their legislation, but the usefulness of omnibus measures for enacting tough bills or for raising the visibility of popular measures led to their continued use. A number of modest provisions were packaged into a big anticrime bill, and omnibus budget measures were used to pass Clinton's economic program.

The most important and most prevalent omnibus measures in the 1980s and 1990s were budget related. The deficits that resulted from the Reagan tax cut guaranteed that budget politics would remain at center stage for the foreseeable future. In its attempts to control the deficit, Congress used the budget process, including in the budget resolution instructions to committees to change the laws under their jurisdiction to bring them into line with the budget resolution. The resulting provisions were then packaged into an omnibus reconciliation bill.

Because the purpose was deficit reduction, the reconciliation instructions usually required committees to cut spending or raise taxes, confronting them with difficult decisions. Deep policy divisions between Republican presidents and House Democrats exacerbated the difficulties of reaching agreements.

In 1993 and 1995 central leaders used the budget process to try to enact comprehensive policy changes that in both years involved making some very difficult decisions. Clinton's economic program cut the deficit by $500 billion over five years and increased spending on high-priority programs; accomplishing that entailed tax increases, which are never popular, and a cut in spending for numerous lower-priority programs. The Republicans' 1995 program envisioned balancing the budget in seven years while also cutting taxes, which would require draconian cuts in domestic spending. It also included revamping major programs such as Medicare, Medicaid, and welfare. The budget process offered the only realistic hope for enacting either party's proposals. Wrapping the provisions into one omnibus bill cuts down the number of battles that need to be won—an important consideration in a system with a bias toward the status quo. Leaders can ask members to cast a handful of tough votes, but not dozens. With an omnibus bill, the stakes are so high, it is harder for members to vote against their party leaders. In 1993, for example, reluctant Democrats were warned that they would bring down the Clinton presidency if they contributed to the defeat of his economic program. In 1995 Newt Gingrich repeatedly warned his members that the Republican Party's ability to govern was at issue; that his own reputation and clout were at stake was clear to his members.

Divided government brought sharp differences in policy preferences between the president and the congressional majority. Combined with the painful decisions that huge budget deficits dictated, those differences have sometimes stalemated normal legislative processes.[7] But the cost of failing to reach an agreement on budget issues was just too high, so when normal processes, even if supplemented by the more active role of majority party leaders, were incapable of producing legislation, the president and Congress had to find another way. The new device was the summit—relatively formal negotiations between congressional leaders and high-ranking administration officials representing the president or, as in 1995, the president himself. Between 1987 and 1990, four summits took place, and three concerned budget issues. Normal legislative processes foundered in the face of policy disagreements between the Democratic congressional majority and President Reagan in 1987 and between Congress and President Bush in 1989 and 1990, but the threat of severe automatic spending cuts dictated by the Gramm-Rudman Act, or the threat of an economic crisis, or both made a failure to reach agreement too costly. Aid to the Nicaraguan contras, another contentious issue, was the subject of the fourth summit.[8]

When the congressional majority and the president are of the same party, normal processes, supplemented by informal consultation and negotiations, suffice to produce agreement on essential legislation such as budget bills. No summits were needed during the 103d Congress with the Democrats in control of both branches. Normal processes are more likely to fail when both policy and electoral goals are in conflict, as they tend to be when government is divided. The conflict between President Clinton and the conservative new Republican majority in the 104th Congress made agreement impossible through anything approaching normal processes. The Republicans attempted to use various legislative strategies to force Clinton to accept their priorities: they threatened to include "must pass" legislation, such as the measure to increase the debt limit, in the reconciliation bill, and they sent Clinton appropriations bills with provisions he had vowed to veto, and, when he did, they refused to pass continuing resolutions to keep the government funded. Clearly, a summit was the only hope of resolving the impasse.

This time, however, the differences between the president and the congressional majority were just too great. Although not reaching a comprehensive agreement was costly for both, the compromises such an agreement would have required entailed sacrificing policy principles and the interests of important constituencies for one or both parties and so were more costly than no agreement.

New Processes and Procedures as Leadership Tools in the House

Traditionally, the legislative process would begin with the referral of a bill to a single committee, which would be largely responsible for its fate. In 1995 the Republicans' bill to abolish the Commerce Department was referred to eleven House committees. Although the number of committees was unusual, the fact that more than one committee was involved was not. In the contemporary House about one bill in five is referred to more than one committee.[9] Major legislation is even more likely to be sent to several committees; between 1987 and 1995, about a third was.

Multiple referral of legislation was not possible before 1975, when the House passed a rule providing for it. The new rule came about for two reasons: the House's inability to realign outdated committee jurisdictions and reform-minded members' desire to increase opportunities for broad participation in the legislative process. The rule was amended in 1977 to give the Speaker the power to set deadlines for committees to report legislation. As revised in 1995, the rule directs the Speaker to designate a lead committee with the most responsibility for the legislation; once that committee has reported, the other committees are required to report under fairly strict deadlines.[10]

For the Speaker, the frequency with which major legislation is multiply referred presents opportunities, but also problems. One problem is that when legislation is referred to several committees, the number of people who must come to agreement is multiplied, complicating and slowing down the legislative process. Often, multiple referral forces the Speaker to be the jurisdictional and substantive mediator, a role that brings with it influence as well as headaches. On contentious legislation, the leaders of the several committees involved may not be able to work out their differences without help. If the party leaders have to get involved, they gain influence over the substance of the legislation. Furthermore, when several committees work on the same piece of legislation, the committee process is more open to influence by party leaders; no one committee can consider such a bill its private business. Multiple referral also gives the Speaker the opportunity to set time limits for the reporting out of legislation. During the first one hundred days of the 104th Congress, when the new Republican majority was attempting to bring all the items in the Contract with America to the floor, that power gave added weight to Speaker Gingrich's stringent informal deadlines.

Although legislation is routinely considered by more than one committee, sometimes bills bypass committee consideration altogether. Skipping committee review was a rare occurrence before the 1980s; for example, in 1969 and 1970 and in 1975 and 1976, committees were bypassed on only 2 percent of the major legislation. By the late 1980s, however, almost 20 percent of major measures were never considered by a committee in the House. The frequency dropped to 6 percent in the 103d Congress; it then rose to 11 percent in 1995, but, as we shall see, that relatively low rate is somewhat misleading.

To force legislation to the floor for consideration, a majority of the House membership can bypass a nonresponsive committee by using the discharge procedure. Any member may file a discharge petition, and, when half the House members—218—have signed the petition, the measure is taken away from the committee and considered on the floor. In the 97th Congress, the 102d (1991–1992), and again in the 103d, a constitutional amendment to require a balanced federal budget was brought to the floor through the discharge procedure. Each time, the committee of jurisdiction—the House Judiciary Committee—opposed the measure and had refused to consider or report it. The discharge route, however, is seldom successful.[11]

The majority party leadership usually makes the decision to bypass a committee, but the rationale for doing so varies widely. In early 1987, at the beginning of the 100th Congress, the Democratic Party leadership brought two big bills—a clean water bill and a highway-mass transit bill—directly to the floor because it wanted to score some quick victories. Both had gone through the full committee process and had passed by large margins in the preceding Congress, but had died because of President Reagan's opposition.

In some rare cases, the majority party leadership believes the issue to be too politically delicate for the committee or committees of jurisdiction to handle. In 1988 Speaker Jim Wright, D-Texas, entrusted the drafting of the House Democrats' plan for contra aid to a task force headed by the deputy whip; no committee was involved. The political risks inherent in opposing the president on a highly visible foreign policy issue, as House Democrats were doing, were too great to leave the decision making to a committee.

On the first day of the 104th Congress, knowing that press coverage would be at a maximum, the new Republican leadership wanted to make a big splash. The House passed the Congressional Accountability Act, which applied a number of federal laws to Congress itself. The bill was a part of the Contract with America, and it had passed the House during the previous Congress. Most of the items in the Republicans' contract went through the formal committee process—if very quickly—but they had actually been drafted before Congress began (the contract was put together in the summer of 1994), and the Republican leadership was unwilling to brook changes of any magnitude. The unfunded mandates bill, for example, was referred to four committees on January 4, the first day of the session. The Government Reform and Oversight Committee ordered it reported on January 10, having spent one meeting, its first of the session, marking up the bill; the Rules Committee followed suit two days later; on January 19 floor consideration began. The Republicans' promise of action on all the items in the first one hundred days allowed for little real deliberation in committee, and the leaders feared Republicans would be accused of not keeping their promises if significant changes were made.

This method of passing legislation is a radical change from the way things used to be done. In the prereform House, autonomous committees crafted legislation behind closed doors and usually passed it unchanged on the floor with little help from the party leadership. As a matter of fact, party leadership intrusion into the legislative process on matters of substance was considered illegitimate. As House members became less willing to defer to committees and more willing to question committee bills on the floor, as multiple referral destroyed committees' monopoly over legislation in their area of jurisdiction, and as the political climate became harsher and the political stakes higher, committees became less capable of crafting legislation that could pass the chamber without help. In responding to their members' demands for assistance, majority party leaders were drawn more deeply into the substantive aspects of the legislative process and, in effect, changed how the process works. Now party leaders often involve themselves well before legislation is reported from committee.

Moreover, party leaders frequently take a role in working out substantive adjustments to legislation *after* it has been reported from committee. In the prereform 91st Congress, no major legislation was subject to such postcommittee adjustments; in the 94th, 4 percent was—all budget resolutions. In the early 1980s, the frequency jumped to almost one major measure in four and, in the late 1980s and early 1990s, averaged a little more than one in three. In 1995 almost half of major measures underwent some sort of postcommittee adjustment.

When party leaders become involved in making postcommittee adjustments to legislation, their objective is to craft a bill that most majority party members can support and one that can pass the House. They may also want to amass enough votes to deter a veto or to send a message to the Senate. In addition, leaders must make sure that the legislation is defensible in the court of public opinion, that it enhances rather than harms the party's image.

Controversy and saliency often prompt the need for postcommittee adjustments. Supporters may find that their bill as it emerged from committee does not command enough votes to pass. For example, the leadership found that a majority of the House considered the 1988 welfare reform bill too expensive as reported from committee. The leaders realized the bill would be radically amended or fail if it went to the floor without change. This was a bill that many Democrats were committed to, that the committees had put a great deal of effort and time into drafting, and that the leadership believed would enhance the party's image. It could not just be allowed to die. After extensive negotiations, the leadership came up with a strategy: an amendment would be offered to cut the program enough to satisfy those Democrats who believed they needed to vote for cuts, but not so much that the legislation's erstwhile supporters could no longer vote for it. The amendment was offered on the floor and, once it passed, the bill did also.

During Clinton's first two years as president, the House leadership found it necessary to make some minor postcommittee adjustments to amass the necessary support for several of his programs; the national service program and the Goals 2000 education legislation, for example, required such finetuning. On the most important legislation of his second year, however, even major adjustments were not enough to win the day. Different versions of comprehensive health care legislation were reported by three committees (one committee reported two bills), and the party leadership attempted to put together a single bill that could pass, but was unsuccessful. The issue and the Clinton approach had become too controversial.

In the 104th Congress, the Republican majority leadership often found it necessary to make postcommittee adjustments in legislation. To pass a big rescission bill (a bill cutting already appropriated spending) in 1995, the leadership had to agree to drop restrictive anti-abortion language and to accept a "lockbox" provision mandating that the savings go to deficit reduction, not to fund tax cuts. The first was necessary to get the votes of GOP moderates, the second to pick up some votes from conservative Democrats.[12] When the constitutional amendment imposing term limits on members of Congress emerged from the Judiciary Committee in a form that the majority of Republicans found unacceptable, the Rules Committee, at the direction of the leadership, dropped the committee draft and substituted another version.[13]

Legislation that is multiply referred often requires postcommittee adjustments. When the committees involved cannot come to an agreement among themselves, the party leadership may have to negotiate enough of an agreement to avoid a bloody battle on the House floor. In 1990 the Ways and Means Committee and the Education and Labor Committee shared jurisdiction over child care legislation. The two committees took very different approaches to the problem and failed to reach an agreement. The party leadership intervened to break the stalemate, and that intervention involved making substantive adjustments to the legislation. In 1995 the House leadership produced a welfare reform bill by combining bills passed by three committees and, in the process, altered some controversial provisions.[14]

The House considers most major legislation under a special rule that sets the conditions for floor debate. The variety in contemporary rules means that the legislative process differs quite substantially depending upon the choice of rule. Rules differ in many ways, but the most important is how amendments are to be treated. Rules can range from allowing no amendments, in which case the legislative battle is focused solely on the measure (or sometimes on the rule) and is clearly defined in time, to allowing all germane amendments, meaning that the amending process may stretch on for days and be unpredictable. Rules also can make otherwise nongermane amendments in order. Many rules allow some but not all germane amendments—sometimes listing them, sometimes requiring they be printed in the *Congressional Record* before floor consideration begins, and sometimes allowing all germane amendments that can be offered in a given time.

In the contemporary House, major legislation is likely to be brought to the floor under a complex, restrictive rule. In the prereform era, only tax bills were considered under a closed rule that allowed no amendments. As late as the 95th Congress (1977–1978), 85 percent of the rules were open, meaning that all germane amendments were allowed.[15] As legislation became more vulnerable to alteration on the floor, Democrats began demanding that their leadership use the control over the Rules Committee they had been given in the reform era to protect legislation and, where possible, to shield members from having to cast difficult votes. In response, the Democratic leadership began to use restrictive rules more frequently. Rules that restrict the offering of germane amendments accounted for two-thirds of the rules granted for initial consideration of legislation in the 102d Congress and for 70 percent in the 103d.

When only major measures are examined, the trend is even stronger. In the 1970s more than 80 percent of the rules for major legislation were simple open rules. In the early 1980s about 60 percent of major measures received simple open rules; the rest were considered under closed or, more frequently, some form of hybrid complex rule. By the late 1980s and continuing in the 1990s, 75 percent or more of major measures were considered under complex (or, rarely, closed) rules. From the early 1980s on, almost all the complex rules restrict amending activity.

During the 1980s and early 1990s Democratic Party leaders developed special rules into powerful, flexible tools that can be tailored to the problem a particular bill presents. A rule that restricts amendments in any way reduces uncertainty and gives the bill's proponents the advantage. Strategy can be planned more efficiently. Carefully crafted rules can sometimes structure choices to bring about a particular outcome. The welfare reform legislation discussed earlier illustrates how. Most Democrats—enough to constitute a clear majority of the House—favored passing a welfare reform bill; they believed it constituted good public policy. Many, however, believed that for reelection reasons they had to go on record as favoring a reduction in what the program was going to cost. By allowing a vote on an amendment to make moderate cuts, but barring one on an amendment that slashed the program, the rule gave members the opportunity to demonstrate fiscal responsibility but ensured that legislation most Democrats favored would be enacted.

The power and flexibility of special rules as they have evolved make them useful in many circumstances. The uncertainty that the 1970s reforms begot and the problems that majority Democrats faced in legislating during the adverse political climate of the 1980s and early 1990s stimulated their development. But the upward trend in the use of special rules did not end when political circumstances changed. The legislative opportunity and the pressure to deliver under difficult circumstances that the election of a Democratic president represented led the Democratic leadership to intensify its employment of such rules during the 103d Congress.

The rule for the reconciliation bill implementing Clinton's economic program in 1993 provides an example of how useful a strategically structured rule can be. That rule allowed a vote only on a comprehensive Republican substitute; amendments to delete various unpopular elements of the package—the BTU tax and the tax on high income recipients' Social Security payments—were not made in order. Passage was crucial for the young Clinton administration and for the Democratic Party, but the constraints imposed by the huge deficit and the need to reduce it made it difficult to put a package together and hold it together. The rule was intended to focus debate on the broad philosophical differences between the two parties' approaches to the problem of reducing the deficit and to protect Democrats from having to cast one tough vote after another. Many would have found it hard to explain to the folks back home why they had voted against amendments striking unpopular tax provisions, especially in response to thirty-second attack ads. If the Republicans were allowed to offer amendments, the Democrats would be forced to choose between casting a series of politically dangerous votes or letting a carefully constructed compromise—the passage of which, most believed, was crucial to the future of the country and the party—be picked apart on the floor.

When in the minority, Republicans had labeled restrictive rules dictatorial and illegitimate and had promised not to use them if they took control.[16] In the 104th Congress, however, they were committed to passing an ambitious agenda in a short time. The usefulness of restrictive rules for promoting the party's legislative objectives overcame any Republican objections based on principle or the fear of seeming hypocritical. To be sure, the restrictions were sometimes of a different nature: Republicans often limited amending activity by restricting the time for consideration rather than specifying the number or kind of amendments that could be offered. Overall, the proportion of restrictive rules declined. In 1995 about half of all rules for the initial consideration of legislation were restrictive. However, when only major measures are considered, the picture is different; in 1995, 77 percent of rules for the consideration of major measures were restrictive.

In 1995 Republicans used a cleverly constructed restrictive rule to protect their rescission bill. It specified that anyone wishing to restore a spending cut in the bill had to offset the cost by cutting something else in the same section of the bill; in other words, no money could be transferred to social programs from defense spending or from disaster relief for California.

The Triumph of Individualism and the New Legislative Process in the Senate

The contemporary legislative process in the Senate is shaped by senators' rampant individualism and their leaders' attempts to do their jobs within that context. Senators now routinely exploit the enormous prerogatives Senate rules give the individual to further their own agendas.

In an institutional setting where every member is able—and often willing—to impede the legislative process, leaders must accommodate individual members to legislate successfully. The increase in postcommittee adjustments to legislation in the Senate reflects this accommodation. Rare in the 1970s even on major legislation—only 2 percent of major measures underwent postcommittee adjustments in the 91st and 94th Congresses—the frequency jumped to about 20 percent in the 1980s and then to more than 33 percent in the early 1990s. In 1995 more than 60 percent of major legislation was subject to postcommittee adjustments. Although the negotiations that produce these modifications are sometimes undertaken by committee leaders or other interested senators, the party leaders often become involved.

Senate individualism is most evident on the floor. Senators can use their power to offer as many amendments as they choose to almost any bill, not only to further their policy preferences but also to bring up issues leaders might like to keep off the floor, to make political points, and to force their political opponents in the chamber to cast tough votes. Senators regularly use their amending prerogatives for all these purposes. Because, in most cases, amendments need not be germane, Barbara Boxer, D-Calif., was able to force onto the floor the issue of holding open hearings on the sexual harassment charges against Bob Packwood, R-Ore., even though Majority Leader Dole wanted to keep it off. Boxer offered it as an amendment to a defense authorization bill. For years, Jesse Helms, R-N.C., has been bringing up and forcing votes on amendments on hot button issues such as abortion, pornography, homosexuality, and school prayer. He often does not expect to win, but to provide ammunition for the electoral opponents of senators who disagree with him.

Senators' use of their amending prerogatives has resulted in many bills being subjected to a barrage of amendments on the floor. In the 1950s the proportion of legislation subject to high amending activity (ten or more amending roll calls) was tiny: for the 84th (1953–1954) and 86th (1959–1960) Congresses, it averaged 2.7 percent. In the 1960s and 1970s it rose to a mean of 8.2 percent per Congress, and in the 1980s it averaged 14.9 percent.[17] In the 1980s and 1990s major legislation was considerably more likely to be subject to such amending marathons; on about 30 percent of major legislation, more than ten amendments were offered on the floor and pushed to a roll call vote.

Bills that are controversial or broad in scope or that, at least in the view of the majority party, have to pass are most likely to be the target of large numbers of amendments. For example, more than forty amendments were offered and pushed to a recorded vote on each of the following: the Democrats' major trade bill in 1988, the 1993 budget resolution that carried Clinton's economic program, and the Republicans' unfunded mandates bill in 1995. Such high amending activity presents problems for the Senate as a legislature and for its majority leadership, which is charged with floor scheduling and coalition building. It creates uncertainty about the schedule and about policy outcomes. How long floor consideration of a contentious measure will take may be impossible to predict. Under a barrage of amendments, compromises can be difficult to hold together. Opponents, after all, attempt to write amendments that will split the majority coalition. The majority leader has no mechanism such as the House special rule that can be used to fend off these amendments.

To lend some predictability to floor proceedings, the majority leader frequently negotiates unanimous consent agreements to govern the consideration of major legislation. Such an agreement limits floor time and may limit the amendments allowed; however, one senator's objection can kill a proposed unanimous consent agreement, so all senators' interests must be accommodated.

Senators' willingness to use their privilege of unlimited debate has had a major impact on the legislative process in the Senate. In the 1950s, filibusters occurred at a rate of about one per Congress; the rate rose to just under five per Congress in the 1960s and continued to rise at an accelerated pace in the 1970s and 1980s. The 103d Congress saw thirty filibusters.[18] Major legislation often encounters some extended debate-related problem identifiable from the public record. In the late 1980s and early 1990s just under 30 percent did; in the first Congress of the Clinton presidency, almost 50 percent of major measures encountered such problems, and in 1995, 44 percent did.

Written into the budget act are rules limiting debate on budget resolutions and reconciliation bills. Because such measures are protected from a filibuster, they become even more attractive as a vehicle for major policy change. The budget act, however, also restricts that strategy through the Byrd rule, named for Sen. Robert Byrd, D-W.Va. The rule prohibits "extraneous matter" in a reconciliation bill.[19]

Given senators' willingness to exploit their right of extended debate, the majority leader, in scheduling legislation and often in crafting it, has little choice but to be responsive to small groups of members or even to individuals. On legislation of secondary importance, before a recess, or late in the session, one senator's objection will suffice to keep a bill off the floor. When a great deal of legislation is awaiting floor consideration, the majority leader cannot afford the time for a filibuster, so even an ambiguous threat to filibuster serves as a veto. This reality has become semi-institutionalized in the practice of holds. Any senator can inform the leader that he or she wishes to place a hold on a measure—a bill, a presidential nomination, or a treaty. Leaders assert that use of this device only guarantees that the senator will be informed before the measure is scheduled for floor consideration; however, if the hold represents a veiled threat to filibuster the measure and if other matters are more pressing, it often constitutes a de facto veto.

The mere threat to filibuster is often sufficient to extract concessions from the supporters of a measure. A number of the Contract with America items that sped through the House were held up in the Senate until their supporters made significant compromises—for example, a bill to impose a moratorium on all new regulations was transformed, under a filibuster threat, into a measure giving Congress forty-five days to review new regulations. In the 103d Congress a number of Clinton's priorities also ran into troubles in the Senate, not because they lacked the support of a majority but because the sixty votes to cut off debate could not be amassed. Supporters had to make concessions on national service legislation and the voter registration bill (motor voter), for example, to overcome a filibuster or a filibuster threat.

Sometimes a large minority defeats outright legislation supported by a majority. Clinton's stimulus package succumbed to this fate in 1993. Senate Majority Leader George Mitchell, D-Maine, attempted to invoke cloture a number of times, but, even though majorities supported cutting off debate, he was not able to put together the necessary sixty votes. In 1995 Senate Democrats forced Majority Leader Dole to abandon his own bill overhauling federal regulatory procedures; he mustered a majority on several cloture votes but fell short of the sixty needed. In the 103d Congress, of nineteen major measures that failed to become law, twelve were killed by the Senate alone; eight of those ran into filibuster-related problems.

The majority leader's leverage depends not on procedural powers, of which he has few, but on his central position in the chamber; on really difficult and contentious issues, he has a better chance than anyone else in the chamber of negotiating a deal that can get the necessary votes. Consequently his leverage is dependent on senators wanting legislation, but if a substantial minority prefers no legislation to a deal, he has little recourse.

New Legislative Processes: An Assessment

By the end of the first hundred days of the 104th Congress, the House had voted on every measure in the Contract with America, as Republicans had promised, and had passed all but the term limits constitutional amendment, which required a two-thirds vote. In the Senate only five measures—some parts of the preface and of two of the ten planks of the contract—had reached the floor, and only four, mostly relatively uncontroversial measures, had passed. By the end of 1995 just five contract items had become law.[20]

The contract items fared differently in the House and Senate in part because the distribution of preferences differed in the two chambers: moderates made up a larger proportion of the Senate Republican membership than of the House Republican membership, and Senate Republicans had not endorsed the contract. Even more important, however, are the differences in chamber rules and in the tools leaders have available. In the House many of the modifications and innovations in the legislative process allow the party leadership to tailor the process to the problems a particular measure raises and use them to get the measure passed. In the Senate changes in the legislative process have created more problems than opportunities for the majority party leadership.

A brief examination of the legislative process on welfare reform, one of the major contract items, illustrates the differences. In the House three committees—Ways and Means, Education and Economic Opportunity, and Agriculture—reported their provisions by early March. Under strict instructions from the party leadership, Republican committee chairs had pushed the measures through their committees with limited debate and on largely party line votes. The leadership then combined the provisions from the three committees, making alterations where they seemed advisable. The bill was brought to the floor under a tight rule barring votes on several amendments that would have split Republicans. Pro-life Republicans, who feared that provisions cutting off benefits to teenage unwed mothers would encourage abortions, were denied a chance to offer amendments deleting such provisions. The rule was narrowly approved, and the bill passed on a 234–199 party line vote.

The Senate Finance Committee did not report a bill until May 26. Problems within the majority party quickly became apparent: Republicans from the South and Southwest, who represent fast-growing states that offer relatively low welfare benefits, objected to funding formulas based on past welfare expenditures; some conservative senators decried the dropping of House provisions barring unwed teenage mothers from receiving welfare; and Republican moderates believed the legislation did not provide enough money for child care and would allow states to cut their own welfare spending too much.

Because of the saliency and hot-button character of the issue, no one, including most Democrats, wanted to vote against a welfare reform bill, and, had the Republican leadership been able to force an up-or-down vote, the committee bill might well have passed. But because Dole had no way of protecting the legislation from a filibuster or a barrage of amendments on the floor, he had to deal. He, along with Finance Committee Chairman Packwood, took on the task of rewriting the bill. In early August, after several months of negotiations, Dole unveiled a revised bill aimed at satisfying the various factions. The new proposal was a modified version of the Finance Committee bill and incorporated in revised form three other pieces of legislation—the food stamps overhaul from the Agriculture Committee and the child care and job training bills approved by the Labor and Human Resources Committee. Adding these provisions provided a greater scope for compromise.

Floor debate began August 7, and it soon became evident that problems still existed and the bill would not pass before the scheduled recess. Republicans blamed the Democrats, charging that they intended to offer fifty amendments. In fact, the GOP was still split. On September 6, after the recess, Dole brought the bill back to the floor, but he still lacked a secure winning coalition and continued to make changes to placate various groups of Republicans. He began talking with Democrats and moderate Republicans, and on September 15 a compromise was reached; among other provisions, it added substantial funds for child care. On September 19 Dole offered for himself and the minority leader the Dole-Daschle amendment, which incorporated the compromise, and it passed, 87–12, with mostly hardline conservative Republicans opposed. Acceptance of the amendment moderated the Senate welfare bill, which was already more moderate than the House bill. The Senate passed the bill as amended 87 to 12, with only one Republican voting in opposition.

In the House, then, the new legislative process has on balance provided the majority party leadership with effective tools for facilitating the passage of legislation. Backed by a reasonably cohesive majority party, House leaders can engineer passage of legislation quickly and in a form consonant with the preferences of the members of the majority party. In the Senate, as in the House, the party leadership has become more central to the legislative process, but, unlike the Speaker, the Senate majority leader has gained few new tools for dealing with a more unruly membership. The need to accommodate most senators and to build supermajority coalitions to pass legislation in the Senate almost always means the process is slower and often results in more broadly based (or weakening) compromises. Sometimes, it results in no legislation at all. In the contemporary Congress, the legislative process in the two chambers is more distinct in form and in results than ever before.

Notes

1. For an elaboration of this argument, see Barbara Sinclair, *Unorthodox Lawmaking* (Washington, D.C.: CQ Press, forthcoming).
2. Donald E. Matthews, *U.S. Senators and Their World* (New York: Vintage, 1960); Norman Ornstein, Robert Peabody, and David Rohde, "The Changing Senate: From the 1950s to the 1970s," in *Congress Reconsidered,* 1st ed., ed. Lawrence C. Dodd and Bruce I. Oppenheimer (New York: Praeger, 1977); Barbara Sinclair, *The Transformation of the U.S. Senate* (Baltimore: Johns Hopkins University Press, 1989).
3. On House change, see Dodd and Oppenheimer, *Congress Reconsidered*; Barbara Sinclair, *Majority Leadership in the U.S. House* (Baltimore: Johns Hopkins University Press, 1983); Steven Smith, *Call to Order: Floor Politics in the House and Senate* (Washington, D.C.: Brookings, 1989); David Rohde, *Parties and Leaders in the Postreform House* (Chicago: University of Chicago Press, 1991); Roger H. Davidson, ed., *The Postreform Congress* (New York: St. Martin's Press, 1991).
4. Barbara Sinclair, *Legislators, Leaders and Lawmaking* (Baltimore: Johns Hopkins University Press, 1995).
5. Major legislation is defined as those measures Congressional Quarterly contemporaneously identifies as major legislation plus those measures on which key votes occurred, again according to CQ. This definition yields approximately forty-five to fifty-five major measures per Congress. The following Congresses have been coded: 91st (1969–1970), 94th (1975–1976), 97th (1981–1982), 100th (1987–1988), 101st (1989–1990), and 103d (1993–1994); when data are presented in the text, they are for these Congresses. Data for the 104th are based on all major measures as defined above that received floor consideration in at least one chamber in 1995.

6. On the budget process, see Allen Schick, *Congress and Money* (Washington, D.C.: Urban Institute, 1980); James Thurber and Samantha Durst, "The 1990 Budget Enforcement Act: The Decline of Congressional Accountability," in *Congress Reconsidered,* 5th ed., ed. Dodd and Oppenheimer (Washington, D.C.: CQ Press, 1993).
7. John Gilmour, *Reconcilable Differences?* (Berkeley: University of California Press, 1990); Barbara Sinclair, "Governing Unheroically (and Sometimes Unappetizingly): Bush and the 101st Congress," in *The Bush Presidency: First Appraisals,* ed. Colin Campbell and Bert Rockman (Chatham, N.J.: Chatham House, 1991); Barbara Sinclair, "Trying to Govern Positively in a Negative Era: Clinton and the 103rd Congress," in *The Clinton Presidency: First Appraisals,* ed. Colin Campbell and Bert Rockman (Chatham, N.J.: Chatham House, 1996).
8. For details on these negotiations, see Sinclair, *Legislators, Leaders and Lawmaking.*
9. Roger Davidson and Walter Oleszek, "From Monopoly to Management: Changing Patterns of Committee Deliberation," in *The Postreform Congress;* Garry Young and Joseph Cooper, "Multiple Referral and the Transformation of House Decision Making," in *Congress Reconsidered,* 5th ed.
10. C. Lawrence Evans and Walter Oleszek, "Congressional Tsunami? Institutional Change in the 104th Congress" (paper delivered at the annual meeting of the American Political Science Association, Chicago, Aug. 31–Sept. 3, 1995), 14–15.
11. Richard Beth, "Control of the House Floor Agenda: Implications from the Use of the Discharge Rule, 1931–1994" (paper delivered at the annual meeting of the American Political Science Association, New York, Sept. 1–4, 1994).
12. ΣGeorge Hager, "House GOP Pushes Budget Cuts as Political Stakes Mount," *Congressional Quarterly Weekly Report,* March 18, 1995, 796–797.
13. "Term Limits: Procedure OK'd on Floor Vote," *Congressional Quarterly Weekly Report,* March 18, 1995, 787.
14. Jeffrey Katz and David Hosansky, "Provisions of House Welfare Bill," *Congressional Quarterly Weekly Report,* March 18, 1995, 815.
15. Stanley Bach and Steven S. Smith, *Managing Uncertainty in the House of Representatives* (Washington, D.C.: Brookings, 1988); Don Wolfensberger, "Comparative Data on the U.S. House of Representatives," compiled by the Republican staff of the House Rules Committee, Nov. 10, 1992.
16. Richard B. Cheney, "An Unruly House," *Public Opinion* 11 (January 1989): 41–44; William Connelly and John Pitney, *Congress' Permanent Minority? Republicans in the U.S. House* (Lanham, Md.: Rowman and Littlefield, 1994).
17. Based on data for even numbered Congresses from the 88th to the 96th and all Congresses from the 97th through the 99th. See Sinclair, *Transformation of the U.S. Senate.*
18. "A Look at the Senate Filibuster," DSG Special Report, June 13, 1994, No. 103–28, Appendix B (compiled by the Congressional Research Service). Data for the 103d Congress are from Richard Beth, "Cloture in the Senate, 103rd Congress," memorandum, Congressional Research Service, June 23, 1995. For pertinent caveats about the data, see Richard Beth, "What We Don't Know About Filibusters" (paper presented at the annual meeting of the Western Political Science Association, Portland, Ore., March 15–18, 1995).
19. Charles Tiefer, *Congressional Practice and Procedure* (Westport, Conn.: Greenwood Press, 1989), 891–894.
20. " 'Contract with America' Update," *Congressional Quarterly Weekly Report,* Jan. 6, 1996, 52.

11. Partisanship, Bipartisanship, and Crosspartisanship in Congress Since the New Deal

Joseph Cooper and Garry Young

The strength of party voting in the contemporary Congress contrasts sharply with voting patterns over the past half-century and is one of the defining features of the politics of the 1990s. The aim of this chapter is to put this development in historical perspective in order to trace its emergence, measure its dimensions, and assess its significance and prospects.

Students of Congress, both in the press and in the universities, have long emphasized the role of parties in their accounts of congressional politics. Indeed, the character and importance of congressional parties seemed so clear and obvious that traditionally parties have been treated as givens with little recognition of any need for deeper conceptual understanding. As a result, through most of this century, analysts of the role of congressional parties have seen them as simple, generic entities and focused on the factual or empirical task of assessing variation in their impact on procedure and decision making in different periods of American history and/or different arenas of policy.

Such an approach, however, provides an inadequate framework for understanding the role and importance of congressional parties. This is particularly true in periods of transition. In recent decades the rapid pace of change has exposed the costs of conceptual weakness. In the 1970s political scientists began to challenge the importance of congressional parties on both empirical and theoretical grounds.[1] It is no accident that this challenge arose in a period when low levels of party voting coincided with a new theoretical perspective on politics. This perspective assumed politics to be individualistic and particularistic. It pictured members as self-interested actors who were primarily concerned with reelection, and congressional decision making as a process primarily defined by the desire of members to maximize discrete services and benefits to their constituencies. In so doing it has raised basic and searching questions regarding the stability of voting coalitions, the basis of collective action, and the importance of parties.

This challenge continues, and the result has been an extensive debate in the academic literature over the role of party as a determinant of policy outcomes and organizational structure in Congress.[2] But there has been another important consequence of limited conceptual understanding that has not been widely recognized. The ways in which we understand a phenomenon constrain and shape the ways we measure it. In other words, measurement is dependent on theory; the assumptions and boundaries of conceptual understanding have decisive impacts on the power and relevance of measurement. It is not surprising, then, that in recent decades there has also been a debate in the academic literature over how to approach and measure congressional voting and whether the strength of party voting has increased or declined in the twentieth century.[3]

Goals and Assumptions

The present state of conceptualizing and measuring the role of congressional parties provides a necessary context for realizing the goals of this chapter. To understand the impact of party on congressional procedures and decision making over the past half-century and to bring that experience to bear on current trends, we must cease treating party and party voting as givens. This chapter therefore relies on a theory of vote structuring that we have developed and on several new measures of congressional voting patterns derived from it. However, as is always true, both our goals and approach rest on certain assumptions that we need to make clear before we present our theory or measures.

First, party voting is based on a variety of forces. The most important of these are the commonalities of principle, view, and interest that unite fellow partisans across their respective constituencies.[4] These factors provide indispensable "glue" for uniting members in support of particular bills on the basis of similar stances or orientations to policy, shared viewpoints on concrete policy issues, and compatible interests. In addition, the degree of interconnection among the electoral fortunes of fellow partisans, the organizational leverage and rewards that are available to party leaders, and the political skills of these leaders provide important reinforcements for building stable and effective majority coalitions. Indeed, under modern conditions it is doubtful that without the aid of all these factors, leaders could manage the high potential for chaos and paralysis endemic in legislative processes of collective choice and collective action.

Second, given the nature and basis of party voting, its strength varies over time and between the houses. Foremost in importance as a source of variation is variation in the breadth and depth of the commonalities of view, interest, and electoral fortune that provide the glue or incentives for collective action. The binding force of this glue rises and falls in response to broader, dynamic forces in the electoral and party systems. Similarly, the nature and distribution of organizational power are not fixed, but vary with the degree of shared purpose and need among majority partisans and with institutional size, culture, and workload. As a result, stark differences in the leverage that structure confers on party leaders, and in their ability to exploit or increase it to enhance party voting, exist both in different time periods and between the two houses. Finally, the skills of party leaders serve as a source of variation, not simply as a matter of personality, but also as a matter of institutional context. In all cases, dependence on the skills of party leaders and their ability to be effective is bounded by the potential for agreement among partisans and the nature and distribution of organizational power.[5]

Third, general or aggregate measures of party voting provide valid and instructive evidence for understanding congressional processes and decision making. The apparent complexity of policy issues and divisions in recent decades should not lead analysts to believe that voting outcomes should be studied only in particular policy areas without direct attention to party. There is value in the analysis of voting in discrete policy areas, especially if it is done historically. Still, it is true both deductively and empirically that there is a strong relationship between the overall strength of partisanship and the character of outcomes in particular policy areas.[6] Similarly, the primacy many contemporary students of Congress place on individual preferences does not mean that party must be seen as an irrelevant or residual force.[7] Nor does it mean that no attention need be given to direct measures of its overall impact. There is value in analyzing voting on the basis of dynamic, spatial modeling without reference to party to establish the nature and scope of overarching patterns of individual preferences. A focus on patterns of preference or ideological orientation can measure the consistency and strength of the glue that underlies party voting and can identify differences in the coherence and distance of the forces that determine voting patterns in particular Congresses and across time. But it cannot easily discriminate among these forces and can deal with the role of party only generally and, even then, in largely inferential terms. Such an approach does not provide an adequate framework for examining the actual impact of party on majority building and the distribution of organizational power.[8]

Fourth, even in legislative systems characterized by two parties, such as Congress, party voting needs to be seen as a complex, not a simple, phenomenon.[9] For the purposes of this chapter, we posit two interrelated dimensions of congressional voting. One is horizontal in character and concerns the overall strength of party voting as compared to other broad voting patterns. This dimension necessarily involves both measures of the frequency of competing voting patterns and measures of their strength. The other dimension is vertical in character and concerns the strength of broad voting patterns in their own distinct spheres or fields of action. In the case of party, this dimension pertains to the strength or effectiveness of the party majority in organizing and controlling roll call votes when majorities of each party oppose one another. Concern with the strength of party voting is thus common to both dimensions in assessing the role and importance of party. However, because each dimension approaches partisan strength differently, each encompasses a different set of the components of party voting. The first dimension equates strength with the level or degree of partisan structuring relative to other voting patterns. So defined, the components of party voting it involves, aside from frequency, are simply intraparty unity and interparty division. In contrast, the second dimension equates strength with effectiveness in controlling outcomes on partisan votes. So defined, it includes components of party voting, such as the majority's vote margin, patterns of support and defection, and the stability of majority support, that are as critical to partisan control as levels of partisan unity and division. In sum, then, this dimension does not involve frequency, but it does involve components of party voting above and beyond those that determine the sheer degree of mobilization into opposing forces.

A Theory of Vote Structuring

We shall elaborate, illustrate, and apply our approach to party voting in the remainder of this chapter. Our first task must be to place party voting within the framework of a more general theory of vote structuring in Congress. Although a host of traditional measures of party voting exist, the utility of these measures has been hampered by lack of attention to the varied dimensions and components of party voting. As we noted, party voting has been treated as a given. Such treatment is blind to the complex character of party voting and implicitly assumes it to be simple and uniform. Measures have therefore typically been seen as roughly equal and generally serviceable without adequate recognition of their fit or power. The result has been not only a certain randomness in measuring party voting, but also a failure to confront the fact that existing measures do not capture pivotal aspects of party voting—for example, changes in trends regarding the overall strength of partisanship and bipartisanship relative to one another or the size and impact of stable party support.

The nature of the problem suggests the strategy for solving it. We need not abandon the familiar aggregate measures of party voting that have been extensively relied upon by many analysts for over a half-century.[10] But we do need to put them in theoretical perspective so that we understand their strengths and weaknesses. Having done so, we will be able to use them appropriately as well as respond to their deficiencies by combining them in new theoretically informed ways. As we have indicated, to accomplish this we must go back to fundamentals and identify a set of basic propositions regarding the structuring of votes. These axioms will provide a framework for analyzing the impact of party and guiding both the use of old measures and the construction of new ones.

Our approach posits three basic voting patterns—partisanship, bipartisanship, and crosspartisanship. We begin by distinguishing perfect partisanship from perfect bipartisanship. Figure 11-1 illustrates the differences. In a perfect partisan vote the forces that unite and divide the two parties fully structure the vote. In such a case 100 percent of the majority party votes together and in an opposite direction from 100 percent of the minority party. Conversely, in a perfect bipartisan vote the forces that unite members across party lines (including indifference as well as principle, view, and interest) fully structure the vote. In this case 100 percent of both the majority and minority parties vote in the same direction (a unanimous vote).

Obviously, perfect partisan votes and perfect bipartisan votes are rare. But conceptually they provide important parameters. This is true not only at the extremes. The voting situation halfway between these points also provides a critical benchmark. In this situation both parties split evenly in voting direction so that 50 percent of each party votes yea and 50 percent votes nay. Such splits are evenly balanced between partisanship and bipartisanship and, though far more theoretical than real, provide a very useful point of departure for dealing with the types of votes that commonly occur. Insofar as votes incline toward perfect par-

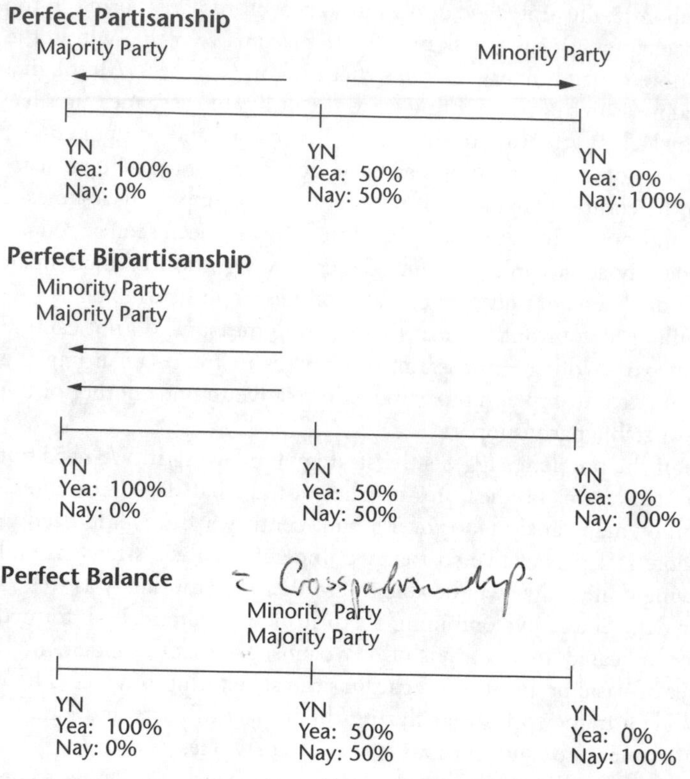

tisanship and involve more than 50 percent of one party opposing more than 50 percent of the other, we can regard such votes as partisan and measure both their frequency (their number as a proportion of all votes) and their potency or strength (the average amount of partisan structuring that occurs on such votes). Combining the two we will have an overall measure of the degree to which party structures voting in any particular Congress. The same is true of votes that incline in a bipartisan direction and involve more than 50 percent of each party voting in the same direction.

This framework also has the advantage of allowing us to identify and distinguish a third voting pattern that we have termed crosspartisanship. The fact that party majorities rarely totally oppose one another or totally vote together means that varying degrees of intraparty division persist and resist partisan structuring on partisan votes and bipartisan structuring on bipartisan votes. As a result, partisan votes not only involve patterns of voting in which party majorities oppose one another, but also patterns in which party minorities vote with majorities of the other party. Similarly, bipartisan votes not only involve patterns of voting in which party majorities vote together, but also patterns in which party minorities vote together. What we have termed or identified as crosspartisanship thus pertains to the residual voting patterns on partisan and bipartisan votes and reflects the degree to which party minorities vote with majorities or minorities of the opposite party in ways that are distinctive from partisan or bipartisan voting patterns. It may be noted that in theory the pattern we have termed perfect balance in Figure 11-1 is a distinctive and independent voting pattern in its own right and equivalent to perfect crosspartisanship. However, as has been noted, exactly equal voting divisions between and within the parties virtually never occur and, in the case of crosspartisanship as elsewhere, serve primarily as a benchmark for conceptualizing and measuring the strength of the voting patterns that do occur. As we shall demonstrate, our approach allows us to derive an overall measure of crosspartisanship once we have secured overall measures of partisanship and bipartisanship.

The basic problem we must solve, therefore, is to create overall measures of partisanship and bipartisanship by combining measures of the frequency or incidence of partisan and bipartisan votes with measures of the degree of structuring on these votes. Measurement of the relative frequency of partisan and bipartisan votes is easily understood and requires only data on the percentage of partisan and bipartisan votes. But measurement of the degree of partisan structuring on partisan votes and the degree of bipartisan structuring on bipartisan votes, separate and apart from the frequency of these types of votes, is not immediately clear. More explanation is required if we are to understand how we can combine frequency and structuring to create an overall measure of structuring.

Figures 11-2 and 11-3 serve this purpose by using the first New Deal Congress—the 73d (1933–1935)—as an example. In this Congress the average voting division on partisan votes in the House was 85.4 percent of Democrats voting against 88.7 percent of the Republicans. These scores are the traditional party unity scores, and they also mean that on average 14.6 percent of the Democrats and 11.3 percent of the Republicans voted against their fellow partisans and in the same direction as the majority of the opposing party. Given these figures, we can easily calculate the degree to which partisanship structures the decision-making outcomes on partisan votes. On such votes 100 percent of one party voting against 100 percent of the other provides 100 percent partisan structuring and a 50 percent-50 percent vote split between the parties serves as the zero point because the level or degree of division within the parties cannot be less than 50 percent versus 50 percent. Therefore, the amount of partisan structuring is not equivalent to the unity scores. As Figure 11-2 illustrates, these scores, while useful, treat a scale that in fact ranges only from 50 percent to 100 percent for each party as a full 100-point scale for each party. Instead, the measurement of structuring requires a single 100-point scale for both parties that recognizes the 50 percent-50 percent break as the zero point. Structuring is equivalent, then, to the sum of the amount to which each majority votes in an opposite direction past the

Figure 11-2 Vote Structuring on Party Votes, 73d House (1933–1935)

Scores
(Party Majorities Opposed)

Unity			Simple Structuring	
	Democrat	Republican	Partisan Structuring	Crosspartisan Residual
Voted with majority of own party	85.4%	88.7%	74.1%	25.9%
Voted against majority of own party	14.6%	11.3%		

Scales for Scores

Unity

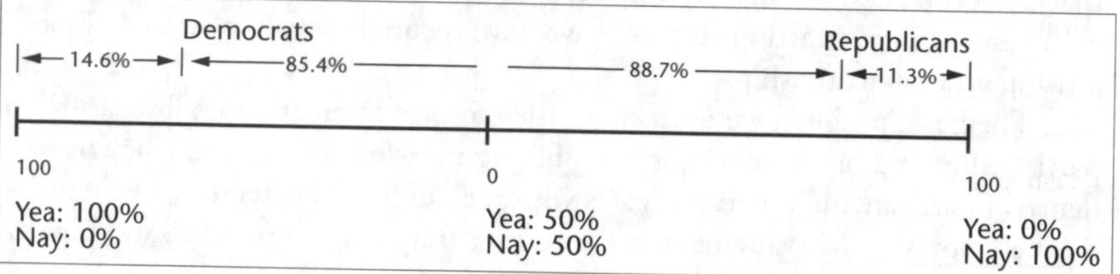

Partisan Structuring

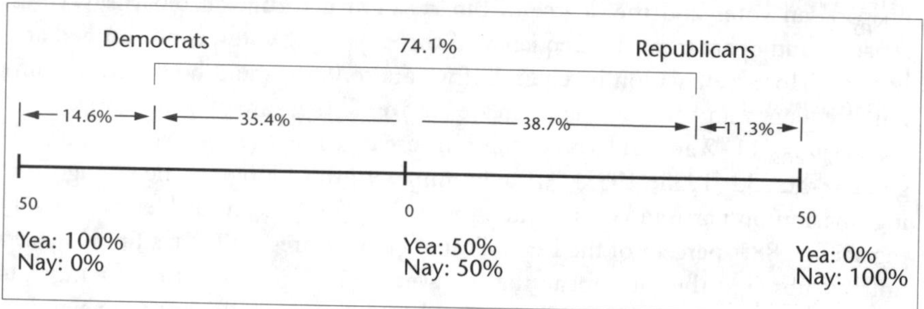

50 percent-50 percent break that constitutes the zero point. Such a score (74.1 percent in this case) should be and is, in fact, equivalent to the sum total of defection in both parties subtracted from 100 percent. To distinguish this score from the overall partisan structuring score, we shall call it the simple partisan structuring score.

As for bipartisan votes in this House, on average 81.4 percent of the Democrats joined with 78.3 percent of the Republicans to form bipartisan majorities, and 18.6 percent of the Democrats joined with 21.7 percent of the Republicans to form opposing bipartisan minorities. Here too, these figures allow us to calculate the degree to which bipartisan factors united the parties and structured the outcomes on bipartisan votes. On such votes 100 percent of one party

Figure 11-3 Vote Structuring on Bipartisan Votes, 73d House (1933–1935)

Scores
(Party Majorities Allied)

	Unity		Simple Structuring	
	Democrat	Republican	Bipartisan Structuring	Crosspartisan Residual
Voted with majority of own party	81.4%	78.3%	59.7%	40.3%
Voted against majority of own party	18.6%	21.7%		

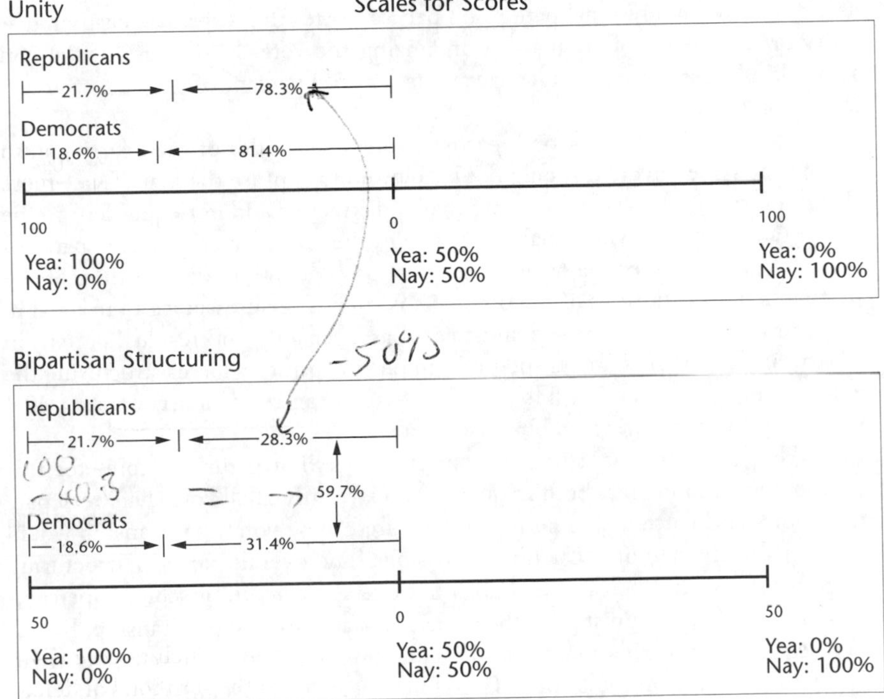

voting in the same direction as 100 percent of the other provides 100 percent bipartisan structuring, and 50 percent of one party voting in the same direction as 50 percent of the other serves as the zero point because division within each party cannot be less than 50 percent versus 50 percent. Again, the actual amount of bipartisan structuring is equivalent, not to the unity scores per se, but to the sum total of agreement between the two majorities past a 50 percent-50 percent level of agreement, 59.7 percent in this case (see Figure 11-3). This score should be and is the same as the sum total of minority defection in both parties subtracted from 100 percent. Again, we shall distinguish it from the overall bipartisan structuring score by calling it the simple bipartisan structuring score.

Let us turn now to measuring crosspartisanship. As we have suggested, crosspartisanship pertains to the degree of intraparty division on both partisan and bipartisan votes. On partisan votes the fact that minorities in each party vote in opposite directions should not be allowed to confuse the issue. This voting pattern is quite different from what we have defined as partisan voting. It involves defectors who are not voting with a majority of their fellow partisans against a majority of the opposing party, but rather with a majority of the opposing party against a majority of their own party. In addition, it is distinguishable from what we have defined as bipartisan voting in which majorities of each party vote together. We therefore regard it as a crosspartisan voting pattern and treat it as a distinctive and residual pattern on partisan votes that expresses partisan disunity or weakness, not strength in organizing the vote. In the case of the 73d House this crosspartisan residual accounts for 25.9 percent of the vote structuring on partisan votes.

Similarly, the fact that on bipartisan votes, minorities of each party join to vote in the same direction should not be allowed to confuse the issue. Once more this is a form of crosspartisan voting that is distinctive and not equivalent to the bipartisan pattern in which majorities vote in the same direction or the patterns on party votes in which majorities vote in opposite directions or minorities of one party join with majorities of the other. As is true of the crosspartisan residual in partisan votes, it is best viewed and treated as a separate and residual pattern in bipartisan votes that counters and undermines the primary forces structuring the vote. In the case of the 73d House this crosspartisan residual accounts for 40.3 percent of the structuring on bipartisan votes.

We are now in a position to construct overall structuring scores for this House that will integrate both frequency and strength. If all votes had been partisan votes and partisanship perfectly structured these votes, partisanship would account for all the vote structuring possible. The overall partisan structuring score would be 100 percent, and all other overall structuring scores 0 percent. Under equivalent circumstances the same point applies to bipartisanship. But all Houses involve combinations of partisan and bipartisan votes as well as less than perfect structuring on these votes. Therefore, to secure an overall picture of structuring, we must adjust the strength of the simple structuring scores and their crosspartisan residuals on each type of vote to the actual frequency of that type of vote.

In the 73d House, 72.7 percent of the votes were partisan votes and 27.3 percent of votes were bipartisan votes. As a result, even if partisanship perfectly structured partisan votes, it could account for only 72.7 percent of the vote structuring in this House because 27.3 percent of the votes involved majorities of both parties voting together. Conversely, bipartisanship can account for no more than 27.3 percent of the vote structuring in this House. Moreover, as Figures 11-2 and 11-3 illustrate, structuring was not perfect on either type of vote and thus both the simple partisan structuring score (74.1 percent) and its residual (25.9 percent) and the simple bipartisan structuring score (59.7 percent) and its residual (40.3 percent) have to be adjusted to reflect the actual incidence of the two types of votes. This can be done by multiplying these scores by the percentage of partisan or bipartisan votes as appropriate and dividing by 100. When we do so, we get an overall partisan structuring score of 53.87 percent (72.7 x 74.1 ÷ 100), an overall bipartisan structuring score of 16.3 percent (27.3 x 59.7 ÷ 100), an overall partisan residual of 18.83 percent (72.7 x 25.9 ÷ 100), and an overall bipartisan residual of 11 percent (27.3 x 40.3 ÷ 100). The sum of the two crosspartisan residuals is 29.83 percent, which provides an overall measure of crosspartisan structuring. The three overall structuring scores for the 73d House are thus 53.87 percent, 16.3 percent, and 29.83 percent. They sum to 100 percent or the total amount of structuring possible.

Trends in House Voting Since the New Deal

Earlier in this chapter we distinguished between vertical and horizontal dimensions of vote structuring. We saw the horizontal dimension as pertaining to the relative strength of partisan voting as compared to other voting patterns. We saw the vertical dimension as pertaining to the strength or effectiveness of particular voting patterns in their own spheres or fields of action. Our theory of vote structuring provides a basis for measuring both the horizontal and vertical dimensions of congressional voting. The overall scores provide comparative measures of the relative strength of partisanship, bipartisanship, and crosspartisanship and allow us to trace trends in party voting with far more precision than has been possible formerly. In addition, the simple or unadjusted partisan and bipartisan structuring scores and their crosspartisan residuals, when combined with measures of margin, support, and stability, provide a basis for assessing success or effectiveness on partisan and bipartisan votes treated as separate or discrete arenas of politics and majority building.

We turn first to the House and to a horizontal or comparative analysis of voting patterns. Figure 11-4 provides data on overall vote structuring scores in the House from the 73d Congress (1933–1935) through most of the 104th Congress (1995–1997), the first Republican Congress in forty years. This figure, as well as others we use, classifies Houses into types on the basis of overall structuring scores for the whole course of congressional history. Both to permit analysis of the data we present and to put this data in even broader historical perspective, we need to begin by explaining our classification scheme.

The most basic criterion involves the balance between the sum of the overall partisan and bipartisan structuring scores and the overall crosspartisan score. When the former is larger than the latter, partisan and bipartisan majorities structure more than half of the voting on roll call votes. In contrast, when the overall crosspartisan score is larger, varied sets of crosspartisan minorities restrict

Figure 11-4 House Overall Structuring Scores, 1933–1997

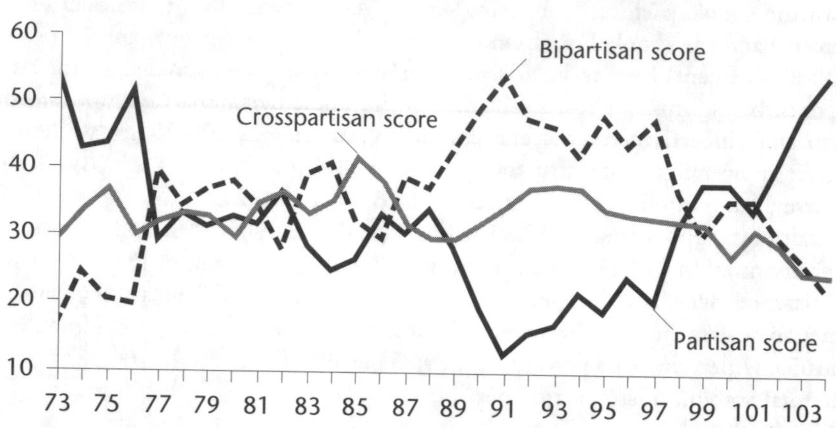

Congress	Type	PS	BS	XS	Congress	Type	PS	BS	XS
73 (1933–35)	P	53.9	16.3	29.8	89 (1965–67)	CB	28.1	42.2	29.7
74 (1935–37)	P	42.5	23.9	33.5	90 (1967–69)	B	19.1	48.8	32.2
75 (1937–39)	P	43.2	20.0	36.7	91 (1969–71)	B	12.2	53.3	34.5
76 (1939–41)	P	50.9	19.2	29.9	92 (1971–73)	B	15.5	47.2	37.3
77 (1941–43)	CB	28.9	39.0	32.2	93 (1973–75)	B	16.7	45.8	37.5
78 (1943–45)	CB	33.0	33.9	33.2	94 (1975–77)	B	21.2	41.7	37.1
79 (1945–47)	CB	30.9	36.2	32.9	95 (1977–79)	B	18.5	47.5	34.0
80 (1947–49)	CB	32.6	37.6	29.8	96 (1979–81)	B	23.5	43.2	33.4
81 (1949–51)	CX	31.2	34.1	34.7	97 (1981–83)	B	20.2	47.0	32.8
82 (1951–53)	CX	36.1	27.6	36.3	98 (1983–85)	CB	31.1	36.4	32.5
83 (1953–55)	CB	28.1	38.8	33.1	99 (1985–87)	CP	37.6	30.2	32.2
84 (1955–57)	B	24.5	40.4	35.1	100 (1987–89)	CP	37.6	35.3	27.2
85 (1957–59)	X	26.1	32.2	41.6	101 (1989–91)	CB	33.6	35.3	31.1
86 (1959–61)	CX	32.7	29.4	38.0	102 (1991–93)	CP	40.9	30.2	28.9
87 (1961–63)	CB	30.2	38.2	31.6	103 (1993–95)	P	48.4	26.6	24.9
88 (1963–65)	CB	33.6	36.6	29.8	104 (1995–97)	P	53.5	21.9	24.6

Source: Data compiled by authors from roll call votes made available by ICPSR (73d–101st); and Keith Poole (102d–104th). Data for the 104th Congress are up to June 5, 1996.

Key: **PS**=Partisan Score; **BS**=Bipartisan Score; **XS**=Crosspartisan Score
P=Partisan; **CP**=Constrained Partisan; **B**=Bipartisan; **CB**=Constrained Bipartisan
X=Crosspartisan; **CX**=Constrained Crosspartisan

partisan and bipartisan majorities to structuring less than half of the voting on roll call votes. Voting patterns may then be seen as more disorganized than organized, and such Houses may be termed factional.

There are no factional Houses after the 1850s, the last time in which one of the two major parties in the political system was replaced by a new party.[11] Therefore, we have only structured Houses to analyze. To frame this analysis, we distinguish several types and subtypes. Houses in which the overall partisan structuring score is higher than the overall bipartisan or crosspartisan scores are termed partisan. Houses in which the overall bipartisan structuring score is the highest score are termed bipartisan. Houses in which the overall crosspartisan score is the highest, but still less than the sum of the overall partisan and bipartisan scores, are termed crosspartisan. Such Houses, while not factional, border on being captive to minorities at least in one area of voting. Within these categories, Houses can be further distinguished in terms of whether the highest overall score is 50 percent or more larger than the lowest overall score. When this is not the case, Houses are termed constrained partisan, constrained bipartisan, or constrained crosspartisan because differences between the highest score and the other scores are limited in range. The 88th House (1963–1965) provides a good example with scores of 33.6, 36.6, and 29.8.

Organized in these categories, the data in Figure 11-4 clearly show the trends in House voting patterns over the past half-century. The period begins in the early 1930s with Houses in which party is the predominant force organizing or structuring the vote. Over the course of the 1930s, however, the strength of the New Deal coalition weakens, and the force of party as an organizing force abates. Houses in which party remains important, but is no longer the predominant force structuring the vote, characterize the 1940s, 1950s, and 1960s. Further steep decline occurs in the late 1960s and lasts through the early 1980s. In the period from the 90th through the 97th Congresses (1967–1983), partisanship structuring falls to the same low levels of overall strength that bipartisan structuring assumed in partisan eras, whereas bipartisan structuring rises to the same high levels of overall strength as partisan structuring in those eras. In the early 1980s, however, the trend changes direction and partisan structuring begins to grow steadily in overall strength. The result is that by the mid-1990s partisanship has climbed back to the same overall levels of strength it had in the early 1930s. In contrast, bipartisanship declines to its levels in the 1930s.

Effectiveness in House Voting Since the New Deal

Our discussion of overall structuring provides only part of the analysis needed to understand the importance of party voting. As indicated earlier, there are two interrelated dimensions, not one. We need to turn to the vertical dimension and examine the strength or effectiveness of partisanship and bipartisanship in their own spheres of action, rather than treating them horizontally as competing forces across all votes. Indeed, in the past analysis has focused on the vertical dimension alone, especially as it relates to party. In shifting our perspective, we can profit from our analysis of overall structuring. That analysis treated frequency and strength as factors that interact to define discrete patterns of overall structuring. Analysis of our second voting dimension can therefore begin by examining the internal dynamics of the overall partisan and bipartisan structuring scores. In doing so we separate what we previously combined by treating partisan and bipartisan votes as self-contained arenas of politics and the relationship between frequency and strength on these votes as an open question.

We address partisan politics first. Table 11-1 provides data for assessing the role of party in majority building on votes that split the parties. There is a broad relationship between the frequency of votes in which more than 50 percent of one party opposes more than 50 percent of the other and the degree of simple partisan structuring. High levels of partisan votes are associated with high levels of partisan structuring on partisan votes and vice versa. As party becomes a more potent force in shaping positions on policy issues, more votes tend to become partisan votes and the impact of party on the character of unity and division on such votes increases.

Still, partisan structuring on partisan votes is far from entirely dependent on their frequency. The varied gradations in overall structuring scores within and among our categories of Houses strongly suggest that the determinants of frequency and simple partisan structuring are different in nature and/or effect. As a result, there are irregularities in their relationship and in the character and success of partisan majority building in different types of Houses. For example, as Table 11-1 indicates, in constrained bipartisan Houses, partisan votes and partisan structuring appear far less related than in partisan or bipartisan Houses.

The character and determinants of majority building on partisan votes thus need further analysis. Our primary measure of strength on partisan votes remains the simple partisan structuring score. Any score close to 50 percent indicates substantial weakness in partisan structuring. Although a structuring score of 50 percent on partisan votes can reflect an actual vote split in which as many as 75 percent of one party oppose 75 percent of the other, it should be remembered that a 50 percent-50 percent split defines the zero point in structuring on partisan votes. Therefore, a simple structuring score of 50 percent on partisan votes means that partisans voting with their colleagues and against the other party accomplish only 50 percent of the structuring that might be obtained.

However, as we have noted, the sheer degree of partisan division or mobilization is not the only kind of strength that matters, and it does not alone determine a party majority's ability to control partisan votes. Patterns of support and defection, vote margin, and the stability of core party support also serve as determinants of the effectiveness of the party majority in majority building. We need to supplement the simple partisan structuring score with other measures, if we are to assess the degree to which majority building can be based on the party majority and avoid reliance on crosspartisan coalitions that involve substantial amounts of minority party support.

High levels of support and low levels of defection are associated with high simple structuring scores and vice versa. Nonetheless, the simple structuring scores obscure differences in patterns of cohesion within the parties because they are insensitive to which party is the more unified internally. As we shall see, the concrete features of actual patterns of support and defection play a critical role in determining the degree to which majority building on partisan votes can be based

Table 11-1 House Average Scores on Partisan Votes, 1933–1997

Type (N)	Congress (Dates)	Partisan Vote %	Simple Partisan Structuring (Residual) %	Margin over Majority %	Margin over Majority N	Support-Defection Majority +80%	Support-Defection Majority −60%	Support-Defection Minority +80%	Support-Defection Minority −60%	Semi-certainty %
Partisan (6)	73–76 (1933–41) 103–104 (1993–97)	66.9	72.8 (27.2)	31.8	69.5	76.9	3.0	82.4	3.8	99.9
Constrained partisan (3)	99–100 (1985–89) 102 (1991–93)	58.2	66.4 (33.6)	18.7	41.3	77.1	3.9	59.5	10.2	91.7
Bipartisan (9)	84 (1955–57) 90–97 (1967–83)	37.2	50.8 (49.2)	18.1	40.0	55.6	22.6	52.4	14.4	65.7
Constrained bipartisan (10)	77–80 (1941–49) 83 (1953–55) 87–89 (1961–67) 98 (1983–85) 101 (1989–91)	48.3	63.7 (36.3)	16.7	36.4	69.6	10.9	65.6	8.8	80.7
Crosspartisan (1)	85 (1957–59)	49.7	52.6 (47.4)	7.0	16.0	52.5	12.0	43.8	15.3	56.4
Constrained crosspartisan (3)	81–82 (1949–53) 86 (1959–61)	55.4	60.4 (39.6)	19.7	42.7	61.8	16.9	65.9	9.1	74.0

Source: Data compiled by authors from roll call votes made available by ICPSR (73d–101st Congresses); and Keith Poole (102d–104th Congresses). Data for the 104th Congress are up to June 5, 1996.

primarily on partisan divisions or rather must be broadly coalitional and depend regularly on attracting substantial minority support. The support-defection columns in Table 11-1 provide data regarding the proportion of majority and minority members who on average voted with a majority of their colleagues 80 percent or more of the time and the proportion who voted with a majority of their colleagues less than 60 percent of the time.

The size of the vote margin the majority party enjoys and the stability of core majority party support also have important effects on the role of the party majority in majority building. The margin over majority columns in Table 11-1 present data on the number and percentage by which the size of the majority party exceeds an absolute majority in the body (218 members). In addition, this table provides what we have called a semicertainty score. This score measures the percentage of an absolute majority supplied by majority party members, whose average level of support on partisan votes is 80 percent or more. For example, in the 73d House (1933–1935) the majority party had 313 members. Of this number, 233 voted with their party on votes that split the parties at least 80 percent of the time. The semicertainty score is thus 233 ÷ 218 x 100 or 106.8 percent.

Table 11-1 indicates that partisan and constrained partisan Houses approach the task of majority building primarily on the basis of party. Note that the simple structuring scores are high, support levels high, and defection levels low. In addition, average margins are high. As a result of all these factors, semicertainty scores are high. Still, in such Houses the importance of margin is reduced because unity is so high. For example, in the Republican-controlled 104th House, the margin over a majority is only 18 members, but the semicertainty score is 103.7 percent due to a 72.8 percent simple structuring score, a majority support score of 95.8 percent, and a majority defection score of 0 percent.

However, partisan Houses have existed only at the very beginning and end of the past half-century. Other types of Houses predominated throughout most of the period, and in many cases party provided only a fragile basis for organizing majorities on votes that split the parties.[12] In bipartisan Houses our data indicate that the construction of majorities behind majority party positions was laborious and dependent on minority support. When simple partisan structuring is low, relative advantage in support and defection becomes more important both in itself and because of the disproportionate costs low levels of support and high levels of defection impose on the larger party. In such situations, if minority party unity is higher than majority party unity, the danger of defeat substantially increases even when the majority party is sizable.

For example, in bipartisan Houses the median majority party margin above an absolute majority was 29 members which translates into a party division of 247 to 188. In votes in which the simple structuring score is only 50 percent, this margin becomes a precarious source of advantage. Even if the vote split is a balanced 75 percent versus 75 percent with 25 percent of each party defecting, the result is to narrow the actual voting division to 232 to 203 and cut the vote margin over an absolute majority to 14. Simple structuring scores under 50 percent seriously threaten defeat if the ratio of support and defection is favorable to the minority party. In our example, if majority party unity falls to 60 percent with 40 percent defecting, and minority party unity decreases only to 70 percent with 30 percent defecting, the simple structuring score falls to 30 and the minority party wins 230–205.

To return to the data in Table 11-1, in bipartisan Houses the average simple structuring scores are roughly 50 percent, levels of stable high support are problematic, and a defection disadvantage exists relative to the minority. Moreover, whereas the median simple structuring score is also roughly 50 percent, the average margin over a majority score of 40 masks considerable variation. As noted, the median score was 29 votes. It is not surprising that the average semicertainty score is only 65.7, indicating that majority construction on the basis of the party majority was difficult and that often the majority party was dependent on minority support to win. Indeed, under these conditions, crosspartisan coalitions, involving a majority of minority members, were quite capable of forming and controlling partisan votes, despite the desires of a majority of the majority party. To offset these difficulties a very large advantage in margin was required, but even then results were limited. The highest semicertainty score in bipartisan Houses (76.5) occurred in the 94th Congress, which was elected in 1974 after the Watergate scandal, and included 291 Democrats or 73 over an absolute majority of 218.

The situation in crosspartisan and constrained crosspartisan Houses appears similar, and that estimate is supported by our Senate data. But these types of Houses are sparse in our time period. More frequent are constrained bipartisan Houses that appear in terms of averages to be in between constrained partisan and bipartisan Houses and that, together with bipartisan Houses, constitute nineteen of our thirty-two cases. In fact, they are, but in complex ways. Half of these Houses had semicertainty scores over 80 percent because of large majority party margins or high majority party unity. Such Houses could operate very much like partisan Houses on votes that split the parties because large margins compensated for high rates of defection, for example, the historic 89th (1965–1967), or because unity was far higher than normal given the proportion of partisan votes, for example, the Republican-controlled 80th (1947–1949). Yet, when these conditions did not obtain, as was the case in the other half of our constrained bipartisan Houses, semicertainty averaged only slightly higher than in bipartisan Houses (70.7), and was not high enough to give party leaders any secure ability to rely primarily on their own partisans in majority building.

We can conclude that in the past half-century neither partisan nor coalitional modes of majority building were dominant in the House when party majorities opposed one another. Rather, different modes governed at different times and shaded into one another depending on a complex array of conditions. The story of bipartisan strength on bipartisan votes in this period is far more straightforward, but also instructive. The relationship between the frequency of bipartisan votes and the strength of bipartisan structuring on such votes is weak.

Figure 11-5 House and Senate Average Scores on Bipartisan Votes, 1933–1997

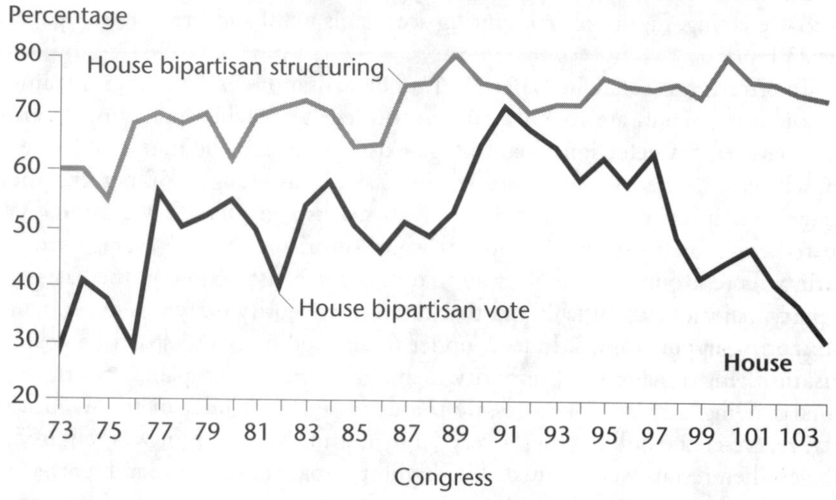

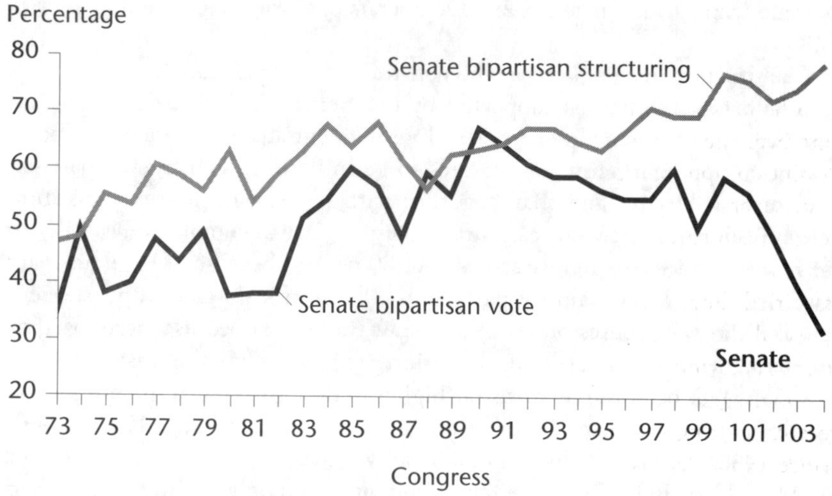

For example, in partisan Houses the average proportion of bipartisan votes is only half that in bipartisan Houses (33 percent to 63 percent), but the average simple bipartisan structuring score is almost 90 percent as large (65 percent to 74 percent). However, the weakness of the relationship is best shown in Figure 11-5, which presents the data historically. Bipartisan structuring scores climb from the 55 percent-60 percent range in the 1930s to the 70 percent-80 percent range in the 1960s and thereafter. During this same period, the frequency of bipartisan votes cycles, increasing to high levels in the late 1960s and then falling back to the levels of the late 1930s. As a result, the frequency of bipartisan votes in the partisan Houses of the 1990s has fallen to the low levels of partisan Houses of the 1930s, but the strength of bipartisan structuring has remained at the high levels of bipartisan Houses in the 1970s.

In the case of bipartisan votes, winning majorities necessarily result, and effectiveness becomes a matter of the strength of the simple bipartisan structuring score. Once again, structuring scores close to 50 percent indicate that majorities of members in both parties voting together accomplish only 50 percent of the structuring that is possible on bipartisan votes. Yet, since the early 1960s, scores of 70 percent or more have prevailed, and these are strong scores. They translate into bipartisan majorities that on average join 85 percent of each party in voting on the same side. As might also be expected, variation in the simple structuring scores in different types of Houses is far less pronounced than in the case of partisan votes. Thus, the decline of the overall bipartisan structuring score in recent Houses does not mean that the strength of bipartisan majorities in their own spheres of action has diminished. Rather, it only reflects a decline in frequency and an associated decline in the overall scope of bipartisanship relative to partisanship.

Trends and Effectiveness in Senate Voting Since the New Deal

When assessed in terms of individual measures, party voting patterns in the Senate over the past half-century appear to be quite similar to the House. The trend lines of measures, such as the partisan vote score or the party unity scores, vary in several respects from those in the House, but still track House trends closely.[13] Such similarity, however, is deceptive because it conceals the effects of lower scores on vote structuring. When party voting is assessed with recognition of its varied dimensions and components, a more accurate picture emerges. Our data reveal the Senate to be quite different from the House both in patterns of overall structuring and in patterns of politics and majority building.

Once again we begin our analysis with a horizontal or comparative analysis of vote structuring. Figure 11-6 presents the overall structuring scores in the Senate since 1933. Because 23 of the 32 cases are crosspartisan, in contrast to only 4 in the House, we have made some further distinctions in this category. Our basic crosspartisan and constrained crosspartisan categories remain the same as in the House. Crosspartisan Senates are Senates in which the overall crosspartisan score is the highest score and is 50 percent higher than the lowest score. Constrained crosspartisan Senates are crosspartisan Senates that do not meet the 50 percent criterion. However, since there are 19 unconstrained or pure crosspartisan cases, we have divided this category into two subcategories: those in which the second highest score is the partisan score and those in which it is the bipartisan score.

Figure 11-6 is organized in terms of these distinctions. It reveals three distinct phases of overall structuring. The first lasts from 1933 to 1953. During

Figure 11-6 Senate Overall Structuring Scores, 1933–1997

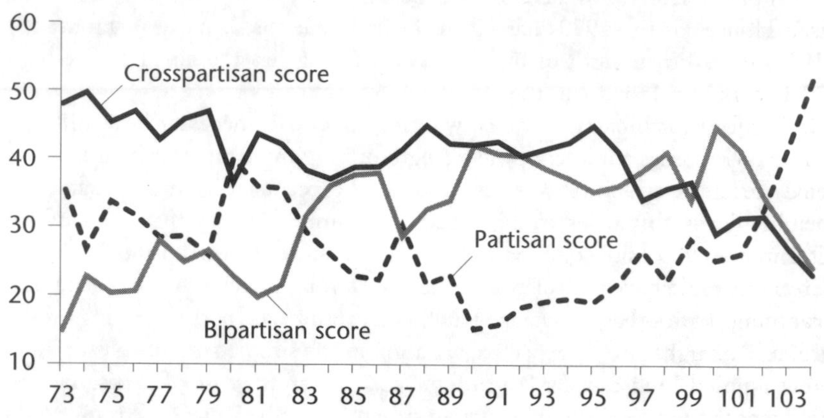

Congress	Type	PS	BS	XS	Congress	Type	PS	BS	XS
73 (1933–35)	X(P)	36.7	15.2	48.1	89 (1965–67)	X(B)	23.4	34.2	42.5
74 (1935–37)	X(P)	27.0	23.1	49.8	90 (1967–69)	X(B)	15.5	42.2	42.3
75 (1937–39)	X(P)	33.9	20.6	45.5	91 (1969–71)	X(B)	16.2	41.0	42.8
76 (1939–41)	X(P)	31.9	20.9	47.1	92 (1971–73)	B	18.7	40.7	40.7
77 (1941–43)	X(P)	28.7	28.3	43.0	93 (1973–75)	X(B)	19.6	38.8	41.7
78 (1943–45)	X(P)	28.9	25.1	46.0	94 (1975–77)	X(B)	20.0	37.4	42.7
79 (1945–47)	X(B)	26.2	26.8	47.1	95 (1977–79)	X(B)	19.5	35.5	45.1
80 (1947–49)	P	40.1	23.2	36.7	96 (1979–81)	X(B)	22.2	36.4	41.4
81 (1949–51)	X(P)	36.2	20.1	43.8	97 (1981–83)	CB	27.0	38.6	34.4
82 (1951–53)	X(P)	35.9	21.8	42.3	98 (1983–85)	B	22.5	41.4	36.1
83 (1953–55)	CX	29.6	31.9	38.5	99 (1985–87)	CX	28.6	34.4	37.0
84 (1955–57)	CX	26.4	36.3	37.3	100 (1987–89)	B	25.6	45.0	29.5
85 (1957–59)	X(B)	23.2	37.9	39.0	101 (1989–91)	B	26.6	41.6	31.8
86 (1959–61)	X(B)	22.7	38.2	39.1	102 (1991–93)	CB	33.1	34.9	32.0
87 (1961–63)	CX	30.5	28.9	41.6	103 (1993–95)	P	42.1	29.8	27.4
88 (1963–65)	X(B)	22.0	32.9	45.1	104 (1995–97)	P	51.9	24.6	23.5

Source: Data compiled by authors from roll call votes made available by ICPSR (73d–101st); and Keith Poole (102d–104th). Data for the 104th Congress are up to June 5, 1996.

Key: **PS**=Partisan Score; **BS**=Bipartisan Score; **XS**=Crosspartisan Score
P=Partisan; **B**=Bipartisan; **CB**=Constrained Bipartisan
X=Crosspartisan; **CX**=Constrained Crosspartisan
X(P)=Crosspartisan with Partisan Score Higher than Bipartisan
X(B)=Crosspartisan with Bipartisan Score Higher than Partisan

these two decades crosspartisan Senates, in which partisan structuring moderately outweighs bipartisan structuring, predominate. This phase is followed by one that lasts three decades, from 1953 to 1983. During this period, crosspartisan Senates, in which bipartisan structuring substantially outweighs partisan structuring, predominate. As in the House, the late 1960s and 1970s constitute the weakest period of party strength in the past half-century. However, once again a significant reversal in trend begins in the early 1980s. The overall crosspartisan score steadily declines to far lower levels. As a result, the Senate moves into a bipartisan mode in the 1980s with stronger partisan scores than in the 1970s, and in the 1990s partisanship emerges as the primary force in overall structuring for the first time since the 67th Congress (1921–1923).

The importance of these findings relates not only to overall trends, but also to what different types of Senates signal about the patterns and politics of majority building. However, to pursue this topic we need once again to look at partisanship and bipartisanship vertically, instead of horizontally, and treat them as self-contained arenas of politics. As in our analysis of the House, we begin by examining the internal dynamics of the overall structuring scores and focusing initially on partisan votes. Table 11-2 provides data for the Senate on measures we applied in analyzing the House. In the Senate, as in the House, there is a relationship between the proportion of partisan votes and the degree of simple partisan structuring. But the relationship is more irregular than in the House, which means that partisan structuring is less tied to the frequency of partisan votes. Given the prevalence of crosspartisan Senates, this is not surprising.

If we examine partisan strength and effectiveness more broadly and directly, the average semicertainty scores indicate that reliance on the party majority as a means of building chamber majorities is a normal or defining feature only of partisan Senates. Although there are only three cases in the Senate, the overall signature in terms of simple partisan structuring, levels of support and defection, and vote margin is quite comparable to the House. The remaining bipartisan and crosspartisan cases, both unconstrained and constrained, all appear to involve coalitional modes or postures with respect to majority building.

In unconstrained crosspartisan Senates, which constitute 59 percent of the cases, the need to build crossparty coalitions to secure a chamber majority is especially pronounced. Not only is simple partisan structuring close to a score of 50 percent in both variants of this type and therefore weak, but levels of stable party support are low and defection is high. In such Senates the ability of a majority of the majority party to win usually depended on its ability to attract substantial minority support. Moreover, when margins were low, crossparty coalitions involving majorities of minority members were well positioned to defeat a majority of the majority party. Only when the majority party's margin was extremely high could stable party support become large enough to provide a basis for a partisan mode of majority building. Again the 89th Congress (1965–1967) provides a prime example with a margin of 17 votes over the 51 votes needed for an absolute majority and a semicertainty score of 83.9.

Assessment of the remaining types of Senates is impeded by the limited number of cases. Still, bipartisan, constrained bipartisan, and constrained crosspartisan Senates appear to be more coalitional than partisan in majority building. Although these Senates have higher levels of stable party support to rely upon

Table 11-2 Senate Average Scores on Partisan Votes, 1933–1997

Type (N)	Congress (Dates)	Partisan Vote %	Simple Partisan Structuring (Residual) %	Margin over Majority		Support-Defection				Semi-certainty %
						Majority		Minority		
				%	N	+80%	-60%	+80%	-60%	
Partisan (3)	80 (1947–49) 103–104 (1993–97)	64.2	70.1 (29.9)	6.0	3.0	83.3	3.8	63.8	10.0	88.5
Bipartisan (4)	92 (1971–73) 98 (1983–85) 100–101 (1987–91)	41.5	56.0 (44.0)	7.0	3.5	64.3	12.1	55.4	19.0	69.4
Constrained bipartisan (2)	97 (1981–83) 102 (1991–93)	48.4	61.9 (38.1)	8.0	4.0	65.0	4.7	63.8	16.5	70.6
Crosspartisan all cases (19)		49.5	51.5 (48.5)	22.4	11.1	54.9	20.8	54.5	19.1	67.2
Crosspartisan partisan (8)	73–78 (1933–45) 81–82 (1949–53)	59.6	54.3 (45.7)	27.3	13.4	51.9	21.1	56.1	14.5	66.2
Crosspartisan bipartisan (11)	79 (1945–47) 85–86 (1957–61) 88–91 (1963–71) 93–96 (1973–81)	42.2	49.5 (50.5)	18.8	9.5	57.0	20.5	53.4	22.4	68.0
Constrained crosspartisan (4)	83–84 (1953–57) 87 (1961–63) 99 (1985–87)	49.6	58.0 (42.0)	6.5	3.3	66.7	13.3	51.9	14.5	71.6

Source: Data compiled by authors from roll call votes made available by ICPSR (73d–101st Congresses); and Keith Poole (102d–104th Congresses). Data for the 104th Congress are up to June 5, 1996.

and lower levels of defection to overcome, the fact that 20 percent to 30 percent of each party provides neither stable support nor stable opposition means that majority building depends on circumstance and is quite volatile. Semicertainty scores on average are thus close to those in crosspartisan Senates and rise above 80 only in isolated cases in which margin or unity is unusually high for these types of Senates.

Confirmation of the largely coalitional nature of majority building on party votes until the late 1980s is provided by the character of support and defection scores across time. The percentage of Democrats who voted 80 percent or more of the time with fellow partisans averaged in the 50 percent to 60 percent range until the late 1980s, and the percentage who voted less than 60 percent of the time with fellow partisans did not average below 20 percent until after 1979 or below 15 percent until after 1987. Average support scores for Republicans are similar, but climb above the 50 percent to 60 percent range after 1981. Although average defection scores do not rise above 15 percent before 1967, they climb to over 25 percent in the next fourteen years before again declining to under 15 percent after 1981.

We may conclude that although the Senate well merited its popular depiction as a "club" in the first half of the period from 1933–1997, its character as a club constituted only a form of coalitional politics, not its essence. As the patterns of norms and behaviors that made it a club eroded in the 1960s and 1970s, divisions within the parties continued and even intensified until trends began to reverse in the 1980s and 1990s in response to change in the centers of policy gravity and regional composition of both parties.[14] Reliance on partisanship as a primary mode of building majorities on partisan votes finally emerged, but at a slower and more hesitant pace than in the House.

In contrast, Senate voting patterns on bipartisan votes are similar to those in the House. The relationship between the proportion of bipartisan votes and bipartisan structuring, as measured by the simple bipartisan structuring score on such votes, is weak. Again, this can be seen in the average scores of the various types of Senates, but it is best seen in the historical data presented in Figure 11-5.[15] The proportion of such votes does not rise above 50 percent until 1953, but climbs to levels of 60 percent or more in the late 1960s. A slow decline begins in the early 1970s and by the 1990s levels are back to where they were in the 1930s. Yet, simple bipartisan structuring climbs, with some limited oscillation, from scores in the 45 percent to 55 percent range in the 1930s to scores in the 70 percent to 80 percent range in the 1990s.

As in the House, bipartisan structuring scores of 70 percent or more testify to high degrees of strength and effectiveness in majority building. They are equivalent to 85 percent of both parties voting together. Senate bipartisan scores also vary less among different types of Senates than the partisan scores. The primary difference from House patterns is one of lag. The House consistently attains scores of 70 percent or more by the end of the 1950s, whereas the Senate matches these levels only in the early 1980s.

Conclusion

That both the House and Senate have become more partisan in recent years is common knowledge. But understanding the nature and meaning of this change is difficult. We close, then, by commenting on the significance of our findings in terms of the theoretical and historical perspectives that have generated them.

First, although partisan Houses and Senates have emerged in the 1990s, it is far from certain that the country has entered a partisan era. Partisan Houses and Senates can be relatively isolated occurrences. For example, the emergence of a partisan Senate in the 80th Congress (1947–1949) was an aberration and not a return to a period like that from 1897 to 1915, when nine consecutive Senates classify as partisan in terms of their overall structuring scores. Similarly, the partisan Houses of the 1930s were neither preceded by nor followed by partisan Houses. In contrast, in the period from 1895 to 1917, eleven consecutive Houses fit our partisan category.

Second, whether partisanship will persist for an extended period of time is far more dependent on the external dynamics of the political system than on the internal processes and politics of Congress. Our findings are in line with the changing character of the party system nationally. It is no accident that the trend toward more partisanship started in both houses in the early 1980s when Ronald Reagan became president. Reagan's presidency changed the basic agenda of politics and policy from acceptance and extension of the role and responsibilities of the federal government to rejection and contraction. Nor is it any accident that the emergence of partisan Houses and Senates in the 1990s is associated with changes in the regional composition of the parties, both nationally and in Congress. New policy agendas not only result from new patterns of politics but also shape their character through a continuing process of response and counterresponse. Finally, it is not surprising that increasing partisanship, sparked by new policy agendas and patterns of politics, would generate more precise and adversarial definitions of the features of that agenda—Newt Gingrich's Contract with America—as vehicles for promoting and capitalizing on partisanship to gain electoral success, policy advantage, and institutional power.

All these ingredients are part of the traditional recipe for realigning American politics and transforming a minority party into a majority party on a continuing basis. What is not clear is how amenable current conditions of American politics are—in terms of issue divisions, party allegiance, and media campaigns—to wholesale, stable, and consistent patterns of change. Despite what historical precedents suggest about the organizing force of plurality elections or current trends indicate about the nationalization of politics, it is far from certain that a traditional realignment will once again occur and succeed in recreating a strong and stable partisan equilibrium. What is clear is that such transformations are not accomplished in one fell swoop. They take several elections, in which distinct components of the task are solved sequentially, as a minority party first defeats the majority party and then hones its policy agenda and implements it in a way that succeeds in attracting the continuing allegiance of a permanent majority coalition in the electorate.

There are, in short, different stages and a need to proceed successfully from one to the other as, for example, Roosevelt did from 1932 to 1938. The fate of partisanship in Congress is therefore yet to be determined; it is highly contingent on the skills of political leaders as well as objective conditions and even chance. The next critical benchmark is the election of 1996. Although both the House and the Senate have become partisan for the first time in many decades, the irony is that in very significant ways this fact is irrelevant. The presence of divided government has meant that a stable partisan majority still cannot produce major policy outcomes by adopting a partisan mode of operation. In the House a veto requires not merely 218 votes to overcome (if all members vote) but 291, and in the Senate 67 votes are required (if all members vote) not merely 51. These are very difficult levels to obtain in partisan Congresses unless majority margins are extremely high. Moreover, in the Senate, practice with respect to the filibuster has changed so that the 60 votes required to impose cloture are also required to win any major policy battle. As a result, the passage of major legislation still requires forms of behavior and negotiation that are coalitional, but in a context in which the character of party divisions provides poor incentives for such behavior. The public's disgust with paralysis may spur action when elections approach, but such a response is only the flip side of the political maneuvering to gain electoral advantage that dominates policy making and usually stymies action.

This pattern of politics is not unprecedented and can contribute to launching a new era of partisan politics. But such efforts must succeed. Whereas divided government with coalitional Congresses is neither unstable nor incapable of passing major legislation, divided government with partisan Congresses may well be unstable and is probably limited to marking a stage in which an opportunity for realignment exists but is far from guaranteed.

The election of 1996 will be a significant one for the future of American politics. If Republicans gain control of the presidency as well as Congress, change in the immediate future will proceed in accord with the traditional, overarching rhythms of American politics.[16] If the election maintains divided control, divided government will persist in a context in which conflict over policy goals and patterns of political incentives undermine coalitional policy making.[17] The very presence of divided government reflects deep public ambivalence about policy direction. When combined with heightened partisanship, it cripples partisan rule, but provides narrow grounds for bipartisan cooperation aside from public distaste for conflict. A politics marked by halting and limited responses to critical national needs and intense competition to assign blame is likely. Such a politics cannot fail to be damaging both to the preservation of the current two-party system and to the power of Congress.[18] Indeed, if the parties cannot find some common ground as a basis for cooperation and action, it is not inconceivable that weakness or breakdown in the party system would occur and again, as it did in the nineteenth century, produce factional Congresses in which the power of majorities of any kind to organize policy making would be seriously impaired. It is possible that the 1996 election will produce neither of these two results, but rather once again create a unified government under Democratic leadership. Because it is difficult to see such a result as a stage in a traditional realignment, what will be at issue is whether the basic contours of an aging party system can be sustained and incrementally attain a more stable and viable form. What would be required are forms of adaptation that cannot be foreseen and would in all likelihood be quite novel.

Third, the levels of bipartisanship and crosspartisanship in any era provide defining factors in the processes and politics of Congress and are critical to any adequate treatment of partisanship. We have therefore been careful to distinguish voting in which majorities of both parties vote in the same direction from voting in which minorities in each party vote in the same direction or with majorities of the opposing party. We have reserved the term bipartisan for the first pattern and seen the other two as variants of crossparty voting. Clearer specification of bipartisanship and crosspartisanship has enhanced our ability to assess both the character of vote structuring in a Congress and patterns of majority building and success on partisan and bipartisan votes per se.

Important findings result. An overall look at the relative strength of partisan, bipartisan, and crosspartisan vote structuring allows us to identify different types of Congresses, and such categories provide useful foundations for assessment and analysis. These categories serve to perfect understanding of persistent differences in the politics of the House and Senate and provide a firmer foundation for examining their causes and effects. They also aid in identifying shifting eras of congressional politics, and the nature of these shifts testifies to broader changes in the political system.

Our discussion of realignment illustrates the point with respect to partisanship, but there are some significant points to be made regarding bipartisanship as well. Judging by House data, there were few bipartisan Congresses in the nineteenth century. Such Congresses appear to be a distinctive feature of the twentieth century and tied to the expanded role of government and the distributive consequences of such a role. Their emergence reveals the overall strength of bipartisanship and the weakness of party over the past half-century, especially in the 1970s.

Similarly, partisanship and bipartisanship can be analyzed as separate arenas of politics in different types of Congresses and over time. Patterns of majority building can be related to the type of Congress, and institutional structure and leadership style related to differences in voting patterns. We did little of the latter in this chapter, but it is worth noting that if stable patterns of partisanship persist in the Senate, the breakdown in informal limits on minority obstruction may well lead the Senate to act more like the House and adopt changes that enhance the ability of the party majority to pass its program.

This is not to imply that simple uniform relationships exist. The independence that also characterizes the connection between frequency and structuring has complex and important consequences both at overall and simple levels of structuring. Bipartisan structuring provides a prime illustration. Although the bipartisan component of overall structuring has receded as partisan Houses and Senates have reemerged, in both bodies the simple structuring scores on bipartisan votes have stabilized at levels that are high for this century and unprecedented for the nineteenth century. Partisan Congresses now are different from such Congresses in the past, and the strength of bipartisanship on bipartisan votes clearly contains important clues about the nature of modern American politics.[19] The lesson all students of Congress must learn is that partisanship is part of a more intricate pattern of politics in Congress and must be analyzed as such if both it and the pattern are to be understood.

Notes

1. Analysis in the decades preceding the 1970s recognized weakness in the actual operation of congressional parties, but accepted their importance and sought to define and/or extend their role. For a pathbreaking and far more fundamental challenge to the importance of party in Congress, based on reelection as the key to motivation and particularistic benefits as the key to politics, see David R. Mayhew, *Congress: The Electoral Connection* (New Haven: Yale University Press, 1974). For developments in party theory since the 1970s, see Joseph Cooper and Rick K. Wilson, "The Role of Congressional Parties," in *Encyclopedia of the American Legislative System,* ed. Joel H. Silbey et al. (New York: Charles Scribner's Sons, 1994), 3: 899–931.
2. In the 1990s obstacles to the development of party theory have been posed by difficulties in accommodating the role of committees, as defined in prior solutions to collective action problems, and by the claim that preferences, analyzed in terms of median voter theory, constitute a necessary and sufficient basis for explanation. See Kenneth A. Shepsle and Barry R. Weingast, "Positive Theories of Congressional Institutions," *Legislative Studies Quarterly* 19 (May 1994): 149–181; and Keith Krehbiel, "Where's the Party," *British Journal of Political Science* 23 (1993): 235–266. However, important work in defense of party has been done by David H. Rohde, *Parties and Leaders in the Postreform House* (Chicago: University of Chicago Press, 1991); D. Roderick Kiewiet and Mathew D. McCubbins, *The Logic of Delegation: Congressional Parties and the Appropriations Process* (Chicago: University of Chicago Press, 1991); Gary W. Cox and Mathew D. McCubbins, *Legislative Leviathan: Party Government in the House* (Berkeley: University of California Press, 1993); and John H. Aldrich, *Why Parties? The Origin and Transformation of Party Politics in America* (Chicago: University of Chicago Press, 1995).
3. See Melissa P. Collie, "Voting Behavior in Legislatures," *Legislative Studies Quarterly* 9 (February 1984): 3–51. In the 1990s controversy has centered on the dimensionality of congressional voting and on the issue of preference outliers. See Keith T. Poole and Howard Rosenthal, "Patterns of Congressional Voting," *American Journal of Political Science* 29 (February 1991): 228–278; Clyde Wilcox and Aage Clausen, "The Dimensionality of Roll-Call Voting Reconsidered," *Legislative Studies Quarterly* 16 (August 1991): 393–407; and John Londregan and James M. Snyder Jr., "Comparing Committee and Floor Preferences," *Legislative Studies Quarterly* 19 (May 1994): 233–267. On party voting per se, see Gary W. Cox and Mathew D. McCubbins, "Party Cohesion on Roll-Call Voting in the U.S. House of Representatives," *Encyclopedia of the American Legislative System,* 3: 931–947.

4. See Joseph Cooper, David W. Brady, and Patricia A. Hurley, "The Electoral Basis of Party Voting: Patterns and Trends in the U.S. House of Representatives, 1887–1969," in *The Impact of the Electoral Process,* ed. Louis Maisel and Joseph Cooper (Beverly Hills: Sage Publications, 1977), 133–165; and Cooper and Wilson, "The Role of Congressional Parties," 915–916.
5. For elaboration of the points made in this paragraph, see Joseph Cooper, "Strengthening the Congress: An Organizational Analysis," *Harvard Journal of Legislation* 2 (April 1975): 301–368; and "Congress in Organizational Perspective," in *Congress Reconsidered,* 1st ed., ed. Lawrence C. Dodd and Bruce I. Oppenheimer (New York: Praeger, 1977), 140–163. See also David W. Brady, Joseph Cooper, and Patricia A. Hurley, "The Decline of Party in the U.S. House of Representatives, 1887–1968," *Legislative Studies Quarterly* (August 1979): 394–396. For relevant work in the 1990s, see Rohde, *Parties and Leaders in the Postreform House*; and Sarah Binder, *Minority Rights, Majority Rule: The Partisan Basis of Procedural Choice in Congress, 1789–1994* (New York: Cambridge University Press, forthcoming).
6. See Barbara Sinclair, *Congressional Realignments, 1925–1978* (Austin: University of Texas Press, 1982); and Melissa P. Collie, "The Rise of Coalition Politics: Voting in the U.S. House, 1933–1980," *Legislative Studies Quarterly* 13 (August 1988): 321–343.
7. See David W. Rohde, "Parties and Committees in the House: Member Motivations, Issues, and Institutional Arrangements," *Legislative Studies Quarterly* 19 (August 1994): 341–361; and Cooper and Wilson, "The Role of Congressional Parties," 909–926.
8. See Poole and Rosenthal, "Patterns of Congressional Voting." It is worth considering whether the dispute between unidimensional and multidimensional approaches to congressional voting is more a matter of perspective, standards, and tools than underlying reality. Poole and Rosenthal can well point out the incongruity of Clausen insisting on unidimensionality in discrete areas of policy while denying it at an aggregate level. However, the flip side is that patterns that can be seen as unidimensional at the aggregate level may still have varying effects in discrete areas of policy both statically and dynamically.
9. For a critique of an earlier formulation, see Cox and McCubbins, "Party Cohesion on Roll-Call Votes," 933–934. This article provides a detailed rationale for an overall structuring score that is multiplicative as well as a simple score that is not.
10. See Collie, "Voting Behavior," 7–13. In this chapter we rely on measures of the party vote and of various forms of unity or cohesion. We do not make use of the index of cohesion or the index of likeness, but rely on measures of difference in the form of structuring scores of our own construction.
11. For added confirmation, see Poole and Rosenthal, "Patterns of Congressional Voting," 229.
12. On the emergence and character of the House from 1940 through the 1960s, see Joseph Cooper and David W. Brady, "Institutional Context and Leadership Style: The House from Cannon to Rayburn," *American Political Science Review* 75 (June 1981): 411–425. Barbara Sinclair and David Rohde have done valuable work on the character of the House in recent decades. See Barbara Sinclair, *Majority Leadership in the U.S. House* (Baltimore: Johns Hopkins University Press, 1983); and Sinclair, *Legislators, Leaders and Lawmaking: The U.S. House of Representatives in the Postreform Era* (Baltimore: Johns Hopkins University Press, 1995). See also David W. Rohde, "Parties and Leaders in the Postreform House."
13. See Samuel C. Patterson and Gregory A. Caldeira, "Party Voting in the U.S. Congress," *British Journal of Political Science* 18 (1988): 111–131; and Patricia A. Hurley and Rick K. Wilson, "Partisan Voting Patterns in the U.S. Senate, 1877–1986," *Legislative Studies Quarterly* 14 (May 1989): 225–251.

14. See Barbara Sinclair, *The Transformation of the U.S. Senate* (Baltimore: Johns Hopkins University Press, 1989). See also Nelson W. Polsby, "Goodbye to the Senate's Inner Club," in *Congress in Change,* ed. Norman J. Ornstein (New York: Praeger, 1975), 208–216.
15. In the Senate, as in the House, a comparison of partisan and bipartisan types also illustrates the point. The average simple bipartisan structuring score for both partisan and bipartisan Senates is 72 percent. Yet the average proportion of bipartisan votes is 35 percent in the former and 59 percent in the latter.
16. For a recent analysis of the dynamics and impacts of realignment, see David W. Brady, *Critical Elections and Congressional Policy Making* (Stanford, Calif.: Stanford University Press, 1988).
17. For an assessment of the causes and effects of divided government, see Bruce I. Oppenheimer, "The Importance of Elections in a Strong Congressional Party Era: The Effect of Unified vs. Divided Government," in *Do Elections Matter?* 3d ed., ed. Benjamin Ginsburg and Alan Stone (London: M. E. Sharpe, 1996), 120–141. See also James Thurber, ed., *Divided Democracy* (Washington, D.C.: CQ Press, 1991).
18. See Lawrence C. Dodd, "Congress and the Politics of Renewal: Redressing the Crisis of Legitimation," in *Congress Reconsidered,* 5th ed., ed. Lawrence C. Dodd and Bruce I. Oppenheimer (Washington, D.C.: CQ Press, 1993), 417-446. See also Cooper, "Strengthening the Congress," 338–345.
19. See Poole and Rosenthal, "Patterns of Congressional Voting," 265, for added confirmation that conflict between the parties is far milder in the twentieth century than it was in the nineteenth. It is also worth noting that "universalism" (votes in which 90 percent of the House vote in the same direction) does not explain variation in the frequency of bipartisan votes or the strength of simple bipartisan structuring on such votes. Universalistic votes constitute a stable proportion of bipartisan votes, and levels of bipartisan structuring remain stable when universalistic votes are removed from the number of bipartisan votes.

12. Congressional Caucuses in the 104th Congress

Susan Webb Hammond

By 1995 the Republican freshmen were a united group, determined to bring about congressional reform and to support the new House Speaker, Newt Gingrich of Georgia, and the Contract with America. They had organized in December 1994 before the 104th Congress convened. They met regularly with Speaker Gingrich, developed proposals for congressional change, and became an important voting bloc. The Tuesday Lunch Bunch, a group of moderate Republicans, also met regularly with the Speaker, at times to discuss modifying the proposals the freshmen supported. Conservative Republicans founded the Conservative Action Team to counteract the Tuesday Lunch Bunch and to build support for their positions. The Coalition, founded by moderate-to-conservative Democrats who sought to use their strength as a centrist group to influence legislation, began in February 1995. The bipartisan Arts Caucus adapted to new regulations and continued to gather and distribute information on arts issues to its members.

What do these groups have in common? They are all congressional caucuses, organized groups of members that operate outside the formal congressional structures. They all continued after the 1994 elections brought major changes to Congress: a switch in party control, more centralized House leadership, and new regulations aimed at caucuses. This chapter describes caucuses, the 1995 rules changes that affected them, and their activities during the 104th Congress.

At the beginning of the 104th Congress, it was widely reported that the House of Representatives had "abolished" congressional caucuses. But a year later, in January 1996, 129 caucuses existed. Some caucuses active in the 103d Congress *had* disbanded, but 111 continued, and 18 new caucuses had been established; 116 of them operated in the House.[1] What actually happened to the caucuses and why? The answer depends on what the various caucuses do, where they fit into the organization of Congress, how they help or do not help members and groups of members, what was truly abolished and, finally, on the role of Congress in the political system. This chapter addresses each of these points.

What Are Caucuses?

Caucuses are voluntary groups of members of Congress who organize to affect the policy process. They are created and operate outside the established structure of Congress. They do not have recognition in chamber rules or line-item appropriations as, for example, committees do. Bills are not referred to caucuses, nor can they "report" legislation for consideration by the Senate or the

House. Nevertheless, as this essay demonstrates, caucuses are often deeply involved in policy matters and legislative decision making.

Unlike committees and leadership offices within the formal congressional system, caucuses are made up of members of Congress who choose to join; seniority does not matter, nor does the "balancing" of regional and other geographic concerns. Most caucuses are bipartisan, and in the 104th Congress, 28 percent were bicameral with members from both the House and Senate. Each caucus can, however, set membership criteria. A caucus may choose to operate only in the House or the Senate or to accept only Democrats or only Republicans.

Although they are not part of the formal congressional system, caucuses are formally organized. All have chairs or co-chairs; many have other officers. Caucus members' personal staff, or very occasionally committee staff, work on caucus issues and concerns. Caucuses are continuing organizations—they do not end when a Congress ends—with a clearly defined membership and goals.

An important advantage of operating outside the formal structure is the ease of establishing or abolishing caucuses. A caucus can be started by one or more representatives or senators making an announcement and sending a "Dear Colleague" letter describing caucus purposes and inviting other members of Congress to join. After that, interested members organize, choose officers, and designate staff contacts in members' offices, and the work of the caucus can begin. Caucus members can in similar fashion decide to disband the group. In contrast, creating or disbanding a committee must be approved by the full House or Senate, and changes in party leadership groups must be approved by all Republicans or all Democrats in the chamber. This ease of organization means that through caucuses senators and representatives can respond quickly to events, crises, or newly emerging concerns in the polity at large. As issues become less salient, the caucuses dealing with them can become less active or dissolve.

Why Caucuses and Why Now?

Today's caucuses are a congressional adaptation to external demands—crises, long-term trends, and emerging issues—and to the inability of the formal system of Congress to handle these demands rapidly and flexibly. Caucuses are also linked to members' individual goals.

The development of caucuses reveals a great deal about member and institutional responsiveness and congressional change. The first caucus of the contemporary era was the Democratic Study Group (DSG), established in 1959. In the next decade members founded two more caucuses, the (Republican) Wednesday Group and Members of Congress for Peace through Law, later renamed the Arms Control and Foreign Policy Caucus. Ten groups were established between 1970 and 1974, and then the pace began to accelerate. Members founded another fifty-seven by 1980. By 1990, 114 additional new caucuses had been launched. In January 1996, at the opening of the second session of the 104th Congress, 129 caucuses were active, and the status of another 27 could not be determined, although some of them appeared to be operating. Eighty-nine of the caucuses established since 1959 had been disbanded.[2] Of the 129 caucuses active in 1996, 24 operated only within the Senate. The other 105 operated within the House or were bicameral.

Caucuses were generally House-based and partisan, concentrating on internal congressional organization or a broad range of issues until about 1975, when a general shift in focus and membership occurred. Most caucuses created since then are bipartisan, bicameral, and often deal with a single issue or a single industry. Senators began to establish caucuses a decade later than their House colleagues, and there have always been fewer Senate caucuses. Besides the bicameral caucuses, there are also a number of parallel House and Senate caucuses.

Why have caucuses proliferated in recent years, and why does proliferation continue? The reasons include the responsibilities and organizational characteristics of Congress; the demands on Congress from the political system; the deficiencies in the formal congressional structure, which was unable or unwilling to handle changing demands; the members' goals; the links between caucuses and the institution's formal structures; and the help caucuses provide their members and the institution to carry out responsibilities and achieve goals.

Congress's responsibilities as an institution include lawmaking and representation, and they are often at odds. Lawmaking is a protracted process involving subcommittee, committee, and floor action within each chamber; it also requires coordination—to reach agreement on the final product—between the two chambers. Lawmaking requires centralization to build majorities from disparate points of view. Representation, a permanent concern, can breed members' independence from their party or leadership; it encourages decentralization.

Congress has responded to the tension between lawmaking's centralization and representation's decentralization by making changes in its organization and how resources are allocated. During the 1970s, reforms, particularly in the House, increased individual members' resources: they could hire more staff, and subcommittee chairs and ranking minority members could appoint aides. At the same time, House leaders were given additional centralizing and coordinating tools to carry out their responsibilities. For example, the Speaker could refer bills to more than one committee and set time limits on their consideration. Ad hoc committees could be created to put together a final version of a multiply referred bill. During the 1980s party leaders began to use these more, and party unity increased.[3]

Legislatures are different from most other organizations. Congress does not select its membership, and, because people outside the organization elect the members, the senators and representatives are accountable to them, not to the institution and its leaders. Members' success may depend on how Congress helps or hinders them in achieving their goals—representation, policy outcomes, and power in the institution—for which constituents hold them accountable.[4]

In recent years, constituents' expectations have grown. They communicate more frequently via letters, telephone calls, faxes, and e-mail. The rise of single-issue interest groups that demand specific policy responsiveness has increased the workload of representatives individually and of Congress as an institution. At the same time, the issues with which the national government, including Congress, are concerned also have grown in number and complexity.

Respondents cite the rise in the public's expectations as one of two major reasons for caucus formation.[5] The other is Congress's inability to process the demands. Respondents blame deficiencies in the leadership and the committee system for the failure to respond as speedily and effectively as members would like. Rep. Robert Edgar, D-Pa., who was chair of the Northeast-Midwest Congressional Coalition in the 97th Congress, explained this linkage in testimony before a subcommittee of the House Rules Committee. "Chief among the reasons [for caucus formation] were factors such as: failure of the parties and other congressional leadership structures to adjust to an era in which more educated, better informed members are requiring better leadership on increasingly complex public policy issues."[6] The Hispanic Caucus, noted a participant, was formed to "overcome the inaccessibility of the House leadership." A senior staffer, reflecting on the proliferation of caucuses, echoed these comments. "Caucuses are not as much a cause as an effect of changing party structures. Caucuses serve a real purpose for members who want to get something done, and who do not necessarily have a united party to work behind."

Members have also sought coordination of information, strategy, and voting clout on specific issues. Here, too, the internal structure of Congress—a decentralized committee system and leadership often perceived as unresponsive—has contributed to caucus formation. A senior staffer described the founding of the industrial innovation caucus: "There was a recognition that committee jurisdictions did not dovetail neatly with this issue. We needed another vehicle. So we turned to the idea of a caucus to try to mobilize congressional interest and opinion across committee jurisdictions." A participant in a party caucus noted the increase in workload and the need for coordination:

> Congress is faced with an incredible amount of work . . . and you've got to find ways of joining together to decrease that load and at the same time get it done. A caucus serves that purpose. It combines interests. It combines expertise. A caucus is a base for working in the future as a coalition on particular issues.

A respondent from another caucus agreed:

> On issues where there's more than just an authorization and appropriation required—border control, children and family, space—it's probably the only way that members can discuss broad policy matters with other members. I don't know any other vehicle in the House for doing that. What should we be doing? How can the problem be solved? Does it take money? If so, how much?

The pace of caucus formation picked up during the 1970s, as members, operating with larger and more equitably distributed resources within a decentralized institution, searched for ways to respond to the growing external demands. Caucuses continued to operate, and to be established, in the 1980s and

1990s because members found that they could help members achieve their goals as well as the institution's. Caucuses offered members a new way to take collective action. Members also derive tangible benefits from caucus activities: they gain information, are identified as "leaders," and are able to demonstrate that they care about an issue of importance to constituents. Caucus actions, such as agenda setting and coalition building, help members achieve individual policy, reelection, and institutional power goals. Caucuses also serve institutional purposes. They are a mechanism for adapting to changed demands or issues and for responding to constituent concerns in a representative system.[7]

Although they are not part of the formal system of committees and party leaders, caucuses are linked to it in various ways. Caucus members are also members of committees and of party groups such as the whip organization and the party policy and research committees. They are therefore decision makers in the formal system and prefer to supplement rather than oppose that system. A senior staffer, describing a small regional caucus, said, "It's an ad hoc group that fulfills an important function and does not have pretensions to being another committee. And, you know, it's not there to challenge the committee system." A senior participant in another caucus agreed: "If you want to get anything done, the best thing to do is to go to the committee [not work outside the system] . . . the committee decides which bill comes out." Although on occasion caucuses oppose party leaders or committees, they also offer leaders and committees information, assistance in coalition building, and access to a bloc of votes.

Types of Caucuses

All caucuses carry out similar activities: gathering and analyzing information, influencing the issue agenda, developing legislation, monitoring the executive's implementation, and coordinating members' activity on issues of concern. But caucuses also differ. If they are grouped on the basis of membership, six types can be distinguished. The caucuses within each group are alike because members share a common characteristic such as party and ideology or representation of constituency industries (see Table 12-1).

Four types are constituency based. Members of the *national constituency* caucuses are perceived, and perceive themselves, as representing certain groups nationwide—blacks, women, Hispanics, Vietnam-era veterans.

Regional caucuses bring together members in adjoining states or congressional districts to work on matters of particular interest to an area: the Northeast and Midwest, New England, the western states, or districts within a state.

State/district caucus members are from states or congressional districts with widely diffused characteristics such as rural or ethnic populations or family farms. The Rural Caucus, the Agricultural Forum, the High Altitude Coalition, and the two Irish caucuses are typical.

Members of *industry* caucuses are from districts or states with specific industries or businesses: coal, textiles, steel, or beef, for example.

Table 12-1 Congressional Caucuses, by Type

Type	Typical Examples
Intraparty	The Coalition Conservative Opportunity Society Democratic Study Group Tuesday Lunch Bunch Wednesday Group Class clubs
Personal interest	Arts caucuses Constitutional Caucus Constitutional Forum Congressional Family Caucus Senate Children's Caucus Human rights caucuses Military Reform Caucus Population and Development Coalition
Constituency concerns, national	Congressional Black Caucus Congressional Hispanic Caucus Congressional Caucus for Women's Issues Vietnam Veterans Caucus
Constituency concerns, regional	Congressional Border Caucus Northeast-Midwest Congressional Coalition Congressional Sunbelt Council Tennessee Valley Authority Caucus Western Caucus Western States Senate Coalition
Constituency concerns, state/district	Congressional Caucus on Armenian Issues Export Caucus Task Force on Industrial Innovation and Productivity Irish caucuses Rural Caucus Suburban Caucus
Constituency concerns, industry	Automotive Caucus Boating Caucus Depot Caucus Steel caucuses Textile Caucus Travel and Tourism Caucus

Party caucuses are formed by intraparty groups whose members share a similar ideology. The Democratic Study Group was established by liberal Democrats; the members of the Republican Wednesday Group, which takes its name from its weekly meeting day, are moderate and liberal members of the GOP. Class clubs are established in the House by newly elected freshmen of each Congress; the Republican Freshman Class of the 104th Congress and the Democratic Class of 1992 Caucus (freshmen Democrats in the 103d Congress) fall into this category. Party caucuses are partisan and chamber-specific.

Members of *personal interest* caucuses share interest in an issue—the environment, space, human rights, the Internet, or the arts, for example.

Party, personal interest, national constituency, and many regional caucuses are concerned with a broad range of issues. The DSG has worked on civil rights legislation, congressional reorganization, campaign finance, and foreign policy issues. In the Reagan administration the caucus opposed the reregistration (to the United States) of Kuwaiti oil tankers in the Persian Gulf to protect them from Iraqi attack. The caucus developed and won House approval of legislation to require a ninety-day delay in the reflagging. During the 1990s it has published research reports and analyses on a broad range of legislative issues including crime, taxes, energy policy, defense, the balanced budget amendment, unemployment benefits, and family leave. The House Wednesday Group has published in-depth research on the North American Free Trade Agreement, market-oriented environmental policies, and immigration. The Northeast-Midwest Congressional Coalition, a regional caucus, has worked on environmental, trade, defense contract, and census count issues. The Hispanic Caucus, a national constituency caucus, has been active on immigration, health, education, small business, the census count, and federal personnel appointment issues.

In contrast, state/district and industry caucuses have a narrower focus. Although they may interact with diverse groups—railroads, shippers, and passengers in the case of the Senate Rail Caucus, for example—these caucuses concentrate on *one* issue. The Travel and Tourism Caucus is typical. Its activities have included working on National Tourism Week legislation, arranging briefings on the federal government's tourism marketing programs, planning National Tourism Week, proposing and supporting the U.S. Travel and Tourism Administration in the Department of Commerce, and then in 1995 opposing congressional efforts to abolish it.

Caucus Activities

Caucuses carry out activities typical of the formal congressional system, in part because formal party and committee structures are not entirely effective. In doing so they fulfill institutional functions and assist members in achieving their individual goals.

Information Gathering and Exchange

All caucuses gather, analyze, and exchange information. Many provide their members with information on pending issues or legislation scheduled for floor debate; some also conduct studies of emerging issues. At regular (often weekly) meetings, members report on legislation in their committees. Briefing sessions and written materials provide current and in-depth information on pending matters. The focus varies by caucus category: regional caucuses analyze appropriations, for example, from a regional perspective; industry caucuses report a tariff proposal's impact on a particular industry; the Congressional Caucus for Women's Issues concerns itself with the effect of legislative proposals on women, the caucus's national constituency.

Some caucuses bring together members, and on occasion constituent groups, that have conflicting viewpoints, such as producers and consumers, or labor and industry interests. Caucus members say that these meetings offer the participants information and an opportunity to hear different points of view.

Influencing Agendas

Caucuses influence both congressional and executive branch agendas. They *set agendas* by pushing an issue to consideration by congressional committees, the full House or Senate, or an executive branch department or agency. The Military Reform Caucus, for example, proposed new approaches—and therefore new agenda items—to defense appropriations. The women's caucus placed women's health issues on the agendas of committees and the National Institutes of Health.

Groups also *maintain* agendas by keeping issues salient. Prior to the 104th Congress, the Conservative Democratic Forum (also known as the Boll Weevils) kept a balanced budget amendment on the agenda of House committees and tried to place it directly on the agenda of the House floor. Different types of caucuses work in various ways to influence agendas. National constituency caucuses seek to place issues on public agendas to facilitate their placement on congressional agendas. Fifty-seven percent of the personal interest caucuses focus primarily on the congressional agenda, as does a similar percentage of the party caucuses. The more narrow their interests the more likely are the constituency caucuses to concentrate on influencing the executive branch's agenda: one-third of the industry caucuses do so.

Other Activities

Caucuses also develop legislation, drafting bills for committee consideration, and amendments that are introduced by caucus members during floor debate. In the mid-1970s the DSG drafted (and the Democratic Caucus adopted) the "subcommittee bill of rights," which provided staff, monies, and fixed jurisdictions for House subcommittees. In 1985 the women's caucus formulated and introduced a family leave bill. A later version was approved by Congress and became law during the 103d Congress. The Pro-Life Caucus, chaired by Christopher Smith, R-N.J., regularly drafts amendments to authorization or appropriations measures to prohibit the use of federal funds for abortion.

Some caucuses also seek their colleagues' votes to support the groups' positions, and successful caucuses frame issues to appeal to the largest possible number. The women's caucus followed this strategy in gathering support for its parental leave bill by emphasizing that the legislation would help families, not just women. At the time of floor voting, a few caucuses operate their own whip systems, while others assign to each caucus member several noncaucus colleagues to contact for support. On occasion, one caucus will act with another on a common concern, as when the chairman of the Steel Caucus, during floor debate, asked Steel Caucus members to support a Textile Caucus bill.[8]

Although major changes occurred at the start of the 104th Congress, caucuses continued. We turn now to a review of those changes and discuss how caucuses fared in the 104th.

Caucuses in the 104th Congress

At the start of the 104th Congress, caucuses came under attack in the House. Although all House members have joined and been active in congressional caucuses, some representatives had expressed concern about the accountability of caucus operations and about caucus influence on policy making. The House has more caucuses than the Senate, with larger memberships and more complex structures. Senate caucuses tend to be informal; they are more likely to rely on the efforts of individual senators to put issues on a committee agenda or build a floor coalition than on caucus staff or members' group activity. So the changes came in the House.

During the late 1970s and through the 1980s, the Committee on House Administration (now the Committee on House Oversight) required periodic reports on caucus staff, income, and expenditures. The committee banned close ties between caucuses and "affiliated" institutes outside of Congress and forbade raising any income from sources outside Congress. However, after the House bank scandal during the 102d Congress, members became more sensitive about accountability and looked for ways to rebuild constituent confidence rather than reinforce cynicism. To begin, members asked for audits of the legislative service organizations (LSOs). The LSOs were a small group of caucuses, most of which were given office space in congressional buildings. They were allowed to pay staff and office expenses from monies transferred from members' personal office expense accounts. The audits turned up some apparent irregularities in reporting and expenditures, so, as a new broom swept through Congress after the 1994 elections, caucus accountability became a major issue.[9]

A second factor that led to changes was the leadership. Newt Gingrich had devised a brilliant strategy for his party to win control of the House: an agenda of reform called the Contract with America, on which Republican candidates would run and, once elected, would vote into law. When he became Speaker, Gingrich centralized power by choosing committee chairs himself and making subcommittees less independent of committee chairs (and, therefore, of the Speaker). Changing the way caucuses operated could contribute to the centralization of power within the House and facilitate party leaders' efforts to unify the party. It is ironic that one of the reasons Gingrich was elected Speaker was his visibility—and effectiveness—as leader of the Conservative Opportunity Society, a caucus of "firebrand" conservative Republicans that he helped found in 1983.

A caucus had helped the Speaker get his job, but caucuses had the potential to hinder him. Caucuses can fragment a party or the unity of a voting majority. Fragmentation of party unity is more likely to occur if like-minded members organize, as they do in caucuses. If a caucus opposes the leadership, an entire bloc of votes may be lost. Caucuses can also be effective forums for bringing about change and for influencing legislative decision making, possibly in opposition to the leadership. Furthermore, Republican leaders had moved to centralize the formal congressional system, but caucuses worked outside that system. Making caucus operations more difficult might limit their ability to oppose the leadership.

Another factor was partisanship. The membership of several well-organized and influential LSOs was entirely Democratic (the Democratic Study Group) or primarily Democratic (the Congressional Black Caucus). Eliminating a caucus office and staff would likely affect Democratic groups more. So some, but not all, of the incentive to eliminate LSOs was partisan, and the Republicans controlled the new Congress.

In January 1995, when the House debated and adopted its rules for the 104th Congress, a Republican proposal to end LSOs was introduced as part of H. Res. 6. This resolution, which made changes in House rules and procedures, was, according to Rep. Gerald Solomon, R-N.Y., the "initial fulfillment of the Contract with America to restore, renew, and reform the people's House."[10] Section 222 of the bill abolished the LSOs: "The establishment or continuation of any legislative service organization . . . shall be prohibited in the 104th Congress." The Committee on House Oversight was directed "to ensure an orderly termination and accounting for funds of any legislative service organization in existence on January 3, 1995," the first day of the 104th Congress. During debate, members argued that eliminating LSOs would save money. Rep. C. W. Bill Young, R-Fla., noted:

> These members' caucuses which represent special interests cost the taxpayer $5 million a year and take up a large amount of office space. In fact, elimination of the LSOs and their 97 staff positions along with the committee staff reductions may free up enough space so that we can sell off an entire House office building.[11]

Others disputed these claims and argued that representation and efficiency would suffer. Rep. Norman Mineta, D-Calif., said:

> If [caucus] work requires that each caucus member duplicate within his or her individual office the work that could be done more efficiently and at a lower cost by one person working for an LSO, then so be it. . . . The ironclad commitment we have made to effectively providing . . . representation will not waiver.[12]

By a party-line vote of 227–201, House members refused to send the bill back to committee and then approved Title II of the bill, including Section 222, by voice vote.[13]

What has been the result? Caucuses still exist, and new caucuses have been established since January 1995. Some caucuses active in the 103d Congress have disbanded. All of the twenty-eight caucuses that had LSO status in the 103d Congress lost it, but twenty-five continued as regular informal caucuses. A new category has been created: caucuses may now register with the House Oversight Committee as congressional member organizations (CMOs).[14] CMOs are permitted to share official resources; for example, two caucus members can pay half of the salary of a staff aide who handles caucus matters and is part-time in each office. CMOs must report to the House Oversight Committee their purpose, officers, and staff. Caucuses not registering as CMOs are termed "informal congressional groups" and operate as non-LSO caucuses did previously: coordinating research, information, and strategy among members with staff working out of caucus members' personal offices.

At the end of the first session of the 104th Congress, 37 of the 116 groups operating in the House were registered as CMOs. Most were continuing caucuses that decided to register for CMO status. Nearly half (eleven) of the twenty-five former LSOs registered as CMOs. Seven of the CMOs were newly established caucuses, founded in 1995 during the first session of the 104th Congress.

Has anything changed? Some things have, some have not. For those caucuses that focused on the exchange of information among members, or that operated with members' personal staff handling caucus work, not much has changed. For the caucuses that were set up as LSOs with a separate office and staff, carrying on their operations and coordinating the work of staff has become more difficult. Many in this group have cut back on research and the production of information. And well into the 104th Congress, former LSOs were continuing to adapt and adjust structures and activities. But overall, caucuses continue to try, with some success, to influence policy and to affect legislative decision making.

Caucuses in Action: Three Case Studies

The fates of three caucuses illustrate the continuity of the caucus system. Two of them, the Coalition and the Republican Freshmen Class of the 104th Congress, are party caucuses. They were established early in 1995 during the first session of the 104th Congress and are examples of members' ability and desire to respond to changes in the political environment by forming caucuses. The Coalition is a group of conservative-to-moderate Democrats. In the 104th Congress, the group focused particularly on budget and welfare legislation, two issues prominent on the congressional and national agenda. The Republican Freshman Class was formed soon after the 1994 election. Freshmen have formed class clubs since the mid-1970s. Two factors made the 104th freshmen Republican group influential: its size—seventy-three, a very large class—and its ideological unity. As is typical of the intraparty groups, both caucuses directed their efforts primarily toward affecting their respective party's agenda and actions. The third caucus is an ongoing, bipartisan, national constituency caucus, the Congressional Black Caucus. The CBC lost its LSO status after these were abolished and was reconstituted as a CMO. Although the CBC lost a caucus office and central staff, its chair and members continued to speak out on issues, to offer alternative legislative proposals, and to seek policy outcomes supported by the group.

The Coalition

The Coalition, also called the Blue Dog Democrats, was established in February 1995 to develop and pursue "middle-of-the-road" policy proposals, particularly on welfare and budget matters.[15] It is a small caucus—about two dozen members who generally have more conservative voting records than those of their party colleagues; on some issues in previous Congresses they had deserted their party to vote with the Republicans.

Observers expected the Republicans to woo the group for votes. With a narrow margin of 230 to 204, the Republicans could not afford to lose any Republican votes, and on some issues they might need the Blue Dog votes. Observers also expected that the Coalition would work occasionally with Republicans to shape legislative provisions sufficiently palatable to the caucus to gain its support. Coalition member Charles Stenholm of Texas, as chair of the Conservative Democratic Forum, had been a leader in earlier Congresses in drafting and seeking support for a balanced budget amendment—which was now part of the Contract with America. In previous years, caucus members had pushed other initiatives that became part of the GOP agenda. Nevertheless, the Coalition said it had "no intention of joining the Republican ranks," but viewed its establishment as representing "a declaration of independence from the Democratic leadership."[16] (Later in the session, five Coalition members changed parties to join the Republicans.) In late February 1995 the Coalition introduced its own welfare reform bill, drafted by a co-chair, Nathan Deal of Georgia. In October the Coalition introduced an alternative federal budget. Both became important in House consideration of these issues.

The Coalition was indeed wooed by both sides. During the first six weeks of the Republican-controlled 104th, before the caucus was established, Coalition members had sided with Republicans on 72 percent of the votes, in contrast to the rest of the Democrats who supported the Republican majority 15 percent of the time.[17] However, many of the votes early in the session were on Contract with America items, which passed with bipartisan support. Some of them had been proposed and supported by Democrats in the past. Soon after the Coalition's formation was announced, members met with the Tuesday Lunch Bunch, a group of moderate Republicans, to discuss upcoming issues, especially welfare reform and the budget, and to explore possible cooperation on votes. In November 1995, during negotiations on the 1996 budget, Republican leaders met with some members of the Coalition to explore the possibility of developing a centrist, bipartisan compromise, but without result.

On the Democratic side, President Clinton met with the Coalition in February 1995, shortly after it was founded. Democratic congressional leaders met with the group on various issues and included it in party deliberations. Representative Deal's welfare bill was adopted by the congressional Democrats as their party's answer to Republican proposals.

In October 1995 the caucus offered an alternative federal budget. It occupied a middle ground, reaching a balanced budget in seven years, which appealed to Republicans; proposed smaller cuts for social programs than the Republican budget, which appealed to Democrats; and did not include tax cuts to balance the budget, which appealed to some Democrats, even though the president had called for modest tax cuts. The budget proposal received a great deal of publicity and gathered bipartisan support. When offered as an alternative budget during House floor debate, the bill got votes from both sides of the aisle, but did not pass. In December, after Clinton vetoed the Republican-passed budget bill, he and his White House aides scrutinized the Coalition's alternative budget as a possible compromise solution to the budget impasse. Coalition proposals remained important in the debates as Congress worked on budget and welfare reform issues during the second session of the 104th.

The Coalition was successful because it occupied a crucial center position on some vital issues. The caucus was able to influence members' perceptions of issues and to affect the debate about legislative content, not only because of its centrist position, but also because of the track record of its members in providing carefully drafted bills. By offering an alternative budget, for example, it shifted the debate from whether to adopt the Republican or the Democratic position—which confronted members with an either-or vote and the possibility of gridlock—to finding a middle position that could be supported by a broad centrist group.

The Republican Freshman Class of the 104th Congress

The Republican Freshman Class, like the Coalition, is a party caucus. During the 104th Congress it worked within the House Republican Party to pursue caucus (and caucus members') goals. Many in the group ran in 1994 on a reform platform, and, once in the House, they pursued reform in two ways: through congressional reforms such as reduced staffing, term limits for the Speaker and committee chairs, provisions for more accountability, and campaign finance reform; and through governmental and programmatic reform such as regulatory and unfunded mandate changes. The freshmen wanted to cut the budget and reduce the size of government; they supported the balanced budget amendment, tax cuts, the line-item veto, campaign finance reform, and the elimination of some cabinet departments. Many of these ideas were part of the Contract with America, which the Republican freshmen loyally supported. Other goals, such as term limits for party leadership positions, members discussed among themselves in early December 1994, and then backed as a group after the Speaker made a formal proposal. Caucus members were ideologically conservative—more so than some of their party colleagues—and, although they supported the leadership on early votes, they also pushed the Speaker and other Republican leaders to pursue the contract agenda and not to compromise on it.

The freshmen organized early, and for most of the Congress spoke with one voice and voted as a bloc. They developed some proposals as a group and lent support to others' ideas. Their numbers and their unity made them a significant force. Moreover, they formed a bloc the Speaker could not afford to lose on crucial votes, which gave them clout on the substance of issues prior to floor votes and on negotiations on legislative provisions.

At times, the caucus position—on budget issues, for example—narrowed the bargaining options available to the Speaker because he needed the freshmen votes. One freshmen strategy was to try to influence bargaining by speaking out before and during negotiations. For example, in December 1995 during the budget negotiations, a group of them announced they would not vote for any budget that increased spending above the amount in the GOP budget package—$12 trillion over seven years.[18] A second strategy was to make sure everyone knew that they were unified in opposition to a legislative provision and if necessary would vote as a group against it.

In September 1995, two-thirds of the freshmen voted against the 1996 Department of Defense appropriations bill. They opposed several provisions, including funds for conversion of military facilities and industries to nonmilitary activities, the Seawolf submarine, and tacit support for sending U.S. troops to Bosnia, but they were particularly upset that an antiabortion provision had been "gutted" by the conference committee. Rep. Robert Livingston, R-La., chair of the House Appropriations Committee, accused the freshmen of opposing the defense bill "for all sorts of reasons. Some are valid, some are not." This in turn infuriated the freshmen, who then felt freer to vote against the bill.[19] In the end, Democrats and conservative Republicans combined to defeat the measure. (A revised bill was later approved.)

The Republican Freshman Class was also a driving force behind the introduction, and House approval of, a bill forbidding the president to send U.S. troops to Bosnia unless Congress appropriated money to pay for the mission. The *Congressional Quarterly Weekly Report* noted that the vote "showed that the GOP freshmen and their allies, in contrast to many of their elders in both parties, were unafraid to challenge the president in his role as commander in chief."[20]

The caucus had ready access to the Speaker and other party leaders, with whom they generally shared a vision of smaller government and programmatic change. But at times Gingrich had to plead for party unity and their support on a legislative provision that was more moderate than they wanted. He prevailed, but his actions illustrate how caucuses, particularly unified caucuses, can be both a help and a hindrance to leaders.

Several factors came together to give the freshmen their influence. They were a large group (almost one-third of the Republicans in the House); they were well organized; they had a specific agenda and ideological unity; and they did not hesitate to speak out. They used the media well to gain publicity for their positions and to increase their influence. For example, Rep. Mark Souder, R-Ind., in the midst of the budget negotiations, told *Wall Street Journal* reporter John Harwood, "We're not scared about shutting down the government [if there is no acceptable budget compromise]."[21] Given its narrow majority, the Republican leadership could not afford to lose many freshman votes on important, often controversial, legislation—and much of the 104th Congress's legislation was both.

The Congressional Black Caucus

The Congressional Black Caucus is one of the long-established congressional caucuses, and formerly was an LSO. Founded in 1970, its membership increased from nine that year, to twenty by the mid-1980s, to thirty-nine during the 103d Congress (1993–1994), and to forty in the 104th. Over the years most members have been Democratic representatives, but in recent Congresses the caucus has been bicameral, when Sen. Carol Moseley-Braun, D-Ill., joined and bipartisan, when Rep. Gary Franks, R-Conn., joined in 1992 and Del. Victor Frazer, Ind.-V.I., in 1994. Rep. J. C. Watts, R-Okla., first elected in 1994, did not join the caucus.[22]

The CBC was influential in the 103d Congress. Its members chaired three standing committees and eighteen subcommittees and held seats on the major committees. The caucus influenced legislation on crime prevention, gun control, and economic issues, including empowerment zones. The votes of the thirty-eight Democratic members of the caucus were crucial to House passage of President Clinton's budget bill in 1993. The CBC held up consideration of a modified line-item veto bill by threatening to side with Republicans against the rule allowing consideration of the bill and delayed a supplemental appropriations bill until it was paired with a vote to fund a program of summer jobs for young people. As an LSO, the CBC had a separate caucus office and staff, with funds from its members' office allotments. All that changed with the 104th.

Rep. Donald Payne, D-N.J., was elected the new chair of the caucus in December 1994, before the 104th Congress convened. It was not yet clear what the status of the LSOs might be, but members knew they were under attack. Even so, members competed for the chair, with Payne winning over Rep. Alcee

Hastings, D-Fla. The election of a new chair was an indication that the caucus would persist despite a change in status. Payne succeeded Rep. Kweisi Mfume, D-Md., who had led the group in the 103d Congress. After his election, Payne noted the determination of the caucus to carry on its work: "The Congressional Black Caucus will change as it has to, so that it will not become obsolete. Members of the caucus . . . will be energized, because we've met adversities all through our history." He also noted that the caucus expected to work with other national constituency LSOs (the Hispanic Caucus and the Congressional Caucus on Women's Issues) during any transition.[23]

At the start of the 104th Congress, the CBC had to adjust to the loss of influential positions by many Democratic caucus members, as well as the loss of LSO status. The Democratic committee and subcommittee chairs of the 103d had become ranking minority members on these committees in the 104th. In addition, some caucus Democrats lost seats on the major House committees, such as Appropriations, Ways and Means, and Rules, as committee rosters were adjusted to reflect the new party ratios in the House.

Caucus membership was also changing. There had been excitement over the 1992 and 1994 elections, which brought a larger number of black members to Congress. At the same time, some caucus differences became apparent. Before the 1990s, most CBC members were liberal Democrats who represented northern urban districts; they shared similar concerns and positions. In the 1990s, party, regional, and constituency differences surfaced as more caucus members represented rural and suburban districts, especially in the South.[24]

The caucus spent the first months of the 104th Congress deciding how to organize and operate and which issues to address. Members were determined that the caucus continue to be "the conscience of Congress." Payne had noted just before the 104th convened, "Our moral leadership will be more crucial in the months ahead of us than ever before. We have always been a voice for the most vulnerable members of our society."[25] During floor debate in January 1995, dismay was evident as Payne and other Democrats opposed the abolition of LSOs. He argued, "[Section 222 to eliminate LSOs] is not about reform. It is a blatant move to put a gag on minorities and others who may differ in opinion from the new majority party."[26] Weekly caucus meetings continued, at which members shared information. CBC members were serving on many different committees, and members were able to bring wide-ranging information to meetings. But coordination of staff work had become more difficult, and it was harder to provide members with specialized information and to organize committee and floor strategy. Payne appointed a transition committee to weigh the post-LSO options, and eventually the caucus applied for CMO status, which enabled members to share official resources (especially staff) for caucus work.

The CBC began to focus on funds for programs that met the needs of members' constituents and that Republicans proposed cutting—summer jobs, student aid, and low income heating assistance, for example—and on policies like affirmative action. It continued to develop policy alternatives, as it had done in previous Congresses, and turned attention particularly to changing or moderating legislative proposals with which it disagreed.

In September 1995, near the end of the first session of the 104th Congress, the CBC held its annual Legislative Conference. Black elected officials and others from across the country came to Washington for a weekend of seminars, discussions, and social events. By that time, the caucus had found its footing, but members were still searching for structures and processes to carry forward caucus purposes in a new and different political situation. Later in the 104th Congress, the caucus received further blows: one of its stars, Representative Mfume, resigned from the House to head the NAACP; two other caucus members resigned from the House; and Supreme Court decisions and the subsequent redrawing of state congressional districts threatened the loss of some majority-minority districts as members headed into the 1996 elections. Several members predicted that Mfume's resignation presaged a shift of strategy by the caucus—a reaching out to the grassroots and more emphasis on working with the private sector—as the CBC adapted to a changed congressional structure and a different political and issue context in the nation.

The caucus continued to serve as a communication and information exchange mechanism and it remained committed to influencing policy. Members still sat on important committees and held senior committee positions, but caucus influence was diminished from the previous Congress. In the 104th, the CBC sought to affect policy primarily by opposing funding cuts for programs critical to caucus members' national constituency and by modifying legislative proposals the caucus opposed. Although effective, it was primarily a defensive posture.

Conclusion

What can be concluded about caucuses from these three case studies? First, caucuses still exist and have important functions. Although House rules eliminated one specific type, the LSO, caucuses as a whole adapted their structures and operations. For the former LSOs, concerns did not change, but the adaptation of structure and shift in some activities was difficult and took time and effort. Throughout the 104th Congress, caucus evolution and adaptation was ongoing. Caucuses, including former LSOs, pursued their goals much as they did in previous years.

The case studies illustrate the operations and the adaptability of caucuses. The Congressional Black Caucus restructured and continues. The Republican Freshman Class reflected concerns important to its constituents. The Coalition focused on two major issues of 1995 and 1996: welfare reform and a balanced budget. Caucuses operate outside the formal structures, but caucuses want to work on their policy concerns with party leaders, and leaders need caucuses' support and votes.

The forces that drove caucus establishment and operation in the 1970s and 1980s persist in the 1990s. Caucuses enable members to focus on shared policy concerns. They are easy to establish and are an efficient way for members to pool their efforts in understanding policy questions and working on policy outcomes. As the case studies reviewed here show, caucuses are often successful in influencing policy by shaping the parameters of debate, affecting the substance of legislation, or rounding up the votes in support of or in opposition to a bill or amendment. Caucuses continue because they help members achieve personal goals of policy, representation, and power in the institution, and because caucus activities are one way Congress as an institution carries out its responsibilities. Neither of these aspects is likely to change any time soon, and, therefore, caucuses are likely to thrive.

Notes

For a more detailed study of caucuses, see Susan Webb Hammond, *Congressional Caucuses in National Policymaking* (Baltimore: Johns Hopkins University Press, forthcoming, 1997). This chapter draws on research for the larger project. I am grateful to the American Enterprise Institute, the Everett McKinley Dirksen Congressional Leadership Research Center, and American University for grants that assisted the research, to the Brookings Institution for appointments as a guest scholar, and to Carol de Frances, Timothy Huelskamp, Martha Kropf, and Scott Rudolph for research assistance. This chapter has benefited from comments by Sarah Binder, Chris Foreman, David Hammond, Eric Patashnik, and Catherine Rudder.

1. Data are derived from Sula P. Richardson, "Informal Congressional Groups and Member Organizations of the 104th Congress: An Informational Directory," *CRS Report for Congress,* Congressional Research Service, Library of Congress, Dec. 5, 1995.
2. Data are derived from author's data and Congressional Research Service reports. Data on the 104th Congress are reported in Richardson, "Informal Congressional Groups and Member Organizations of the 104th Congress."
3. See David W. Rohde, *Parties and Leaders in the Postreform House* (Chicago: University of Chicago Press, 1991).
4. See Richard F. Fenno, *Congressmen in Committee* (Boston: Little, Brown, 1973); and David Mayhew, *Congress: The Electoral Connection* (New Haven: Yale University Press, 1974).
5. Semifocused interviews were conducted with members of Congress, caucus staff directors, and House leadership aides. Quotations are not attributed, as all respondents were promised anonymity.
6. House of Representatives, Committee on House Administration, Ad Hoc Subcommittee on Legislative Service Organizations, *Hearing,* Committee Print, 97th Cong., 2d sess., June 24, 1982, 57.
7. See Burdett A. Loomis, "Congressional Caucuses and the Politics of Representation," in *Congress Reconsidered,* 2d ed., ed. Lawrence C. Dodd and Bruce I. Oppenheimer (Washington, D.C.: CQ Press, 1981), for discussion of the latter point.
8. *Congressional Record,* daily ed., 99th Cong., 2d sess., Oct. 10, 1985, H20798.
9. The Congressional Accountability Act, H.R. 1 (P.L. 104–1), passed by the House Jan. 5, 1995, on a 429–0 vote, made Congress subject to private-sector labor laws such as overtime pay and was also a result of this concern.
10. *Congressional Record,* daily ed., 104th Cong., 1st sess., Jan. 4, 1995, H31.

11. Ibid., H44.
12. Ibid., H89.
13. H. Res. 6, Rules of the House (Title I: Contract with America: A Bill of Accountability; Title II: General—Section 222, Abolition of Legislative Service Organizations). *Congressional Record,* daily ed., Jan. 4, 1995, H30 (Section 222), H83–89 (debate), H89–90 (motion to recommit and voice vote on adopting Title II, including Section 222).
14. Congressional Member Organization (CMO) Regulations, Committee on House Oversight, Feb. 8, 1995.
15. Members used the term Blue Dog Democrats to distinguish themselves from Yellow Dog Democrats—"a dying breed of southern Democrat so loyal to the party that, it's said, they would vote for a yellow dog over a Republican." Jackie Calmes, "Conservative 'Blue Dog' Democrats in the House," *Wall Street Journal,* March 28, 1995, A28.
16. Gabriel Kahn, " 'The Coalition,' A Virtual Third Party for House, To Draft Own Legislation," *Roll Call,* Feb. 16, 1995, A1.
17. *Congressional Quarterly Weekly Report,* Feb. 18, 1995, 496.
18. Quoted in Morton Kondracke, "Pennsylvania Avenue," *Roll Call,* Dec. 18, 1995, 5.
19. Quoted in Jeff Shear, "United They Stand," *National Journal,* Oct. 28, 1995, 2646–7.
20. Jan. 20, 1996, 127.
21. *Wall Street Journal,* Oct. 31, 1995, A20.
22. Sen. Edward Brooke, R-Mass., had worked with the CBC during his years in the Senate, but had never formally joined it.
23. Craig Winneker, "CBC Plans to Form Task Force on the Future," *Roll Call,* Dec. 19, 1994, 7.
24. It is difficult to separate the effect on the caucus of the loss of LSO status from other factors like the loss of committee and subcommittee chair positions and emerging caucus differences. It is clear that loss of LSO status made caucus operation more difficult.
25. Kenneth J. Cooper, "Black Caucus Tries to Cushion the Fall From Its Height of Influence," *Washington Post,* Dec. 16, 1994, A2.
26. *Congressional Record,* daily ed., 104th Cong., 1st sess., Jan. 4, 1995, H85.

Part V
Congress, the Executive, and Public Policy

13. Assessing Congress's Role in the Making of Foreign Policy

Eileen Burgin

Alexis de Tocqueville wrote that "in the control of society's foreign affairs democratic governments do appear decidedly inferior to others."[1] The "inferior" qualities causing Tocqueville unease are most acute in Congress, the most democratic branch of the United States government. Tocqueville's concerns undoubtedly strike a responsive chord in many Americans: over the past two decades criticizing Congress's actions has become nothing less than a national pastime. Indeed, Congress often appears as a gadfly, if not the sole culprit, hindering U.S. foreign relations; few commentators defend Congress's activities, or even hint at a silver lining.[2]

Observers of Congress and foreign policy highlight a full spectrum of problems with congressional participation. At the extremes, Jim Lindsay classifies critics as "irreconcilables" and "skeptics."[3] Irreconcilables argue that Congress overreacted to an "imperial presidency," and now an "imperial Congress" "fetters" an "imperiled presidency."[4] Those who contend that the president has become Congress's servant maintain, in part, that 535 secretaries of state micromanage foreign policy.[5] At the opposite end of the critics' spectrum are skeptics who believe that although Congress may bark it does not bite. Harold Koh argues, for instance, that "Congress has *persistently* acquiesced in what the President has done."[6] Barbara Hinckley claims that congressional assertiveness is simply a "myth," perpetuated by "a host of surface activities."[7] Critics' complaints also cover other aspects of congressional foreign policy activity that fall between the extremes of an imperial or impotent Congress. Congressional involvement may be problematic because of institutional inadequacies (for example, inefficiency), inconstancy, ignorance, or, perhaps most important, members' reelection orientations.[8] Commentators may stress, for example, that an inconstant, ignorant, or parochially minded Congress encourages, or even dictates, policies that are "inexcusable from the standpoint of genuine concern for national security."[9]

Certainly, criticizing Congress in the foreign policy field is easy as well as amusing, for colorful anecdotes and intuitively appealing stories of misguided acts are not lacking, regardless of which party controls Congress. But is the situation as bad as critics contend? The central argument here, simply stated, is that while many of the criticisms have some merit, Congress does have a significant role to play in the foreign policy arena and may even make effective contributions to forming U.S. foreign policy. Congress is neither imperial nor impotent; Congress is not so institutionally inadequate, inconstant, or ignorant to warrant grave concern; and, although members of Congress may be obsessed with reelection, their parochial interests do not automatically translate to congressional contamination of foreign policy making. I therefore advocate that we strive not to exaggerate vices and overlook virtues. We also must remember that Congress is not the only branch that makes flawed decisions or is "remote from . . . perfect wisdom and perfect virtue,"[10]—just consider the actions of the Reagan administration in the Iran-contra scandal.[11]

In this essay, I first examine the constitutional framework in the foreign policy arena and, more specifically, Congress's constitutional powers. Next, I explore how Congress exercises its constitutional prerogatives; understanding how Congress asserts itself is crucial for evaluating its actions. Then I describe the various types of criticisms of congressional foreign policy involvement. Finally, I evaluate critics' concerns and offer a more balanced assessment.[12]

Constitutional Framework

> *Something of the wonder that suffuses a child upon learning that a mighty oak sprang from a tiny acorn fills one who peers behind the tapestry of conventional learning and beholds how meager are the sources of presidential claims to monopolistic control of foreign relations.*[13]
>
> Raoul Berger

Presidential claims to monopolistic power in foreign affairs *are* inaccurate.[14] Our constitutional system of "separated institutions sharing powers" did not intend to create an omnipotent executive.[15] Rather, the Framers designed two active and combative branches, with many overlapping foreign policy roles. In so doing, the Founders sought to safeguard against the arbitrary exercise of authority. As James Madison wrote, "Ambition must be made to counteract ambition."[16] Indeed, thwarting ambition was so important that the Framers chose that goal over efficiency in conflicts between the two. Justice Louis Brandeis observed, "The doctrine of the separation of powers was adopted . . . not to promote efficiency but to preclude the exercise of arbitrary power."[17]

In terms of specific constitutional grants of authority, the president has fewer prerogatives related to foreign policy than does Congress. The president is "Commander in Chief of the Army and Navy"; the president has the power, with the Senate's "Advice and Consent," to "make Treaties" and to "appoint Ambassadors"; and the president receives "Ambassadors and other public Ministers." In addition, some of the president's general authority is relevant: the president is vested with the "executive Power," takes an oath to "preserve, protect, and defend the Constitution," and "shall take Care that the Laws be faithfully executed."

The specific issues within Congress's constitutional purview, in contrast to those within the president's purview, are vast.[18] Congress is the lawmaking branch: it may "make all Laws which shall be necessary and proper for carrying into Execution" its enumerated powers, about half of which pertain to foreign affairs. Congress's constitutional prerogatives in five substantive policy areas related to foreign policy stand out. First, Congress has substantial power over the purse. This power derives from the authority to determine how funds should be spent ("No Money shall be drawn from the Treasury, but in Consequence of Appropriations made by Law"), along with the power to raise revenue ("To Lay and collect Taxes, Duties, Imposts, and Excises, to pay the Debts and provide for the common Defence and general Welfare"). Madison regarded the power of the purse as "the most complete and effectual weapon with which any constitution can arm the immediate representatives of the people."[19] Second, in Article 1, Section 8, Congress's national security or war powers are enumerated: Congress is given the power to "declare War," to "raise and Support Armies," to "provide and maintain a Navy," to "make Rules for the Government and Regulation" of the armed forces, to "provide for calling forth the Militia," and finally to "provide for organizing, arming, and disciplining the Militia." In discussing Congress's war powers, Michael Glennon goes so far as to say that the president's powers "are paltry in comparison with, and are subordinate to, [the] grants to Congress."[20] Even Alexander Hamilton, a consistent advocate for a strong executive, stressed that the president was less threatening than the British king, for Congress, not the president, has power that "extends to the *declaring* of war and to the *raising* and *regulating* of fleets and armies."[21] Third, Congress has the power to "regulate Commerce with foreign Nations," ensuring congressional prerogatives over foregn trade apart from the taxing powers. The last two substantive policy areas in which Congress is granted power fall under the Senate's purview: the Senate is given the power of "Advice and Consent" on both treaties and ambassadorial appointments.

This list of specific constitutional grants of authority pertaining to foreign policy should not be misleading; ambiguities, areas of concurrent power, and omissions exist. Important foreign policy prerogatives lie in what Justice Robert Jackson coined a "zone of twilight."[22] (For instance, consider questions regarding which branch deploys military forces and regulates covert action as well as the role of executive agreements and executive privilege.) With such uncertainty surrounding two vigorous and ambitious branches, therefore, it is not surprising that the Constitution created, as Edward Corwin stated, "an invitation to struggle for the privilege of directing American foreign policy."[23] In the consequent "tug for more of the foreign policy blanket," various influences beyond constitutional powers often have been significant: these include historical precedents, presidents broadly construing their constitutional authority, crises confronting the nation, and Supreme Court decisions.[24]

Congress's Powers in Practice

Given Congress's ample—albeit sometimes ambiguous and shared—constitutional powers, we may consider how Congress asserts itself in the foreign policy field. The most basic congressional method for exercising foreign policy prerogatives is legislation. Binding legislative tools—bills, joint resolutions, and amendments to these measures—only succeed in a technical sense (that is, by becoming law) when a majority of a quorum in both houses agree, assuming that two-thirds majorities are not necessary to override a presidential veto. (Treaties require a two-thirds majority in the Senate, and nominations require a simple Senate majority.) But Congress does not limit itself to a purely legislative strategy in the foreign policy arena, as most observers would have us believe; rather, Congress supplements its legislative authority with informal or nonlegislative mechanisms such as consultations, public appeals through the press, and hearings. Congress uses its two means of influence independently and symbiotically. Legislative and nonlegislative vehicles often are inextricably intertwined: the tools are employed in tandem; legislation mandates the use of informal mechanisms; and nonlegislative tools serve as the precursor to formal legislation. Members wield both kinds of instruments regarding all substantive foreign policy areas in which Congress exercises constitutional authority.

Legislative Tools

Binding legislation is the traditional congressional mechanism for trying to influence foreign policy and exercise constitutional prerogatives. Many binding foreign policy measures are issue-specific and reactive in nature. Rather than attempting to make broad procedural and structural changes that may not affect the particular subject engendering congressional interest and concern, issue-specific legislation directly addresses a current foreign policy problem.

Issue-specific measures include bills and joint resolutions that fulfill constitutional prerogatives in a straightforward manner. Senate approval of nominations and treaties, trade policy (especially that aimed at specific countries), and authorization and appropriations measures may be examples of such legislation. In 1986, for instance, Congress imposed trade sanctions against South Africa, overriding President Reagan's veto to do so.[25] More recently, Congress took the lead on issue-specific legislation when it passed—and saw enacted into law without President Clinton's signature—the fiscal 1996 defense spending package, containing money for several unrequested items such as the B-2 stealth bomber, transport ships, and fighter jets.[26] In addition, Congress uses its power of the purse to determine how money contained in foreign aid bills will be spent.

It passes legislation that earmarks most of the available funds.[27] Congress responds to special executive requests for funds as well, as it did in 1993 and 1994 when passing assistance bills proposed by Clinton for Russia and the other newly independent states.[28]

Some issue-specific legislation contains restrictive provisions. These provisions typically involve Congress exercising negative powers to prohibit certain actions or to decrease the room for executive interpretation. The so-called Boland amendments, and more generally U.S. policy during the Reagan years regarding aid for the Nicaraguan contras, illustrate restrictive legislation: through the power of the purse, Congress attempted to restrict not only the amount of contra aid funds but also the purposes for which the funds could be used.[29] Another case in point concerns U.S. policy toward Somalia early in the Clinton presidency—in 1993 Congress passed restrictive legislation forbidding money to be used for military action after March 31, 1994, unless Congress legislatively granted a presidential request for an extension. Through this legislation, Congress established a deadline for troops to leave Somalia.[30]

Issue-specific legislation also may be directive. In other words, Congress gives the president what he wants, but adds hurdles, mandating that the executive undertake certain activities. The most common requirements are issue-specific executive reports; in the early 1990s the Congressional Research Service (CRS) identified close to seven hundred foreign policy reporting requirements.[31] Reports enable Congress to achieve a number of objectives. Through reporting requirements, Congress can monitor the executive branch without tying its hands. Congress also requires reports to force the executive to acknowledge certain facts. For example, Congress passed an amendment to the fiscal 1991 foreign aid appropriations bill obligating President Bush to report on any military cooperation since 1986 between the U.S.-aided noncommunist resistance in Cambodia and the Khmer Rouge, cooperation considered to be "common knowledge" outside administration circles.[32] Reports also permit Congress to remain part of the process, at least nominally. In authorizing the use of force against Iraq in January 1991, for instance, Congress directed the president before using force to report to Congress his determination that "all appropriate diplomatic and other peaceful means" to obtain Iraqi compliance with United Nations resolutions had not been and would not be successful.[33]

In addition to issue-specific legislation, Congress passes prospective-procedural legislation. Prospective-procedural legislation moves beyond the triggering event to influence foreign policy making in a non-case-specific manner. Prospective-procedural legislation attempts to improve the future functioning of the foreign policy system by altering the policy process or broad procedural and structural mechanisms. Ultimately, prospective-procedural legislation may establish a framework for Congress to assert its institutional prerogatives; it often creates a convenient, policy-neutral foil for criticizing future executive actions as well.

The classic prospective-procedural measure is the War Powers Resolution, passed over Richard Nixon's veto in 1973. This law, which sought to design a formula for congressional-executive codetermination for troop involvement abroad, included three principal procedures: (1) presidential consultation with Congress "in every possible instance . . . before introducing United States Armed Forces into hostilities or into situations where imminent involvement in hostilities is clearly indicated by the circumstances"; (2) executive reports to Congress within forty-eight hours when armed forces are sent into one of several situations without a declaration of war—the reporting requirements under Section 4(a)(1) trigger a sixty-day clock for presidential withdrawal of troops; and (3) congressional action regarding military ventures, including how Congress may extend, sustain, or terminate the use of force.[34] The War Powers Resolution contains three provisions common to many prospective-procedural measures, namely, consultations, reports, and independent congressional action.

Prospective-procedural legislation sometimes includes provisions delegating authority to the executive branch. Yet in delegating authority, Congress strives to ensure congressional influence. The Omnibus Trade and Competitiveness Act of 1988 illustrates the point. A CRS report explained that, although the law delegates power, "it provides a greater, participatory role for the Congress" in ways such as the following: it requires "increased consultation"; it requires an "annual statement" from the U.S. trade representative; it gives Congress "leverage" to ensure adequate executive branch consultations "during trade negotiations"; it "provides for congressional withdrawal of fast-track procedures"; and it significantly changes the trade remedy provisions, "primarily by limiting the discretion of the President and making action by the executive branch more likely."[35]

Nonlegislative Tools

In studies of Congress and foreign policy, nonlegislative tools—or more precisely, non-legally binding tools—receive little attention.[36] Yet we cannot evaluate critics' concerns without understanding the less traditional ways in which Congress exercises power. All non-legally binding instruments can influence policy, and influence it without the widespread consensus needed for passing, and overriding presidential vetoes on, bills and joint resolutions. Most informal mechanisms influence policy in several ways. First, nonlegislative vehicles may provide members with a forum to sway public, congressional, executive, or even a foreign government's opinion. If successful in swaying opinion, members may affect agendas, decision making, and critical actions abroad, as well as in the legislative and executive branches. Second, non-legally binding tools may allow legislators to influence policy by offering them the opportunity to inform or educate—whether it be constituents, the American public, other members of Congress, or the people and officials in other nations. Third, through nonlegislative instruments members may send out signals about possible future legislative and nonlegislative moves, thereby achieving desired results by generating anticipated reactions in the executive branch and in foreign governments. Because other actors may base their behavior and decisions on expectations of what Congress will do, these signals may prompt responses obviating the need for further congressional action.[37] In addition to influencing policy, nonlegislative mechanisms may enable members to pursue personal political objectives, such as winning reelection, maintaining or gaining power in Congress, and seeking higher elected office.

Many factors help define which legislative and nonlegislative tools Congress employs. The nature of a congressional response may depend upon the specifics of an issue, for instance, content, surrounding controversy, timing, and duration.[38] A short-lived foreign policy problem occurring during a lengthy congressional recess—such as the 1989 Panama invasion, for example—tends to stimulate less legislative activity than a long-lived issue occurring during a legislative session; simple logistics compel members to rely upon nonlegislative tools.[39] Factors within Congress, ranging from institutional and structural considerations to more personal ones, also affect congressional action. More specifically, the committee (or committees) with jurisdiction over an issue, the role of the majority party leadership, and the personality and power of the individual leaders on a subject may influence the type of action taken.[40] The use of legislative and nonlegislative instruments may reflect the impact of divided government as well.

While various considerations affect the nature of a congressional response, it should be remembered that legislative and nonlegislative mechanisms usually become part of one process of Congress asserting its power in foreign policy. In the effort to pressure the government of South Africa to dismantle apartheid, Congress had laid the groundwork for legislation over several years through the use of many non-legally binding instruments. Then in 1985, to preempt legislative action that was mere hours away, President Reagan issued an executive order imposing economic sanctions, but less stringent measures than called for by Congress. Culminating action taken over several years, Congress in 1986 passed sanctions legislation.[41]

To illustrate further how non-legally binding tools may influence policy, I now briefly review nine specific indirect mechanisms. The following discussion also highlights the number and variety of ways in which Congress may influence foreign policy and, consequently, the flaws implicit in limiting an analysis to legally binding legislative tools.

Nonbinding legislation. Although they are called "legislation," simple and concurrent resolutions lack the binding, mandatory effect of bills and joint resolutions and do not require presidential action. In fact, nonbinding legislation resembles nonlegislative tools in intended and actual impact. When the House approved a nonbinding resolution requesting a host of documents on the proposed economic rescue plan for Mexico in March 1995, for instance, the action did not force President Clinton to change his proposal, but it publicly demonstrated his lack of support.[42] Nonbinding provisions also may be directed at other countries: the passage of a provision in the 1994 State Department authorization called on, but did not require, Clinton to provide weapons to the besieged Bosnian Muslims. Through this language, Congress communicated to combatants the extent of congressional displeasure and the possibility of binding legislative retribution because, in the words of Rep. Henry Hyde, R-Ill., Americans are "moral players in the world."[43]

Informal advice. Informal advice covers everything from suggestions made by members during routine White House telephone calls to inform them of impending action to exchanges that occur at regular meetings or because of member observance of treaty negotiations and foreign elections. At a breakfast meeting Clinton held with important foreign policy members in April 1994, for example, legislators suggested a solution to the administration's problem of how to pay for the mounting pile of peacekeeping bills.[44]

Consultation. Consultation with the executive branch presents a more formal means of influence than informal advice. Often consultation occurs in response to legislative requirements, such as those in the 1988 Omnibus Trade and Competitiveness Act. Because in theory consultation furnishes members with a meaningful chance to share their views and influence policy (perhaps by blocking proposals before they become a fait accompli), Congress tries to mandate increased consultation in a range of policy areas.

Direct dealings with foreign governments. Members' direct dealings with foreign governments come in two forms. First, members regularly meet with foreign personnel stationed in Washington embassies, with other dignitaries visiting Washington, and with officials abroad when members travel. For instance, in February 1993 legislators met with Bosnia's visiting foreign minister, Haris Silajdzic, and Rep. Frank McCloskey, D-Ind., even asserted at a joint news conference with Silajdzic that the United States had responded to Serbian atrocities with "hypocritical diplomacy."[45] Second, occasionally members engage in personal or private diplomacy. Most such diplomatic efforts follow an executive's invitation, as with the eleventh-hour attempt in 1994 by Sen. Sam Nunn, D-Ga.—along with former president Jimmy Carter and the former head of the Joint Chiefs of Staff, Gen. Colin Powell Jr.—to resolve the Haiti problem without bloodshed.[46] Not all personal or private diplomacy has an executive link, but truly independent "lone ranger diplomacy" is much less common.[47]

Public appeals through the press. Activities such as press conferences, interviews, op-ed pieces, and less formal photo opportunities are all regularly used means of influence. For instance, in August 1993 Sen. Robert Byrd, D-W.Va., sought to modify the Clinton administration's peacekeeping policy in Somalia, which he thought might lead to military involvement in operations the American people neither supported nor understood. Byrd therefore published an article in the *New York Times* outlining his concerns.[48] In contrast, Rep. Joseph Kennedy II, D-Mass., along with five members of the Congressional Black Caucus, chose a photo opportunity in their fight against and endeavor to alter U.S. policy toward Haiti in 1994: they protested in front of the White House and were arrested while doing so.[49]

Hearings. A wide range of committees and subcommittees hold hearings on foreign policy issues; most committees have some jurisdiction over these matters. In addition to the objectives common to all nonlegislative vehicles, hearings provide Congress with a vehicle to conduct oversight. Consider the hearings by several committees in December 1990 concerning what appeared to be an impending war in the Persian Gulf. At the time of the hearings, President Bush had already altered the nature of the U.S. mission from defensive to offensive by nearly doubling the troops in Saudi Arabia—without congressional approval while Congress was in recess. He also had received UN Security Council authorization to use "all necessary means" to force Iraqi compliance with UN resolutions. Given Congress's exclusion from these actions, the hearings furnished members with an avenue to become more active players: the committees attempted to influence policy and conduct oversight, and many committee members sought personal benefits, such as increased visibility, from participation.[50] The 1987 Iran-contra hearings, although substantively very different kinds of hearings, offered members similar opportunities.[51]

Floor statements. Speeches in the House and Senate occasionally go beyond simple "position taking" aimed at constituents.[52] A case in point is the three-day speech in 1987 by Senator Nunn, the chair of the Armed Services Committee, about the Reagan administration's reinterpretation of the antiballistic missile (ABM) treaty. When Reagan officials attempted to justify forging ahead with strategic defense initiative ("star wars") technology, in part by reinterpreting the ABM treaty, Nunn took to the floor, critically and exhaustively analyzing the reinterpretation. Nunn's decision to use floor statements as part of his strategy to influence events underscores this nonlegislative vehicle's potential.[53]

Letters. Members also write letters to the executive, although this tool is less publicized than most other nonlegislative tools. Substantively, much correspondence resembles the letter fifty Senate Republicans and one Senate Democrat, led by Majority Leader Bob Dole, R-Kan., sent to Clinton in October 1995 urging him to request congressional authorization in advance of any troop deployment to Bosnia. The letter writers, many of whom might have been so-called swing votes, hoped to send an unequivocal signal and exert pressure on the administration.[54]

Lawsuits against the president. Perhaps the most unusual nonlegislative measure is the lawsuit. When members attempt to use this avenue, they rarely succeed. The Supreme Court usually refuses to deal with claims, rebuffing members primarily on the basis of the political question doctrine, which is a device federal courts use to insulate themselves from what are deemed to be essentially political disputes. And when the Court does rule on the merits of a case, it tends to favor the president.[55]

The Negative Ledger Entries

Having examined Congress's constitutional powers and its exercise of these prerogatives, we now shall look at observers' criticisms in greater detail. In this section I review critics' diverse concerns about Congress's actions. After considering somewhat contradictory arguments by commentators at the spectrum's extremes—an "imperial" Congress or an "impotent" Congress?—I address other criticisms of congressional foreign policy involvement.

An Imperial Congress?

Critics who see an imperial Congress fettering an imperiled presidency complain about the legislative and nonlegislative devices used to exert influence. Legislative and nonlegislative vehicles allow Congress to micromanage the executive, observers contend, by taking over the detailed administration of foreign policy and curtailing the president's flexibility. For instance, earmarking in foreign aid gives Congress the opportunity to make specific decisions that constrain the executive's ability to spend appropriated funds as necessary. And restrictive measures such as the Boland amendments present similar problems; repeating a common refrain, Douglas Jeffrey argues that "the congressional majority foreordained something like the Iran-Contra 'scandal' by attempting to hog-tie the president with the Boland Amendment."[56] Congress also allegedly micromanages when it holds a president "hostage" through restrictive legislation that limits or withholds funds. And Congress may act in an imperial manner by forcing the president to surrender power to Congress, as it did with the 1996 Cuban sanctions bill in which President Clinton relinquished the authority to decide when to lift the Cuban embargo.[57] Observers maintain that reporting requirements in directive and prospective-procedural legislation offer further evidence of congressional meddling. President Bush complained, for example, that the Pentagon alone spent $50 million and five hundred man-years in fiscal 1989 writing reports to satisfy Congress.[58] Along the same lines, Secretary of Defense William Perry strongly objected to the Republican-dominated Congress's proposal in 1995 to create a commission to assess defense needs, saying that it undermined executive branch power.[59] Critics also contend that nonlegislative mechanisms are notorious for hampering and undermining the executive: hearings capriciously interfere with administration officials' time through requested testimony and pry into executive matters; informal advice and consultations may circumscribe executive freedom of action; and private diplomacy undercuts the president in his dealings and negotiations with foreign governments. Commentators argue that an imperial Congress oversteps its constitutional prerogatives as well. The War Powers Resolution is these critics' favorite illustration of an unconstitutional law that hamstrings the presidency.[60]

An Impotent Congress?

Critics at the opposite end of the spectrum see an impotent Congress. An impotent Congress almost always loses to the president in foreign policy making because it complies with or acquiesces in what the president wants or has done, even if clearly contrary to Congress's stated will.[61] Three related points are particularly relevant to this argument.

First, critics stress that laws are not self-executing, and administrations often exploit weaknesses.[62] Commentators say the War Powers Resolution is a case in point: the executive branch typically construes consultation obligations narrowly, holding informational briefings in which it presents a fait accompli and fails to solicit legislators' counsel, rather than actually seeking members' "advice and opinions" when "a decision is pending." Moreover, the executive circumvents the law's sixty-day clock by submitting reports "consistent with" the act instead of pursuant to the relevant section, as Congress intended.[63] Critics also point to Congress's attempt to influence military aid to El Salvador in the early 1980s as an example of executive noncompliance. Kenneth Sharpe writes, "The administration . . . provided false and misleading information in order to certify that the conditions required for aid existed, despite overwhelming evidence to the contrary."[64] And when Congress used the power of the purse to limit military appropriations to El Salvador, Sharpe explains that President Reagan violated the laws' intent and circumvented Congress by increasing military assistance through the president's special defense drawdown authority and the authority to reallocate funds.[65] So these critics argue that even appropriations cutoffs do not ensure good executive behavior. And since Congress frequently attaches cutoffs to continuing appropriations measures to deter vetoes, the provisions are subject to yearly reconsideration.[66] Complaints about executive branch noncompliance with the Intelligence Oversight Act of 1980 also abound. The CIA's failure to inform Congress adequately about the agency's role in the 1984 mining of Nicaraguan harbors, for instance, prompted this protest from Rep. Norman Y. Mineta, D-Calif.: "We've dug, probed, cajoled, kicked and harassed to get facts from the CIA, but Casey wouldn't tell you that your coat was on fire unless you asked him."[67]

Second, these commentators contend that the legislative cry has more resonance than substance—the hallmark of binding legislation is ambiguities, loopholes, and giveaways to the executive. The Intelligence Oversight Act, according to critics, illustrates the common problems. An impotent Congress passed loosely written legislation that codified executive practice, rather than clearly revamping the intelligence oversight system and establishing ironclad requirements.[68] Instead of a blanket requirement on prior notification of all intelligence activities, for instance, Congress allowed the executive to act without prior notice in some cases as long as appropriate committees were informed "in a timely manner." Another ambiguity or loophole, critics complain, concerns covert operations affecting "vital" U.S. interests—in such cases only eight congressional leaders must be notified.[69] Similarly, the Nuclear Proliferation Prevention Act of 1994, including its new sanction denying Export-Import Bank loans, credits, and insurance to countries that have "willfully aided or abetted" states in acquiring nuclear weapons or "unsafeguarded special nuclear material," allows the president to waive the sanctions if doing so is in the "national interest." The national interest standard remains a relatively easy threshold to meet.[70] Along the same lines, Barbara Hinckley claims that "paper oversight" also exemplifies the common problems with binding legislation: "What appears to be oversight—the persistent demand for reports to Congress from the executive branch— . . . is used for a very different purpose. . . . It becomes a routine response, a kind of paper oversight, predictable by the executive and manageable by it. . . . The reports proliferate, but the . . . policy does not change."[71] And even legislation with a veto-proof majority may contain giveaways: the bill aimed at forcing relocation of the U.S. Embassy in Israel from Tel Aviv to Jerusalem by mid-1999, which became law without Clinton's signature, provides a way out for the president in the form of a funding limitation waiver if the president determines that national security interests warrant it.[72]

Third, critics maintain that presidential evasion of statutes typically prompts weak congressional responses.[73] Congress usually suffers from collective-action troubles, these commentators argue, unable to defeat, let alone override, the executive; a critical mass is rarely willing to rein in any president—and especially a popular president—on foreign policy issues. Observers contend that concerns about being blamed for policy failures make members powerless. Even when a president openly flouts a law's spirit—such as the War Powers Resolution, the Intelligence Oversight Act, or the military aid restrictions to El Salvador—Congress has been unable to muster the requisite will to demand faithful execution of the law.

An Institutionally Inadequate Congress?

Still other commentators stress the significance of institutional inadequacies in evaluating Congress's foreign policy participation; these inadequacies make it difficult, if not impossible, for Congress to be an effective foreign policy player. Several institutional inadequacies stand out. Most important, critics argue that Congress is an inefficient body that cannot act quickly. The glacial pace of the legislative process is legendary, these commentators maintain. Procedural mechanisms available to senators on the floor, for instance, may stymie Congress's ability to respond promptly to a problem. Gregg Easterbrook in the *Atlantic Monthly* criticized Congress for what he saw as a fiasco in the congressional response to the African famine crisis. The House passed a simple $60 million emergency aid package to assist drought victims, but, because the Senate attached thirty-six nongermane amendments to it and the House-Senate differences then needed to be resolved, the measure was not enacted into law until four months later.[74] The proliferation of filibusters and the threat of filibusters also shows the system's inefficiencies, observers contend. The ability of one member to halt Senate action further illustrates institutional inadequacies. For example, Sen. Jesse Helms, R-N.C., froze Senate Foreign Relations Committee business (including ambassadorial nominees and START II approval) for four months over a dispute with the Clinton administration regarding State Department reorganization.[75] Members of the House employ stalling tactics as well: in July 1995, during consideration of the foreign operations appropriations bill, Democrats demanded roll call votes on repeated procedural motions and forced hours of debate on each amendment.[76]

Critics note that Congress's structure often makes it difficult for the body to exercise power with dispatch. The internal organization of Congress is "collegial and sequential," whereas the executive is "hierarchical and centralized."[77] Committee redundancy also slows the legislative process on major issues. Commentators stress the similar impact of the decentralized nature of Congress, the breakdown of the seniority system, and the increase in staff people; when all members think they can be "players," movement is gradual.

Critics concerned about institutional inadequacies detect other weaknesses. Commentators underscore the deficient tools Congress uses to influence policy. Excessive reliance on blunt legislative instruments, they argue, eliminates the flexibility a president needs on complex foreign policy issues and may reveal U.S. strategy and policy to other governments.[78] Along these lines, another institutional inadequacy plaguing Congress is the lack of secrecy. This problem takes two forms. Some observers complain that Congress acts publicly; in other words, Congress is institutionally ill-suited to participate in the foreign policy arena where subtle nuance is paramount.[79] The more typical grievance about the lack of secrecy, however, is that members leak classified information. During the Iran-contra hearings, Oliver North even justified lying to Congress because he said Congress could not be trusted with sensitive intelligence material.[80]

An Inconstant Congress?

Critics who lament Congress's inconstancy believe that Congress is an unreliable policy-making body because it does not have long-term policy vision; Congress lacks the steadfastness in a course that Tocqueville identified as an indispensable quality to foreign relations.[81] This problem appears especially acute with legislative vehicles. Critics contend that shifts on policy questions—sometimes due to Congress's responsiveness to public opinion swings—result in foreign policy instabilities and program management inefficiencies. The twists and turns on contra aid policy in the 1980s, according to the minority report from the Iran-contra investigation, exemplify "vacillating congressional policy" and "constantly changing laws."[82] In 1985, less than two months after reaffirming its yearlong opposition to contra aid, Congress reversed itself and allowed the legal flow of assistance to resume; about six months after resuming contra aid, Congress voted down a $100 million aid package the Reagan administration had requested; and less than six months later, Congress approved the president's $100 million aid package.[83] Similarly, on defense policy Barry Blechman states that Congress sacrifices "overall consistency and coherence of national policy for narrow interests and short-term objectives."[84] In addition to causing instability, this inconstant Congress harms U.S. policy because it leads to inefficiencies in program management; frequent shifts in course are costly and counterproductive, as well.[85]

An Ignorant Congress?

The lack of expertise, according to another criticism, may be Congress's fatal flaw in the foreign policy realm. Foreign policy issues are often complex matters requiring an appreciation of what Richard Nixon called the "interrelationship of international events."[86] Commentators argue that members lack such an appreciation of foreign affairs. Most people elected to Congress have little experience in foreign policy. And while in Congress, members do not obtain the knowledge necessary to make informed decisions on these complicated issues.[87] Not only do time constraints curtail legislators' ability to master foreign policy issues, but Congress also lacks the executive's foreign policy apparatus. Observers examining the decisions of first-term Republicans in the 104th Congress have become even more concerned about members' lack of expertise, as on several occasions these members have been swayed more by talk radio voices than by foreign policy experts, even those from their own party.[88] These critics maintain that legislative and nonlegislative tools just enable members to intrude upon executive actions beyond their ken.

A Reelection-Oriented Congress?

Other commentators advocate the "self-interest axiom," namely, that members are "single-minded seekers of reelection."[89] Critics detect several disturbing effects of the reelection orientation on congressional foreign policy involvement. First, they suggest that because members focus only on their own political futures, not on substantive policy problems, Congress cannot be an effective and judicious foreign policy participant and will contaminate U.S. policy. The subtle prevalence of this type of criticism, with its implicit assumption that members are so anxious about reelection that it is difficult for them to make "wise" foreign policy decisions, is noteworthy.

Second, commentators contend that reelection-oriented members inappropriately consider and evaluate complex foreign policy issues through narrow, parochial lenses; in other words, reelection-oriented members may serve as "delegates" rather than "trustees," losing sight of broad policy issues in responding to constituents' detailed concerns. Some new members even publicly discuss this phenomenon. As Rep. David Funderburk, R-N.C., a first-term member in the

104th Congress on the International Relations Committee, explained, "We [first-term members] look at international relations through the prism of our districts."[90]

Third, a reelection-oriented Congress, critics maintain, impedes U.S. foreign policy making because the desire to be reelected leads to an uncreative, stagnant Congress unable to pass innovative legislation. Innovation signifies risks; risks suggest responsibility; responsibility may imply blame; and blame may be registered at the polls. Consequently, members may focus excessively upon "safe" foreign policy issues, exploiting them for publicity at home.[91]

A More Balanced Assessment

Before evaluating critics' concerns by assessing what Congress does, several points merit underscoring. We must not consider commentators' complaints about Congress according to whether we agree or disagree with what Congress tries to accomplish. If we allow our values and policy preferences to intrude on these judgments, our assessments will be ever changing and essentially meaningless. An accurate evaluation cannot be based on criticisms serving as smoke screens for dissatisfaction with a Democratic Congress's interaction with a Republican administration or vice versa. We saw such a flip-flop in the narrow war powers area, for instance, after Clinton became president—many House Republicans abandoned their previously adamant defense of presidential prerogatives and demanded advance congressional approval for various U.S. troop deployments. In addition, we must remember that although different elements in American society may favor different foreign policy decisions and outcomes, there is no single position that necessarily serves the "national interest." Such judgments are inevitably subjective and should be divorced from an analysis of this kind. Similarly, responsiveness to public opinion is not tantamount to a policy hindering the national interest, as some observers imply. Another caveat relates to the Constitution. In many cases the Founders envisioned, and the constitutional framework created, the very structures, procedures, and processes about which critics complain; therefore, commentators essentially are expressing dissatisfaction with the constitutional system. Yet rather than considering the rationale for the framework or honestly addressing the objections to the Constitution, critics usually imply that Congress has erred. Finally, while in this section I offer another side to their complaints, the critics are correct that problems exist—many of their concerns are valid. Nonetheless, the conclusions drawn about Congress's ability to participate effectively in foreign policy making tend to be much less valid than some of the specific criticisms about Congress's actions.

An Influential, but Not Dictatorial, Congress

Congress is neither imperial nor impotent. Despite Congress's vast constitutional grants of authority in foreign affairs, the executive branch currently is the more powerful in this arena, enjoying substantial "informal and extraconstitutional techniques" for managing foreign affairs.[92] Even though Congress does not control foreign policy making, it is not impotent. Congress is a foreign policy player, influencing policy directly and indirectly. As a discussion of Congress's use of legislative and nonlegislative instruments illustrates, fixations with Congress's alleged powerlessness and imperialism obscure more than they illuminate.

Contrary to what certain critics suggest, legislative tools sometimes achieve intended results. Examples of Congress influencing policy, checking the president, or imposing wishes on the executive through issue-specific, reactive measures, as described previously, are not lacking. Congress forced South African sanctions on a reluctant administration in 1986 by overriding Reagan's veto. (In 1993 Congress repealed these sanctions, in recognition of South Africa's efforts to create a democracy as well as other dramatic changes in the country.) More recently, Congress imposed its wishes on Clinton in the fiscal 1996 defense appropriations bill: Clinton permitted the bill to become law in 1995 without his signature, although he opposed provisions in the legislation, including money for unrequested weapons, increases in spending on programs such as antimissile defenses, conditions on U.S. peacekeeping operations, and restrictions on abortions at overseas military hospitals. "Clinton's push to send more than 20,000 troops to enforce the Nov. 21 Balkan peace agreement, and the political reality that the Republican-controlled Congress would be reluctant to provide some $2 billion for the deployment if the White House rejected the spending bill, forced the president to accept the legislation."[93]

Congress also may accomplish its objectives through issue-specific, reactive legislation containing restrictive provisions. In general, restrictive "congressional action on human rights [targeting Latin American countries] did affect [Reagan's] conduct," according to David Forsythe. "Security or economic assistance was blocked, limited, or delayed."[94] And in the case of the U.S. role in the UN peacekeeping mission in Somalia, even after Clinton agreed, under congressional pressure, to withdraw most U.S. forces by March 31, 1994, Congress attached restrictive language to the fiscal 1994 defense appropriations bill, cutting off funding for the Somalia operation after the March deadline.[95]

Directive legislation, too, can be an effective tool. A 1988 CRS study found that Congress may accomplish its objectives through reporting requirements by raising a subject's priority within an agency.[96] Requiring human rights reports did just that. An investigation by the bipartisan panel of the National Academy of Public Administration (NAPA) discovered "almost universal agreement" that human rights reports have had a "significant" effect.[97] These reports may keep Congress better informed, making the executive more accountable and less likely to disregard a congressional majority.[98] The reporting requirements in the fiscal 1991 foreign aid appropriations bill regarding the use of U.S. aid in Cambodia similarly furnished Congress with what it wanted—Bush officials were unable to deny that cooperation existed between the U.S.-aided noncommunist resistance and the Khmer Rouge, and this admission served as the foundation for restrictive measures regarding aid.[99]

Congress also may achieve its goals through prospective-procedural laws. The NAPA study concluded that "had Congress not carved out a larger formal role for itself in foreign military sales decisions [through the 1974 Nelson-Bingham amendment, modified in the Arms Export Control Act], the United States would have sold more arms abroad than it had during the 1970s and through the mid-1980s. Moreover, larger numbers and more sophisticated weapons would have been sold to Middle Eastern countries that have historically been enemies of Israel."[100] The NAPA study stressed the Goldwater-Nichols Act accomplishments as well: it "made Congress a stronger and more active player in defense organization and process issues," even "without the [executive's] full support and cooperation."[101]

In addition to achieving intended results, binding legislation influences policy and presidential actions in unanticipated, yet significant, ways. Thus, even if a president circumvents a law or ignores its spirit and intent, the measure is not necessarily useless. The War Powers Resolution is a case in point. Although widely regarded as a failure—because of presidential violations and congressional inability to demand compliance—the law has provided members with a framework for asserting prerogatives and a convenient foil for criticizing executive military actions.[102] Consider House Republican members' 1993 use of the War Powers Resolution—a law many of them denounced when their party held the White House—in attempts to force Clinton to remove all U.S. troops from Somalia by January 31, 1994.[103] And as seen in the Persian Gulf crisis of 1990 and 1991, the War Powers Resolution's impact is far less direct than the law's sponsors intended under some of the mechanistic procedures they created, but the impact remains real to participants, who found that the law provided them with the requisite "push in the behind."[104] Moreover, the existence of the War Powers Resolution has affected presidential decisions about whether, how, and for how long to commit troops.[105]

Beyond accomplishing its objectives by passing legislation, Congress also often achieves desired results by threatening legislative actions, particularly when it exhibits the consensus and will to pass a measure. Because Congress was on the verge of passing (and overriding Reagan's expected veto of) a South African sanctions bill in 1985, Reagan attempted to preempt congressional action by issuing an executive order that addressed many of Congress's concerns. Congress forced Reagan to alter his approach of "constructive engagement" and succeeded in influencing policy without passing the bill.[106] And from the president's vantage point, he forestalled congressional action, at least temporarily. To assess Congress's legislative influence accurately, therefore, one must look past the scorecard of legislation enacted into law.

Congress's means of influence are not limited to legislative vehicles—those enacted and those simply threatened—as some critics imply. Congress also affects foreign policy through nonlegislative tools. Nonlegislative tools offer members opportunities to influence agendas, decision making, and actions by swaying opinions, informing and educating, and generating anticipated reactions. Several examples illustrate the potential effect of nonlegislative tools. When Bush failed to offer a far-reaching new defense strategy in response to the end of the cold war, members in early 1990 began using a variety of nonlegislative devices. In floor statements, public appeals through the press, and committee hearings, "legislators excoriated Bush's 'business as usual' FY 91 [budget] request, and highlighted the need for a quick and dramatic revision of U.S. military strategy." Congress's "evident willingness" to act spurred Bush; he subsequently offered a revised proposal "sufficiently consistent with the congressional demands for change."[107] Nonlegislative activism also influenced Clinton's policy on the Mexican loan plan in 1995. After weeks of intensive congressional-executive negotiations, the Clinton administration decided not to have supportive members formally introduce a legislative proposal because through an array of nonlegislative acts the rank-and-file members of both parties had demonstrated their "utter unwillingness" to back the plan.[108] Legislators' direct dealings with foreign governments sometimes have dramatic results as well: after a January 1991 meeting with members, for instance, the Saudi ambassador, Prince Bandar Bin Sultan, apparently suggested postponing the huge U.S. arms deal to Saudi Arabia because of concern about significant congressional opposition.[109]

In evaluating Congress's influence, critics also must recognize that the legislature's effectiveness varies by issue. Consequently, it is misleading to stress Congress's impotence based only on its actions in crisis situations. Congress often appears unable to wield any weapon—let alone its most potent weapon, the power of the purse—when faced with a fait accompli such as an undeclared war, for Congress then would be responsible for stranding soldiers in the field. Furthermore, presidential power is at its greatest under such crisis conditions. Yet on "strategic" policy (for example, specifying "goals and tactics") and "structural" policy (for example, "procuring, deploying, and organizing military personnel and material"), Jim Lindsay and Randall Ripley argue that Congress's influence increases.[110] Especially when a "policy vacuum" exists, Congress is more apt to be able to assert itself successfully.[111]

The preceding discussion illustrates that Congress is a player in the foreign policy arena and can influence policy. Sometimes legislation achieves intended results; sometimes legislation succeeds in unexpected ways; sometimes the threat of legislation generates desired actions; and sometimes nonlegislative mechanisms accomplish members' goals. Despite successes, critics who see an impotent Congress correctly raise a few problems, albeit they overstate the extent and consequences of these problems. In particular, binding legislation is not flawless. Presidents at times ignore the letter and intent of laws, and Congress may fail to confront presidents with such violations. Moreover, because of the need to garner adequate support to pass legislation and because of poor drafting, laws may have loopholes and ambiguities. Limits on Congress's effectiveness thus exist;

nevertheless, we have seen that Congress can be an effective foreign policy participant and should not be considered impotent.

The fact that Congress is not impotent, however, does not validate claims of an imperial Congress. Four points deserve further attention in this regard. First, critics significantly exaggerate the degree to which Congress engages in micromanagement. Critics typically fail to offer evidence documenting that this activity is as extensive as they suggest, instead extrapolating from a few specific examples to imply that Congress micromanages everything. Although Congress at times uses the purse strings to assert itself, and although members at times undertake actions of "lone ranger diplomacy," for instance, it is misleading to draw sweeping conclusions from isolated occurrences. Indeed, the president has substantial flexibility on most issues, especially on those relating to crisis situations. Similarly, complaints about Congress increasing demands on the executive through nonlegislative means are overblown—the number of hearings and requested testimonies on defense activities, for example, has been relatively stable.[112] Critics also exaggerate the burden of reporting requirements. It is unlikely that $50 million in reporting expenses strained a $300 billion Pentagon budget, for instance, as Bush suggested.[113]

Second, the criticism of an imperial Congress is often disingenuous. The argument may serve as a smoke screen for critics unhappy with the constitutional structure because it allows a Congress controlled by their unpreferred party to check a president from their preferred party, thereby hindering the "national interest." In other words, this grievance may stem both from perceived policy and partisan disagreements with a particular Congress and a concomitant belief that the president knows best. Many of the critics who today denounce the imperial Congress applauded when more liberal legislators sought to block policies during the Reagan and Bush years. In arguing against a Republican initiative urging Clinton to bring U.S. troops home from Somalia two months before the agreed-upon deadline, for instance, Rep. Lee Hamilton, D-Ind., invoked a favorite Republican refrain from years past: "If that's not micromanagement, I don't know what is."[114] Furthermore, for Congress to have any ability to shape broad policy contours, it must become enmeshed in policy debates. If protests were sincere, moreover, executive branch officials complaining about micromanagement through reporting requirements would make significant and numerous suggestions to abolish reports when so asked. But only Congress has worked to abolish unnecessary reports.[115] Also suggestive of the hypocrisy here is the occurrence of presidential requests for Congress to require some reports.[116] The executive reaction to cases of congressional "intrusion" further illustrates the criticism's hollowness. Despite administration cries that Congress undermines the president and curtails his flexibility, the executive may in fact desire congressional action. The White House may appreciate being able to blame Congress for carrying out an action the president wanted done but could not do. [117] In dealing with foreign governments, "good cop" presidents may find congressional power over the purse handy, warning a head of state of severe "bad cop" retribution if certain conditions are not fulfilled.[118]

Third, an imperial Congress is an unrealistic possibility under our constitutional framework. Just to form a consensus among a majority of both bodies is often so difficult that it is unlikely that Congress could pass measures forcing the president to be Congress's "servant." Recall, for example, the seemingly intractable House-Senate dispute over abortion limitations in the fiscal 1996 foreign operations appropriations bill, with the Republican House firmly favoring restrictions and the Republican Senate just as adamantly agreeing with Clinton in opposing those restrictions.[119] The compromise ultimately pieced together in this case provided each side with clear victories and defeats.[120] And even if majorities in both houses defy a president, mustering the requisite two-thirds to override a veto is improbable—Congress has overridden only one foreign policy veto since the War Powers Resolution in 1973. Congress did not even come close, for instance, to overriding Clinton's veto of the critical fiscal 1996 defense authorization bill in January 1996.[121] And when Clinton ultimately signed a modified authorization bill the following month, he simultaneously mounted a multifront effort to gut the bill's provision requiring the armed services to discharge HIV-positive service members, including ordering the Justice Department not to defend the provision when challenged in court.[122] Even when Congress kills a president's proposal, as it did with Clinton's 1995 plan to provide $40 billion in loan guarantees for Mexico, presidents retain alternative methods to achieve their aims. In this case, the Clinton administration devised a new initiative that did not require congressional approval: by turning to the Treasury Department's Exchange Stabilization Fund, the International Monetary Fund, the Bank for International Settlements, Latin American countries, and Canada, Clinton found the money for Mexico.[123]

Fourth, when congressional micromanagement occurs, it sometimes happens in reaction to executive actions that invite a response—that is, a refusal to discharge the constitutional obligation to "take care that the laws be faithfully executed." As Louis Fisher states, if an administration chooses "to sabotage statutory programs and . . . implement White House policy instead of public law, the light for congressional intervention turns green."[124] Rather than an insidious Congress waiting to pounce on an unsuspecting executive, a reactive Congress may be responding to executive misdeeds.

A Deliberative Congress (Not Necessarily Inefficient or Indiscreet)

Institutional inadequacies do indeed exist. At times, Congress may move too slowly, members may manipulate procedural devices and delay action on urgent measures, and individual legislators may leak classified information. These flaws, however, do not render Congress unable to contribute effectively to foreign policy making. Congress is, and was designed to be, a deliberative body. The Founders did not intend Congress to be the paragon of efficiency—they preferred to preclude the arbitrary exercise of power. Nonetheless, although Congress is a deliberative body not designed for fast action, and although it does move more slowly than may be desirable in some cases, it also can act quickly upon occasion.

When speed is paramount, Congress can enact and follow expedited procedures.[125] In considering whether to authorize the use of force in the Persian Gulf in January 1991, for instance, Congress responded promptly to Bush's request for congressional action. Bush asked, in a letter of January 8, for a resolution stating support for the "use of all necessary means to implement" the UN resolution. The House and Senate each considered two separate resolutions, finishing action on January 12, four days after Bush's request and three days before the January 15 UN deadline.[126] Congress's speed, regardless of how one feels about its final vote, is noteworthy. Congress also may operate under so-called fast-track rules—as in the case of the North American Free Trade Agreement (NAFTA)—which subject a measure only to an up-or-down vote in each chamber.

Along these lines, procedural delays often can be managed. When controversial nongermane amendments in the Senate bogged down the African famine relief bill in March 1984, the drought victims did not have to wait four months for U.S. aid (until House-Senate disagreements were resolved), as critic Easterbrook suggested. Congress ensured that food aid would not be delayed by attaching emergency food aid to an urgent low-income energy supplemental aid bill, which was enacted into law within weeks.[127] In the House, too, majority party leaders manipulate rules and procedures to thwart others' efforts to delay or kill measures they favor. In 1983 they moved the unpopular $8.4 billion International Monetary Fund quota increase through the House; they attached the bill to a popular housing measure and brought the package to the floor in such a way that it could not be debated for more than one hour or amended.[128]

Sometimes, however, Congress is simply inefficient. In certain cases this inefficiency is problematic; at other times it is beneficial. In other words, an efficient Congress is not tantamount to a wise Congress— "deliberation often prevents error."[129] Open debate in formulating legislation may help ensure that policies reflect public attitudes and have the public support needed to sustain them over the long term. And on major controversial issues, prolonged congressional deliberation not surprisingly mirrors the public debate. Even widespread committee participation, as part of the deliberative process, may not be harmful; broad involvement may counter the often narrow executive decision making and the possibility that policies will fall prey to the distortions of "groupthink." Furthermore, there are few instances in which speed is as critical as commentators would have us believe. Even in crisis situations, a decision rarely needs to be made so quickly that Congress cannot participate.

Congress also is not a sieve, leaking whatever comes its way. In fact, the executive branch leaks significantly more information than does Congress.[130] Near the beginning of his first term as vice president, Bush considered leaks to be the Reagan administration's "biggest failure." "Everything from classified intelligence reports to accounts of a spat between Secretary of State Alexander Haig and Defense Secretary Caspar Weinberger [had] found its way into the press."[131] The two leaks that Oliver North mentioned in the Iran-contra hearings to support his contention that Congress could not be trusted came from the executive branch, not from Congress; North himself had leaked one of the stories.[132]

A Flexible Congress Able to Grapple with Some Long-Term Issues

Congress can be shortsighted, but, contrary to conventional wisdom, it is not always so. Congress at times strives for both consistency and a long-term approach to problems. Through issue-specific legislation Congress may confront the underlying causes of crises. While passing legislation dealing with the African famine emergency in the mid-1980s, Congress also addressed related long-term problems.[133] In addition, with prospective-procedural measures Congress may attempt to construct a broad framework in a specific policy area to ensure constancy of approach over an extended period of time. For example, the 1980 Intelligence Oversight Act requires that the House and Senate intelligence committees receive prior notification of covert operations, unless the president determines that an operation affects vital U.S. interests. In that case, prior notification is limited to eight specified congressional leaders.[134] And the 1988 Omnibus Trade and Competitiveness Act requires, among other things, increased consultation with Congress (even during trade negotiations) and annual reports from the U.S. trade representative on policy objectives and actions taken to achieve the objectives.[135]

Obviously, though, Congress is at times inconstant and myopic. But this inconstancy is not necessarily problematic, as it may allow for flexibility.[136] Congressional policy shifts often simply reflect eroding public support for unwavering policy approaches. And it is not axiomatic that such responsiveness to public opinion, even if it yields inconstant policies, hurts the "national interest," as critics assume. The ability to mirror public ambivalence is one of Congress's attributes; a president may be less apt to appreciate prevailing attitudes and less able to respond.[137]

Congress is not the only branch that struggles with inconstancy and a proclivity for shortsightedness. Presidents also can be guilty of myopia and inconstancy. According to Maynard Glitman, chief negotiator for the Intermediate-Range Nuclear Forces (INF) Treaty and former ambassador to Belgium, "Presidents may be more prone to short-sightedness than Congress, whose members have almost guaranteed life tenures." Incoming presidents, on the other hand, "often approach issues in the context of a four-year term"; that is, to "make a mark," they must act quickly.[138] Consider Reagan's inconstancy and shortsightedness on the matter of terrorism. At the very time he was advocating a policy of not dealing with terrorists, he was doing just that in the Iran-contra affair, secretly trading arms for hostages.[139] Or recall Clinton's early policy shifts on Haiti: in 1992 candidate Clinton denounced Bush's policy of summarily returning Haitians rescued or intercepted at sea, but on January 14, 1993, President-elect Clinton announced that he would continue the controversial interception policy.[140] Albeit the relative level of inconstancy and myopia between Congress and the president cannot easily be gauged, it is important to appreciate that this problem is not exclusive to Congress—it is unfair to level criticisms only against Congress that similarly apply to the executive.

A Congress with Foreign Policy Expertise

The majority of members are not foreign policy specialists. Members may enter Congress with little knowledge of foreign policy issues, and while there they may not become well schooled in these matters. Nonetheless, ignorance is not a serious defect in the foreign policy realm: Congress as an institution has, and uses, foreign policy expertise.

The congressional leaders on foreign policy issues who frequently influence the legislative agenda, the parameters of debates, the votes of rank-and-file members, and the policy outcomes tend to be members with much more expertise than the average member and with more expertise than critics concede. With larger and more highly qualified staffs and with the increase in foreign travel, these members have become better informed. And because of long service in Congress, members may "possess a degree of expertise and kind of institutional memory rarely found in the upper echelon of Executive Departments."[141] Representative Hamilton, for example, a leader in the foreign policy field, was elected to the House in 1965; he has served through seven presidents and nine secretaries of state. Senior congressional aides also typically remain on the job much longer than secretaries and assistant secretaries. Hamilton's "foreign policy alter ego," Michael Van Dusen, has been on the representative's staff since 1971.[142] And because other members often rely on the expertise of knowledgeable members and staff, such as Hamilton and Van Dusen, Glitman found that "it is not necessary for everybody to be an expert."[143] During Senate consideration of the INF Treaty, for instance, Glitman stressed that senators looked to Senator Nunn, who was known for his and his staff's specialized knowledge.

And when members disregard the experts, the consequences are not necessarily problematic. As Samuel Huntington explained, "The more important a policy issue is, the less important becomes detailed technical information and the more relevant becomes broad judgments on goals and values, i.e., political judgments, where presumably the congressman's competence is greatest."[144] In other words, members may not always need a sophisticated appreciation of the "interrelationship of international events," as Nixon suggested.

A Reelection-Oriented Congress—No Cause for Alarm

Most members are reelection oriented. Because a legislator's survival in office hinges on adequate district support, a member tries to respond to perceived constituent—particularly supportive constituent—pressures.[145] But the consequences of the reelection orientation are not as negative as critics believe. Although in some foreign policy cases a reelection obsession and a consequent fear of retribution at the polls may prompt individual members to undertake questionable actions and to be uncreative and risk-averse, Congress is not critically harmed by this phenomenon.

Commentators exaggerate the ramifications of members' reelection orientation. Congress may not pander to special constituent interests as consistently as critics contend—consider Congress's independence from the pro-Israel lobby in the fall of 1991, when this powerful lobby was actively supporting the proposed $10 billion loan guarantees to Israel.[146] Pivotal legislators backed Bush's request that Congress delay action on the loan guarantees until early 1992 because of concerns that granting them at that time "could jeopardize plans for an Arab-Israeli peace conference."[147] PAC money as well tends not to govern congressional vote outcomes. Although it may influence a few members' votes, more generally it buys access.[148] The effects of parochialism on specific issues also may be overblown, for critics sometimes ignore the multidimensional aspects of policy questions. Critics may not consider, for instance, that members often face parochial and policy-related cross-pressures, as illustrated by the dilemma Rep. Anna Eshoo, D-Calif., faced in the NAFTA vote:

> She can vote against NAFTA and jeopardize her position as a Clinton-style, white-collar "New Democrat" who believes in free trade and promotes her district's Silicon Valley and its high-skill, high-paying jobs as the future of the U.S. economy. Or she can vote for the pact and risk alienating organized labor, environmentalists, human rights activists, and other NAFTA opponents that have formed her core constituency over the years.[149]

As Eshoo herself recognized, "I could lose my seat, regardless of the way I vote."[150]

Critics similarly overstate the impact of the electoral orientation on individual members' involvement and therefore on the actions of Congress as a whole. Responsiveness to constituents is primarily symbolic; constituents affect whether members participate much more than how extensively they participate.[151] Members' perceptions of supporters' preferences generally do not lead members to engage in forms of involvement likely to affect the outcome of a debate; instead, their perceptions prompt activities that simply may help electorally. Hence, the impact of responsiveness to constituents is minimal in terms of actual policy formation. Congressional foreign policy leaders and activists are driven not by constituents but by personal policy interests, committee and leadership position, and the desire for influence.[152]

Commentators also assume that members allow parochial concerns to sidetrack national objectives, essentially because the public does not encourage actions consistent with the national interest. Yet judgments about the national interest inevitably are subjective; it is therefore not axiomatic that constituents promote policies contrary to the good of the nation. As Rep. Patsy T. Mink, D-Hawaii, wrote after time in Congress and the State Department, "It is folly to believe . . . that good foreign policy necessarily stands above the pressures of . . . constituent interests. Politics is the art of reconciling and educating, not of avoiding, those interests."[153] A foreign policy, to be pursued effectively over an extended period of time, typically requires a foundation of legitimacy, and it may gain that legitimacy through public backing. Representative Hamilton explained that "congressional support is a primary expression of the people's approval. The President is not likely to gain the support of the American people if he cannot gain the [Congress's] support."[154]

Finally, it is noteworthy that the Framers recognized that self-interest would be a significant motive and sought strong constituent links. According to Madison, "Duty, gratitude, interest, ambition itself, are the cords by which [representatives] will be bound to fidelity and sympathy with the great mass of the people."[155] Consequently, the standard for judging the use of legislative and non-legislative vehicles should not be purity of motives—purity of motives is not a precondition for a tool to be helpful or for Congress to contribute to foreign policy making.

Summary

Congress is, and will remain, a participant in the foreign policy making process. And contrary to what critics contend, that prospect is a positive feature of our system of government. Considering how Congress exercises its constitutional prerogatives, we have seen that the criticisms of congressional participation in foreign policy making are often overblown and misguided; effective congressional participation in foreign affairs is not an oxymoron for the reasons critics have identified. Congress is neither imperial nor impotent; Congress is not so institutionally inadequate, inconstant, or ignorant to render it incapable of contributing to foreign policy making; and members' interests in reelection do not disqualify Congress from playing a productive role. Although it is convenient and intuitively appealing to use Congress as a receptacle for blame, little here suggests that such an orientation is correct. In fact, Congress often contributes effectively to foreign policy making, offering strengths such as greater deliberation of policies, discretion, flexibility, expertise, and representation of public sentiment. Perhaps it is time to appreciate some of Congress's virtues rather than simply harping on its vices.

Notes

1. Alexis de Tocqueville, *Democracy in America,* ed. J. P. Mayer, trans. George Lawrence (Garden City, N.Y.: Doubleday, 1969), 228.
2. For two recent works that offer a more positive perspective, see James M. Lindsay, *Congress and the Politics of U.S. Foreign Policy* (Baltimore: Johns Hopkins University Press, 1994); and Kenneth R. Mayer, *The Political Economy of Defense Contracting* (New Haven: Yale University Press, 1991).

3. James M. Lindsay, "Congress and Diplomacy," in *Congress Resurgent: Foreign and Defense Policy on Capitol Hill,* ed. Randall B. Ripley and James M. Lindsay (Ann Arbor: University of Michigan Press, 1993), 261–281.
4. L. Gordon Crovitz and Jeremy A. Rabkin, eds., *The Fettered Presidency* (Washington, D.C.: American Enterprise Institute, 1989); Gordon S. Jones and John A. Marini, eds., *The Imperial Congress* (New York: Heritage Foundation, 1988); and quote of former president Gerald R. Ford in Marvin Stone, "Presidency: Imperial or Imperiled?" *U.S. News and World Report,* Jan. 15, 1979, 88.
5. See Herman A. Mellor, "Congressional Micromanagement: National Defense," in *The Imperial Congress,* 107–129; and commentary by Richard N. Perle, in *Fettered Presidency,* 103–104.
6. Harold Hongju Koh, "Why the President (Almost) Always Wins in Foreign Affairs: Lessons of the Iran-Contra Affair," *Yale Law Journal* 97 (June 1988): 1297. Emphasis added.
7. Barbara Hinckley, *Less than Meets the Eye: Foreign Policy Making and the Myth of the Assertive Congress* (Chicago: University of Chicago Press, 1994), 174.
8. For instance, see Les Aspin, "Congress versus the Defense Department," in *The Tethered Presidency,* ed. Thomas M. Franck (New York: New York University Press, 1981), 245–263; I. M. Destler, "Executive-Congressional Conflict in Foreign Policy: Explaining It, Coping with It," in *Congress Reconsidered,* 3d ed., ed. Lawrence C. Dodd and Bruce I. Oppenheimer (Washington, D.C.: CQ Press, 1985), 343–363; and J. William Fulbright, "The Legislator as Educator," *Foreign Affairs* 57 (Spring 1979): 719–732.
9. Robert Higgs used the phrase in reference to a "selfish, parochial, and wasteful" Congress. Higgs, "Hard Coals Make Bad Law: Congressional Parochialism Versus National Defense," *Cato Journal* 8 (Spring/Summer 1988): 80.
10. *Federalist Papers,* No. 6 (New York: The New American Library, 1961), 59.
11. Even Rep. Dick Cheney, a staunch supporter of the "fettered presidency" school of thought, admonished John Poindexter during the Iran-contra hearings: "The reason for not misleading the Congress is a practical one. It is stupid." House Select Committee to Investigate Covert Arms Transactions with Iran and Senate Select Committee on Secret Military Assistance to Iran and the Nicaraguan Opposition, *Joint Hearings on the Iran-Contra Investigation,* 100th Cong., 1st sess., 1987, 246.
12. Most issues discussed in this essay are recent. Three factors encouraged this concentration. First, as Thomas E. Mann states, the "pace of congressional involvement [in foreign policy making] actually accelerated during the presidency of Ronald Reagan." See Mann, "Making Foreign Policy: President and Congress," in *A Question of Balance: The President, the Congress, and Foreign Policy,* ed. Thomas E. Mann (Washington, D.C.: Brookings, 1990), 1. For a different view, see Hinckley, *Less than Meets the Eye.* Second, scholars already have lavished much attention on congressional assertiveness in the immediate post-Vietnam period. For example, see Thomas M. Franck and Edward Weisband, *Foreign Policy by Congress* (New York: Oxford University Press, 1979); James L. Sundquist, *The Decline and Resurgence of Congress* (Washington, D.C.: Brookings, 1981); Charles W. Whalen Jr., *The House and Foreign Affairs: The Irony of Congressional Reform* (Chapel Hill: University of North Carolina Press, 1982). Third, reader familiarity with recent issues is likely to be greater.
13. Raoul Berger, *Executive Privilege: A Constitutional Myth* (Cambridge: Harvard University Press, 1973), 131.
14. Note that the term "foreign affairs" is not used in the Constitution.
15. Richard E. Neustadt, *Presidential Power: The Politics of Leadership with Reflections on Johnson and Nixon* (New York: Wiley, 1976), 101.

16. *Federalist Papers,* No. 51, 322.
17. *Myers v. United States,* 272 U.S. 52 (1926), 293.
18. See for instance, Cecil V. Crabb Jr. and Pat M. Holt, *Invitation to Struggle: Congress, the President, and Foreign Policy,* 4th ed. (Washington, D.C.: CQ Press, 1992), 39–55; and Mann, "Making Foreign Policy," 4–7. There is another argument stating that presidents have inherent constitutional powers, making them dominant in conducting foreign policy. See Committees Investigating the Iran-Contra Affair, *Minority Report of the Congressional Committees Investigating the Iran-Contra Affair,* 100th Cong., 1st sess., 1987, H.Rept. 100–433, S.Rept. 100–216, pt. 2, ch. 2.
19. *Federalist Papers,* No. 58, 359.
20. Michael J. Glennon, *Constitutional Diplomacy* (Princeton: Princeton University Press, 1990), 72.
21. *Federalist Papers,* No. 69, 418. Emphasis in original.This is not to imply that there are not differing interpretations of the war power. See David Gray Adler, "The Constitution and Presidential Warmaking: The Enduring Debate," *Political Science Quarterly* 103 (Spring 1988): 1–36; J. Terry Emerson, "The War Powers Resolution Tested: The President's Independent Defense Power," *Notre Dame Lawyer* 51 (1975): 187–216; and Abraham D. Sofaer, *War, Foreign Affairs and Constitutional Power: The Origins* (Cambridge: Ballinger, 1976).
22. *Youngstown Sheet and Tube Company v. Sawyer,* 343 U.S. 579 (1952), 637.
23. Edward S. Corwin, *The President: Office and Powers, 1787–1957,* 4th rev. ed. (New York: New York University Press,1957), 171.
24. The quoted phrase is Louis Henkin's in "Foreign Affairs and the Constitution," *Foreign Affairs* 66 (Winter 1987/88): 285.
25. House Committee on Foreign Affairs, *Congress and Foreign Policy, 1985–1986,* 1987, Committee Print, 24–36.
26. Donna Cassata, "Clinton Accepts Defense Bill in Bid for Bosnia Funds," *Congressional Quarterly Weekly Report,* Dec. 2, 1995, 3672.
27. John Felton, "Foreign Aid System Criticized as Cumbersome, Ineffective," *Congressional Quarterly Weekly Report,* Feb. 11, 1989, 272.
28. Jeremy D. Rosner, *The New Tug-of-War: Congress, the Executive Branch, and National Security* (Washington, D.C.: Brookings, 1995).
29. See Cynthia J. Aronson, *Crossroads: Congress, the Reagan Administration, and Central America* (New York: Pantheon Books, 1989).
30. Louis Fisher, *Presidential War Power* (Lawrence: University Press of Kansas, 1995), 154.
31. Pamela Fessler, "Complaints Are Stacking Up as Hill Piles on Reports," *Congressional Quarterly Weekly Report,* Sept. 7, 1991, 2562.
32. Ibid., 2564.
33. PL 102–1.
34. See PL 93–148. Reprinted in House Committee on Foreign Affairs, Subcommittee on Arms Control, International Security and Science, *The War Powers Resolution: Relevant Documents, Correspondence, and Reports,* 100th Cong., 2d sess., May 1988, Committee Print, 1.
35. House Committee on Foreign Affairs, *Congress and Foreign Policy, 1988,* 1989, Committee Print, 94–95.
36. For some exceptions, see Thomas M. Franck and Clifford A. Bob, "The Return of Humpty-Dumpty: Foreign Relations Law After the *Chadha* Case," *American Journal of International Law* 79 (October 1985): 912–960; Susan Webb Hammond, "Congress in Foreign Policy," in *The President, the Congress and Foreign Policy,* ed. Edmund S. Muskie, Kenneth Rush, and Kenneth W. Thompson (Lanham, Md.: University Press of America, 1986), 67–91; Lindsay, *Congress and the Politics of U.S.*

Foreign Policy; and James M. McCormick, "Decision Making in the Foreign Affairs and Foreign Relations Committees," in *Congress Resurgent,* 115–153.

37. Lindsay describes the phenomenon of anticipated reactions well: "Just as chess players consider their opponent's possible moves and plan several steps ahead, Congress and the executive branch anticipate one another's behavior and modify their own behavior accordingly." See James M. Lindsay, "Congress and Foreign Policy: Why the Hill Matters," *Political Science Quarterly* 107 (Winter 1992–1993): 613–619. Admittedly, though, the effect of anticipated reactions cannot be evaluated perfectly. Mark A. Peterson writes, "[T]he processes are so complex, the participants are so varied and numerous, and executive decisions about legislative issues are often not discrete events." Peterson, *Legislating Together* (Cambridge: Harvard University Press, 1990), 46.
38. For a discussion of the effect of issue-related factors on the influences affecting a representative's participation in foreign policy issues, see Eileen Burgin, "Representatives' Involvement in Foreign and Defense Policy Issues: Do Issue Characteristics Affect Participation?" *Congress and the Presidency* 22 (Spring 1995): 57–84.
39. For background on the timing and duration of the Panama incursion, see Eileen Burgin, "Congress, the War Powers Resolution, and the Invasion of Panama," *Polity* 25 (Winter 1992): 216-242.
40. See McCormick, "Decision Making in the Foreign Affairs and Foreign Relations Committees"; and Barbara Sinclair, "Congressional Party Leaders in the Foreign and Defense Policy Arena," in *Congress Resurgent,* 207–231.
41. House Committee on Foreign Affairs, *Congress and Foreign Policy, 1985–86,* 16–36.
42. Carroll J. Doherty, "House Seeks Data on Mexico Aid," *Congressional Quarterly Weekly Report,* March 4, 1995, 698.
43. *Congressional Quarterly Almanac, 1994* (Washington, D.C.: Congressional Quarterly, 1995), 457.
44. Rosner, *The New Tug-of-War,* 88–89.
45. *Congressional Quarterly Almanac, 1993* (Washington, D.C.: Congressional Quarterly, 1994), 495.
46. Carroll J. Doherty, "President, Rebuffing Congress, Prepares to Launch Invasion," *Congressional Quarterly Weekly Report,* Sept. 17, 1994, 2578–83.
47. Lindsay, "Congress and Diplomacy."
48. Robert Byrd, "The Perils of Peacekeeping," *New York Times,* Aug. 19, 1993.
49. Mary E. Kortanek, "Democrats Push Clinton To Toughen Embargo," *Congressional Quarterly Weekly Report,* April 23, 1994, 1015.
50. For a brief discussion of the hearings, see Crabb and Holt, *Invitation to Struggle,* 155–157.
51. For conflicting views of the hearings, see William S. Cohen and George J. Mitchell, *Men of Zeal,* rev. ed. (New York: Penguin, 1989); and Harold Hongju Koh, *The National Security Constitution: Sharing Power After the Iran-Contra Affair* (New Haven: Yale University Press, 1990), chap. 1.
52. The phrase is David R. Mayhew's. See Mayhew, *Congress: The Electoral Connection* (New Haven: Yale University Press, 1974), 61–73.
53. In the *Congressional Record,* 100th Cong., 1st sess., see the following: March 11, 1987, S2967–S2986; March 12, 1987, S3090–S3095; and March 13, 1987, S3171–S3173.
54. Pat Towell, "U.S. Readies for Peace Talks; Lawmakers Remain Wary," *Congressional Quarterly Weekly Report,* Oct. 28, 1995, 3319.
55. See Thomas M. Franck, "Courts and Foreign Policy," *Foreign Policy* 83 (Summer 1991): 66–86; and Koh, *The National Security Constitution,* chap. 6.

56. Douglas A. Jeffrey, "Executive Authority Under the Separation of Powers," in *Imperial Congress,* 62.
57. Carroll J. Doherty, "Congress Ignores Objections in Push to Punish Castro," *Congressional Quarterly Weekly Report,* March 9, 1996, 632–633.
58. Fessler, "Complaints Are Stacking Up," 2562.
59. Carroll J. Doherty and David Masci, "Sharply Divided House Panel Votes to Curb U.N. Missions," *Congressional Quarterly Weekly Report,* Jan. 28, 1995, 291–292.
60. For instance, see Caspar W. Weinberger, "Dangerous Constraints on the President's War Powers," in *Fettered Presidency,* 95–101.
61. Koh, *The National Security Constitution,* 117.
62. For instance, see Sharpe, "The Post-Vietnam Formula Under Siege," 556–559.
63. These arguments are reviewed in Burgin, "Congress, the War Powers Resolution, and the Invasion of Panama."
64. Sharpe, "Post-Vietnam Formula Under Siege," 556.
65. Ibid., 556–559.
66. Koh, *National Security Constitution,* 129.
67. Martin Tolchin, "Congress: Of C.I.A. Games, and Disputed Rules," *New York Times,* May 14, 1984. Casey is William J. Casey, CIA director in the Reagan administration.
68. Koh, *National Security Constitution,* 58–59.
69. For a review of the act's provisions, see Congressional Research Service, "Covert Actions: Congressional Oversight," IB87208, Oct. 14, 1988.
70. Carroll J. Doherty, "Reports of Chinese Shipments Put Clinton on the Spot," *Congressional Quarterly Weekly Report,* Feb. 17, 1996, 396–397.
71. Hinckley, *Less than Meets the Eye,* 145.
72. Carroll J. Doherty, "Bill to Relocate Embassy Heads to President," *Congressional Quarterly Weekly Report,* Oct. 28, 1995, 3318.
73. For instance, see Koh, *National Security Constitution,* 131–133.
74. Gregg Easterbrook, "What's Wrong with Congress?" *Atlantic Monthly,* December 1983, 57–84.
75. Carroll J. Doherty, "Senate Slashes Agency Budgets, Confirms 18 Ambassadors," *Congressional Quarterly Weekly Report,* Dec. 16, 1995, 3821.
76. Carroll J. Doherty, "Uproar Over Democrat's Switch Snarls House Foreign Aid Bill," *Congressional Quarterly Weekly Report,* July 1, 1995, 1936.
77. Glennon, *Constitutional Diplomacy,* 28.
78. For instance, see Franck and Weisband's discussion of two congressional actions: (1) the decision to allow bombing in Cambodia only until August 15, 1973 (or for forty-five more days); and (2) the cutoff of military aid to Turkey in 1974, with the cutoff's implementation suspended for almost two months, theoretically to allow executive flexibility. *Foreign Policy by Congress,* 16-23, 35–45.
79. The Bush administration voiced such complaints about congressional handling of China's most-favored-nation status. See Eduardo Lachica, "Senate Imposes Curbs on China's Trade Status," *Wall Street Journal,* Feb. 26, 1992, sec. A.
80. See Cohen and Mitchell, *Men of Zeal,* 183.
81. Tocqueville, *Democracy in America,* 229.
82. Committees Investigating the Iran-Contra Affair, *Minority Report,* 438, 511.
83. On the shifts described here, see Philip Brenner and William M. LeoGrande, "Congress and Nicaragua: The Limits of Alternative Policy Making," in *Divided Democracy,* ed. James A. Thurber (Washington, D.C.: CQ Press, 1991), 222–233.
84. Barry M. Blechman, *The Politics of National Security: Congress and U.S. Defense Policy* (New York: Oxford University Press, 1990), 21.
85. Ibid., 56–57.

86. Report to Congress, Feb. 18, 1970, *Public Papers of the Presidents of the United States: Richard Nixon, 1970,* 179.
87. For instance, a Bush White House official explained why any House measure on most-favored-nation status for China would be unacceptable: "It is just too hard to educate that many members." David S. Cloud, "White House Looks to Senate to Maintain China Status," *Congressional Quarterly Weekly Report,* June 1, 1991, 1434.
88. Carroll J. Doherty, "New Generation Challenges Established Orthodoxy," *Congressional Quarterly Weekly Report,* Feb. 3, 1996, 306–308.
89. The argument, in its initial and general form (that is, not relating to foreign policy), appears in Morris P. Fiorina, *Congress: Keystone of the Washington Establishment,* 2d ed. (New Haven: Yale University Press, 1989); and Mayhew, *Congress: The Electoral Connection.*
90. Doherty, "New Generation Challenges Established Orthodoxy," 307–308.
91. Fulbright, "The Legislator as Educator," 719–732.
92. Crabb and Holt, *Invitation to Struggle,* 19–23.
93. Cassata, "Clinton Accepts Defense Bill."
94. David P. Forsythe, *Human Rights and U.S. Foreign Policy: Congress Reconsidered* (Gainesville: University of Florida Press, 1988), 157.
95. *Congressional Quarterly Almanac, 1993,* 486–493.
96. Fessler, "Complaints Are Stacking Up," 2565.
97. National Academy of Public Administration, *Beyond Distrust: Building Bridges Between Congress and the Executive* (Washington, D.C.: National Academy of Public Administration, 1992), 47.
98. Forsythe, *Human Rights and U.S. Foreign Policy,* 140.
99. Fessler, "Complaints Are Stacking Up," 2564.
100. National Academy of Public Administration, *Beyond Distrust,* 60.
101. Ibid., 45–46.
102. Burgin, "Congress, the War Powers Resolution, and the Invasion of Panama."
103. *Congressional Quarterly Almanac, 1993,* 492–493.
104. Eileen Burgin, "Rethinking the Role of the War Powers Resolution: Congress and the Persian Gulf War," *Journal of Legislation* 21 (1995): 23–47.
105. See, for instance, testimony of Rep. Dante Fascell, D-Fla., in Senate Committee on Foreign Relations, Special Subcommittee on War Powers, *The War Power After 200 Years: Congress and the President at a Constitutional Impasse,* 100th Cong., 2d sess., July, August, and September 1988, 942–943; House Committee on Foreign Affairs, *The War Powers Resolution: A Special Study of the Committee on Foreign Affairs,* 97th Cong., 2d sess., April 1982, Committee Print, 278–280; and Christopher Madison, "Despite His Complaints, Reagan Going Along with Spirit of the War Powers Law," *National Journal,* May 19, 1984, 989–993.
106. House Committee on Foreign Affairs, *Congress and Foreign Policy, 1985–1986,* 22–23.
107. Paul N. Stockton, "Congress and the Defense Policy-Making for the Post–Cold War Era," in *Congress Resurgent,* 235–259.
108. Carroll J. Doherty, "Collapse of Mexican Loan Plan Exposes Leaders' Limitations," *Congressional Quarterly Weekly Report,* Feb. 4, 1995, 372–374.
109. Rochelle Stanfield, "Weighing Arms Sales for Saudis," *National Journal,* Jan. 12, 1991, 79.
110. James M. Lindsay and Randall B. Ripley, "How Congress Influences Foreign and Defense Policy," in *Congress Resurgent.*
111. Stockton, "Congress and Defense Policy-Making for the Post–Cold War Era."
112. General Accounting Office, *Legislative Oversight: Congressional Requests for Informa-*

tion on Defense Activities, Report to Chair of the Armed Services Committee (Washington, D.C.: Government Printing Office, 1986).

113. Fessler, "Complaints Are Stacking Up," 2562.
114. *Congressional Quarterly Almanac, 1993,* 493.
115. Fessler, "Complaints Are Stacking Up," 2566.
116. Facing the possibility of an aid cutoff to Jordan because of Jordan's support for Iraq in the 1991 Persian Gulf war, Bush sought a provision allowing $27 million in military assistance to Jordan if he reported that it had both terminated Iraqi aid and backed the Middle East peace efforts. Ibid., 2565.
117. Blechman, *Politics of National Security,* 132–133.
118. Recall Bush's response to congressional threats about allies' paltry contributions at the beginning of the Persian Gulf crisis: he welcomed legislative efforts aimed at increasing prosperous nations' contributions. Crabb and Holt, *Invitation to Struggle,* 280.
119. Carroll J. Doherty, "Abortion Imbroglio Stalls Foreign Aid Bill," *Congressional Quarterly Weekly Report,* Dec. 16, 1995, 3820.
120. Carroll J. Doherty, "Family-Planning Compromise Helps Foreign Aid Pass," *Congressional Quarterly Weekly Report,* Jan. 27, 1996, 227.
121. Pat Towell, "Leaders Pursue Compromise As Override Vote Fails," *Congressional Quarterly Weekly Report,* Jan. 6, 1996, 61–62.
122. Congressional Quarterly, "Clinton Assails HIV Provision as Unconstitutional," *Congressional Quarterly Weekly Report,* Feb. 10, 1996, 362.
123. Doherty, "Collapse of Mexican Loan Plan," 372–374.
124. Louis Fisher, "Micromanagement by Congress: Reality and Mythology," in *Fettered Presidency,* 155.
125. Franck and Bob, "Return of Humpty-Dumpty," 943–944; Lee H. Hamilton, "Congress and the Presidency in American Foreign Policy," *Presidential Studies Quarterly* 18 (Summer 1988): 509.
126. Carroll J. Doherty, "Bush Is Given Authorization To Use Force Against Iraq," *Congressional Quarterly Weekly Report,* Jan. 12, 1991, 65–71.
127. *Congressional Quarterly Almanac, 1984* (Washington, D.C.: Congressional Quarterly, 1985), 429–439.
128. House Committee on Foreign Affairs, *Congress and U.S. Foreign Policy, 1983,* 110–133.
129. Hamilton, "Congress and the Presidency in American Foreign Policy," 509.
130. Ibid.
131. "Reagan Runs Up Against the Real Washington," *U.S. News and World Report,* May 25, 1981, 43.
132. Cohen and Mitchell, *Men of Zeal,* 184–186.
133. House Committee on Foreign Affairs, *Congress and Foreign Policy, 1985–1986,* 147.
134. James M. McCormick and Steven S. Smith, "The Iran Arms Sale and the Intelligence Oversight Act of 1980," *PS: Political Science and Politics* 20 (Winter 1987): 29–37.
135. House Committee on Foreign Affairs, *Congress and Foreign Policy, 1988,* 94–95.
136. Stockton, "Congress and Defense Policy-Making for the Post–Cold War Era."
137. Ibid., for a discussion of presidential problems in responding to such shifts.
138. Maynard Glitman, interview with author, University of Vermont, Burlington, March 5, 1992. Glitman entered the Foreign Service in 1956.
139. Cohen and Mitchell, *Men of Zeal*; and Walter Pincus, "President Was Told Arms Were Key to Iran's Help," *Washington Post,* Nov. 14, 1986, sec. A.
140. *Congressional Quarterly Almanac, 1993,* 499.

141. Francis O. Wilcox, "Cooperation vs. Confrontation: Congress and Foreign Policy Since Vietnam," *Atlantic Community Quarterly* 22 (Fall 1984): 277.
142. Christopher Madison, "Hamilton's Foreign Policy Alter Ego," *National Journal,* Dec. 22, 1990, 3097.
143. Glitman, interview with author.
144. Samuel P. Huntington, *The Common Defense: Strategic Programs in National Politics* (New York: Columbia University Press, 1961), 130–131.
145. See Eileen Burgin, "Influence of Constituents: Congressional Decision Making on Issues of Foreign and Defense Policy," in *Congress Resurgent.*
146. Christopher Madison, "A Not-So-Sure Thing," *National Journal,* Sept. 14, 1991, 2200–3.
147. Ibid. Bush subsequently altered his stance: on August 11, 1992, Bush and Prime Minister Yitzhak Rabin announced a U.S.-Israeli agreement on loan guarantees.
148. For instance, see Mayer, *Political Economy of Defense Contracting.* For a different perspective on this issue, see Richard L. Hall and Frank W. Wayman, "Buying Time: Moneyed Interests and the Mobilization of Bias in Congressional Committees," in *American Political Science Review* 84 (September 1990): 797–820.
149. David S. Cloud, " 'Undecideds' Are Final Target in Battle Over Trade Pact," *Congressional Quarterly Weekly Report,* Nov. 6, 1993, 3011.
150. Ibid.
151. Burgin, "Influence of Constituents."
152. Eileen Burgin, "Representatives' Decisions on Participation in Foreign Policy Issues," *Legislative Studies Quarterly* 16 (November 1991): 521–546.
153. Patsy T. Mink, "Institutional Perspective: Misunderstandings, Myths, and Misperceptions: How Congress and the State Department See Each Other," in *Tethered Presidency,* 74.
154. Hamilton, "Congress and the Presidency in American Foreign Policy," 509.
155. *Federalist Papers,* No. 57, 353.

14. Centralization, Devolution, and Turf Protection in the Congressional Budget Process

James A. Thurber

"Gingrich had always understood that the struggle over the budget would be the most important—and the most perilous—stage in the revolution. The dry figures that Congress and the President would clash over would define the role of government. The budget reached into every recess of the government; it set policy in thousands of areas. The budget battle was where most of the political differences would be settled. The Hundred Days were just the prelude."[1]

After two historic federal government shutdowns, thirteen stopgap spending measures, several presidential vetoes, and seven months of fighting, neither the White House nor the Republican Congress had a clear victory. The winner of the fiscal year (FY) 1996 budget battle had to await the 1996 election results, when the voters decided. If the outcome was uncertain until November 5, the origins of the problem were not. They can be traced to twenty years of partisan struggles over federal spending, deficits, the national debt, and congressional budget process reforms.

The congressional budget process has been transformed dramatically since 1974, when Congress passed a major reform act. Budget reforms under Presidents George Bush and Bill Clinton resulted in substantial deficit reductions, but did not satisfy the demand for reform. Dozens of proposals were considered under Democrats and Republicans in the most recent Congresses.[2] The drive to balance the budget, the line-item veto act, and the unfunded mandate reform act were all part of budget reforms in 1995 led by the Republican Contract with America.[3] Changing the rules of the budget game has been part of congressional politics since 1974 and continues to dominate it as the United States moves into the twenty-first century.

After a brief description of congressional budget reform since 1974, this chapter describes and evaluates the historic battle over the budget during 1995 and 1996, analyzes the impact of reforms on presidential and congressional budget power, and concludes with a discussion about the ability of Congress to make tough budget decisions through a centralized and decentralized process.[4]

Budget Reforms

To combat deficits and improve accountability, Congress has passed four major budget reforms since 1974: the Congressional Budget and Impoundment Control Act of 1974, the Balanced Budget and Emergency Deficit Control Act

Major Congressional Budget Reforms, 1974–1996

1974 Congressional Budget and Impoundment Control Act

Created House and Senate Budget Committees; established the congressional budget process requiring an annual congressional budget resolution setting expenditures, estimating revenues and deficit (or surplus); founded Congressional Budget Office. Provided procedures for congressional review of impoundments (rescissions) and deferrals.

1980 Reconciliation Process

Reconciliation used for the first time at the beginning of the congressional budget process. Reconciliation procedures, established in the 1974 Congressional Budget Act, require Congress to change revenues and spending to the level set in a budget resolution. House and Senate committees are required to recommend legislation changing existing law to bring the spending, revenues, or the debt limit into conformity with the budget resolution.

1985 Balanced Budget and Emergency Deficit Control Act (Gramm-Rudman-Hollings and *1987 Amendments)*

Set fixed deficit reduction targets and the sequestration of budgetary resources if the projected deficit was greater than the target.

1990 Budget Enforcement Act

Substantially amended Gramm-Rudman-Hollings by shifting from fixed to adjustable deficit targets, caps on discretionary spending, established pay-as-you-go rules for revenues and direct spending, and passed new budgetary rules for direct and guaranteed loans.

1995 Unfunded Mandates Act

A majority of unfunded mandates from Congress to state and local government were deemed unlawful under this act.

1996 Line Item Veto

Through an amendment to Title X of the 1974 Budget and Impoundment Control Act, a new enhanced expedited rescission gave the president the authority to veto part of an appropriations act.

Box 14-1

of 1985 and 1987, and the Budget Enforcement Act of 1990 (BEA), which is Title XIII of the Omnibus Budget Reconciliation Act of 1990 (OBRA).[5] Box 14-1 outlines some of their major characteristics. Supporters suggested that their passage would promote more discipline, reduce deficits, and make the process more efficient. However, in the years since their adoption, concern has not abated, and 1995 brought a new round of budget reform efforts.

The 1974 Reforms

The most important postwar change in the budget process was the 1974 Congressional Budget and Impoundment Control Act, also referred to as the Congressional Budget Act.[6] The act created standing House and Senate Budget Committees responsible for setting overall tax and spending levels and required Congress to establish levels of expenditures and revenues every year. The legislation includes three important provisions. First, to ensure completion before the start of each fiscal year, the act established a timetable that set deadlines for action on budget-related legislation. Second, the act required the annual adoption of concurrent budget resolutions. Initial resolutions establish targets for total budget authority, outlays, and revenues for the upcoming fiscal year, and a final "binding" resolution puts ceilings on budget authority and outlays and a floor on revenues. Third, the act instituted a reconciliation process to conform revenue, spending, and debt legislation to the final budget resolution.[7] Under reconciliation, the Budget Committees may direct other committees to determine and recommend actions deemed necessary to conform to the budget resolutions. They may require House and Senate committees to report legislation that meets budget targets.[8] They may also direct legislative committees to make changes in existing laws to achieve the desired budget reductions. These changes are submitted to each house "without any substantive revision."

Reconciliation was to be a relatively brief, simple exercise, included in the second concurrent resolution and applied only to appropriations. However, the Budget Committees turned the process around and included directions for the authorizing and appropriating committees in the first resolutions for FY 1981. Despite the original intent, the strategy worked. The Budget Committees successfully required spending reductions of about $6.2 billion and revenue increases of $4.2 billion. The FY 1981 reconciliation bill established an important precedent and resulted in savings for fiscal years 1981 through 1985 of more than $50 billion in outlays and additional revenues of $29 billion. Reconciliation permits actions to be taken in tandem, such as spending cuts and tax increases, that would never survive alone. However, the problem of large deficits remained.

Gramm-Rudman-Hollings I and II

By the early 1980s projected budget deficits were in the $200 billion range, far higher than ever before.[9] In response, Congress enacted the Balanced Budget and Emergency Deficit Control Act of 1985, known as Gramm-Rudman-Hollings (GRH I), and of 1987 (GRH II).

GRH revised established deadlines for the major aspects of the budget process to increase efficiency and focus attention on reducing the deficit.[10] The central enforcement mechanism is sequestration, automatic spending cuts that occur if the federal budget does not fall within $10 billion of the deficit targets.[11] The GRH deficit targets for each fiscal year are listed in Table 14-1. If the proposed budget did not meet the targets, the president was required to make spending cuts evenly divided between domestic and defense programs until the targets were met. However, interest payments and most entitlement programs were "off-budget," partially or totally exempt from the potential cuts.

GRH I gave the General Accounting Office (GAO) the responsibility for triggering sequestration. In 1986 the Supreme Court declared part of the legislation unconstitutional because it gave the GAO, a legislative support agency, executive functions.[12] Congress responded with the passage of GRH II, which directed the Office of Management and Budget (OMB), an executive agency, to trigger sequestration. GRH II also revised the original targets in accordance with more realistic economic assumptions.

The GRH plan failed to deliver long-term progress toward a balanced budget. Neither the president nor Congress considered long-term budgetary goals. Even after the GRH II revisions, the new targets were well out of reach as early as 1990. Sequestration was supposed to threaten the interests of all policy makers enough to make them want to avoid it, but did not work. Comparing the projected impact of sequestration with the potential impact of cuts from regular legislation, policy makers decided that their interests were best served by delaying the passage of bills until after sequestration occurred.[13] Two other factors contributed to the failure of GRH. First, sequestration could be avoided by using overly optimistic assumptions as substitutes for real policy changes. Second, before passage of the 1990 BEA, Congress evaluated the budget only once a year to ascertain whether it was meeting GRH targets. After this evaluation, legislation could be adopted that raised the deficit in the current and following years.[14]

The 1990 Reforms

Because previous reforms failed to meet their intended goals, Congress changed the rules again with passage of OBRA 1990. The bipartisan agreement was intended to bring more control over spending, allow more efficient negotiated compromises, reduce deficits, and provide political cover for unpopular election-year decisions.[15]

The 1990 BEA reforms further centralized power within Congress and required "zero-sum" choices: that is, trading reductions in one program for increases in another, or tax cuts for some taxpayers in exchange for increases for others. In December 1990 the Congressional Budget Office (CBO) estimated that BEA provisions promised to reduce the cumulative deficit by about $496

Table 14-1 Deficit Reduction Targets and Actual Deficits, Fiscal Years 1986-1996

	Deficit Reduction Targets (in billions of dollars)					
Fiscal Year	1985 GRH Limits	1987 GRH Limits	1990 BEA Limits	CBO Deficit Projections[a]	Actual Deficits	Deficit (% GDP)
1986	$172	—	—	—	$221	5.4
1987	144	—	—	—	150	3.7
1988	108	$144	—	—	155	3.9
1989	72	136	—	—	152	3.8
1990	36	100	—	—	195	4.9
1991	0	64	$327	$331	269	5.5
1992	—	28	317	425	290	5.5
1993	—	0	236	348	255	4.6
1994	—	—	102	318	203[a]	3.8
1995	—	—	83	162	164[a]	3.2
1996	—	—	—	176[a]	115[b]	1.8[b]

Sources: CBO estimates of the deficit taken from *An Analysis of the President's Budgetary Proposals for Fiscal Year 1991* (Washington, D.C.: Congressional Budget Office, March 1990), 8; and *The Economic and Budget Outlook: An Update* (Washington, D.C.: Congressional Budget Office, July 1990), x; and *Update* (August 1994), 31.

Note: The budget figures include Social Security, which is off-budget but is counted for the purposes of the balanced budget act targets. For comparability with the targets, the projections exclude the Postal Service, which is also off-budget.

[a] These deficit figures are from CBO, *The Economic and Budget Outlook: Fiscal Years 1997-2006* (May 1996), 134.

[b] The deficit for fiscal year 1995 was estimated as $115 billion as of July 16, 1996, in a letter from the CBO to Rep. John R. Kasich, R-Ohio, chairman of the House Budget Committee.

billion for 1991 through 1995.[16] The most visible change was the elimination of fixed deficit targets, but other innovations had a major impact on the budgetary powers of both Congress and the president.[17]

The 1990 BEA required a specified amount of savings for each of five years covered by a multiyear budget plan. Through FY 1993, sequestration was linked to discretionary spending ceilings in three categories of government programs—defense, domestic, and international—rather than the entire budget.[18] These ceilings were perhaps the most significant aspect of the BEA reforms. Each ceiling was enforced by a sequestration applied across-the-board to all of the programs *within* a category that exceeded its spending limits, a process called categorical sequestration. It would be triggered only if the spending limits of any or all of the categories were exceeded due to changes in legislation. If the limits were exceeded because of changes in economic conditions, sequestration would not be triggered.

Another characteristic of the BEA was "look back" legislation, which required that any amount added to the current year's deficit by policy changes made after the final budget evaluation would also be added to the following year's deficit target. Doing so eliminated incentives for post-snapshot budget changes, but reduced the flexibility of fiscal policy. There were exemptions for emergencies, such as the Persian Gulf War.

Rather than return to fixed deficit targets and the enforcement rules used prior to the 1990 act, President Clinton sought further deficit reduction. The goal was to reduce cumulative deficits by a total of $500 billion between fiscal years 1994 and 1998. With few changes, Congress passed the 1993 OBRA, which codified a new five-year deficit reduction plan. The BEA's enforcement procedures were extended through 1998. Categorical spending ceilings continued through fiscal years 1994 and 1995.

The 1990 BEA and 1993 OBRA budgets also included a major reform called the pay-as-you-go (PAYGO) procedure. PAYGO automatically cuts nonexempt entitlement spending to make up for any increase in the deficit caused by the passage of legislation that increases entitlement benefits, or extends benefits to more people, or leads to revenue reductions.[19] PAYGO made the budget process a zero-sum game, the most important consequence of the 1990s budget reforms. PAYGO was not necessarily intended to reduce the deficit, but to limit growth in spending and deficits.[20] Under PAYGO, the ceiling for each year's new budget was set as if every program had been frozen at the previous year's amount. Proposals to increase expenditures for existing programs or add expenditures for new programs had to include tax increases or spending cuts to produce the revenues required. Otherwise, there would be a special reconciliation process to eliminate any net revenue loss and a sequester to eliminate any deficit increase. Legislation could be exempted if there was an emergency need. The 1990 budget agreement also required that all new revenues go to deficit reduction. The primary impact of PAYGO was to discourage spending, which, in turn, reduced the deficit in absolute dollars as well as a percentage of gross domestic product. The difficulty of either raising taxes or cutting popular existing mandatory programs effectively curtailed creation of new programs.

A number of the programs that are part of the budget were not to be counted against the spending limits of their categories. Moreover, Social Security receipts and disbursements were completely off-budget, and none of their transactions were counted for estimations of the deficit or the calculations for sequestration.[21] The Social Security Trust Fund was also protected by "fire wall" points of order against legislation that would reduce trust fund balances.[22]

House and Senate points of order against "budget busting" provisions are an important enforcement mechanism in the BEA. Under the 1990 act, legislation was subject to a point of order for breaching either the budget-year levels or the sum of the five-year levels set in a budget resolution. To prevent temporary savings and timing shifts, budget resolutions in each year are for five years.

The 1990 budget pact also led the House and Senate to create different procedures for the appropriators. House appropriations were allowed to proceed on May 15 even in the absence of a budget resolution. Senate committees other than the Appropriations Committee were allowed to proceed in the absence of a new budget resolution if their bills conformed to the out-year allocations in the most recent budget resolution. This procedure established more spending control by the Appropriations Committees, but allowed the House and Senate to move bills even if the budget resolution is late.

Consequences of Budget Reform

The impact of the budget reforms of the 1990s can be evaluated in terms of the degree of centralization; the control by the president versus Congress over the budget; the amount of openness in the decision-making process; the extent of complexity in decision-making rules; and the timeliness of the process.[23] Generally, the 1990s reforms establish more budget control, expand the power of the Appropriations Committees, and, because the reforms establish a zero-sum budget game, they diminish the influence of other committees. At the same time, the budget process is made more accessible and accountable to the public, interest groups, and the administration by publicly revealing the tradeoffs that must be made in spending.

Scorekeeping is the process of accounting for the cost of authorizations and appropriations bills and determining whether they are consistent with the budget resolution. The 1990 BEA shifted this function from the CBO to the OMB. This change was a major gain for the president and a loss for Congress. The shift made the budget process less complex, more open, yet more time-consuming because of the conflicts over cost estimates. Subsequently, however, the House Democratic Caucus revised the 1990 budget agreement by transferring scorekeeping authority to the CBO and the Joint Committee on Taxation. President Bush objected to the move, but the revision held, retaining within the legislative branch the power of scorekeeping.[24]

When the game is too hard, however, members of Congress change the rules.[25] When they dislike budget outcomes or process reforms, they simply make revisions. Although the BEA supporters had many policy goals, they supported change out of fear of the negative impact of an FY 1991 GRH sequestration (an estimated 20 percent cut across the board), as well as a perception that the underlying causes of the deficit were complex and uncontrollable in the short term. The changes led to ever-increasing centralization and a better grasp of the scope of budget problems by the budgeteers and those affected by their work.

The Republican Revolution and the 1996 Budget

The election of Republican majorities in the House and Senate in 1994 had an immediate and dramatic impact on the congressional budget process and the war over federal government spending and taxing.[26] The Republican congressional budget ignored President Clinton's preferences and directly confronted hundreds of special interests with its proposals to balance the budget by 2002, slow the growth of Medicare, devolve power over Medicaid to the states, reform welfare by cutting the growth in entitlement programs, cut education funding, reduce environmental regulations, eliminate the Departments of Commerce, Energy, and Education (and abolish hundreds of other federal programs), and cut taxes by $245 billion. President Clinton confronted the Republican budget by vetoing the Balanced Budget Act of 1995 and numerous appropriations bills. The ensuing standoff between Congress and the president resulted in a shutdown of the federal government for an unprecedented number of days. Final passage of the FY 1996 budget was almost seven months late.

In assessing the budget process in the 104th Congress, the most central factors to stress are the impact of divided party government, the policy and ideological conflicts between the Republican Congress and the Democratic president, and the consequent effort of the Republicans to approach budgetary politics in a highly centralized manner. The 1994 election brought divided party government and little consensus between the president and Congress.[27] As a general rule, divided party control of Congress and the presidency is believed to be inefficient and irresponsible.[28] Government that is divided is viewed as creating a power gridlock where neither party acquiesces to the other on important legislative issues, such as the budget. The historic divided party government battles over the budget in 1995 and 1996 seem to fit that model. Behind the battle and final agreement over the FY 1996 budget is a story of centralization and decentralization of the budget decision-making process in the House and Senate and the power of the president to persuade.

Assessing the Budget Showdown

To achieve the goals of a balanced budget by 2002, House Republican budgeting and appropriating in the first session of the 104th Congress was centralized, disciplined, and top-down. It was designed to limit deliberations and the power of agencies and their supportive interest groups, and to discourage individualism by members of Congress.[29] However, the concentrated power of the House budget process began to devolve into the more traditional decentralized decision-making system as the 1996 election created incentives for members to represent local rather than abstract partisan interests. The revolutionary budget cutters evolved into pragmatic constituency program protectors.

In the 1996 battle over cutting domestic discretionary spending and entitlement programs, members pursued "strategic protection" of individual interests over a more broadly defined public interest. The Republican Senate, whether led by Sen. Robert J. Dole of Kansas or later by Sen. Trent Lott of Mississippi, changed little from the way the Democrat leaders budgeted and appropriated federal dollars. The central role of the committees, especially the appropriations subcommittees, stayed the same under the Republican Senate leadership. The institution remained decentralized and more individualistic, with less party discipline than among the House Republicans.

Table 14-2 House Votes on Selected Reforms in the First One Hundred Days of the 104th Congress

Reform Measure	Vote
Congressional Accountability Act	429–0
Cutting committees and staff	416–12
Budget reform	421–6
Term limits for Speaker, committee chairs	355–74
Ban on proxy voting	418–13
Open meetings for public and press	431–0
Three-fifths vote for tax increases	79–152
Audit House books	430–1
Balanced Budget Amendment	300–132
Line-item veto act	430–1
Unfunded mandate reform act	418–0

Source: Congressional Quarterly Weekly Report, various issues, January 1995 to April 1996.

In the House, where three-fifths of the Republicans were elected in the 1992 and 1994 elections, many said they owed their seats to GOPAC, the Contract with America, and Newt Gingrich, R-Ga. Naturally, they backed him in the centralized budget process. Because of a strong, unified House Republican Party, which ran on a common ideology—the contract—Speaker Gingrich effectively consolidated power and dominated the budget process to the detriment of the president (and the Senate) until January 1996.[30] The symbiotic relationship between the House GOP freshmen and the Speaker paid off in their strong support for his prolonged negotiations over the FY 1996 budget.

Speaker Gingrich helped to build party unity in the House by using the Contract with America as an agenda-setting device (see Table 14-2).[31] He also supported several important reforms in the organization and structure of the House and basic budget policy. Table 14-2 lists eleven votes on selected budget and centralizing reforms, based on the contract and Republican Conference rule changes. Most of the votes had strong bipartisan support except the balanced budget amendment and the requirement to have a three-fifths vote for all new tax increases. With the adoption of these reforms, Gingrich gained more power to control budget policy. He effectively appointed all of the chairs of House committees, ignoring seniority in several cases, including the Appropriations Committee. Chairmen have said they owe their positions to him (and the Republican Conference) rather than seniority. The House restricted the power of the chairs by placing term limits of six years on their positions. The Speaker also successfully pushed through a ban on proxy voting by the chairs, which tended to undermine their ability to act independently of the Speaker in the budget process. Gingrich effectively made all freshmen committee assignments, putting freshmen on the four most important committees: Rules, Ways and Means, Budget, and

Appropriations, where six of eleven open Republican appointments went to freshmen. Putting freshmen on these committees as well as the Commerce Committee and appointing freshmen to three subcommittee chairmanships helped Gingrich build loyal GOP freshmen support both on the Budget Committee and in the House as a whole.

Speaker Gingrich's consolidated power and discipline over the Republican members of the House came close to matching that of Thomas Brackett Reed and Joseph G. Cannon around the turn of the twentieth century. His centralization forced President Clinton to threaten vetoes, build coalitions in the Senate to moderate the actions of the House, and to simplify his activist domestic agenda and move toward the Republican Party position in a number of areas. Gingrich and the conservative House Republicans changed the policy agenda and focused on balancing the budget, tax cuts, and slowing the growth in entitlement programs.

The House Republican leadership's centralization of the budget and appropriations processes also had the effect of increasing the power of some interest groups and reducing the power of others. The centralized budget process did not hurt those interest groups that agreed with the shrinking of the federal government. Lobbyists from some of the most important groups in U.S. politics—for example, the National Federation of Independent Business—were given direct access to the House leadership and special assignments to help pass provisions of the Contract with America and the new budget. Revealing is *Time* writer Jeffrey H. Birnbaum's comment about having lobbyists playing such roles:

> Welcome to the underside of the Republican revolution. To an extent unusual even for parasitic Washington, the House GOP leadership has attached its fortunes to private lobbyists, and is relying on their far-flung influence to pass its agenda. Representative John Boehner's (R-Ohio) Thursday Group is the top of the pyramid of that sophisticated effort, serving as command central for a series of multimillion-dollar campaigns on behalf of the Contract with America. The stakes of the enterprise—and the potential rewards for the lobbyists—are huge.[32]

Groups such as environmentalists and agricultural interests that did not want to see the role of the federal government reduced were left out of the Republican agenda. For example, when the House Agriculture Committee failed to approve the Republican leadership's cuts in farm spending in FY 1996, the leadership pulled the bill and sent it to the Budget Committee, which did not have farm interests pressuring it, for insertion into the budget reconciliation package. The agricultural subsidy interests were major losers, leading one observer to conclude, "Cross the Republican House leaders and be prepared to reap the whirlwind. They will threaten your livelihood, take your bill away and then do what they want anyway, all in the name of progress."[33]

During the early battles over the FY 1996 budget, the abiding obsessions of John R. Kasich, R-Ohio, chairman of the House Budget Committee, as reported by David Maraniss and Michael Weisskopf, were his confrontations with members over the historic slashes in federal spending. "When he fell asleep, his

Table 14-3 Party Unity and Presidential Support Among Republican and Democratic Freshmen and Veterans, 104th Congress

	House		Senate	
Member Status	Unity	Support	Unity	Support
Overall	88%	48%	88%	58%
Freshman	93	31	93	33
Veterans	87	52	87	61
GOP freshmen	94	23	93	33
GOP veterans	92	25	90	38
Democratic freshmen	87	78	NA	NA
Democratic veterans	82	75	84	82
Budget committee				
GOP freshmen	96	21	87	36
GOP veterans	92	26	94	34
Demcratic freshmen	92	79	NA	NA
Democratic veterans	78	72	85	83

Source: The data are from *Congressional Quarterly Weekly Report,* various issues. All party unity and presidential support scores are for the 104th Congress, 1st sess.

restless mind encountered the same nocturnal furies—fellow members of Congress who appeared before him red-faced and screaming: 'How could you do this to us! We didn't know about this! '"[34] However, Chairman Kasich was acting with the direction and assistance of the House Republican leadership. A further example of House Republican leadership management of the drive to cut spending in 1995 was the micromanagement of the appropriations subcommittee bills. Interviews with House majority leadership staff revealed that most of the "backdoor" spending provisions and "backdoor de-authorizations" in the House appropriations bills were "cleared" by House Republican leadership prior to consideration in the House Appropriations Committee (usually in the office of Majority Leader Richard K. Armey of Texas) to the ire of Appropriations Committee members.[35] Neither the House Democrats nor President Clinton's White House were included in these decision-making sessions.

The discipline and strong party loyalty of Republicans during the 104th Congress are clearly shown in Tables 14-3 and 14-4. The exceptionally high party support scores among the GOP freshmen and the Republicans on the Budget Committee in Table 14-3 reveal their allegiance to Gingrich's leadership and the drive to balance the budget in seven years, an important element of the contract. Table 14-3 shows the underlying pattern of party discipline that made the GOP budget-cutting strategy possible in the first session of the 104th Congress.

Budget Committee members, as well as rank and file Republicans, showed higher party loyalty than their Democratic counterparts. Comparing party, as

Table 14-4 Party Unity and Presidential Support Among Republican and Democratic Budget Committee Members

Member Status	102d Congress		104th Congress	
	Unity	Support	Unity	Support
House Budget GOP	79%	70%	93%	24%
House Budget Dems	82	31	80	73
Senate Budget GOP	87	83	91	34
Senate Budget Dems	78	37	85	83

Source: The data are from *Congressional Quarterly Weekly Report,* various issues. All party unity and presidential support scores are for the 104th Congress, 1st sess. All 102d Congress voting scores are for both sessions.

well as the 102d Congress to the 104th Congress—two periods of divided government—the pattern of strong and consistent support for the party position by the Republicans in the 104th Congress is clear (see Table 14-4).

The loyalty of the Republican Budget Committee members, an essential factor in the Republicans' budget strategy, was especially impressive compared to Democrats and the 102d Congress, when Republican president George Bush faced a Democratic-controlled House and Senate. The House and Senate GOP members of the Budget Committees in the 104th Congress had party unity scores of 93 percent and 91 percent, respectively, compared to the House and Senate Democrats with party unity scores of 80 percent and 85 percent. The thirteen-point difference between the House Republican and Democratic Budget Committee members is especially revealing if one compares the difficulties of passing the budget resolutions in the most recent Congresses. Republicans passed the fiscal year 1996 and 1997 budgets with relative ease compared to the internal party warfare that occurred with the Democratic Party in the 102d and 103d Congresses. The party unity scores of House GOP Budget Committee members rose dramatically from the 102d Congress when they had a score of 79 percent. One reason for the increase was Speaker Gingrich's concentration of decision making in the budget process in the 104th Congress. The group with the highest party unity score (96 percent) of Budget Committee members was the House freshmen GOP in the 104th Congress, first session, loyal supporters of Gingrich and the Contract with America. They were a consistent force behind Speaker Gingrich's drive to balance the budget in seven years.

Another measure of party loyalty is the vote for or against a president's legislative agenda. Presidential support scores, which are calculated from roll call votes on the floor of the House and Senate, measure the backing by members of Congress for the president's publicly stated legislative agenda. The presidential support scores of congressional Democrats were particularly low compared to GOP support for President Bush in the 102d Congress. Congressional Democrats generally, and Democratic Budget Committee members in particular, had low party unity and presidential support scores, making it difficult for President Clinton to build a coalition around his centrist FY 1993 budget. The close vote in the House for Clinton's FY 1993 budget (with a majority of one vote) and the absence of a natural coalition among House Democrats is apparent in the low support scores among the veteran Democrats. The House Democratic party unity average of 82 and presidential support score average of 75 and Senate Democratic party unity average of 84 and presidential support of 82 are significantly lower than Republican party unity and support of President Bush in the 102d Congress. These scores also revealed the split in the Democratic Party between the conservative southern Democrats and other more liberal Democrats.

Although there was strong Republican Party discipline in the House, Speaker Gingrich's revolutionary rhetoric did not sit well with the American people—and it still took a two-thirds vote to overcome a presidential veto. The new Republican members began to understand the meaning of the separation of powers between the president and Congress in December 1995. The power of representation and the will of the American public were also central parts of the calculus of the Speaker and the president. The more Newt talked, the higher his negatives grew in the public opinion polls. It appeared that the public did not like the Speaker, nor did they like the government being shut down. The president took advantage of these two facts.

When the confrontation with President Clinton resulted in the second shutdown of the federal government December 15, 1995, Speaker Gingrich drafted a memorandum that listed assumptions and strategies for the battle with the administration. The Gingrich memo stated: "The White House has crossed the line. We want them to understand that if they want a long-term stand-off, we are prepared to stay the course for as long as it takes." The memo listed three assumptions that accurately described the president's strategy:

1. The White House is prepared for a situation in which there is no deal.
2. The White House believes they can beat us in a short-term tactical confrontation.
3. The White House wants a situation in which they can continue to portray us as extremists. They want to blame the government shutdown on us as irresponsible partisans.[36]

Gingrich proposed that the House pass a continuing resolution that would allow federal employees to be paid through January 3, 1996. That would be followed by a series of bills to reopen the government but fund only the programs the Republicans supported. The Speaker's Advisory Group, his top lieutenants, lined up solidly against him, as did all of the other House Republican leaders. Gingrich relented, but took a hard line against the president. His leadership and centralized discipline began to weaken the longer the negotiations with the president continued.

Ultimately, President Clinton and the House Democrats were able to stall and build public support in their extended confrontation with the Republicans. The White House portrayed the House Republicans as extremists who were cutting Medicare, Medicaid, education, spending for environmental enforcement, and other popular programs at levels that were unacceptable to the public. Gingrich's strategy memo turned out to be correct, but it took until April 1996 for the House Republicans to realize it. Clinton used his powers under the Constitution, the veto and the threat of the veto, as well as the power to persuade the public that the Republicans were responsible for shutting down the federal government, to build support for his agenda.

The Republican shutdown strategy failed by mid-December 1995, but it took until April to pass a compromise FY 1996 budget. Rather than forcing the White House to compromise, the shutdown was only obscuring the larger Republican campaign for a balanced budget. Gingrich argued, "Republicans had to aim high to get what they got. Could we have gotten [this far] with a lower profile, less energetic, less aggressive, less far-reaching effort? I don't know. But I think you needed the energy and the momentum and the excitement to really force the debate."[37] In the end, Clinton and the House Democrats had to adjust to the new Republican agenda in the 104th Congress, but the Republicans had to compromise and learn that the president has substantial power through the veto and public opinion in any confrontation with Congress.

The 1997 Budget and the Limits of Party Government

In terms of leadership and party loyalty, the battle over the fiscal 1997 budget was a different story from the fiscal 1996 budget wars. It brought into focus the difficulty of maintaining partisan discipline in the House, an institution that is structurally decentralized and representative of local interests. In attempting to find where moderate Senate Republicans, President Clinton and a disciplined minority party, and hard-core House conservatives, especially the freshmen, could all agree on spending policy, Speaker Gingrich discovered the difficulty of building a winning coalition. To avoid another protracted battle over the budget with the Senate and the president, Gingrich and the House leadership agreed on a "risky strategy of preemptively fattening up the budget resolution and domestic appropriations bills."[38]

The fiscal 1997 budget agreement barely passed on a vote of 216 to 211 on June 12, 1996.[39] The close vote revealed how undisciplined the House can be. Nineteen House conservatives openly defied the Republican leaders and voted against the budget resolution conference report, which carried $4 billion in extra spending for domestic appropriations, money intended to placate both Senate GOP appropriators and the president. In the Senate twenty-three conservative Republicans had originally opposed adding the money, but none of them thought it important enough to oppose the final budget, which passed on a straight party-line vote, 53–46, on June 13.[40]

The freshman-led rebellion in the House was a manifestation of the tensions between the House and Senate Republicans and the problems inherent in leading a naturally individualistic House of Representatives. Sen. Pete V. Domenici, R-N.M., chairman of the Budget Committee, openly sympathized with Democratic budget shortfalls for critical domestic programs. "If I were king, I wouldn't write this budget," Domenici said. "This is as good as we can do this year."[41] Chairman Kasich of the House Budget Committee spoke almost the same words, but they meant something different. He was supporting the conservative freshmen who wanted even less spending when he stated, "It's not what I want, but it's the best we can get."[42] The fiscal 1997 budget conference report carried the heart of the House GOP agenda to remake government by balancing the budget by 2002, cutting taxes at least $122 billion over six years, and making deep reductions in projected spending from welfare, health insurance programs for the poor and the elderly, and domestic discretionary appropriations, but not in many other domestic programs with strong constituencies.

The zero-sum budget game in Congress got tighter as a result of the Contract with America agenda, which required major cuts in social programs and taxes and a balanced budget in seven years, but the 1997 federal budget showed again how easy it is to slip away from the hard budget cuts.[43] Roy T. Meyers reinforces this point in *Strategic Budgeting:*

> Persistent fiscal stress now guarantees that funding for many programs will be threatened each year. Consequently, most advocates of existing programs feel they must develop strategies of protection. Advocates of proposed programs must also find strategies to counter the inevitable bias against new spending when times are tight.[44]

The "strategies of protection" for the fiscal 1997 budget included more money for domestic programs to help meet the demands of members during an election year. House and Senate Republicans' original seven-year budget plan, approved in June 1995, would have cut government outlays for nondefense programs from $277.6 billion in 1995 to $258.4 billion in 1997. Under the Republican working plan in July, however, the target was missed by more than $15 billion. As of mid-July 1996, federal outlays for FY 1997 were projected to be at least $273.8 billion and were likely to end up higher.[45] The fiscal hardliners in the House (mostly freshmen) lost a close vote on the "fattened" Senate 1997 budget resolution, but only after Speaker Gingrich and the Republican leadership worked hard on the floor to prevent defections. More moderate Senate Republicans had forced the House to add back $4 billion and reserve another $1.3 billion in case Congress opted to adopt a continuing resolution, a measure that would continue funding the federal departments into 1997 at the fiscal year 1996 level, instead of enacting individual appropriations bills. House Republicans had no such trouble on their high-profile budget and reconciliation bill votes in 1995. They had few defectors and won with comfortable victories.

By early October 1996, it was clear that the House Republicans had evolved from revolutionaries to pragmatists when putting together the budget for fiscal year 1997. Faced with President Clinton's refusal to back away from his domestic spending priorities and worried about being blamed by the public if a budget deadlock produced another government shutdown just before the election, Republicans retreated on a number of budget fronts. They broke their target for balancing the budget in seven years by exceeding their domestic spending ceiling by $15.6 billion ($487.4 billion to $503 billion) to accommodate Democratic spending priorities such as federal aid to education and environmental protection. President Clinton's strategy of blaming the Republicans for cuts in education, the environment, Medicare, and Medicaid, and for shutting down the government over the budget impasse had worked for the budget negotiations. The Republican retreat on the FY 1997 budget revealed a clear picture of the political obstacles that occur when spending cuts are proposed. Despite the Republican criticism of the federal government in the 104th Congress, there appeared to be few programs that lacked a vocal constituency. When cuts were suggested by the Republicans, lobbyists, associations, and grassroots support quickly emerged for federal aid to education, public broadcasting, the arts, environmental enforcement, water projects, veterans hospital construction, inland waterways, and a variety of other federal programs with well-organized constituencies.

The Republican drive to cut spending faced the realities of an election year in the early spring of 1996. One observer concluded, "As the Republican 'revolution' to trim government spending moves into its second summer, the revolutionaries have begun to feel the squeeze. Burned by the negative public reaction to federal shutdowns last winter and harried by constituents eager for more services, many Republican lawmakers are rediscovering government."[46] In the House the tough 1997 spending ceilings set by the Republican leadership for Army Corps of Engineers water projects and other programs in the energy and water development appropriations bill triggered a mini-revolt by Rep. John T. Myers, R-Ind., an Appropriations subcommittee chairman. Myers refused to send his bill to the full Appropriations Committee until House leaders had agreed to add $1.1 billion to his allocation. But his bill was still below the level of the Senate subcommittee bill. Moreover, Speaker Gingrich directed that annual appropriations bills be analyzed specifically in terms of their impact on Republican incumbents and California, a crucial state in the 1996 election.

The Republican House members had changed from their almost revolutionary fervor to the more usual pragmatic protection of favorite programs, revealing a reassertion of power by the appropriations subcommittee chairs, the authorizing committee chairs, and the more senior and moderate Republicans who were protecting spending to help reelect GOP members.[47]

Early in the fight over the FY 1996 budget, the conservative Republicans' tough budget-cutting rhetoric had drowned out the usual pleas for federal projects and programs to benefit the folks back home. However, *New York Times* reporter David E. Rosenbaum concluded that nobody "won" the battle over the FY 1996 budget:

> In many respects, the battle over this year's budget ended with a whimper. The agreement between President Clinton and the Republican Congress involves only one-tenth of the $1.6 trillion Federal budget and will remain in effect only for the next five months. It does not deal at all with the giant benefit programs like Social Security, Medicare, Medicaid and welfare that consume about two-thirds of all Federal spending. Nor does it make any changes in tax policy.[48]

The debate over the FY 1997 budget revealed a shift back to the usual election year protection of program spending that helps reelect incumbents. In 1996 the highly centralized House of a year earlier became more like the more decentralized Senate. The internal struggle demonstrated the shift when, in early July, a skirmish broke out between congressional appropriators and the GOP leaders. The appropriators wanted to be left alone to move their bills, and the GOP leaders were pushing them to pass a "standby" bill that would ensure an on-time adjournment before the election even if all the appropriations bills were not passed.[49] In mid-July Robert Livingston, R-La., chairman of the House Appropriations Committee, appeared to beat the leadership and a proposal by Majority Leader Armey to pass a continuing resolution (CR) before the August recess. Sen. Mark O. Hatfield, R-Ore., chairman of the Senate Appropriations Committee, called the suggestion by Armey and Senate Majority Leader Lott "negative" and "sort of defeatism." When Hatfield was asked if the party leaders had made any persuasive arguments that he should back the CR bill, he replied, "I didn't hear it. Of course, I wear hearing aids."[50] The battle among President Clinton, the congressional Republican Party leaders, and the Republican rank and file over the FY 1997 budget was fully engaged as the 1996 election approached. A *New York Times* editorial summarized the legacies of the 104th Congress:

> With Newt Gingrich leading the parade, the new Republican majority swaggered into Washington in January of last year convinced that their radical agenda had popular appeal. In the beginning, their confidence did not seem misplaced. They dominated the national debate and instituted significant reforms of congressional procedures. Then they overreached. They shut down the government in an effort to win huge spending cuts, and all they really got for their pains was a reputation—cleverly manipulated by President Clinton—for callousness. Now, as the 104th passes into history, the very Republicans who had defied Mr. Clinton are trying to build a more moderate legislative record to take to the voters.[51]

The 104th Congress completed its budgetary battle with the president, averting a second government shutdown, through pragmatic compromise on domestic spending. Desperate to campaign back home, the Republicans took no chances in triggering a last-minute confrontation with the president. In the end, President Clinton and the congressional Democrats held the upper hand.

Conclusion

Dramatic policy outcomes did not result from the passage of budget reform legislation: deficits and entitlements kept growing.[52] Instead, change came about because of a transformational election that provided the motivation for Congress and the president to attempt to balance the budget within a specific number of years. Since the end of World War II, the real growth in government spending had happened almost automatically through pluralistic incrementalism. The collective strength of special interests persuaded Congress and the president to add more programs and more spending. Interest groups, agencies, and committees successfully practiced "strategic protection" of their favorite spending programs securing their "fair share" of increase as they did before the major congressional budget process reforms were implemented. The budget game got tighter after passage of each reform, starting in 1974, but no major groups were significantly disadvantaged by the reforms until the Republican 104th Congress established the priority of cutting the size of federal government spending. No major programs were cut by a president or Congress until the partisan change came in both the House and Senate after the 1994 election. No congressional committees tried to abolish major programs under their jurisdiction until the 104th Congress. Presidential and congressional spending priorities were not greatly changed as a direct result of the 1974 budget process reforms, GRH I or II, or the 1990 Budget Enforcement Act. Spending change came with the centralization of the House in 1995 and the electoral promise by the House Republicans to balance the budget in seven years, cut taxes, and reduce the size of the federal government.

The emphasis of the 1990 BEA reforms was on spending, not deficits, but the budget battles of the 104th Congress were fought over deficits and program cuts. Presidential budget strategies have concerned spending priorities and cuts in programs within zero-sum limits defined by the reforms of the 1990s and the realities of a more conservative and centralized leadership in the House. These reforms made spending trade-offs more visible and imposed more control over the process. The centralization of power over the budget process in the House in the first session of the 104th Congress and the increased discipline of the congressional Republican Party reduced the power of the president until the Republicans were blamed for the government shutdown. Ironically, the shutdown of the federal government over the budget and Speaker Gingrich's highly visible confrontation with the White House helped to resuscitate the Clinton presidency.

The Budget Enforcement Act, the Balanced Budget Act, and other reforms of the 1990s insulated Congress from accountability and made it difficult to assign responsibility for the growth of the federal budget or the size of the deficit. The reality of the congressional budget process in the 104th Congress was the opposite. It was open and transparent; the policy differences between the Democrats and the Republicans, the president and Congress were clear.

Further centralization or decentralization of the congressional budget process will come as a result of elections, as it did in 1994. In the end, the desires of the American electorate will have the strongest impact on the battle over the federal budget. Congressional interpretation of the voters' wishes happens every two years when voters have reacted to the outcome of the previous two-year budget war and the new spending and taxing priorities that resulted. The final decision about the structure of the budget, how to balance it, and further reform is up to the electorate. Ultimately, the voters must make the critical decision about spending, taxing, and what kind of government and society they want.

Notes

Research for this chapter is partially based upon interviews with White House staff, House and Senate members, congressional staff, and other informed observers. I am grateful for the time they gave and for their observations. I especially thank Rep. Robert Livingston, R-La., Rep. David Obey, D-Wis., Dan Meyer, chief of staff to Speaker Newt Gingrich, R-Ga., and Dr. Patrick J. Griffin, assistant to the president for legislative affairs, for sharing their information and insights about the appropriations process and the budget negotiations between Congress and President Clinton's White House in 1995 and 1996. I also thank the School of Public Affairs and the Center for Congressional and Presidential Studies at American University for supporting this research. Special thanks also go to Larry Dodd for his helpful suggestions for this chapter.

1. Elizabeth Drew, *Showdown: The Struggle Between the Gingrich Congress and the Clinton White House* (New York: Simon and Schuster, 1996), 203.
2. See Joint Committee on the Organization of Congress, *Background Materials: Supplemental Information Provided to Members to the Joint Committee on the Organization of Congress,* S. Rept. 103–155 (Washington, D.C.: U.S. Government Printing Office, 1993); and JCOC, *Organization of Congress: Final Report,* H. Rept. 103–413/S. Rept. 103–215, 3 vols.
3. See in the 104th Congress: H.J. Res. 1, Balanced Budget Amendment; H.R. 2, Line-Item Veto Act; and H.R. 5, Unfunded Mandate Reform Act.
4. Some of the data and observations in this chapter are based on my analysis in "Congressional-Presidential Battles to Balance the Budget," in *Rivals for Power,* ed. James A. Thurber (Washington, D.C.: CQ Press, 1996).
5. For a discussion of these reforms, see James A. Thurber, "The Impact of Budget Reform on Presidential and Congressional Governance," in *Divided Democracy: Cooperation and Conflict Between the President and Congress,* ed. James A. Thurber (Washington, D.C.: CQ Press, 1991), 145–170; James A. Thurber, "Budget Continuity and Change: An Assessment of the Congressional Budget Process," in *Studies in U.S. Politics,* ed. D. K. Adams (Manchester, England: Manchester University Press, 1989), 78–118; Louis Fisher, "Ten Years of the Budget Act: Still Searching for Controls," *Public Budgeting and Finance* 5 (Autumn 1985); Harry Havens, "Gramm-Rudman-Hollings: Origins and Implementation," *Public Budgeting and Finance* 6 (Autumn 1986): 424; Lance T. LeLoup, Barbara Luck Graham, and Stacy Barwick, "Deficit Politics and Constitutional Government: The Impact of Gramm-Rudman-Hollings," *Public Budgeting and Finance* 7 (Spring 1987): 83–103; and Raphael Thelwell, "Gramm-Rudman-Hollings Four Years Later: A Dangerous Illusion," *Public Administration Review* 50 (March/April 1990): 190–197.
6. One of the important reforms instituted by the 1974 Budget Act was the creation of the Congressional Budget Office (CBO). This agency serves as Congress's principal source of information and analysis on the budget and on spending and revenue legis-

lation. The CBO's specific mandate is, first, to assist the House and Senate Budget Committees and the spending and revenue committees, and, second, to respond to requests for information from other committees and individual members of Congress. Prior to the creation of the CBO, Congress had to rely on the president's budget estimates and economic forecasts and the Joint Economic Committee's annual analysis of the economy and fiscal policy.

7. Thurber, "Budget Continuity and Change," 80.
8. See Allen Schick, *Reconciliation and the Congressional Budget Process* (Washington, D.C.: American Enterprise Institute, 1981); D. Tate, "Reconciliation Breeds Tumult as Committees Tackle Cuts: Revolutionary Budget Tool," *Congressional Quarterly Weekly Report,* May 23, 1981, 887–891.
9. Another measure of budget deficit problems is the imbalance of outlays and receipts as a percentage of the gross national product (GNP). The deficit is coming down as a percentage of GNP. For example, outlays were 24.3 percent of GNP, and receipts were 18.1 percent of GNP in 1983; 23.7 percent outlays to 18.4 percent receipts in 1986; and 22.2 percent outlays to 19.2 percent receipts in 1989. See Congressional Budget Office, *The Economic and Budget Outlook: Fiscal Years 1991–1995* (January 1990), Appendix E, Table E-2, at 123.
10. These deadlines significantly altered prior budget process deadlines. Notably, the new deadlines have been delayed or modified informally each year since GRH I and GRH II were passed.
11. See Rudolph G. Penner and Alan J. Abramson, *Broken Purse Strings: Congressional Budgeting 1974–1988* (Washington, D.C.: Urban Institute Press, 1988), 97.
12. *Bowsher v. Synar,* 478 U.S. 714, decided July 7, 1986.
13. House, Committee on the Budget, *The Fiscal Year 1991 Budget,* 101st Cong., 2d sess., Feb. 2, 1990, committee print.
14. See Senate, Committee on Governmental Affairs, "Proposed Budget Reforms: A Critical Analysis," in *Proposed Budget Reform: A Critical Analysis,* 100th Congress, 2d sess., prepared by Allen Schick (Washington, D.C.: Congressional Research Service and the Library of Congress, April 1988): 52.
15. John E. Yang and Steven Mufson, "Package Termed Best Circumstances Permit," *Washington Post,* Oct. 29, 1990, A4.
16. Congressional Budget Office, *The 1990 Budget Agreement: An Interim Assessment,* December 1990.
17. Detailed explanations of the Omnibus Budget Reconciliation Act of 1990 (OBRA) and Title XIII of that act, the Budget Enforcement Act of 1990, can be found in Richard Doyle and Jerry McCaffery, "The Budget Enforcement Act of 1990: The Path to No Fault Budgeting," *Public Budgeting and Finance* 10 (Spring 1991); and Congressional Budget Office, *The 1990 Budget Agreement.*
18. Budget Enforcement Act of 1990, P.L. No. 101–508, sec. 13101, 1990 U.S.C.C.A.N. (104 Stat.) 1388–574.
19. Budget Enforcement Act of 1990, sec. 13204, 1388–616.
20. Congressional Budget Office, *Pay-as-You-Go Budgeting,* a staff memorandum, March 1990.
21. Budget Enforcement Act of 1990, sec. 13301, 1388–573.
22. Budget Enforcement Act of 1990, secs. 13302 and 13303, 1388–623. The "fire wall" points of order provisions provided for in the 1990 Budget Enforcement Act differ between the House and the Senate. In the House the provision "creates a 'fire wall' point of order (as freestanding legislation) to prohibit the consideration of legislation that would change the actuarial balance of the Social Security trust funds over a five-year or fifteen-year period. In the case of legislation decreasing Social Security revenues, the prohibition would not apply if the legislation also included an equiva-

lent increase in Medicare taxes for the period covered by the legislation." The Senate "also creates a fire wall to protect Social Security financing but does so by expanding certain budget enforcement provisions of the Congressional Budget Act of 1974. The Senate amendment expands the prohibition in Section 310(g) of the budget act to specifically protect Social Security financing, prohibits the consideration of a reported budget resolution calling for a reduction in Social Security surpluses, and included Social Security in the enforcement procedures under Sections 302 and 311 of the budget act. The Senate amendment also requires the secretary of Health and Human Services to provide an actuarial analysis of any legislation affecting Social Security, and generally prohibits the consideration of legislation lacking such an analysis." Conference Committee Report, final draft, 101st Cong., 2d sess. (1990), sec. 6, "Treatment of Social Security," 10.

23. See Thurber, "Budget Continuity and Change," 78–118; and James A. Thurber and Samantha Durst, "Delay, Deadlock, and Deficits: Evaluating Congressional Budget Reform," in Thomas D. Lynch, ed., *Federal Budget and Financial Management Reform* (Westport, Conn.: Greenwood Press, 1991).
24. President George Bush, press release, Dec. 21, 1990.
25. I would like to thank James V. Saturno, Government Division, Congressional Research Service, Library of Congress, for this observation.
26. For an analysis of the impact of the 1994 election on Congress, see James A. Thurber, "Remaking Congress After the Electoral Earthquake of 1994," in *Remaking Congress: Change and Stability in the 1990s,* ed. James A. Thurber and Roger H. Davidson (Washington, D.C.: CQ Press, 1995), 1–9. Some observations in this chapter were made by James A. Thurber, in "Republican Centralization of the Congressional Budget Process," in Lawrence C. Dodd, ed., *Extension of Remarks: The New Republican Congress: Explanations, Assessments, and Prospects,* Legislative Studies Group, American Political Science Association, December 1995, 3–4.
27. See James A. Thurber, "Representation, Accountability, and Efficiency in Divided Party Control of Government," *PS: Political Science and Politics* 24 (December 1991): 653–657, for a discussion of the impact of divided party government on congressional decision making.
28. See David W. Brady, "The Causes and Consequences of Divided Government: Toward a New Theory of American Politics?" *American Political Science Review* 87 (March 1993): 189–194. For an opposing view on the negative effects of divided government, see David R. Mayhew, *Divided We Govern* (New Haven: Yale University Press, 1991).
29. See Jeff Shear, "Power Loss," *National Journal,* April 20, 1996, 874–878, for a description of the conflict between the House Appropriations Committee and the House Republican leadership over control of the budget and appropriations processes.
30. See James G. Gimpel, *Fulfilling the Contract: The First 100 Days* (Boston: Allyn and Bacon, 1996).
31. For further discussion of these reforms, see Thurber and Davidson, *Remaking Congress.*
32. Jeffrey H. Birnbaum, "The Thursday Regulars," *Time* magazine, March 27, 1995, 31.
33. Guy Gugliotta, "Democratic Tactics Prove Useful to GOP Leaders," *Washington Post,* Sept. 17, 1995, A4.
34. David Maraniss and Michael Weisskopf, *Tell Newt to Shut Up!* (New York: Touchstone, 1996), 36.
35. Reported in interview with House Republican leadership staff, February 1996.
36. Maraniss and Weisskopf, *Tell Newt to Shut Up!* 167.

37. Helen Dewar and Eric Pianin, "Concession Supersedes Revolution," *Washington Post,* Sept. 29, 1996, A14.
38. See George Hager, "House GOP Rebels Make Sure Accord Doesn't Come Easy," *Congressional Quarterly Weekly Report,* June 15, 1996, 1653.
39. Ibid., 1653–6.
40. See the vote on H. Con. Res. 178, "Fiscal 1997 Budget Resolution/Conference Report," in *Congressional Quarterly Weekly Report,* June 15, 1996, 1717.
41. Hager, "House GOP Rebels Make Sure," 1655.
42. Ibid.
43. See Thurber, "Remaking Congress After the Electoral Earthquake of 1994," 1–8; and James A. Thurber, "Thunder from the Right: Observations About the Elections," *The Public Manager* (Winter 1994–95): 13–16.
44. Roy T. Meyers, *Strategic Budgeting* (Ann Arbor: University of Michigan Press, 1994), 1.
45. Dan Morgan, "GOP Congress's Budget Deep-Freeze Begins to Melt," *Washington Post,* July 22, 1996, A10.
46. Ibid., A1.
47. For a discussion of the House appropriators' reassertion of power, see Shear, "Power Loss."
48. David E. Rosenbaum, "Ammunition for the Fall," *New York Times,* April 26, 1996, 1.
49. See George Hager, "Appropriators Rebuff 'CR' Pushed by GOP Leaders," *Congressional Quarterly Weekly Report,* July 13, 1996, 1951.
50. Ibid.
51. Editorial, *New York Times,* Sept. 29, 1996, E14.
52. See James A. Thurber, "If the Game Is Too Hard, Change the Rules: Congressional Budget Reform in the 1990s," *Remaking Congress,* 130–144.

15. The Contract with America: Origins and Assessments

John B. Bader

On September 27, 1994, more than three hundred Republican candidates for the House of Representatives, both incumbents and challengers, gathered on the west side of the U.S. Capitol building. With flags fluttering under an intensely blue sky and cameras recording each choreographed moment, party leaders, including Rep. Newt Gingrich of Georgia, began a series of exhortative speeches. "If the American people accept this contract," Gingrich boldly predicted, "we will have begun the journey to renew American civilization. . . . Together we can help every human across the planet seek freedom, prosperity, safety and the rule of law. That is what is at stake."[1] Then, a few at a time, the large group of women and men walked confidently to a table to sign an ambitious document called the Contract with America. Candidates signing this contract pledged to address a ten-point agenda in the first one hundred days of a Congress led by a Republican majority.

That agenda, which included items such as a balanced budget constitutional amendment and term limits for members of Congress, seemed as audacious as the notion that it would be enacted by a Republican majority in the House. When the 1994 elections gave Republicans their first majority in forty years, their party leaders did not back down from the promise of fulfilling their contract. In fact, they insisted they had a mandate to do just that. "This election was an election of ideas," said Republican National Committee Chairman Haley Barbour shortly after the election. "Voters clearly understood what they were doing when they voted for us."[2] Gingrich and other Republican leaders, such as Rep. Dick Armey of Texas, relentlessly pursued this agenda in the first one hundred days of the 104th Congress. They acknowledged that only a minority of voters had heard of the contract, but they insisted that candidates had run on it and that large popular majorities supported each item and the principles they embodied. Republicans argued that they had the legitimate authority to bring these priorities to a vote. And they did so with a vengeance.

It is hard to say without speculating what long-term effects the contract will have on American politics and public policy, but easy to accept that it has had a profound impact in the short run. It may have been critical to a historic election, and it certainly dictated the tone and substance of political debate in 1995 and 1996. Plus, it is a great story, filled with audacious personalities and risky strategies. For these reasons, the Contract with America is an obvious target for political analysis. What does it mean? Where did it come from? Why and how did Republicans choose the issues they did? This essay attempts to trace the contract's origins using a framework originally developed to understand how Democratic leaders set priorities during many years of divided government.[3]

Setting Agendas in Divided Government

Some might think the Contract with America was a unique example of agenda setting by party leaders in Congress. Few can recall another time when a leader like Newt Gingrich took such a high-profile approach to choosing and publicizing a set of issues for which the party would be held accountable. Others would be skeptical that party leaders could play any meaningful role, although some scholars have argued otherwise.[4] In fact, we need look back only seven years before the contract to find an example of aggressive agenda setting by congressional leaders. During the 100th Congress (1987–1988) Speaker Jim Wright of Texas effectively pushed his agenda—including highway reconstruction, clean water, and relief for homelessness—toward enactment. The 100th Congress is well remembered as one of the most productive in the modern era.

The similarity between Newt Gingrich and Jim Wright is ironic: Gingrich relentlessly pursued allegations that Wright had violated ethical standards, and these charges eventually led to Wright's resignation in 1989. But two more important points should be made. First, the experiences of Wright and Gingrich underscore the importance of divided government, meaning that Congress and the presidency are controlled by different political parties. In this setting, the majority or "opposition" party in Congress has little incentive to follow the president's lead on priorities. Wright, a Democrat, had no compelling reason to listen to Ronald Reagan, a Republican often hostile to the more liberal Democratic agenda. Gingrich had little inclination to subscribe to Bill Clinton's agenda for similar partisan and ideological reasons. He and his associates developed the contract to apply if Republicans took the majority and returned the government to split partisan control, which occurred after the 1994 elections. So, Wright and Gingrich operated under a partisan system that encourages majority party leaders in Congress to develop agendas independently of the president.

Second, the Contract with America represents a tradition in Congress encouraged by years of split partisan rule. Divided government has become a regular feature of American politics. It characterizes 59 percent of the postwar period (thirty of the fifty-one years between 1945 and 1996) and 79 percent of the years between 1969 and 1996 (twenty-two of twenty-eight years). Divided government returned in 1995 after only two years of unified control by Democrats. Given the regularity of this arrangement, it is easy to see that Gingrich would not be the first leader to choose issues; nor was Wright the only other. Agenda setting is a regular part of majority party leadership in divided government, as the lists in Table 15-1 of priority issues from six periods suggest.[5] While agenda setting reached new heights and became more visible with the development of the contract, it evolved over a long time.

Table 15-1 Party Leadership Priorities for Select Congresses, 1969–1990, and the Contract with America, 1995–1996

91st (1969–1970)	94th (1975–1976)	97th (1981–1982)
Tax reform	Tax cuts	Social Security
Welfare reform	Lower interest rates	Clean air amendments
Crime	Budgeting	Emergency housing aid
National environmental policy	Emergency housing	Trade: domestic content
Social Security increase	Tax reform	Emergency jobs: labor supplement
Clean air	Consumer Protection Agency	Tax cuts
Education: ESEA extension	National health insurance	Budget cuts
Wage and price controls	Highway construction	Defense spending increase
Defense spending cuts	Energy: conservation, taxes	Crime
Military in Cambodia		Gas tax/highways/transit
Selective Service reform		Tax increases: TEFRA
Clean water		Interest rates: control of Federal Reserve
100th (1987–1988)	**101st (1989–1990)**	**Contract with America**
Highway construction	Nonlethal aid to contras	Balanced budget amendment/Line item veto
Clean water	Disabled discrimination	Revised crime bill
Homelessness	Child care	Welfare reform
Farm disaster relief	Clean air	Family tax cuts/adoption
Trade	Sanctions against China	Tax credit for children
Catastrophic health insurance	Capital gains tax cut	UN troop restrictions
Welfare reform	Budget deficit reduction	Tax cuts for elderly
Campaign finance reform	Debt ceiling	Capital gains/small business
Peace in Nicaragua	Minimum wage increase	Tort reform
Budget: reconciliation	Campaign finance reform	Term limits for Congress
Housing: FHA	Oil spill liability	Congressional reform
Budget: resolution	Airline buyout restrictions	
	Congressional pay increase	
	High technology	

Sources: Almanacs (Washington, D.C.: Congressional Quarterly, Inc., various years); *Congressional Quarterly Weekly Reports;* archival materials; interviews; *TV Guide;* and other materials for the Contract with America.

Note: Lists are not in rank order.

Whatever the incentives, leaders do not set priorities willy-nilly if they want those choices to be meaningful and influential. They cannot push members too hard or force them in a direction they do not wish to go. The urge to act independently of the president is checked by the need to make decisions that fit the institutional and political environment. Leaders choose priorities to instigate change, but they are bound by the status quo. It is a difficult path to follow, a difficult dilemma to resolve. I have found that they generally succeed in this endeavor by setting strategic goals and by finding issues that promise to advance those goals.[6] Leader goals include: highlighting partisan differences, demonstrating bipartisan agreement, showing deference to others, asserting congressional independence, proving competence in solving problems, and providing policy leadership.[7] The choice of a particular goal reflects the political environment at the time, such as the nature of presidential relations, and the institutional constraints of the House and Senate.

After setting their goals, leaders evaluate or *define* issues by several criteria: the strength of the issue's backers (called "policy entrepreneurs"), the amount of support in Congress, the level of public enthusiasm, the presence of a triggering event, and an estimate of the associated costs.[8] The priority-setting process involves finding issues with particular characteristics that promise to advance one or several strategic goals. Party leaders choose those issues as priorities, so decisions can be understood as a matching process between goals and issues. Agenda setting in Congress is a strategic exercise.

The evidence from numerous interviews and material gathered from staff memos, advertising, and media coverage suggests that the goal-issue framework helps us understand how and why the Republican leadership developed the Contract with America. Like Democrats, the Republicans chose their priorities strategically. They began with basic principles. They set their goals to fit those principles, their personal propensities, and current political conditions. They then searched for issues that promised to fulfill those goals. To do so, issues had to have strong support among Republican candidates and widespread popularity with voters. The framework holds up rather nicely to the challenge of providing insight to this most recent example of leadership priority setting.

That is not to say that Republicans make decisions for the exact same reasons as Democrats or that their view of issues is identical. The contract embodies goals that are far more partisan in nature. The issues listed there give more weight, for example, to public opinion. These are important differences worth examining. But the overall schema of finding issues that meet certain needs seems to describe Republican decision making processes as well as it did Democratic.

Beginnings

House Republicans met in Salisbury, Maryland, in January 1994. They thought the situation looked promising for gaining the majority. The presidency was now in Democratic hands, freeing them of the obligations that had bound them to George Bush's agenda. Gingrich, who had a well-deserved reputation as a tough partisan, was set to become floor leader because Bob Michel of Illinois was retiring. And President Clinton had made some strategic blunders early in his administration—gays in the military, tax increases, ethics charges, health care reform, and reversals in foreign policy. The Salisbury Conference, explains participant Rep. Deborah Pryce of Ohio, was a time to take "a hard look at who we were as a party, where we were going and what we stood for."[9] If Republicans were to gain control of Congress, they needed a way to mobilize political support. Conference participants believed that they could do this by agreeing to certain "guiding principles" that would suggest strategies for gaining support. They settled on five politically conservative values: individual liberty, limited government, economic opportunity, personal responsibility, and security at home and abroad.

Shortly thereafter, Gingrich met with Armey, Tom DeLay of Texas, Robert Walker of Pennsylvania, and Bill Paxon of New York, all members of the House Republican Conservative Opportunity Society. They came to two conclusions: they had a chance to regain the majority and they needed a positive agenda to supplement any attacks they might make against Clinton. This agenda would be based upon the five Salisbury principles. Gingrich asked Armey to head the development of a ten-item agenda that they could bring to a floor vote in the first one hundred days of a Republican-controlled House. Gingrich believed the number ten had a "mythic quality" in American culture. And since Franklin Roosevelt's presidency, one hundred days has become the standard—no matter how unreasonable—for legislative success. Finally, Gingrich argued that House Republicans should organize a large gathering during the fall election period to unveil this agenda, an idea based upon a similar event held by GOP supporters of the Kemp-Roth tax cut plan in 1980.

The Contract with America began with people and principles long before it became policy. From the start, the process of developing the contract was a *deductive* one, moving from broader principles influenced by ideology and personal experience to specific strategies shaped by changing circumstances to concrete policy initiatives. This deductive process precisely describes the way Democratic Party leaders have chosen priorities, a process captured by the goal-issue matching model. Such observations, then, encourage the use of this model to understand the details of the contract's development. To further that exercise, we need to identify which goals Republican leaders were seeking to advance when they chose the contract issues. By identifying those goals, we can better understand the selection process.

The Goals of the Contract

House Republican leaders developed the Contract with America for two main reasons. First, they wanted to capture a majority in Congress and to shake off years of frustration and neglect. To accomplish this goal, they needed to highlight differences with the Democratic Party. This partisan goal drove the process to find issues on which Republicans could campaign. The contract may not have been a campaign "gimmick," as many critics charged, but it was designed principally to drive a wedge between the parties. Second, leaders like Gingrich and Armey wanted the contract to prove that Republicans were competent problem-solvers who could be trusted to run Congress in an open and honest manner. The

GOP would pursue this policy goal vigorously and doggedly to restore the party's reputation for innovation. These two leader goals—partisan differences and policy competence—provided the impetus for the contract and dictated which issues Republican leaders would choose as priorities.

The two goals are closely related. Republicans felt they could make a strong case to voters for rejecting Clinton and congressional Democrats, but they needed to show that they offered an appealing alternative. John Boehner, the conference chair, says that the contract began as a campaign project, but he and other leaders knew that negative feelings toward Democrats do not translate into positive feelings for the Republican Party. They needed a magnet to generate enthusiasm and support. As Armey writes, "Standing up against the Clinton administration's tax-and-spend assault on American families will be worth a lot to Republicans in the November elections, but standing up for a positive agenda to help restore the American dream and the integrity of government will be worth a lot more."[10] That agenda would support the notion that Republicans could do the job and do it better than Democrats had. Furthermore, they would do the job in a way that could be clearly evaluated. The contract would establish a checklist of accomplishments on which the party could be judged. The promise of competence and accountability was uniquely Republican, they argued, not Democratic. It would justify their election over Democrats and their continued control of Congress.

However related, the goals of highlighting differences and proving competence can be considered independently. Republican leaders emphasized party differences in the contract to underscore three important political points: that Republicans rejected the presidential leadership of Bill Clinton; that the Republican Party would operate the House differently from Democrats over a forty-year reign; and that the GOP was highly unified, disciplined, and determined.

Weakened by two years of miscalculations, Clinton was an easy target for the Republican leadership. The president had failed to deliver, Republicans argued, on promises such as health care reform and a middle class tax cut and he should be held accountable. In contrast, the GOP would accomplish more in one hundred days than Clinton had in two years. The "White Book," a briefing packet prepared by the RNC for candidates, underscores these differences with a list of failures entitled "Clinton's First 100 Days" and explains their strategic significance:

> The House Republican "Contract with America" will show the country the fundamental differences between President Clinton's misguided policies and the Republicans' common sense goals. By outlining the Republicans' agenda for the first 100 days of a Republican-controlled Congress, the American people will better be able to distinguish between the failed policies of the Democrats and the positive proposals being offered by House Republicans.

Highlighting differences with House Democrats and their leadership was a goal from the inception of the contract. In a June 8, 1994, draft letter from Gingrich, Armey, and National Republican Congressional Committee Chairman Bill

Paxon to GOP candidates, that goal is made clear: "The purpose of this event [the contract unveiling] is to show the American people that the House GOP is different from the Democrats who have controlled the House for the last 40 years." The opening lines of the signed contract say, "This year's election offers the chance, after four decades of one-party control, to bring to the House a new majority that will transform the way Congress works."

A final partisan point GOP leaders wished to make was that Republicans are a cohesive and determined group. The corollary to showing the Democrats in a negative light was to give Republicans a positive vision around which they could rally. Gingrich believed that Republicans could take advantage of Democratic weakness only if his party was united. As already noted, developing a set of unifying principles was the purpose of the Salisbury Conference. But the leaders wanted something more than ideological unity. They wanted a sense of team spirit, a common belief that their party was strong, vibrant, and worthy of holding power. Candidates meeting at the contract unveiling excitedly swapped "war stories." At the least, the event gave individuals running for separate seats the sensation of unified purpose and may have marked the beginning of the solidarity for which freshmen of the 104th Congress became so well known. Republicans needed to feel like a majority party if they were going to take the majority. The contract was designed as an *integrative exercise in self-definition*.

In addition to highlighting partisan differences, Republican leaders wanted the contract to prove their competence in policy making. This goal is less politically charged and less divisive than showing differences, a point made to the leadership by polling consultants. These consultants urged the leadership to downplay partisanship, as it would only exacerbate voter cynicism. GOP leaders already had decided that a partisan strategy alone was insufficient to win support, and that they needed a plan for governance that would prove Republicans and Congress could competently deal with the nation's problems. Following the failures of Presidents Bush and Clinton as well as the gridlock and partisan conflict in Congress, this was a difficult case to make. But Gingrich said that with the contract, Republicans "would actually have a game plan" that could focus the energies and attention of its new members and its new committee chairs, which would increase the likelihood of success. And, Boehner argued, it could help in another way: "It's both the credibility of the party and the credibility of the institution that can benefit from this. . . . [The public] will think that this is a place where innovation takes place."

Republican leaders believed that more than institutional credibility was at stake, however. Their success would "restore the bonds of trust between the people and their elected representatives," reads the text of the signed document. The contract was burdened with the heavy responsibility of "repairing the disconnect" between government and a suspicious citizenry.[11] This goal may seem unreasonably ambitious given an American culture built around distrust of collective efforts, but that was the mission envisioned in the contract. A leadership staff member explains:

> One of the goals was to demonstrate to the American people that we are worthy of their trust to govern. Getting control for the first time in 40 years is a big responsibility that we are asking for, an untested proposition for most Americans. We wanted to let them know what to expect. We understand you would not otherwise know what to expect.

Data from focus group research suggested to the leadership that the contract could show voters what to expect and give them a way to keep score. Voters were invited to save the *TV Guide* version of the contract, to check off each item as "done," and to "throw us out" if the contract was broken. Supporters of Ross Perot's independent candidacy for president in 1992—a critical group of swing voters—found the enforcement clause particularly appealing. It made Republicans explicitly accountable. And it could prove them to be competent trustees of power.

Searching for Issues

The Republican search for particular issues to include in the contract, like those conducted by Democratic leaders, can best be understood as a systematic, comprehensive, and pluralistic *gathering process.* GOP leaders and staff gathered input from a variety of sources. They listened to other House members, challengers to Democratic seats, Senate Republicans, interest groups, and the public. They then compiled an exhaustive list of new and traditional GOP issues from these inputs and began a winnowing process based on which issues best fit their strategic needs. Those needs provided the criteria for selection. As they were motivated to show partisan differences and policy competence, they needed issues that had high levels of support within the Republican Party, particularly in the House. These issues would help them show how unified the party was and, because they could build majorities easily, prove they could get the job done. Issues with widespread popular support also fit these goals, as Republican leaders wanted the contract to make a high-profile statement about their party and Congress.

Armey and his staff began the process by conducting a survey of the Republican Conference and other GOP House candidates. Respondents to the seven-page survey were advised that their input would shape the contents of the not-yet-named contract, that the "canvass seeks to get your assessment of the desirability and political feasibility of more than 60 potential legislative initiatives." They were also asked to rank a list of twelve issues, vaguely described by terms such as "real congressional reform," "pro-family tax reforms," "cut spending now," and "strengthening our national defense and foreign policy." More than 100 members and 150 challengers answered this survey, and leadership staff members tabulated the responses to find which issues had the greatest consensus.

A member/challenger survey of this kind has no precedent. Democratic leaders regularly but informally polled their members, often relying on the whip system to give them a sense of enthusiasm. On rare occasions, such as the salary increase debate in 1989, Democrats conducted a formal poll of their membership. But Democrats had never conducted a member survey for the explicit purpose of developing an agenda.

By surveying their immediate constituents, the GOP leaders made it clear that support in Congress was the pivotal variable in choosing agenda items. "Unity was a big factor," said an aide to Armey. Leaders wanted an agenda with clear conservative leanings that had the support of the membership. Tom DeLay, who became House majority whip, said that the leadership wanted issues that could be completed within one hundred days. "We weren't going to promise something we couldn't do," he said.[12] For that, they would need to have near unanimity to avoid time-consuming debate. Health care reform, tax reform, and education would require more time, so they are mentioned as future issues in the contract *TV Guide* ad. By the same token, they wished to avoid issues that would divide the party. The member survey asked if voluntary school prayer should be included, but leaders saw the potential for an internal party battle over the issue. Abortion met the same fate. Where there were divisions among respondents, leaders looked for issues that made bolder, more populist statements. Many senior members opposed term limits, but its wide popularity and its determined backing by newer members and challengers assured it a spot in the contract.

Republican leaders also took public opinion seriously when developing the Contract with America. Gingrich insisted that every issue have at least public approval ratings of 60 percent to 70 percent. "Politics is about public opinion and gathering public support," he said in defending the use of popularity in choosing issues.[13] The voting public, after all, would determine the outcome of the 1994 election, so it made good strategic sense to be sure the public backed every item on the contract. Indeed, Republicans defended their "mandate" after the election on the basis that most Americans wanted those issues addressed even if they had not heard of the contract itself. Popularity proved particularly important in the selection of congressional reforms, the balanced budget amendment, and term limits. Gingrich was understandably pleased, therefore, to see such popularity confirmed after the election. "I was incredibly excited on Friday to pick up *USA Today*," he said in early December 1994, "and read the very front page: 'Public backs GOP agenda.'"[14]

But the use of polling should not be overstated. Republican leaders commissioned polls only after selecting the issues for the contract to be sure they were popular. Luntz Research of Arlington, Virginia, conducted a poll of one thousand registered voters that confirmed public enthusiasm for the contract. Frank Luntz insists that this was a confirming activity, not one used in development. Leaders included defense issues, he points out, even though such issues had less support than school prayer, which was excluded.

Instead, Republicans used polling data principally for marketing research. Ed Goeas of the Tarrance Group, another polling company, wrote the Republican Conference on August 30, 1994, to stress the importance of congressional reform. Voters wanted certain reforms, he said, not extensive changes, so reforms need to be well specified. Such polls determined the order of the contract items, with the most popular—the balanced budget amendment—at the top and the second most popular—term limits—at the bottom. Consultants assured leaders that people remember the first and last item of any given list. Other issues were listed in descending order of popularity. Public opinion research also affected the wording of the contract. Luntz ran a focus group of independent voters in Denver, Colorado, which suggested the use of the term "citizen legislators" to describe term limits, the use of a toll-free number to get more information, and the repetition of the enforcement clause to "throw them out" if they failed. Democratic leaders have become quite sophisticated in the use of polling, but the use of such data to develop a marketing strategy for advancing an agenda was quite new—and quite effective.

GOP leaders solicited the input of others in the development of the contract, but the responses had little impact. DeLay reportedly consulted more than one hundred interest groups. Lobbyists were invited to speak before the working groups. But there is little evidence that these exercises had much effect on the outcome. Policy entrepreneurs—those people backing specific issues—generally did not matter as leaders weighed collective interests over individual demands. House leaders also paid little real attention to Senate concerns. The Senate Republican leader, Robert Dole of Kansas, publicly expressed little enthusiasm for the contract items.

Finally, leaders apparently gave little weight to cost while developing the contract. Rep. John Kasich of Ohio made an effort to consider cost, as Republicans wanted to avoid accusations that they would add to the federal budget deficit. Kasich suggested the use of "dynamic scoring" in projecting budget costs, whereby the effects of program changes would be taken into account. But cost considerations do not appear to have mattered much in the selection process. The Democrats made this point a focus of their criticism. The media also latched onto budgeting figures in their comments. The *National Journal* called Republicans the "Santa Clauses," and a *New York Times* editorial called the contract "Reaganism in a rear-view mirror . . . not only reckless but deceptive."[15] Even Republicans in office had difficulty with the numbers. Sen. Hank Brown of Colorado said, "All these tax cuts are good ideas, but whether they will be enacted depends on the key question of where the money comes from."[16] Republican staff members on the Budget Committee estimated net costs at $190 billion over five years. Such numbers suggest that GOP leaders did not weigh costs heavily. They also suggest that agendas like the contract cannot both further political ends and respect the bottom line.

The process of developing the Contract with America shows that Republican party leaders made an effort to listen to many voices before deciding on a limited set of priorities. It also shows that they weighed variables differently as a result of pursuing goals that demanded party consensus and strong public approval. They needed consensus to enact legislation, popularity to elect a majority to Congress. Overall, leaders paid closest attention to support in Congress

Table 15-2 The Contract with America, with Goals and Issue Dimensions

Issue	Primary Leader Goal	Secondary Leader Goal	Entrepreneur Strength	Support in Congress	Public Opinion	Cost	Trigger
Reform Congress	Competence	Differences	None	Moderate	High	Moderate	Moderate
Balanced budget	Differences	Competence	None	Moderate	High	Low	Low
Crime	Differences	Competence	None	High	Moderate	Low	Moderate
Welfare reform	Differences	Competence	Low	High	Moderate	Moderate	None
Strengthen families	Differences	Competence	None	High	Moderate	None	None
Tax cuts for families	Differences	Competence	Moderate	High	Low	Moderate	None
Strong defense	Differences	Independence	None	Moderate	Low	None	High
Senior citizens	Competence	Differences	None	High	Moderate	Moderate	Low
Business incentives	Differences	Leadership	High	Moderate	Low	Moderate	Low
Tort reform	Competence	Deference	Moderate	High	Low	Low	Low
Term limits	Differences	Competence	Low	Moderate	High	None	Moderate
OVERALL	Differences	Competence	Low	High	Moderate	Low	Low

through member surveys. Public opinion had the next strongest impact. Leaders only considered issues with high approval ratings and then shaped the campaign to fit polling research. Other variables, such as cost and entrepreneur strength, mattered little, presumably because they were motivated principally by political goals. Leaders paid little or no attention to triggering events. Table 15-2 summarizes findings on the selection process by listing the issues in the Contract with America and their associated goals and issue dimensions.

The discussion so far suggests that leaders from both parties set priorities by finding issues that advance strategic goals. They first set goals to fit personal and political circumstances, and then they search for issues—defined along five dimensions of varying importance—that match a "profile" suggested by their goals. That process is careful, lengthy, and systematic. So, the Republican contract not only fits a tradition of priority setting by opposition party leaders, but also it was created in much the same way its Democratic predecessors developed their agendas.

Republican Variations on a Democratic Tradition

Similarities between Democratic priorities and the Contract with America extend beyond the general manner in which they were chosen, because both sets of leaders faced similar partisan arrangements. Divided government isolates members of the opposition party, forcing them to protect and to reassert their prerogatives. They must answer policy challenges by the president and take advantage of the opportunity to take the initiative. Clinton's 1992 victory allowed congressional Republicans to set their priorities without regard to the president's concerns, just as Democrats had done during decades of split partisan control. By exploiting Clinton's weakness to seize the initiative, Republicans followed the path of Democrats who had taken advantage of similar failings by Presidents Ford, Reagan (in his later years), and Bush. Presidents continue to have little say in the priorities of opposition leaders in Congress.

The institutional independence of divided government provides opportunity, but it also brings responsibility. Thinking as a majority party, Republicans realized that they needed to prove they deserved the power they sought, just as Democrats needed to show their competence at problem solving. Republicans rediscovered that they could initiate policies on their own, but they knew that their goals would not be realized unless they could successfully address serious problems. Only then could they take credit. That is why both leaders from both parties stress the importance of support within Congress. As Figure 15-1 shows, support was an important factor in every item on the contract. Based on previous findings, that echoes the primary weight that Democratic leadership put on consensus (see Figure 15-2).[17]

Neither party shows much regard for fiscal concerns in choosing priorities, as Figures 15-1 and 15-2 suggest. The authors of the contract made minimal efforts to contain costs or worry about how much discretion they had. Critics

Figure 15-1 Relative Importance of Issue Dimensions for All Items on the Republican Contract with America

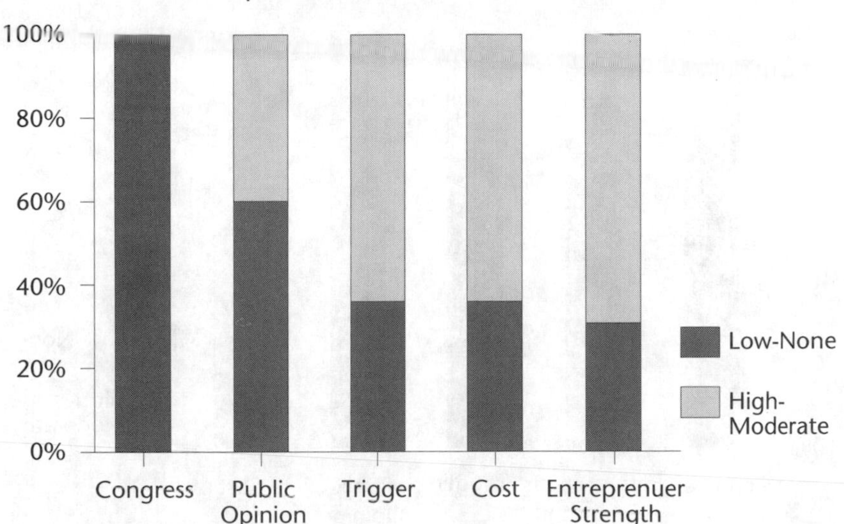

Sources: Drawn from John B. Bader, *Taking the Initiative: Leadership Agendas in Congress and the "Contract with America"* (Washington, D.C.: Georgetown University Press, 1996). Congressional Quarterly *Almanacs; Congressional Quarterly Weekly Reports;* archival materials; and interviews.

Note: In y% of cases, x dimension was of high or moderate importance.

claimed the initiatives would cost nearly $1 trillion. These claims did not matter to Republicans any more that it did to Democrats when they chose issues. Dollar figures rarely determine political success, a fact well known by both parties on Capitol Hill.

There are important and revealing differences, however, between the Republican contract and Democratic priorities from previous Congresses. The most obvious is that Gingrich and other GOP leaders developed and promoted their priorities publicly. Their high-profile efforts, culminating in the September 27 event, contrast sharply with the quiet nature of most Democratic attempts to set priorities. Mindful of the decentralized nature of Congress, Democratic leaders developed priorities largely for internal use. Identifying these priorities was sometimes an exercise in reconstructive historiography. The Republican list, on the other hand, is available in many easily obtainable forms. It appeared in *TV Guide,* a magazine with a circulation of millions. Times Books published a version of the contract in book form in late 1994, calling it the "Bold Plan by Rep. Newt Gingrich, Rep. Dick Armey, and the House Republicans to Change the Nation." These efforts should leave little doubt that Republicans meant the contract to win the election and prove their worthiness in the most public way possible.

Figure 15-2 Relative Importance of Issue Dimensions for All Democratic Leadership Priorities, in Select Congresses, 1969–1990

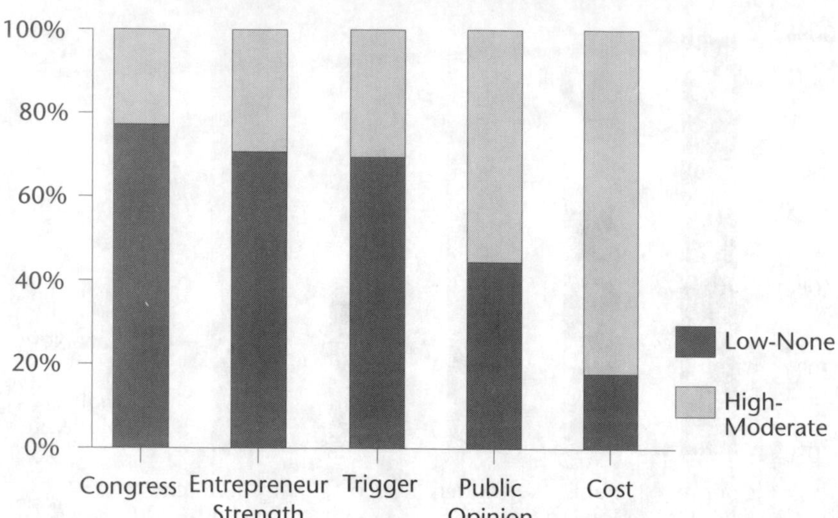

Sources: Drawn from John B. Bader, *Taking the Initiative: Leadership Agendas in Congress and the "Contract with America"* (Washington, D.C.: Georgetown University Press, 1996). Congressional Quarterly *Almanacs; Congressional Quarterly Weekly Reports;* archival materials; and interviews.

Note: In y% of cases, x dimension was of high or moderate importance.

Figures 15-1 and 15-2 show more substantive differences. Republicans gave more weight to public opinion in their choice of priorities than did Democrats. In more than 60 percent of contract items, public opinion was of moderate to high importance, compared to just over 40 percent for Democrats. The 1994 GOP victories may be explained in part by their close attention to public sentiment and because Democrats may have been "out of touch." Republicans also used public opinion research to develop a very sophisticated marketing plan to push their agenda and get their candidates elected. Democrats consistently fail to use these techniques, as the 1994 defeats seemed to testify.

Republican leaders paid little attention to policy entrepreneurs' or to triggering events, important considerations for Democrats. This difference may be attributed to each party's experiences. Democratic leaders, as longtime managers of the legislative process, have had to cope with the many policy demands of an active membership. That was the norm. The GOP leadership seemed to have quieted these demands in favor of the collective interests of the party, which may reflect the party's history as a minority party that was excluded from serious policy debates. Leaders were confident that their committee chairs would not push

Figure 15-3 Distribution of Primary Republican Leader Goals in the Contract with America, 1994

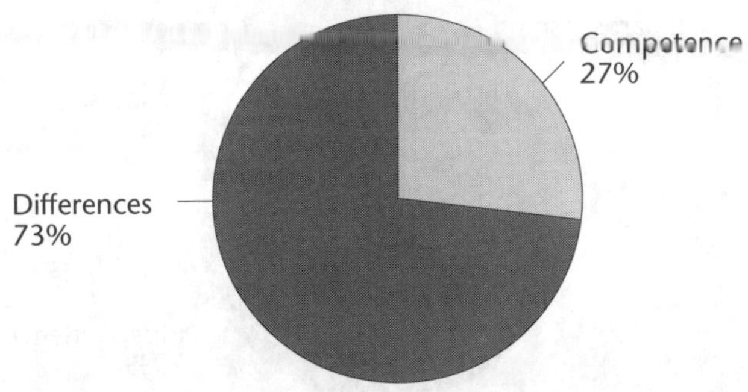

their own agendas because they all believed in the causes embodied in the contract.

A similar point can be made about the unimportance of triggering events in the development of the contract. Democratic leaders appear to be highly sensitive to changes in the political environment, while Gingrich and his colleagues chose their priorities in relative quiet. Again, that changed as Republicans in Congress had to respond to the new circumstances. The contract may not have been a "normal" act of governance, in the sense that it was developed while out of power, far from the daily responsibilities of legislating.

Figure 15-3 shows the distribution of primary goals in the choice of GOP priorities on the contract. It offers another important difference between the parties. Democrats pursued a wide variety of goals when setting priorities, as Figure 15-4 shows, most notably showing competence and reasserting independence. Over time, more and more Democratic priorities demonstrated the desire for bipartisanship, blurring distinctions between the parties. But Figure 15-3 shows that 73 percent of contract items primarily highlight party differences, more than three times that for Democratic priorities in five Congresses.

Such partisanship reflects both the strategic need of Republican leaders to take control of Congress and their highly partisan background. Gingrich saw no benefit to being bipartisan. These leaders also added an ideological dimension generally missing with Democrats. The Contract with America was a conservative plan of action based on conservative principles. It helped unite Republicans on common themes. Democrats have shown little desire to apply ideological litmus tests to issues largely because they lack consensus on ideology in the first place. They cannot point to an experience like the Salisbury Conference because they could never agree on principles. While Democratic priority decisions would be highly strategic, the resulting lists lack the cohesiveness of the contract.

Figure 15-4 Distribution of Primary Democratic Leader Goals in Five Selected Congresses, 1969–1990 (percentage of total cases)

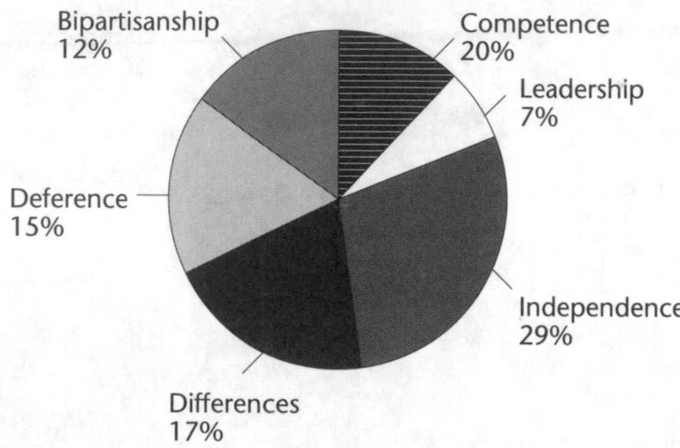

The Impact

What impact will the Contract with America have? Was it a success? It may fit a tradition of priority setting in Congress, but did it change the way policy is made in America? Did it build trust and restore confidence, as Republicans hoped it would? Some of these questions can be answered now. Republican leaders promised action within the first one hundred days of the 104th Congress, so we are free to evaluate their efforts. But the more important questions concerning changes in the political system can be answered only tentatively for now.

In the strictest sense, the House leadership successfully fulfilled the entire contract. The contract states that a Republican-led House will vote on each of its items within the first one hundred days of the 104th Congress. They did that, with several days to spare, itself an impressive task. The House of Representatives is not known for such quick action. Predecessors of Gingrich and Armey generally worked for two years to pass their priorities. Such decisive speed suggested the advent of a new era of American politics, in which Congress innovates and party leaders drive the legislative process. Gingrich became a ubiquitous, if somewhat notorious, figure in Washington. The speakership took on great force. And the contract set a new standard of decision making.

Before we proclaim a new day of congressional power and party government, however, we need to put the success of the contract in context and to evaluate it systematically. That evaluation should be based on a standard applied to other actors and to other instances of priority setting, namely how far an initiative has gone through the legislative process. A floor vote alone does not affect policy or the political process in the long run. Enactment is the final proof of power for party leaders, whose responsibilities and reputation center on the pas-

Table 15-3 Legislative Success Rates for Agenda Items, Comparing the Contract with America, 1995–1996, with Democratic Leadership Priorities, Selected Congresses, 1969–1990

	Contract with America (21 Cases [a])	Democratic Leader Priorities (59 Cases)
Passed at least one chamber	95% (20 cases)	92% (54 cases)
Passed both chambers	62 (13)	81 (48)
Became law/passed/ratified	38 (8)	75 (44)
Passed only one chamber	33 (7)	10 (6)
Neglected/rejected by both chambers	5 (1)	8 (5)
Bills vetoed	24 [b] (6)	14 (8)
Vetoes overridden	0 (0)	25 (2)
Vetoes sustained	100 (6)	75 (6)

Sources: Almanacs (Washington, D.C.: Congressional Quarterly, various years); Congressional Quarterly Data Base, August 1, 1996, for Contract with America items.

[a] Although the original contract lists eleven items, it does include several subissues, which subsequently appeared as separate bills in the legislative process.

[b] Veto of H.R. 4, which included language on two contract items, welfare reform and a provision to strengthen child support enforcement. Counted as a single veto.

sage of legislation. Tracking legislative progress can give a good measure of the contract's short-run impact.

By this standard, the Contract with America was not impressive when compared to the success of previous leadership priorities. I came to this conclusion by tracking the legislative progress of contract items through the entire 104th Congress, long after the one hundred-day deadline passed. As several GOP priorities, such as strengthening families and providing business incentives, became manifest in several different bills, each of the bills had to be tracked. Table 15-3 shows that 95 percent of contract items passed at least one chamber. Alone, that is an impressive figure, suggesting that party leaders had a great deal of power. That kind of legislative power is not new to majority leaders, however: 92 percent of Democratic leadership priorities passed at least one chamber in the ten years under previous study.[18] There is no significant difference between parties by this measure either in success or in how often leadership priorities are rejected by both chambers (8 percent for Democrats versus 5 percent for Republicans).

The contract does not fare nearly as well, however, using other measures. Eighty-one percent of Democratic priorities passed both chambers and 75 percent became law, but only 62 percent of contract items had passed both and only 38 percent had become law by the end of the Congress. Fully 33 percent passed only one chamber—the House—but then got no further in the process. Only 10 percent of Democratic priorities met a similar early death. Republicans were unable to override Clinton's vetoes of contract legislation, while Democrats overcame 25 percent of presidential vetoes.

These figures may be surprising to those who concluded that Newt Gingrich controlled the legislative process. In fact, he was no more successful than previous majority leaders in divided government and lagged far behind in his ability to see priorities become law. These failures remind us of the limitations of leadership in Congress. Gingrich may have had the loyalty of House Republicans, many of whom give him credit for winning the majority and giving their concerns priority. But he had little influence in the Senate, which proved to be the greatest obstacle to the ultimate success of the contract. The House leaders may have been wrong to ignore bicameral relations when developing their priorities. The Senate, with a vocal minority and a large faction of moderate Republicans, treated the contract skeptically and very slowly. House Republicans also seemed to have overlooked the need to win presidential approval when making law. Whatever contract items made it past the Senate were withheld for fear of a veto. The failure to seriously consider presidential relations may be a consequence of inexperience in the majority party as well as the desire to highlight partisan differences.

The long-term impact of the contract can be measured along partisan and institutional dimensions. The House Republican Party clearly benefited at first from the development and execution of the contract. Through GOPAC, a conservative political action committee, Gingrich recruited, campaigned for, and enlisted one freshman class after another, beginning in 1986. As a result, he had a large base of support among these young, devoted, enthusiastic conservatives. The contract helped to solidify his support and gave this cohort the positive, substantive focus it lacked. It is not surprising that this group could not accept any changes to the agenda. They were the first to criticize any sign of backing down from the promises they made to voters. However consistent this might be, it caused the leadership problems as it dealt with the realities of legislating and compromise. Some freshmen protested when leaders abandoned provisions to require a three-fifths vote on tax increases, but to no avail. And they proved to be a constant irritant to party leaders during the budget negotiations of the winter of 1995–1996. The cost of unity can be high if compromise is the vocabulary of lawmaking.

Dissension can become a problem for a party so determined to remain unified on a given agenda. Both parties have become more homogeneous over time, but each has a group of dissenters who operate outside the ideological mainstream. For the Republicans in early 1995 it was Mark Hatfield, the senior senator from Oregon, who voted against the balanced budget amendment, causing its defeat by a single vote. Some Republicans were furious. Connie Mack of Florida and Rick Santorum of Pennsylvania wanted Hatfield stripped of his Appropriations Committee chairmanship. Majority Leader Dole was embarrassed. And the Republican Party looked fragmented and intolerant. Party leaders may have listened to members when setting their priorities, but members will continue to reserve the right to act independently without sanction.

It seems unlikely that the Contract with America will keep the Republican Party cohesive and focused in the long run. By early 1996, their "revolution" had lost much of its energy. GOP members spun away from a centralized agenda as new problems emerged and as they dealt with divisive spending questions. If history provides any insights, Congress is a fundamentally decentralized institution that does not follow a single piper for very long. Powerful presidents with full agendas, like Lyndon Johnson and Ronald Reagan, faced ultimate failure and loss of control. Ambitious party leaders have met the same fate.

The Contract with America did have an effect on the institution of Congress. The years leading up to 1994 provided an ever-growing list of congressional abuses and mistakes. The public was frustrated and angry, turning to quick solutions like term limits and a balanced budget amendment to reassert some control over their legislators. Republican leaders designed the contract partly to restore confidence and trust in Congress. They thought a clear agenda would give voters a means to hold members of Congress accountable. To some extent they succeeded in this endeavor, although only for a short time. Approval ratings of Congress went from roughly 10 percent to more than 40 percent in the first weeks of the 104th Congress. That improvement echoes a similar jump in the early months of the highly productive 100th Congress, led by Gingrich's nemesis, Jim Wright. The public apparently feels better about a Congress that innovates, initiates, and legislates. Those feelings did not last in the face of bitter budget debates and government shutdowns, but the upsurge in approval reversed a very long and potentially delegitimizing trend. (For more on public opinion toward Congress, see Chapter 3.)

Whether the institutional changes are structural and lasting remains an open question, however. Reforms passed on the first day of the 104th Congress altered the institutional landscape by cutting staff and increasing accountability. But the majority shift itself probably had a greater impact. Hundreds of Democratic staff lost their jobs as the members and committee chairs lost their seats. The Republican victory brought in new chairs and a new generation of staff members, who changed the tenor of policy making on Capitol Hill. But these personnel changes may not alter the decentralized nature of Congress, which most likely will resurface after efforts to pass the contract have ended. Gingrich may have created the sense of centralized leadership, but previous Speakers who have tried to maintain such control—from "Uncle Joe" Cannon to Wright—have been curbed or rejected. Gingrich, damaged politically during the budget crises, seems to be no exception.

Has the Contract with America changed our political system? In some ways, it has. Republican control revived Congress, shaking up the House after forty years of single-party rule. If turnover is a natural part of a democratic system, then this shift was healthy and necessary. The contract also revived the notion that Congress can innovate. It reminded the public that members of Congress can initiate policy without presidential guidance and that action is appropriate in a separated system. The national press paid renewed attention to congressional actions as a result of the contract. Media attention surrounding it and the ensuing public discussion restored some confidence in an institution that is the linchpin of the federal system. This kind of revival must take place from time to time, as it has throughout our history. The contract was just the most recent effort to keep the system alive.

But in more substantive ways, the impact of the contract may be fleeting. Newt Gingrich and the Republican leadership did not radically change Congress as an institution. Memories of the contract faded as press coverage diminished and as the country turned its attention to other matters and to the contest for the presidency. The Republicans did not introduce a process of priority setting that was entirely new. Majority leaders have set priorities under divided government for decades. They have done so in ways that are just as strategic, although not as public, as Republican efforts to develop the contract. There are substantive and ideological differences, to be sure. But the deductive process of setting goals and matching them to redefined issues is a regular feature of party leadership in divided government.

Notes

1. Quoted by the *New York Times,* Sept. 28, 1994, A16.
2. Quoted by *USA Today,* Dec. 2, 1994, 7A.
3. See John B. Bader, "Congressional Party Leadership and Policy Priorities Under Divided Government, 1969–1990" (paper delivered at the annual meeting of the American Political Science Association, New York, Sept. 1–4, 1994); and Bader, *Taking the Initiative: Leadership Agendas in Congress and the "Contract with America"* (Washington, D.C.: Georgetown University Press, 1996).
4. Some of the literature on congressional leadership supports an emphasis on party leaders and their priorities. David Truman (*The Congressional Party: A Case Study,* New York: Wiley, 1959, 104, 132) writes that Senate leaders can effectively combine "fragments of power" to affect agendas earlier than consideration on the floor. Ralph Huitt ("The Internal Distribution of Influence: The Senate," 1965, reprinted in his *Working Within the System,* Berkeley: University of California Press, 1990, 108) points out that such leadership requires personal skill and tenacity. This is not to say that

party leaders can set priorities or even lead very easily. Huitt's model is Lyndon Johnson, inarguably the most skilled majority leader in the modern era. And Samuel Patterson ("Party Leadership in the U.S. Senate," *Legislative Studies Quarterly* 14, August 1989, 401–410) points to a host of challenges facing leaders: a more individualistic context, wavering party loyalty, an unstable succession pattern, unclear roles, and problematic external relations. Nevertheless, party leaders in the Senate do not have to have the same style to deal with these challenges. Huitt ("Democratic Party Leadership in the Senate," *American Political Science Review* 55, June 1961, 333–344) argues that if Senate leaders adapt to and then exploit their complex environment, they can strongly affect decision making. These Senate studies—both of divided government—may not specifically address agenda setting, but their findings suggest that leaders can play a major role if the circumstances warrant it.

Scholars of the House have examined agenda setting more directly and find a more pronounced role for the leadership. David Rohde (*Parties and Leaders in the Postreform House,* Chicago: University of Chicago Press, 1991, 93–94) argues that the House Speaker's ability to shape the agenda expanded during the reform era as a result of new powers to make multiple referrals, to appoint Rules Committee members, and to set schedules. Rohde generally finds that party leaders have successfully adapted to the challenges of the postreform Congress, using skill and available institutional tools to influence policy.

Barbara Sinclair has been particularly persistent in her exploration of policy-making roles for party leaders. In one study ("Majority Party Leadership Strategies for Coping with the New U.S. House," *Legislative Studies Quarterly* 6, August 1981: 413), she speculated that the election of a Republican president would give Democratic Party leaders more discretion in picking policy battles. No longer obligated by partisan ties to advance the president's agenda, they could move more freely. She later argued (*Majority Leadership in the U.S. House,* Baltimore: Johns Hopkins University Press, 1983, 29) that leaders can structure choices—akin to priority setting—by using positive inducements such as committee assignments, easier schedules, and office perquisites. This work generally casts serious doubt on widely held expectations by scholars such as James Sundquist that party leaders cannot lead. Sundquist writes (*The Decline and Resurgence of Congress,* Washington: Brookings, 1981, 427) that "no one can speak with authority for Congress as a whole, or even for either house." While the obstacles are many, leaders in fact do fill a variety of roles very effectively.

In a more recent round of research, Sinclair ("House Majority Party Leadership in the Late 1980s," in *Congress Reconsidered,* 4th ed., ed. Lawrence C. Dodd and Bruce I. Oppenheimer, Washington, D.C.: CQ Press, 1989, 307–329; and "The Emergence of Strong Leadership in the 1980s House of Representatives," *Journal of Politics* 54, August 1992, 657–684) finds that House majority leadership had become stronger in the 1980s, most noticeably under Jim Wright's speakership in the 100th Congress (1987–1988). Wright's aggressive leadership in developing and shepherding a large policy agenda through Congress presents an interesting question to Sinclair and to me: Was Jim Wright an anomaly? Her findings suggest he was not. Over the last two decades, party leaders gradually have become more involved, more policy-oriented, and more media-conscious. Sinclair argues that this increased activity resulted from divided government politics, greater legislative complexity (which forces members to seek help), shrinking innovation opportunities (from budget deficits), and increased party unity ("The Emergence of Strong Leadership," 669, 681). So, Wright's leadership does have precedent, with threads reaching back several years. In sum, "party leadership did become stronger over this period (1969 to 1988)" (Ibid., 682).

5. In addition to listing Contract with America items taken from campaign literature, I have reconstructed leadership priorities for five Congresses by examining media accounts, legislative histories, and archival materials such as memoranda and party publications.
6. The link between goals and agendas has been explored before, although not regularly and not fully. Frank Baumgartner and Bryan Jones (*Agendas and Instability in American Politics,* Chicago: University of Chicago Press, 1993, 237) mention goals briefly in their study of agendas, noting that political leaders seeking to make a name for themselves have an incentive to push proposals. "Successful political leaders," they write on page 237, ". . . are often those who recognize the power of political ideas sweeping through the system and who take advantage of them to favor particular policy proposals." In his study of presidential agenda setting, Paul Light (*The President's Agenda: Domestic Policy Choice from Kennedy to Carter [with Notes on Ronald Reagan],* Baltimore: Johns Hopkins University Press, 1983, 63–69) argues persuasively that "goals affect the president's choice of domestic issues" (page 80) but does not use this framework consistently. John Kingdon (*Agendas, Alternatives, and Public Policies,* Boston: Little, Brown, 1984, 41–43) discusses goal achievement as the principal motive behind agenda setting in Congress. Kingdon cites Richard Fenno's troika of goals (reelection, policy, influence) (*Congressmen in Committees,* Boston: Little, Brown, 1973, 1). Barbara Sinclair, in a unique study of congressional agenda change over time ("Agenda, Policy, and Alignment Change from Coolidge to Reagan," in *Congress Reconsidered,* 3d ed., ed. Lawrence C. Dodd and Bruce I. Oppenheimer, Washington, D.C.: CQ Press, 1985, 291–314), argues that constituent concerns drive agenda setting: "congressional alignments will change when the signals the representative receives from the constituency change" (page 313). But only Calvin Mouw and Michael MacKuen's study, "The Strategic Agenda in Legislative Politics," *American Political Science Review* 86, March 1992, 87–105, makes a consistent connection between goals and agendas: "Members of Congress have different types of career objectives and choose agenda strategies accordingly" (page 91). They show that politicians set agendas strategically to advance electoral, policy, and personal goals (pages 91, 96). In these cases and in other goal-based studies, the goal framework nevertheless seems to get lost along the way. This is understandable, given that motives can be difficult to identify empirically.
7. Fenno, *Congressmen in Committees,* 1, first articulated a typology of goals for members of Congress that remains the fountainhead for this line of research. Many scholars have used Fenno's typology (such as John Kingdon, "Models of Legislative Voting," *Journal of Politics* 39, August 1977, 563–595; Light, *The President's Agenda*; Sinclair, *Majority Leadership in the U.S. House*; and Mouw and MacKuen, "The Strategic Agenda in Legislative Politics"), while others have stressed electoral goals when explaining congressional behavior (notably David Mayhew, *Congress: The Electoral Connection,* New Haven: Yale University Press, 1974; and R. Douglas Arnold, *The Logic of Congressional Action,* New Haven: Yale University Press, 1990). Fenno provides a useful idea for linking these goals to the priority-setting process. He developed his own typology (reelection, influence, good policy) to explain differences between committees in Congress. One committee helps members achieve one set of goals; another committee advances other goals. "The opportunity to achieve the three goals varies widely among committees," he writes on page 1. "House members, therefore, match their individual patterns of aspiration to the diverse patterns of opportunity presented by House committees." Following this logic of "matching," we can see that certain issues fill different needs or goals.
8. Some research, mostly from policy studies on agenda setting, emphasizes "issue definition." It explores how political elites understand policy issues and how they can

reshape that definition to suit their needs, an idea many attribute to E. E. Schattschneider (*The Semisovereign People: A Realist's View of Democracy in America*, New York: Holt, Rinehart and Winston, 1960, 62–77). Most notable among these studies are: Frank Baumgartner and Bryan Jones, "Agenda Dynamics and Policy Subsystems," *Journal of Politics* 53 (November 1991): 1044–74; and Paul A. Sabatier, "An Advocacy Coalition Framework of Policy Change and the Role of Policy Oriented Learning Therein," *Policy Sciences* 21 (1988): 129–168.

9. Quoted by Suzy DeFrancis in "Fulfilling the Promise: A Reader's Guide to the New Republican Congress and its Contract with America," *Rising Tide*, January/February 1995, 20.
10. From "A Contract with America: What Republicans Stand For—in Writing," written with Pete Dupont, *Rising Tide*, November/December 1994, 15.
11. From the RNC "White Book," 1.
12. Quoted by the *Washington Post*, Dec. 20, 1994, A8.
13. Ibid., A14.
14. Quoted by *Congressional Quarterly Weekly Report*, Dec. 10, 1994, 3522.
15. *National Journal*, Oct. 22, 1994, 2451; and editorial, *New York Times*, "The GOP's Deceptive Contract," Sept. 28, 1994, A20.
16. Quoted by *Congressional Quarterly Weekly Report*, Nov. 19, 1994, 3337.
17. See Bader, "Congressional Party Leadership," and *Taking the Initiative*.
18. Ibid.

Part VI
Congress and Political Change

16. Abdicating Congressional Power: The Paradox of Republican Control

Bruce I. Oppenheimer

During the first one hundred days of the 104th Congress, many observers, including political scientists and journalists, marveled at the reforms instituted by the new Republican majorities, especially in the House of Representatives. The achievements included not only the votes on the items in the Contract with America, but also internal changes. Comparisons were made with the first one hundred days of the New Deal, the passage of many Great Society programs in 1965 following Lyndon Johnson's landslide victory, and the post-Watergate reforms of the 94th Congress. Although I disagree with many of these evaluations, there is, in fact, an important similarity between the 104th Congress and its well-known predecessors: after years of frustration over issues of process and policy, a political minority that becomes the majority enacts nonincremental reforms and policy changes with unusual speed and cohesion. In doing so, the reformers often ignore all warnings, viewing them as attempts by the old guard to block policy change and sidetrack reform efforts. Even if these suspicions are correct, the reformers push changes beyond what is needed to achieve their goals, and they produce unanticipated, and usually undesired, consequences. In this regard the Republicans in the 104th Congress are remarkably similar to the overachievers in earlier Congresses.

I argue here that the consequences of the Republican takeover of Congress in 1995 have been misunderstood. The lasting impact of the Republicans' reforms will be redistribution of power from Congress to the executive branch, especially to the presidency. In this, I differ from those who have concluded that Congress has enhanced its role as a policy leader or that the president has to prove his relevancy to the struggle over policy.[1] Rather, the longer-term consequences will be a significant, and perhaps permanent, shift of power from Congress to the executive branch.

In developing this argument, I first discuss why political reformers tend to push changes beyond what is necessary to achieve their immediate goals, and the reasons why congressional Republicans were susceptible to this pitfall. Second, I briefly examine a number of reforms the House and Senate Republicans made during the 104th Congress to demonstrate that these reforms individually contribute to a reduction in congressional influence and collectively will have a marked effect on the struggle over policy between Congress and the president. I analyze the reduction in congressional committee staffs and the enactment of enhanced rescission authority, two of the more visible examples of the congressional giveaway. Even the critics of these changes have not fully anticipated their consequences. Third, I discuss the irony of these changes: ideological conservatives are weakening the branch of the national government that historically has resisted the growth of federal power. Finally, I explore whether these changes will have a permanent effect on the power relationships between Congress and the president or whether they are a point in the pendulum swing of what James Sundquist has described as the decline and resurgence of Congress.[2] I suggest that it is possible that the pendulum may have moved to a point of no return.

Why Reformers Go to Excess

Two factors tend to cause political reformers to behave excessively when they win control of government, behavior I call the "reformers' pitfall." Reformers usually start as outsiders: if they were insiders and had sufficient governing power, they would have been able to institute the changes they favored. Advocating reforms is one strategy in building electoral support, but the proposed reforms have to be extensive enough to garner media and broader public attention. Reformers know that they cannot excite the electorate by claiming that only modest changes or adjustments are needed. In short, reformers understand that a platform of incrementalism will not capture the public. At the very least, the rhetoric and reform proposals need to be extreme and need to convey a sense of urgency. Those in power are often portrayed as corrupt; not only must they be replaced, but the institutions and processes also require a major reworking. To further their ends, reformers adopt the language of crisis and impending disaster.[3] While some activists in the reform movement, and especially converts to it, believe the rhetoric, others lock themselves into supporting the proposals as part of their campaign for office. Upon winning power, however, the centrists within the reform movement who understood the pragmatic purposes of the campaign rhetoric may find it difficult to restrain the true believers. After years out of power, the reformers are so energized by their victory that differences among them are put aside, at least for a time. Acting with more cohesion than they actually feel, they take advantage of the moment to achieve their overall goals and, in so doing, enact much of their reform agenda. In the end, what is enacted tends to reflect the rhetoric and commitments of the candidates more than the actual changes needed. Whether the reformers actually achieve their intended goals is a separate question.

A second and more subtle reason why reformers make changes that are greater than necessary to achieve their goals is that they fail to understand the inertia governing institutions. The truth is that institutions resist change. Congress's structure, with its elaborate set of committees, subcommittees, rules, and procedures; the long tenure of many members who have a stake in the status quo; and extensive behavioral norms and precedents, such as a seniority system, presents formidable obstacles to change.[4] Accordingly, many conclude that change is difficult and that major alterations are necessary to shift the institutional status quo. Congress is viewed as a nine hundred pound gorilla: it resists change and does not respond to subtlety. After all, if it were responsive, it would already have complied with the requests of those seeking modifications. Reformers therefore assume that big changes are required to produce the desired results.

In spite of these arguments, I believe reformers often misread the way inertia works in political institutions. Some years ago, I had a conversation with Richard Bolling, D-Mo., who was the chair of the House Rules Committee. Bolling had a good deal of practical experience with congressional reform efforts, and he put forth a different view of institutional inertia. Bolling contended that political institutions such as Congress rest in a delicate balance and that it does not always require major reform to shift the inertia and, in turn, produce changes in the institution.[5] Instead, modest alterations often can do the trick. Extensive reforms, moreover, are likely not only to alter the inertia, but also to produce unforeseen effects.

Bolling could relate this view to the problems the reforms of the first half of the 1970s had created for legislating in the House. By pushing democratization so strongly through the subcommittee bill of rights, among other reform vehicles, the advocates of change created a situation in which managing a party's legislative program, especially on the House floor, became chaotic and unpredictable. The unanticipated consequences far outweighed those that were predicted.[6]

Although either of these two factors may be sufficient to produce excessive changes and unanticipated consequences, together they may have a reinforcing effect. Indeed, there are examples outside the congressional literature suggesting that the reformers' pitfall occurs in other institutions as well. There is ample support for this perspective in the urban politics literature. Once they were in office, big city reformers who had fought the bosses of the urban machines made major changes to ensure that the bases of the machines' influence and the sources of corruption were permanently removed. But the impact of these reforms went well beyond what the insurgents had planned. Wallace Sayre and Herbert Kaufman, for example, conclude that, although the reformers in New York City overcame the antidemocratic tendencies of the machine, in doing so they created many nonpolitical agencies "insulated by rule or practice from the intervention by party leaders or supervision by elected officials. . . . The consequences of this trend have been a strengthening of the tendencies toward a multicentered system of power in the city and a weakening of the influence of party leaders and elected officials, especially the Mayor. The direct beneficiaries of the movement have been the nongovernmental interest groups that constitute the intimate 'constituencies' of the nonpolitical agencies."[7] By ensuring that the bosses would no longer control city government, the reformers also insulated it from the broader public as well. Ironically, reformers often sow the seeds of their own defeat. Congressional reformers, be they liberal Democrats of the 1970s or conservative Republicans of the 1990s, are not unlike these city reformers. They cannot restrain the energy of their movements.

Why Republicans Were Vulnerable to the Pitfall

By the time the Republicans took over the House and Senate in 1995, they were particularly susceptible to the reformers' pitfall, especially in the House, where they had spent forty consecutive years in the minority. The most senior House Republicans in the 104th Congress were first elected eight years after their party became the minority. Not only had they spent a long time as the minority, but also the job had grown more frustrating. When the House Democrats were divided between northern liberals and southern conservatives, the Republican minority was pivotal on a range of issues. Their support was sought in building majority coalitions, and they had a hand in designing legislation. But by 1982 the two parties had become stronger and more homogeneous. The House had become a more partisan institution, and the role for Republicans often was limited to obstruction.[8]

The majority party wrote the legislation, and the Republicans felt that they were locked out of committee negotiations until the Democrats came to an agreement among themselves. To limit the Republicans' ability to obstruct, Democratic leaders increasingly resorted to restrictive rules for the consideration of legislation on the House floor. Rather than being allowed to offer amendments to build a majority around their substitute, Republicans were frequently confined to an up-or-down vote on their alternative to the Democrats' bill.[9] As committee staffs became more partisan, Republicans regularly complained about receiving less than their fair share of staff allocations.

To these internal frustrations there was added an external one. Recognizing the reelection success of incumbents and seeing the Democrats' majority as having some permanence, political action committees (PACs), even those with policy ties to Republicans, were giving a higher percentage of their campaign contributions to incumbent House members and to Democrats. This was especially noticeable after 1982, when Republicans lost the House seat gains they had made during Ronald Reagan's landslide of 1980.[10] Even their friends appeared to have deserted them.

In fairness to these PACs, there seemed to be little hope that the Republicans would end their minority status anytime soon. Republicans mistakenly blamed incumbency and Democratic gerrymandering of districts for their fate. In fact, incumbents of both parties were advantaged. One-party control of redistricting was limited to a handful of states and was done by Republicans as well as Democrats. And most important, Republicans were not faring significantly better in open-seat contests than in races where incumbents were running. Simply relying on the same tactics did not seem to hold much hope for winning control of the House.

In response to these conditions, a more confrontational approach, as advocated by the Conservative Opportunity Society, became more attractive. Inside the House, Republicans took a less conciliatory attitude toward the Democratic majority. The selection of a new set of Republican leaders epitomized this change. When the whip position became open in 1989, Newt Gingrich of Georgia defeated the more moderate Edward Madigan of Illinois by two votes. Gingrich was clearly at odds with the more consensual approach of Minority Leader Bob Michel of Illinois, whom he increasingly overshadowed. A Republican freshman observed: "We're not interested in being a better minority. Newt personifies that message."[11] The more aggressive strategy inside the House was matched by a new external strategy. Republicans campaigned for Congress by attacking the institution: they pointed to the corrupting effect of one-party domination and continued that attack as the minority party in office. Even before 1994, Republicans had started to nationalize their congressional campaigns against the Democratic majority and the institution.

In contrast, Senate Republicans had enjoyed majority status for six years in the 1980s. Even after they returned to minority status in 1987, they continued to play a larger role in the legislative process than their House counterparts because of the rules and norms of the Senate. Nevertheless, partisanship was also on the increase in the Senate. The Republicans made regular use of party-directed filibusters in the 103d Congress to derail legislation. Barbara Sinclair wrote in 1989, "The Senate has been subjected to a litany of criticism during the last few years, and senators have been prominent among the toughest critics."[12] Although Republican senators were somewhat more restrained in their criticisms of the Senate than their fellow partisans in the House were of their chamber, institutional loyalty had largely disappeared.

The Republican attack on Congress was further fueled by the longest continuous period of divided government in the nation's history. During the twelve years of the Reagan and Bush administrations—with Democratic House majorities throughout and Senate majorities for half the time—there was little respite from presidential and Republican attacks on Congress. Although a degree of conflict between the institutions is built into the constitutional system, divided government exacerbated the level of Congress-bashing within the two houses. The level of criticism coming from the White House often went beyond mere policy disagreements to attack the legitimacy of congressional action. As one analysis concluded, the White House "on many occasions deliberately ignored or defied congressional intent, frequently exercising a kind of executive veto of legislative provisions."[13] Moreover, with the White House in GOP hands, congressional Republicans were limited to criticizing the Democratic-controlled Congress for policy shortcomings or failures. Once Bill Clinton became president, congressional Republicans could direct some of their fire elsewhere. But for twelve years their sights, as well as those of Republican presidents, were aimed at Congress.

The Democrats also contributed to the scenario. Scandals involving the House bank and post office, resignations of a Speaker and a majority whip faced with ethical problems, and the indictment of the Ways and Means Committee chair lent credibility to Republican charges and intensity to the reformers' themes. Tinkering would not be enough to address the problems.

Finally, Republicans may have been particularly vulnerable to the reformers' pitfall because their victory was unexpected, involving the election of so many new members. Until just before the election, few observers thought the Republicans had a realistic chance of winning the House. Once there, the Republican freshmen had no time to be socialized to the institution. They had little stake in House status quo; indeed, they had campaigned against the institution. Add to their number the more than fifty members who had only served a single term. Together these first- and second-termers comprised a majority of House Republicans. These newcomers, it may be fair to assume, were more committed to the rhetoric of reform than their more experienced colleagues. In the Senate the eighteen Republicans first elected since 1992 were only a third of the party's membership. In addition, half of them had served in the House, so they were not newcomers to Congress.[14]

When these conditions are combined we find a long-standing minority party, frustrated by its limited legislative role, escalating its criticism of the institution as a means of gaining majority status, reinforced by years of Republican presidential attacks that were echoed by Republicans in Congress, winning an unexpected victory by electing a large number of newcomers. It is difficult to imagine how the reformers' pitfall of excess could have been avoided.

The Reforms and Their Consequences

The Republicans' behavior, especially in the House, was consistent with these expectations. They acted quickly. Within the first one hundred days of the 104th Congress, the House voted on all the items in the Contract with America and passed all of them except the term limits constitutional amendment. Throughout the first session, Republican House members acted with a level of cohesion not observed in modern Congresses. During 1995 House Republicans' party unity support score averaged 93 percent (controlling for absences). Differences among them took a back seat. As Sherwood Boehlert, a moderate New York Republican noted, "We've been on the outside looking in as a minority for the last forty years. We'd like to maintain majority status in the next generation at least." To do so meant demonstrating an ability to enact legislation, which required sticking together.[15]

Senate Republicans, many of whom had not signed onto the contract and who were constrained by Democratic filibuster threats, nevertheless managed to pass legislation dealing with congressional accountability, unfunded mandates, paperwork reduction, and the line-item veto. Although the Senate did not vote on a number of items in the contract during the first hundred days, only the balanced budget constitutional amendment, requiring a two-thirds majority, was defeated. The cohesion level of Senate Republicans did not reach that of their House counterparts, but they still scored a 91 percent average unity support score during 1995. No party in the modern Senate even approached that level.

In addition to passing contract items, the Republicans made substantial changes in the House rules and the way they organized and operated the institution. Three standing committees were abolished. Speaker Gingrich selected committee chairs, and he did not adhere to seniority in doing so. Term limits were placed on leadership positions: committee or subcommittee chairs were limited to six years, and the Speaker could serve no more than eight consecutive years. Committee staffs were cut by one-third. Proxy voting in committee was abolished. Much of the subcommittee bill of rights was reversed.[16]

Except for making deep cuts in committee staff and budgets and reducing the number of subcommittees on three standing committees, the Senate Republicans' changes were less severe and more gradual. But by mid-July 1995, the Senate Republican Conference had adopted a package of reforms consistent with some of those put in place by House Republicans. Among the provisions were term limits on committee chairs, six-year limits on leadership positions other than majority leader and president pro tempore, and a rule limiting members to chairing a single committee or subcommittee, with the exception of Appropriations.[17] The impetus for and backing of these changes came most strongly from Republicans elected since 1992. However, Senate Republicans stopped short of taking action against the Appropriations Committee chair, Mark Hatfield of Oregon, who had voted against the balanced budget constitutional amendment. Conservatives and newer senators had urged that Hatfield be stripped of his chairmanship.

The Republican majorities in the House and Senate did not achieve everything they promised or intended. In addition to the balanced budget amendment, a term limits constitutional amendment was defeated. And it was not until well into 1996 that House and Senate conferees resolved their differences on line-item veto legislation, which would not go into effect until 1997. Not wanting to get bogged down early, the House leadership also deferred action on major jurisdictional restructuring of its standing committees. But, for the most part, the Republicans worked quickly and cohesively to enact a substantial part of their agenda during the early months of the 104th Congress.

Congress seemed to be operating differently. The workload was handled. Conflict was overridden. The leaders appeared to be capable of marshaling their troops. And the institution seemed to be offering policy leadership for the country, especially if the president was not or could not. Under such circumstances, how could one conclude that the effect of the reforms instituted by the Republicans would be to weaken Congress vis-à-vis the president?

To answer this question, let us first examine some of the changes for the potential impact they may have on Congress's influence as an institution rather than on the internal workings of Congress. To address the tendency for some members to become entrenched in power positions, for example, Republicans limited the terms of committee chairs and of the Speaker. Consequently, committee chairs may lose substantial influence in negotiations with the executive branch. Before the advent of these restrictions, executive agency and White House officials knew there was no limit on how long they might have to deal with a given chair. Failure to be cooperative, to bargain in good faith, or to uphold commitments with a committee chair could have substantial repercussions. But now committee chairs become automatic lame ducks, especially once they have completed four of their six-year terms of service. At one time, knowing that John Dingell, D-Mich., would chair the Commerce Committee indefinitely gave him and the committee a certain amount of bargaining influence with others. His term-limited Republican successor, Tom Bliley of Virginia, and other Republican committee chairs will not have that.

Newt Gingrich may serve no more than eight consecutive years as Speaker. The consensus interpretation of this change is that the limit will have no effect. After all, only Tip O'Neill, D-Mass., served longer than eight consecutive years as Speaker. And, as congressional scholar Tom Mann correctly observed, "Eight years is not a short time."[18] But what will be the effect on the Speaker's influence as the end of the term approaches as compared to a Speaker who operates without a term limit? I would argue that the Speaker will exercise less influence both inside and outside the House and that the external weakness will be the more apparent. By removing a source of congressional influence, even these two seemingly minor changes may be sufficient to shift the inertia and alter the delicate balance that exists between the institutions.

Second, to return decision-making authority to the states and limit federal control, the 104th Congress passed, and President Clinton signed, legislation to prohibit enactment of unfunded mandates. Ironically, this law almost exclusively limits the legislative branch. Executive agencies must perform cost-benefit analyses of new regulations, but are not prohibited from placing mandates on states.[19] And there are seemingly no restrictions on courts, even though many of the most onerous federal mandates from a fiscal perspective have been placed on states in response to court orders on prison overcrowding and on equalization in elementary and secondary education. The legislation may or may not have the effect its proponents desired, but it clearly limits the powers of Congress to a far greater extent than the executive branch or the courts. Accordingly, states and localities may prove far more responsive to those branches than to Congress.

If the limiting of chair and Speaker terms and the unfunded mandates legislation may have effects on congressional influence beyond what was anticipated, other reforms may have even more significant repercussions. In particular, two of the more sweeping changes—the reductions in congressional committee staffs and the passage of enhanced rescission authority (more popularly, but inexactly, described as line-item veto)—deserve serious attention.

Reductions in Committee Staff

One area Republicans attacked was the high cost of running Congress, including the members' perquisites and what they considered the bloated staffing of the institution. They saw the congressional bureaucracy as symptomatic of the institution's corruption. Reducing costs was in keeping with the idea that Congress should return to being a "citizen legislature," meeting only part of the year with members who treat service as part time and noncareer. Moreover, as national government functions were returned to states and localities and to the private sector, the workload of Congress would naturally decrease.

The main targets of Republican reform efforts here were the standing committee staffs. There were practical reasons for targeting them instead of the members' office staffs. First, cutting members' staffs would bring the goals of individual members into conflict with the institutional goal of reducing costs and staffing. The literature on previous congressional reform efforts notes that when individual and institutional reforms goals conflict, reform efforts are likely to fail.[20] Second, committee staff reductions could be completed almost entirely at the expense of Democratic committee staff positions. Because Democrats were moving into the minority, nearly all the dismissed committee staffers would be those who worked for them. Republicans, as the majority party, would have more staff than before, despite the overall reductions.

Few could argue that congressional staffs had not become too large. The cut that occurred in 1995 was not the first time the issue had been addressed. As the data in Table 16-1 indicate, Republicans cut Senate committee staffs by around 15 percent after becoming the majority in 1981. (As in 1995, Democrats absorbed all the cuts.) Democrats, in response to criticism about their administration of Congress, cut committee staffs in the House and the Senate by around 10 percent at the start of the 103d Congress. The committee staffing cuts in 1995 were far greater, however. House committee staff dropped more than 38 percent, from 2,046 in 1994 to 1,246 in 1995. Senate committee staff positions decreased nearly 25 percent, from 958 to 732. Other staff reductions were achieved through the abolishment of the Office of Technological Assessment and cuts in the General Accounting Office budget.

These nonincremental reductions returned committee staffs to a size not seen since the early 1970s. For example, in the Senate the staff size in 1995 approximates that of 1971. Although the 1995 House committee staffing level appears to be at a level midway between the 1974 and 1975 totals, two important qualifications should be noted. First, after 1972 the staff of the House Information System, which operates the body's computer system, was included in the staff of the House Administration Committee (now House Oversight). Second, the House Budget Committee staff was created in 1975 to perform functions not being carried out by any other committee. If one removes these two groups from the 1995 figures, the House committee staff total drops nearly to the 1973 level.

Table 16-1 Standing Committee Staffs, 1970–1995

Year	House	Senate	Year	House	Senate
1970	702	635	1983	1,970	1,075
1971	729	711	1984	1,944	1,095
1972	817	844	1985	2,009	1,080
1973	878	873	1986	1,954	1,075
1974	1,107	948	1987	2,024	1,074
1975	1,460	1,277	1988	1,976	970
1976	1,680	1,201	1989	1,986	1,013
1977	1,776	1,028	1990	1,993	1,090
1978	1,844	1,151	1991	2,201	1,030
1979	1,909	1,269	1992	2,178	1,008
1980	1,917	1,191	1993	2,118	897
1981	1,843	1,022	1994	2,046	958
1982	1,839	1,047	1995	1,246	732

Sources: For 1970 through 1993 the data in this table come from Norman J. Ornstein, Thomas E. Mann, and Michael J. Malbin, *Vital Statistics on Congress, 1995–1996* (Washington, D.C.: Congressional Quarterly, 1996), 137. Data for 1994 and 1995 were supplied by Norman Ornstein and Amy Schenkenberg of the American Enterprise Institute.

But, in the early 1970s Congress was responding to what was seen as its woefully understaffed condition, a situation in which Congress was beginning to reassert itself in dealing with an imperial presidency and a well-staffed executive bureaucracy. James Sundquist asserts that the increase in staffing was a direct result of Congress's effort to cope with its workload and to "be far more assertive in the legislative process vis-à-vis the executive branch."[21] For Congress to be able to hold its own against a more powerful executive branch, committee and support organization staff were essential ingredients.

It follows that cutting staffs back to the levels of the early 1970s will place serious limitations on the long-term governing role of Congress, even if it succeeds in cutting the legislative branch appropriation. Although Sundquist favors a strong presidency and is generally critical of Congress's efforts to exert policy leadership, he argues that the congressional staff increases were critical in preventing executive domination.

> [S]taff can be reduced only if, and to the extent that, the Congress is willing to return to the attitudes and practices that prevailed when staff was small—if it returns, in a phrase, to the norm of deference, of individual members to committees, of juniors to seniors, of the legislative branch to the executive. . . . [C]ongressional staff grew slowly during the long period when Congress permitted each accretion of governmental power to be lodged primarily in an expanding executive. That the legislature has been, in the 1970s, by far the fastest growing branch of government is a direct reflection of its reassertion of authority vis-à-vis the president.[22]

It is one thing to argue that congressional staff had expanded beyond a necessary level and needed to be trimmed as part of the overall effort to downsize government. It is quite another to return committee staff to the size it was a quarter century ago and expect it to be adequate to the task of coping with the executive. Even if conservatives succeed in reducing the size of the federal government, or, more realistically, its rate of growth, drastic cuts of committee and support agency staff are premature. It is improbable that the United States will return to a national government of size and scope similar to the 1950s or even the 1970s. Nevertheless, committee staffs have been reduced as if that were already the case.

It is too soon to know the full impact of the staffing cuts. However, there have been indications that congressional committees are finding it necessary to rely on lobbyists to an unusual extent in drafting legislation. In a period of divided party control, we might not observe a growing reliance on the executive branch, but, without sufficient staff, Congress eventually will rely more heavily on executive branch information, expertise, and conclusions. The ability will be compromised to challenge the executive branch, to perform meaningful oversight, and to design legislation with sufficient specificity to ensure a limit on executive discretion in its interpretation. Ironically, in preserving personal staffs (as opposed to committee staffs), the Republican reformers have protected that part of the congressional bureaucracy that is least skilled in withstanding executive dominance.

Enhanced Rescission

Of all the reforms instituted during the 104th Congress, enhanced rescission clearly has the most profound effect on the balance between Congress and the president. Lacking the ability to enact a line-item veto constitutional amendment, Republican reformers in the House formulated a legislative alternative to give the president the ability to cut wasteful pork barrel spending that finds its way into appropriations bills. They agreed on the most extreme of the alternatives under consideration. As one might expect, the Senate considered more modest approaches, but in the end accepted an amended version of the House's stronger enhanced rescission mechanism. It may well give the president more power than would have been granted under a line-item veto.[23]

If the enhanced rescission mechanism survives constitutional challenges, it will operate in the following manner beginning in January 1997. It allows the president, within five days, excluding Sundays, of signing an appropriations bill, to send Congress a list of individual items to be canceled. The cancellations take effect unless Congress within thirty days passes a bill disapproving any or all of them. In addition, the president has the power to veto the disapproval bill, and it requires a two-thirds vote of each house to override the veto. In other words, the president's rescission could be sustained by one-third plus one member of either chamber. (The president has similar authority in dealing with provisions in tax bills that benefit one hundred or fewer individuals or ten or fewer businesses. In addition, the president has some ability to cancel new or expanded entitlements.)

Unlike a line-item veto, the enhanced rescission mechanism gives the president more precise authority. Instead of just being able to rescind spending for lump-sum categories in appropriations bills, which are often fairly broad in coverage, the president may use the fuller descriptions contained in committee reports that accompany the bills or in the statements of bill managers as the vehicle for rescissions. Compared to the appropriations bill, these materials provide far greater detail on the spending outlined in the bill. The president may have the ability, for example, to veto spending for a particular public works project instead of being forced to veto the item providing funds for all harbor dredging projects. Because it can be exercised in a more precise fashion than the line-item veto, enhanced rescission is a more powerful tool. Rescinding spending for a whole program would likely engender the opposition of many members of Congress whose districts and states would be affected. But by eliminating funding for smaller units of programs, the president will make it difficult for members to build coalitions to oppose the rescission.

Why will enhanced rescission affect the power balance that currently exists between Congress and the president? How much impact will it have? Proponents and opponents of various forms of item veto agree that it will give some additional power to the president. The advocates favor giving the president additional authority, thinking that the reform will mean only a modest influence transfer, one that a president would be reluctant to abuse. They also point to Congress's ability to respond if abuses occur. In general, proponents are willing to accept the consequences because it may help control pork barrel spending. They do not see enhanced rescission as a panacea to the deficit problem, but they believe Congress is incapable of self-restraint.

During floor debate on the bill, S 4, Sen. John McCain, R-Ariz., articulated the proponent perspective in discussing the effect on the deficit of the Budget and Impoundment Control Act of 1974, which constrained the president's ability to impound appropriated funds.

> From the earliest times in our history, when impoundment was practiced by the President of the United States, until 1974, the President of the United States, for all intents and purposes, had a line-item veto power. In other words, he had the authority to not spend moneys and use so-called impoundment authority. In 1974, Mr. President, the Budget Impoundment Act was enacted.
>
> Mr. President, it is not a coincidence . . . that beginning around 1974–75, the deficit began to rise. . . . [T]he overall trend is not only significant but it is clearly alarming.
>
> What happened, Mr. President? I think it is clear the real restraint on the appropriations process and the appropriations of funds, which really had no real fiscal governing on it, took place, and we went from fundamentally a rather small deficit and accumulated debt to one which, as we know now, is approaching \$5 trillion.[24]

Later, he contended that "the Budget and Impoundment Control Act of 1974 weakened executive power by allowing the Congress the legal option of ignoring the spending cuts recommended by the President through simple inaction."[25]

However, even proponents were generally willing to admit that a line-item veto of some form would transfer significant power from the legislative to the executive branch. But as McCain argued, "Congress would not submit to extortion from a President with line-item veto authority. They would expose the President's coercion, and overturn any offensive rescission."[26]

Opponents of enhanced rescission viewed the transfer of power as more consequential and a potential source of abuse, but recognized the futility of their argument given the push for reform. Robert Byrd, D-W.Va., viewed the transfer as a "disturbing proposition," but felt that "when a Senator starts to talk about the shifting of power from the legislative branch to the executive branch his words in great measure fall upon deaf ears insofar as his colleagues are concerned."[27] Later in the debate, Paul Sarbanes, D-Md., expressed the overriding concern with the line-item veto, that it would not be used as a tool to manage government spending but instead would give the president leverage with members of Congress on other issues:

> The danger, of course, is that these line-item veto proposals open up the opportunity for the Executive branch, for the President, to bring to bear enormous pressure upon Members of Congress and, therefore, markedly affect the dynamics between the two branches. What the various forms of the line-item veto would do, unless very carefully restrained, is enable a President to link votes on matters unrelated to the appropriation bill to a specific item in the appropriation measure.
>
> Members may well be confronted with a situation in which the Executive says, "I see this item in this bill and it is a good item; it makes a lot of sense; it is obviously very important to your state or to your district; and I certainly do not want to exercise my veto over it; but I am very concerned about the position you are taking"—and then he mentions some totally unrelated issue, perhaps a nomination to the Supreme Court, perhaps a foreign policy matter involving very important issues of war and peace, or other issues on the domestic front.[28]

During debate in the House, David Obey, D-Wis., expressed similar concerns more bluntly. Noting that Lyndon Johnson had federal officials check on him for writing a letter urging an end to the Vietnam War, Obey suggested:

> [I]f you have that kind of tendency on the part of any President to use whatever Executive power is around, what happens the next time we have a Mexican loan bailout before us and you have a two-thirds requirement to overturn a President's decision? And that President goes to you, or me, and says, "If you do not vote for that proposition, that $40 billion proposition, I am going to yank every single thing out of your State, and I have got one-third loyalists in this House, and, baby, you will not get a dime."[29]

In fact, neither the reassurances of the proponents nor the hypothetical fears of the opponents fully capture the potential power transfer that enhanced rescission offers a president. If it were used as bluntly to coerce members as the opponents suggest, then Congress might well react. But a skilled president is likely to use this power in a subtler, but even more effective, fashion. No explicit coercive threat need be made. After the president demonstrates the capacity to veto projects in particular districts and states, House members and senators will be sensitized to the power enhanced rescission confers.[30] From that point on, it is unlikely that the president will need to threaten a member. When the president asks Senator X for support on a given bill, Senator X will already know that failure to vote with the president carries with it the potential of vetoed projects. The power of rescission authority will not come from specific *quid pro quo* threats. Instead, knowing the president has the ability to rescind funds for projects in their constituencies, members will be more responsive to presidential requests, and potential power becomes actual power.[31] In the case of enhanced rescission, the exercise of power will occur because of the anticipated response of members rather than the actual use of the rescission power. If anyone raises a *quid pro quo* arrangement, it is likely to be the member of Congress, who asks the president for a guarantee that a particular project will not be subject to rescission, not the president or the president's agent. Under these circumstances it will be difficult for members to claim that the president is using enhanced rescission to coerce them. Is it any wonder that many governors who have some form of line-item veto rarely use it? Power derives from its potential use, whether threatened or not, rather than from its exercise.

True, there are two supposed safeguards in the enacted version of enhanced rescission. One is a "lockbox" provision that prevents the transfer of money saved from a rescission from being used to fund another program. Instead, the savings from a rescission are dedicated to deficit reduction. The lockbox mechanism supposedly discourages the president's exercise of rescission authority because the money cannot be used for other purposes. But this safeguard does not reduce the effectiveness of enhanced rescission in getting cooperation from members on issues about which the president is concerned.

The other safeguard is that the enhanced rescission bill contains a sunset provision. Unless Congress renews it, the president's rescission authority ceases in 2005. In addition, Congress can repeal enhanced rescission at any time, assuming that the president signs such legislation or that the House and Senate can override a presidential veto. (Clearly, this is the weakness of enhanced rescission when compared to a line-item veto constitutional amendment.) The potential for losing enhanced rescission may restrain a president's use of it. But if the real impact of enhanced rescission on presidential power is not visible, it will be difficult for opponents to make a case against its renewal. Moreover, members may realize that costs will be incurred if they oppose renewal and lose.

Perhaps the best safeguard for Congress would be for the Supreme Court to find enhanced rescission unconstitutional. Even if that should occur, the other reforms—staff reductions, term limitations for committee chairs and leaders, and restrictions on legislative mandates on states—will still have a substantial impact on the balance of power between the branches.[32]

The Irony of the Republican Reforms

It may come as no surprise if the Republicans' congressional reforms produce far more unintended than intended consequences. That result would be consistent with many political reform efforts. The greater irony will be the effect of the unanticipated consequences. One of the major Republican policy goals has been to reduce the size and importance of the federal government by moving policy decisions back to states and localities and by transferring many federal government functions to the private sector.

In weakening Congress vis-à-vis the president and the executive branch, however, Republicans have weakened the branch of the national government that historically has resisted federal government growth. They have given power to the executive, the branch that historically has tried to strengthen the national government and increase the federal role. For much of the twentieth century, Congress has been the stumbling block for presidents of both parties who proposed new federal programs. Every Democratic president up to and including Clinton, with his administration's failure to enact national health care, has felt the frustration of a legislative institution reluctant to expand the federal role. Republican and Democratic presidents alike have been disposed toward new federal programs and bureaucracies. The creation of the Environmental Protection Agency and the greatest expansion of Social Security coverage and benefits were initiated by the Nixon administration. A Congress dominated by southern Democrats and Republicans was more responsible for delaying extensions of the New Deal than was the Eisenhower administration.

Republican presidents from Eisenhower through Ford did not oppose a strong national government, nor did George Bush. If the 1990 budget struggle is any example, Bush was not nearly as conservative about the role of government as were House Republicans. President Reagan is the only clear exception.

In addition to their failure to understand the effects their reforms would have on the balance between Congress and the president, Republicans made the mistake of weakening Congress before they achieved their policy goals. Even a Democratic president may find it politically advantageous to make the national government somewhat leaner, but that does not mean returning the federal government to a pre–Great Society level any more than it meant that Eisenhower would have reversed the New Deal. In part, with the broad constituencies to which a president must be responsive—as opposed to the narrower interests often represented by House members and senators—the reduction of the national government is not likely to be in the president's electoral interests.

Why then did Republicans choose to weaken Congress and strengthen the president and executive branch? Several explanations can be offered. First, they may not have been totally aware of what they were doing to the institutional balance. Although Senator McCain's statements indicate that Republicans recognized that the president would be strengthened with enhanced rescission authority, they may have underestimated its magnitude.

A second, and perhaps a more plausible, explanation is that Republicans, like most politicians, are not very good historians — Speaker Gingrich's previous career notwithstanding. They tend to generalize from the recent past. Two aspects of the recent past have been the relative success of Republican presidential candidates and the tendency during the divided party governments of the Reagan and Bush years for Congress to be ideologically more liberal than the president. True, the 1992 election may have dampened the belief in the former, but holding to the latter makes the mistake of treating the 1981–1993 period as the rule when it is the exception. The frequency and duration of divided party control are phenomena of the late twentieth century, and they have made a real difference only since the mid-1980s, when congressional parties became stronger.[33] Historically, Congress has been more conservative than the president in terms of expanding the role of the federal government for most of this century, including since 1993. As Sundquist observed, "In the Reagan years, the country witnessed an unprecedented political configuration — an activist conservative president determined to roll back the welfare state encountering increasing resistance from a moderate Congress more disposed to defend the status quo."[34] Republicans have mistaken the "unprecedented" for the norm.

Will Congress Be Able to Assert Itself Again?

Assuming that the recent reforms weaken Congress and strengthen the president, is there reason for concern? After all, many scholars and pundits would contend that this situation is just a phase of the pendulum swing between Congress and the president. In the post–New Deal context, they would argue that nothing fundamental has changed. If the president becomes too strong, Congress reasserts itself, and then the excesses and shortcomings of Congress asserting itself cause a swing back to the president. Although at times the adjustments are slower than some would like and may not reach an ideal equilibrium, the pendulum does not swing out of control.

Some evidence lends support to this point of view. The reassertion of Congress's role in the post-Vietnam, post-Watergate era is testimony to the safeguards that keep the system in balance. Congress enacted war powers legislation, limited the president's impoundment authority, adopted a new budget process, beefed up its staff, and made frequent use of the legislative veto. By the early 1980s there was some reaction to a Congress that was perceived as unable to supply policy leadership and too meddlesome in activities that were the legitimate activity of the executive branch.

During the same period, Congress adjusted to the excesses of its own internal reforms. As noted, mechanisms were developed to provide greater party leadership control after the wave of decentralizing and democratizing reforms of the early 1970s. These adjustments indicate that when congressional members become aware of unanticipated consequences of reform, they are capable of correcting the dysfunctional aspects.

However, there is reason to question whether the current reform wave is analogous to these two examples. Future Congresses may find it more difficult to react to the unanticipated consequences of the 104th's reforms. As long as concern with balancing the federal budget continues, who in Congress will be willing to take responsibility for allowing staffs to grow again? Republicans would open themselves up to considerable public criticism for going back on their commitments. Should the Democrats regain majority party status, they would also find it politically difficult to increase staff sizes. The same might well hold for any effort to remove limits on the terms of committee chairs. The current wave of internal reforms differs from that of the 1970s because it is more public. The democratization of Congress in the 1970s was not used as a vehicle in campaigns for office, and most citizens paid little attention to it, so congressional Democrats could make adjustments without electoral consequences.

Much the same might be said of the vehicles Congress used to reassert itself in the 1970s. They were not campaign material. In contrast, the line-item veto has been a major public issue for some time. Once enacted in the form of enhanced rescission, it may be very difficult politically to propose altering or repealing it. To do so would open one to the charge of favoring wasteful pork barrel spending. Moreover, it will be difficult to claim that the power is being abused because its exercise will be largely unseen.

Will the recent wave of reforms permanently change the balance between the institutions? Just as the decline of Congress following the New Deal "appears . . . to have been a natural historic trend, flowing from the fundamentals of the political system,"[35] so the lasting impact of the Republican revolution of the 1990s could be a major shift in the institutional balance. Now, as then, Congress may let strong presidents "have an increasing share of the totality of decision-making."[36] And we should not expect presidents, whether liberal or conservative, to willingly give back power that has been granted.

Notes

1. For example, in Donna Cassata, "Swift Progress of 'Contract' Inspires Awe and Concern," *Congressional Quarterly Weekly Report,* April 1, 1995, 909–912, a number of prominent political scientists are quoted as supporting this point of view. Richard Fleisher observes: "The 104th Congress has shown us that the conventional wisdom that Congress is dependent on leadership from the president is overstated." William Connelly goes even farther in concluding: "They wrested control of the political agenda away from the president and raised new questions about the political system and the role of government." And David Mayhew claimed: "Not only is the president not taking a major part, he's largely on the other side." But, keep in mind that these scholars may have been quoted out of context.
2. James L. Sundquist, *The Decline and Resurgence of Congress* (Washington, D.C.: Brookings, 1981).
3. An analysis of GOPAC tapes indicates that Republican reformers were well aware of the importance of language. One video offers lists of words and phrases to be used in

various forms of written and oral communication. See "Language: A Key Mechanism of Control," *Extra! Update,* February 1995, 3.

4. The causes, indicators, and consequences of institutionalization are most fully articulated by Nelson W. Polsby in "The Institutionalization of the House of Representatives," *American Political Science Review* 62 (March 1968): 144–168.
5. Bolling may not have always practiced what he preached. But the conversation occurred rather late in his House career. It was in the context of his having just taken a set of offices in the Longworth Building from the Select Committee on Congressional Operations and its chair, Jack Brooks, D-Texas, and getting them for use by the Rules's subcommittees. Bolling said that he had never been concerned with something as minor as office space; in fact, unlike most members, Bolling used a small room in his office suite for himself and kept the two larger rooms for staff. But he said that after taking the offices from Brooks, he realized that other members viewed the ability to control space as an important indicator of power.
6. For a detailed discussion of the internal reforms of the early and mid-1970s, see Lawrence C. Dodd and Bruce I. Oppenheimer, "The House in Transition," in *Congress Reconsidered,* 1st ed., ed. Lawrence C. Dodd and Bruce I. Oppenheimer (New York: Praeger, 1977), 21–53.
7. Wallace S. Sayre and Herbert Kaufman, *Governing New York City* (New York: Norton, 1960), 732–733.
8. John B. Bader and Charles O. Jones, "The Republican Parties in Congress: Bicameral Differences," in *Congress Reconsidered,* 5th ed., ed. Lawrence C. Dodd and Bruce I. Oppenheimer (Washington, D.C.: CQ Press, 1993), 291–314.
9. Steven S. Smith, *Call to Order* (Washington, D.C.: Brookings, 1989).
10. Gary C. Jacobson, "Parties and PACs in Congressional Elections," in *Congress Reconsidered,* 4th ed., ed. Lawrence C. Dodd and Bruce I. Oppenheimer (Washington, D.C.: CQ Press, 1989), 116-133.
11. Janet Hook, "Gingrich's Selection as Whip Reflects GOP Discontent," *Congressional Quarterly Weekly Report,* March 25, 1989, 625–627.
12. Barbara Sinclair, *The Transformation of the U.S. Senate* (Baltimore: Johns Hopkins University Press, 1989), 101.
13. *Renewing Congress: A Second Report* (Washington, D.C.: American Enterprise Institute and Brookings, 1993), 78.
14. Some of these new senators with previous House service were among the most vehement of the Senate reformers. See David S. Cloud, "Santorum Pushing Senate To Be More Like House," *Congressional Quarterly Weekly Report,* Oct. 28, 1995, 3255–57.
15. Dan Carney, "As Hostilities Rage on the Hill, Partisan-Vote Rate Soars," *Congressional Quarterly Weekly Report,* Jan. 27, 1996, 199–201.
16. For a description and analysis of the internal changes at the start of the 104th Congress, see C. Lawrence Evans and Walter J. Oleszek, "Congressional Tsunami? Institutional Change in the 104th Congress" (paper delivered at the annual meeting of the American Political Science Association, Chicago, Aug. 31–Sept. 3, 1995).
17. Ibid.
18. Janet Hook, "Gingrich Backs Speaker Limits," *Congressional Quarterly Weekly Report,* Dec. 17, 1994, 3548.
19. Executive agencies can be sued for not doing cost-benefit studies, but not for the quality of the studies.
20. This general point is made by Lawrence C. Dodd in "Congress and the Quest for Power," in *Congress Reconsidered,* 1st ed. In *Congress Against Itself* (Bloomington: Indiana University Press, 1977), Roger H. Davidson and Walter J. Oleszek present a nice example of this conflict in their study of the Bolling Committee and its efforts to restructure committee jurisdictions in the House.

21. Sundquist, *Decline and Resurgence of Congress,* 413.
22. Ibid., 413–414.
23. The name given to the law, the Line-Item Veto Act, is not an accurate description.
24. *Congressional Record,* daily ed., March 16, 1995, S4075.
25. Ibid., S4078.
26. Ibid.
27. *Congressional Record,* daily ed., March 21, 1995, S4224.
28. *Congressional Record,* daily ed., March 22, 1995, S4314.
29. *Congressional Record,* daily ed., Feb. 3, 1995, H1180.
30. S 4 assists in this regard by requiring that the president include information on the states and congressional districts affected by the rescissions.
31. Peter Bachrach and Morton Baratz, "Two Faces of Power," *American Political Science Review* 56 (December 1962).
32. I have not discussed the two major components of the Contract with America that were not enacted—constitutional amendments on term limits and requiring a balanced budget. Without too much difficulty one could argue that they too would have weakened Congress.
33. Bruce I. Oppenheimer, "The Importance of Elections in a Strong Congressional Party Era: The Effect of Unified vs. Divided Government," in *Do Elections Matter?* 3d ed., ed. Benjamin Ginsberg and Alan Stone (Armonk, N.Y.: M. E. Sharpe, 1996).
34. James L. Sundquist, *Constitutional Reform and Effective Government* (Washington, D.C.: Brookings, 1992), 14.
35. Sundquist, *Decline and Resurgence of Congress,* 457.
36. Ibid.

17. Congress and the Emerging Order: Conditional Party Government or Constructive Partisanship?

Lawrence C. Dodd and Bruce I. Oppenheimer

The 1996 elections confirmed the growing perception that Congress and American politics are entering a new partisan era. Only twice between 1930 and 1994—in 1946 and 1954—had Republicans won simultaneous majorities in the House of Representatives and the Senate. Both times majority status lasted only two years. When the Republicans swept the 1994 elections, it was reasonable to wonder whether the Republican majorities would endure beyond the 104th Congress.

Initial analyses of the changing political and electoral landscape in early 1995 suggested, in fact, that a new Republican era was emerging.[1] The expectation was that the Republicans would add to their gains in 1996. This conclusion was based on several factors. First, following their party's debacle in 1994, a sizable number of Democratic House members and senators announced their intention to retire at the end of the 104th Congress, creating a disproportionate ratio of Democratic to Republican open seats. Second, as the majority party, Republican incumbents began to enjoy an advantage in attracting PAC contributions. Third, some Democratic incumbents in the South, Southwest, and West had barely survived the 1994 landslide and faced renewed challenges from Republicans. Fourth, there was the widespread assumption that President Bill Clinton had been crippled by the 1994 elections and would lose in 1996. A Republican presidential victory would produce congressional gains as well. Finally, these prospects would discourage strong Democratic House and Senate candidates from contesting seats in 1996 but encourage Republicans.[2] The Republicans were expected to increase their seat total by twenty to thirty in the House and by eight or more in the Senate. Combined with the election of a president in 1996, Republicans would consolidate their party's dominance of American politics.

The rapid House passage of most of the Contract with America items in the early months of 1995 and the Republicans' cohesive move on other issues seemed to reinforce the perception of a developing era of Republican dominance. But just as the party was on the verge of dominating national government, it went too far, produced two government shutdowns, and generated a rebound by the president and the Democratic Party that threatened to reverse Republican control, particularly in the House. A strategic retreat in the last six months of the 104th Congress enabled the Republicans to avert disaster.

The Republicans succeeded in retaining control of Congress in 1996, although more closely than the final seat count in the House would suggest, and broke their historic pattern of rapid exit from majority status. They did so despite the reelection of the Democratic president in an electoral college landslide and a well-financed attack by labor and the national Democratic Party. These results demonstrated that the 1994 election had not been a fluke. It had been rooted in some deeper shifts in electoral politics and the support base of the two parties. Indeed, a new political order appeared to be developing in Congress. What was left unclear by the 1996 results, however, was the precise nature of this new order and how it would affect the operation of Congress.

In this chapter we discuss some factors that could define the new order. We focus, in particular, on whether the unified, aggressive partisanship seen during the first session of the 104th Congress is likely to remain dominant in the future. By reinstating homogeneous and conservative Republican majorities in both houses, the 1996 election raises the prospect that "conditional party government," which scholars John Aldrich and David Rohde have persuasively argued was the general characteristic of the 103d and 104th Congresses and particularly dominant in 1995, could typify the emerging period as well.[3] Conditional party government would be characterized by high Republican Party cohesion and aggressive leadership coordination of member voting on crucial issues in committee and on the floor, all in pursuit of the party's dominant policy positions, even if some policy domains with high public saliency escape party control.

At issue is whether conditional party government is the inherent and dominant model for the new era. The 1996 election yielded some results that reinforce, and even mandate, a continuance of conditional party government fitting with the model that Aldrich and Rohde have proposed. Other aspects of the election, when combined with broader contextual factors, suggest that conditional party government may have peaked midway through the 104th Congress and mitigate against its further development. Instead, competing forms of rational behavior may arise and result in more muted, complicated forms of partisanship. The Republicans may decide to focus less on enacting the dominant or median policy position of party members and concentrate their efforts on constructing a productive legislative record that demonstrates their ability to govern, even if that effort requires a moderation in their party's policy stance and less aggressive partisanship.

Our purpose in this chapter is to clarify the implications of the 1996 election and related contextual factors for the creation of a new partisan order in Congress. We first discuss the nature of conditional party government and some alternative models of partisan behavior. Next, we examine the 1996 election results in some detail and identify their general implications for partisanship in the new Congress, particularly when they are combined with expectations about the 1998 election. We then concentrate on four specific constraints on conditional party government facing the Republicans and consider whether party members might have some collective incentives to move away from the highly partisan forms of policy making that characterize conditional party government. In conclusion, we suggest that a party intent on keeping control of Congress may have to move beyond strict conditional party government and embrace a constructive partisanship that demonstrates its ability to govern a heterogeneous society within the rules established by a separation of powers constitution. A failure to learn how to govern constructively could cripple the party's ability to solidify control of Congress and the national government despite some considerable advantages that would seem to predict success.

The Creation of Conditional Party Government

Because parties contest elections, organize Congress, and control the distribution of institutional resources, it is natural to assume that the new era will be shaped by the nature of partisanship that develops in Congress and American politics. The strongest form of partisanship is traditional party government in which the parties control nominations and electoral resources, present candidates who promise to adhere to the party agenda, and run issue-oriented, party-dominated campaigns. In a parliamentary system, in which the winning party controls both the legislature and the government ministries, the party implements its agenda and governs by relying on the cohesive loyalty of party members. Party loyalty is reinforced by the rewards and resources controlled by party leaders, particularly the prime minister.[4]

National party government of this sort is seldom if ever possible in the United States because regional complexity, national size, and social diversity make it unlikely that a large group of citizens and politicians will share homogeneous policy preferences across all salient policy issues facing the nation.[5] State control of election laws, the widespread use of party primaries, and party organization based in states all make it difficult for a national party to prescribe nominations to Congress or ensure agreement among members on a policy agenda. Separation of powers, bicameralism, and the presidency further complicate the system, so that party leaders cannot exercise firm control over the government and its resources. Built in to the American system are institutional divisions that make unified party government across policy domains unlikely at best and short-lived should it ever occur. However, as discussed by Joseph Cooper and Garry Young in Chapter 11, other forms of partisanship occur with some frequency in the American context. These forms of partisanship shape the political order and give distinctive character to political eras.

Beginning in the 1980s and coming into full flower in the 1990s is a model of party behavior, referred to as conditional party government, that is less encompassing than traditional party government in parliamentary systems, but considerably more developed than party government has been in the past eighty years in this country. Conditional party government exists when a party pursues the dominant or median position of its members across a broad (though not exhaustive) array of policy areas. Aldrich and Rohde posit that conditional party government emerges when the parties' officeholders are in relatively homogeneous agreement on policy, but the two parties hold distinctly separated or polarized positions.[6] Under these conditions of high intraparty agreement and high interparty difference, members (usually in the majority party) will cede substantial authority to their party leaders so the leaders can facilitate the coordination and cooperation of their members in behalf of the common agenda.

In some policy areas, homogeneous preferences may not exist. Those areas fall outside the parameters of party government, building conditionality into it and accounting for the lack of party cohesion and strong leadership coordination. Still, strong party leadership acts aggressively to realize party policies in areas where the party approaches preference homogeneity. Although it is difficult to do justice to Aldrich and Rohde's argument in a few sentences, this summary captures the core of their elegant model.

As opposed to traditional party government, in which leaders hold rank and file together to support a comprehensive program so that the prime minister can govern despite intraparty division and difficult national crises, conditional party government allows leaders to act only where the party is highly united. It is therefore limited in scope to those areas of "natural" agreement and limited in time to periods of agreement. Under conditional party government, the party caucus gives its leaders authority, and the caucus can bring a leader down without changing the shape of national government or facing new elections. Under traditional party government, the leader has independent constitutional authority and personal power derived from the national party organization. When parliament replaces the leader, it generally constitutes a repudiation of the present government and the need for new elections. As this contrast demonstrates, congressional leaders are more subject to the whims of their party's members, while parliamentary leaders can be removed only with great difficulty and by forces outside of the legislature or by the willingness of the majority party members to bring down the government and face new elections. Conditional party government is not only a weaker and more transient form of partisanship than traditional party government, but also it leaves congressional party leaders in a considerably more vulnerable and defenseless position, compared to parliamentary leaders.

Conditional party government exists when a majority party can construct and enact legislative programs that reflect the median or dominant policy preferences of the party's members within a legislative chamber rather than the median preference of all the members. High levels of cohesive party voting are achieved in behalf of the party position and in opposition to a minority party position. In the strictest case of conditional party government, the governing majority depends on the votes of the majority party and does not need support from the minority party.

In the process of constructing and passing party legislation, leaders use strategies, rewards, and sanctions to move members who deviate from the party median in their committee and floor behavior back to the median position. Leaders can do so because party members have electoral, policy, and influence goals that conditional party government may serve.[7] In particular, when issue polarization exists in the electorate that parallels agenda differences between the legislative parties, conditional party government can serve multiple member goals. It builds a base for reelection by enacting policies desired by majorities in members' constituencies and enables members to achieve their personal policy preferences. Conditional party government ensures that the party retains majority status in the legislature, when its policy positions reflect the dominant policy concerns of a polarized electorate, and that its members maintain their personal power within the institution.

Because conditional party government can be attempted only when a party has reasonable preference homogeneity, it has not been the norm for American parties during much of the twentieth century. Rather, the parties were characterized by internal divisions and preference heterogeneity: the Democratic Party was divided between a conservative southern wing and liberal northern wing, and the Republican Party was divided between its liberal eastern establishment and more conservative western members. However, as southern conservative voters left the Democrats in response to the expansion of civil rights and joined the Republicans, and as northern liberal Republican voters left their increasingly conservative party to join the national Democrats, the social conditions became right for conditional party government. In response, from the mid-1970s to the late 1980s, the Democrats, growing more liberal, strengthened their party leaders and organization within Congress, and the Republicans resorted to policy and procedural obstruction, especially in the House, to block liberal policy making. Conditional party government blossomed in the 1990s, first in 103d Congress when the Democrats tried to use their control of Congress to enact President Clinton's legislative agenda, then in the 104th Congress when the Republicans attempted to use their control to enact the Contract with America.

At issue for the 105th Congress and thereafter is whether conditional party government will prove to be the dominant pattern in a new partisan order or a transitory phase that is followed by a return to a more muted partisanship. In their chapter, Cooper and Young detail alternative forms of partisan behavior that could replace conditional party government. These more muted forms of partisan behavior could include a constrained partisanship in which the majority party votes cohesively and dominates the legislative process, but does so in pursuit of a moderated party agenda that is more centrist than the party; a cross-party coalition in which the legislative majority depends on a coalition between a slight majority of one party and a slight majority of the other; or a bipartisan coalition in which large majorities of both parties support the median position of the legislature.

A number of factors may mitigate against conditional party government. In particular, voters can send messages in elections that limit a party's mandate, or produce close election results that undercut leaders' ability to maintain firm control of congressional policy making by relying solely on their own party. Such developments may require party leaders to pursue more constrained, bipartisan, or crosspartisan strategies so that the majority party can fulfill its governing responsibilities such as the passage of taxing and spending legislation or the rapid response to pressing crises. We now will consider whether the 1996 elections may have imposed such constraints on congressional Republicans and limited their opportunity for conditional party government.

The 1996 Election and Conditional Party Government

In 1996 the Democrats made a net gain of about ten House seats, but the Republicans maintained a narrow majority and gained two seats in the Senate. The change in numbers was smaller than many might have expected. For several weeks before the election it appeared that the Democrats might benefit from a Clinton landslide and regain the House. *Congressional Quarterly Weekly Report* found 174 competitive races in its preelection roundup, 27 more than at a similar point in 1994.[8] The Senate seemed highly unpredictable with fourteen open seats being contested and an unusually high number of races in which there was no clear favorite.[9]

The small net change in the partisan composition of the two houses camouflages some significant points about the results. Looking first at the House, we see considerably more turnover in membership than the net figures suggest. In addition to the fifty new members elected in open-seat House contests and two new members who won seats where incumbents had been defeated in primaries, at least twenty-one incumbents were defeated in the general election.[10] Included in this number were thirteen Republican freshmen and several second-term members. Still, House incumbents who sought reelection won at about a 94 percent rate. The rate of return was higher than in either 1990 or 1992, but lower than the rates for 1984 through 1988.

Although Republicans can take comfort in retaining their House majority, they did not do so without a scare. The class elected in 1994 barely dodged a bullet. Of the fifty-seven who were reelected, twenty-two won with 53 percent or less of the vote.[11] On average, contested Republican incumbents received 60.7 percent of the vote, less than 1 percent higher than Democratic incumbents received in the 1994 elections.[12] Democratic incumbents fared better, suffering only three losses and averaging 66.7 percent of the vote.

For the third election in a row, there were a large number of competitive contests. In more than eighty House contests, the winner received less than 55 percent of the vote, and more than sixty of these races involved incumbents. There may be a large number of House members who feel uncertain that they have a policy mandate from their constituents, especially the junior Republicans who were the backbone of conditional party government in 1995.

In the Senate only one incumbent was defeated in the general election. Perhaps there would have been more if some who chose to retire had sought reelection. But the results indicate how competitive the contests were. In twenty-one of the thirty-four races, the winner received 55 percent or less of the total vote. Compared with the House, a larger percentage of Senate seats remains competitive. The 55–45 seat distribution between the two parties provides Senate

Table 17-1 Partisan Distribution of Senate Seats, 1990–1996, and Contested Seats, 1998 (by region)

Congress	Party	East	Midwest	South	West	Total
102d	Democrats	15	14	17	10	56
	Republicans	9	10	9	16	44
103d	Democrats	16	15	15	11	57
	Republicans	8	9	11	15	43
104th*	Democrats	14	13	10	10	47
	Republicans	10	11	16	16	53
105th	Democrats	14	13	8	10	45
	Republicans	10	11	18	16	55
106th	Democrats	3	5	5	5	18
(contested)	Republicans	3	4	4	5	16

Note: East: Conn., Del., Maine, Md., Mass., N.H., N.J., N.Y., Pa., R.I., Vt., W.Va. Midwest: Ill., Ind., Iowa, Kan., Mich., Minn., Mo., Neb., N.D., Ohio, S.D., Wis. South: Ala., Ark., Fla., Ga., Ky., La., Miss., N.C., Okla., S.C., Tenn., Texas, Va. West: Alaska, Ariz., Calif., Colo., Hawaii, Idaho, Mont., Nev., N.M., Ore., Utah, Wash., Wyo.

*For the purpose of this table Richard Shelby (Ala.) who switched parties shortly after the election is counted as a Republican, but Ben Nighthorse Campbell (Colo.) who switched parties after the session began is counted as a Democrat in calculating the partisan composition of the 104th Congress.

Republicans with a more comfortable majority than their House counterparts, especially given the prospects for the 1998 elections, discussed later in the chapter. We argue that the seat split is likely to play a larger role in the partisan tendencies in the House, but that the competitiveness of individual contests affects the form partisanship takes in the Senate.

Another important feature of the election was the continued change in the geographic distribution of party strength. As Tables 17-1 and 17-2 show, in both the House and the Senate a marked transformation has occurred in the bases of Republican strength over the last decade. The Republican House and Senate majorities have been built almost entirely on the party's success in the South. In the three other regions partisan splits remained relatively stable. Republicans held a majority of House and Senate seats in the 104th Congress and increased their southern majorities in the 105th Congress by nine seats in the House and two seats in the Senate. Democrats made net gains in the 1996 House races in the East, Midwest, and West and held constant in those regions in the Senate. For the Republicans to maintain their majority in the 105th Congress, they had to win southern open seats that had been previously held by Democrats.

These Republican gains in the South continue the trend toward a homogeneous, conservative party in Congress, in part because Republicans elected from the South are almost always conservative. In addition, most of the retiring Democrats from the South who have been replaced by Republicans were in the

Table 17-2 Partisan Distribution of House Seats, 1990-1996 (by region)

Congress	Party	East	Midwest	South	West	Total
102d	Democrats	66	68	85	48	267
	Republicans	41	45	44	37	167
	Other	1				1
103d	Democrats	57	61	85	55	258
	Republicans	42	44	52	38	176
	Other	1				1
104th	Democrats	54	46	64	40	204
	Republicans	45	59	73	53	230
	Other	1				1
105th*	Democrats	60	50	54	43	207
	Republicans	39	55	83	50	227
	Other	1				1

*At the time this table was constructed the partisan outcome of two House seats in Texas was undetermined and awaited a runoff election. For the purposes of this table the seats are credited to the party of the candidate leading after the November election with one seat going to each party. In addition, the results in several districts were not final. Therefore, the figures for the 105th Congress may change slightly.

moderate to conservative end of their party. This means that the Democrats in the House and the Senate are also more ideologically homogeneous, but toward the liberal side. To the degree that Democratic numbers increase outside the South, the additions are likely to continue the moderate to liberal trend. Moreover, as was the case in 1996, some of the defeated nonsouthern Republicans were moderates, and their defeat increases the conservative dominance of the party. The 1994 election continued the decline in the ideological heterogeneity of the two parties in Congress while increasing their distinctiveness. And although it produced a modest amount of net change in partisan composition, the 1996 election reinforced this trend. These are precisely the conditions that would lead theorists to expect a greater manifestation of conditional party government.

Finally, the 1996 election produced high membership turnover for the third Congress in a row. A sizable part of the turnover was due to voluntary departures. Retirements from the House mean that most of the elderly members have departed, and many of the politically ambitious junior members have already taken a crack at winning higher office. After three elections from 1986 to 1990, in which a total of thirty-two incumbents were defeated in primaries or general elections, the elections of 1992 through 1996 averaged thirty-five incumbent defeats. These numbers demonstrate that the competitive appearance of House races can result in the defeat of incumbents. But many of the Democrats who survived 1994 and Republicans who survived 1996 may prove difficult to defeat in future elections because they will be wary of straying too far from the policy preferences of their constituents. (This pattern may be similar to the one that occurred following the large number of incumbent defeats in 1980 and 1982.) Unless a large number of members who support term limits volunteer to leave after a prescribed number of years, Congress may be entering a period when retirements will again drop and few incumbents are defeated. Much as in the mid-1980s, the result will be little movement in the partisan composition of the House. Even if there is a strong partisan trend in a given election, most incumbents may be able to insulate themselves from it. And open-seat races may be so few in number that neither party is able to take much advantage of the partisan swing.

However, unlike the mid-1980s, when the Democrats enjoyed a comfortable House majority, the partisan balance of the 105th House is extremely close. Even small seat shifts could result in a new majority party. One effect of this close division is that the parties will not feel that their positions are ascribed and unchanging. The majority knows that it can easily become the minority and vice versa. The small partisan majority may also affect whether conditional party government is viable.

The Senate is somewhat different. First, the class up for election in 1998 contains a large number of potential retirees as well as senators who were unaffected by the partisan swings of 1994 and 1996. Many are Democrats who were fortunate enough to run in 1986, a good year for their party, and in 1992, an election without a strong partisan swing. Second, of the senators in this class who may retire rather than run for reelection several are southern Democrats. Third, because Senate seats are generally more competitive than House seats, senators may not be sufficiently insulated against partisan trends. (Those who ran for reelection in 1994 and 1996 managed to survive with only three incumbents being defeated.) Finally, in 1998 eighteen Democrats and sixteen Republicans may be running, making the Democrats slightly more vulnerable. The mix of seats is such that only six are in the East, the region with the strongest Democratic congressional contingent (see Table 17-1). The 1998 election has the potential to strengthen the homogeneity of both parties in the Senate.

To these conditions add the fact that 1998 will be a midterm election with a Democratic president, meaning that the Republicans are in a good position to expand their Senate majority. The chances for expansion are more favorable than in the House. But while the Republican Senate majority may be more comfortable than the Republican House majority and increases may make the parties more homogeneous, the competitiveness of individual Senate races as well as the rules of the Senate may continue to inhibit the development of conditional party government there. One needs to remember that in the Senate of the 106th Congress, whatever its partisan composition, nineteen of its Republican members, should they seek reelection in the year 2000, will have to face the voters in potentially competitive contests.

In sum, the 1996 elections and the upcoming elections of 1998 and 2000 create a context that may provide incentives and disincentives for conditional party government. Together with the experiences of conditional party government in the 103d and 104th Congresses and the reelection of a Democratic president, they provide the parameters for evaluating the direction of partisanship in the foreseeable future. To assess the partisan pattern likely to emerge, let us examine the impact of this context on the behaviors of members, parties, and leaders.

Constraints on Conditional Party Government

Under what conditions might congressional parties be homogeneous and polarized and yet be restrained from aggressive pursuit of conditional party government? Aldrich and Rohde acknowledge that complicating circumstances can limit members' ability to realize their personal goals through the pursuit of conditional party government and push them toward other strategies of governing, even when the parties are relatively homogeneous and polarized. Here we will discuss four such circumstances and consider how they might undermine the emergence of conditional party government as the dominant mode of partisan behavior in Congress. We begin by considering the effects of close seat division between the parties and then assess the impact of competitive seats, the structure of policy conflict, and trust in the leadership.

Close Seat Distribution Between Parties

Our first concern is with how the partisan distribution of seats in Congress can influence the creation of conditional party government. It is generally argued that a large majority makes it unlikely that a governing party can maintain internal cohesion or sustain strong leadership coordination of party activities.[13] Such a majority will tend to emerge in a landslide party victory that brings in a number of members from outside the party's political base and who therefore deviate in critical ways from the party's dominant policy positions. The result is a heterogeneous and factionalized membership that is not amenable to cohesive and coordinated party government.

When a governing party has a modest majority, the possibility for conditional party government increases. Such a majority may naturally be more homogeneous than a large majority because it is unlikely to contain deviant members elected in a party landslide. Yet it is not so large that policy victory is always guaranteed. The party may need leaders strong enough to negotiate with small groups of members at committee and floor stages to ensure their support, to craft legislation that reflects the party's median policy concerns, and to pay close attention to procedural issues to overcome the obstacles generated by opponents.

It does not follow, however, that close party seat divisions facilitate conditional party government. As the seats controlled by each party approach an equal number, the modest cushion of votes enjoyed by the governing party disappears and it must rely on a narrow majority to govern. Under such circumstances, a governing party may have to construct a near consensual level of membership coordination and vote cohesion, which can be difficult to achieve even in conditions of membership homogeneity and party polarization. The loss of support from just a few party members can defeat a party's bills or force leaders to rely on votes from the other party, undercutting the majority party's claim to full credit for the legislation.

The leaders' fear of losing on critical policy votes in a closely divided legislature gives increased bargaining leverage to party moderates. Their policy positions are more centrist than those of the party as a whole, but the party cannot win without them. Centrists can bargain for moderating policy positions before they agree to vote with the party. As the party becomes more moderate, it moves away from the median position of party members and toward the median policy preferences of the legislature as a whole. This movement undercuts the party's ability to govern in behalf of its dominant policy orientations and shifts the legislature away from conditional party government with its strongly partisan voting patterns and toward more muted and complicated forms of partisanship, including a more constrained partisanship, cross-party coalitions, or bipartisanship.

Close party division within a legislature therefore threatens conditional party government. It can do so, moreover, even when parties hold distinct policy positions and attain a high degree of homogeneity.

This concern is particularly relevant to the 105th Congress because the close seat divisions between the two parties, particularly in the House, could complicate the Republican Party's ability to sustain the strong form of conditional party government of the 104th. The Republican seat loss in 1996 moved the party from a relatively modest majority, where an eighteen- to twenty-seat shift would have been required to move the Republicans to minority status, to a more narrow majority, where an approximately ten-seat switch could push them into the minority. This close margin, together with the fact that the Republicans' seat loss came after their aggressive effort at conservative party government, could embolden some less conservative Republicans to push for moderation or to join with Democrats on critical votes. For example, such movement occurred at the end of the 104th Congress on the vote to increase the minimum wage. Even in the Senate, where the Republicans increased their majority to a 55–45 seat division, they still are short of the sixty seats needed for a filibuster-proof majority. This realization may allow Republican centrists to moderate their party's policy positions on those issues where a relatively united Democratic Party would be prepared to engage in a filibuster against conservative Republican policies. The problems for conditional party government caused by the close party divisions are reinforced, moreover, by a second consideration: the competitiveness of district elections.

Competitive Seats

The willingness of members to support conditional party government may depend on how competitive members' districts are. When members serve districts whose constituents generally support their party and its policy positions, the members may cooperate with party leaders, occasionally take some controversial stands that constituents might oppose, and vote cohesively with the party's median position. But when members come from competitive districts with a substantial presence of independents or supporters of the opposition party, they may face some significant reelection costs for supporting conditional party government. These members will be inclined to pay close attention to the median position of the constituency, which would lie between the two parties, rather than the median position of their legislative party. While the median position of a constituency cannot dominate members' voting decisions—because the legislators also need to win primary elections and therefore must please voters of their own party—the competitive nature of the district will require the members to find ways to moderate their policy behavior to appeal to their broader constituency. Such calculations should lead them to deviate from strict adherence to the median position of their party and to push for moderation of the party's policy behavior.

Many of the junior Democrats who survived the 1994 election and junior Republicans who survived in 1996 may be particularly sensitive to these considerations and press for policy moderation. After all, if they cannot maintain support of a majority of their constituents, they cannot be reelected, pursue their general policy goals, or gain institutional power in Congress.

When members from competitive districts push for party moderation, they have special bargaining leverage. While the leaders and most members may want to enact the party's dominant policy position, they have a collective stake in the reelection of the members from competitive districts. These members could be defeated if they supported the party's dominant policies or perhaps if the policies were implemented even without their support. With their defeat, a party may lose its control of the legislature. For this reason, party leaders and other members must be sensitive to the policy concerns of electorally vulnerable members, particularly if they are numerous or if control rests on a small number of seats.

The existence of competitive seats complicates the creation of conditional party government on two levels. On the individual level, members may hesitate to go along with the party because they need to reach out to centrist voters in their constituencies. On the collective level, even if they are safe in their own seats, members may fear that an aggressive pursuit of party government could lead to the defeat of vulnerable party incumbents and to the party's loss of legislative control.

A consideration of individual and collective costs suggests that the Republican Party could face moderating pressures in the 105th Congress and thereafter because of competitive seats. In the Senate, where the party's margin of control looks relatively safe in the near term, individual members may push for party moderation because they come from heterogeneous and competitive states and could face difficult reelection contests. Most House members should feel relatively safe, based on their victory margins in 1996 and the number of homogeneous districts, but they may be somewhat concerned that the party has such a small majority that it could lose control in 1998 were the members from competitive seats to lose reelection. These collective considerations may moderate the House Republicans at least through the 1998 elections. If the party picks up a substantial number of seats, as almost always happens in midterm elections for the party opposed to the president, the House might become more aggressive in its policy making, as it did in 1995, while Senate Republicans may moderate further as a large number of them approach reelection in 2000.

All these considerations assume that the structure of policy conflict in the nation will remain roughly the same as in the 1996 elections, so the parties will not suddenly be confronted with divisive internal struggles or external public opinion shifts that could alter their base electoral support. Let us now turn to a closer assessment of that assumption.

The Structure of Policy Conflict

The creation of conditional party government in Congress is always fragile and tentative because it can occur only as long as no serious intraparty divisions develop on pressing policy questions. Party members may be willing to give their leaders considerable resources if they can help the party govern effectively in areas of agreement and if they believe that the leaders will not pressure members in areas outside of general agreement. In actual practice, it is virtually impossible for party members to limit leaders' use of power to the areas of general agreement. Skillful leaders understand that they can undermine their hold on power if they use it cavalierly; therefore, members can generally trust the leaders to focus only on the issues on which there is preference homogeneity. If conditions develop in which party leaders might violate that trust, support for strong leaders and conditional party government may dissipate.

The greatest threat to conditional party government comes from the emergence of salient policy issues that are critical to the party's governing success and on which party members seriously disagree. In such situations, party leaders may be tempted to use their power to create a cohesive and effective governing party, and perhaps they may even feel compelled to do so to demonstrate the party's ability to govern and maintain its national support. If leaders insist on unity in areas of deep intraparty division, they can generate rebellion. This is precisely what occurred in 1910 when progressive Republicans, angered by Speaker Joseph Cannon's use of his leadership power to push conservative policies, joined with Democrats to strip the speakership of most of its power.[14]

The question facing the congressional Republicans is whether the nation has entered a period in which its policy conflicts are polarized along partisan lines, so that Republicans can freely embrace conditional party government, or whether some intense "wedge" issues will emerge that are central to the governing responsibility of a majority party but also divisive. Perhaps the most critical test the Republicans face in this regard is their ability to sustain a coalition between southern social conservatives, whose concern over segregation and traditional values divided the Democratic Party for decades and kept it from pursuing conditional party government, and the traditional fiscal conservatives who have long been the backbone of the party.

As Theodore Lowi argues in *The End of the Republican Era*, the move of the southern conservatives to the Republican side has introduced a social conservatism into that party, ranging across issues such as race relations, abortion, school prayer, gay rights, and government assistance for the underprivileged, that is distinctly different from the economic conservatism of most northern and western Republicans.[15] Southern social conservatism envisions a government that supports traditional moral values and uses its power in behalf of them, but that opposes using government for social goals such as reducing poverty and social betterment. Traditional economic conservatives in the Republican Party have wanted a government that supports capitalist enterprise, limits its regulatory role in economic matters, and restrains its taxation of business. These Republicans are usually social moderates who accept diversity in personal values and lifestyles and support some degree of government action in behalf of minorities, the disadvantaged, and general societal improvement.[16] The detrimental effects of this intraparty division can be seen at the presidential level where social conservatives have demanded party platforms and presidential nominees firmly committed to pro-life policies and similar moral positions. The result has been an abandonment of the party in presidential elections by many traditional Republicans who support more moderate social positions and the humiliating defeat of two Republican presidential candidates in the 1990s.

Because congressional majorities are built on a district-by-district basis across the nation, the Republicans have been able to finesse their intraparty division by emphasizing different forms of conservatism in different regions. It is also the case that the social conservatism of many southern Republicans has magnified their economic conservatism, so that even in areas of greatest party agreement, fiscal policy and regulatory restraint, the southern and southwestern Republicans tend to emphasize a strong hostility toward government, and northern and western Republicans tend to accept some government involvement in economic and social policy. This division is apparent across a variety of issues: minimum wage increases, environmental protection, education policy, welfare reform, and entitlement control. All of these policy conflicts, moreover, involve issues that are central to effective governance in the late twentieth century.

As the Republican Party solidifies its position as the nation's governing congressional party following the 1996 elections, its members will have to build a governing record that confronts social, economic, and moral issues on a continuing basis, and they will have to do so despite the fault line between southern and nonsouthern members. The Republicans may be able to unite against President Clinton and the Democrats by focusing on scandals or a mishandled policy crisis and thereby avoid policy questions that would touch off their internal differences. But Clinton won a landslide victory in the electoral college and could be in a position to undertake popular policy initiatives that might accentuate divisions among Republicans and generate cross-party or bipartisan policy behavior in Congress, at least on some important issues. In contrast to 1995, when Republicans dominated the policy agenda, Clinton began his second term in a good position to provide policy leadership rather than defer to the Republicans, if he can avoid being crippled by scandal or a policy crisis. Clinton's leverage was reinforced, moreover, by the close intraparty seat divisions in Congress and by the presence of a number of Republican incumbents who serve competitive constituencies.

Potential policy divisions within the Republican Party in the 105th Congress and thereafter could create difficult governing tasks for its party leaders and complicate the continuation of conditional party government. Let us now consider whether members will continue to trust party leaders with the authority that is necessary to coordinate and lead the party in the face of internal policy disputes and contextual pressures.

Willingness to Trust Party Leaders

As House and Senate Republicans enter a period in which their policy unity could come under increased pressure, the success of the party depends on their ability to facilitate policy agreement and to defuse disagreements in policy areas where governing failure could hurt the party and the nation. Party leaders need strong resources at least as much as they did in the 104th Congress. The question is whether party members will continue to cede party leaders the formal and informal authority necessary to coordinate and lead the party. In the face of the various policy pressures and personal calculations we have discussed, are members willing to trust their party leaders with power?

Members may trust party leaders with strong resources when a leader or leadership team closely reflects the dominant characteristics of party members. When the leadership resembles the members, the rank and file can more easily believe that the leaders understand the members' concerns and will be attentive to their interests. For this reason, congressional parties often prefer a centrist leader and attempt to construct leadership teams that reflect the parties' regional and ideological diversity. A classic example of such balance was the Democrats' selection of a Texas Speaker, Sam Rayburn, and a Massachusetts majority leader, John McCormack, during the 1950s and early 1960s. This balance helped hold the House Democrats together during the early years of the civil rights movement. During much of the 1970s and 1980s, the Democrats reversed the pattern but maintained regional balance by putting a Bostonian, Thomas P. "Tip" O'Neill, in the speakership and a Texan, Jim Wright, as majority leader. In the early 1990s the House Republicans created a similar balance by selecting Bob Michel of Illinois as minority leader and Newt Gingrich of Georgia as minority whip.

In the 105th Congress, one potential factor constraining members' trust of party leaders could be the predominance of southern Republicans in positions of leadership: Senate Majority Leader Trent Lott of Mississippi, House Speaker Gingrich, House Majority Leader Dick Armey of Texas, and House Majority Whip Tom DeLay of Texas. The dominance of southerners in the leadership may make it difficult for the party to be attuned to the sentiments of nonsouthern Republicans and increases the prospect that they will misjudge how party actions will resonate outside of the South. It is possible that the southern orientation of the House leaders contributed to Gingrich's miscalculations about how the country would react to government shutdowns over the budget impasse. The continued dominance of southerners could dispose the other members to question leadership decisions and support efforts to constrain leadership power. An unwillingness to trust the leaders and a move against their power could erupt into a broad-based rebellion if a wedge issue should arise that divides the party along regional lines, throws northern and western members (particularly those who are social moderates) into an alliance with Democrats, and isolates the Republicans' southern leaders.

A second factor that could shape members' willingness to invest power in the leaders is the generational aging of the congressional party. The vast powers given to Speaker Gingrich at the beginning of the 104th Congress came after decades in the minority and at a time in which a majority of Republican members were in their first or second terms, did not yet have extensive seniority, personal resources, or congressional experience, and felt indebted to Gingrich for the role he had played in their recruitment and election. Some of these members were defeated in 1996, and the remaining members may feel less indebted to Gingrich and the other leaders who created the hostile environment in which they ran. In addition, as members advance in their careers, they generally develop a vested interest in power positions and discretionary control of personal resources. They become more likely to support a fragmentation of power than its centralization. Should the Republicans remain the majority congressional party and return most of their current members over the next four to eight years, the party's growing number of mid-career and senior members may be concerned with acquiring greater personal influence in Congress and be less prone to support centralized leaders and policy coordination. This generational aging of the congressional Republicans could undercut conditional party government.

Finally, the willingness of party members to maintain strong leadership resources will depend on the performance of the leaders. Clearly, Speaker Gingrich hurt himself during 1995 with his verbal gaffes, manic intensity, and effort to dominate national politics, particularly through the use of government shutdowns. However, he demonstrated an ability to recognize his own failings and to learn from them, so that his party survived the 1996 elections partly because of his success in moderating his fellow Republicans and producing a legislative record at the end of the 104th Congress. Gingrich showed a willingness to move away from strict conditional party government when its continued pursuit threatened the Republicans' retention of majority status. He was joined in this effort in the summer of 1996 by Majority Leader Lott.

Gingrich and Lott together showed the benefits that can accrue to a party when leaders use their powers in a skillful manner to create a constructive governing record that is sensitive to the varied interests of party members, attentive to the nation's shifting policy moods, and focused on productive governance. Perhaps the most notable example of this effort came in welfare reform, where the party moderated its previous positions and passed a bill the president said he could sign. The Republicans entered the 1996 elections with a major policy accomplishment that appealed to its base supporters and independent voters and helped refurbish the party's tarnished image. While their performance in the last six months of the 104th Congress may not accord as strongly with conditional party government as their performance during their first year in power, the skillfulness of the party leaders in generating a constructive legislative record while respecting intraparty differences may have reassured members that the leaders could be trusted with a second chance. It is doubtful that such trust would exist in the 105th Congress had Gingrich not moderated during 1996 and had Lott not embraced a cooperative stance.

At the beginning of the 105th Congress, the Republican leaders appear to head homogeneous House and Senate parties that are distinctly different in policy preferences from the Democratic minority. The homogeneous and polarized character of the Republican caucuses in both houses seems to be primed for another round of aggressive conditional party government much like that witnessed in 1995. In fact, it is possible that the Republicans have a more conservative membership coming out of the 1996 elections than they did following the 1994 victory. This more consensual conservatism would seem to push the party toward an aggressive partisanship. And yet the leaders face constraints on the creation of conditional party government, including the close partisan divisions in the two chambers, the presence of a number of vulnerable members, the underlying policy cleavages within the party, and limits on members' faith in the party leaders. These constraints suggest that even if the leaders wanted to pursue conditional party government, their task might prove difficult unless they focused on attacks against President Clinton that resonated with the national public and provided the party a unifying focus.

Perhaps most critical, the Republicans face the paradoxical lesson of the 104th Congress: aggressive assertion of a legislative party's dominant policy positions is not always the best way to ensure sustained party control of Congress. It is not always in the party's long-term interest, even when parties are as homogeneous and polarized as they were in the 104th Congress. Moderation and a focus on constructing a productive legislative record, even cooperating with the opposition president, may pay significant partisan dividends. The Republicans' embrace of this lesson in the last months of the 104th Congress may have been momentary, or it may have been the product of a learning process that led them to understand the benefits that come with pursuing a moderated partisanship and constructive congressional government. In such pursuit, moreover, the constraints on conditional party government that we have discussed may be a godsend to party leaders that helps them reinforce the need for moderation and legislative productivity to their members. We now consider this possibility more fully.

Learning to Govern

When one party dominates a legislature for a long time—best illustrated by the Democrats' control of the House of Representatives for four decades—both parties may suffer a loss of perspective and a diminution of their ability to govern.[17] In such circumstances, the majority party can become arrogant and bullying and disregard the rights of the minority. The seemingly permanent minority party may take on a hostile, obstructionist role that serves to justify further majority limits on minority rights. The result can be a cycle of arrogance and obstruction that generates extensive partisan hostility, aggravates the conflict between the parties, and diverts them from a shared concern with productive governance.

The detrimental effect of one-party dominance can be aggravated further by the separation of powers system and divided government. If the majority party in the legislature truly believes that it is the nation's permanent majority party, it may refuse to cooperate with the president when he is a member of the opposite party and instead hold out for the return of unified government. The minority party, if it believes that it is locked out of legislative power through traditional reelection strategies, may augment its obstructionism and attempt to discredit the legislative majority by stressing its inept and unethical governing practices and by attacking the institution itself. Any semblance of institutional comity may disappear and a breakdown in productive governance may result.[18] This scenario is a fairly accurate depiction of Congress and national politics during much of the 1980s and early 1990s when Democratic control, particularly in the House, was a foregone conclusion.

When parties occasionally alternate in majority control of the House and Senate, a different type of behavior has a chance to arise. Perhaps most important, party members may begin to think in terms of their collective interests in governing because they realize that their party has a realistic opportunity to gain power or to lose it. As members focus on their shared interest in gaining and maintaining control—a major focus in the mid-1990s—they also come to recognize that the voters may hold accountable the party and its members for their collective performance in office. A legislative party may be judged by what it has accomplished in policy terms. In the United States policy success comes only as legislation clears the two coequal houses of Congress and is enacted into law with the president's signature or with a congressional override of the president's veto.

To achieve policy success and maintain governing control of a chamber, an American legislative party must cooperate with the other house of Congress and other branch of government, and in so doing must compromise with the ideological factions or parties that control them.[19] Under a separation of powers system, the persistent adherence by a legislative majority party in one chamber to the dominant or median position of its members, and a consequent refusal to compromise, may undermine the party's ability to create a productive governing record and retain chamber control. Certainly, a legislative party may at first try to unite its members around a core policy position to create a bargaining position that the party can defend as it enters negotiations with the other chamber or with the president. But eventual moderation that takes into account the position of the other chamber and the president may prove essential if the party is to create a productive record that members can stress in their reelection campaigns. If the other chamber or the presidency is controlled by the opposition, a legislative party may have to move toward a relatively centrist policy stance as legislation approaches final votes, even if the party's members hold homogeneous and polarized positions. Ironically, a legislative party that moderates its policies as a strategy for retaining chamber control may need leaders who are as powerful and skilled as they would be under conditions of conditional party government. They will need both power and skill to coordinate the moderation of members' positions during inter-institutional negotiations and final legislative passage.[20]

The alternation of parties in power also has other moderating effects. Because each party at times occupies the minority position, parties may learn to appreciate and respect minority rights and to behave more cordially toward one another. As parties experience being in the majority, they also learn to appreciate and respect the responsibilities that come with governing. They may see the legislative struggle less as a partisan game with no holds barred and more as a policy-making process that has real consequences. In addition, with majoritarian experience, a party learns how to organize a legislature and plan legislative schedules. It understands how to make smooth transitions into power when it again controls the legislature. It also learns the importance of coalition building to sustain critical functions of government such as the appropriations and budget processes and foreign policy decision making.

True, when a party first comes to power after a long period in the minority, the moderating effects of party alternation may be difficult to discern. The initial behavior of the new majority and minority parties, at such moments, is not necessarily a good guide to the long-term effects of party alternation. A party long in the minority may flex its muscles on attaining majority status and act in an arrogant or even vindictive manner; a party long in the majority may necessarily try to give the new majority a taste of its old obstructionist medicine. The nation witnessed both patterns in the first year of the 104th Congress as the House Republican juggernaut rolled and as Democrats retaliated by filing procedural complaints and harassing Speaker Gingrich with ethical charges. But as the reality of the new situation dawns, particularly if that reality entails the possibility of long-term periodic alternation in power, the parties may shift toward comity and norms of procedural and even programmatic moderation.

Much depends on how the parties interpret their shifting fortunes. If a new majority party thinks it is heading for long-term majority party dominance, it may keep up its bullying and try to break the minority. And if the minority thinks it is heading toward oblivion, it may try to provoke the majority party into destructive behavior that will change the minority's fortunes. When the parties experience and foresee long-term alternation in power, moderation becomes possible, particularly if pressures for moderation are reinforced by constraints such as close seat divisions between the parties and competitive seats. The possibility for moderating effects depends on whether the voters hold relatively moderate positions and on whether they accept the possibility of parties alternating in power. Any chance for moderation and constructive partisanship probably will be destroyed if the public polarizes into extreme positions or if a controversial issue divides the nation and the parties.

The nation watched the moderating process at work in the 104th Congress. During the first year, the Republicans believed they were on the verge of creating party dominance of national politics. They took a hardline stance on budget negotiations designed to break the Democratic president and assert the Republican agenda. The president and congressional Democrats responded by testing the Republicans' resolve and Speaker Gingrich's emotional tenacity. The negative public response to the subsequent government shutdowns made it clear that neither party had a firm long-term hold on the voters' loyalty and that voters were not going to rally around the Republicans' attack on government. Rather than responding to the government shutdowns in a polarized fashion, the public's frustrated response was that they wanted sensible government and that they would punish the party deemed responsible for continued gridlock. It was at this point that the move toward moderation and legislative productivity began in the 104th Congress.

A central question for the 105th Congress and those to follow is how the congressional party leaders and the president interpret the results of the 1996 election. It is tempting for the Republicans to believe that by surviving the 1996 elections they now are guaranteed increased control of the House and the Senate in 1998 because of the customary midterm vote swings against the president's party. The Republicans look at their various structural and financial advantages and may believe that they are on the verge of their own forty years of congressional control. Convinced of such a result, they could again pursue aggressive strategies of conditional party government, or their experiences in the 104th Congress could give them pause.

At the beginning of the 104th Congress, virtually all political analysts were certain that the president and the Democrats were doomed. This did not prove to be the case, and, had various Democrats not retired from Congress based on this assumption, the party might well have regained control in 1996. Rather than jump to conclusions again about the Republicans' solidification of power, analysts might recognize that the 1990s are years of extensive transformation in the nation's social and economic life and in its governing agenda. Such periods can be characterized by unusual behavior. It should be noted, in fact, that the one time since the emergence of the current two-party system that a president's congressional party *gained* seats in a midterm election was in 1934 when the nation was involved in another period of societal change, political experimentation, and agenda shift. It might be more appropriate for the Republicans to conclude that the 1996 elections gave them a second chance and to recognize that how well they use this opportunity to demonstrate their governing competence could determine their fate in 1998 and after. The Democratic president and his party might likewise see the election results as giving them a second chance to demonstrate that they have learned to move beyond the liberal expansionism of the Great Society and Clinton's health care proposals and to embrace the modest government innovations and centrist policy making that citizens appear to want.

In pursuing their second chance, the Republicans face the various constraints on conditional party government we have discussed, but they also have another opportunity to learn how to govern in a constructive and productive manner. The constraints pose serious challenges to the party's ability to govern and suggest that continued party alternation in power is distinctly possible. But these constraints also provide Republican party leaders with the opportunity to experiment with more moderated forms of partisanship, to work at creating a constructive relationship between both houses of Congress and the president, and to produce a record of legislative accomplishment and governing success. If they make good, their record will reflect their conservative commitments and respond to the centrist and moderating tendencies inherent in a heterogeneous society and a separation of powers constitutional system. If they can create a productive legislative record, in cooperation with a president and congressional Democrats who are attentive to their own moderating lessons, the Republicans may convince citizens that they can be trusted as a majority congressional party and should stay in control of Congress. Ironically, to do so, the Republicans may be required to move away from conditional party government and toward a more moderated and constructive partisanship.

Conclusion

Throughout American history, majority parties have succeeded in maintaining congressional control not by adopting conditional party government, particularly on a strict and continuous basis, but by embracing constructive partisanship. As Cooper and Young indicate, strong united partisanship within Congress is a relatively rare experience, particularly since the rise of a professionalized Congress and careerist legislators. When it exists, it decays rapidly as a majority party faces the difficulties of governing a heterogeneous society within a separation of powers system. It is unusual in such a society for policy conflicts to remain polarized in ways that reinforce the distinctiveness of the two parties. It is far more common for cross-cutting conflicts to arise that divide the two parties internally along some major salient issues and create overlapping agreement or commonality across their members. The cohesiveness of the New Deal Democrats lasted barely six years before concern about executive usurpation of power and fears about national government intervention into southern segregation combined to split them and give rise to a long-term coalition of southern Democrats and Republicans.[21] Likewise, the Great Society coalition of Lyndon Johnson lasted only about eighteen months before preoccupation with the Vietnam War split the party again. The Democrats survived both periods of division not by trying to impose party government, or even by pursuing conditional party government, but by using a broad range of partisan strategies designed to demonstrate their ability to contribute to effective national governance.

A majority party concerned with keeping control of Congress must demonstrate the ability to address the cross-cutting policy conflicts of a heterogeneous society and manage the governing complexities created by bicameralism and a separation of powers system. As salient cross-cutting issues arise that are central to governing, party members restrict the formal powers and leeway of congressional leaders, although probably less so in periods of divided government and alternating control than under long-term united government. Under such conditions, party success relies less on the absolute formal power of leaders and their creation of conditional party government and more on their skill in constructing shifting coalitions within and across the majority and minority parties and in generating policy results that voters will embrace. Such constructive partisanship sustains a majority party in office and creates a reputation that enables it to regain control after a loss. A party that learns to engage in constructive partisanship can continue to contest for majority control of Congress even in the presence of the internal divisions and restricted leadership power that are normal byproducts of political life in a heterogeneous nation with a separation of powers arrangement.

The Democratic Party proved successful in pursuing constructive partisanship and contesting for control of Congress as the presumptive majority party for more than six decades. It did so, moreover, in the face of one of the nation's most severe cleavage issues, the division between the North and the South over segregation and race relations. The party's success reflected the skillfulness of leaders such as Sam Rayburn and John McCormack in the House and Lyndon Johnson in the Senate. Lacking the substantial formal powers of Speaker Cannon or Speaker Gingrich, these leaders nevertheless constructed the shifting coalitions that allowed the Democrats to demonstrate productive legislative records and sustain public support despite their internal divisions and the deep national conflict over civil rights. Particularly impressive was their ability to create a productive record (including a civil rights bill) in the second term of Dwight Eisenhower, a Republican president. Their success positioned the party to win both Congress and the presidency in 1960. Throughout these years, the Democrats did not present themselves as a unified party offering party government in behalf of a distinct policy agenda. Instead, they appeared as a governing party that cared about specific policy issues, but would attempt to manage the nation's policy problems as they arose. Ironically, the Democrats lost their preeminent position as the presumptive congressional majority in the 1990s at a point when they became a more homogeneous party characterized by conditional party government. With apparent party unity, strengthened party leaders, and a vigorous young president, they created strong expectations that their united control of government could effectively address the nation's health care problems. They failed because they could not overcome the divisions built into national policy making by our separation of powers system. The public judged their unified governing effort a failure and delivered them a devastating electoral defeat.

The test facing Republicans in Congress is whether they can learn to engage in constructive partisanship, face inevitable cross-cutting policy conflicts and frustrating constitutional obstacles, and still find partisan strategies by which to build a productive record of governance. The key is for the party to present itself as capable of not just passing legislation, but of contributing to constructive national governance. The proven ability to participate in governance—that is, to manage the nation's crises and maneuver through divisive periods of cross-cutting conflict over long periods of time—is central to the public's faith in a party and willingness to entrust it with a sustained majority in Congress. In the 104th Congress the Republicans had an extraordinary opportunity to demonstrate their governing ability, but they almost destroyed the public's faith in the party. Given a second chance, the Republicans can move to create a productive governing record in league with the Democratic president, much as did Rayburn and Johnson with Eisenhower. Fortunately for them, they do not face a divisive issue such as civil rights that would greatly complicate their governing efforts. The intriguing question is how effectively they have learned their lesson.

Notes

1. See, for example, Gary Jacobson and Thomas P. Kim, "After 1994: The New Politics of Congressional Elections" (paper presented at the annual meeting of the Midwest Political Science Association, Chicago, April 18–20, 1996); and the essays in Philip A. Klinkner, ed., *Midterm: Election of 1994 in Context* (Boulder: Westview, 1996).
2. Gary Jacobson and Samuel Kernell, *Strategy and Choice in Congressional Elections* (New Haven: Yale University Press, 1983).
3. For useful statements by John Aldrich and David Rohde on the theory of conditional party government, see "Theories of the Party in the Legislature and the Transition to Republican Rule in the House" (paper presented at the annual meeting of the American Political Science Association, Chicago, Aug. 31–Sept. 3, 1995). See also Aldrich's book, *Why Parties? The Origin and Transformation of Political Parties in America* (Chicago: University of Chicago Press, 1995); and David Rohde, *Parties and Leaders in the Postreform House* (Chicago: University of Chicago Press, 1991). For earlier work that foreshadows the theory of conditional party government, see Joseph Cooper and David Brady, "Institutional Context and Leadership Style: The House from Cannon to Rayburn," *American Political Science Review* 75 (1981): 411–425.
4. For relevant discussion, see Leon Epstein, *Political Parties in Western Democracies* (New York: Praeger, 1967).
5. Pendleton Herring, *The Politics of Democracy* (New York: Norton), 1940.
6. See the discussion, for example, by John Aldrich and David Rohde in "The Republican Revolution and the House Appropriations Committee" (paper presented at the annual meeting of the Southern Political Science Association, Atlanta, Nov. 7–9, 1996), 1–2.

7. The stress on reelection, policy, and influence goals by Aldrich and Rohde owes a debt to the initial work on member goals by Richard Fenno Jr. in *Congressmen in Committees* (Boston: Little, Brown, 1973).
8. Juliana Gruenwald and Deborah Kalb, "No Longer Ascendant, GOP Hopes to Keep Majority," *Congressional Quarterly Weekly Report,* Oct. 19, 1996, 2964–8.
9. Alan Greenblatt and Robert Marshall Wells, "Senate Elections: Still Anybody's Call," *Congressional Quarterly Weekly Report,* Oct. 19, 1996, 2954–9.
10. These numbers do not reflect the final recounts in two races in Washington State and the final runoff decisions in two Texas races, which occurred after this essay went to press.
11. *New York Times,* Nov. 7, 1996, B2.
12. *CQ Monitor,* Nov. 7, 1996.
13. Frank Sorauf, *Party and Representation* (New York: Atherton Press, 1963).
14. Kenneth W. Hechler, *Insurgency: Personalities and Politics in the Taft Era* (New York: Columbia University Press, 1940).
15. Theodore Lowi, *The End of the Republican Era* (Norman: University of Oklahoma Press, 1995).
16. For an excellent elaboration of these contrasts between regions and some empirical illustration, see Russell L. Hanson, "Liberalism and the Course of American Social Welfare Policy," in Lawrence C. Dodd and Calvin Jillson, *The Dynamics of American Politics* (Boulder: Westview Press, 1994).
17. For discussion relevant to this point, see Morris Fiorina, *Divided Government* (New York: Allyn and Bacon, 1995); David Mayhew, *Divided We Govern* (New Haven: Yale University Press, 1991); and Lawrence C. Dodd, "Re-Envisioning Congress" (paper presented at the annual meeting of the American Political Science Association, San Francisco, Aug. 29–Sept. 1, 1996).
18. Eric Uslaner, *The Decline of Comity in Congress* (Ann Arbor: University of Michigan Press, 1993).
19. Even when a party's members in the two houses of Congress appear relatively close in their ideological positions, as would seem the case with the House and Senate Republicans in the 105th Congress, senators (whose state constituencies tend to be relatively heterogeneous) may see policy questions differently from House members (whose districts tend to be smaller and more homogeneous). Substantial differences may exist in the bills that emerge from the two chambers and substantial compromise between the chambers may be required. Likewise, a party's president may respond to different constituent and institutional considerations from those of the congressional parties, so that legislative-executive compromise is necessary.
20. Party leaders may be able to maintain their strong powers under conditions of periodic party alternation because a party's movement in and out of power can make it more difficult for rank and file members to build up entrenched power as committee chairs or policy leaders and because parties tend to maintain relatively strong leadership structures while in the minority to fight more effectively for influence and work more cohesively to regain control.
21. James T. Patterson, *Congressional Conservatism and the New Deal* (Lexington: University of Kentucky Press, 1967).

Suggested Readings

✧ ✧ ✧

Aberbach, Joel D. "Changes in Congressional Oversight." *American Behavioral Scientist* 22 (1979): 493–515.

___. *Keeping a Watchful Eye.* Washington, D.C.: Brookings, 1990.

Abramowitz, Alan I. "A Comparison of Voting for U.S. Senators and Representatives in 1978." *American Political Science Review* 74 (1980): 637–640.

___. "Explaining Senate Election Outcomes." *American Political Science Review* 82 (1988): 385–404.

___. "Incumbency, Campaign Spending, and the Decline of Competition in U.S. House Elections." *Journal of Politics* 53 (1991): 34–56.

Abramowitz, Alan I., and Jeffrey A. Segal. *Senate Elections.* Ann Arbor: University of Michigan Press, 1992.

Abramson, Paul, John H. Aldrich, and David W. Rohde. "Progressive Ambition Among United States Senators: 1972–1988." *Journal of Politics* 49 (1987): 3–35.

Aldrich, John. *Why Parties? The Origin and Transformation of Political Parties in America.* Chicago: University of Chicago Press, 1995.

Aldrich, John, and David Rohde. "The Republican Revolution and the House Appropriations Committee" (paper presented at the annual meeting of the Southern Political Science Association, Atlanta, Nov. 7–9, 1996).

Alesina, Alberto, and Howard Rosenthal. "Partisan Cycles in Congressional Elections and the Macroeconomy." *American Political Science Review* 83 (1989): 373–398.

Ansolabehere, Stephen, and Alan Gerber. "The Effects of Filing Fees and Petition Requirements in U.S. House Elections." *Legislative Studies Quarterly* 21 (1996): 249–264.

Arnold, R. Douglas. *Congress and the Bureaucracy.* New Haven: Yale University Press, 1979.

___. *The Logic of Congressional Action.* New Haven: Yale University Press, 1990.

Asher, Herbert B. "The Learning of Legislative Norms." *American Political Science Review* 67 (1973): 499–513.

Bach, Stanley, and Steven S. Smith. *Managing Uncertainty in the House: Adaptation and Innovation in Special Rules.* Washington, D.C.: Brookings, 1988.

Baker, Ross K. *House and Senate.* New York: Norton, 1989.

Bauer, Raymond A., Ithiel de Sola Pool, and Lewis A. Dexter. *American Business and Public Policy.* New York: Atherton, 1963.

Benjamin, Gerald, and Michael Malbin, eds. *Limiting Legislative Terms.* Washington, D.C.: CQ Press, 1992.

Berkman, Michael. "State Legislators in Congress: Strategic Politicians, Professional Legislatures, and the Party Nexus." *American Journal of Political Science* 38 (1994): 1025–55.

Bianco, William T. *Trust: Representatives and Constituents.* Ann Arbor: University of Michigan Press, 1994.

Bibby, John F., and Roger H. Davidson. *On Capitol Hill.* 2d ed. Hinsdale, Ill.: Dryden Press, 1972.

Binder, Sarah A. "The Partisan Basis of Procedural Choice: Allocating Parliamentary Rights in the House, 1789–1900." *American Political Science Review* 90 (1996): 8–20.

Binder, Sarah A., and Steven S. Smith. *Politics or Principle: Filibustering in the United States Senate.* Washington, D.C.: Brookings, 1997.

Bolling, Richard. *House Out of Order.* New York: Dutton, 1965.

___. *Power in the House.* New York: Dutton, 1965.

Bond, Jon R., Cary Covington, and Richard Fleisher. "Explaining Challenger Quality in Congressional Elections." *Journal of Politics* 47 (1985): 510–529.

Bond, Jon R., and Richard Fleisher. *The President in the Legislative Arena.* Chicago: University of Chicago Press, 1990.

Born, Richard. "Changes in the Competitiveness of House Primary Elections, 1956–1976." *American Politics Quarterly* 8 (1980): 495–506.

Bosso, Christopher. *Pesticides and Politics: The Life Cycle of a Public Issue.* Pittsburgh: University of Pittsburgh Press, 1988.

Brady, David W. *Congressional Voting in a Partisan Era: A Study of the McKinley Houses.* Lawrence: University Press of Kansas, 1973.

___. *Critical Elections and Congressional Policy Making.* Stanford, Calif.: Stanford University Press, 1988.

Brady, David W., Joseph Cooper, and Patricia A. Hurley. "The Decline of Party in the U.S. House of Representatives, 1887–1968." *Legislative Studies Quarterly* 4 (1979): 381–407.

Bullock, Charles S., III. "House Careerists: Changing Patterns of Longevity and Attrition." *American Political Science Review* 66 (1972): 1295–1305.

___. "Redistricting and Congressional Stability, 1962–1972." *Journal of Politics* 37 (1975): 569–575.

___. "House Committee Assignments." In *The Congressional System: Notes and Readings.* 2d ed. Edited by Leroy N. Rieselbach. North Scituate, Mass.: Duxbury Press, 1979.

Burrell, Barbara C. *A Woman's Place Is in the House.* Ann Arbor: University of Michigan Press, 1994.

Cain, Bruce, John Ferejohn, and Morris Fiorina. *The Personal Vote: Constituency Service and Electoral Independence.* Cambridge: Harvard University Press, 1967.

Canon, David T. *Actors, Athletes, and Astronauts: Political Amateurs in the United States Congress.* Chicago: University of Chicago Press, 1990.
Canon, David, Matthew Schousen, and Patrick Sellers. "The Supply Side of Congressional Redistricting: Race and Strategic Politicians, 1972–1992." *Journal of Politics* 58 (1996): 846–862.
Clausen, Aage R. *How Congressmen Decide.* New York: St. Martin's Press, 1973.
Clem, Alan L., ed. *The Making of Congressmen: Seven Campaigns of 1974.* North Scituate, Mass.: Duxbury Press, 1976.
Collie, Melissa. "Incumbency, Electoral Safety and Turnover in the House of Representatives, 1952–1976." *American Political Science Review* 75 (1981).
Collie, Melissa, and Brian E. Roberts. "Trading Places: Choice and Committee Chairs in the U.S. Senate, 1950–1986." *Journal of Politics* 54 (1992): 231–245.
Cook, Elizabeth Adell, Sue Thomas, and Clyde Wilcox, eds. *The Year of the Woman: Myths and Reality.* Boulder: Westview Press, 1994.
Cooper, Joseph. *The Origins of the Standing Committees and the Development of the Modern House.* Houston: Rice University Studies, 1971.
___. "Strengthening the Congress: An Organizational Analysis." *Harvard Journal on Legislation* 2 (1975): 301–368.
Cooper, Joseph, and David W. Brady. "Institutional Context and Leadership Style: The House from Cannon to Rayburn." *American Political Science Review* 75 (1981).
___. "Toward a Diachronic Analysis of Congress." *American Political Science Review* 75 (1981).
Cooper, Joseph, and G. Calvin Mackenzie. *The House at Work.* Austin: University of Texas Press, 1981.
Cover, Albert D. "One Good Term Deserves Another: The Advantage of Incumbency in Congressional Elections." *American Journal of Political Science* 21 (1977): 523–541.
___. "Contacting Congressional Constituents: Some Patterns of Perquisite Use." *American Journal of Political Science* 24 (1980): 125–134.
Cover, Albert D., and David R. Mayhew. "Congressional Dynamics and the Decline of Competitive Congressional Elections." In *Congress Reconsidered.* 2d ed. Edited by Lawrence C. Dodd and Bruce I. Oppenheimer. Washington, D.C.: CQ Press, 1981.
Cox, Gary, and Mathew McCubbins. *Parties and Committees in the U.S. House of Representatives.* Berkeley: University of California Press, 1990.
___. *Legislative Leviathan: Party Government in the House.* Berkeley: University of California Press, 1993.
Cox, James, Gregory Hager, and David Lowery. "Regime Change in Presidential and Congressional Budgeting: Role Discontinuity or Role Evolution." *American Journal of Political Science* 37 (1993): 88–118.
Davidson, Roger H., ed. *The Postreform Congress.* New York: St. Martin's Press, 1992.

Davidson, Roger H., David M. Kovenock, and Michael K. O'Leary. *Congress in Crisis: Politics and Congressional Reform.* Belmont, Calif.: Wadsworth, 1966.

Davidson, Roger H., and Walter J. Oleszek. *Congress Against Itself.* Bloomington: Indiana University Press, 1977.

———. *Congress and Its Members.* 5th ed. Washington, D.C.: CQ Press, 1996.

Davidson, Roger H., Walter J. Oleszek, and Thomas Kephart. "One Bill, Many Referrals: Multiple Referrals in the U.S. House of Representatives." *Legislative Studies Quarterly* 13 (1988): 3–28.

De Boef, Suzanna, and James A. Stimson. "The Dynamic Structure of Congressional Elections." *Journal of Politics* 55 (1993): 630–648.

Deering, Christopher J. *Congressional Politics.* Chicago: Dorsey, 1989.

Deering, Christopher J., and Steven S. Smith. *Committees in Congress.* 3d ed. Washington, D.C.: CQ Press, 1997.

Degregorio, Christine, and Kevin Snider. "Leadership Appeal in the U.S. House of Representatives: Comparing Officeholders and Aides." *Legislative Studies Quarterly* 20 (1995): 491–511.

Dexter, Lewis A. *How Organizations Are Represented in Washington.* Indianapolis: Bobbs-Merrill, 1969.

———. *The Sociology and Politics of Congress.* Chicago: Rand McNally, 1969.

Dion, Douglas, and John Huber. "Procedural Choice and the House Committee on Rules." *Journal of Politics* 58 (1996): 25–53.

Dodd, Lawrence C. "Congress and the Quest for Power." In *Congress Reconsidered.* 1st ed. Edited by Lawrence C. Dodd and Bruce I. Oppenheimer. New York: Praeger, 1977.

———. "The Expanded Roles of the House Democratic Whip System." *Congressional Studies* 6 (1979).

———. "Congress, the Constitution, and the Crisis of Legitimation." In *Congress Reconsidered.* 2d ed. Edited by Lawrence C. Dodd and Bruce I. Oppenheimer. Washington, D.C.: CQ Press, 1981.

———. "The Cycles of Legislative Change." In *Political Science: The Science of Politics.* Edited by Herbert F. Weisberg. New York: Agathon Press, 1986.

———. "Re-Envisioning Congress: Some Reflections on the Republican Revolution." (paper prepared for delivery at the annual meeting of the American Political Science Association, San Francisco, Aug. 29–Sept. 1, 1996).

Dodd, Lawrence C., and Richard L. Schott. *Congress and the Administrative State.* 2d ed. Boulder: Westview, 1994.

Eckhardt, Bob, and Charles L. Black Jr. *The Titles of Power: Conversations on the American Constitution.* New Haven: Yale University Press, 1976.

Edwards, George C., III. *Presidential Influence in Congress.* San Francisco: Freeman, 1980.

Endersby, James W., and Karen M. McCurdy. "Committee Assignments in the U.S. Senate." *Legislative Studies Quarterly* 21 (1996): 219–234.

Epstein, David, and Peter Zemsky. "Money Talks: Deterring Quality Challengers in Congressional Elections." *American Political Science Review* 89 (1995): 295–308.

Erikson, Robert S. "The Advantage of Incumbency in Congressional Elections." *Polity* 3 (1971).

___. "Is There Such a Thing as a Safe Seat?" *Polity* 8 (1976): 623–632.

___. "The Puzzle of Midterm Loss." *Journal of Politics* 50 (1988): 1011–29.

Eulau, Heinz, and Paul Karps. "The Puzzle of Representation." *Legislative Studies Quarterly* 2 (1977): 233–254.

Evans, C. Lawrence. *Leadership in Committee.* Ann Arbor: University of Michigan Press, 1991.

Evans, C. Lawrence, and Walter J. Oleszek. *Congress Under Fire.* Boston: Houghton Mifflin, 1997.

Evans, Diana. "Policy and Pork: The Use of Pork Barrel Projects to Build Policy Coalitions in the House of Representatives." *American Journal of Political Science* 38 (1994): 894–917.

Fenno, Richard F. Jr. *The Power of the Purse.* Boston: Little, Brown, 1966.

___. *Congressmen in Committees.* Boston: Little, Brown, 1973.

___. "If, as Ralph Nader Says, Congress Is 'the Broken Branch,' How Come We Love Our Congressmen So Much?" In *Congress in Change.* Edited by Norman J. Ornstein. New York: Praeger, 1975.

___. *Home Style: House Members in Their Districts.* Boston: Little, Brown, 1978.

___. *The United States Senate: A Bicameral Perspective.* Washington, D.C.: American Enterprise Institute, 1982.

___. *Senators on the Campaign Trail: The Politics of Representation.* Norman: University of Oklahoma Press, 1996.

Ferejohn, John A. *Pork Barrel Politics.* Stanford, Calif.: Stanford University Press, 1974.

Fiorina, Morris P. *Representatives, Roll Calls, and Constituencies.* Lexington, Mass.: Lexington Books, 1974.

___. *Congress: Keystone of the Washington Establishment.* New Haven: Yale University Press, 1977.

___. *Divided Government.* New York: Allyn and Bacon, 1995.

Fiorina, Morris P., David W. Rohde, and Peter Wissel. "Historical Change in House Turnover." In *Congress in Change.* Edited by Norman J. Ornstein. New York: Praeger, 1975.

Fishel, Jeff. *Party and Opposition.* New York: David McKay, 1973.

Fisher, Louis. *President and Congress: Power and Policy.* New York: Free Press, 1972.

___. *The Constitution Between Friends: Congress, the President, and the Law.* New York: St. Martin's Press, 1978.

Flemming, Gregory N. "Presidential Coattails in Open-Seat Elections." *Legislative Studies Quarterly* 20 (1995): 197–211.

Fowler, Linda L. *Candidates, Congress, and American Democracy.* Ann Arbor: University of Michigan Press, 1993.

Fowler, Linda L., and Robert D. McClure. *Political Ambition: Who Decides to Run for Congress?* New Haven: Yale University Press, 1989.

Fox, Harrison W. Jr., and Susan Webb Hammond. *Congressional Staffs: The Invisible Force in American Lawmaking.* New York: Free Press, 1977.

Franklin, Daniel P. *Making Ends Meet.* Washington, D.C.: CQ Press, 1993.

Frantzich, Stephen E. "Computerized Information Technology in the U.S. House of Representatives." *Legislative Studies Quarterly* 4 (1979): 255–280.

Freeman, J. Leiper. *The Political Process.* New York: Random House, 1955.

Friedman, Sally. "House Committee Assignments of Women and Minority Newcomers." *Legislative Studies Quarterly* 21 (1996): 73–82.

Froman, Lewis A. Jr. *The Congressional Process: Strategies, Rules and Procedures.* Boston: Little, Brown, 1967.

Gamm, Gerald, and Kenneth Shepsle. "The Emergence of Legislative Institutions: Standing Committees in the House and Senate, 1810–1825." *Legislative Studies Quarterly* 14 (1989): 39–66.

Gibson, Martha. "Issues, Coalitions and Divided Government." *Congress and the Presidency* 22 (1995): 155–166.

Gilmour, John B. *Reconcilable Differences.* Berkeley: University of California Press, 1990.

Gilmour, John B., and Paul Rothstein. "A Dynamic Model of Loss, Retirement, and Tenure in the U.S. House." *Journal of Politics* 58 (1996): 54–68.

Glazer, Amihai, and Bernard Grofman. "Two Plus Two Plus Two Equals Six: Tenure of Office of Senators and Representatives, 1953–1983." *Legislative Studies Quarterly* 12 (1987): 555–563.

Goehlert, Robert U., and John R. Sayre. *The United States Congress: A Bibliography.* New York: Free Press, 1982.

Goldenberg, Edie N., and Michael W. Traugott. *Campaigning for Congress.* Washington, D.C.: CQ Press, 1984.

Goodwin, George Jr. *The Little Legislatures.* Amherst: University of Massachusetts Press, 1970.

Hall, Richard L. "Participation and Purpose in Committee Decision Making." *American Political Science Review* 81 (1987): 105–127.

———. *Participation in Congress.* New Haven: Yale University Press, 1993.

Harris, Joseph. *Congressional Control of Administration.* Washington, D.C.: Brookings, 1964.

Hechler, Kenneth W. *Insurgency: Personalities and Politics in the Taft Era.* New York: Columbia University Press, 1940.

Henry, Charles P. "Legitimizing Race in Congressional Politics." *American Politics Quarterly* 5 (1977): 149–176.

Herrnson, Paul S. *Party Campaigning in the 1980s.* Cambridge: Harvard University Press, 1988.

———. *Congressional Elections: Campaigning at Home and in Washington.* Washington, D.C.: CQ Press, 1995.

Hershey, Marjorie R. *The Making of Campaign Strategy.* Lexington, Mass.: Lexington Books, 1974.

Hibbing, John R. "Ambition in the House: Behavioral Consequences of Higher Office Goals Among U.S. Representatives." *American Journal of Political Science* 30 (1986): 651–665.

___. *Congressional Careers.* Chapel Hill: University of North Carolina Press, 1991.

Hibbing, John R., and John R. Alford. "Economic Conditions and the Forgotten Side of Congress: A Foray into U.S. Senate Elections." *British Journal of Political Science* 12 (1982): 505–513.

Hibbing, John R., and Elizabeth Theiss-Morse. *Congress as Public Enemy: Public Attitudes Toward American Political Institutions.* Cambridge: Cambridge University Press, 1995.

Hinckley, Barbara. *The Seniority System in Congress.* Bloomington: Indiana University Press, 1971.

___. *Stability and Change in Congress.* New York: Harper, 1971.

___. "The American Voter in Congressional Elections." *American Political Science Review* 74 (1980): 641–650.

___. *Less than Meets the Eye.* Chicago: University of Chicago Press, 1994.

Hoadly, John F. "The Emergence of Political Parties in Congress, 1789–1803." *American Political Science Review* 74 (1980): 757–779.

Holtzman, Abraham. *Legislative Liaison.* Chicago: Rand McNally, 1970.

Huitt, Ralph K., and Robert L. Peabody. *Congress: Two Decades of Analysis.* New York: Harper, 1969.

Huntington, Samuel P. "Congressional Responses to the Twentieth Century." In *The Congress and America's Future.* 2d ed. Edited by David B. Truman. Englewood Cliffs, N.J.: Prentice-Hall, 1973.

Hurley, Patricia, and Kim Quarle Hill. "The Prospects for Issue-Voting in Contemporary Congressional Elections." *American Politics Quarterly* 8 (1980): 425–448.

Jackson, John. *Constituencies and Leaders in Congress.* Cambridge: Harvard University Press, 1974.

Jacobson, Gary C. *Money in Congressional Elections.* New Haven: Yale University Press, 1980.

___. "The Marginals Never Vanished: Incumbency and Competition in Elections to the U.S. House of Representatives, 1952–81." *American Journal of Political Science* 31 (1987): 126–141.

___. *The Politics of Congressional Elections.* 4th ed. New York: Longman, 1996.

___. *The Electoral Origins of Divided Government.* Boulder: Westview Press, 1990.

Jacobson, Gary C., and Samuel Kernell. *Strategy and Choice in Congressional Elections.* New Haven: Yale University Press, 1983.

Jewell, Malcolm E. *Senatorial Politics and Foreign Policy.* Lexington: University of Kentucky Press, 1962.

Jewell, Malcolm E., and Samuel C. Patterson. *The Legislative Process in the United States.* 3d ed. New York: Random House, 1977.

Jillson, Calvin, and Rick K. Wilson. *Congressional Dynamics: Structure, Coordination, and Choice in the First American Congress, 1774–1789.* Stanford, Calif.: Stanford University Press, 1994.

Johannes, John R. *Policy Innovation in Congress.* Morristown, N.J.: General Learning Press, 1972.

Jones, Charles O. "Representation in Congress: The Case of the House Agricultural Committee." *American Political Science Review* 55 (1961): 358–367.

___. "The Role of the Congressional Subcommittee." *Midwest Journal of Political Science* 6 (1962): 327–344.

___. *The Minority Party in Congress.* Boston: Little, Brown, 1970.

___. "Will Reform Change Congress?" In *Congress Reconsidered.* 1st ed. Edited by Lawrence C. Dodd and Bruce I. Oppenheimer. New York: Praeger, 1977.

Katz, Jonathan, and Brian Sala. "Careerism, Committee Assignments, and the Electoral Connection." *American Political Science Review* 90 (1996): 21–33.

Kazee, Thomas. "The Decision to Run for the U.S. Congress: Challenger Attitudes in the 1970s." *Legislative Studies Quarterly* 5 (1980): 79–100.

___. ed. *Who Runs for Congress? Ambition, Context, and Candidate Emergence.* Washington, D.C.: CQ Press, 1994.

Keefe, William J. *Congress and the American People.* Englewood Cliffs, N. J.: Prentice-Hall, 1980.

Keefe, William J., and Morris S. Ogul. *The American Legislative Process.* 4th ed. Englewood Cliffs, N.J.: Prentice-Hall, 1977.

Kelly, Sean Q. "Democratic Leadership in the Modern Senate: The Emerging Roles of the Democratic Policy Committee." *Congress and the Presidency* 22 (1995): 113–140.

Kiewiet, Roderick, and Mathew D. McCubbins. *The Spending Power.* Berkeley: University of California Press, 1991.

Kingdon, John W. *Candidates for Office.* New York: Random House, 1968.

___. *Congressmen's Voting Decisions.* New York: Harper, 1973.

Krasno, Jonathan S. *Challengers, Competition and Reelection: Comparing Senate and House Elections.* New Haven: Yale University Press, 1994.

Krehbiel, Keith. "Are Congressional Committees Composed of Preference Outliers?" *American Political Science Review* 84 (1990): 149–164.

___. *Information and Legislative Organization.* Ann Arbor: University of Michigan Press, 1990.

Krehbiel, Keith, Kenneth A. Shepsle, and Barry R. Weingast. "Why Are Congressional Committees Powerful?" *American Political Science Review* 81 (1987): 929–948.

Kuklinski, James H. "District Competitiveness and Legislative Roll Call Behavior: A Reassessment of the Marginality Hypothesis." *American Journal of Political Science* 21 (1977): 627–638.

LeLoup, Lance T. *Budgetary Politics.* Brunswick, Ohio: Kings Court Press, 1977.

LeLoup, Lance T., and Steven Shull. "Congress Versus the Executive: The 'Two Presidencies' Reconsidered." *Social Science Quarterly* 59 (1979): 704–719.

Lindsay, James M. *Congress and the Politics of U.S. Foreign Policy.* Baltimore: Johns Hopkins University Press, 1994.

Loewenberg, Gerhard, and Samuel Patterson. *Comparing Legislatures.* Boston: Little, Brown, 1979.

Longley, Lawrence D., and Walter J. Oleszek. *Bicameral Politics: Conference Committees in Congress.* New Haven: Yale University Press, 1989.

Lowi, Theodore J. *The End of Liberalism.* New York: Norton, 1969, 1979.

___. *The End of the Republican Era.* Norman: University of Oklahoma Press, 1995.

Maass, Arthur. *Congress and the Common Good.* New York: Basic Books, 1983.

Maisel, Louis S. *From Obscurity to Oblivion: Running in the Congressional Primary.* Knoxville: University of Tennessee Press, 1982.

Maltzman, Forrest. "Meeting Competing Demands: Committee Performance in the Post-Reform House." *American Journal of Political Science* 39 (1995): 653–682.

Manley, John F. *The Politics of Finance.* Boston: Little, Brown, 1970.

Mann, Thomas E. *Unsafe at Any Margin: Interpreting Congressional Elections.* Washington, D.C.: American Enterprise Institute, 1978.

___. ed. *A Question of Balance: The President, the Congress, and Foreign Policy.* Washington, D.C.: Brookings, 1990.

Mann, Thomas E., and Norman J. Ornstein. *The New Congress.* Washington, D.C.: American Enterprise Institute, 1981.

___. *Renewing Congress: A Second Report.* Washington, D.C.: American Enterprise Institute and Brookings, 1993.

Mann, Thomas E., and Raymond E. Wolfinger. "Candidates and Parties in Congressional Elections." *American Political Science Review* 74 (1980): 616–632.

Matthews, Donald R. *U.S. Senators and Their World.* New York: Vintage Books, 1960.

Mayhew, David R. *Party Loyalty Among Congressmen.* Cambridge: Harvard University Press, 1966.

___. *Congress: The Electoral Connection.* New Haven: Yale University Press, 1974.

___. *Divided We Govern.* New Haven: Yale University Press, 1991.

McAdams, John C., and John R. Johannes. "Congressmen, Perquisites, and Elections." *Journal of Politics* 50 (1988): 412–439.

Meernik, James. "Presidential Support in Congress: Conflict and Consensus in Foreign and Defense Policy." *Journal of Politics* 55 (1993): 569–587.

Mezey, Michael L. *Congress, the President, and Public Policy.* Boulder: Westview Press, 1989.

Moe, Terry M. "An Assessment of the Positive Theory of Congressional Dominance." *Legislative Studies Quarterly* 12 (1987): 475–520.

Mondak, Jeffrey. "Competence, Integrity, and Electoral Success of Congressional Incumbents." *Journal of Politics* 57 (1995): 1043–69.

Nelson, Garrison. "Partisan Patterns of House Leadership Change, 1789–1977." *American Political Science Review* 71 (1977): 918–939.

Niemi, Richard, and Laura Winsky. "The Persistence of Partisan Redistricting Effects in Congressional Elections in the 1970s and 1980s." *Journal of Politics* 54 (1992): 563–572.

Norpoth, Helmut. "Explaining Party Cohesion in Congress: The Case of Shared Party Attributes." *American Political Science Review* 70 (1976): 1157–71.

Ogul, Morris S. *Congress Oversees the Bureaucracy.* Pittsburgh: University of Pittsburgh Press, 1976.

Oleszek, Walter J. *Congressional Procedures and the Policy Process.* 4th ed. Washington, D.C.: CQ Press, 1996.

Oppenheimer, Bruce I. *Oil and the Congressional Process: The Limits of Symbolic Politics.* Lexington, Mass.: Lexington Books, 1974.

———. "The Rules Committee: New Arm of Leadership in a Decentralized House." In *Congress Reconsidered.* 1st ed. Edited by Lawrence C. Dodd and Bruce I. Oppenheimer. New York: Praeger, 1977.

———. "Split-Party Control of Congress, 1981–1986: Exploring Electoral and Apportionment Explanations." *American Journal of Political Science* 33 (1989): 653–669.

———. "The Representational Experience: The Effect of State Population on Senator-Constituency Linkages." *American Journal of Political Science* 40 (1996): 1280–99.

Orfield, Gary. *Congressional Power: Congress and Social Change.* New York: Harcourt, 1975.

Ornstein, Norman J. *Congress in Change: Evolution and Reform.* New York: Praeger, 1975.

Ornstein, Norman J., and Shirley Elder. *Interest Groups, Lobbying and Policymaking.* Washington, D.C.: CQ Press, 1978.

Ornstein, Norman J., Thomas E. Mann, and Michael J. Malbin. *Vital Statistics on Congress, 1995–1996.* Washington, D.C.: Congressional Quarterly, 1995.

Ornstein, Norman J., and David W. Rohde. "Shifting Forces, Changing Rules, and Political Outcomes: The Impact of Congressional Change on Four House Committees." In *New Perspectives on the House of Representatives.* Edited by Robert L. Peabody and Nelson W. Polsby. Chicago: Rand McNally, 1977.

Owens, John E. "Curbing the Fiefdoms: Party-Committee Relations in the Contemporary U.S. House of Representatives." In Lawrence D. Longley and Attila Agh, eds. *The Changing Roles of Parliamentary Committees.* Appleton, Wis.: Research Committee of Legislative Specialists, 1997.

Parker, Glenn R. "Some Themes in Congressional Unpopularity." *American Journal of Political Science* 21 (1977): 93–110.

———. "The Advantage of Incumbency in House Elections." *American Politics Quarterly* 8 (1980): 449–464.

———. *Homeward Bound: Explaining Changes in Congressional Behavior.* Pittsburgh: University of Pittsburgh Press, 1986.

___. *Institutional Change, Discretion and the Making of the Modern Congress.* Ann Arbor: University of Michigan Press, 1992.

Parker, Glenn R., and S. L. Parker. "Factions in Committees: The U.S. House of Representatives." *American Political Science Review* 73 (1979): 85–102.

Patterson, James T. *Congressional Conservatism and the New Deal.* Lexington: University of Kentucky Press, 1967.

Payne, James L. "The Personal Electoral Advantage of House Incumbents, 1936–1976." *American Politics Quarterly* 8 (1980): 465–482.

Peabody, Robert L. *Leadership in Congress: Stability, Succession, and Change.* Boston: Little, Brown, 1976.

Peabody, Robert L., and Nelson W. Polsby, eds. *New Perspectives on the House of Representatives.* 3d ed. Chicago: Rand McNally, 1977.

Peters, John G., and Susan Welch. "The Effects of Charges of Corruption on Voting Behavior in Congressional Elections." *American Political Science Review* 74 (1980): 697–708.

Peters, Ronald M. Jr. *The American Speakership.* Baltimore: Johns Hopkins University Press, 1990.

Peterson, Mark A. *Legislating Together: The White House and Capitol Hill from Eisenhower to Reagan.* Cambridge: Harvard University Press, 1990.

Pierce, John C., and John L. Sullivan. *The Electorate Reconsidered.* Beverly Hills, Calif.: Sage, 1980.

Polsby, Nelson W. "Institutionalization in the U.S. House of Representatives." *American Political Science Review* 62 (1968): 144–168.

___. *Congress and the Presidency.* 3d ed. Englewood Cliffs, N.J.: Prentice-Hall, 1976.

Polsby, Nelson W., Miriam Gallagher, and Barry Rundquist. "The Growth of the Seniority System in the House of Representatives." *American Political Science Review* 63 (1969): 787–807.

Powell, Lynda W. "Issue Representation in Congress." *Journal of Politics* (1982).

Price, David E. *Who Makes the Laws?* Cambridge, Mass.: Schenkman, 1972.

Price, H. Douglas. "Congress and the Evolution of Legislative Professionalism." In *Congress in Change.* Edited by Norman J. Ornstein. New York: Praeger, 1975.

Ragsdale, Lyn. "The Fiction of Congressional Elections as Presidential Events." *American Politics Quarterly* 8 (1980): 395–398.

Ragsdale, Lyn, and Timothy E. Cook. "Representatives' Actions and Challengers' Reactions: Limits to Candidate Connections in the House." *American Journal of Political Science* 31 (1987): 45–81.

Ragsdale, Lyn, and Jerrold G. Rusk. "Candidates, Issues, and Participation in Senate Elections." *Legislative Studies Quarterly* 20 (1995): 305–328.

Reid, T. R. *Congressional Odyssey: The Saga of a Senate Bill.* San Francisco: Freeman, 1980.

Rieselbach, Leroy N. *The Roots of Isolationism.* Indianapolis: Bobbs-Merrill, 1966.

———. *Congressional Politics: The Evolving Legislative System.* 2d ed. Boulder: Westview, 1995.

———. *Congressional Reform: The Changing Modern Congress.* Washington, D.C.: CQ Press, 1994.

Ripley, Randall B. *Party Leaders in the House of Representatives.* Washington, D.C.: Brookings, 1967.

———. *Majority Party Leadership in Congress.* Boston: Little, Brown, 1969.

———. *Power in the Senate.* New York: St. Martin's Press, 1969.

Ripley, Randall B., and Grace N. Franklin. *Congress, the Bureaucracy, and Public Policy.* 5th ed. Belmont, Calif.: Wadsworth, 1991.

Ripley, Randall B., and James M. Lindsay, eds. *Congress Resurgent: Foreign and Defense Policy on Capitol Hill.* Ann Arbor: University of Michigan Press, 1993.

Rohde, David W. *Parties and Leaders in the Postreform House.* Chicago: University of Chicago Press, 1991.

Rohde, David W., and Kenneth A. Shepsle. "Democratic Committee Assignments in the U.S. House of Representatives." *American Political Science Review* 67 (1973): 889–905.

Rothman, David J. *Politics and Power.* New York: Atheneum, 1969.

Rudder, Catherine E. "Committee Reform and the Revenue Process." In *Congress Reconsidered.* 1st ed. Edited by Lawrence C. Dodd and Bruce I. Oppenheimer. New York: Praeger, 1977.

Saloma, John S., III. *Congress and the New Politics.* Boston: Little, Brown, 1969.

Schick, Allen. *Making Economic Policy in Congress.* Washington, D.C.: American Enterprise Institute, 1983.

Schiller, Wendy J. "Senators as Political Entrepreneurs: Using Bill Sponsorship to Shape Legislative Agendas." *American Journal of Political Science* 39 (1995): 186–203.

Schneider, Jerrold E. *Ideological Coalitions in Congress.* Greenwood, Conn.: Greenwood Press, 1979.

Schwarz, John E., and L. Earl Shaw. *The United States Congress in Comparative Perspective.* Hinsdale, Ill.: Dryden Press, 1976.

Seidman, Harold. *Politics, Position, and Power.* 2d ed. London: Oxford University Press, 1975.

Shepsle, Kenneth A. *The Giant Jigsaw Puzzle.* Chicago: University of Chicago Press, 1978.

Shepsle, Kenneth A., and Barry R. Weingast, eds. *Positive Theories of Congressional Institutions.* Ann Arbor: University of Michigan Press, 1995.

Sinclair, Barbara Deckard. "Determinants of Aggregate Party Cohesion in the U.S. House of Representatives." *Legislative Studies Quarterly* 2 (1977): 155–175.

———. *Majority Leadership in the U.S. House.* Baltimore: Johns Hopkins University Press, 1983.

———. *The Transformation of the U.S. Senate.* Baltimore: Johns Hopkins University Press, 1989.

___. *Legislators, Leaders, and Lawmaking: The U.S. House of Representatives in the Postreform Era.* Baltimore: Johns Hopkins University Press, 1995.

Smith, Steven S. *Call to Order: Floor Politics in the House and Senate.* Washington, D.C.: Brookings, 1989.

___. *The American Congress.* Boston: Houghton Mifflin, 1995.

Stimson, James A., Michael B. MacKuen, and Robert S. Erikson. "Dynamic Representation." *American Political Science Review* 89 (1995): 543–565.

Stone, Walter J. "The Dynamics of Constituency: Electoral Control in the House." *American Politics Quarterly* 8 (1980): 399–424.

Strahan, Randall. *New Ways and Means: Reform and Change in a Congressional Committee.* Chapel Hill: University of North Carolina Press, 1990.

Sundquist, James L. *Politics and Policy.* Washington, D.C.: Brookings, 1968.

___. *The Decline and Resurgence of Congress.* Washington, D.C.: Brookings, 1981.

Swain, Carol M. *Black Faces, Black Interests: The Representation of African Americans in Congress.* Cambridge: Harvard University Press, 1993.

Swift, Elaine K. *The Making of an American Senate: Reconstitutive Change in Congress, 1787–1841.* Ann Arbor: University of Michigan Press, 1996.

Talbert, Jeffery, Bryan D. Jones, and Frank R. Baumgartner. "Nonlegislative Hearings and Policy Change in Congress." *American Journal of Political Science* 39 (1995): 383–405.

Thomas, Sue. *How Women Legislate.* New York: Oxford University Press, 1994.

Thurber, James A., ed. *Rivals for Power: Presidential-Congressional Relations.* Washington, D.C.: CQ Press, 1996.

Thurber, James A., and Roger H. Davidson. *Remaking Congress: Change and Stability in the 1990s.* Washington, D.C.: CQ Press, 1995.

Truman, David B. *The Governmental Process.* New York: Knopf, 1951.

Turner, Julius. *Party and Constituency: Pressures on Congress.* Rev. ed. Edited by Edward V. Schneier Jr. Baltimore: Johns Hopkins University Press, 1970.

Unekis, Joseph, and Leroy N. Rieselbach. *Congressional Committee Politics: Continuity and Change.* New York: Praeger, 1984.

Uslaner, Eric M. "Policy Entrepreneurs and Amateur Democrats in the House of Representatives." In *Legislative Reform: The Policy Impact.* Edited by Leroy N. Rieselbach. Lexington, Mass.: Lexington Books, 1978.

___. *The Decline of Comity in Congress.* Ann Arbor: University of Michigan Press, 1993.

Vogler, David J. *The Third House.* Evanston, Ill.: Northwestern University Press, 1971.

___. *The Politics of Congress.* 6th ed. Madison, Wis.: Brown and Benchmark, 1993.

Wahlke, John C., Heinz H. Eulau, W. Buchanan, and L. C. Ferguson. *The Legislative System: Explorations in Legislative Behavior.* New York: Wiley, 1962.

Wayne, S. J. *The Legislative Presidency.* New York: Harper, 1978.

Weingast, Barry. "Floor Behavior in the U.S. Congress: Committee Power Under the Open Rule." *American Political Science Review* 83 (1989): 795–815.

Weisberg, Herbert F. "Evaluating Theories of Congressional Roll Call Voting." *American Journal of Political Science* 22 (1978): 554–577.

Westefield, L. P. "Majority Party Leadership and the Committee System in the House of Representatives." *American Political Science Review* 68 (1974): 1593–1604.

Wildavsky, Aaron. *The Politics of the Budgetary Process.* Boston: Little, Brown, 1964.

Wilson, Rick. "Forward and Backward Agenda Procedures: Committee Experience and Structurally Induced Equilibrium." *Journal of Politics* 48 (1986): 390–409.

Wilson, Woodrow. *Congressional Government.* 1885. Reprint, Gloucester, Mass.: Peter Smith, 1973.

Wolfinger, Raymond E., and Joan Heifetz Hollinger. "Safe Seats, Seniority, and Power in Congress." *American Political Science Review* 59 (1965): 337–349.

Wright, Gerald C., and Michael B. Berkman. "Candidates and Policy in United States Senate Elections." *American Political Science Review* 80 (1986): 567–588.

Wright, Gerald C. Jr., Leroy Rieselbach, and Lawrence C. Dodd, eds. *Congress and Policy Change.* New York: Agathon, 1986.

Wright, John. "PACs, Contributions, and Roll Calls: An Organizational Perspective." *American Political Science Review* 75 (1985): 400–414.

Young, James S. *The Washington Community, 1800–1828.* New York: Columbia University Press, 1966.

Index

✧ ✧ ✧

Page references followed by *t*, *f*, or *n* indicate tables, figures, or notes, respectively.